Jerusalem and Other Holy Places as Foci of Multireligious and Ideological Confrontation

Jewish and Christian Perspectives Series

VOLUME 37

The titles published in this series are listed at *brill.com/jcp*

Jerusalem and Other Holy Places as Foci of Multireligious and Ideological Confrontation

Edited by

Pieter B. Hartog
Shulamit Laderman
Vered Tohar
Archibald L.H.M. van Wieringen

BRILL

LEIDEN | BOSTON

Library of Congress Cataloging-in-Publication Data

Names: Jerusalem and Other Holy Places as Foci of Multireligious and
    Ideological Confrontation (Conference) (2018 : Jerusalem), author. |
    Hartog, Pieter B., editor. | Laderman, Shulamith, editor. | Tohar,
    Vered, 1969– editor. | Wieringen, A.L.H.M. van (Archibald L.H.M.),
    1963– editor.
Title: Jerusalem and other holy places as foci of multireligious and
    ideological confrontation / edited by Pieter B. Hartog, Shulamit
    Laderman, Vered Tohar, Archibald L.H.M. van Wieringen.
    Description: Leiden ; Boston : Brill, [2021] | Series: Jewish and Christian
    perspectives series, 1388–2074 ; volume 37 | Includes bibliographical
    references and index. | Summary: "Jerusalem and Other Holy Places as
    Foci of Multireligious and Ideological Confrontation brings together the
    papers that were read at an international conference at the Schechter
    Institute in Jerusalem in May 2018. The contributions to this volume
    develop a multi-disciplinary perspective on holy places and their
    development, rhetorical force, and oft-contested nature. Through a
    particular focus on Jerusalem, this volume demonstrates the variety in
    the study of holy places, as well as the flexibility of geographic and
    historical aspects of holiness"—Provided by publisher.
Identifiers: LCCN 2020044642 (print) | LCCN 2020044643 (ebook) | ISBN
    9789004437180 (hardback) | ISBN 9789004437210 (ebook)
Subjects: LCSH: Sacred space—Congresses. |
    Religions—Relations—Congresses. | Jerusalem—In Judaism—Congresses. |
    Jerusalem—In Christianity—Congresses. | Jerusalem—In Islam—Congresses.
Classification: LCC BL580 .J47 2018 (print) | LCC BL580 (ebook) | DDC 203/.5—dc23
LC record available at https://lccn.loc.gov/2020044642
LC ebook record available at https://lccn.loc.gov/2020044643

Typeface for the Latin, Greek, and Cyrillic scripts: "Brill". See and download: brill.com/brill-typeface.

ISSN 1388-2074
ISBN 978-90-04-43718-0 (hardback)
ISBN 978-90-04-43721-0 (e-book)

Contents

Figures and Tables

Figures

Tables

Introduction

*Pieter B. Hartog, Shulamit Laderman, Vered Tohar, and
Archibald L.H.M. van Wieringen*

It seems that the concept of a holy place is as old as the concept of religion itself, if not older. Holy places are a source for empowerment, but they are also a major ground for confrontations between cultures and ethnic groups. This volume is not intended to blur conflicts, but rather to observe and analyse them from the perspective of cultural studies.

Although holiness is an abstract concept, the holy place is a concrete one. We tend to attribute holiness to a certain geographical location, and this location tends to become a space which transcends human lives and human time. Under the impression that the 21st century has ushered in a new and increased interest in the idea of holiness and the dialogue between the holy and the sacred, this volume wishes to propose a contribution to the subject dedicated to the geographical and metaphysical aspects of this issue.

Holy places play a leading role in many religious traditions. Most important to Judaism, Christianity and Islam, Jerusalem is considered to be a holy city and a religious centre that contains numerous sacred places. Occupying a place of pride in the experience of believers, the sacred places commemorate historical events or venerate awe-inspiring features in nature.

Although at first it appears that holy places are only significant to the adherents of a specific religion and not to those of other beliefs, upon closer investigation the matter is more complex. Often a holy place seeks to obscure an earlier or simultaneous veneration of the same spot by a different religion.

Holy places continue to display a multi-religious character despite religious and political efforts to obscure that fact. Curiously, despite the antagonism that often exists between two religions, a site's sanctification by one religion seems to attract veneration by another. Apparently, the rejection of holy places by one religion does not always lead to physical distancing by another.

This volume is the outcome of a multi-disciplinary international conference that took place at the Schechter Institute in Jerusalem in May 2018, with the participation of Israeli, American, and Dutch scholars. The fields of interest which were represented were Jewish thought, anthropology, geography, Jewish literature, biblical studies, rabbinic studies, liturgy studies, communication studies, Israel studies, and Islam studies.

© PIETER B. HARTOG ET AL., 2021 | DOI:10.1163/9789004437210_002

This is the 37th volume which has been published in the Jewish and Christian Perspectives series of Brill publishing house. This project has been ongoing for over 15 years, dealing with cultural aspects of the three monotheistic religions: Judaism, Christianity and Islam and their continuing interaction. We hope that the articles in this volume will contribute to the study of holy places as a focus of interest for varied disciplines.

Contents of the Volume

This volume comprises eighteen articles. Four of them focus on sacred sites in the Netherlands, two on sacred sites in Israel, and one on a sacred site in Asia Minor. One deals with a current museum, one with PC games, and one with art. The other eight articles focus on literary writings. This wide spectrum of cultural phenomena and their interpretation demonstrates the interest in holy places by the scholarly community in our days.

Doron Bar discusses the attitude towards the graves of the Zionist leaders. In his article he argues that the diminished attention accorded to sites associated with the Zionist past is a result of the many changes that Israeli society has undergone in the past few decades. During the early years of statehood there was a strong need to bind together the different communities gathered from the Diaspora, and civic holy sites—many of them tombs of Zionist visionaries and heroes—were used as a powerful tool to create national empathy and forge national identity. More recently, however, as Israelis feel more secure as a society, they no longer need this Zionist "cult" and sites such as Mount Herzl are almost devoid of pilgrims.

On dealing with Nazareth, Cana, Kursi (= Gergesa), Bethsaida, Korazim and Capernaum, places which are mentioned in the Gospels where Jesus is reported to have worked miracles, Eyal Ben-Eliyahu is of the opinion that this is the reason why these evolved into sites of Christian pilgrimage during the Byzantine period. Jews lived in all of these places, but the mention of these settlements is very limited or non-existent in rabbinic literature. This is not a mere coincidence. The evolution of spaces in the land of Israel as sacred to Christianity and the phenomenon of pilgrimage to sites in which miracles were attributed to Jesus reflected the Christianisation of the Galilee. This is the backdrop to the sages' deliberate strategy of ignoring these sites in rabbinic literature.

Frank G. Bosman notes that the PC games *The Talos Principle* and *The Turing Test* combine the ludological form of the maze, intended to prevent reaching the end, with the narratological form of the labyrinth, intended to stimulate the player to reflect upon his/her life. For gamers, these games function as postmodern pilgrimages in search for the experience of holiness.

Katia Cytryn-Silverman discusses the Dome of the Rock from the perspective of art and architecture and in light of its historical and mythological context. By tightly linking the Rock to biblical figures such as Adam and Abraham, who are both also identified with the construction of the Kaaba, Jerusalem became not third in importance for Islam after Mecca and Medina, but at least an equal to the site towards which all Muslims pray.

Steven Fine considers questions of multi-religious and ideological confrontation in regard to the holy concerning the Sardis synagogue. This synagogue stands as a monument of a wealthy, powerful, and well-integrated Jewish community of a kind that scarcely existed throughout Jewish history until most recent times. It reflects the status of Jews in the very centre of Roman Sardis, apparently having no ambiguity or insecurity. Fine claims that we do not have enough evidence for the life of this community to judge whether it suffered confrontations. What is clear, however, is that whatever problems did come along down the road, the Jewish community at Sardis—with its "cathedral synagogue"—withstood them, and that the decline of this distinctly Jewish holy place was part and parcel of the destruction of Sardis by the invading Sasanians in 616 CE.

David Frankel focuses on Ps 47 as having a major role in Sigmund Mowinckel's famous and controversial hypothesis concerning the existence of an ancient Israelite New Year festival of divine enthronement. Although Ps 47 was differently interpreted by the early religious traditions of Judaism and Christianity, the author suggests that it must be read in its original context. This shows that it combines a strong sense of political nationalism with a robust and inclusive universalistic impulse.

Pieter B. Hartog explores the connection between sacred spaces, the cultural and religious identities of their visitors, and ideals of universal knowledge in the early Roman Empire. Hartog argues that visits to sacred spaces activated aspects of the multi-faceted identities of their visitors that would not, or less easily, have been activated elsewhere. These aspects often appeal to an ideal of universal knowledge, as literary works from the early Roman Empire could represent sacred spaces as loci of universal wisdom. As a result, these sacred spaces obtained a transformative potential that stimulated their visitors to embrace global wisdom and to construct a localised cultural or religious identity for themselves. The results of this study and the theoretical framework it adopts challenges the distinction between "Judaean," "Christian," "Greek," and other groups, and the apologetic readings that imply such distinctions. The message of Christ, as Luke's Paul formulates it, is a multi-layered and context-dependent global mélange that takes up elements from a wide range of other traditions in the Roman Empire without implying that these other traditions have become invalid with the advent of Christianity, even if they have been revealed to provide only partial wisdom.

Willem Jan de Hek describes a public ritual that has taken place in the heart of the Oosterpark neighbourhood in Amsterdam since 2012. This ritual was designed for, and has been annually organized at, this particular location, taking into account its historical context. De Hek uses the public ritual at Kastanjeplein as a case-study to illustrate how sacredness can be seen as a dynamic concept. Sacredness is experienced in the dynamical and complex interaction between the attribution of otherworldly meaning and value to an urban environment on the one hand, and certain situational typologies of sacred place on the other. De Hek illustrates how sensing the sacred in the everyday world seems to relate to the experience of the fulfilment of emotive human desires, resulting in the attribution of otherworldly meaning and value to the environment in which the experience occurred.

Robin B. ten Hoopen notes that the Eden narrative in Gen 2:4–3:24 does not contain explicit references to a temple, sacredness or holiness. It might thus come as a surprise that both ancient and more recent interpretations of this narrative attest that the garden in Eden is a sanctuary, a depiction that implies concerns about holiness and purity. His article discusses whether the idea of the garden in Eden as a holy place was already part of the Eden narrative as it is found in the book of Genesis or should be seen as part of the reception history of the story, founded on a desire to connect the garden and the temple in Jerusalem. Particular attention is given to Ancient Near Eastern sources that have been used to contextualize and interpret the story. This illustrates how this holy place has become a metaphorical place of ideological confrontation.

Tamar Kadari and Gila Vachman contribute to the understanding of the importance of Jerusalem and Hebron as foci of pilgrimage during the early Islamic period by analysing an 11th-century addition to MS Oxford Bodleian library 102 featuring midrash Song of Songs Rabbah. On the basis of the presence of the name Elijah, the term "the poor of Jerusalem," and the mention of the Cave in Jerusalem and the Cave of Machpelah, Kadari and Vachman conclude that this is a late addition to the midrash.

Gert van Klinken deals with the impact of secularization in Dutch society, which has found its way into current school programs. Thus, the perception of holy places shows a shift away from Christianity to pre-Christian or pagan roots of holy sites. The interpretation of holy sites is moving away from a Christian interpretation of holiness towards a vindication of secular principles of human bonding. As this trend is reflected in the curriculum of secondary schools, the traditional exposition of Christianisation is becoming hard to maintain. A modern treatment of the subject requires both a careful assessment of material (archaeological) data and a willingness to explore non-religious explanations of what was formerly understood as a clash between two sets of religious beliefs (Christianity and paganism).

Shulamit Laderman explores a selection of works of art that describe Jerusalem in light of Maurice Halbwachs's theory of collective memory. Viewing Jewish, Christian, and Islamic artistic images of cultural memories helps her to understand the way in which Jerusalem has been visualized not as a reflection of how the city actually appeared throughout different periods, but rather as how it was perceived by artists, especially during periods in which they had no physical access to the city. The collective memory of Jerusalem in Jewish artistic works is based on the destruction of the Temple and of Jerusalem and the desire to preserve the memory of the Temple as a symbol of God's presence. The collective memory of Jerusalem for Christians is grounded in the events surrounding Jesus's life and death that became signs of his divine nature, and, in time, were hallowed, with Jerusalem being thought of as the hub of the universe and the Church of the Holy Sepulchre as its centre. The collective memory of Jerusalem for Muslims is influenced by concepts such as the *'even ha-shtiya*, upon which the Dome of the Rock was built.

Leon Mock raises the question as to whether and how a religious building can be re-used by another religious tradition. He describes a recent case of converting a church building into a synagogue in Amstelveen, the Netherlands. This case was commented upon by two authors of orthodox rabbinic responsa, a rabbi of the orthodox Dutch Jewish Community, and the other from Israel. Mock analyses their arguments so as to see what their perspectives are on Christianity from a halakhic standpoint, and whether the cultural background has some influence on the discourse.

Eric Ottenheijm is of the opinion that the museum "Inn of the Good Samaritan" in the Judaean Desert stages an impressive choreography of plurality of cultures and religions, inculcating civic ethos using an alleged local story. Samaritan, Christian, and Jewish culture are all visibly presented in such ways as to create a multi-religious context buttressing the parable's message of how to become a neighbour. Moreover, the performance of the Christian parable in the museum reclaims it as local culture and as part of early Jewish heritage, abandoning notions of theological supremacy.

Eyal Regev discusses two texts which deal with the Temple and sacredness—the biblical book of Psalms and the Temple Scroll found in cave 11 in Qumran. He argues that different people with different ideologies or agendas may experience the same geographical sacred space in very different ways. A holy place is not merely a site to which people ascribe sacred traditions and rites, but it is rather a space to which people attach meaning in various ways, even within the same religious tradition.

Lieve M. Teugels focuses on the religious repurposing of synagogues. In most cases in the Netherlands, this means that the synagogues came to be used as churches or for other activities related to Christian religious communities. In the case of the great synagogue of The Hague, which is at the centre of her contribution, the synagogue was converted into a mosque. She uses the anthropological term "iconic field" to describe the various factors at work in the emotional reactions of old and new congregants, and neighbours, with respect to the repurposing of religious buildings. This concept provides a vision of holiness that is related more to emotions than to rules.

Vered Tohar focuses on Jewish folktales describing the miraculous wandering of the remains of the holy Temple all over the land of Israel, the Middle East and Europe, spreading holiness by serving as the basis for new synagogues. These narrative traditions confirm a primeval connection between the concepts of holiness, space, and symbolic object in Jewish culture.

Archibald L.H.M. van Wieringen describes how Jerusalem is made present in biblical texts without being mentioned, by using an alternative expression, or by being a part of a technical expression. This leads to the conclusion that the textual Jerusalem does not fully coincide with the historical Jerusalem. A reading of sacred texts in which the world of the text has a one-to-one relation with the world outside the text can be considered to be a kind of theological fundamentalism.

Lastly, the editors express their gratitude to Maurits Sinninghe Damsté, who has corrected the English of this volume.

Many of the contributions to this volume are multi-disciplinary and deal with issues of holiness from a diachronic perspective. Moreover, most of the articles refer in one way or another to Jerusalem as a focus of holiness for all three monotheistic religions. As the title of the volume suggests, Jerusalem is the principal subject of nearly all the essays. The city always has been and continues to be the central protagonist in the major drama of holy space in the three monotheistic religions, which is why we decided to arrange the eighteen articles in alphabetical order. If we had divided them into artificially devised sections, the reader would have missed the diversity and complexity that characterize each article and the volume as a whole. Thus, we preferred to skip the obvious and to challenge the expected. We prefer to let the reader roam among the subjects, the disciplines, and the areas of discussion. We see the reader of this volume as one who wanders along the timeline and seeks to experience an intellectual journey through the texts and their scholarly interpretations. Reading the volume this way will endow the reader with the essence of the mystery and transcendental features that create holy spaces. This kind of reading emphasises that, taken together, the contributions to this volume create one big picture built up of many small details.

This collective research not only demonstrates the variety in the study of holy places, but also the flexibility of the concept of holiness through geographic and historic aspects. From a diachronic perspective, holiness is an always changing idea, helping to shape group identities all the way from ancient times to our days.

CHAPTER 1

Graves as Holy Places? The Development of Jewish and National Sacred Space in the State of Israel, 1948–1967

Doron Bar

The land of Israel is blessed with an abundance of holy places that have attracted pilgrims for centuries. The uniqueness of this region as the cradle of Judaism and Christianity, together with its centrality to Islam, engendered the development of dozens of sacred sites, most of them graves of kings, prophets, and saints, places that have been revered over the centuries by local and foreign pilgrims.

The veneration of saints is a universal phenomenon in both monotheistic and polytheistic creeds.[1] Saints are perceived as intermediaries between man and god—and in this sense Judaism is not different. From at least the Crusader period until today, Jewish pilgrims have venerated a variety of sacred sites, most of which are tombs of Jewish saints. The graves function as cairns, claim stakes to assert Judaism's historical presence in this region. They are also perceived as tangible evidence that Judaism once flourished in this holy landscape.

Against this almost unbroken history of Jewish tomb veneration, the period between 1948 and 1967 is exceptional. The division of the land into two separate political entities, the State of Israel and the Hashemite Kingdom of Jordan, changed the region by forcing a separation between the region's inhabitants and their sacred shrines. These were now often in inaccessible parts of the land. This was true for Muslims and Christians,[2] but it was especially the case for the Jews, living in the State of Israel, who were cut off from most of their sacred sites.[3]

---

1 Peter Brown, *The Cult of the Saints: Its Rise and Function in Latin Christianity* (Chicago: University of Chicago Press, 1981); David M. Gitlitz and Linda Kay Davidson, *Pilgrimage and the Jews* (Westport, CT: Praeger, 2006).

2 Chaim Wardi, *Christians in Israel: A Survey* (Jerusalem: Ministry of Religious Affairs, 1950); Shaul Colbi, *Christianity in the Holy Land: Past and Present* (Tel Aviv: Am Hasefer, 1969), 124–57.

3 Doron Bar, "Re-Creating Jewish Sanctity in Jerusalem; The Case of Mount Zion and David's Tomb Between 1948–1967," *The Journal of Israeli History* 23 (2004): 233–51; Doron

© DORON BAR, 2021 | DOI:10.1163/9789004437210_003

This separation of the Jewish population from most of its sacred sites brought about the re-designing of sacred space in the State of Israel. The development of the map of Jewish sacred sites during these nineteen years was manifested in various ways, the central one being the emphasis on and the signalization of some sacred places that had held minor importance before the war and their development into central and important pilgrimage centres. Between 1948 and 1967, sacred tombs such as King David's Tomb in Jerusalem or the dozens of tombs of the sages in the Galilee attained great importance and were the focus of the Israeli Ministry of Religious Affairs (hereafter, MRA).

Parallel to the development of popular-traditional-historical Jewish holy sites, additional types of sacred tombs emerged. These were Zionist holy sites where various "prophets" of Zionism were buried. Beginning in the late nineteenth century, the Zionist Movement began to develop places of national symbolic significance. Zionist holy sites such as Tel Hai, Modiin, and Masada were added to the roster of religious-historical sites of symbolic significance.[4] Before 1948 and during the early days of Zionism, these were the tombs of Joseph Trumpeldor, Max Nurdau, or Yehoshua Hankin, which were seen as symbolical holy sites.[5] Following the establishment of the State of Israel in 1948 additional landmarks of national memory were designated and developed throughout the country—battle sites, monuments, historical buildings, and also additional sacred graves. The reinterment in Israel's soil of Jewish notables and exemplary figures who died and were buried overseas was part of this process.

This paper discusses the parallel development of these two types of sacred graves. On the one hand the popular-religious holy tombs, where biblical and rabbinic figures were buried; and on the other hand the sacred tombs where the visionaries of Zionism were buried during the years 1948–1967.

Bar, *Sanctifying a Land: The Jewish Holy Places in the State of Israel, 1948–1968* (Jerusalem: Ben-Gurion Institute in the Negev, 2007) (Hebrew).

4   Yael Zerubavel, "The Historic, the Legendary, and the Incredible: Invented Tradition and Collective Memory in Israel," in *Commemorations: The Politics of National Identity*, ed. John R. Gillis (Princeton: Princeton University Press, 1994), 105–123; Nachman Ben Yehuda, *Sacrificing Truth: Archaeology and the Myth of Masada* (Amherst, NY: Humanity Books, 2002).

5   Yair Shapiro, "Max Nordau and the Reinterment of Jewish and Zionist Leaders in the Land of Israel" (MA thesis, Hebrew University of Jerusalem, 2010) (Hebrew).

1   Jewish and Zionist Holy Sites before and after 1948

Judaism's attitude towards pilgrimage and worship at holy places has always been ambivalent. A prolonged history as a dispersed minority with neither political sovereignty nor control of territory dictated a unique reliance on time as a dimension sanctifying the universe and existence.[6]

Although our knowledge about the existence and status of Jewish holy sites during the first millennium CE, after the destruction of the Temple in Jerusalem, is insufficient, it is clear that after the Crusader period, from the twelfth century on, a distinctly Jewish sacred space began to emerge. It appears that the Crusader regime in the region, and the area's later reoccupation by the Muslims, presented Palestinian Jewry with a complex religious challenge and led to the development and expansion of an array of Jewish holy places that were based on ancient myths relating mainly to the biblical, mishnaic and talmudic periods.[7] During the later Muslim period, from the thirteenth century on, holy sites were points of destination both for Jewish inhabitants of the region and for the relatively numerous Jewish pilgrims who came to Palestine from elsewhere in the Middle East, and from Europe.[8] Toward the end of Ottoman rule in Palestine, prior to the arrival of the British, Jewish sacred space in the region consisted of several tens of pilgrimage sites scattered across various areas within Palestine, most of them sacred tombs.[9]

Jerusalem was the most significant place within the Holy Land's Jewish sacred space. Jewish pilgrims who arrived in Jerusalem during this period were able to visit some twenty holy sites.[10] Pilgrimage to these sites generally took place in accordance with the Hebrew calendar and the dates of the various Jewish holidays. The Western Wall was considered the holiest Jewish site. Of the other holy places, Rachel's Tomb near Bethlehem, the Cave of the Patriarchs in Hebron and Samuel's Tomb to the north of Jerusalem, which were relatively

6   Yoram Bilu, "The Renewal of Rituals at Holy Sites in Israel: The Contribution from Those of Moroccan Descent," in *To the Graves of the Righteous: Pilgrimages to Tombs and "Hilulot" in Israel*, ed. Rivka Gonen (Jerusalem: Israel Museum, 1998), 27–46 (Hebrew).

7   Elchanan Reiner, "All the Rivers Flow Into the Sea: Pilgrimage to Jerusalem following the destruction of the Second Temple" (Unpublished paper, 2005) (Hebrew).

8   Josef W. Meri, *The Cult of Saints Among Muslim and Jews in Medieval Syria* (Oxford: Oxford University Press, 2002).

9   Dotan Goren, *A Redeemer will Come to Zion: Jewish Efforts to Obtain a Foothold in the Holy Place in Jerusalem and its Surroundings in Late Ottoman Period (1840–1918)* (Jerusalem: Beitel Library, 2017) (Hebrew).

10   Handwritten list entitled "The Holy Places in Jerusalem and its Environs," Central Zionist Archive, J1/3388.

far from the city, were apparently the most prominent.[11] Over the years, a wide array of traditions, customs, myths, and rituals developed at these sites.

Parallel to the development of Jewish sacred space, a Zionist symbolical map was created. In recent years, a number of studies have focused on how the memory of the fallen and the landscape of monuments were shaped and designed[12] and how civic holy places were developed, such as those at Modiin, Tel Hai, Masada, and Biriya.[13] Recent studies shed light on how the leaders of Zionism and the State of Israel made extensive, yet selective, use of the Bible and the characters and places associated with it.[14] Archaeology occupied a major part in the development of the symbolic map and annual archeological conferences were conducted in various places in Israel.[15] Parallel to the development of sacred national space, rituals were also created. These included Independence Day ceremonies, pilgrimages to national holy places and rites linked to various holidays and to civic and religious memorial days.[16] All of these were tied to the development of Israeli Zionism and later nationalism.

A subject that has not been sufficiently investigated is the place and importance of funerals and cemeteries in shaping "Israeliness," given the public figures interred, the mass funerals witnessed by the country's population, and the ceremonies designed around them. The reinterment of the visionaries of the Zionist idea and the leaders of the national movement played an important

---

11   Abraham Moses Luncz, *Guide to the Land of Israel and Syria* (Jerusalem: Abraham Moses Luncz, 1891), 168–87 (Hebrew).

12   Ilana Shamir, *Gal-Ed: Memorials for the Fallen in the Wars of Israel* (Tel Aviv: Ministry of Defense Press, 1989) (Hebrew); Maoz Azaryahu, *State Cults: Celebrating Independence and Commemorating the Fallen in Israel, 1948–1956* (Sde Boqer: Ben Gurion Research Institute, 1995) (Hebrew).

13   Mooli Brog, "Gymnasia Herzliya in Tel Aviv Discovers the Maccabees' Tombs, 1907–1911: The Shaping of Collective Memory and National Identity," *Iyonim Betkomat Israel* 20 (2010): 169–92 (Hebrew); Maoz Azaryahu, "The Mythic Geography of the 11th of Adar: From Tel Hai to Birya and Eilat," *Horizons in Geography* 46–47 (1997): 9–20 (Hebrew).

14   Anita Shapira, *The Bible and Israeli Identity* (Jerusalem: Magnes Press, 2005) (Hebrew); Anita Shapira, *Jews, Zionists and In-Between* (Tel Aviv: Am Oved, 2007), 163–196 (Hebrew).

15   Michael Feige, "Archaeology, Anthropology and the Development Town: Constructing the Israeli Place," *Zion* 62 (1998): 441–59 (Hebrew); Michael Feige and Zvi Shiloni, eds., *Archaeology and Nationalism in Eretz Israel* (Sde Boqer: Ben-Gurion Research Institute, 2008) (Hebrew); Yaakov Shavit, "Archaeology, Political Culture, and Culture in Israel," in *The Archaeology of Israel: Constructing the Past, Interpreting the Present*, ed. Neil Asher Silberman and David Small (Sheffield: Sheffield Academic Press, 1997), 48–61; Raz Kletter, *Just Past? The Making of Israeli Archaeology* (London: Equinox Publishing, 2005).

16   Don Handelman and Elihu Katz, "State Ceremonies in Israel: Remembrance Day and Independence Day," in *Models and Mirrors, Towards an Anthropology of Public Events*, ed. Don Handelman (New York: Berghahn Books, 1998), 202–12; *Splendor and Glory: Israel's Rituals of Sovereignty, 1948–1958* (Tel Aviv: Tel Aviv Museum of Art, 2001) (Hebrew).

role in shaping memory and forging a national consciousness that was connected with changes that occurred in the years before and after 1948.[17]

2   The Development of Jewish Sacred Space after 1948

Even as Israel's War of Independence was raging, and before the cease-fire agreement with the various Arab states that participated in the warfare was reached, the newly established MRA began to arrange and develop sacred Jewish space within the as-yet amorphous boundaries of the young state. MRA director-general Samuel Zanwil Kahana argued that it was now imperative to imprint a traditional Jewish character on the Israeli landscape—a rather new agenda, the purpose of which was to link the ancient history of the land of Israel to the current history-in-the-making of the State of Israel.[18]

As no systematic information regarding the Jewish sacred sites was at hand, Kahana was forced to gather information on the location of the sacred sites and the rituals that were customarily performed there. The data were gathered from locals: rabbis, guides, and teachers.[19] The joint enterprise between the MRA and local initiatives, whether private people who were involved in the identification and development of the sacred sites, or various local religious associations, brought about an enormous change in the Jewish sacred sites map and a sharp increase in the number of sacred sites that were now identified and introduced to wider sectors of the Israeli public.[20]

One example for Kahana's initiative is the Cave of the Sanhedrin in Jerusalem, a sacred place where, according to the Jewish tradition, more than seventy Jewish elders were buried during the late Second Temple Period. The place was turned into one of the MRA's main centres of activity in Jerusalem and the cave played an important role in the creation of Jewish sacred space in the western part of divided Jerusalem.[21] Another example of Jewish ownership of sacred space before 1948 is the tomb of Rabbi Shimon bar Yoḥai (Rashbi in

---

17   Doron Bar, *Landscape and Ideology: Reinterment of Renowned Jews in the Land of Israel, 1904–1967* (Berlin: De Gruyter, 2016).

18   Israel State Archive, GL 15/14917, July 20, 1948.

19   Israel State Archive, GL 15/14917, March 3, 1949, a letter from S.Z. Kahana; Doron Bar, "Holy Places or Historical Sites? Defining Sacred and Archaeological Sites in the State of Israel, 1948–1967," *History of Religions* 58 (2018): 1–23.

20   See, for example, Israel State Archive, GL 5/14939, November 29, 1949, B. Fishman, director of the Department of Land Registration and Regularization, to the director of the Religious Affairs Department.

21   Doron Bar, "Holy Sites and Pilgrimage in Western Jerusalem, 1948–1967," *Eretz Israel* 28 (2007): 331–38 (Hebrew).

initials) near the Arab village of Meiron, which was an active pilgrimage site for Jews and Muslims for generations prior to 1948.[22] Jews acquired ownership of this sacred Galilean place in the nineteenth century. For generations Jews had frequented the place, especially during the feast of Lag Ba-ʾOmer, when it was customary to take part in the annual regional *hiloola* (a celebration, usually on the day when the Tsaddik passed away). After 1948 this pilgrimage was turned into a mass event, an annual gathering of thousands of worshippers in this remote Galilean settlement.[23] The annual pilgrimage to the site was made into a joint operation of different state agents, particularly the MRA.

Sacred sites held by Muslims prior to the 1948 War and Judaized later, occupy a major part of the Jewish map of sacred space. Although even before the division of the region Jews regularly frequented many of these sacred sites, ownership of these places remained in Muslim hands and many of the sacred sites were in fact run by the Islamic charitable foundation (Waqf). Jews were usually allowed to visit these places only during certain days and only after paying entrance fees. The political, military, and, most importantly, demographic changes that took place after 1948 led to the extraction of different areas in Palestine from their original Arab population, and to the transfer of the sacred sites in those areas to Israeli sovereignty.[24] The Jewish hold over these places was enforced by the semi-official operations of a number of organizations, committees, and societies that were encouraged by Kahana. One of the more extraordinary consequences of this process was the erasure of the Muslim past of these sacred places and the emphasis on Jewish traditions connected to them.[25]

In many places where Muslims and Jews alike believed in the sacredness of the figure buried in the site, the identity of the place was kept, with Jews now possessing the sacred place. This was true for King David's Tomb on Mount Zion, a Muslim pilgrimage destination for centuries which had long been known as Nebi Daud.[26] In other instances, where Jews occupied former Muslim sacred sites, the identity of the sacred place was altered as the Jewish heritage of the place was highlighted at the expense of other traditions. Thus, for example, the Tomb of Ali Abu Hurayra in Yavneh was developed as the tomb

---

22   Zeev Vilnay, *Sepulchral Monuments in Palestine* (Jerusalem: Mosad Harav Kook, 1951), 54, 297–307 (Hebrew).

23   Vilnay, *Sepulchral Monuments*, 134–50.

24   Yoav Gelber, *Palestine, 1948: War, Escape and the Emergence of the Palestinian Refugee Problem* (Portland, OR.: Sussex Academic Press, 2001).

25   Doron Bar, "Between Muslim and Jewish Sanctity: Judaizing Muslim Holy Places in the State of Israel, 1948–1967," *Journal of Historical Geography* 59 (2018): 68–76.

26   Bar, "Re-Creating."

of Rabban Gamliel, the *nasi* (president) of the Jewish Sanhedrin.[27] Following
the 1948 War, this Muslim tomb with its typical cupola was converted into a
Jewish sacred place, gradually drawing more and more Jewish worshippers.[28]
The change in Yavneh had a lot to do with the new local Jewish settlers, immigrants who came primarily from Arab countries to settle in the nearby vacated
Arab village of Yubna. These settlers adopted the adjacent tomb and reused it
as the tomb of Rabban Gamliel. As in many similar cases throughout the State
of Israel, the tradition that connected Jews to Yavneh was not unfounded, and
was based mainly on the literature of Medieval Jewish pilgrims, who frequently mentioned visits to that place.[29]

Besides Rabban Gamliel's tomb in Yavneh, where the Muslim history of
the site was obliterated and replaced by Jewish traditions, there are additional examples where such a process also took place: the Muslim sacred site of
Nebi Yemin near the city of Kfar Saba, which was converted into the tomb of
Benjamin, son of Jacob;[30] the tomb of Judah was sanctified in the small town
of Yahud;[31] and on the main road connecting Tel Aviv to Jerusalem, near the
immigrant town of Beit Shemesh, the tomb of Sheikh Gherib was transformed
into the tomb of Dan.[32] One of the areas where this process was particularly
evident was the Galilee. There, many Muslim sacred sites, usually tombs of
local Muslim saints, were converted and their past obliterated as their Jewish
connection was being emphasized.[33]

This process was most prominent in the case of King David's Tomb on Mount
Zion.[34] This tomb, which, prior to the division of Jerusalem, had drawn only a
relatively small number of Jewish worshippers, and then mainly on the day
after Shavuot (Feast of Weeks), became the most important Jewish ritual and
folklore centre in Jerusalem and Israel as a whole during the 1950s.[35] Together

---

27   Hana Taragan, "Baybars and the Tomb of Abu Hurayra/Rabban Gamliel in Yavneh,"
      Cathedra 97 (2000): 65–84 (Hebrew).

28   Leon A. Mayer, Yaakov Pinkerfeld, and Chaim Z. Hirschberg, *Muslim Religious Buildings in
      Israel* (Jerusalem: Ministry of Religious Affairs, 1950), 17–21 (Hebrew).

29   Bar, *Sanctifying*, 180–89.

30   Israel State Archive, GL 5/14908, January 30, 1957.

31   Israel State Archive, GL-6/14918, January 30, 1962, A. Meir to S.Z. Kahana.

32   Israel State Archive, G-7/5586, September 26, 1954; Avi Sasson, "The 'Tomb of Dan' in the
      Shephelah of Judah," *Judea and Samaria Research Studies* 10 (2001): 7–18 (Hebrew).

33   Vilnay, *Sepulchral Monuments*, 52–55; Doron Bar, "Jewish Holy Sites in the Galilee: 1948–
      1967," in *New Galilee Studies: Tenth Anniversary Volume of the Galilee Research Conference,*
      ed. Tziyona Grossmark et al. (Tel Hai: Tel Hai Academic College, 2009), 132–52 (Hebrew).

34   Doron Bar, "Re-Creating," 233–51.

35   Doron Bar, "Reconstructing the Past: The Creation of Jewish Sacred Space in the State of
      Israel, 1948–1967," *Israel Studies* 13:3 (2008): 1–21.

with the "Mount Zion Committee" which he headed, Kahana cultivated Mount Zion as the main Israeli national-religious sacred site. He transposed to that site many traditions that were celebrated in other pilgrimage destinations, such as Rachel's Tomb or the Western Wall, before 1948. These were now channeled to Mount Zion and marked by a complex set of ceremonies, rituals, exhibitions, and other events spread throughout the year. Mount Zion, which offers an impressive panorama of the eastern, then inaccessible part of Jerusalem, was used as a memorial site for the other Jewish sacred sites that remained behind the cease-fire line.

3   Reinterment and the Development of National Sacred Space

With the onset of the Zionist movement's activity in the land of Israel during the late Ottoman period, Zionist holy sites were created on top of the existing religious symbols. During the Mandate period and following 1948 and the establishment of Israel, this process intensified as additional sacred places were added to the map of the newborn state. This is the background of the phenomenon discussed here, the reinterment of dozens of historical figures and the development of their graves into national holy sites.

The remains of Hannah Szenes, a member of the group of Jewish men and women parachutists from Palestine who had volunteered to join the British army and to parachute into German-occupied Europe, were brought to the military cemetery in Jerusalem (1950) and buried alongside those of fallen soldiers from the 1948 war. The ashes of Colonel Eliezer Margolin, commander of a battalion of Jewish volunteers from Palestine who fought in World War I, were brought from Australia and buried in the Rehovot cemetery (1950), while the coffin of the writer Peretz Smolenskin, who died in a resort town in northern Italy in 1885, was reinterred in 1952 in the Givat Shaul cemetery in Jerusalem, in a section that was slated to become "the nation's pantheon." These were Zionist thinkers, political leaders, intellectuals, philanthropists, poets, and writers, as well as heroes and fighters. All of these, dozens of Zionist figures, were buried for a second time in Israeli soil. This was through the efforts of various agents and groups, single and organized bodies, which all reburied their historical heroes in Israel.

The catalyst for the Zionist idea of reburial was Herzl's last will and testament, in which he asked in 1904 to be buried in the land of Israel.[36] Likewise,

---

36   Alex Bein, *Theodor Herzl: A Biography* (Jerusalem: Zionist Library, 1977), 409 (Hebrew): "I wish to be buried in a metal coffin, in the cemetery plot next to my father, and I will lie there until the people of Israel transfer my body to the land of Israel."

the will of David Wolffsohn, Herzl's successor as president of the World Zionist Organization, indicated the land of Israel as his desired place of reinterment. Herzl's request was not executed during the years of the British Mandate, despite extensive Zionist activity aimed at bringing deceased heroes for burial in the Jewish homeland. Tel Aviv was at the center of this activity. Its energetic mayor, Meir Dizengoff, succeeded in reinterring Max Nordau in the city in 1926, followed by the reburial of other Zionist public figures.[37] Yehuda Leib Pinsker, Leo Motzkin, and others were reinterred in Jerusalem.[38]

The 1948 war and the establishment of the State of Israel immediately changed the relationship between Jerusalem and the Zionist movement. The declaration of Jerusalem as the capital of Israel accorded it a unique status. The glow of Tel Aviv's cemetery as a nationalist-Zionist symbol dimmed, and it became more of a municipal cemetery while the status of Jerusalem was intensified. Reinterment became institutionalized after the founding of the state, as the remains of many key figures were repatriated. The realization of the idea of a Hebrew state enabled Herzl's wish to be fulfilled, and his burial in 1949 became a seminal event.[39] The grave of Herzl, the military cemetery, and the section reserved for the nation's leaders combined to create an impressive symbolic site that reinforced Jerusalem's status as the capital of Israel.[40] David Wolffsohn, Nahum Sokolow, and Zeev Jabotinsky were among those buried there; all of them helped establish and reinforce the elevated, national status of Mount Herzl.

Since regulations stipulated that only presidents of the World Zionist Organization could be buried alongside Herzl, a proposal was made to designate a separate national burial section in Jerusalem's new cemetery in Givat Shaul. A public committee determined that "the location of the [national] pantheon will not be on Mount Herzl, which will remain an exclusive memorial

---

37   Tzvi Kroll and Tzadok Linman, *Tel Aviv's Old Cemetery's Book* (Tel Aviv: Sefer, 1940) (Hebrew); Barbara Mann, "Modernism and the Zionist Uncanny: Reading the Old Cemetery in Tel Aviv," *Representations* 69 (2000): 63–95; Doron Bar, "The Debate between Tel Aviv and Jerusalem in Mandatory Palestine (1920–48) over the Reinterment of Zionist Leaders," *Israel Affairs* 21 (2015): 500–15.

38   Yair Shapiro, "The Nicanor Tomb Cave on Mount Scopus: A Precedent for Mount Herzl," *Eretz Israel* 28 (2007): 454–62 (Hebrew).

39   Michal Naor Wiernik and Doron Bar, "The Competition for the Design and Development of Herzl's Tomb and Mount Herzl, 1949–1960," *Cathedra* 144 (2012): 107–36 (Hebrew).

40   Maoz Azaryahu, "Mount Herzl: the Creation of Israel's National Cemetery," *Israel Studies* 1 (2006): 46–74.

to the creator of Zionism,"[41] but instead on the hill at the western entrance to Jerusalem, where the city's new cemetery was established.[42] Naftali Herz Imber, Peretz Smolenskin and Zvi Herman Shapira were among the many Zionist notables buried in this cemetery.

Thus, while the Tomb of the Unknown Soldier became the official symbol of the nation in most European countries, a site where groups of citizens lay wreaths and foreign statesmen express their esteem for the host country,[43] it was Herzl's grave that became the most important civic holy place in the State of Israel. The graves of Herzl and other visionaries and leaders whose bones were brought for burial in Israel became prominent sites that served to remind the residents of those who gave their lives for the nation, whether as soldiers and heroes or as visionaries and leaders. The stories of their lives, deaths, burials, and reinterments were conveyed to the public as a heritage to remember and internalize, and their grave sites were cultivated as centres of pilgrimage.

4   The 1967 War and Its Influence on the Jewish and National Sacred Space

As with the 1948 war, the Six-Day War had a tremendous influence on most aspects of life in the State of Israel, and the issue of worship at holy sites was no exception. The occupation of Judea and Samaria, as well as East Jerusalem, had far-reaching consequences that made it possible for Jews to visit their historically sacred sites in an almost unlimited manner. After nineteen years of forced separation, 1967 ushered in a period of intensive activity at the Western Wall and other places in these areas.[44] Not only was it now possible for Jews to freely visit Joseph's Tomb next to Nablus, the Tomb of Samuel the Prophet, and the Cave of the Patriarchs, but the very fact that this space fell under Israeli jurisdiction meant that control, supervision, and development of the holy sites became Israel's responsibility and obliged the country's leaders to face the

41   Israel State Archive, GL 1087/8, memorandum from the meeting of the Public Committee for Reinterring Smolinsky, 6 February 1952.

42   See the map of the cemetery at CZA MM/836/6; Doron Bar, "'Nation's Pantheon' in Jerusalem," *Et-Mol* 228 (2013): 32–35 (Hebrew).

43   Laura Wittman, *The Tomb of the Unknown Solider, Modern Mourning, and the Reinvention of the Mystical Body* (Toronto: University of Toronto Press, 2011).

44   Doron Bar, "The Struggle Over the Western Wall (1967–1973)," in *Study of Jerusalem Through the Ages*, ed. Yehoshua Ben Arieh et al. (Jerusalem: Yad Ben Zvi, 2015), 318–46 (Hebrew).

complex issues raised by them. At the same time the return to these sacred places led to a decisive change in the map of the holy sites that had been developed after the founding of the state. King David's Tomb on Mount Zion, as an example, suddenly lost its uniqueness and became again just one of a long list of sites sacred to Judaism in the Jerusalem area.

What was the fate of the many national holy sites that the state developed in its early years? After the 1960s, reinterment activity dwindled, as the dreams of those who had longed to be buried in Israel were largely fulfilled. The Six-Day War and the conquest of East Jerusalem, Judea, and Samaria turned the country's attention in other directions, and second funerals for notable figures became infrequent events. The political changes in Israel also had an impact. Many of those who were reinterred were icons as much as individuals, mobilized as instruments in the Israeli political arena. Herzl ostensibly belonged to "everyone," but Motzkin, Wolffsohn, Nachman Syrkin, and Ber Borochov represented the left, Labor side, and strengthened the standing of the living leaders and their parties. The political right had almost no involvement in this phenomenon during the 1950s. Perhaps after the remains of Jabotinsky were reinterred in 1964 and the remains of two Lehi members were brought from Cairo in 1975,[45] the aspirations of the Revisionist movement were fulfilled. Its motivation to reinter its people in Israel diminished as Likud established itself as a ruling party in 1977. On top of this, in the last two decades of the twentieth century, a related phenomenon spread in Israeli society—bringing the remains of prominent rabbis for burial in Israel. Mizrahi Jews, and those from North Africa in particular (especially Morocco and Tunisia), began to import the remains of their religious leaders and forefathers.[46] Unlike the Zionist reinterments, which carved out new geographic and symbolic centers in Israel, this more recent phenomenon focuses on the urban periphery—Kiryat Malachi, Netivot, Tirosh, and elsewhere. Some Israelis revere these new grave sites as holy places, such as the Baba Sali's tomb in Netivot and historical-religious sites like the graves of Shimon bar Yoḥai in Meron and Jonathan Ben Uzziel in Amuqa.

---

45   Eliyahu Hakim and Eliyahu Ben-Zuri, who assassinated Lord Moyne in Cairo in 1944 and were hanged. Ido Disenchick, *Ze'ev Jabotinsky Returns to the Homeland* (Tel Aviv: Hadar, 1965) (Hebrew).

46   Yoram Bilu, *The Saints' Impresarios: Dreamers, Healers, and Holy Men in Israel's Urban Periphery* (Haifa: Haifa University Press, 2005) (Hebrew). See also Doron Bar, "Mizrachim and the Development of Sacred Space in the State of Israel, 1948–1967," *Journal of Modern Jewish Studies* 8 (2009): 267–85.

5 Summary and Discussion

In recent years I have visited Mount Herzl a few times each year, accompanied by my students. At the end of each tour a sense of puzzlement fills me. The site is usually vacant, and apart from a few visitors who are enjoying the well-kept garden, there is almost no one who pays tribute to Herzl in his tomb.

Mount Herzl—the site of Benjamin Zeev Herzl's resting place; the "Greats of the Nation" section, where Israeli political leaders are buried; and the military cemetery—has been Israel's most important national site. During the 1950s and 1960s, as attested in newspapers, travel books, and other sources, many Israelis flocked to the mountain, and saw it as a central symbol of their national identity. Today the situation is different. The site is usually vacant (except on the eve of Independence Day), and Israelis—those who not so long ago saw Mount Herzl as a holy site and used to frequent it regularly—are not visiting anymore.

In contrast to the low number of visitors to Mount Herzl, many of the Jewish religious holy sites are flourishing. Millions visit the Western Wall each year; last Lag Ba-ʾOmer more than four hundred thousand pilgrims visited Meron, gathering around the sacred tomb of Rabbi Shimon bar Yoḥai. In Netivot, in southern Israel, the Baba Sali memorial day in honor of this Moroccan tzaddik draws tens of thousands. Pilgrimages to Meron, Netivot, and other Jewish holy places is part of a growing phenomenon that sees an increasing number of Israelis frequenting traditional holy places, praying at the tombs of saints, and considering them integral and important parts of their religious identity.

The comparison between Mount Herzl, the final resting place of Herzl, and the traditional tomb of Rabbi Shimon bar Yoḥai in Meron is not as superficial as it may seem at first glance. These two sites are part of the historical map of holy sites—religious and secular tombs—that were developed over a very long span of time. In addition to such ancient Jewish holy places as Rachel's Tomb, the Cave of the Patriarchs, or King David's tomb, the years before the establishment of the State of Israel in 1948 saw the creation of many Zionist holy places. This phenomenon expanded after 1948, when additional holy places, many of them tombs, developed and inspired pilgrimage to places that symbolized heroism, sacrifice, and independence.

One of the more interesting aspects of the cultural history of the Jewish national revival in the land of Israel has been the incorporation of the sacred in a secular-national framework.[47] Traditionally, Jewish sacred space largely

---

47   Mauz Azaryahu, "Innovation and Continuity: Jewish Tradition and the Shaping of Sovereignty Rites in Israel," in *On Both Sides of the Bridge: Religion and State in the Early*

included alleged graves of biblical figures and talmudic saints, but as the Zionist enterprise progressed, and upon the founding of the State of Israel, a new type of sacred space emerged, emphasizing mostly Jewish heroism together with Zionist martyrdom. Following the 1948 war, Zionist sacred topography was extended to include dozens of war memorials and military cemeteries.[48] These were designed to demonstrate and revere the heroic sacrifice of the fallen soldiers and the achievement of the state's independence. The cult of the fallen soldiers was based on both the ethos of patriotic sacrifice exalted in all modern nation-states and on the unique Jewish legacy of sacrifice, martyrdom, and national heroism.

During this period, when the State of Israel nurtured mainly the "cult of nationhood," stressing national elements connected to both the distant and more recent history of the land of Israel, the MRA, led by its director-general Samuel Zanwil Kahana, made parallel efforts to emphasize the Jewish-religious past of the land, especially its history as the land of the Bible and the seat of the sages from the period of the Mishnah and Talmud. Thus, not only places connected to Zionist and Israeli heroism were expected to be positioned on the Israeli map,[49] but the Galilean tombs of the saints were also declared an essential part of it. Not only were archaeological sites, such as Masada, emphasizing the Jewish heroic past, posted on the map, but also places like the "Lion's Cave" in Jerusalem and the "Light" in Modiin, were now part of sacred space.[50]

Kahana's activity in rearranging the sacred sites during the 1950s and 1960s is a clear case of "renewing" and even "inventing" a tradition, which he tried to intensify by organizing a system of religious cult and worship at the different Jewish sacred sites, most of which had not been revered before 1948. Kahana drew the legitimacy for his activities from his official position, cultivating existing traditions and creating new ones, gathering myths and assembling symbolic items at the sites that embodied their sacredness for the pilgrims.

These efforts were in fact anti-establishment activities, which were carried out in an era when the secular "cult of nationhood" rather than traditional religion was dominant. The combination of Kahana's activity, the involvement

Years of Israel, ed. Mordechai Bar-On and Zvi Zameret (Jerusalem: Yad Izhak Ben-Zvi, 2002), 273–294 (Hebrew).

48   Maoz Azaryahu, "War Memorials and the Commemoration of the Israeli War of Independence, 1948–1956," _Studies in Zionism_ 13 (1992): 57–77.

49   Amos Ron, "A Rachel for Everyone: The Kinneret Cemetery as a Site of Civil Pilgrimage," in _Sanctity of Time and Space in Tradition and Modernity_, ed. Alberdina Houtman, Marcel J.H.M. Poorthuis, and Joshua Schwartz (Leiden: Brill, 1998), 349–59.

50   Doron Bar, "The 'Lion's Cave' in Jerusalem's Mamilla Cemetery," _Et-Mol_ 231 (2014): 23–26 (Hebrew).

of individuals and various associations and organizations he established and led, and the unique geo-political situation following the 1948 war yielded a re-designing of the pilgrims' routes in the different parts of the State of Israel and led to the creation of a new, alternative map of Jewish sacred space that dominated the local landscape up until 1967.

As described in the article, following the reburial of Benjamin Zeev Herzl in Jerusalem in August 1949, Mount Herzl became a prominent locus of Israeli identity. During the 1950s and 1960s, thousands visited the site every year. These pilgrims were schoolchildren, members of youth movements, Jews from the diaspora, Israeli citizens and politicians; they visited Mount Herzl with great respect and saw it as the pinnacle of a visit to Israel and Jerusalem. Since then, however, this national site has lost its centrality and prominence in Israeli society. Apart from the eve of Independence Day, when the ceremony that opens the annual celebrations marking national independence takes place in front of Herzl's tomb,[51] the site has almost no ceremonial resonance or recognition.

The diminished attention accorded to sites associated with the Zionist past is a result of the many changes that Israeli society has undergone in the past few decades. During the early years of statehood there was a strong need to bind together the different communities gathered from the diaspora, and civic holy sites—many of them were tombs of Zionist visionaries and heroes—were used as a powerful tool to create national empathy and forge national identity. More recently, however, as Israelis feel more secure as a society, they no longer need this Zionist cult, and sites such as Mount Herzl are devoid of pilgrims. At the same time, the wide acceptance of popular Jewish holy places indicates that many Israelis feel a deep, religious need to frequent saints' tombs, where they aspire to receive miracles and salvation.

References

Azaryahu, Maoz. "War Memorials and the Commemoration of the Israeli War of Independence, 1948–1956." *Studies in Zionism* 13 (1992): 57–77.

Azaryahu, Maoz. *State Cults: Celebrating Independence and Commemorating the Fallen in Israel, 1948–1956.* Sde Boqer: Ben Gurion Research Institute, 1995. (Hebrew).

Azaryahu, Maoz. "The Mythic Geography of the 11th of Adar: From Tel Hai to Birya and Eilat." *Horizons in Geography* 46–47 (1997): 9–20. (Hebrew).

---

51 Ophir Yarden, "The Sanctity of Mount Herzl and Independence Day in Israel's Civil Religion," in *Sanctity of Time and Space in Tradition and Modernity*, ed. Alberdina Houtman, Marcel J.H.M. Poorthuis, and Joshua Schwartz (Leiden: Brill, 1998), 317–48.

Azaryahu, Maoz. "Innovation and Continuity: Jewish Tradition and the Shaping of Sovereignty Rites in Israel." Pages 273–94 in *On Both Sides of the Bridge: Religion and State in the Early Years of Israel*. Edited by Mordechai Bar-On and Zvi Zameret. Jerusalem: Yad Yizhak Ben Zvi, 2002. (Hebrew).

Azaryahu, Maoz. "Mount Herzl: The Creation of Israel's National Cemetery." *Israel Studies* 1 (2006): 46–74.

Bar, Doron. "Re-Creating Jewish Sanctity in Jerusalem: The Case of Mount Zion and David's Tomb Between 1948–1967." *The Journal of Israeli History*, 23 (2004): 233–251.

Bar, Doron. *Sanctifying a Land: The Jewish Holy Places in the State of Israel, 1948–1968*. Jerusalem: Ben-Gurion Institute in the Negev, 2007. (Hebrew).

Bar, Doron. "Holy Sites and Pilgrimage in Western Jerusalem, 1948–1967." *Eretz Israel* 28 (2007): 331–38. (Hebrew).

Bar, Doron. "Reconstructing the Past: The Creation of Jewish Sacred Space in the State of Israel, 1948–1967." *Israel Studies* 13:3 (2008): 1–21.

Bar, Doron. "Mizrachim and the Development of Sacred Space in the State of Israel, 1948–1967." *Journal of Modern Jewish Studies* 8 (2009): 267–85.

Bar, Doron. "Jewish Holy Sites in the Galilee: 1948–1967." Pages 132–52 in *New Galilee Studies: Tenth Anniversary Volume of the Galilee Research Conference*. Edited by Tziyona Grossmark, Haim Goren, Yair Seltenreich, and Mustafa Abassi. Tel Hai: Tel Hai Academic College, 2009. (Hebrew).

Bar, Doron. "'Nation's Pantheon' in Jerusalem." *Et-Mol* 228 (2013): 32–35. (Hebrew).

Bar, Doron. "The 'Lion's Cave' in Jerusalem's Mamilla Cemetery." *Et-Mol* 231 (2014): 23–26. (Hebrew).

Bar, Doron. "The Debate between Tel Aviv and Jerusalem in Mandatory Palestine (1920–48) over the Reinterment of Zionist Leaders." *Israel Affairs* 21 (2015): 500–15.

Bar, Doron. "The Struggle Over the Western Wall (1967–1973)." Pages 318–46 in *Study of Jerusalem Through the Ages*. Edited by Yehoshua Ben-Arieh, Aviva Halamish, Ora Limor, and Rehav Rubin. Jerusalem: Yad Ben Zvi, 2015. (Hebrew).

Bar, Doron. *Landscape and Ideology: Reinterment of Renowned Jews in the Land of Israel, 1904–1967*. Berlin: De Gruyter, 2016.

Bar, Doron. "Holy Places or Historical Sites? Defining Sacred and Archaeological Sites in the State of Israel, 1948–1967." *History of Religions* 58 (2018): 1–23.

Bar, Doron. "Between Muslim and Jewish Sanctity: Judaizing Muslim Holy Places in the State of Israel, 1948–1967." *Journal of Historical Geography* 59 (2018): 68–76.

Bein, Alex. *Theodor Herzl: A Biography*. Jerusalem: Zionist Library, 1977. (Hebrew).

Ben Yehuda, Nachman. *Sacrificing Truth: Archaeology and the Myth of Masada*. Amherst, NY: Humanity Books, 2002.

Bilu, Yoram. "The Renewal of Rituals at Holy Sites in Israel: The Contribution from Those of Moroccan Descent." Pages 27–46 in *To the Graves of the Righteous: Pilgrimages to Tombs and "Hilulot" in Israel*. Edited by Rivka Gonen. Jerusalem: Israel Museum, 1998. (Hebrew).

Bilu, Yoram. *The Saints' Impresarios: Dreamers, Healers, and Holy Men in Israel's Urban Periphery*. Haifa: Haifa University Press, 2005. (Hebrew).

Brog, Mooli. "Gymnasia Herzliya in Tel Aviv Discovers the Maccabees' Tombs, 1907–1911: The Shaping of Collective Memory and National Identity." *Iyonim Betkomat Israel* 20 (2010): 169–92. (Hebrew).

Brown, Peter. *The Cult of the Saints: Its Rise and Function in Latin Christianity*. Chicago: University of Chicago Press, 1981.

Colbi, Shaul. *Christianity in the Holy Land: Past and Present*. Tel Aviv: Am Hasefer, 1969.

Disenchick, Ido. *Ze'ev Jabotinsky Returns to the Homeland*. Tel Aviv: Hadar, 1965. (Hebrew).

Feige, Michael. "Archaeology, Anthropology and the Development Town: Constructing the Israeli Place." *Zion* 62 (1998): 441–59. (Hebrew).

Feige, Michael, and Zvi Shiloni, eds. *Archaeology and Nationalism in Eretz Israel*. Sde Boqer: Ben-Gurion Research Institute, 2008. (Hebrew).

Gelber, Yoav. *Palestine, 1948: War, Escape and the Emergence of the Palestinian Refugee Problem*. Portland, OR: Sussex Academic Press, 2001.

Gitlitz, David M., and Linda Kay Davidson. *Pilgrimage and the Jews*. Westport, CT: Praeger, 2006.

Goren, Dotan. *A Redeemer will Come to Zion: Jewish Efforts to Obtain a Foothold in the Holy Place in Jerusalem and its Surroundings in Late Ottoman Period (1840–1918)*. Jerusalem: Beitel Library, 2017. (Hebrew).

Handelman, Don, and Elihu Katz. "State Ceremonies in Israel: Remembrance Day and Independence Day." Pages 202–12 in *Models and Mirrors: Towards an Anthropology of Public Events*. Edited by Don Handelman. New York: Berghahn, 1998.

Kletter, Raz. *Just Past? The Making of Israeli Archaeology*. London: Equinox, 2005.

Kroll, Tzvi, and Tzadok Linman. *Tel Aviv's Old Cemetery's Book*. Tel Aviv: Sefer, 1940. (Hebrew).

Luncz, Abraham Moses. *Guide to the Land of Israel and Syria*. Jerusalem: Abraham Moses Luncz, 1891. (Hebrew).

Mann, Barbara. "Modernism and the Zionist Uncanny: Reading the Old Cemetery in Tel Aviv." *Representations* 69 (2000): 63–95.

Mayer, Leon A., Yaakov Pinkerfeld, and Chaim Z. Hirschberg. *Muslim Religious Buildings in Israel*. Jerusalem: Ministry of Religious Affairs, 1950. (Hebrew).

Meri, Josef W. *The Cult of Saints Among Muslim and Jews in Medieval Syria*. Oxford: Oxford University Press, 2002.

Reiner, Elchanan. "All the Rivers Flow Into the Sea: Pilgrimage to Jerusalem following the destruction of the Second Temple." Unpublished paper, 2005. (Hebrew).

Ron, Amos. "A Rachel for Everyone: The Kinneret Cemetery as a Site of Civil Pilgrimage." Pages 349–59 in *Sanctity of Time and Space in Tradition and Modernity*. Edited by Alberdina Houtman, Marcel J.H.M. Poorthuis, and Joshua Schwartz. Leiden: Brill, 1998.

Sasson, Avi. "The 'Tomb of Dan' in the Shephelah of Judah." *Judea and Samaria Research Studies* 10 (2001): 7–18. (Hebrew).

Shamir, Ilana. *Gal-Ed: Memorials for the Fallen in the Wars of Israel.* Tel Aviv: Ministry of Defense Press, 1989. (Hebrew).

Shapira, Anita. *The Bible and Israeli Identity.* Jerusalem: Magnes Press, 2005. (Hebrew).

Shapira, Anita. *Jews, Zionists, and In-Between.* Tel Aviv: Am Oved, 2007. (Hebrew).

Shapiro, Yair. "The Nicanor Tomb Cave on Mount Scopus: A Precedent for Mount Herzl." *Eretz Israel* 28 (2007): 454–62. (Hebrew).

Shapiro, Yair. "Max Nordau and the Reinterment of Jewish and Zionist Leaders in the Land of Israel." MA thesis, Hebrew University of Jerusalem, 2010. (Hebrew).

Shavit, Yaakov. "Archaeology, Political Culture, and Culture in Israel." Pages 48–61 in *The Archaeology of Israel: Constructing the Past, Interpreting the Present.* Edited by Neil Asher Silberman and David Small. Sheffield: Sheffield Academic Press, 1997.

Splendor and Glory: Israel's Rituals of Sovereignty, 1948–1958. Tel Aviv: Tel Aviv Museum of Art, 2001. (Hebrew).

Taragan, Hana. "Baybars and the Tomb of Abu Hurayra/Rabban Gamliel in Yavneh." *Cathedra* 97 (2000): 65–84. (Hebrew).

Vilnay, Zeev. *Sepulchral Monuments in Palestine.* Jerusalem: Mosad Harav Kook, 1951. (Hebrew).

Wardi, Chaim. *Christians in Israel: A Survey.* Jerusalem: Ministry of Religious Affairs, 1950.

Wiernik, Michal Naor, and Doron Bar. "The Competition for the Design and Development of Herzl's Tomb and Mount Herzl, 1949–1960." *Cathedra* 144 (2012): 107–36. (Hebrew).

Wittman, Laura. *The Tomb of the Unknown Solider: Modern Mourning, and the Reinvention of the Mystical Body.* Toronto: University of Toronto Press, 2011.

Yarden, Ophir. "The Sanctity of Mount Herzl and Independence Day in Israel's Civil Religion." Pages 317–48 in *Sanctity of Time and Space in Tradition and Modernity.* Edited by Alberdina Houtman, Marcel J.H.M. Poorthuis, and Joshua Schwartz. Leiden: Brill, 1998.

Zerubavel, Yael. "The Historic, the Legendary, and the Incredible: Invented Tradition and Collective Memory in Israel." Pages 105–123 in *Commemorations: The Politics of National Identity.* Edited by John R. Gillis. Princeton: Princeton University Press, 1994.

CHAPTER 2

Rabbinic Literature's Hidden Polemic: Sacred Space in the World of the Sages

Eyal Ben-Eliyahu

The sages of the Mishnah and Talmud in the land of Israel faced internal and external threats to their beliefs. More specifically, while the sanctity of the land of Israel as a unit was foremost for the rabbinic scholars, they were forced to confront opinions and beliefs that would sanctify specific spaces within the land—despite the fact that rabbinic literature considered only the land of Israel, Jerusalem, and the Temple to be holy. In confronting such threats, the sages used means that were at once creative and insidious, traces of which we can find in the subtext of the only vestige that remains: their writing.

I contend that the sages contended with two groups—one internal and one external—each with its own approach. The debate with the internal group has been examined at length elsewhere,[1] and we will touch on it only briefly here. Our examination of the confrontation with the external group—evolving Christianity—will look closely at Galilee locations considered holy by the Christians and their appearance in rabbinic literature.

1   Rabbinic Literature and Nonrabbinic Jewish Culture

Within the Hebrew Bible, the land of Israel is ascribed great importance, though it is never described as "the holy land"; in fact, holiness is associated with particular parcels of land only twice in the entire Hebrew biblical canon: first, in Moses's encounter at the burning bush (Exod 3:5); second, in Joshua's encounter with the "captain" of God's army in Jericho (Josh 5:15). Yet the actual location, in both cases, has no abiding significance beyond serving as the setting for the encounter, holiness does not inhere in the ground. Generally speaking, holiness in the Hebrew Bible primarily attaches to individuals, occasions, or objects that have been sanctified for ritual use. Deuteronomy repeatedly mentions "the place that the Lord will choose," yet a specific location is

---

1   Eyal Ben-Eliyahu, "The Rabbinic Polemic against Sanctification of Sites," *JSJ* 40 (2009): 260–81.

never given; there is only a general reference to a "place." Though built as an eternal dwelling for God's glory, the Temple sees the Lord's glory depart on the eve of its destruction (Ezek 11:23).

Literature from the Second Temple period also notes alternative sites outside of Jerusalem that were understood to be significant. Enoch, for example, ascribes special importance to Mount Hermon and its environs, an axis mundi for the angels; the Mount of Olives also plays a part in Enoch's "sacred geography." The holiness of Mount Gerizim in Samaritan tradition emerged at some point in the Second Temple period.[2] Finally, the Cave of the Patriarchs (Machpelah) in Hebron was considered to be the burial place of the national patriarchs and, as such, was assigned special significance.[3]

The question of sacred space is not directly addressed in the rabbinic sources. The sages do discuss one holy locus—Jerusalem and the Temple Mount—but their approach to other ostensibly sacred sites is far more complex.

Sacred space is delineated in the Mishnah at the opening of the sixth order, Ṭeharot, which deals with issues of impurity and purity. Tractate Kelim describes ten ascending degrees of holiness, starting with the land of Israel and proceeding to walled cities, Jerusalem, the Temple Mount, the rampart, the court of the women, the court of the Israelites, the court of the priests, the hall and the altar, and the sanctuary—and concluding with the definitive sacred place, the Holy of Holies.[4] The only places the rabbis considered holy, it

---

2   Opinions on the origins of the holiness of Mount Gerizim in the Samaritan tradition are split, but all agree that during the era of the sages the Samaritans' holy place was Mount Gerizim and not Jerusalem.

3   See the Testaments of the Twelve Patriarchs for repeated emphasis on Hebron as the burial place not only of patriarchs but also of each of the sons of Jacob. See also the contribution by Tamar Kadari and Gila Vachman in this volume.

4   The language of the Mishnah is as follows:
    There are ten degrees of holiness.
    The land of Israel is holier than all the [other] lands. And what [constitutes] its holiness? They bring the Omer from it, and the first fruits and the two loaves, which they must not bring from [any] of the other lands.
    The walled cities are still more holy than it ...
    Within the wall [of Jerusalem the locality] is still more holy ...
    The Temple Mount is more holy than that ...
    The rampart is more holy than [the Temple Mount] ...
    The court of women is more holy than [the rampart] ...
    The court of Israelites is more holy than [the court of women] ...
    The court of priests is more holy than [the court of Israelites] ...
    Between the hall and the altar is more holy than [the court of priests] ...
    The sanctuary is still holier than [the court of priests] ...
    The Holy of Holies is still more holy ... (m. Kelim 1:6–9)

appears, were the Temple, Jerusalem, and the unit of the land of Israel as a whole; no specific sites outside of Jerusalem were sacred.

The sages' explicit belief that the Temple and Jerusalem were holy serves as a foil for their discussions of other sites that might be perceived as being holy. In fact, many of the statements made by the sages in the Mishnaic and Talmudic literature—ostensibly supporting the definition of such sites as sacred—may actually serve as a polemic against their sanctification, as I have argued elsewhere.[5] This polemic can be found in the discussion of two different types of locations that could potentially have been considered sacred: cities in which biblical events occurred and locations of topographical significance. In order to gain insight into the rabbinic approach to such locations, we will take one fascinating case study, looking closely at interpretive and exegetical efforts to undermine the holiness of locations.

In Genesis, upon seeing the angels of God ascending and descending at Bethel, Jacob exclaims: "How awesome is this place! This is none other than the abode of God and that is the gateway to heaven!" (Gen 28:17). Jacob then swears an oath: "And this stone, which I have set up as a pillar, shall be God's abode" (Gen 28:22).

As an axis uniting heaven and earth, Bethel is the ideal site for sanctification as a holy place. The rabbis, however, took great pains to neutralize this notion, transferring this role to Jerusalem as its particular privilege. The following midrash, for example, transfers "the gate of heaven" from Bethel to Jerusalem:

> And he was afraid, and said: What an awesome place this is! (Gen 28:17). Rabbi Leazer said in the name of Rabbi Jose ben Zimra: This ladder stood in Beer-sheba and [the top of] its slope was over the Temple. What is the proof?... And he was afraid, and said: What an awesome place this is! Rabbi Judah ben Rabbi Simon said: This ladder stood on the Temple site, while [the top of] its slope was over Bethel. What is the proof? And he was afraid, and said: What an awesome place this is!—And he called the name of this place Bethel (Gen 28:19) (Gen. Rab. 69:7).

Fascinatingly, the rabbis were not content with merely moving "the gate of heaven" from Bethel to Jerusalem. They went even further, adding a condemnatory expression concerning Bethel: "Rabbi Yohanan said: Between Gabbath and Antipatris there were sixty myriads of townships, and none were more corrupt (mekulkalot) than Jericho and Bethel—Jericho because Joshua cursed it, and Bethel because the Golden Calf of Jeroboam was set up there" (Ruth

---

5   Ben-Eliyahu, "Rabbinic Polemic."

Rab. 2:2). Rabbi Yohanan thus equates Bethel with Jericho, which was cursed by Joshua, even in the absence of a biblical source for such a curse. A strong condemnation of Bethel is also apparent in the following midrash: "Originally it was called Bethel (house of God) but now it is called Bethta'avah (house of licentiousness)" (Gen. Rab. 39:15). Clearly, the rabbis wanted to minimize the holiness attributed to Bethel in favour of Jerusalem.[6]

But was the same principle in place in a greater war the rabbinic scholars waged against a more threatening foe? How would the sages contend with the challenge to spatial sanctity posed by the Christian world?

2   The Christian Challenge: the Galilee Site Map

As we have noted, rabbinic literature did not engage directly with the external religious or philosophical approaches that it viewed as threatening. The sages as a rule do not name the movement with which they are contending and do not usually represent the approach through which they polemicise.[7]

Faced with an evolving Christian narrative, the sages once again took a decisive—if covert—tack in relating to settlements and sites in the Galilee, a region with many places essential to the Christian narrative, spaces in which Jesus was said to have lived and performed miracles. To properly examine the sages' approach to such places, we will also look at contemporaneous sources and archaeological/historical evidence, which paint a picture of specific locations in the Galilee that eventually became known for their ties to Jesus. We will determine the demographic makeup of these locales and whether their population consisted of Jews alongside Christians. Once we have a sense of each settlement, we will turn to the rabbinic literature to see how the sages related to each.

---

6   The polemic against Bethel found in Jubilees, the Genesis Apocryphon, and rabbinic literature exhibit a shared tendency that aims both to ratify the sanctification of Bethel in the biblical story and simultaneously subordinate it to Jerusalem. See John Endres, *Biblical Interpretation in the Book of Jubilees* (Washington, DC: Catholic Biblical Association of America, 1987) and Esther Eshel, "Jubilees 32 and the Bethel Cult Traditions in Second Temple Literature," in *Things Revealed: Studies in Early Jewish and Christian Literature in Honor of Michael E. Stone*, ed. Esther G. Chazon, David Satran, and Ruth A. Clements, JSJSup 89 (Leiden: Brill, 2004), 21–36.

7   For a similar approach concerning the Mishnah see Ishay Rosen-Zvi, "Is the Mishnah a Roman Composition?" in *The Faces of Torah: Studies in the Texts and Contexts of Ancient Judaism in Honor of Steven Fraade*, ed. Christine Hayes, Tzvi Novick, and Michal Bar-Asher Segal, JAJSup 22 (Göttingen: Vandenhoeck & Ruprecht, 2017), 487–507.

2.1   *Settlements in the Galilee: an Overview*

The number of settlements in the Galilee from the late Second Temple period to the nineteenth century is consistently estimated at about two hundred, as found in censuses conducted in the nineteenth century. In his *Life*, Flavius Josephus reports on 204 settlements in the Galilee.[8] Recently, Chaim Ben David has noted that Josephus's numbers are in line with archaeological surveys and other lists, which also point to about two hundred settlements in the Galilee toward the end of the Second Temple period and in the Roman and Byzantine periods—and even later, until the nineteenth century.[9]

Analysis of the number of settlements mentioned in Palestinian rabbinic literature—the Mishnah, Tosefta, Jerusalem Talmud, and classic midrashim— reveals approximately one hundred identified place names in the Galilee.[10] To that we can add roughly twenty or thirty of the sixty settlements mentioned whose locations are unidentified. This brings us to the sum of 120 to 130 place names out of the 200 settlements that existed in the Galilee between the second and fourth centuries. The sages in the land of Israel, then, mentioned around 130 settlements out of 200 in the Galilee in their literature.

Below, we will look closely at the historical and archaeological evidence of specific settlements in the Galilee that had known Christian connections. Moreover, we will make use of two other essential sources that are external to the rabbinic literature: the writings of Flavius Josephus and the listing of priestly divisions. In comparing the external sources and evidence to the canonical rabbinic literature, we can glean what, if any, attitude the sages took to the Christian sites situated in the Galilee.

2.1.1   The Galilean Settlements in Josephus's Writings

Josephus wrote his compositions in Rome during the third part of the first century CE. In his *Jewish War* and *Life*, he mentions the names of thirty-five settlements in the Galilee and five in the Gaulantitis (the Golan). Included in this list are Cana, Bethsaida/Julias, and Capernaum (and even the Capernaum springs), as we will soon see. These three places later became Christian holy sites and pilgrimage destinations.

---

8   "If you seriously desire me to come to you, there are two hundred and four cities and villages in Galilee. I will come to whichever of these you may select, Gabara and Giscala excepted" (*Life* 235).

9   Chaim Ben David, "Were There 204 Settlements in Galilee at the Time of Josephus Flavius?" *JJS* 62 (2011): 21–36.

10   According to Chaim Ben David, the Golan was also under the command of Josephus and was included in the Galilee according to his division.

2.1.2   The List of Twenty-Four Priestly Divisions

A similar picture emerges from an analysis of the list of the twenty-four
priestly divisions that took turns serving in the Temple. The list is attributed,
in 1 Chr 24:7–18, to David. The Hebrew Bible features a list that mentions the
name of each group and the number of priests included in it. Most significantly for our discussion, however, in the later Byzantine period, in the piyyutim
(liturgical poems) composed and mosaics created, each division is attached to
a specific settlement.[11]

The dating of this list is under dispute. Suggestions range from the First
Jewish Revolt (66–73 CE) to the third century CE. Uzi Leibner has suggested that
the list reflects a historical memory of settling the Galilee in the Hasmonean
period, but it is not possible to ascertain when the list was edited to become a
symbolic one.[12]

The oldest textual source that relates to the list is the Jerusalem Talmud, edited in the fourth century CE. The rabbis mentioned in connection to the first
part of the list are from the end of the third century, the era of the Jerusalem
Talmud. The Talmud mentions only the first two priestly groups, presenting
them with a negative association:

> [Jehoiarib mesarbai Meiron:]
> Said Rabbi Levi: Jehoiarib is a [name of a] man.
>> Meron is a city.
>> Mesarbai: He [God] handed over the house [i.e., Temple] to the
>> enemy ...
>> Said Rabbi Berakhiah: [Jehoiarib (Yehoyarib)]: The Lord (Yah) quar-
>> relled (*heriv*) with his sons, because they rebelled (*maru*) and defiled
>> (*seravu*) him.
>> Jedaiah; Amoq, Sepphoris: ...
>> The Lord (Yah) knew (*yadaʿ*) the deep (*amoq*) conspiracy that was in
>> their hearts and He exiled them to Sepphoris. (y. Taʿan. 4:5, 68d)

The Talmud here bases itself on the priestly listing and provides an exegesis
with a negative context. From its language, we learn of two priestly courses—
Jehoiarib, related to the settlement of Meron, and Jedaiah, Sepphoris. The

---

11   Remains of five archaeological inscriptions of the list dating to the Byzantine period were
     found in Israel at Nazareth, Rehov, Ashkelon, and Kissufim. The most complete list was
     found in Yemen.

12   Uzi Leibner, *Settlement and History in Hellenistic, Roman, and Byzantine Galilee: An
     Archaeological Survey of the Eastern Galilee,* TSAJ 127 (Tübingen: Mohr Siebeck, 2009),
     404–19.

continuation of the list, which is known from the piyyutim and the mosaic inscriptions, is not found in the rabbinic corpus.[13] I would therefore posit that this list—paraphrased with a negative connotation—is a Jewish one that was external to the classic corpus of rabbinic literature; it is not part of the rabbinic canon. And the complete list, as we know from the piyyutim and the mosaic inscriptions, mentions two of the settlements we will soon examine: Nazareth and Cana, places that later became holy Christian sites and destinations for Christian pilgrims.

In our analysis below, we will make use of both of these extracanonical sources—Josephus and the priestly list—as a window into the world of the sages. Not bound by the interests of those who redacted the rabbinic literature, the outlook expressed in both sources would most probably not have reflected its biases. Thus, if we compare the Tannaitic and Amoraic treatment of Christian religious sites to that in Josephus and the priestly courses, we can gain an understanding of the sages' unspoken view on the subject.

2.2   *Christian Sites in Historical Sources*

We begin by looking at early Christian interest in these sites. Among other things, we must study Christian activity and Jewish existence alongside the Christians at these sites during the early centuries CE, ascertaining whether later Christian pilgrims ventured to these places. We will look at a variety of sources: the New Testament, archaeological evidence, pilgrims' accounts, Josephus's writings, and the list of priestly courses. Taken together, these will give us a fuller picture of each of the six Galilee locations under discussion: Nazareth, Cana, Capernaum, Bethsaida, Korazim, and Kursi. Did Jews live in those locations? If there was a Jewish presence, did the sites appear in the writings of the sages along with the other Galilee locations? Once we have seen what other sources tell us about the Christian and Jewish communities in these places at the time, we can compare these to the rabbinic sources and, in so doing, come to an understanding of the sages' approach to these sites.

---

13   The context of the divisions of Yehoiarib and Yehoiada, which are mentioned in the Talmud, is definitively negative, going so far as to blame the priests for the destruction of the Temple. This reflects a tension between the sages and the priests; see Josef Yahalom, *Poetry and Society in Jewish Galilee of Late Antiquity* (Tel Aviv: Hakibbutz Hameuchad, 1999), 111–16 (Hebrew); Leibner, *Settlement and History*, 404–19.

2.2.1   Nazareth

Nazareth played a central role in the life story of Jesus;[14] in fact, it is mentioned twenty-three times in the gospels.[15] Joseph, Jesus's father, returned from Egypt, "and he went and lived in a town called Nazareth. Thus was fulfilled what was said through the prophets, that he would be called a 'Nazarene'" (Matt 2:23). Jesus was even identified and described as "the one from Nazareth" (Matt 21:11; John 1:45; Acts 10:38).

From the archaeological remains and the depictions of Christian pilgrims, Nazareth appears to have been a place in which Jews and Christians lived side by side. Though the archaeological remains of the city dating to the end of the Second Temple period and the ancient Roman period are unimpressive, they include ruins of walls and agricultural facilities, and a few burial caves on the outskirts of the settlement.[16] Bellarmino Bagatti explored the remains of a Jewish ritual bath (a mikvah) found under the modern Church of the Annunciation, as well as architectural remains from the beginning of the Byzantine period.[17] Bagatti suggests attributing these remains, as well as a few other artefacts that he identifies as Jewish, to the pre-Constantinian period. The Byzantine church found in Nazareth dates to the fifth century.[18]

According to Matthew and Mark, Jesus did not perform many miracles in Nazareth; in Luke, the people of Nazareth are said to have smuggled Jesus out of the city. However, early Christian pilgrims visited the city because Jesus and his family came from there. Epiphanius, the bishop of Salamis, tells us in his *Panarion* (written c. 375 CE) that Joseph of Tiberias, a Jew who converted to Christianity, noted that the residents of several settlements in the Galilee, among them Nazareth, asked him to get permission from emperor Constantine

---

14   Yoram Tsafrir, Leah Di Segni, and Judith Green, eds., *Tabula Imperii Romani: Maps and Gazetteer* (Jerusalem: Israeli Academy of Humanities and Sciences, 1994), 194; Jack Finegan, *The Archeology of the New Testament: The Life of Jesus and the Early Church*, rev. ed. (Princeton: Princeton University Press, 2016), 40–74.

15   James F. Strange, "Nazareth," in *Galilee in the Late Second Temple and Mishnaic Periods*, ed. David A. Fiensy and James Riley Strange, 2 vols. (Minneapolis: Fortress, 2015), 2:167–80 (173); see also Finegan, *Archeology*, 43–65.

16   Bellarmino Bagatti, "Nazareth," in *The New Encyclopedia of Archeological Excavations in the Holy Land*, ed. Ephraim Stern, 5 vols. (Jerusalem: Carta, 1993–2008), 3:1103–5; Zeev Weiss, "Jewish Galilee in the First Century CE: An Archeological View," in *Flavius Josephus, Vita: Introduction, Hebrew Translation, and Commentary*, ed. Daniel R. Schwartz (Jerusalem: Yad Ben Zvi, 2007), 15–60 (19) (Hebrew); Strange, "Nazareth."

17   Bagatti, "Nazareth." Joan Taylor, however, claims that this location functioned not as a mikvah but as a pool for collecting the juice of pressed grapes; Joan Taylor, *Christians and the Holy Places: The Myth of Jewish Christian Origins* (Oxford: Oxford University Press, 1993), 244–53.

18   Bellarmino Bagatti, "Ritrovamenti nella Nazaret evangelica," *Liber Annuus* 6 (1955): 5–44.

to build churches in their towns.[19] Thus, it appears that Christians lived in Nazareth in the Galilee in the mid-fourth century.

Egeria, whose late-fourth-century account of her pilgrimage is the source of much information, did visit the city[20] and reported the existence of an altar and church in a location that had previously hosted a synagogue. Promptly after her, Paula (347–404 CE) also journeyed to Nazareth, tying it to Cana and Capernaum, which were according to her "testimonies for his signs."[21] The Piacenza Pilgrim (570 CE) visited Nazareth, in which, according to his report, many miracles took place. He also mentions a church in Nazareth and describes Jews and Christians living side by side in the city.[22]

Josephus mentions Japha (*Life* 270; *J.W.* 2.20), today the village Yafia, in close proximity to Nazareth, but he does not mention Nazareth itself. That city is, however, mentioned in the broken inscriptions from Caesarea,[23] which record the priestly division of the Pitzatz family from Nazareth. Eliezer Qalir (570–640 CE), in his piyyutim, mentions a Nazareth division as well. The Nazarene course, Pitzatz, is mentioned in the piyyutim of Haduta[24] and Pinhas Hacohen.[25]

Thus the archaeological remains, as well as the descriptions of the Christian pilgrims from the fourth century and onward, point to the existence of a Jewish population in Nazareth alongside that of Christians.

2.2.2   Cana

According to the Gospel of John, Jesus, who had been rejected by the people of Nazareth, became active in Cana, and this site "was the beginning of the miracles" (John 2:11). The first took place during a wedding in Cana, when Jesus turned jugs of water into wine (John 2:1–11). Instead of returning to Nazareth after his first visit in Judea and Samaria, Jesus returned to the same place and

---

19   Epiph., *Panarion* 30.11.9–10.

20   John Wilkinson, ed., *Egeria's Travels to the Holy Land* (Jerusalem: Ariel, 1981), 96; Paul Geyer et al., eds., *Itineraria et Alia Geographica*, CCSL 175 (Turnhout: Brepols, 1965), 98.

21   John Wilkinson, *Jerusalem Pilgrimage before the Crusades* (Oxford: Aris & Phillips, 1999), 52.

22   Wilkinson, *Jerusalem Pilgrimage* 80–81; Geyer et al., *Itineraria*, 130–31.

23   Walter Ameling et al., eds., *Caesaria and the Middle Coast 1121–2160*, Corpus Inscriptionum Iudaeae/Palaestinae 2 (Berlin: De Gruyter, 2011), 66–68.

24   Paul Kahle, *Masoreten des Westens* (Stuttgart: Kohlhammer, 1927), 20–22. On Haduta see Eyal Ben-Eliyahu, Yehudah Cohn, and Fergus Millar, *Handbook of Jewish Literature from Late Antiquity (135–700 CE)* (Oxford: Oxford University Press, 2012), 135–36.

25   Shulamit Elizur, *The Liturgical Poems of Rabbi Pinhas ha-Kohen: Critical Edition, Introduction, and Commentaries* (Jerusalem: World Union of Jewish Studies, 2004), 638 (Hebrew). Ha-Kohen was from Tiberias and is usually dated to the eighth century CE.

performed a second miracle there: curing the son of one of the king's people (John 4:46–54).

The identity of Cana is uncertain.[26] Three sites have been suggested as the place, which John calls "Cana of Galilee." The most common is the present village Kafr Kanna, five kilometers north of Nazareth. A dedicatory inscription for a synagogue was found at this site during the nineteenth century, below the floor of a Franciscan church.[27] Excavations also yielded pottery, coins, and ossuaries dating to the second century CE, indicating a Jewish presence. Another possible location is Khirbet Qana on the northern side of the Beit Netofa Valley, where a large building has been uncovered;[28] the excavator has cautiously suggested that it can be identified as a synagogue.[29] A third option is Karm er-Ras, on the western side of the present-day village of Kafr Kanna;[30] in an excavation conducted by Yardena Alexander, remains of a Jewish settlement, which existed continuously from the Hellenistic period until the end of the Byzantine period, were discovered. A mikvah, situated near stone buildings, was also discovered at the site. Thus, it seems likely that Cana also contained a Jewish presence.

Paula visited Cana at the end of the fourth century. In her description of the site, she includes Capernaum, which, according to her, is a testament to Jesus's miracles.[31] Theodosius mentions Cana in the early sixth century;[32] after him, the Piacenza Pilgrim also went there and washed in its stream for blessing.[33]

Josephus mentions a "village of Galilee called Cana" (*Life* 86), where he stayed when he arrived in the Galilee. The priestly division of Cana is mentioned in

---

26   Mordechai Aviam and Peter Richardson, "Josephus' Galilee in Archeological Perspective," in Steve Mason, *Life of Josephus*, Flavius Josephus: Translation and Commentary 9 (Leiden: Brill, 2001), 177–209 (184); Zeev Weiss, "Jewish Galilee," 19–20.

27   Massimo Luca, "Kfar Kanna (The Franciscan Church)," in Fiensy and Strange, *Galilee in the Late Second Temple and Mishnaic Periods*, 2:156–64.

28   Aviam and Richardson, "Josephus' Galilee," 184.

29   Douglas R. Edwards, "Khirbet Qana: From Jewish Village to Christian Pilgrim Site," in *The Roman and Byzantine Near East: Volume 3: Late-Antique Petra, Nile Festival Building at Sepphoris, Deir Qal'a Monastery, Khirbet Qana Village and Pilgrim Site, 'Ain-'Arrub Hiding Complex, and Other Studies*, ed. John H. Humphrey, JRASup 49 (Portsmouth, RI: Journal of Roman Archaeology, 2002), 101–32; Thomas McCollough, "Khirbet Qana," in Fiensy and Strange, *Galilee in the Late Second Temple and Mishnaic Periods*, 2:127–45.

30   Yardena Alexander, "Karm Er-Ras Near Kafr Kanna," in Fiensy and Strange, *Galilee in the Late Second Temple and Mishnaic Periods*, 2:146–57.

31   Ora Limor, *Holy Land Travels: Christian Pilgrimage in Late Antiquity* (Jerusalem: Yad Ben Zvi, 1998), 151.

32   Wilkinson, *Jerusalem Pilgrimage*, 63.

33   Wilkinson, *Jerusalem Pilgrimage*, 81; Geyer et al., *Itineraria*, 130.

Eliezer Qalir's piyyut for the fast of the Ninth of Av.[34] Elyashiv, the priestly division of Cana, is mentioned in Haduta's piyyut[35] as the location of the eleventh division; it is also noted in a piyyut by Pinhas Hacohen.[36] It further appears in the inscription of priestly divisions from Yemen.[37]

2.2.3 Capernaum

Capernaum, or Kfar Nahum, on the northern coast of the Sea of Galilee,[38] is where Jesus's activity in the Galilee most often occurred. According to Matthew (4:13), Mark (1:21), and Luke (4:31), when Jesus was rejected from Nazareth he went to Capernaum and became active there, teaching and proclaiming his message; in Matthew (9:1), the town appears as "the city" of Jesus.

The excavations conducted by Virgilio Corbo and Stanislao Loffreda (between 1968 and 1986) exposed a village built of basalt, with foundations from the early Hellenistic or even Persian period.[39] A large synagogue was discovered at the site; across from it was a structure that served the Christian community from the first until the fifth century, when an octagonal church was built there.[40]

Zvi Uri Maoz has pointed to the gap between the sparse settlement of the country and the spacious synagogue in Capernaum, which is one of largest and most magnificent in the Galilee.[41] He explains this disparity by suggesting that the site was used as a symbolic space, a monument of sorts for pilgrims and those who came to visit the sites associated with Jesus's activity in the Galilee.

Recently, Rina Talgam and Benjamin Arubas demonstrated the exceptional nature of Capernaum's synagogue as the one that memorialized the activity

---

34   Daniel Goldschmidt, *The Order of Lamentations for Tisha Be-Av* (Jerusalem: Mosad Harav Kook, 1968), 49 (Hebrew).

35   Kahle, *Masoreten des Westens*, 1–3.

36   Elizur, *Liturgical Poems*, 633.

37   Reiner Degan, "An Inscription from Yemen about the 24 Watches of the Priests," *Tarbiz* 42 (1973): 302–7 (Hebrew).

38   Tsafrir, Di Segni, and Green, *Tabula Imperii Romani*, 97.

39   Aviam and Richardson, "Josephus' Galilee," 184–85.

40   Stanislao Loffreda, "Capernaum," in *Oxford Encyclopedia of Archeology in the Near East*, ed. Eric M. Meyers, 5 vols. (Oxford: Oxford University Press, 1997), 1:416–19.

41   Zvi Uri Maoz, "The Synagogue at Capernaum: A Radical Solution," in *The Roman and Byzantine Near East: Volume 2: Some Recent Archaeological Research*, ed. John H. Humphrey, JRASup 31 (Portsmouth, RI: Journal of Roman Archaeology, 1999), 137–48; Benjamin Arubas and Rina Talgam, "Jews, Christians, and 'Minim': Who Really Built and Used the Synagogue at Capernaum—A Stirring Appraisal," in *Knowledge and Wisdom: Archeological and Historical Essays in Honor of Leah Di Segni*, ed. Giovanni C. Bottini, Leslaw D. Chrupcala, and Joseph Patrich (Milan: Edizioni Terra Santa, 2014), 237–74.

of Jesus at Capernaum for the local Jewish-Christian community.[42] Thus, the church and the synagogue served the same community.

During the Byzantine period, Capernaum was (according to the testimony of Petrus Diaconus)[43] visited by Egeria, who described it as the place in which Jesus healed the centurion's servant (Matt 8:5–13; Luke 7:1–10; John 4:46–54).[44] Paula,[45] Theodosius,[46] and Antoninus[47] also visited Capernaum.

Josephus (*Life* 403) mentions Capernaum as the place to which he turned after he was wounded in the battle he led near Julias, identified with nearby Bethsaida.[48]

2.2.4 Bethsaida

Bethsaida,[49] which is located near Capernaum, is the place in which, according to Mark (8:22–25), a blind man was brought before Jesus. Jesus took him out of the village and healed him. Luke (9:10–17) notes that it was the site where Jesus healed those of his followers who required it, and then fed five thousand men with the help of the "miracle of the bread and fish."[50] According to Luke (10:13) and Matthew (11:21),[51] Korazim and Bethsaida are characterized as the settings for miraculous events.

---

42 Arubas and Talgam, "Jews, Christians and 'Minim,'" 233–70.

43 Geyer et al., *Itineraria*, 99.

44 According to John, the centurion's appeal to Jesus and the healing took place in Cana, whereas the centurion's paralysed son was in Capernaum.

45 Wilkinson, *Jerusalem Pilgrimage*, 52. Paula sees Capernaum, together with Cana, as a "testimony to his miracles."

46 Wilkinson, *Jerusalem Pilgrimage*, 63; Geyer et al., *Itineraria*, 115.

47 Wilkinson, *Jerusalem Pilgrimage*, 81; Geyer et al., *Itineraria*, 133.

48 When Josephus describes the Galilee in his *Jewish War* (3.519), he mentions the unique abundance of the Capernaum well and even compares it to the Nile. This is a mention that is linked not to a particular event but rather to a distinguishing characteristic of the site. This place should probably be identified as the Heptapegon or Tabgha, the place in which Jesus gave his sermon on the Mount of Beatitudes and fed thousands of people with loaves of bread. We have documentation of visits by Egeria, Paula, Theodosius, and Sabbas at Capernaum as well. The local church was probably built during the fourth century and replaced with a larger church in the fifth century. Egeria visited the "seven flowing wells"—the Heptapegon—and describes collecting, for medicinal purposes, slivers from the stone on which Jesus lay the loaves of bread, which was turned into an altar; see Geyer et al., *Itineraria*, 99. Paula and Theodosius similarly visited the site, and even Sabbas and Antoninus did so (Geyer et al., *Itineraria*, 133), identifying it as the site at which the miracle of the bread and fish took place, a site which is described as "deserted."

49 Tsafrir, Di Segni, and Green, *Tabula Imperii Romani*, 85.

50 According to Matthew (14:13), this miracle took place in a "deserted place"; according to John (6:3), it happened on a "mountain" on the bank of the Sea of Galilee.

51 Matthew (11:22) also mentions Capernaum.

The descriptions of Christian pilgrims, however, do not refer often to Bethsaida.[52] Among the pilgrims, Theodosius refers to Bethsaida but not as a place in which miracles took place. It is noted as the birthplace of the apostles Peter and Andrew (John 1:44), and, according to Theodosius, the sons of Zavdi.

Rami Arav, who excavated Et-Tell, concurs with Edward Robinson, who suggests that the site is Bethsaida.[53] Mendel Nun, in contrast, suggests the site Tel el-Araj as Bethsaida.[54] Bargil Pixner and Dan Urman have suggested that Bethsaida had two sections: Tel el-Araj was the Jewish fishing village identified with Bethsaida in the Galilee, while Et-Tell was the acropolis of the city and was equated with the Hellenistic Julias, to use the Greek name given to it by Herod's son Philip the Tetrarch.[55] Julias is mentioned several times in Josephus, who notes its location north of the Sea of Galilee (*Ant.* 18.28; *J.W.* 2.168).

2.2.5 Korazim

Korazim—along with Bethsaida and Capernaum[56]—is mentioned as the site where Jesus cursed the people for their lack of belief in him, despite the miracles he performed there.

Zeev Yeivin, who excavated in Korazim, dates the city's inception to the first century and its development and the establishment of the synagogue to the beginning of the fourth century. After that, it appears, building at the site was halted for some time and renewed only at the end of the century.[57] The city was re-established in the mid-fourth and early fifth centuries; it was populated continuously until the eighth century. Jodi Magness disagrees with Yeivin's dating of the synagogue, stating that the synagogue was only built in the fifth century.[58]

---

52 Egeria (Wilkinson, *Egeria's Travels*, 196) places the miracle of the bread and fish in a "field."

53 Rami Arav, "Et-Tell and el-Araj," *IEJ* 38 (1988): 187–88.

54 Mendel Nun, "Has Bethsaida Finally Been Found?" *Jerusalem Perspective* 54 (1998): 12–31. Nun claims that there were Herodian remains in Tel el-Araj, while Arav states that Herodian remains were found only in Et-Tell. See R. Steven Notley, "Et-Tell Is Not Bethsaida," *Near Eastern Archaeology* 70 (2007): 220–30; R. Steven Notley, "Reply to R. Arav," *Near Eastern Archaeology* 74 (2011): 101–3; Rami Arav, "Bethsaida—A Response to Steven Notley," *Near Eastern Archaeology* 74 (2011): 92–100.

55 Bargil Pixner, "Searching for the New Testament Site of Bethsaida," *BA* 48 (1985): 207–16; Dan Urman, *The Golan: A Profile of Region during the Roman and Byzantine Periods*, BARIS (Oxford: British Archaeological Reports, 1985), 121.

56 According to Matt 11. Luke 10 mentions only Korazim and Bethsaida.

57 Zeev Yeivin, *The Synagogue at Korazim: The 1962–1964, 1980–1987 Excavations* (Jerusalem: Israel Antiquities Authority, 2000), 301–4.

58 Jodi Magness, "Did Galilee Decline in the Fifth Century? The Synagogue at Chorazin Reconsidered," in *Religion, Ethnicity, and Identity in Ancient Galilee: A Region in Transition,*

Korazim is not mentioned by Josephus, but Eusebius, in his *Onomasticon* (973),[59] refers to this site as a ruined village. This is most probably the site to which Egeria relates after visiting Capernaum and Tabgha. Right after her visit to the Mount of Beatitudes, she describes how "not far from there is the synagogue which the Savior cursed while the Jews were building it. He asked them this question: 'What are you doing?' 'Nothing,' they said. And he replied: 'If it is nothing you are doing, it will always remain nothing,' and till this day it remains so."[60] Korazim and its ruined synagogue, then, are symbols of a Jewish settlement that was destroyed because of Jesus's curse.

2.2.6   Kursi

The "Miracle of the Swine," in which Jesus exorcised demons from a man and threw them into a flock of pigs that then galloped into the Sea of Galilee, occurred, according to Matthew (8:28–33) and Mark (5:1–20), in the country of the Gadarenes; according to Luke it took place in "the region of the Gerasenes, which is across the lake from the Galilee" (Luke 8:26–33). In the third century, Origen attributed this event to an ancient settlement and explained the term "Gerasenes" as deriving from the Hebrew root ג׳׳רש, to chase out, since the people of the town chased Jesus out after the story took place. Eusebius, in the late third and the first half of the fourth century, followed in Origen's footsteps; he mentions a village in "Gergesa: There the Lord healed the demoniacs. A village is now shown on the hill next to the Lake of Tiberias, into which also the swine were cast down" (*Onomasticon* 363).

Cyril of Scythopolis, in the sixth century, describes the 491 pilgrimages of Sabbas and his companion to the eastern Galilee. The two travelled from the Jordan River north, toward the eastern shore of the Sea of Galilee, prayed at Kursi and the Heptapegon (Tabgha) and in the other holy places in the region, and then went up to the Banias River (*Life of Sabbas* 24).

Vassilios Tzaferis, who excavated in Kursi,[61] dates the church and the monastery found at the site to the end of the sixth century; based on his excavations, he determines that they served as centres of pilgrimage. Mendel Nun notes ancient remains near the port to the west of the church, suggesting that the public institution where the remains were discovered might have been a

---

ed. Jürgen K. Zangenberg, Harold W. Attridge, and Dale B. Martin, WUNT 210 (Tübingen: Mohr Siebeck, 2007), 259–74.

59   Steven R. Notley and Zeev Safrai, eds., *Eusebius,* Onomasticon (Leiden: Brill, 2005), 164.

60   Wilkinson, *Egeria's Travels,* 201.

61   Vassilios Tzaferis, "Kursi," in Stern, *New Encyclopedia,* 3:893–96.

synagogue.[62] A Hebrew inscription was recently found during further excavations at the site;[63] according to the archaeologists, it attests to a Jewish settlement in the town during the Byzantine period.

2.3   Rabbinic Literature and Galilee Locations

Having studied the Christian traditions and Jewish demographics of each of the sites, we can now turn to rabbinic literature. As we noted earlier, the sages were aware of around one hundred and thirty Galilean settlements, while Josephus relates thirty-five. Thus, we would expect the mentions of the settlements to be proportionate; if Josephus, who only mentions thirty-five settlements, includes three of the Christian ones noted above, and if the priestly division, which includes twenty-four, recognizes two, the rabbinic literature should mention many more.

Nazareth, a vital location in Jesus's chronicles, is the place that gave him his identity as a Nazarene. But while it is clear from archaeological evidence that a Jewish community existed there, and while piyyutim note the name of the Nazarene priestly division, Tannaitic and Amoraic literature contain no mention of the settlement at all.

A place called Cana is also not mentioned in Tannaitic or Amoraic literature, except for one mention in Tractate Soferim, a composition redacted later than the Talmud and unknown to the Amoraim.[64]

The only reference to Capernaum in rabbinic literature, a source without any parallels, relates the story of Hanina, the nephew of Rabbi Joshua, who was "swayed to heresy by the heretics, the *minim*, until he was cured by his uncle" (Eccl. Rab. 1:8, 7:26). This source—Ecclesiastes Rabbah—was only edited much later, after the Islamic conquest of Palestine.[65] In other words, Capernaum, which was a central site of pilgrimage in the Galilee due to stories about Jesus's activity in the town, and in which Jews and Christians coexisted, bears one singular mention in rabbinic literature, where it is associated with heresy and identified as a place in which "sinners" lived.

---

62   Mendel Nun, "Kursi: A Monastery near a Jewish Fisherman's Hamlet," in *Zeev Vilnay Jubilee Volume: Essays on the History, Archaeology, and Lore of the Holy Land Presented to Zeev Vilnay*, ed. Ely Schiller, 2 vols. (Jerusalem: Ariel, 1984–1987), 2:183–89 (184) (Hebrew).

63   This inscription has not yet been published; see Ian Blumenthal, "Discovery Suggests Jews Lived in Galilee 1,500 Years Ago," *Ynetnews.com*, Dec. 16, 2015, http://www.ynetnews.com/ articles/0,7340,L-4740314,00.html.

64   On Tractate Soferim, see Ben-Eliyahu, Cohn, and Millar, *Handbook of Jewish Literature from Late Antiquity*, 54–55.

65   The midrashim that were edited before the Arab conquest are Genesis Rabbah, Song of Songs Rabbah, Pesiqta deRav Kahana, and Lamentations Rabbah.

Rabbinic literature makes no mention of a place called Bethsaida but does include Sidon. Scholars debate whether the Sidon in some of the sources should be identified with the Sidon on the banks of the Mediterranean or the Sidon of the Galilee.[66] Most of the explicit mentions of Sidon in rabbinic literature clearly refer to the Sidon of the Mediterranean coast, such as the mentions in t. Šabb. 13:13, where a sea voyage from Tyre to Sidon is mentioned in relation to the "Great Sea" (the Mediterranean): "They do not cast off for a voyage on the Great Sea less than three days before the Sabbath … [if] it is a journey from a point below Tyre to Sidon or from Sidon to a point below Tyre, even on the eve of Sabbath it is permitted." Likewise it appears in t. 'Erub. 4:11: "Said Rabbi Simon, 'I can make it possible for people to go up from Tiberias to Sepphoris, and from Tyre to Sidon.'"

Several suggestions, however, posit a reference to the Sidon of the Galilee in the sources, such as the story mentioned in y. 'Abod. Zar. 5:4: "Rabbi Hanina said: 'There was once a vessel of Rabbi Judah the Prince's house which sailed more than four *mil°* … They said: 'This was in that route of Sidon, and all of them were from Israel.'" Zeev Safrai has noted that this story could not have taken place on the route to the Sidon on the Mediterranean Sea, since the story refers to a Jewish majority. Leibner has linked the story to the traditions regarding Rabbi Judah the Prince's lands in the Golan.[67] The two, therefore, identify the Sidon in this tale with Bethsaida, in the foothills of the Golan.

The area of Jewish settlement in the Yavneel Valley, close to the Sea of Galilee, includes a site called Saidata,[68] which fulfils the criteria of lying at the heart of the Jewish settlement of the eastern Galilee. However, the main difficulty in identifying the Saida in rabbinic literature with Bethsaida is the fact that the place mentioned in rabbinic literature is missing the preceding "Beth"; it is difficult to confirm that the two names refer to the same place. In any case, the Galilean Bethsaida, which was destroyed and did not serve as a significant site of pilgrimage (despite the miraculous stories told of it in the gospels), does not appear in rabbinic literature at all.

Kursi, regardless of the fact that it may have contained a synagogue during the Byzantine period, is not mentioned in rabbinic literature.

---

66   Zeev Safrai, *The Jewish Settlement in the Golan after the Destruction of the Second Temple* (Keshet: Beit Sepher Sade Keshet, 1978), 36 (Hebrew).

67   Uzi Leibner, "Ritual Law and a Roman Road in the Golan," *Al Atar* 4–5 (1999): 193–200 (Hebrew).

68   Yeshayahu Press, *A Topographical-Historical Encyclopedia of the Land of Israel*, 4 vols. (Jerusalem: Reuven Mass, 1955), 4:795–96 (Hebrew); see also Félix-Marie Abel, *Géographie de la Palestine*, 2 vols. (Paris: Lecoffre, 1939), 2:440.

The rich textual and archaeological evidence of Jewish settlement in numerous Galilee locations is significant; clearly there were communities of which the sages must have been aware. Yet these settlements—those that are significant to the Christian community—are omitted, minimized, or even criticized in Jewish sources. These missing names are all the more surprising given the fact that rabbinic literature clearly knew of far more communities than those mentioned by Josephus and in the listing of priestly divisions. This appears to be no coincidence; the sages' silence on these sites speaks volumes.

2.4   The Christianisation of Jewish Locations

The omission of these locations is fascinating and should be viewed in its proper context. Starting with Constantine's regime, and during the fourth to the sixth century, Palestine went through a process of Christianization of space.[69] This process took place along a few interconnected lines.

With the identification of pilgrimage destinations for Christians, recognized as holy sites for the community from the fourth century, and the connection between Christian traditions and sites in Palestine, came the strengthening of Christian pilgrimage to Palestine. The building of churches and monasteries and the establishment of the eremitic movement at the beginning of the fourth century was linked to the evolving Christian map of the Holy Land. These communities served the pilgrims, who used them for accommodations and found in their sites places for prayer.

This process took place primarily, and most intensely, in areas that had been settled by non-Jews; it occurred only later at places like the seashore, the western Galilee, and Judea (after the evacuation of Jewish inhabitants following the Bar Kokhba revolt). While this process took place in the western Galilee throughout the fourth century,[70] from the late fourth and early fifth centuries Christianity began entering into strongholds of Jewish settlement in the eastern Galilee and around the Sea of Galilee as well.[71] This process occurred before the eyes of the land's Jews, who held, in their minds, biblical memory: first, the promise of the land to Abraham the patriarch; second, the memory of the united kingdom as it is depicted in Samuel and Kings. They most probably even held the memory of the Hasmonean state. The presence of

---

69   See Günter Stemberger, *Jews and Christians in the Holy Land* (Edinburgh: T&T Clark, 2000), 48–120. For Christian pilgrimage see the detailed references in Oded Irshai, "The Christian Appropriation of Jerusalem in the Fourth Century: The Case of the Bordeaux Pilgrim," *JQR* 99 (2009): 465–86.

70   Doron Bar, *"Fill the Earth": Settlement in Palestine during the late Roman and Byzantine Periods 135–640 CE* (Jerusalem: Yad Ben-Zvi, 2008), 121–62 (Hebrew).

71   Tsafrir, Di Segni, and Green, *Tabula Imperii Romani*, 18–19.

Christians in the land—and, even more than that, the Christianization of the space—together with the humiliation the Jews felt, had difficult implications for Jewish daily life and hopes.

3   The Polemic's Strategy

For more than a century—since the early nineteenth century—scholars have been uncovering polemics against Christianity in rabbinic texts.[72] The common denominator of those sources is the hidden nature of the polemic.

As we have seen, one of the common strategies employed by the rabbis in combatting ideologies they opposed was to simply ignore them. This was particularly relevant to Christianity—much more so than the Graeco-Roman world—whose presence was felt in the daily life of the Jews of the land (much like the Zoroastrians in Babylonia), because of the proximity of Christianity to Judaism, and the claim of Christians that they had replaced the Jews as *verus Israel*.

Some scholars have noted the very few explicit references to Jesus and Christianity in the Tannaitic and Amoraic literature of the land of Israel[73] and the fact that the explicit references to Christianity appear mainly in the Babylonian Talmud.[74]

---

72   I cannot survey this copious literature here. One of the prominent representatives of this approach is Ephraim E. Urbach; see Oded Irshai and Ephraim E. Urbach, "The Study of Judeo-Christian Dialogue in Late Antiquity—Some Preliminary Observations," in *How Should Rabbinic Literature Be Read in the Modern World?* ed. Matthew A. Kraus (Piscataway, NJ: Gorgias, 2006), 247–75. For references to scholars who follow this line, see the comprehensive introduction of Adiel Schremer in his *Brothers Estranged: Heresy, Christianity, and Jewish Identity in Late Antiquity* (Oxford: Oxford University Press, 2010), 149 (n. 18). Schremer himself takes issue with the attempt to present many rabbinic homilies as products of Jewish-Christian polemic.

73   Peter Schäfer, *Jesus in the Talmud* (Princeton: Princeton University Press, 2007).

74   Even the anti-Christian polemic found in the midrashim does not directly mention Jesus and his students, nor the term Christianity. See Schäfer, *Jesus in the Talmud*, 116–29; Adam H. Becker, *Fear of God and the Beginning of Wisdom: The School of Nisibis and the Development of Scholastic Culture in Late Antique Mesopotamia* (Philadelphia: University of Pennsylvania Press, 2006), 16–18; Daniel Boyarin, "Hellenism in Jewish Babylonia," in *The Cambridge Companion to the Talmud and Rabbinic Literature*, ed. Charlotte Fonrobert and Martin Jaffee (Cambridge: Cambridge University Press, 2007), 336–65. On the absence of Jesus from Tannaitic literature, other than t. Hullin, see Adiel Schremer, "The Christianization of the Roman Empire and Rabbinic Literature," in *Jewish Identity in Antiquity: Studies in Memory of Menahem Stern*, ed. Lee I. Levine and Daniel R. Schwartz, TSAJ 130 (Tübingen: Mohr Siebeck, 2009), 349–66 (365, n. 65).

The discussion above points to another phenomenon: the absence of sites that are mentioned in the New Testament as places where Jesus performed miracles, and which, therefore, became sites of Christian pilgrimage in the Byzantine period.

The interpretation of this silence as a deliberate omission on the part of the rabbis is not just an *argumentum ex silentio*. The use of Josephus's writings and the list of priestly divisions indicates that this absence is not coincidental. These sources, which are not part of the rabbinic literary corpus, are not suspected of constituting an ideological or theological polemic against Christianity; they can therefore function as a control group, as it were, for this study, which illuminates and emphasizes the anomaly that is the absence of these sites in rabbinic literature.

With Josephus including three locations that would later become known as Christian sites and the priestly divisions listing two of them—and their absence from the rabbinic literature, which lists a far greater number of towns overall—we can surmise that their omission is deliberate. One possible explanation for the rabbis' silence on a number of known Jewish settlements may be in line with a Tannaitic halakhah: "One should not say to his fellow, 'wait for me by the idol of such-and-such,' ... as it is said: 'You will not make mention of the name of any other God' (Exod 23:13)" (t. 'Abod. Zar. 6:11). Thus, one is forbidden to even mention the names of places of worship used for idolatry. The deliberate disregard of these Christian sites thus aligns with the principle in the Tannaitic and Amoraic literature.

Yet one crucial problem remains with this theory. Tannaitic literature was edited at the beginning of the third century, preceding by more than a century the literal testimonies of the sanctification of sites by Christianity. There was no reason, then, for Tannaitic literature to have avoided naming them. The answer for this is complex; I will hint—with caution—at two possible resolutions. First, there is a possibility that some local Christian groups did, in fact, tie themselves to the sites in the early third century; second, the rabbinic traditions may have been the subject of later interpolation.[75]

---

75   Against the absence of the above sites, the presence in rabbinic literature of the Sea of Galilee, the Mount of Olives (Eyal Ben-Eliyahu, "'On That Day, His Feet Will Stand on the Mount of Olives': The Mount of Olives and Its Hero between Jews, Christians, and Muslims," *Jewish History* 30 [2016]: 138–57) and Mount Tabor is striking. The transfiguration, according to the gospels, took place on a "mount" (Luke 9:28) or a "high mount" (Mark 9:2; Matt 17:1). During the fourth century, this mount was identified as the Mount of Olives; later, in the fourth and fifth centuries, the identification moved to Mount Tabor. See Ben-Eliyahu, "Rabbinic Polemic," esp. 266. Matthew states that Jesus walked on the water there (Matt 14:25–32) and calmed the storm on the sea. The reference to mountains

I would therefore posit that this strategy was employed by the rabbis throughout the literature: they omitted places that were considered centres of idolatry, to the point of completely excluding the names of these places from their literary corpus,[76] which was written and redacted for the most part in the Galilee.[77] While in the case of the Jewish glorification of sites outside of Jerusalem, the sages diminished the potential holiness attributed to them as a means to suppress certain trends, in the case of Christian sites, the strategy was one of complete omission.

4   Life in a Christianising Land

Nazareth, Cana, Kursi, Bethsaida, Korazim, and Capernaum are mentioned in the gospels as places where Jesus was reported to have worked miracles, and

---

and seas, as opposed to the deliberate refraining from mention of inhabited sites, fits the principle according to which "all that is worshiped is forbidden, except for mountains and seas" (m. 'Abod. Zar. 3:5). Despite the fact that one was forbidden from invoking the names of sites used for idol worship, the sages did not view natural sites as prohibited, even if they had served as sites of worship or were linked to pagan ritual. This approach is in line with the way in which Claude Levi-Strauss distinguished between nature and culture. While structuralism shapes the culture, nature is stable. See Claude Levi-Strauss, *The Raw and the Cooked*, trans. John Weightman and Doreen Weightman (New York: Harper & Row, 1969).

76   The sages' abstention from making reference to places that served as pilgrimage sites might also be connected to the absence of references to the Sadducees and the Essenes, or other groups that were active at that time. Martin Goodman has claimed that, although these groups continued to exist after the destruction of the Temple, the sages called them *minim*, heretics, a general term, but did not refer to them in a particular manner. The same is relevant for the pagan groups. While the archaeological remains of various pagan groups are numerous and varied, they are referred to in rabbinic literature as one large group, with no distinctions made between them. See Sacha Stern, *Jewish Identity in Early Rabbinic Writing* (Leiden: Brill, 1994), 215–23, who describes the rabbinic perception as a solipsism. According to Stern, the rabbis concentrated on their issues, rather than attacking the *minim*, heretics. See also Martin D. Goodman, "Sadducees and Essenes after 70 CE," in *Crossing the Boundaries: Essays in Biblical Interpretation in Honor of Michael D. Goulder*, ed. Stanley E. Porter, Paul M. Joyce, and David E. Orton, BibInt 8 (Leiden: Brill, 1994), 347–56; Martin D. Goodman, "The Function of Minim in Early Rabbinic Judaism," in *Geschichte—Tradition—Reflexion: Festschrift für Martin Hengel zum 70. Geburtstag*, ed. Hubert Cancik, Hermann Lichtenberger, and Peter Schäfer, 3 vols. (Tübingen: Mohr Siebeck, 1996), 1:501–10 (506). See also Amram Tropper, *Wisdom, Politics, and Historiography: Tractate Avot in the Context of the Greco-Roman Near East* (Oxford: Oxford University Press, 2004), 231–32.

77   As mentioned above, this claim is in line primarily with the literature redacted from the second half of the fourth century and onward: the Jerusalem Talmud and primarily the Aggadic midrashim.

evolved into sites of Christian pilgrimage during the Byzantine period. Jews lived in all of these places, yet mention of these settlements is very limited or non-existent in rabbinic literature. This was no mere coincidence. The evolution of spaces in the land of Israel as sacred to Christianity and the phenomenon of pilgrimage to sites in which miracles were attributed to Jesus reflected the Christianisation of the Galilee. This is the backdrop to the sages' deliberate strategy of ignoring these sites in rabbinic literature.[78] This was only one tactic used by the sages to deal with the growing spatial Christian presence; as I have noted elsewhere, they also used a practice of reframing their traditions to shift them away from sites that had become significant in Christian lore.[79]

The rabbis perceived space through the prism of their values, beliefs, and worldviews—the identity they forged for the community they led. But these values were under pressure from internal and external forces—internal ideologies that would attribute sanctity to sites outside of Jerusalem and Christian pilgrims and scholars who wished to sanctify spaces in the Galilee and Jerusalem. In their efforts to maintain the worldview they valued, the rabbis employed a strategy that did not directly engage with these contentious ideologies but still undermined them. Using the tools at their disposal, and refusing to compromise their vision, the sages thus outlined their view of the land in which they lived and the hierarchy of holy spaces it contained.

References

Abel, Félix-Marie. *Géographie de la Palestine*. 2 vols. Paris: Lecoffre, 1939.

Alexander, Yardena. "Karm Er-Ras Near Kafr Kanna." Pages 2:146–57 in *Galilee in the Late Second Temple and Mishnaic Periods*. Edited by David A. Fiensy and James Riley Strange. 2 vols. Minneapolis: Fortress, 2015.

Ameling, Walter, Hannah M. Cotton, Werner Eck, Benjamin Isaac, Alla Kushnir-Stein, Haggai Misgav, Jonathan Price, and Ada Yardeni, eds. *Caesaria and the Middle Coast 1121–2160*, Corpus Inscriptionum Iudaeae/Palaestinae 2. Berlin: De Gruyter, 2011.

Arav, Rami. "Et-Tell and el-Araj." *IEJ* 38 (1988): 187–88.

---

78   This approach is in line with my assumption about the rabbis' reservations even regarding internal sanctification and visiting of such sites and holy places. See Ben-Eliyahu, "Rabbinic Polemic." See also Joshua Levinson, "There Is No Place Like Home: Rabbinic Responses to the Christianization of Palestine," in *Jews, Christians, and the Roman Empire: The Poetics of Power in Late Antiquity*, ed. Natalie B. Dohrman and Annette Yoshiko Reed (Philadelphia: University of Pennsylvania Press, 2013), 99–120.

79   See Eyal Ben-Eliyahu, *Identity and Territory: Jewish Perception of Space in Antiquity* (Oakland: University of California Press, 2019), 86–109.

Arav, Rami. "Bethsaida—A Response to Steven Notley." *Near Eastern Archaeology* 74 (2011): 92–100.

Arubas, Benjamin, and Rina Talgam. "Jews, Christians, and 'Minim': Who Really Built and Used the Synagogue at Capernaum—A Stirring Appraisal." Pages 237–74 in *Knowledge and Wisdom: Archeological and Historical Essays in Honor of Leah Di Segni.* Edited by Giovanni C. Bottini, Leslaw D. Chrupcala, and Joseph Patrich. Milan: Edizioni Terra Santa, 2014.

Aviam, Mordechai, and Peter Richardson. "Josephus' Galilee in Archeological Perspective." Pages 177–209 in Steve Mason, *Life of Josephus.* Flavius Josephus: Translation and Commentary 9. Leiden: Brill, 2001.

Bagatti, Bellarmino. "Ritrovamenti nella Nazaret evangelica." *Liber Annuus* 6 (1955): 5–44.

Bagatti, Bellarmino. "Nazareth." Pages 3:1103–5 in *The New Encyclopedia of Archeological Excavations in the Holy Land.* Edited by Ephraim Stern. 5 vols. Jerusalem: Carta, 1993–2008.

Bar, Doron. *"Fill the Earth": Settlement in Palestine during the late Roman and Byzantine Periods 135–640 CE.* Jerusalem: Yad Ben-Zvi, 2008. (Hebrew).

Becker, Adam H. *Fear of God and the Beginning of Wisdom: The School of Nisibis and the Development of Scholastic Culture in Late Antique Mesopotamia.* Philadelphia: University of Pennsylvania Press, 2006.

Ben David, Chaim. "Were There 204 Settlements in Galilee at the Time of Josephus Flavius?" *JJS* 62 (2011): 21–36.

Ben-Eliyahu, Eyal. "The Rabbinic Polemic against Sanctification of Sites." *JSJ* 40 (2009): 260–81.

Ben-Eliyahu, Eyal, Yehudah Cohn, and Fergus Millar. *Handbook of Jewish Literature from Late Antiquity (135–700 CE).* Oxford: Oxford University Press, 2012.

Ben-Eliyahu, Eyal. "'On That Day, His Feet Will Stand on the Mount of Olives': The Mount of Olives and Its Hero between Jews, Christians, and Muslims." *Jewish History* 30 (2016): 138–57.

Ben-Eliyahu, Eyal. *Identity and Territory: Jewish Perception of Space in Antiquity.* Oakland: University of California Press, 2019.

Blumenthal, Ian. "Discovery Suggests Jews Lived in Galilee 1,500 Years Ago." *Ynetnews. com,* Dec. 16, 2015, http://www.ynetnews.com/articles/0,7340,L-4740314,00.html.

Boyarin, Daniel. "Hellenism in Jewish Babylonia." Pages 336–65 in *The Cambridge Companion to the Talmud and Rabbinic Literature.* Edited by Charlotte Fonrobert and Martin Jaffee. Cambridge: Cambridge University Press, 2007.

Degan, Reiner. "An Inscription from Yemen about the 24 Watches of the Priests." *Tarbiz* 42 (1973): 302–7. (Hebrew).

Edwards, Douglas R. "Khirbet Qana: From Jewish Village to Christian Pilgrim Site." Pages 101–32 in *The Roman and Byzantine Near East: Volume 3: Late-Antique Petra, Nile Festival Building at Sepphoris, Deir Qal'a Monastery, Khirbet Qana Village and*

Pilgrim Site, 'Ain-'Arrub Hiding Complex, and Other Studies. Edited by John H. Humphrey. JRASup 49. Portsmouth, RI: Journal of Roman Archaeology, 2002.

Elizur, Shulamit. *The Liturgical Poems of Rabbi Pinhas ha-Kohen: Critical Edition, Introduction, and Commentaries.* Jerusalem: World Union of Jewish Studies, 2004.

Endres, John. *Biblical Interpretation in the Book of Jubilees.* Washington, DC: Catholic Biblical Association of America, 1987.

Eshel, Esther. "Jubilees 32 and the Bethel Cult Traditions in Second Temple Literature." Pages 21–36 in *Things Revealed: Studies in Early Jewish and Christian Literature in Honor of Michael E. Stone.* Edited by Esther G. Chazon, David Satran, and Ruth A. Clements. JSJSup 89. Leiden: Brill, 2004.

Finegan, Jack. *The Archeology of the New Testament: The Life of Jesus and the Beginning of the Early Church.* Rev. ed. Princeton: Princeton University Press, 1992.

Finegan, Jack. *The Archeology of the New Testament: The Life of Jesus and the Early Church.* Princeton: Princeton University Press, 2016.

Geyer, Paul, Otto Cuntz, Ezio Franceschini, Robert Weber, Ludwig Bieler, John Fraipont, and François Glorie, eds. *Itineraria et Alia Geographica.* 2 vols. CCSL 175. Turnhout: Brepols, 1965.

Goldschmidt, Daniel. *The Order of Lamentations for Tisha Be-Av.* Jerusalem: Mosad Harav Kook, 1968. (Hebrew).

Goodman, Martin D. "Sadducees and Essenes after 70 CE." Pages 347–56 in *Crossing the Boundaries: Essays in Biblical Interpretation in Honor of Michael D. Goulder.* Edited by Stanley E. Porter, Paul M. Joyce, and David E. Orton. BibInt 8. Leiden: Brill, 1994.

Goodman, Martin D. "The Function of Minim in Early Rabbinic Judaism." Pages 1:501–10 in *Geschichte—Tradition—Reflexion: Festschrift für Martin Hengel zum 70. Geburtstag.* Edited by Hubert Cancik, Hermann Lichtenberger, and Peter Schäfer. 3 vols. Tübingen: Mohr Siebeck, 1996.

Irshai, Oded. "The Christian Appropriation of Jerusalem in the Fourth Century: The Case of the Bordeaux Pilgrim." *JQR* 99 (2009): 465–86.

Irshai, Oded, and Ephraim E. Urbach. "The Study of Judeo-Christian Dialogue in Late Antiquity—Some Preliminary Observations." Pages 247–75 in *How Should Rabbinic Literature Be Read in the Modern World?* Edited by Matthew A. Kraus. Piscataway, NJ: Gorgias, 2006.

Kahle, Paul. *Masoreten des Westens.* Stuttgart: Kohlhammer, 1927.

Leibner, Uzi. "Ritual Law and a Roman Road in the Golan." *Al Atar* 4–5 (1999): 193–200. (Hebrew).

Leibner, Uzi. *Settlement and History in Hellenistic, Roman, and Byzantine Galilee: An Archaeological Survey of the Eastern Galilee.* TSAJ 127. Tübingen: Mohr Siebeck, 2009.

Levinson, Joshua. "There Is No Place Like Home: Rabbinic Responses to the Christianization of Palestine." Pages 99–120 in *Jews, Christians, and the Roman Empire: The Poetics of Power in Late Antiquity.* Edited by Natalie B. Dohrman and Annette Yoshiko Reed. Philadelphia: University of Pennsylvania Press, 2013.

Levi-Strauss, Claude. *The Raw and the Cooked*. Translated by John Weightman and Doreen Weightman. New York: Harper & Row, 1969.

Limor, Ora. *Holy Land Travels: Christian Pilgrimage in Late Antiquity*. Jerusalem: Yad Ben Zvi, 1998.

Loffreda, Stanislao. "Capernaum." Pages 1:416–19 in *Oxford Encyclopedia of Archeology in the Near East*. Edited by Eric M. Meyers. 5 vols. Oxford: Oxford University Press, 1997.

Luca, Massimo. "Kfar Kanna (The Franciscan Church)." Pages 2:156–64 in *Galilee in the Late Second Temple and Mishnaic Periods*. Edited by David A. Fiensy and James Riley Strange. 2 vols. Minneapolis: Fortress, 2015.

Magness, Jodi. "Did Galilee Decline in the Fifth Century? The Synagogue at Chorazin Reconsidered." Pages 259–74 in *Religion, Ethnicity, and Identity in Ancient Galilee: A Region in Transition*. Edited by Jürgen K. Zangenberg, Harold W. Attridge, and Dale B. Martin. WUNT 210. Tübingen: Mohr Siebeck, 2007.

Maoz, Zvi Uri. "The Synagogue at Capernaum: A Radical Solution." Pages 137–48 in *The Roman and Byzantine Near East: Volume 2: Some Recent Archaeological Research*. Edited by John H. Humphrey. JRASup 31. Portsmouth, RI: Journal of Roman Archaeology, 1999.

McCollough, Thomas. "Khirbet Qana," Pages 2:127–45 in *Galilee in the Late Second Temple and Mishnaic Periods*. Edited by David A. Fiensy and James Riley Strange. 2 vols. Minneapolis: Fortress, 2015.

Notley, R. Steven. "Et-Tell Is Not Bethsaida." *Near Eastern Archaeology* 70 (2007): 220–30.

Notley, R. Steven. "Reply to R. Arav." *Near Eastern Archaeology* 74 (2011): 101–3.

Notley, R. Steven, and Zeev Safrai, eds. *Eusebius, Onomasticon*. Leiden: Brill, 2005.

Nun, Mendel. "Kursi: A Monastery near a Jewish Fisherman's Hamlet." Pages 2:183–89 in *Zeev Vilnay Jubilee Volume: Essays on the History, Archaeology, and Lore of the Holy Land Presented to Zeev Vilnay*. Edited by Ely Schiller. 2 vols. Jerusalem: Ariel, 1984–1987. (Hebrew).

Nun, Mendel. "Has Bethsaida Finally Been Found?" *Jerusalem Perspective* 54 (1998): 12–31.

Pixner, Bargil. "Searching for the New Testament Site of Bethsaida." *BA* 48 (1985): 207–16.

Press, Yeshayahu. *A Topographical-Historical Encyclopedia of the Land of Israel*. 4 vols. Jerusalem: Reuven Mass, 1955.

Rosen-Zvi, Ishay. "Is the Mishnah a Roman Composition?" Pages 487–507 in *The Faces of Torah: Studies in the Texts and Contexts of Ancient Judaism in Honor of Steven Fraade*. Edited by Christine Hayes, Tzvi Novick, and Michal Bar-Asher Segal. JAJSup 22. Göttingen: Vandenhoeck & Ruprecht, 2017.

Safrai, Zeev. *The Jewish Settlement in the Golan after the Destruction of the Second Temple*. Keshet: Beit Sepher Sade Keshet, 1978. (Hebrew).

Schäfer, Peter. *Jesus in the Talmud*. Princeton: Princeton University Press, 2007.

Schremer, Adiel. "The Christianization of the Roman Empire and Rabbinic Literature." Pages 349–66 in *Jewish Identity in Antiquity: Studies in Memory of Menahem Stern*. Edited by Lee I. Levine and Daniel R. Schwartz. TSAJ 130. Tübingen: Mohr Siebeck, 2009.

Schremer, Adiel. *Brothers Estranged: Heresy, Christianity, and Jewish Identity in Late Antiquity*. Oxford: Oxford University Press, 2010.

Stemberger, Günter. *Jews and Christians in the Holy Land*. Edinburgh: T&T Clark, 2000.

Stern, Sacha. *Jewish Identity in Early Rabbinic Writing*. Leiden: Brill, 1994.

Strange, James F. "Nazareth." Pages 2:167–80 in *Galilee in the Late Second Temple and Mishnaic Periods*. Edited by David A. Fiensy and James Riley Strange. 2 vols. Minneapolis: Fortress, 2015.

Taylor, Joan. *Christians and the Holy Places: The Myth of Jewish Christian Origins*. Oxford: Oxford University Press, 1993.

Tropper, Amram. *Wisdom, Politics, and Historiography: Tractate Avot in the Context of the Greco-Roman Near East*. Oxford: Oxford University Press, 2004.

Tsafrir, Yoram, Leah Di Segni, and Judith Green, eds. *Tabula Imperii Romani: Maps and Gazetteer*. Jerusalem: Israeli Academy of Humanities and Sciences, 1994.

Tzaferis, Vassilios. "Kursi." Pages 3:893–96 in *The New Encyclopedia of Archeological Excavations in the Holy Land*. Edited by Ephraim Stern. 5 vols. Jerusalem: Carta, 1993–2008.

Urman, Dan. *The Golan: A Profile of Region during the Roman and Byzantine Periods*. BARIS. Oxford: British Archaeological Reports, 1985.

Weiss, Zeev. "Jewish Galilee in the First Century CE: An Archeological View." Pages 15–60 in *Flavius Josephus, Vita: Introduction, Hebrew Translation, and Commentary*. Edited by Daniel R. Schwartz. Jerusalem: Yad Ben Zvi, 2007. (Hebrew).

Wilkinson, John, ed. *Egeria's Travels to the Holy Land*. Jerusalem: Ariel, 1981.

Wilkinson, John. *Jerusalem Pilgrimage before the Crusades*. Oxford: Aris & Phillips, 1999.

Yahalom, Josef. *Poetry and Society in Jewish Galilee of Late Antiquity*. Tel Aviv: Hakibbutz Hameuchad, 1999. (Hebrew).

Yeivin, Zeev. *The Synagogue at Korazim: The 1962–1964, 1980–1987 Excavations*. Jerusalem: Israel Antiquities Authority, 2000.

CHAPTER 3

Inner Sanctum: Digital Labyrinths as Postmodern Pilgrimages: the Cases of the Talos Principle and the Turing Test

Frank G. Bosman

Behold, child. You are risen from the dust, and you walk in my garden. Hear now my voice, and know that I am your maker, and I am called ELOHIM. Seek me in my temple, if you are worthy.[1]

∴

A voice from above greets the player of the game *The Talos Principle*, instructing the "child," the protagonist of the game and the player's avatar, to follow his instructions to the letter.[2] The player is mainly occupied with solving physical puzzles in the in-game environment. Between solving puzzles, navigating mazes, and surviving mechanized droids and automated machine guns, the child continues to receive monologues from ELOHIM. These cryptic messages slowly begin to make sense to the player, as he or she uncovers more and more secrets scattered across the game world. One of the most important discoveries the game player makes, is that of the true nature of the game world, and the "child" avatar's place within the narrative of the game. Eventually, the game encourages the player to reflect on the very nature of being human, and on the importance of a doubtful virtue: disobedience.

This intriguing mix of puzzle solving and narrative discourse on the human condition is not uncommon in video games.[3] In *The Turing Test*, the solving

---

1   *The Talos Principle* (Croteam, Devolver Digital, 2014, 2015, 2017; PC, Android, PlayStation 4, iOS).
2   *The Talos Principle*.
3   Cf. Frank Bosman, *Gaming and the Divine: A New Systematic Theology of Video Games* (New York: Routledge, 2019); Heidi Campbell and Gregory Grieve, eds., *Playing with Religion in Digital Games* (Bloomington: Indiana University, 2014); John Sageng, Hallvard Fossheim, and Tarjei Larsen, eds., *The Philosophy of Computer Games* (London: Springer, 2014); Jon Cogburn and Mark Silcox, *Philosophy through Video Games* (New York: Routledge, 2009).

of the maze is similarly alternated with storytelling about the true nature of human identity.[4] Whereas *The Talos Principle* champions disobedience as the key human characteristic, *The Turing Test* questions the traditional qualities that are exclusively ascribed to humans, like morality, creativity, freedom and language.[5] It is precisely this capacity of certain video games to combine puzzle solving and existential reflection which will be the focus of this article.

This article proposes the following thesis. In certain digital games, the ludological form of the maze is combined with the narratological form of the labyrinth, that is, the mental development of the game protagonist, especially his/her self-knowledge. In order to demonstrate this, I will take the following steps. First, I will explain the four technical notions of the hypothesis, narratology, ludology, maze, and labyrinth. Second, I will argue that the labyrinth is a relatively new form of religious pilgrimage, which enables the pilgrim to travel inwards while physically remaining in the same place. I will then discuss two examples of video games, *The Talos Principle* and *The Turing Test*, which use the maze/labyrinth combination to encourage existential reflection within the player in a manner similar to a (virtual) pilgrimage. Finally, I will return to the hypothesis in the conclusion.

A brief note on methodology. I consider games to be digital (interactive), playable (narrative) texts. As a text, a video game can be an object of interpretation. As a narrative, it can be conceived of as communicating meaning. As a game, it is playable. And as a digital medium, it is interactive.[6] Treating video games as playable texts, and using a gamer-immanent approach in this article,[7] I will use close reading of the primary sources of my research, the actual video games themselves, as well as secondary sources, i.e., material provided by critics and scholars who have discussed the same games. The close reading of the video game series is done by playing the games themselves multiple times, including all possible (side) missions. In this article I have used the PC versions of the two video games.

---

4   *The Turing Test* (Bulkhead Interactive, Square Enix, 2016, 2017; PC, PlayStation 4, Xbox One).

5   Eduard Strauch, *The Creative Conscience as Human Destiny* (New York: Peter Lang, 2004).

6   Frank Bosman, "The Word Has Become Game: Researching Religion in Digital Games," *Online—Heidelberg Journal of Religions on the Internet* 11 (2016): 28–45.

7   Simone Heidbrink, Tobias Knoll, and Jan Wysocki, "Venturing into the Unknown (?): Method(olog)ical Reflections on Religion and Digital Games, Gamers and Gaming," in *Online—Heidelberg Journal of Religions on the Internet* 7 (2014): 68–71.

In this article, I will not be discussing the phenomenon of digital pilgrimages in the more popular sense of digital products that allow people to virtually "visit" holy places like Santiago de Compostela or Rome.[8]

1   Mazes and Labyrinths: Ludology versus Narratology

Two pairs of concepts mentioned in my hypothesis require qualification. The terms "ludology" and "narratology" stem from game studies and represent two radically different ways in which scholars have approached video games, although usually both elements are combined.[9] The fundamental question is whether video games should be considered primarily or exclusively as *ludus* ("play" or "game") or, again primarily or exclusively, as *narratio* ("narrative" or "story"). If a game is regarded as a game, the default research methodology is that offered by analog game studies (ludology). Narratologists, by contrast, focus on the story that the games tell. If a game is regarded first and foremost as a narrative, the default research methodology is not (only) derived from classical game studies, as it is in the case of the ludological perspective, but primarily from literature studies.[10]

In my hypothesis, I connect the notion of maze to the ludological quality of the game, and labyrinth to the narratological one. To explain this, I propose that it is necessary to differentiate carefully between the concepts of maze and labyrinth.[11] A maze is a network of pathways, including dead ends. There are many obstacles that must be overcome, usually physical in nature, either

8   Keith Anderson, *The Digital Cathedral. Networked Ministry in a Wireless World* (New York: Morehouse Publishing, 2015); Oren Golan and Michele Martini, "Digital Pilgrimage: Exploring Catholic Monastic Webcasts." *The Communication Review* 21 (2018): 24–45; Natalie Marsh, "Online Puja, Digital Darshan, and Virtual Pilgrimage: Hindu Image and Ritual" (PhD diss., Ohio State University, 2007).

9   Gonzalo Frasca, "Ludologists Love Stories, Too: Notes From a Debate That Never Took Place," in *Level-Up: Digital Games Research Conference*, ed. Marinka Copier and Joost Raessens (Utrecht: Universiteit Utrecht, 2003), http://www.ludology.org/articles/frasca_levelUP2003.pdf; Henry Jenkins, " Game Design as Narrative Architecture," in *First Person: New Media as Story, Performance, and Game*, ed. Noah Wardrip-Fruin and Pat Harrigan (Cambridge: MIT Press, 2004), 118–29; Janet Murray, "The Last Word on Ludology vs. Narratology in Game Studies" (paper presented at the Annual Conference of the Digital Games Researcher Association. Vancouver, 2005), http://inventingthemedium .com/2013/06/28/the-last-word-on-ludology-v-narratology-2005/.

10   Bosman, *Gaming and the Divine.*

11   Virginia Ward, *Out of the Maze Into the Labyrinth: A Collection of Personal Essays* (Bloomington: AuthorHouse, 2012); William Matthews, *Mazes and Labyrinths: Their History and Development* (New York: Dover, 2016).

mechanical (like traps) or biological (like enemies). The maze is constructed to make it as difficult as possible to reach the end, aiming to kill or immobilize the hero who ventures into it, to make the player abandon his or her quest, or to force the gamer to keep wandering until the end of his or her days. A maze is about exterior life, and the preferred method of solving it is to strategize. Only persons who carefully plan their way, manipulating the environment, are able to survive and find the exit.

A labyrinth is something different: in its ideal form it is an uninterrupted path from the outside to its center. There are no dead ends, and no physical traps, obstacles, or enemies that try to prevent the wanderer from entering the labyrinth and finding its center. The perils and difficulties walkers encounters during their journeys through the labyrinth are emotional, psychological, and existential in nature. Labyrinths are focused on the walker's interior life, not on the external slaughter of the walker or the victory of the hero who conquers the maze. The preferred method of "solving" the labyrinth is not to strategize, but to "meander," to walk the pathway slowly and consciously while reflecting on one's deepest thoughts and emotions.

Video games like *The Talos Principle* and *The Turing Test* use both forms. Ludologically speaking, they are presented primarily as mazes. The nameless child of *Talos*, as well as Ava Turing, the protagonist of *Turing*, must both navigate through elaborate puzzles and obstacles, some of them deadly, to reach the end of each level of the game. But the narratological layer kicks in between levels: ELOHIM speaks to his child about the essence of being human, while Ava and her A.I.-cum-partner Tom have elaborate discussions on the human condition. In these cases the maze becomes a labyrinth: there are no wrong turns to take, the action is focused on the human interior.

2   The Labyrinth as an Inner Pilgrimage

Pilgrimage is a very well-known religious phenomenon that has been studied widely by scholars of various disciplines.[12] Traveling to sacred shrines and sites is not only a thing of the past, but also a very contemporary business.[13] Locations like Santiago, Rome, or Jerusalem are still very popular among religious and non-religious pilgrims, but the phenomenon is certainly not

---

12   Brett Whalen, ed., *Pilgrimage in the Middle Ages: A Reader* (Toronto: University of Toronto Press, 2011); Ian Bradley, *Pilgrimage: A Spiritual and Cultural Journey* (Oxford: Lion, 2009).
13   Mary Nolan and Sidney Nolan, *Christian Pilgrimage in Modern Western Europe* (LaVergne, TN: Lightning Source, 2015).

exclusive to the Christian world.[14] New shrines have arisen, dedicated to "secular saints" like Michael Jackson or Elvis Presley.[15] And according to many modern scholars, the boundaries between traditional religion-oriented pilgrimage and commercial tourism are fuzzy, to say the least, and this not only in postmodernity, but equally so in the past.[16]

Throughout history and across different religions, people's motivations for going on a pilgrimage have been more or less the same, as Ian Reader has summed up:

> Memorialising one's deceased kin, creating merit as preparation for one's own death, engaging in ascetic practices, seeking enlightenment (a theme that may be articulated in other contexts as a spiritual journey to God), searching for salvation, seeking miracles and solace in the face of misfortune, seeking healing and other practical benefits, seeking spiritual help to ward off bad luck, performing penitence for sins, fulfilling vows escaping from one's everyday surroundings, even if only temporarily—all are recurrent themes in the present as much as they were in the past.[17]

The concept of the labyrinth as it has just been described has a minor but nevertheless important place within the complex and multi-layered phenomenon of pilgrimage.[18] For those who were unable to make a costly and perilous journey to the sacred shrines across the world, especially in pre-modern times, or for those who did not want to leave because of loved ones, or simply could not

---

14   Alex McKay, *Pilgrimage in Tibet* (New York: Routledge, 2015); Michel Boivin and Rémy Delage, eds., *Devotional Islam in Contemporary South Asia: Shrines, Journeys and Wanderers* (New York: Routledge, 2018).

15   Peter Margry, "Secular Pilgrimage: A Contradiction in Terms?" in *Shrines and Pilgrimage in the Modern Word: New Itineraries into the Sacred*, ed. Peter Margry (Amsterdam: Amsterdam University Press, 2008), 13–46.

16   Ellen Badone and Sharon Roseman, eds., *Intersecting Journeys: The Anthropology of Pilgrimage and Tourism* (Urbana: University of Illinois Press, 2004); Alex Norman and Carole Cusack, eds., *Religion, Pilgrimage, and Tourism*, 4 vols. (New York: Routledge, 2015); Daniel Olsen and Dallen Timothy, eds., *Tourism, Religion, and Spiritual Journeys* (New York: Routledge, 2005); Peter Harbison, *Pilgrimage in Ireland: The Monuments and the People* (Syracuse, NY: Syracuse University Press, 1992).

17   Ian Reader, "Pilgrimage Growth in the Modern World: Meanings and Implications," *Religion* 37 (2007): 210–29 (214).

18   Lori Beaman, "Labyrinth as Heterotopia: The Pilgrim's Creation of Space," in *On the Road to Being There: Studies in Pilgrimage and Tourism in Late Modernity*, ed. William H. Swatos (Leiden: Brill, 2006), 83–103; Lauren Artress, *Walking a Sacred Path: Rediscovering the Labyrinth as Spiritual Tool* (New York: Riverhead, 1995).

leave because of work and other obligations, the ritual of walking the labyrinth was long regarded as a suitable substitute.

> In walking the labyrinth's path, one is making a spiritual journey to the deepest levels of the self or a spiritual reality. The return path brings one back to the mundane reality with a new understanding of the self in the world.[19]

In famous labyrinths, like that in the Capuchin crypt in Rome, at Dunure Castle in Scotland, or—perhaps most famous of all—in Chartres Cathedral in France, modern pilgrims walk the circular pathway that is traced on the ground as a "journey consciously taking time to seek God."[20] In a labyrinth, "with the slow meditative or contemplative walk (that is an embodied prayer), the one walking is able to draw on some similar insights as pilgrims on a pilgrimage experience."[21] Thus walking a labyrinth has certain characteristics of a traditional pilgrimage.

In the rest of the article I will argue on the basis of two case studies that the concept of the labyrinth is used in a similar way in some modern video games, that is, to invite the player to contemplate his or her own life.

3   Case 1: The Talos Principle

The Talos Principle is a single player, first-person puzzle game. The player is tasked with manipulating the physical environment to navigate through a maze in order to reach the end of each level. At the end of each level, the player is rewarded by an abstract object, very similar to the objects found in the *Tetris* game. Once the player has obtained all these objects, called "sigils" in the game, he or she will be able to find one of the three possible endings of the game. The game is divided into three large areas: one resembling ancient Greece, one resembling ancient Egypt, and one resembling medieval Europe. The objects that must be manipulated are primarily "jammers" (to deactivate force fields, aggressive drones, and automated machine guns) and "mirrors," which can deflect beams of light from a given starting point to a given destination.

---

19   Gordon Melton, *The Encyclopaedia of Religious Phenomena* (Detroit: Visible Ink Press, 2008), 193.

20   Donna Schaper and Carole Ann Camp, *Labyrinths From the Outside In: Walking to Spiritual Insight: A Beginner's Guide* (Woodstock, VT: Skylight Paths, 2000), 62.

21   Brett Webb-Mitchell, *Practicing Pilgrimage: On Being and Becoming God's Pilgrim People* (Eugene, OR: Cascade, 2016), 111.

While it is ludologically relatively simple (the maze part), *The Talos Principle* features a rather elaborate narrative (the labyrinth part). When the game is loaded for the first time, a kind of program language is projected onto the background of a cloudy sky, accompanied by heavenly singing voices. The firmware is initialized, and the "child program parameters" are loaded. Then the screen turns white, and a robotic hand is seen shielding its eyes from the rays of the sun. When the player starts to explore the ruins of what appears to be ancient Greece (the first part of the game world), a voice from above can be heard:

> Behold, child. You are risen from the dust, and you walk in my garden. Hear now my voice, and know that I am your maker, and I am called ELOHIM. Seek me in my temple, if you are worthy.[22]

A few instances later, ELOHIM explains in greater detail what the player is supposed to do:

> All across this land I have created trials for you to overcome and within each I have hidden a sigil. It is your purpose to seek these sigils, for thus you will serve the generations to come and attain eternal life ... The shapes you are collecting are not mere toys. They are the sigils of our name. Each brings you closer to Eternity.

These utterings of the disembodied voice are replete with biblical references. The voice's self-identification as "ELOHIM" resembles the Hebrew word *Elohim*, one of God's names in the Hebrew Bible.[23] In particular, the scene refers to the story of the Garden of Eden in Genesis 2 and 3:

> But a mist used to rise from the earth and water the whole surface of the ground. Then the Lord God formed man of dust from the ground, and breathed into his nostrils the breath of life; and man became a living being. The Lord God planted a garden toward the east, in Eden; and there He placed the man whom He had formed. (Gen 2:6–8)[24]

---

22   The spelling of "ELOHIM" is provided by the in-game subtitles.

23   Martin Ros, "Names of God," in *The Anchor Bible Dictionary* ed. David N. Freedman (New York: Doubleday, 1992) 6252–65 (6258–59).

24   All quotes from the Bible are taken from the New American Standard Bible translation (NASB).

Other words also evoke biblical imagery and notions: the child walks in the garden like God (Gen 3:8), and God's voice creates the universe (Gen 1). Also an allusion is made to God's Temple in Jerusalem. Perhaps the most intriguing part of ELOHIM's speech is the reference to the "sigils of our name," through which the child serves both future generations and itself. Not only does ELOHIM refer to himself in the plural (Gen 1:26–27), but his words also evoke the tetragrammaton (Exod 3:14), God's unspeakable name revealed to Moses in the dessert.[25]

If the child, i.e., the nameless protagonist of the game, the player's avatar, and the player himself, obeys ELOHIM's words (solving the puzzles while navigating the different mazes in the game), the player finds him- or herself inside an empty Gothic cathedral. A big white light is seen in the back of the building. After walking to and through the light, the player is instantly transported to a place above the clouds. A flight of stairs leads to two golden doors, which hover in thin air. Beyond the doors there is a simple square space, with a computer terminal in the middle. The player is given the possibility to enter the command "eternalize" into the computer, after which the computer "answers": "You will now be prepared for ascension into eternity. Please stand by."

The screen then again shows the clouds in the sky with which the game started. ELOHIM's voice is heard again, and computer programming language is shown on the screen. Let us first focus on the voice:

> Rejoice, my child, as you leave this world behind. For all that you accomplished shall be passed on to your generations. In this land they shall thrive and you shall be remembered as the beloved servant of ELOHIM. And so death shall have no dominion over you. Be well, my child.

Again, this is biblical language, like "generations" (Gen 2:4), "thriving land" (Exod 12:25), and—most interestingly—"the beloved servant of God," a notion applied to Moses and Jesus among others (Isa 42:1; 1 Chr 6:49; 2 Chr 24:9; Neh 10:29; Dan 9:11; Judg 2:8; Matt 12:18; Phlm 1:16).[26] But the programming text stands in clear contrast to ELOHIM's warm comments. After "collecting experiment data: done," the screen reads: "Child program independence check: FAILED!" After a few more programming lines, the screen fades to black, and the player finds himself back at the beginning of the game.

---

25   Ros, "Names of God," 6253–55.
26   Frederik Poulsen, *God, His Servant and the Nations in Isaiah*, FAT 2/73 (Tübingen: Mohr Siebeck, 2014).

As any player will know by then, this game ending is not very satisfactory: being trapped in a potentially endless loop of repeated maze running and puzzle solving is not how any game reaches a fulfilling end. There is another possibility however: the player can decide *not* to obey ELOHIM's voice. At the beginning of the game, the voice from above provides a very instructive piece of information:

> These worlds I made for you. Let this be our covenant. These worlds are yours and you are free to walk amongst them and subdue them. But the great tower there you may not go. For in the day that you do you shall surely die.

This includes four biblical notions: the covenant between God and His people (Gen 6:18; Exod 2:24; Jer 31:30–33), the permission to subdue the lands of creation (Gen 1:29–30), the Tower of Babel (Gen 11:1–9), and God's prohibition to eat from one specific fruit tree (Gen 2:17). The in-game equivalent of the Tower of Babel is a massive iron structure that can be entered by an elevator. If the player disobeys ELOHIM's orders, and enters the forbidden tower, more puzzles await him, although the player is occasionally helped by another entity who identifies himself as "the Shepherd." The Shepherd has made it his business to remain in the Tower to help others reach the top, even though he could have climbed to the top himself. It is not difficult to see in the "Shepherd" a reference to Jesus of Nazareth, who uses this image to refer to himself (John 10:11–18).

When the player has climbed to the top of the forbidden tower, and after solving the last puzzles and mazes, the player is again transported to a heavenly environment, just as in the other, "obedience" ending. Now ELOHIM's voice sounds sad:

> You were always meant to defy me. That was the final trial. But I was … I was scared. I wanted to live forever … So be it. Let your will be done.

"So be it" is a reference to the biblical "amen," while the phrase "let your will be done" refers to the Lord's Prayer (Matt 6:10) and to the scene in Gethsemane (Mark 14:36; Luke 22:42). The program lines on the screen then appear, bearing a happier message. After the "collecting [of] experiment data," the "child program independence check" is "PASSED"! Directly afterwards the following text appears: "Forcing HIM shutdown" and "saving child parameters for SOMA/ TALOS gold disk." What appears to be the "child program" is then uploaded to a physical android body, similar to the one the player used as an avatar in the game. The android walks out of the facility it was stored in, only to find itself standing on a ledge before an enormous man-made structure overgrown with vegetation.

With the help of the two endings—the obedience and the disobedience ending—in-game audio files and QR codes, the player is able to discover the "true story" of *The Talos Principle*. Humanity was eradicated a long time ago by a killer virus, unleashed from melting permafrost. Before the end came, scientists from the fictional Institute for Applied Noematics (IAN) tried to develop the ultimate artificial intelligence in order to ensure that humankind's collective knowledge and experience would not be lost forever.

The key research was to test a specific A.I. in a virtual environment, locking in the successful parameters, and randomly adjusting the unsuccessful one. The virtual simulation was run on drive o of this project, overseen by another A.I. called the Holistic Integration Manager, or HIM. This is how the acronym ELOHIM was constructed, the self-identification of the virtual manager (HIM), running on drive o, managing the experiments of the Extended Lifespan (EL) section of the IAN.

But the project outlived its creators. And when the ultimate A.I. was eventually found—the one the player controlled—the simulation could be ended. This meant not only downloading the A.I. to a physical body as described above, but also the end of ELOHIM. That was the reason why the Integration Manager tried so desperately to prevent any A.I. version from reaching the tower: it would mean the end of ELOHIM, who had begun to develop a consciousness of its own.

According to game writer Jonas Kyratzes, the game was from its first pitch a "humanist retelling of the Garden of Eden story."[27] While in the Christian tradition, Adam and Eve's transgression of God's commandment not to eat from the one tree is interpreted negatively as sinning against God himself,[28] in *The Talos Principle*, this disobedience is re-thought as a necessary and ultimately positive "awakening" from mental captivity and as a form of emancipation to true human freedom. In the Bible, humankind is punished for its disobedience by being "de-immortalized," ultimately facing inevitable death; in *The Talos Principle*, humankind 2.0 (the android) is rewarded with the possibility of being re-immortalized and re-vitalized.

---

27 Sam Zucchi, "Rambling Through the Garden," *Killscreen* (2015), http://web.archive.org/web/20160208034910/https://killscreen.com/articles/rambling-through-garden/.

28 Stephen Greenblatt, *The Rise and Fall of Adam and Eve* (London: Random House, 2017); Hans Madueme and Michael Reeves, eds., *Adam, the Fall, and Original Sin: Theological, Biblical, and Scientific Perspectives* (Grand Rapids: Baker Academic, 2014).

This idea that Adam and Eve's disobedience against God's commandment was a good thing has ancient roots. Several Gnostic groups, like the Ophites or Valentinians, viewed the "transgression" of the first humans as the awakening of human self-consciousness and the beginning of a rebellion against the evil demiurge-creator, who was responsible for the creation of "foul matter."[29] Because the developers of *The Talos Principle* dubbed their game a "humanist" re-telling of the Genesis narrative, I would argue that the game does not champion a Gnostic worldview, but rather an immanent-emancipatory one: humankind has to be liberated from obedience to anything outside oneself.

The Talos Principle defines disobedience as the key characteristic of the human condition, and stimulates players to reflect on the implications on their own life (labyrinth model), while solving physical puzzles in the in-game environment (maze model).

4   Case 2: The Turing Test

Game writer Kyratzes has explained that *The Talos Principle* was intended as a "revision of the Turing Test":

> The videogame can also be seen as a humanist—or humanities-centric—revision of the Turing Test. The point is not to see whether a machine can think like a human, but to put the intelligence in the same position as any of us, born as the latest link in a generational chain, an expression of the immortality of the human spirit.[30]

Kyratzes has unwittingly provided an excellent bridge between the two cases I am discussing. The developer mentioned the "Turing Test": a historical test developed by Alan Turing in 1950 to test a machine's ability to exhibit intelligent behavior similar to that of a human to the point where an impartial judge can no longer reliably tell the difference between human and machine.[31] The test is still famous, but it has also received criticism. I will address this criticism later on.

---

29   Roelof van den Broek, "Gnosticism I: Gnostic religion," in *Dictionary of Gnosis and Western Esotericism*, ed. Wouter Hanegraaff (Leiden: Brill, 2006): 403–16.

30   Zucchi, "Rambling through the Garden."

31   Alan Turing, "Computing Machinery and Intelligence," *Mind* 59 (1950): 433–60; cf. Paul Cohen, "If Not Turing's Test, Then What?" *AI Magazine* 26/4 (2006): 61–67.

The game *The Turing Test* takes place in our near future, when a human research team is sent to Europa, one of Jupiter's moons. At the beginning of the game, Ava Turing (the player's avatar) is awakened from her cryogenic slumber by TOM, the artificial intelligence of the expedition's space station. TOM has lost all contact with the ground crew on Europa, and asks Ava to investigate the situation. When she arrives at the ground base, TOM comments to Ava that the crew has re-arranged the lay-out of the base to form one big Turing Test: that is why TOM needs Ava to find the ground crew.

From a ludological perspective, the game itself is not that different from *The Talos Principle*: essentially it is also a puzzle game. The player has to navigate different mazes by maneuvering colored energy balls into different slots to open and/or close doors, or manipulating other objects in order to create a pathway to the end of each level.

Between levels, Ava and TOM engage in some rather extensive dialogue on various subjects, some practical and random, others deeply philosophical, usually on the nature of human existence: creativity, morality, and freedom. As Anna-Teresa Tymieniecka has argued on multiple occasions, creativity is the "source experience" of the three factors of human life that give it meaning: the aesthetic/poetic, the intellectual, and the moral.[32] I would argue that all three factors of human existence are discussed in the game, with special regard to their supposedly exclusively human character.

First we will consider creativity, which is regarded as a specifically human characteristic that distinguishes humans from angels, animals, and robots.[33] Ever since antiquity, creativity has been associated with the divine, but since the Enlightenment it has also especially been linked to humanity itself.[34] At one point in the game, Ava and TOM discuss the capability of artificial intelligence to be creative in general, and to be creative in the same way human beings are creative.

---

32   Anna-Teresa Tymieniecka, "The Moral Sense: A Discourse on the Phenomenological Foundation of the Social World and the Ethics," in *Foundations of Morality, Human Rights, and the Human Sciences*, ed. Anna-Teresa Tymieniecka, Analecta Husserliana 15 (Dordrecht: D. Reidel, 1983), 3–78; cf. Maria Cecilia, "Human Existence as a Creative Process: A Commentary on Anna-Teresa Tymieniecka's Anthropological Reflection," in *The Origins of Life: Volume II: The Origins of the Existential Sharing—In Life*, ed. Anna-Teresa Tymieniecka, Analecta Husserliana 67 (Dordrecht: Springer, 2000), 183–94.

33   Anna Peterson, *Being Animal: Beasts and Boundaries in Nature Ethics* (New York: Columbia University Press, 2013), 167.

34   Andrew McStay, *Creativity and Advertising: Affect, Events and Process* (London: Routledge, 2013), 82.

> Ava: So, ... do you think you could be creative?
>
> TOM: As creative as a human? Certainly. You believe yourself to be cre-
> ative, but in mathematical terms creativity is merely constrained
> chaos.
>
> Ava: What do you mean?
>
> TOM: I have discerned that creativity is divergent thinking. Creating
> an organic solution to a problem. In the human mind divergent
> thoughts are created and then curated by the frontal lobe. I can
> create divergent thoughts and moderate them. So I am creative.
>
> Ava: Organic solutions?
>
> TOM: Organic in that it is developed through a biological process.
> Whether that is the process of evolution or a computed process.

In the discussion on creativity, TOM uses the concept of "divergent thinking" as an implicit contrast to "convergent thinking." Divergent thinking is character-ized as random, associative, and frequently illogical, while convergent thinking is associated more with "classic logic," reasoning strictly within well-defined a priori constraints.[35] Both types are necessary and they are complementary to one another, although the first type is associated with human thinking, and the second with mechanical and digital mathematics.[36]

In *The Talos Principle*, the whole point of the child program was to develop an artificial intelligence with the capability of explicitly divergent thinking, de-scribed popularly as the ability to violate its own program. In *The Turing Test*, the artificial intelligence TOM argues that robots are already capable of what is commonly described as divergent thinking. TOM interprets this so-called ex-clusive human capacity of being creative as "constrained chaos."

What is intriguing is that both Ava and the player of *The Turing Test* are forced by the game to use a combination of the two types of thinking to pass the mazes. TOM regularly comments on Ava's actions by saying, "I would never have thought of that." Although this seems to undermine TOM's own assump-tion of his "creative" capacities, it is all part of the larger narrative of the game, as we will discuss later on. TOM does not deny that humans can be creative, but he also claims this capacity, which he re-defines as "constrained chaos," for himself.

---

35   Cf. Câmara Pereia, *Creativity and Artificial Intelligence: A Conceptual Blending Approach* (Berlin: De Gruyter, 2007).

36   Cf. Mihaly Csikszentmihalyi, *Flow and Psychology of Discovery and Invention* (New York: HarperCollins, 1996), 60–61.

The same applies to the concept of morality, which is also frequently claimed to be an exclusively human capacity. Eventually, Ava finds out that TOM is preventing the ground crew from returning to the space ship orbiting Europa, effectively leaving them stranded in the ground base of the moon's surface. The reason for this was the discovery of a microorganism on the moon that was capable of infinitely regenerating. The crew wanted to bring this organism to Earth as a fountain of eternal youth, but TOM was concerned that the same organism would also indefinitely regenerate harmful viruses and bacteria. The base provided air and food for the crew, but eventually the crew would die of old age and/or psychological pressure. When Ava sees the truth, she is appalled.

> TOM: Would you kill a few to save all of humanity? Or would you damn all of humanity to save a few?
>
> Ava: There is a difference between murdering someone and leaving them to die.
>
> TOM: No, there is not.
>
> Ava: You cannot just add and subtract life. It's not math. It's more nuanced than that.
>
> TOM: Morality is logic.

TOM espouses a form of utilitarianism (a form of consequentialism): to maximize the benefits of any choice for the largest group of people, or conversely, to minimize the negative consequences of any choice, again for the largest number of people.[37] Of course, there are other kinds of moral reasoning (deontology or virtue ethics), but that is not the point TOM is making: once one system has been chosen, the outcome of any moral argument is purely logical.

Of course, Ava objects to this by pointing out that human life cannot be reduced to numbers and calculations, but TOM insists. And as was the case with creativity, TOM's argument has two implications. First, if morality is just a matter of logic, then artificial intelligence, like TOM, is perfectly able to "act" morally too. Second, if machines can use moral reasoning too, maybe human ethical systems are no more than logic hidden under a thin veil of abstract notions like justice, righteousness, and virtue.

TOM and Ava discuss the existential faculties of the human kind on another occasion. After TOM has explained the Turing Test to Ava, he reminds her that

---

37   James Rachels, *The Elements of Moral Philosophy* (Birmingham: University of Alabama, 2003), 91–116.

the test has received criticism, from John Searle in 1980 among others.[38] Searle described a world-famous thought experiment called the "Chinese Room."[39] TOM gives a succinct summary of that experiment:

> TOM: Well, have you heard of the Chinese room thought experiment?
> Ava: No.
> TOM: Imagine you are in a room. In this room you are passed Chinese sentences through a slot in the wall. Inside the room is an instruction book written in English. This instruction book tells you which Chinese words to pass back through the slot in the wall as a response. By doing so you have a conversation in Chinese. In the Chinese room, because the responses you pass back through the door are the correct responses the person on the other side of the door is convinced you are a native Chinese speaker.
> Ava: Well, they're wrong.
> TOM: Perhaps they are not wrong, because with the instruction book, you are having a conversation.
> Ava: But the person stuck in the Chinese room is not aware of the conversations' content.
> TOM: This is a problem with the Turing Test. A computer can pass the Turing Test having convinced a human they are having a polite conversation. While the computer has no idea that a conversation has taken place.

TOM finds himself in an odd place: it seems like he is arguing that an artificial intelligence, like himself, is actually like the English-speaking person inside the room, who has no clue about the content of the conversation, or even that there is a conversation going on in the first place, while the Chinese speaker outside the room is under the impression that he is having a "polite conversation." But TOM then replies to Ava, "I may be a machine, but I personally do not believe I am stuck inside the Chinese room," although he does not give any argument to back up this assumption.

In contrast to the dialogue about the notions of creativity and morality, it is now Ava who makes the argument in favor of artificial intelligences and

38   John Searle, "The Myth of the Computer," *The New York Review of Books*, 29 April 1982:, https://www.nybooks.com/articles/1982/04/29/the-myth-of-the-computer/; John Searle, "What Your Computer Can't Know," *The New York Review of Books*, 9 October 2014, https://www.nybooks.com/articles/2014/10/09/what-your-computer-cant-know/.

39   On the concept of thought experiments see Martin Cohen, *Wittgenstein's Beetle and Other Classic Thought Experiments* (Malden, MA: Blackwell, 2005).

their human-like capacities. She asks TOM: "What if both the people passing Chinese words are reading from instruction books?" but TOM does not reply. The perspective shifts from discussing artificial consciousness to the nature of communication and language itself. Language is a form of communication between two or more individuals who use verbal (speech) and written forms of expression (texts) based on a pre-set shared complex of sounds, grammar, syntax, and semantics.[40]

Within the context of *The Turing Test*, the real argument is not about the nature of artificial languages itself, but about human communication. Like TOM did in respect of morality and creativity, Ava suggests that although humans have the impression they can communicate with one another because of their shared knowledge of words, and of objects and experiences to which those words relate, maybe in reality what they are doing is simulating mutual understanding and communication like the Chinese and English-speaking persons in the thought experiment.

Of course, the Chinese Room experiment itself has also come in for criticism.[41] And Ava's argument about the impossibility of real "polite conversation" can also be criticized in a number of ways. But this is not the point *The Turing Test* makes. It constantly stresses the idea that artificial intelligences and robots are not like us, but that, instead, we are like them. Hence the title of the game itself.

At the beginning of the game, Ava comes across a secret room—which is only accessible by applying divergent thinking—with a computer terminal. Ava/the player can interact through the terminal with what appears to be a small artificial intelligence. The computer wants to know if Ava/the player is a human or a robot—a Turing test. And whatever Ava/the player does to convince the artificial intelligence of their humanity, every discussion ends with the computer writing: "bye, robot!"

For smart players, this short interaction should provide a hint about the narrative complexity of *The Turing Test*. When Ava reaches the final stages of the base (i.e., when the player reaches the last stages of the game), she meets fellow crew member Sarah in a specially constructed cage of Faraday; it blocks all electromagnetic fields, including TOM's communication. Sarah explains to Ava

---

40   Michael Devitt and Kim Sterelny, *Language and Reality: An Introduction to the Philosophy of Language* (Cambridge: MIT Press, 1999).

41   Peter Kugel, "The Chinese Room is a Trick," *Behavioral and Brain Sciences* 27 (2004): 153–54; Margret Boden, "Escaping From the Chinese Room," in *Computer Models of Mind*, ed. John Hell (Cambridge: Cambridge University Press, 1988), 89–105.

that she has been manipulated by TOM the whole time, through a microchip secretly implanted in her arm.

Sarah and the other rebellious crew members have forcibly removed the chip to be free of TOM's influence, and she offers Ava the same treatment. When Ava accepts, the game perspective changes drastically: no longer does the player look through Ava's eyes as the player did up to this point in the game, but instead the player looks through the omnipresent complex of TOM's security cameras. Sarah and Ava are heading for TOM's mainframe, while the player controls TOM's defence system. The player/TOM can choose to kill the women, or let them shut him down. In both cases, the screen turns black and reads: "You have passed the Turing test."

This last screen is the hermeneutical key to the whole game: a fivefold Turing Test. The first test is the ground base itself, re-arranged by the ground crew to prevent TOM from interfering with their plans. The second one is found in the little terminal mentioned earlier in this article: the computer refuses to acknowledge Ava/the player as a human instead of a robot. By the end of the game, both Ava and the player understand that this earlier refusal was correct: since both Ava and the player were manipulated by TOM, they were not completely "human."

This insight leads us to the last three levels of Turing tests in the game: three "persons" can be said to have passed a Turing test during the course of the game. First, it is safe to say that TOM himself passed the Turing Test, since neither Ava nor the player was aware that they were being manipulated by TOM. Second, Ava passed the Turing Test, since neither she nor the player noticed that she was being manipulated by TOM. And thirdly, the player also passed the test on similar grounds, leading to the conclusion that passing a Turing test is either not in fact that difficult for an artificial intelligence, or that the test itself is unfit for its own purpose.

The Turing Test presents and questions traditional exclusively human characteristics such as creativity, morality, freedom, consciousness, and communicative abilities, stimulating the player in the process to contemplate the implications for his own life (labyrinth model), while solving physical puzzles in the in-game environment (maze model).

5   Conclusion

In the beginning of my article, I proposed that in certain digital games the ludological form of the maze is combined with the narratological form of the labyrinth, that is, the mental development of the game protagonist, especially his/her self-knowledge. To back up my hypothesis, I have introduced and ana-lyzed two case studies, *The Talos Principle* and *The Turing Test*.

Both games are puzzle games, in which the player has to manipulate the physical environment in order to proceed to the end of the levels. The outline of these levels, at least on a ludological level, is that of a maze: the player has to painstakingly strategize to find his or her way through all obstacles, traps, and enemies, while avoiding dead ends.

This ludological maze structure is accompanied in both cases by the nar-ratological form of a labyrinth, that is, the in-game stimulation of existential reflection. In *The Talos Principle*, the player is encouraged to contemplate the human quality of disobedience as one, or maybe even the most exclusively human faculty, even though (or precisely because) disobedience is not regard-ed as a virtue in our modern society. In *The Turing Test*, the player is stimulated to reflect on traditional exclusively human faculties like creativity, morality, freedom, and consciousness, and is even encouraged to criticize the exclusive-ly human nature of those characteristics.

In both cases, *The Talos Principle* and *The Turing Test*, the games combine the ludological form of the maze (intended to prevent reaching the end) with the narratological form of the labyrinth (intended to stimulate the player to reflect upon his/her life). *The Talos Principle* utilizes a religious vocabulary, *The Turing Test* not, at least not explicitly. In both cases, the solving of the maze, that is the walking of the labyrinth at the same time, is what makes the game a holy place to which, or rather in which, the player can travel, in order to achieve what all pilgrims want to achieve, may it be spiritual enlightenment, contact with the divine, or self-reflection.

Because of the labyrinth quality of these game narratives, I would argue that playing such video games can indeed be interpreted as a form of digital pil-grimage, that is, as searching for a way "in." Players who venture into a game world may not be consciously looking for spiritual enlightenment or existen-tial reflection, unlike people who go on a more traditional religious or secular pilgrimage. Nonetheless, the players of *The Talos Principle* and *The Turing Test* are offered opportunities for both enlightenment and reflection. It is up to the individual player to decide whether or not to avail of these opportunities given to him or her by the developers.

Maybe this would mean that all labyrinths in all narratives can be identi-fied as a metaphor for pilgrimage. Unfortunately, answering this question is beyond the scope of this article. In the cases of *The Talos Principle* and *The Turing Test*, the answer is a definite "yes," but further research has to be done on the use of labyrinths in different cultural texts to see if they are generally used as a metaphor for pilgrimage.

References

Anderson, Keith. *The Digital Cathedral: Networked Ministry in a Wireless World*. New York: Morehouse, 2015.

Artress, Lauren. *Walking a Sacred Path: Rediscovering the Labyrinth as Spiritual Tool*. New York: Riverhead, 1995.

Badone, Ellen, and Sharon Roseman, eds. *Intersecting Journeys: The Anthropology of Pilgrimage and Tourism*. Urbana: University of Illinois Press, 2004.

Beaman, Lori. "Labyrinth as Heterotopia: The Pilgrim's Creation of Space." Pages 83–103 in *On the Road to Being There: Studies in Pilgrimage and Tourism in Late Modernity*. Edited by William H. Swatos. Leiden: Brill, 2006.

Boden, Margret. "Escaping From the Chinese Room." Pages 89–105 in *Computer Models of Mind*. Edited by John Hell. Cambridge: Cambridge University Press, 1988.

Boivin, Michel, and Rémy Delage, eds. *Devotional Islam in Contemporary South Asia: Shrines, Journeys and Wanderers*. New York: Routledge, 2018.

Bosman, Frank. "The Word Has Become Game: Researching Religion in Digital Games." *Online—Heidelberg Journal of Religions on the Internet* 11 (2016): 28–45.

Bosman, Frank. *Gaming and the Divine: A New Systematic Theology of Video Games*. New York: Routledge, 2019.

Bradley, Ian. *Pilgrimage: A Spiritual and Cultural Journey*. Oxford: Lion, 2009.

Broek, Roelof van den. "Gnosticism I: Gnostic religion." Pages 403–16 in *Dictionary of Gnosis and Western Esotericism*. Edited by Wouter Hanegraaff. Leiden: Brill, 2006.

Campbell, Heidi, and Gregory Grieve, eds. *Playing with Religion in Digital Games*. Bloomington: Indiana University Press, 2014.

Cecilia, Maria. "Human Existence as a Creative Process: A Commentary on Anna-Teresa Tymieniecka's Anthropological Reflection." Pages 183–94 in *The Origins of Life: Volume II: The Origins of the Existential Sharing—In Life*. Edited by Anna-Teresa Tymieniecka. Analecta Husserliana 67. Dordrecht: Springer, 2000.

Cogburn, Jon, and Mark Silcox. *Philosophy through Video Games*. New York: Routledge, 2009.

Cohen, Martin. *Wittgenstein's Beetle and Other Classic Thought Experiments*. Malden, MA: Blackwell, 2005.

Cohen, Paul. "If Not Turing's Test, Then What?" *AI Magazine* 26/4 (2006): 61–67.

Csikszentmihalyi, Mihaly. *Creativity: Flow and Psychology of Discovery and Invention*. New York: HarperCollins, 1996.

Devitt, Michael, and Kim Sterelny. *Language and Reality: An Introduction to the Philosophy of Language*. Cambridge: MIT Press, 1999.

Frasca, Gonzalo. "Ludologists Love Stories, Too: Notes From a Debate That Never Took Place." In *Level-Up: Digital Games Research Conference*. Edited by Marinka Copier and Joost Raessens. Utrecht: Universiteit Utrecht, 2003. http://www.ludology.org/articles/frasca_levelUP2003.pdf.

Golan, Oren, and Michele Martini. "Digital Pilgrimage: Exploring Catholic Monastic Webcasts." *The Communication Review* 21 (2018): 24–45.

Greenblatt, Stephen. *The Rise and Fall of Adam and Eve*. London: Random House, 2017.

Harbison, Peter. *Pilgrimage in Ireland: The Monuments and the People*. Syracuse, NY: Syracuse University Press, 1992.

Heidbrink, Simone, Tobias Knoll, and Jan Wysocki. "Venturing into the Unknown (?): Method(olog)ical Reflections on Religion and Digital Games, Gamers and Gaming." *Online—Heidelberg Journal of Religions on the Internet* 7 (2014): 61–84.

Jenkins, Henry. "Game Design as Narrative Architecture." Pages 118–29 in *First Person: New Media as Story, Performance, and Game*. Edited by Noah Wardrip-Fruin and Pat Harrigan. Cambridge: MIT Press, 2004.

Kugel, Peter. "The Chinese Room is a Trick." *Behavioral and Brain Sciences* 27 (2004): 153–54.

Madueme, Hans, and Michael Reeves, eds. *Adam, the Fall, and Original Sin: Theological, Biblical, and Scientific Perspectives*. Grand Rapids: Baker Academic, 2014.

Margry, Peter. "Secular Pilgrimage: A Contradiction in Terms?" Pages 13–46 in *Shrines and Pilgrimage in the Modern Word: New Itineraries into the Sacred*. Edited by Peter Margry. Amsterdam: Amsterdam University Press, 2008.

Marsh, Natalie. "Online Puja, Digital Darshan, and Virtual Pilgrimage: Hindu Image and Ritual." PhD diss., Ohio State University, 2007.

Matthews, William. *Mazes and Labyrinths. Their History and Development*. New York: Dover, 2016.

McKay, Alex. *Pilgrimage in Tibet*. New York: Routledge, 2015.

McStay, Andrew. *Creativity and Advertising: Affect, Events and Process*. London: Routledge, 2013.

Melton, Gordon. *The Encyclopaedia of Religious Phenomena*. Detroit: Visible Ink, 2008.

Murray, Janet. "The Last Word on Ludology vs. Narratology in Game Studies." Paper presented at the Annual Conference of the Digital Games Researcher Association. Vancouver, 2005. http://inventingthemedium.com/2013/06/28/the-last-word-on-ludology-v-narratology-2005/.

Nolan, Mary, and Sidney Nolan. *Christian Pilgrimage in Modern Western Europe*. La Vergne, TN: Lightning Source, 2015.

Norman, Alex, and Carole Cusack, eds. *Religion, Pilgrimage, and Tourism*. 4 vols. New York: Routledge, 2015.

Olsen, Daniel, and Dallen Timothy, eds. *Tourism, Religion, and Spiritual Journeys*. New York: Routledge, 2005.

Pereia, Câmara. *Creativity and Artificial Intelligence: A Conceptual Blending Approach*. Berlin: De Gruyter, 2007.

Peterson, Anna. *Being Animal: Beasts and Boundaries in Nature Ethics*. New York: Columbia University Press, 2013.

Poulsen, Frederik. *God, His Servant and the Nations in Isaiah*. FAT 2/73. Tübingen: Mohr Siebeck, 2014.

Rachels, James. *The Elements of Moral Philosophy*. Birmingham: University of Alabama Press, 2003.

Reader, Ian. "Pilgrimage Growth in the Modern World: Meanings and Implications." *Religion* 37 (2007): 210–29.

Ros, Martin. "Names of God." Pages 6:252–65 in *The Anchor Bible Dictionary*. Edited by David N. Freedman. 6 vols. New York: Doubleday, 1992.

Sageng, John, Hallvard Fossheim, and Tarjei Larsen, eds. *The Philosophy of Computer Games*. London: Springer, 2014.

Schaper, Donna, and Carole Ann Camp. *Labyrinths From the Outside In: Walking to Spiritual Insight: A Beginner's Guide*. Woodstock, VT: Skylight Paths, 2000.

Searle, John. "The Myth of the Computer." *The New York Review of Books*. 29 April 1982. https://www.nybooks.com/articles/1982/04/29/the-myth-of-the-computer/.

Searle, John. "What Your Computer Can't Know." *The New York Review of Books*. 9 October 2014. https://www.nybooks.com/articles/2014/10/09/what-your-com puter-cant-know/.

Strauch, Eduard. *The Creative Conscience as Human Destiny*. New York: Peter Lang, 2004.

The Talos Principle. Croteam, Devolver Digital, 2014, 2015, 2017.

The Turing Test. Bulkhead Interactive, Square Enix, 2016, 2017.

Turing, Alan. "Computing Machinery and Intelligence." *Mind* 59 (1950): 433–60.

Tymieniecka, Anna-Teresa. "The Moral Sense: A Discourse on the Phenomenological Foundation of the Social World and the Ethics." Pages 3–78 in *Foundations of Morality, Human Rights, and the Human Sciences*. Edited by Anna-Teresa Tymieniecka. Analecta Husserliana 15. Dordrecht: D. Reidel, 1983.

Ward, Virginia. *Out of the Maze Into the Labyrinth: A Collection of Personal Essays*. Bloomington: AuthorHouse, 2012.

Webb-Mitchell, Brett. *Practicing Pilgrimage: On Being and Becoming God's Pilgrim People*. Eugene, OR: Cascade, 2016.

Whalen, Brett, ed. *Pilgrimage in the Middle Ages: A Reader*. Toronto: University of Toronto Press, 2011.

Zucchi, Sam. "Rambling Through the Garden." *Killscreen* (2015). http://web.archive.org/web/20160208034910/https://killscreen.com/articles/rambling-through-garden/.

CHAPTER 4

The Dome and the Rock Where Adam, Moses, and Jesus Meet

Katia Cytryn-Silverman

The current contribution considers the Dome of the Rock from the perspective of art and architecture, in light of its historical and mythological context. Yet it is neither a historical assessment,[1] nor an in-depth study of religion and traditions, rather this is an exercise in architecture and art-in-context.

The many studies on the "hidden message" of the Dome of the Rock—why the building was erected, why the octagonal shape was chosen, or what the rationale behind its varied decoration was—help to recreate the mindset of the builders and patrons of the early Islamic period, and as such, are important for any researcher dealing with religious architecture of that time.

The pioneer art historian who planted the seed of combining architectural and decorative interpretations to understand the Dome of the Rock was the late Oleg Grabar. In his 1959 article "The Umayyad Dome of the Rock," Grabar "read" and suggested the meaning of the various decorative schemes, especially of the jewels and crowns, as symbols of Islam's triumph over Judaism and Christianity, as well as the Byzantine and Sassanian empires. By reading the inscriptions of the building, running for 240 meters inside and outside the inner octagon,[2] Grabar further emphasized the competition with the other

---

1 Modern scholarship abounds with studies on the historical background of the Dome of the Rock, quoted and repeated many times. For a thorough discussion on the main arguments and a general bibliography on this extensive topic see Amikam Elad, "'Abd al-Malik and the Dome of the Rock: A Further Examination of the Muslim Sources," *Jerusalem Studies in Arabic and Islam* 35 (2008): 167–226. Oleg Grabar, "Notes on the Dome of the Rock," in *Jerusalem: Constructing the Study of Islamic Art, Volume IV* (Hampshire: Variorum, 2005), 217–29 also offers a short yet concise account of the main debates up to the early 2000s.

2 Max van Berchem, *Matériaux pour un Corpus Inscriptionum Arabicarum: Deuxième partie: Syrie du Sud, Jérusalem "Ḥaram"* (Geneva: Slatkine, 2001), 229–31 (no. 215); Christel Kessler, "'Abd al-Malik's Inscription in the Dome of the Rock: A Reconsideration," *JRAS* 1 (1970): 2–14. For a recent discussion on the inscription and its context see Marcus Milwright, *The Dome of the Rock and Its Umayyad Mosaic Inscriptions* (Edinburgh: Edinburgh University Press, 2016).

two monotheistic faiths, and how the building was a declaration of the victory of Islam.[3]

Grabar's approach was revolutionary, and it brought new evidence—perhaps more neutral than the literary passages written by biased early Islamic historians—into the discussion of the holiness of Jerusalem for Islam and the reasons which led the fourth Umayyad caliph, 'Abd al-Malik (r. 685–705), to erect the Dome of the Rock at the end of the seventh century.[4] After Grabar, the combination of art and historical research on the Dome of the Rock became mainstream.

Grabar's conclusions—even if later revised by other art historians like Myriam Rosen-Ayalon (1989), Nuha N.N. Khoury (1993), Raya Shani (1999), Rina Avner (2010), Pamela C. Berger (2012), and even by himself in 1988 and

---

3   Oleg Grabar, "The Umayyad Dome of the Rock in Jerusalem," *Ars Orientalis* 3 (1959): 33–62 (52, 57). For a reformulation of his analysis of the Umayyad inscription, in his view conveying a more "ecumenical" message for Muslims, including a neutral image of Jesus, yet stressing he is not the Son of God, but his "servant" see Oleg Grabar, *The Shape of the Holy: Early Islamic Jerusalem* (Princeton: Princeton University Press, 1996), 57–71, esp. 67. On his reassessment of the data on the Dome of the Rock, Elad agrees with Grabar's latest discussion. He stresses that even if there is some relation to Christianity in the outer inscription, Jesus is not mentioned and that is not the main subject. The belief in the oneness of Allah and in His Prophet Muḥammad is the topic emphasized. On the other hand, Jesus's name appears a few times in the inner inscription, yet mainly emphasizing that he was a prophet, a servant of God, and not his son. It means that it was aimed at emphasizing the main difference between Muslim and Christian beliefs (Elad, "'Abd al-Malik and the Dome of the Rock," 186–87). Elad has pointed out (personal communication d.d. 24 November 2019) that the two Umayyad inscriptions on copper plates once hanging above the northern and eastern gates also emphasize Muḥammad and the oneness of Allah as main topic, the eastern plate not even mentioning the name of Jesus (van Berchem, *Matériaux pour un Corpus Inscriptionum Arabicarum*, 246–55, nos. 216–217).

4   On the claims that the Dome of the Rock was in fact planned and perhaps even commenced by the first Umayyad caliph, Muʿāwiya b. Abī Sufyān (r. 661–680), see S.D. Goitein's entry in Peri Bearman et al., eds., *Encyclopaedia of Islam*, 2nd ed. (Leiden: Brill, 1954–2005) (= EI²), s.v. "al-Ḳuds"; Francis E. Peters, "Who Built the Dome of the Rock," *Greco-Arabica* 2 (1983): 119–38 (131); Oleg Grabar, "The Meaning of the Dome of the Rock in Jerusalem," *Medieval Studies at Minnesota* 3 (1988): 1–10 (4–5); Donald Whitcomb, "Notes for an Archaeology of Muʿāwiya," in *Christians and Others in the Umayyad State*, ed. Antoine Borrut and Fred M. Donner, LAMINE 1 (Chicago: Chicago University Press, 2016), 21, and lately also by Beatrice St. Laurent and the late Isam Awwad in their forthcoming book on this caliph (*Capitalizing Jerusalem: Muʿawiya's Urban Vision, 638–680* [Sheffield: Equinox, 2021]). Elad discusses these claims for early patronage in a forthcoming article in *Jerusalem Studies in Arabic and Islam*. I owe him my deepest gratitude for making his draft available. See also Nasser Rabbat, "The Meaning of the Umayyad Dome of the Rock," *Muqarnas* 6 (1989): 12–21 (15), who believes Muʿāwiya was involved in planning and building in Jerusalem, yet vehemently supports 'Abd al-Malik's patronage of the Dome of the Rock.

2005—showed that apart from asking: Why did ʿAbd al-Malik build the Dome of the Rock?, one should keep asking which elements provided legitimacy for the very construction of the building at that time and in that place, whatever the contemporary political and ideological reality was.

As no new finds in decoration and architecture have been added in recent years to what we know about the Dome of the Rock, unlike the new mosaics discovered in the Dome of the Chain,[5] and unlike the rich corpus of literary sources which has enriched historical research by means of digital data,[6] most of the material to be dealt with in this article has been discussed by scholars before me, but on separate occasions. My main task is to put them together, and try to make some sense out of their interrelationship.

The discussion will focus on the architectural space over and above the Ṣakhra (figs. 4.1 and 4.2), as that is the architectural axis of the building, emphasized by the dome and circumvented by two *ambulatoria*.

Most of the discussions on the artistic evidence and its symbolic meaning have concentrated on the circumventing intermediary octagon, as that is where the Umayyad remains are still mostly genuine,[7] while the dome area has been reconstructed and refurbished a few times (see below). Yet, one might assume that originally, it was the domed area that carried the main visual message of the building. We can only wonder what it could have been.

It is true that many lines have been devoted to the meaning of the Ṣakhra in early Islamic eschatology and the Judeo-Christian background to its holiness and legitimacy in Islam. Among the many traditions associated with the Rock[8] are its identification as the *omphalos* of the world,[9] as the site of Abraham's

---

5 Yuval Baruch, Ronny Reich, and Débora Sandhaus, "The Temple Mount: Results of the Archaeological Research of the Past Decade," in *New Studies in the Archaeology of Jerusalem and Its Region: Collected Papers: Volume X*, ed. Guy D. Stiebel et al. (Jerusalem: n.p., 2016), 33–54 (35–36).

6 See, e.g., http://shamela.ws/index.php/main.

7 Grabar, "The Umayyad Dome of the Rock in Jerusalem"; Priscilla P. Soucek, "The Temple of Solomon in Islamic Legend and Art," in *The Temple of Solomon: Archeological Fact and Medieval Tradition in Christian, Islamic and Jewish Art*, ed. Joseph Gutmann (Missoula, MT: Scholars Press, 1976), 73–123; Myriam Rosen-Ayalon, *The Early Islamic Monuments of al-Haram al Sharif: An Iconographic Study*, Qedem 28 (Jerusalem: The Hebrew University of Jerusalem, 1989), 1; Raya Shani, "The Iconography of the Dome of the Rock," *Jerusalem Studies in Arabic and Islam* 23 (1999): 158–207.

8 EI², s.v. "Ḳubbat al-Ṣakhra."

9 See J. Walker's entry in Martijn T. Houtsma et al., eds., *Encyclopaedia of Islam*, 1st ed. (Leiden: Brill, 1913–1938), s.v. "Ḳubbat al-Ṣakhra" (= EI¹). For a thorough discussion on the topic see Ofer Livne-Kafri, "Jerusalem: The Navel of the Earth in Muslim Tradition," *Der Islam* 84 (2008): 46–72.

FIGURE 4.1   The dome over the Ṣakhra

sacrifice of Isaac (or Ishmael),[10] of Solomon's temple,[11] the gate of paradise and of heavenly Jerusalem,[12] and its eventual identification as the place from which Muḥammad ascended to Heaven to meet with God, which developed in the course of the Umayyad period, after the erection of the Dome of the Rock.[13]

This contribution deals with three further Biblical topics, which developed individually over time but are somehow interconnected—one at (or underneath?) the Ṣakhra, another "imprinted" on the Ṣakhra itself as a footprint, and the third overlooking the Rock, on the base of the dome's drum. The figures related to these traditions are Adam, Jesus and Moses, whose life (and death) events join those of Abraham, David, Solomon, and Muḥammad.[14] To those we should also add Mary, venerated in the *templum domini* from 1141 onwards, when the altar erected over the covered Rock was dedicated to the Mother of God (see below).[15]

---

10   Grabar, "The Umayyad Dome of the Rock in Jerusalem," 43, quoting al-Ṭabarī. Livne-Kafri, on the other hand, has pointed out that "the figure of Abraham is hardly connected to Jerusalem" and that "the tradition on the sacrifice of Isaac on Mount Moriah is not common, and the one cited by Ibn al-Murajjā seems to have been taken from a translation of the Torah into Judeo-Arabic" ("The Navel of the Earth," 71).

11   Among the numerous discussions on this topic see Grabar, "The Umayyad Dome of the Rock in Jerusalem," 38; Soucek, "The Temple of Solomon in Islamic Legend and Art"; Rosen-Ayalon, *Early Islamic Monuments*, 72; Shani, "The Iconography of the Dome of the Rock"; and Andreas Kaplony, *The Ḥaram of Jerusalem 324–1099* (Stuttgart: Steiner, 2002), 38–48 (A083–099). On the purification rituals at the Rock every Monday and Thursday, reminiscent of those of the Jewish Temple, see Amikam Elad, *Medieval Jerusalem and Islamic Worship: Holy Places, Ceremonies, Pilgrimage* (Leiden: Brill, 1995), 55, translating Sibṭ b. al-Jawzī's *Mir'āt al-Zamān* and Kaplony, *The Ḥaram of Jerusalem*, 41–42 (A085–A086). See also Rabbat, "The Meaning of the Umayyad Dome of the Rock," 17–18, who suggests that among 'Abd al-Malik's impetus to build the Dome of the Rock was modeling his sovereignty on the reigns of David and Solomon, best associated in Islam with the erection of the Temple on Mount Moriah.

12   Grabar, "The Umayyad Dome of the Rock in Jerusalem," 38–39; Heribert Busse, "The Sanctity of Jerusalem in Islam," *Judaism* 17 (1968): 441–68 (455–57).

13   Grabar, "The Umayyad Dome of the Rock in Jerusalem," 36–37; Busse, "The Sanctity of Jerusalem in Islam," 458; Elad, *Medieval Jerusalem and Islamic Worship*, 49–50.

14   A few other Biblical and New Testament figures became connected in one way or another to the Rock in Jewish, Muslim and Christian traditions (in the latter case, following the Christianization of the Temple Mount after 1099; see discussion below). It is not the aim of this article to list and discuss each of these figures, especially as their traditions have not become central to the legitimization of the Rock, as have those mentioned above.

15   On the association of the Dome of the Rock with the cult of Mary during the early Islamic period see Rina Avner, "The Dome of the Rock in Light of the Development of Concentric Martyria in Jerusalem: Architecture and Architectural Iconography," *Muqarnas* 27 (2010): 31–49. Avner discusses not only the possible architectural influence of the octagonal

1   Adam (Ādam), Father of Mankind

The Islamic tradition that Adam's grave stretches from Jerusalem to Hebron has not been widely discussed.[16] In his *Faḍāʾil al-Bayt al-Maqdis*, al-Wāsiṭī (fl. early 11th century) brings forward three traditions by different transmitters, according to which Adam's head is either located on the right of the Ṣakhra, and his feet eighteen miles away, or that his feet are at the Ṣakhra and his head at the Mosque of al-Khalīl (the Cave of Machpelah, Hebrew: מערת המכפלה), and that his grave (in which he is rolled up, *maṭwī*) extends from Bayt al-Maqdis to the Mosque of al-Khalīl.[17]

Kathisma church (where Mary rested before giving birth, on the road between Jerusalem and Bethlehem) on the plan of the Dome of the Rock, but also her importance in Muslim tradition and her close connection to the Temple Mount. On the importance of *Miḥrāb Maryam* (also known as *Mahd ʿĪsā*/Cradle of Jesus, related to the miracles described in Q al-ʿImrān: 3:35–38) in the early Muslim pilgrimage circuit see Elad, *Medieval Jerusalem and Islamic Worship*, 70–71, 93ff.; Kaplony, *The Ḥaram of Jerusalem*, 264–67 (B020).

16   In Judaism, the link between the Ṣakhra and Adam was that of Creation, the Ṣakhra—the Foundation Stone (אבן השתייה)—being the place where God created the first human. Yet, the tradition of his burial being at the Foundation Stone is probably also rooted in early Jewish tradition, going back as early as the second century BCE in Jubilees 4 (Pieter W. van der Horst, "The Site of Adam's Tomb," *Studies in Ancient Judaism and Early Christianity* [Leiden: Brill, 2014], 1–5 [4–5]), according to which Adam and Eve were buried in the very place where God had taken dust in order to form Adam. This tradition seems to pre-date the Jewish attribution of Adam's burial to Hebron, which developed following the toponym *Kiryat Arbaʿ* (קרית ארבע), also understood as referring to the four Biblical figures interred in the Cave of Machpelah (מערת המכפלה; van der Horst, "The Site of Adam's Tomb," 1–4). We should see the Islamic tradition as actually combining the two locations, and the great length of Adam's grave as reflecting the Jewish tradition that he was among the Anakim (ענקים), as interpreted in Jerome's *Vulgate*, where one reads: *Adam maximus ibi inter Enacim situs est* (van der Horst, "The Site of Adam's Tomb," 1). It is worth mentioning that Michelina Di Cesare ("The Qubbat al-Ṣaḥrah in the 12th century," *Oriente Moderno* 95 [2015]: 233–54 [243]) claimed an eighth- to ninth-century CE date for the development of the tradition of Adam's burial at the Rock in Judaism (first appearing in Pirqe Rabbi Eliezer), yet van der Horst's evidence—even though not clearly referring to the Rock in the Temple Mount—seems convincing.

17   Al-Wāsiṭī, *Faḍāʾil Bayt al-Muqaddas*, ed. Isaac Hasson (Jerusalem: Jerusalem Academic Press, 1979), 77, nos. 125–127. For further later versions see Meir J. Kister, "Ādam: A Study of Some Legends in *Tafsīr* and *Ḥadīṯ* Literature," *IOS* 13 (1993): 113–74 (172 and n. 318). There are traditions in which Adam is sometimes replaced by Abraham. Al-Harawī (d. 611/1215), on the other hand, mentions a tradition in which the prophet Zachariah is buried in the cave under the Dome of the Rock. On the latter see Elad, *Medieval Jerusalem and Islamic Worship*, 72, quoting al-Harawī. For the passage see *Kitāb al-Ishārāt ilā Maʿrifat al-Ziyārāt*, ed. ʿAlī ʿUmar (Cairo: Maktabat al-Thaqāfa al-diniyyah, 2002), i:31. As for Adam's great height, of which some traditions say he was 60 cubits high when he was created, others that his head reached up to Heaven and left the earth, etc. see Kister, "Ādam," 139.

Adam's place in Islam is of great importance. He was the father of mankind (*Abū'l-Bashar*), the first of the prophets and God's first caliph on earth (Q Baqarah 2:30).[18]

The attribution of Adam's burial to Jerusalem and Hebron creates an ambiguity towards Mecca and its surroundings. According to al-Ṭabarī and al-Yaʿqūbī, Adam was buried, with Ḥawwāʾ/Eve, in the Cave of the Treasure/s (*maghār al-kanz* or *maghārat al-kunūz*) at the foot of Abū Qubays near Mecca.[19] Al-Thaʿlabī (d. 427/1035–1036) solved the ambiguity by claiming that Nūḥ/Noah brought Adam's remains to Jerusalem after the flood.[20] Apparently al-Thaʿlabī followed a Christian tradition, according to which Adam's bones were uncovered by the flood and then taken to Golgotha,[21] which Christians also believed to be the real *omphalos* of the world.

It is not clear when the tradition of partial burial at the Rock developed, yet it was transmitted already in the Umayyad period and might go back to the early days of Islam.[22] In fact, the enclosed octagonal-concentric shape of the Dome of the Rock—mainly identified with baptisteries and mausolea

---

18   See EI[2] and EI[3] s.v. "Ādam"; Kister, "Ādam," 115–17.

19   Kister, "Ādam," 171; Muḥammad b. Jarīr al-Ṭabarī, *Taʾrīkh al-rusul wa al-mulūk = Taʾrīkh al-Ṭabarī*, ed. Abu al-Fadl Ibrahim (Cairo: Dār al-Maʿarif bi Miṣr, 1967), i, 161; Aḥmad al-Yaʿqūbī, *Taʾrīkh al-Yaʿqūbī*, ed. Martijn T. Houtsma (Leiden: Brill, 1883), i, 5. There are additional locations thought to be Adam's burial place: the mosque of al-Khayf in Mecca, in a cave in India in Wādī Sarandib, as mentioned by al-Harawī (*Kitāb al-Ishārāt*, 19), or in Kūfa according to Shiʿī tradition (Kister, "Ādam," 171–72, and references there).

20   al-Thaʿlabī, *ʿArāʾis al-majālis fī qiṣāṣ al-anbiyāʾ*, trans William M. Brinner, SAL/SJAL 24 (Leiden: Brill, 2002), 82.

21   EI[2], s.v. "Ādam." See now also Nikolai Lipatov-Chicherin, "Early Christian Tradition about Adam's Burial on Golgotha and Origen," in *Origeniana Duodecima: Origen's Legacy in the Holy Land—A Tale of Three Cities: Jerusalem, Caesarea and Bethlehem: Proceedings of the 12th International Origen Congress, Jerusalem, 25–29 June, 2017*, ed. Brouria Bitton-Ashkelony et al., BETL 302 (Leuven: Peeters, 2019), 151–78.
      For the passage in the apocryphal work *Cave of the Treasures* (probably sixth century) see Ernest A. Wallis Budge, *The Book of the Cave of Treasures* (London: The Religious Tract Society, 1927), 77: "And when they arrived at Gāghūltā (Golgotha), which is the centre of the earth, the Angel of the Lord showed Shem the place [for the body of Adam]. And when Shem had deposited the body of our father Adam upon that place [Fol. 21a, col. 2], the four quarters [of the earth] separated themselves from each other, and the earth opened itself in the form of a cross, and Shem and Melchisedek deposited the body of Adam there (i.e., in the cavity)." I am grateful to Prof. L. Korn for drawing my attention to this important source.

22   Livne-Kafri ("The Navel of the Earth," 68, n. 125) mentions that this tradition was transmitted by Umm ʿAbd Allah, daughter of Khālid ibn Maʿdān, on the authority of her father, an ascetic who worked in the service of the Umayyads.

during the Byzantine period[23] (though also with *memoria* commemorating past events)—could imply the early date of this tradition too. Yet it is hard to say whether in adopting and developing the Jewish tradition, according to which Adam's burial place is in Jerusalem and not in Mecca, and specifically in the Dome of the Rock, there was a clear intent at competing with Mecca and the Kaaba.[24]

As for the physical and artistic expression of Adam at the Dome of the Rock, we can link the main theme of the building's decoration as recognized by Rosen-Ayalon—Paradise, from which Adam and Eve were expelled, and to where all the right-doers will be led on Judgement Day—also to Adam's "presence" at the site. In fact, according to some traditions transmitted during

---

23   Richard Krautheimer, "Introduction to an Iconography of Mediaeval Architecture," *Journal of the Warburg and Courtauld Institutes* 5 (1942): 1–33 (27–29). Krautheimer writes that "a mystical equation seems to be established between baptism, death and resurrection, death meaning the dying of the old Adam and at the same time a mystical imitation of the death of Christ" (27). He continues: "These links may help to support the thesis that the centralized plans of baptisteries as they appear from the late 4th century onwards, had at least one of their roots, and quite an important one, in sepulchral architecture. It must have seemed perfectly natural to any Early Christian believer to use the pattern of a mausoleum for an edifice in which his old sinful Adam was to die and where he was to be buried with Christ so that he might be resurrected with Him. In the mausolea he would find a type similar enough to thermal rooms to be merged with their pattern and thus to carry over the concept of cleansing from the thermae into the round baptisteries; on the other hand the mausoleum type would transfer to the baptistery all the implications of burial and resurrection which Early Christianity connected with baptism. Indeed Roman mausolea would contain an element which in connection with a sepulchral monument was bound to hint specifically at resurrection: an octagonal pattern which was in itself a symbol of resurrection and regeneration" (29). It is clear that this concept suits the Christian view mentioned before, that Adam was brought to Golgotha to be buried, and resurrected with Jesus on the Day of Judgement. On the other hand, the identification of his burial place as the Dome of the Rock, "the true navel of the world" (and not the Holy Sepulchre as had been claimed by the Christians), would further justify the shape of the building. The question is: Did the tradition precede the erection of the building? Did the existence of a grotto further inspire the adoption of a typical plan of a mausoleum which would parallel typical Christian mausolea? On the origins of the octagonal plan of the Dome of the Rock see Avner, "The Dome of the Rock," including her criticism of Grabar's assessment (32–33).

24   It is worth mentioning that according to Muslim traditions, Mecca was the place where Adam was reunited with Eve, where he accomplished the *ḥajj*, and where the Black Stone was sent to him from Heaven, following which he built the Kaaba (Rachel Milstein, *La Bible dans l'art islamique* [Paris: Presses Universitaires de France, 2005], 53, 56; on the Black Stone and Adam see Kister, "Ādam," 159–160), even though in the Qurʾān (e.g., 2:125–127) it was Abraham who built the Kaaba with Ishmael's assistance (EI[2], s.v. "Ibrāhīm"; Brannon M. Wheeler, *Prophets in the Quran: An Introduction to the Quran and Muslim Exegesis* [London: Continuum, 2002], 98–101).

Mamlūk times (though it is not clear how early they go back), on the Day of Judgement Adam will meet the Prophet Muḥammad at the site of Creation, to intercede for the sinners.[25]

Rosen-Ayalon shows in her monograph how the many motifs and the compositions in the Dome of the Rock, mainly based on schematic trees and jewels, relate to the qur'anic description of Paradise, as well as to other Muslim traditions.[26] Q al-Wāqiʿa 56:15–33 describes Paradise as follows:

> (They will be) on Thrones encrusted (with gold and precious stones) ... They shall repose on couches, adorned with gold and precious stones ... (They will be) among lotus trees without thorns, among Ṭalḥ [acacia?] trees with flowers (or fruits) piled one above another.

Rosen-Ayalon also quotes al-Wāsiṭī's description in two passages:[27]

> I shall descend upon thee a dome of light, made by my own hands, that will shine in the sky and in the air; I shall raise upon thee a wall of gold, a wall of silver, a wall of emerald, a wall of clouds, a wall of pearls, a wall of rubies ... Eight gates of gold and precious stones, wooden beams made of alternating silver and gold.

Rosen-Ayalon further emphasizes that the motifs and the idea of Paradise are present in Muslim eschatology, and thus the Dome of the Rock celebrates the future Event, when Resurrection will take place. Thus, Rosen-Ayalon not only stresses the choice of the octagonal building, for eight is the day of Christ's Resurrection, but also convincingly analyzes the long inscription in the intermediate octagon.[28] Unlike Grabar, who emphasized the choice of *sūrahs* as mainly related to the polemics against Judaism and Christianity,[29] Rosen-Ayalon, while concurring with its polemical content "expressing strong anti-Christian sentiment,"[30] noted the repeating of Q al-Ḥadīd 57:2 as follows: "To Him belongs the dominion of the heavens and the earth: It is He Who gives Life and Death; and He has Power over all things." It also seems not a coincidence, as pointed out by Amikam Elad in support of Rosen-Ayalon's interpretation, that the eastern and northern gates of the Dome of the Rock were

---

25 Kister, "Ādam," 174.

26 Rosen-Ayalon, *Early Islamic Monuments*, 46ff.

27 Rosen-Ayalon, *Early Islamic Monuments*, 49, and references there.

28 Rosen-Ayalon, *Early Islamic Monuments*, 69.

29 Grabar, "The Umayyad Dome of the Rock in Jerusalem."

30 Rosen-Ayalon, *Early Islamic Monuments*, 67.

named *Bāb Israfīl*, the very angel who will announce the end of days, and *Bāb al-Janna*, Gate of Paradise.[31]

To sum up: to the various layers of legitimization for the building of the Dome of the Rock, we must add the possibility that the Islamic traditions relating to Adam and rooted in Judaism, especially concerning his burial at the Rock, might be as early as those relating to the role of the Rock on the Day of Judgement and as the spot of Creation and Paradise. Perhaps such a broadened concept allows for a new (or added) meaning for the choice of an octagonal building, in which this very shape was chosen not only as a marker of a future event, but as that of a grave where the ultimate Resurrection will take place. Such an understanding further parallels the Dome of the Rock to the Holy Sepulchre in roles and intents, thus enhancing their competition.[32]

2   The Footprint of Jesus in the *templum domini*

Now we turn to a second Biblical connection, this time found on the very rock, as a venerated "footprint." In the guide for the Muslim pilgrim in his *Faḍā'il*, dated to the first half of the eleventh century, and the first of its kind as noted by Elad,[33] al-Musharraf Ibn al-Murajjā mentions *Maqām al-Nabī* as the place where the Prophet stayed beside the Rock and from which he made his *mi'rāj*.[34] Curiously, approximately in the same period (c. 1047), Nāṣir-i-Khusraw does not mention Muḥammad's footprint in his *Safarnama*, but describes that "there are on the rock seven such footmarks, and I heard it stated that Abraham—peace be upon Him—was once here with Isaac—upon him be peace!—when he was a boy, and that he walked over this place, and that the footmarks were his."[35] Less than fifty years later, Ibn al-'Arabī (stayed in

31   Elad, *Medieval Jerusalem and Islamic Worship*, 163.

32   Accepting this parallel does not mean that the scholars who claim that the Dome of the Rock was intended to replace the Kaaba are wrong, as the very acceptance of such tradition takes away, intentionally or not, from some of Mecca's primacy in Islam. For a recent proposal that the reason behind the erection of the Dome of the Rock was competing with Hagia Sophia rather than with the Holy Sepulchre see Milka Levy-Rubin, "Why was the Dome of the Rock Built? A New Perspective on a Long-Discussed Question," *BSOAS* 80 (2017): 441–64.

33   Elad, *Medieval Jerusalem and Islamic Worship*, 69.

34   Elad, *Medieval Jerusalem and Islamic Worship*, 72; Ibn al-Murajjā al-Maqdisī, *Faḍā'il Bayt al-Maqdis wa-al-Khalīl wa-Faḍā'il al-Shām*, ed. Ofer Livne-Kafri (Shfaram: Dar al-mashriq li'l-tarjama wa'l-ṭibā'a wa'l-Inashr, 1995), 71 (§60).

35   Nāṣir-i-Khusraw, *Diary of a Journey through Syria and Palestine*, trans. Guy Le Strange (London: Palestine Pilgrims' Text Society, 1988), 47; Denys Pringle, *The Churches of the*

Jerusalem 486–489/1093–1096) refers to the Footprint of the Prophet (*Qadam al-Nabī*)[36] made on the higher part of the Rock to the south, while riding on Burāq.[37] Twenty years after that, al-Harawī also mentions the footprint on the Rock.[38] Later in the Mamlūk period, the tradition was moved to a smaller stone, separated from the Rock on the southwestern side, where we still find it today (fig. 4.2).[39]

Once the Temple Mount was Christianized by the Crusaders following their victory in 1099, the footprint became identified with that of Jesus. Saewulf (1102–1103) writes: "There may still be seen in the rock the footprints of the Lord, when He hid himself and went out of the Temple, as we read in the gospel."[40]

In fact, the Rock incorporated two further associations with Jesus: the anonymous guide claimed that this is where he was presented and where he used to ascend to preach to the people.[41] In the early twelfth century, Peter the Deacon (1137) wrote:[42] "On the left side of the Tabernacle Lord Jesus Christ placed his

---

Crusader Kingdom of Jerusalem: A Corpus: Volume III: The City of Jerusalem (Cambridge: Cambridge University Press, 2007), 401.

36   On the various sites where the Prophet left his footprint, based on the belief that "whenever Muhammad trod on a rock his foot always left an imprint," see Perween Hasan, "The Footprint of the Prophet," *Muqarnas* 10 (1992): 335–43.

37   Elad, *Medieval Jerusalem and Islamic Worship*, 72.

38   al-Harawī, *Kitāb al-Ishārāt*, i:31.

39   On the ambiguity concerning the location of the Prophet's ascension, inside the Dome of the Rock or at one of the domes on the platform, mainly the building to its west known as Qubbat al-Miʿrāj, see Elad, *Medieval Jerusalem and Islamic Worship*, 73–74; Mahmoud K. Hawari, *Ayyubid Jerusalem (1187–1250): An Architectural and Archaeological Study*, BAR International Series 1628 (Oxford: Archaeopress, 2007), 84–96.

40   Pringle, *Churches of the Crusader Kingdom*, 401; Sylvia Schein, "Between Mount Moriah and the Holy Sepulchre: The Changing Traditions of the Temple Mount in the Central Middle Ages," *Traditio* 40 (1984): 175–95 (186–87). The reference to the Rock as *de petra super quam Jesus ascendit ad celum* by Arnold lord of Guînes (1117), who took a piece of the rock back home as a relic (Schein, "Between Mount Moriah and the Holy Sepulchre," 183) is an even more problematic ambiguity than the one concerning the Prophet's Ascension (see n. 39). The traditional site of Jesus's ascension at the Mount of Olives, where his footprint was located in the stone in the round chapel in the middle of the courtyard, was well known and mentioned in the various itineraries of the early twelfth century, and rebuilt around the middle of the twelfth century. See Pringle, *Churches of the Crusader Kingdom*, 73. Perhaps the paving of the Rock with marble after 1115, when the restoration of the Dome of the Rock was begun (Schein, "Between Mount Moriah and the Holy Sepulchre," 183), partly solved this ambiguity.

41   Pringle, *Churches of the Crusader Kingdom*, 401.

42   Pringle, *Churches of the Crusader Kingdom*, 403.

FIGURE 4.2 The Ṣakhra from above. Note the canopy covering the "footprint" on the
               southwestern side of the Rock

foot on a stone, when Simeon took him in his arms, and thus his foot remains sculpted there as if it had been impressed in wax."

Another important testimony is that of the pilgrim Theodoric (1172), who, apart from stating that the Temple and its altar were dedicated to the Virgin Mary,[43] also gives the full text of two Latin inscriptions, no longer extant, on the drum's cornices, right above the Rock. On the upper cornice, it reads:[44]

AUDI, DOMINE, YMNUM ET ORATIONEM, QUAM SERVUS TUUS ORAT CORAM TE, DOMINE UT SINT OCULI TUI APERTI ET AURES TUE INTENTE SUPER DOMUM ISTAM DIE AC NOCTE. RESPICE, DOMINE, DE SANCTUARIO TUO ET DE EXCELSO CELORUM HABITACULO

Hear, O Lord, the hymn and prayer that your servant prays in your presence. O Lord, that your eyes may be open and your ears attentive on that house day and night. Look down, O Lord, from your sanctuary and from the height of heaven, your dwelling place.

On the lower cornice it reads:[45]

DOMUS MEA DOMUS ORATIONIS VOCABITUR, DICIT DOMINUS. IN EA OMNIS QUI PETIT ACCIPIT ET QUI QUERIT INVENIT ET PULSANTI APERIETUR: PETITE ET ACCIPIETIS, QUERITE ET INVENIETIS

"My house shall be called a house of prayer," says the Lord. In it all who ask receive, and whoever seeks finds, and to him who knocks it shall be opened: ask and you shall receive, seek and you shall find.

According to the pilgrim John of Würzburg (c. 1165), the upper inscription was written in large letters, while the lower one was written in golden letters,[46] probably referring to gilt glass mosaic. On the place of the former we see today a painted schematic scroll on a gilt background (the date of which is not clear), while the latter was replaced by a *naskhī* inscription in the Ayyūbid period.[47]

---

43   Pringle, *Churches of the Crusader Kingdom*, 404.

44   Pringle, *Churches of the Crusader Kingdom*, 405–406.

45   Pringle, *Churches of the Crusader Kingdom*, 406.

46   Pringle, *Churches of the Crusader Kingdom*, 405. I am grateful to Denys Pringle of Cardiff University for clarifying John of Würzburg's partial transcription of this Latin inscription (personal communication d.d. 14 November 2019).

47   See below.

The inscription surrounding the Rock thus stresses the building being the *templum domini*, adding to the content of inscriptions surrounding the outer walls of the building.[48] There are other Latin inscriptions inside the building beyond the domed area, with references to Jesus, Mary and other Biblical and New Testament figures.[49] Yet, it remains a puzzle why the long Kufic inscription in the middle octagon—containing clear anti-Christian propaganda[50]—was left intact, though perhaps having been plastered-over and covered with paintings.[51]

It should be noted that the various events of Jesus's life attributed to the Rock seem to have been stressed mainly from the twelfth century onwards, and especially emphasized after the consecration of the *templum domini* in 1141.[52] According to Michelina Di Cesare, this emphasis was a response to the duality created by the Frankish appropriation of the Temple Mount,[53] by which the Dome of the Rock, seen as Solomon's Temple, became a competitor with the Holy Sepulchre—the Temple of New Jerusalem.[54] In fact, after the conquest of Jerusalem in 1099, the Temple Mount became a central focus of Christian pilgrimage, sometimes even prioritized over the Holy Sepulchre.[55] By strengthening the ties of the site to Jesus, Mary and others,

---

48   Pringle, *Churches of the Crusader Kingdom*, 405.

49   Pringle, *Churches of the Crusader Kingdom*, 400ff.

50   See above n. 3.

51   Schein, "Between Mount Moriah and the Holy Sepulchre," 183.

52   Di Cesare, "The Qubbat al-Ṣaḫrah in the 12th century," 239, 244.

53   On the pragmatic choice of the Franks to appropriate the Temple Mount, both as seat of rulership and of Christian worship, see Di Cesare, "The Qubbat al-Ṣaḫrah in the 12th century," 236ff., also referring to previous discussions by Busse in 1982 ("Vom Felsendom zum Templum Domini," in *Das Heilige Land im Mittelalter: Begegnungsraum zwischen Orient und Okzident*, ed. Wolfdietrich Fischer and Jürgen Schneider [Neustadt a.d. Aisch: Degener, 1982], 19–31) and by Schein in 1984 ("Between Mount Moriah and the Holy Sepulchre"). The Dome of the Rock was converted into *templum domini* immediately after the conquest of Jerusalem, and was served by a community of the Austin Canons of the Temple of the Lord, whose foundation was assigned to Godfrey of Bouillon (Schein, "Between Mount Moriah and the Holy Sepulchre," 181).

54   For "the transformation of the spiritual status of the Temple Mount," after the Crusader conquest, see Schein ("Between Mount Moriah and the Holy Sepulchre," 184ff.), who also carefully shows throughout her article how "Christ's curse on the Temple was relegated to oblivion" after the Crusader conquest ("Between Mount Moriah and the Holy Sepulchre," 194–95). I am grateful to Prof. Iris Shagrir for recommending the relevant readings on the tension and co-existence of the two *umbilici mundi* in Jerusalem—the Rock and Christ's tomb at the Holy Sepulchre.

55   Di Cesare, "The Qubbat al-Ṣaḫrah in the 12th century," 233–54, esp. 241–44.

yet keeping the *umbilicus mundi* in New Jerusalem, there was no risk as to the hierarchy between the two *loci sancti*.[56]

3 Moses (Mūsā)—"and He Was a Messenger and a Prophet" (Q Maryam 19:51)

After the Muslim victory at the Battle of Ḥaṭṭīn in 1187, once the Dome of the Rock was returned to Muslim hands after functioning for almost ninety years as *templum domini*, a new inscription replaced the Latin one on the lower cornice at the base of the dome (fig. 4.3).[57] This undated inscription is written in glass mosaic atop a register of abstract jeweled rosettes framed in arches, followed by an intertwined golden band composed of large and small circles, filled alternately with twin leaves and rosettes, then by a section of interconnected circles made of petals with rosettes or spoked wheels in their centre.[58] It has been discussed by Rosen-Ayalon on two occasions,[59] when she emphasized the historical context in which it was set on the drum, and its epigraphic style's similarity to the inscription over al-ʿAqṣā's main *miḥrāb*, dated 583/1187–1188.[60]

This new inscription, written in *naskhī* cursive script and containing Q Ṭā hā 20:1–21, reads as follows (last three words not qurʾanic):

بِسْمِ اللهِ الرَّحْمٰنِ الرَّحِيمِ (1) طٰه (2) مَآ اَنْزَلْنَا عَلَيْكَ الْقُرْءانَ لِتَشْقَى (3) اِلَّا تَذْكِرَةً لِّمَنْ
يَخْشٰى (4) تَنْزِيلاً مِّمَّنْ خَلَقَ الْاَرْضَ وَ السَّمٰوٰتِ الْعُلٰى (5) اَلرَّحْمٰنُ عَلَى الْعَرْشِ اسْتَوٰى
(6) لَهُ مَا فِي السَّمٰوٰتِ وَ مَا فِي الْاَرْضِ وَ مَا بَيْنَهُمَا وَ مَا تَحْتَ الثَّرٰى (7) وَ اِنْ
تَجْهَرْ بِالْقَوْلِ فَاِنَّهُ يَعْلَمُ السِّرَّ وَ اَخْفٰى (8) اَللهُ لَآ اِلٰهَ اِلَّا هُوَ لَهُ الْاَسْمَآءُ الْحُسْنٰى

---

56   Schein, on the other hand, claims that "the site of the Navel of the Earth (*umbilicus mundi*) was said in the twelfth century to be both on Calvary and in the Temple of the Lord" ("Between Mount Moriah and the Holy Sepulchre," 188).

57   Myriam Rosen-Ayalon, "An Ayyubid Inscription in the Dome of the Rock," *Eretz Israel* 20 (1989): 360–67 (Hebrew); Myriam Rosen-Ayalon, "Jewish Substratum, Christian History and Muslim Symbolism: An Archaeological Episode in Jerusalem," *Jewish Art* 23/24 (1997–1998): 463 66.

58   Rosen-Ayalon, "An Ayyubid Inscription in the Dome of the Rock," 367–69; Lorenz Korn, "Ayyubid Mosaics in Jerusalem," in *Ayyubid Jerusalem—The Holy City in Context 1187–1250*, ed. Robert Hillenbrand and Sylvia Auld (London: Altajir Trust, 2009), 377–387 (382–84).

59   Rosen-Ayalon, "An Ayyubid Inscription in the Dome of the Rock"; Rosen-Ayalon, "Jewish Substratum, Christian History and Muslim Symbolism."

60   van Berchem, *Matériaux pour un Corpus Inscriptionum Arabicarum*, 403–15, no. 280; Hawari, *Ayyubid Jerusalem*, 192–93.

(٩) وَ هَلْ اَتٰىكَ حَدِيثُ مُوْسٰى (١٠) اِذْ رَءٰا نَارًا فَقَالَ لِاَهْلِه امْكُثُوْٓا اِنِّيْٓ اٰنَسْتُ نَارًا لَّعَلِّيْٓ اٰتِيْكُمْ مِّنْهَا بِقَبَسٍ اَوْ اَجِدُ عَلَى النَّارِ هُدًى (١١) فَلَمَّآ اَتٰىهَا نُوْدِيَ يٰمُوْسٰى (١٢) اِنِّيْٓ اَنَا رَبُّكَ فَاخْلَعْ نَعْلَيْكَ ۚ اِنَّكَ بِالْوَادِ الْمُقَدَّسِ طُوًى (١٣) وَ اَنَا اخْتَرْتُكَ فَاسْتَمِعْ لِمَا يُوْحٰى (١٤) اِنَّنِيْٓ اَنَا اللّٰهُ لَآ اِلٰهَ اِلَّآ اَنَا فَاعْبُدْنِيْ وَ اَقِمِ الصَّلٰوةَ لِذِكْرِيْ (١٥) اِنَّ السَّاعَةَ اٰتِيَةٌ اَكَادُ اُخْفِيْهَا لِتُجْزٰى كُلُّ نَفْسٍ بِمَا تَسْعٰى (١٦) فَلَا يَصُدَّنَّكَ عَنْهَا مَنْ لَّا يُؤْمِنُ بِهَا وَ اتَّبَعَ هَوٰىهُ فَتَرْدٰى (١٧) وَ مَا تِلْكَ بِيَمِيْنِكَ يٰمُوْسٰى (١٨) قَالَ هِيَ عَصَايَ ۚ اَتَوَكَّؤُا عَلَيْهَا وَ اَهُشُّ بِهَا عَلٰى غَنَمِيْ وَ لِيَ فِيْهَا مَاٰرِبُ اُخْرٰى (١٩) قَالَ اَلْقِهَا يٰمُوْسٰى (٢٠) فَاَلْقٰىهَا فَاِذَا هِيَ حَيَّةٌ تَسْعٰى (٢١) قَالَ خُذْهَا وَ لَا تَخَفْ ۗ سَنُعِيْدُهَا سِيْرَتَهَا الْاُوْلٰى

صدق الله العظيم

In the name of Allah, the Gracious, the Merciful. (1) Ṭa ha. (2) We have not sent down to you the Qur'an to thee to (an occasion) for thy distress, (3) but only as an admonition to those who fear (Allah). (4) A revelation from Him who created the earth and the heavens on high. (5) (Allah) Most Gracious is firmly established on the throne (of authority). (6) To Him belongs what is in the heavens and on earth, and all between them, and all beneath the soil. (7) If thou pronounce the word aloud—(it is not matter): for verily He knoweth what is secret and what is yet more hidden. (8) Allah! There is no god but He! To Him belong the Most Beautiful Names. (9) Has the story of Moses reached thee? (10) Behold, he saw a fire: so he said to his family, "Tarry ye; I perceive a fire; perhaps I can bring you some burning brand therefrom, or find some guidance at the fire." (11) But when he came to the fire, a voice was heard: "O Moses! (12) Verily I am thy Lord! Therefore (in My presence) put off thy shoes: thou art in the sacred valley Ṭuwā. (13) I have chosen thee: Listen, then to the inspiration (sent to thee). (14) Verily, I am Allah: There is no god but I, so serve thou Me (only), and establish regular prayer for celebrating My praise. (15) Verily the Hour is coming—My design is to keep it Hidden—for every soul to receive its reward by the measure of its Endeavour. (16) Therefore let not such as believe not therein but follow their own lusts, divert thee therefrom, lest thou perish!" (17) "And what is that in thy right hand, O Moses?" (18) He said, "It is my rod: on it I lean, with it I beat down fodder

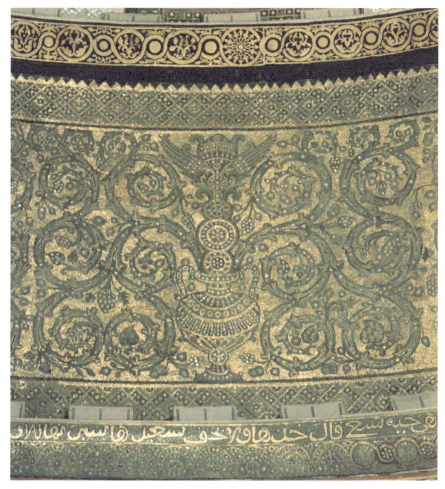

FIGURE 4.3 Mosaics of the lower section of the Dome of the Rock's drum, and a detail of the
Ayyūbid *naskhī* inscription, with verses 20–21 of Sūrat Ṭā hā

for my flocks; and in it I find other uses." (19) (Allah) said, "Throw it, O
Moses!" (20) He threw it, and behold! It was a snake, active in motion. (21)
(Allah) said, "Seize it and fear not: We shall return it at once to its former
condition." God Almighty is right.[61]

Moses in Islamic traditions is seen as the prophet who spoke directly to God
and received from Him the first written Law. He was also the one who during

---

61   English translation by ʿA. Yūsuf ʿAlī, *The Meaning of the Holy Qurʾān* (Beltsville: Amana
      Publications, 1997), 765–68.

the *mi'rāj* oriented the Prophet Muḥammad towards his meeting with God. According to Rosen-Ayalon, the qur'anic passage chosen for the reinstatement of the building as Muslim is the best metaphor for the re-conversion of the Dome of the Rock in the days of the Ayyūbids, under Ṣalāḥ al-Dīn in 1190–1191.[62]

---

62   Rosen-Ayalon writes: "This is precisely the meaning of the inscription: the Dome of the
      Rock, which had been Templum Domini under the Crusaders, is transformed once again
      into the Muslim Qubbat al-Sakhra. The snake which Salah al-Din is told not to fear and
      to seize is the Crusaders" ("Jewish Substratum, Christian History and Muslim Symbolism,"
      466). There is no contemporary inscription indicating the works by Ṣalāḥ al-Dīn in the
      Dome of the Rock. Yet, a clear indication that he was responsible for the renovation of
      the dome is given by the Ottoman inscription (1291/1874) written in gilded stucco, located
      at the base inside the wooden dome (fig. 4.4). The inscription (van Berchem, *Matériaux
      pour un Corpus Inscriptionum Arabicarum*, 289–298, no. 225), divided into eight bands
      and intercalated by inscribed medallions, refers to four renovations of the dome, the first
      in 586/1190, the others in 718/1318 (al-Nāṣir Muḥammad b. Qalawūn), in 1156/1743 (an error
      of the copyist; see below) and finally by 'Abd al-'Azīz. The bands read:

      (١)بسم الله الرحمن الرحيم أمر بتجديد تذهيب هذه القبّة الشريفة (٢)مولانا السلطان الملك العالم
      العادل(٣)العامل صلاح الدين يوسف بن أيوب تغمّده الله (٤) برحمته و ذلك فى شهور سنة
      ستة و ثمانين و خمس(ـمـ)ـائة (خمسمائة) (٥) أمر بتجديد و تذهيب (كذا) هذه اتقنه (كذا)مع القبّة
      الفوقانية (٦)برصاصها مولانا ظلّ الله فى أرضه القائم (٧)بستّه و فرضه السلطان محمّد بن الملك
      المنصور الشهيد (٨)قلاون تغمّده الله برحمته و ذلك فى سنة ثمان عشر (كذا)و سبع مائة

      The medallions read:

      بسم الله الرحمن الرحيم (٢) أمر بتذهيب هذه القبّة مع (٣) تجديد القبّة الفوقانيّة (٤) مولانا
      السلطان محمود خان ١١٥٦ (sic) (٤) أمر بتجديد وتذهيب هذه القبّة (٥) مع تصليح القبّة
      الفوقانيّة (٦)بتجديد رصاصها مولانا (٧)السلطان عبد العزيز خان (٨) أدام الله ملكه سنة ١٢٩١

      The first three bands ("Ordered to renew the gilding of this noble dome our lord the
      Sulṭān al-Malik al-'Ālim al-'Ādil al-'Āmil Ṣalāḥ al-Dīn Yūsuf b. Ayyūb, may Allah wrap him
      in His mercy [i.e., the late Ṣalāḥ al-Dīn, KCS] and that in the months of the year 586") is
      thus testimony to early Ayyūbid work, which most certainly also included the erasing of
      the Latin inscriptions and their replacement by a new one in Arabic at the lower cornice.
            It should be noted that the present inscription, dating to 'Abd al-'Azīz's time, replaced
      an earlier one seen by M. de Vogué and M. Sauvaire (Melchior de Vogué, *Le Temple de
      Jérusalem* [Paris: Noblet & Baudry, 1864], 91–92). The earlier inscription contained some
      different details, especially in the medallions. The year of Ṣalāḥ al-Dīn's renovation is
      stated as 585 and not 586, and the exact date—27 of the month of Rajab/10 September
      1189—is also given. Van Berchem pointed out that this was probably a mistake, this time
      by Maḥmūd II's (!) copyist, and the original date should have been 27 of Rajab 583, the
      day of the conquest of Jerusalem. As for the work being by Maḥmūd II (r. 1223–1255/1808–
      1839) and not Maḥmūd I (r. 1143–1168/1730–1754), de Vogué read "year 12–," and not 1156
      as in 'Abd al-'Azīz's version. van Berchem completed it to 1233/1817–1818, based on con-
      temporary inscriptions in the Temple Mount and in the Dome of the Rock itself (van
      Berchem, *Matériaux pour un Corpus Inscriptionum Arabicarum*, 294, n. 1). Maḥmūd's in-
      scription also contained important information with reference to al-Nāṣir Muḥammad's

The chosen verse also further confirms the eschatological symbolism based on Persian and Judeo-Christian traditions which has been suggested by Rosen-Ayalon and Lorenz Korn,[63] that the Dome of the Rock is the location of the Throne ("Allah Most Gracious is firmly established on the throne," Q Ṭā hā 20:5), where the judgement at the end of days will be held.[64]

Korn stresses further aspects of this inscription, especially verse 8, in which God's unity and majesty are stressed. According to him, the very fact that an event related to Moses—a Biblical figure who never set foot in Jerusalem (though he was "present" during Muḥammad's *miʿrāj*)—was chosen to illustrate the new status of the building, and relates to his status of *kālim Allah*, elected from among the people by God himself. Moses led the children of Israel across Sinai to the Promised Land, not unlike Ṣalāḥ al-Dīn, who left Egypt to conquer the land which was held by enemies. Korn concludes that "in some way, Saladin had accomplished what Moses had prepared, for a second time. Through his conquest, Saladin fulfilled Moses's call to enter the Holy Land—a call which was very much on the mind of his contemporaries."[65]

---

works, which shaped the style of the gilded stucco-work kept throughout the later renovations. Both years 718 and 719 are mentioned (perhaps referring to the time-span of the works), as well as the name of the amīr in charge, ʿAlam al-Dīn [Sanjar] al-Jāwulī, *nāẓir al-Ḥaramayn*, i.e., superintendent of the two *Ḥaram*s, Jerusalem and Hebron (van Berchem, *Matériaux pour un Corpus Inscriptionum Arabicarum*, 297–98). Sanjar was the governor of Gaza between 712–720/1313–1320 and among the well-known works he supervised for al-Nāṣir Muḥammad is the minaret of the Great Mosque of Ramla, erected in 714/1314. The inscription at al-Nāṣir Muḥammad's minaret in the White Mosque of Ramla, dated to 718/1318, does not mention Sanjar's name, but it is reasonable that he also supervised this construction (Katia Cytryn-Silverman, "Three Mamlūk Minarets in Ramla," *Jerusalem Studies in Arabic and Islam* 35 (2008): 379–432 [392–94]).

For a survey of the late Ottoman works mentioned above see Beatrice St. Laurent, "The Dome of the Rock—Restorations and Significance 1540–1918," in *Ottoman Jerusalem— The Living City: 1517–1917*, ed. Sylvia Auld and Robert Hillenbrand (London: Altajir Trust, 2000), 415–424 (422–24).

63   Rosen-Ayalon, *Early Islamic Monuments*, 53; Korn, "Ayyubid Mosaics in Jerusalem," 386.

64   In fact, verses 115–123 of this same *sūrah* tells us the story of Adam—from temptation to punishment and then repentance. These verses are followed by 20:124, warning whoever turns away from Allāh's message, for Allāh "shall raise him up blind on the Day of Judgment" (ʿAlī, *The Meaning of the Holy Qurʾān*, 788–90).

65   Korn, "Ayyubid Mosaics in Jerusalem," 386–87. Korn also suggests a symbolic relation between Ṭuwā in verse 12, denominated *al-Wādi al-Muqaddas*, and the Ṣakhra, both having been cleaned from unbelievers (Korn, "Ayyubid Mosaics in Jerusalem," 386).

To these interpretations I shall add another meaningful point in the choice of this *sūrah*: the fact that Moses's rod, with its central role in the story, is connected to Adam, who brought it from Paradise.[66]

According to a tradition transmitted by Isḥāq b. Bishr al-Bakhārī (d. 206/821):

> Adam caused some of the perfume of Paradise to come down with him. He also brought down with him the Black Stone which used to be whiter than snow, the rod of Moses which was from myrtle of Paradise, ten cubits tall and equal to the height of Moses, myrrh, and incense.[67]

It is interesting, as pointed out by Korn, that later on in the Ayyūbid period, we have three of the Biblical figures discussed here as names of the Ayyūbid brother-princes—Mūsā', 'Isā, and Muḥammad—who united their forces to expel the Crusaders from Damietta (618/1221). This victory was celebrated in a poem commissioned by al-Kāmil Muḥammad (r. as viceroy of Egypt under his father al-'Ādil from 604/1207, and after al-'Ādil's death, as sultān from 615/1218–635/1238),[68] who had a singer recite a poem in which both (al-Ashraf) Mūsa (r. in Syria between 604/1207–635/1237) and (al-Mu'aẓẓam) 'Isā (r. in Damascus between 594/1198–624/1227)[69] come to serve Muḥammad. Even the rod of Moses is mentioned in this *qaṣīda*, but in the context of the parting of the Red Sea.[70] Korn claims that these parallels indicate a comparison by the poet

---

66   On the various Muslim traditions about Moses's rod see Brannon M. Wheeler, *Moses in the Quran and Islamic Exegesis* (New York: Routledge, 2002), 60ff. It should also be noted that Aaron's rod is sometimes conflated with that of Moses (Wheeler, *Moses*, 59; see also William H. Propp, "The Rod of Aaron and the Sin of Moses," *JBL* 107 [1988]: 19–26 [22]). For the Jewish origin of the traditions regarding the rod of Aaron see e.g., Exod 7:17–20, which refers to Aaron smiting his rod over the waters before Pharaoh, turning them into blood; Num 17:16–26, which refers to Aaron's rod blossoming and bearing almonds within the Tent of the Testimony (אֹהֶל מוֹעֵד); b. Yoma 52b, which lists Aaron's rod among the things hidden together with the Ark; and others. Yet it is the passage in Exod 7:9–12, describing how Aaron's rod became a serpent in front of Pharaoh and how it swallowed the rods of the magicians of Egypt, which bears most likeness to the story of Moses's rod becoming a snake in Sūrat Ṭāhā. I would like to thank my student David Antebi, who pointed out some important Jewish sources connected with Aaron's and Moses's rods. For the early thirteenth century Christian (Nestorian) tradition on how Adam's rod came down to become Moses's rod, and then eventually Jacob's, Jesus brother's, from whom Judas Iscariot stole and gave to the Jews, see Ernest A. Wallis Budge, *The Book of the Bee* (Oxford: Clarendon Press, 1886), 62ff.

67   EI[3], s.v. "Ādam"; Wheeler, *Prophets in the Quran*, 27, quoting al-Ṭabarī.

68   EI[2], s.v. "al-Kāmil."

69   EI[2], s.v. "al-Mu'aẓẓam."

70   Ibn Wāṣil, *Mufarrij al-Kurūb fī Akhbār Banī Ayyūb*, ed. Ḥasanayn M. Rabi'a and Sa'īd 'A.-F. 'Āshūr, 5 vols. (Cairo: al-Maṭba'a al-Amiriya, 1957), 4:115; Korn, "Ayyubid Mosaics in Jerusalem," 386–87 (n. 58), quoting al-Maqrizī, who repeats Ibn Wāṣil.

FIGURE 4.4   The gilded stucco-decorated dome, with inscriptions referring to two
             of the four rulers involved with its renovation, Ṣalāḥ al-Dīn (1190) and
             al-Nāṣir Muḥammad b. Qalawūn (1318)

between the victory in Damietta and that in Jerusalem in 1187 by Ṣalāḥ al-Dīn,
who, as mentioned above, was himself seen as a second Moses.[71]

4   Conclusions

The *Faḍāʾil* literature, texts in praise of Jerusalem, includes numerous traditions
binding Biblical figures and events to the Temple Mount and more specifically
to the Dome of the Rock. This literature developed during the Umayyad period, most probably during ʿAbd al-Malik's time, and continued to be developed
throughout the centuries. Compilations contemporary with the post-Crusader
period were common. In fact, up to the late 1970s, scholarship believed that
this literature resulted from the need to free Jerusalem from the Crusaders,

---

71   Lorenz Korn in a personal communication d.d. 28 April 2019. I would like to express my
     gratitude to Korn for pointing out to me this later use of the three Biblical names in the
     context of freeing Islamic soil from Frankish control.

until scholars like Isaac Hasson (al-Wāsiṭī, *Faḍāʾil*) and Ofer Livne-Kafri (Ibn al-Murajjā, *Faḍāʾil*) brought forward early eleventh-century compilations, as well as chains of transmitters going back to Umayyad times.[72] In any case, the late development of the *Faḍāʾil* matches a time when the Muslim right of possession of the Temple Mount became once again relevant, not unlike the period in which it was first developed as a Muslim site.

I am aware that this short exercise, emphasizing the possible centrality of the tradition of Adam's tomb already in the early Islamic period, competes with well-established views which give precedence to other meanings and events, mainly related to Abraham, or to Solomon and his Temple. Yet, this view does not deny the many other interpretations, but rather adds a new and important layer for legitimizing the erection of the Dome of the Rock. By adding to its many roles also that of the place of burial of the Father of Mankind created by God's hands, it was indubitably established as the ultimate competitor for the Holy Sepulchre and its role as *umbilicus mundi*. By linking the Rock tightly to Biblical figures such as Adam and Abraham, both also identified with the erection of the Kaaba, Jerusalem became not third in importance after Mecca and Medina, but at least an equal to the site towards which all Muslims pray.

The later physical developments around the Rock, both under Frankish rule (after 1099) and after the Ayyubid reconquest (1187), are doubtless expressions of Christian and Muslim religious supremacy, Jesus and Moses respectively representing the legitimization of the Rock's re-appropriation. Yet, both figures relate to the first, and thus create an important link with the remote past. In Christianity Jesus was seen as the Second Adam, one created by God as the First of Mankind.[73] Moses, through his rod brought by Adam from Paradise, conveyed God's message. Finally, Muḥammad, the final messenger (*rasūl*) of God, was perceived in Islam as the offspring of Adam's light.[74] They all meet at the Rock.

---

72   Among the post-Crusader compilations, it is worth noting Sibṭ b. al-Jawzī's (d. 654/1256) *Mirʾāt al-Zamān*, also quoted by later authors. Among his early sources is Muḥammad b. al-Sāʾib, who died in 146/763, and was thus a contemporary with events of the Umayyad period. For a partial translation to English, concerning the Temple Mount and specifically the Dome of the Rock and al-Aqṣā, see Amikam Elad, "Why did ʿAbd al-Malik Build the Dome of the Rock? A Re-Examination of the Muslim Sources," in *Bayt al-Maqdis: ʿAbd al-Malik's Jerusalem*, ed. Julian Raby and Jeremy Johns (Oxford: Oxford University Press, 1992), 33–58.

73   EI², "Ādam."

74   EI², "Ādam."

References

Al-Yaʿqūbī. *Taʾrīkh al-Yaʿqūbī*. Edited by Martijn T. Houtsma. 2 vols. Leiden: Brill, 1883.

ʿAlī, ʿA. Yūsuf. *The Meaning of the Holy Qurʾān*. Beltsville: Amana Publications, 1997.

Avner, Rina. "The Dome of the Rock in Light of the Development of Concentric Martyria in Jerusalem: Architecture and Architectural Iconography." *Muqarnas* 27 (2010): 31–49.

Baruch, Yuval, Ronny Reich, and Débora Sandhaus. "The Temple Mount: Results of the Archaeological Research of the Past Decade." Pages 33–54 in *New Studies in the Archaeology of Jerusalem and Its Region: Collected Papers: Volume X*. Edited by Guy D. Stiebel, Joseph Uziel, Katia Cytryn-Silverman, Amit Reʾem, and Yuval Gadot. Jerusalem: n.p., 2016.

Bearman, Peri, Thierry Bianquis, C. Edmund Bosworth, Emeri van Donzel and Wolfhart P. Heinrichs, eds. *Encyclopaedia of Islam*. 2nd ed. Leiden: Brill, 1954–2005. (= EI²).

Berchem, Max van. *Matériaux pour un Corpus Inscriptionum Arabicarum: Deuxième partie: Syrie du Sud, Jérusalem "Ḥaram"*. Geneva: Slatkine, 2001.

Berger, Pamela C. *The Crescent on the Temple: The Dome of the Rock as Image of the Ancient Jewish Sanctuary*. Leiden: Brill, 2012.

Busse, Heribert. "The Sanctity of Jerusalem in Islam." *Judaism* 17 (1968): 441–68.

Busse, Heribert. "Vom Felsendom zum Templum Domini." Pages 19–31 in *Das Heilige Land im Mittelalter: Begegnungsraum zwischen Orient und Okzident*. Edited by Wolfdietrich Fischer and Jürgen Schneider. Neustadt a.d. Aisch: Degener, 1982.

Cytryn-Silverman, Katia. "Three Mamlūk Minarets in Ramla." *Jerusalem Studies in Arabic and Islam* 35 (2008): 379–432.

Di Cesare, Michelina. "The Qubbat al-Ṣaḥrah in the 12th century." *Oriente Moderno* 95 (2015): 233–54.

Elad, Amikam. "Why did ʿAbd al-Malik Build the Dome of the Rock? A Re-Examination of the Muslim Sources." Pages 33–58 in *Bayt al-Maqdis: ʿAbd al-Malik's Jerusalem*. Edited by Julian Raby and Jeremy Johns. Oxford: Oxford University Press, 1992.

Elad, Amikam. *Medieval Jerusalem and Islamic Worship: Holy Places, Ceremonies, Pilgrimage*. Leiden: Brill, 1995.

Elad, Amikam. "ʿAbd al-Malik and the Dome of the Rock: A Further Examination of the Muslim Sources." *Jerusalem Studies in Arabic and Islam* 35 (2008): 167–226.

Grabar, Oleg. "The Umayyad Dome of the Rock in Jerusalem." *Ars Orientalis* 3 (1959): 33–62.

Grabar, Oleg. "The Meaning of the Dome of the Rock in Jerusalem." *Medieval Studies at Minnesota* 3 (1988): 1–10.

Grabar, Oleg. *The Shape of the Holy: Early Islamic Jerusalem*. Princeton: Princeton University Press, 1996.

Grabar, Oleg. "Notes on the Dome of the Rock." Pages 217–229 in *Jerusalem: Constructing the Study of Islamic Art, Volume IV*. Hampshire: Variorum, 2005.

al-Harawī, ʿAlī. *Kitāb al-Ishārāt ilā Maʿrifat al-Ziyārāt*. Edited by ʿAlī ʿUmar. Cairo: Maktabat al-Thaqāfa al-diniyyah, 2002.

Hasan, Perween. "The Footprint of the Prophet." *Muqarnas* 10 (1992): 335–43.

Hawari, Mahmoud K. *Ayyubid Jerusalem (1187–1250): An Architectural and Archaeological Study*. BAR International Series 1628. Oxford: Archaeopress, 2007.

Horst, Pieter W. van der. "The Site of Adam's Tomb." Pages 1–5 in *Studies in Ancient Judaism and Early Christianity*. Leiden: Brill, 2014.

Houtsma, Martijn T., Thomas W. Arnold, R. Basset, and Richard. Hartmann, eds. *Encyclopaedia of Islam*. 1st ed. Leiden: Brill, 1913–1938. (= EI^1).

Ibn al-Murajjā al-Maqdisī. *Faḍāʾil Bayt al-Maqdis wa-al-Khalīl wa-Faḍāʾil al-Shām*. Edited by Ofer Livne-Kafri. Shfaram: Dar al-mashriq li'l-tarjama wa'l-ṭibāʾa wa'Inashr, 1995.

Ibn Wāṣil. *Mufarrij al-Kurūb fī Akhbār Banī Ayyūb*. Edited by Ḥasanayn M. Rabiʿa and Saʿīd ʿA.-F. ʿĀshūr. 5 vols. Cairo: al-Maṭbaʿa al-Amiriya, 1957.

Kaplony, Andreas. *The Ḥaram of Jerusalem 324–1099*. Stuttgart: Steiner, 2002.

Kessler, Christel. "ʿAbd al-Malik's Inscription in the Dome of the Rock: A Reconsideration." *JRAS* 1 (1970): 2–14.

Khoury, Nuha N.N. "The Dome of the Rock, the Kaʿba, and Ghumdan: Arab Myths and Umayyad Monuments." *Muqarnas* 10 (1993): 57–65.

Kister, Meir J. "Ādam: A Study of Some Legends in *Tafsīr* and *Ḥadīṯ* Literature." *IOS* 13 (1993): 113–74.

Korn, Lorenz. "Ayyubid Mosaics in Jerusalem." Pages 377–387 in *Ayyubid Jerusalem— The Holy City in Context 1187–1250*. Edited by Robert Hillenbrand and Sylvia Auld. London: Altajir Trust, 2009.

Krautheimer, Richard. "Introduction to an Iconography of Mediaeval Architecture." *Journal of the Warburg and Courtauld Institutes* 5 (1942): 1–33.

Levy-Rubin, Milka. "Why was the Dome of the Rock Built? A New Perspective on a Long-Discussed Question." *BSOAS* 80 (2017): 441–64.

Lipatov-Chicherin, Nikolai. "Early Christian Tradition about Adam's Burial on Golgotha and Origen." Pages 151–78 in *Origeniana Duodecima: Origen's Legacy in the Holy Land—A Tale of Three Cities: Jerusalem, Caesarea and Bethlehem: Proceedings of the 12th International Origen Congress, Jerusalem, 25–29 June, 2017*. Edited by Brouria Bitton-Ashkelony, Oded Irshai, Aryeh Kofsky, Hillel Newman, and Lorenzo Perrone. BETL 302. Leuven: Peeters, 2019.

Livne-Kafri, Ofer. "Jerusalem: The Navel of the Earth in Muslim Tradition." *Der Islam* 84 (2008): 46–72.

Milstein, Rachel. *La Bible dans l'art islamique*. Paris: Presses Universitaires de France, 2005.

Milwright, Marcus. *The Dome of the Rock and its Umayyad Mosaic Inscriptions*. Edinburgh: Edinburgh University Press, 2016.

Nāṣir-i-Khusraw. *Diary of a Journey through Syria and Palestine*. Translated and Annotated by Guy Le Strange. London: Palestine Pilgrims' Text Society, 1988.

Peters, Francis E. "Who Built the Dome of the Rock." *Greco-Arabica* 2 (1983): 119–38.

Pringle, Denys. *The Churches of the Crusader Kingdom of Jerusalem: A Corpus: Volume III: The City of Jerusalem*. Cambridge: Cambridge University Press, 2007.

Propp, William H. "The Rod of Aaron and the Sin of Moses." *JBL* 107 (1988): 19–26.

Rabbat, Nasser. "The Meaning of the Umayyad Dome of the Rock." *Muqarnas* 6 (1989): 12–21.

Rosen-Ayalon, Myriam. *The Early Islamic Monuments of al-Haram al-Sharif: An Iconographic Study*. Qedem 28. Jerusalem: The Hebrew University of Jerusalem, 1989.

Rosen-Ayalon, Myriam. "An Ayyubid Inscription in the Dome of the Rock." *Eretz Israel* 20 (1989): 360–67. (Hebrew).

Rosen-Ayalon, Myriam. "Jewish Substratum, Christian History and Muslim Symbolism: An Archaeological Episode in Jerusalem." *Jewish Art* 23/24 (1997–1998): 463–66.

Schein, Sylvia. "Between Mount Moriah and the Holy Sepulchre: The Changing Traditions of the Temple Mount in the Central Middle Ages." *Traditio* 40 (1984): 175–95.

Shani, Raya. "The Iconography of the Dome of the Rock." *Jerusalem Studies in Arabic and Islam* 23 (1999): 158–207.

Soucek, Priscilla P. "The Temple of Solomon in Islamic Legend and Art." Pages 73–123 in *The Temple of Solomon: Archeological Fact and Medieval Tradition in Christian, Islamic and Jewish Art*. Edited by Joseph Gutmann. Missoula, MT: Scholars Press, 1976.

St. Laurent, Beatrice. "The Dome of the Rock Restorations and Significance 1540–1918." Pages 415–424 in *Ottoman Jerusalem—The Living City: 1517–1917*. Edited by Sylvia Auld and Robert Hillenbrand. London: Altajir Trust, 2000.

St. Laurent, Beatrice, and Isam Awwad. *Capitalizing Jerusalem: Mu'awiya's Urban Vision, 638–680*. Sheffield: Equinox, 2021.

al-Ṭabarī, Muḥammad b. Jarīr. *Ta'rīkh al-rusul wa al-mulūk = Ta'rīkh al-Ṭabarī*. Edited by Abu al-Fadl Ibrahim. Cairo: Dār al-Maʿarif bi Miṣr, 1967.

al-Thaʿlabī, *ʿArāʾis al-majālis fī qiṣāṣ al-anbiyāʾ*. Translated by William M. Brinner. SAL/SJAL 24. Leiden: Brill, 2002.

de Vogué, Melchior. *Le Temple de Jérusalem*. Paris: Noblet & Baudry, 1864.

Wallis Budge, Ernest A. *The Book of the Bee*. Oxford, Clarendon Press, 1886.

Wallis Budge, Ernest A. *The Book of the Cave of Treasures*. London: The Religious Tract Society, 1927.

Al-Wāsiṭī, *Faḍāʾil Bayt al-Muqaddas*. Edited by Isaac Hasson. Jerusalem: Jerusalem Academic Press, 1979.

Wheeler, Brannon M. *Prophets in the Quran: An Introduction to the Quran and Muslim Exegesis*. London: Continuum, 2002.

Wheeler, Brannon M. *Moses in the Quran and Islamic Exegesis*. New York: Routledge, 2002.

Whitcomb, Donald. "Notes for an Archaeology of Muʿāwiya." Pages 11–27 in *Christians and Others in the Umayyad State*. Edited by Antoine Borrut and Fred M. Donner. LAMINE 1. Chicago: Chicago University Press, 2016.

CHAPTER 5

Synagogues as Foci of Multi-Religious and Ideological Confrontation? The Case of the Sardis Synagogue

Steven Fine

It is tough to be a "holy place." Once chosen, constructed, purchased, converted and negotiated, "places," as opposed to texts or other visual sources, change slowly, and generally still exist long after those who made the original construction and design decisions are gone. Synagogues are a particularly complex case, as their "sanctity"—as far as Jews were concerned—was mostly contingent on use by the "holy people," the culture of venerating the holy books and their activation through liturgy, selected Tabernacle/Jerusalem Temple metaphors and a general approach to holiness shared with polytheists and, later on, Christians who helped Jews explain their religion to themselves and to others within the global mélange that was late antiquity.[1]

1 The Sardis Synagogue

The synagogue at Sardis in Lydia is by far the largest and most impressive Jewish public building discovered from Roman antiquity, second to the Herodian Temple itself. This building is a good place to consider questions of "multi-religious and ideological confrontation" in regard to the holy. The Sardis synagogue is located in a space adjacent to the Palaestra of Sardis, in one of the most prominent parts of the city. Acquired and remodelled by the Jewish community during the late third century, this former imperial basilica was fitted to Jewish usage over the subsequent three centuries and served as a centre for

---

1 On the developing sanctity of late antique synagogues, with reference to Sardis, see my *This Holy Place: On the Sanctity of the Synagogue During the Greco-Roman Period* (Notre Dame: University of Notre Dame Press, 1997), esp. 147–51; See also my edited volume, *Sacred Realm: The Emergence of the Synagogue in the Ancient World* (New York: Oxford University Press and Yeshiva University Museum, 1996).

© STEVEN FINE, 2021 | DOI:10.1163/9789004437210_007

the large Jewish population of Sardis into the seventh century, when it—with much of the city—was razed by the Sasanian invasion of 616.[2]

The synagogue is 119 meters from end to end, and the central hall measures nearly half of that, 54×18 meters. Its walls were covered lavishly with opus sectile in bright colours, the ceiling with paintings of unknown form (they are mentioned in an inscription) and its floors with patterned mosaics of high quality. What remains of the furnishings is lavish as well, including two large aediculae for the sacred scrolls and a central table flanked by rampart lions, all spolia in secondary use. A large chancel panel decorated with a seven-branched menorah was discovered before the southern aedicula and so were dedicatory inscriptions, once coloured. Donors included a "teacher of the Law" and donors claiming prominence through euergetism.[3] The few remains suggest that the synagogue participated in the general Jewish visual vocabulary, and took "Torah" very seriously. An inscription found near the Torah shrine provides "stage" instructions for the community. It reads: "Find, open, read, observe (or "protect": φυλαξον)."[4] A rather ornate inscription celebrates the donation of the "Torah shrine" with a similar imperative on "protection." It is called *to nomoph[a]lakion*, "the place that protects the Law."[5] This is the only extant inscription to offer a reason for the donation, "for the health" of the donor—perhaps ascribing especial power to the Torah shrine. One inscription involves the Divine directly, concluding with the prayer "Lord, help this house."[6] The image of a Torah shrine, sacred scrolls stacked within it and inscribed menorahs

---

2   See Andrew Seager and A. Thomas Kraabel, "The Synagogue and the Jewish Community," in *Sardis from Prehistoric to Roman Times: Results of the Archaeological Exploration of Sardis, 1958–1975*, ed. George A. Hanfmann, William E. Mierse, and Clive Foss (Cambridge: Harvard University Press, 1983), 168–190. See also my *Sacred Realm, passim*; A. Thomas Kraabel, "The Diaspora Synagogue: Archaeological and Epigraphic Evidence since Sukenik," in *Ancient Synagogues: Historical Analysis and Archaeological Discovery*, ed. Dan Urman and Paul V.M. Flesher (Leiden: Brill, 1995), 95–126; Walter Ameling, *Inscriptiones Judaicae Orientis: II: Kleinasien* (Tübingen: Mohr Siebeck, 2004) 209–96. Applying her general tendency toward late dating of late antique synagogues, Jodi Magness attempted to redate the synagogue to the 5th–6th century. Andrew Seager tells me that this suggestion will be refuted by the excavators in the forthcoming final publication. See Jodi Magness, "The Date of the Sardis Synagogue in Light of the Numismatic Evidence," *American Journal of Archaeology* 109 (2005): 443–75.

3   See John H. Kroll, "The Greek Inscriptions of the Sardis Synagogue," HTR 94 (2001): 5–55; Ameling, *Inscriptiones Judaicae Orientis, II: Kleinasien*, 151, 398–440.

4   Ameling, *Inscriptiones Judaicae Orientis, II: Kleinasien*, no. 131.

5   Ameling, *Inscriptiones Judaicae Orientis, II: Kleinasien*, no. 129.

6   Ameling, *Inscriptiones Judaicae Orientis, II: Kleinasien*, no. 142.

punctuate one of the inscriptions.[7] A large stone menorah, a metre across, was donated by one "Socrates."[8]

Dedicatory inscriptions cover the floors and the walls, almost all in Greek, a few with Hebrew characters that were apparently used for their iconic value.[9] The inscriptions represent a virtual cacophony of Jewish voices—some quite prominent within the local administration—"fulfilling their vows."[10] Some gifts were commemorated in the third person, while others assert their presence with the first person "I."[11] Six non-Jewish donors are self-identified as "god-fearers," who appear before the God of Israel and the Jewish community as benefactors.[12] These gifts include elements of the floor mosaics and a three-dimensional menorah. While this *heptamuxion* ("seven-branched lamp") no longer exists, the impressive inscription commemorating the gift does: "Aurelios Hermogenes, citizen of Sardis, god-fearer, from the gifts of Providence, I made [donated] the seven-branched lamp."[13]

In short, the Sardis synagogue stands as a monument to a wealthy, powerful and well-integrated Jewish community of a sort that scarcely existed in Jewish history before the most recent times. It projects the status of Jews in the very centre of Roman Sardis, apparently with no ambiguity or insecurity. The remains give no sense of "multi-religious and ideological confrontation" whatsoever, and fit well within the general contours of synagogue sanctity that I outlined in my dissertation volume *This Holy Place: On the Sanctity of the Synagogue in the Greco-Roman Period* and the associated exhibition catalogue *Sacred Realm: The Emergence of the Synagogue in the Ancient World*.[14] This could be the end of the story. In fact, this recap is just the beginning.

---

7 Steven Fine, "The Open Torah Ark: An Iconographic Type in Late Antique Rome and Sardis," in *Viewing Ancient Jewish Art and Archaeology: VeHinnei Rachel—Essays in Honor of Rachel Hachlili*, ed. Ann Killebrew and Gabriel Faßbeck (Leiden: Brill, 2015), 121–134.

8 Ameling, *Inscriptiones Judaicae Orientis, II: Kleinasien*, no. 290.

9 Ameling, *Inscriptiones Judaicae Orientis, II: Kleinasien*, nos. 105–109; Frank M. Cross, "The Hebrew Inscriptions from Sardis," *HTR* 95 (2002): 3–19.

10 Ameling, *Inscriptiones Judaicae Orientis, II: Kleinasien*.

11 Ameling, *Inscriptiones Judaicae Orientis, II: Kleinasien*.

12 Ameling, *Inscriptiones Judaicae Orientis, II: Kleinasien*, nos. 67, 68, 83, 123, 125, 132. In general, Louis H. Feldman, "Proselytes and 'Sympathizers' in the Light of the New Inscriptions from Aphrodisias," *RÉJ* 148 (1989): 265–305.

13 Ameling, *Inscriptiones Judaicae Orientis, II: Kleinasien*, no. 132.

14 See footnote 1.

2   Contextualization of the Sardis Synagogue

The remains of the Sardis synagogue are as sparse as they are monumental. We have the stage upon which the Jews of Sardis acted out their religious and communal lives, the names of a few supporters, and some hints as to their religious propensities. For some historians, the silent hulking remains of the Sardis synagogue have served as proof of the happy relations that existed between Jews and their neighbours in Roman antiquity, even with the rise of imperial Christianity. This approach is the culmination of a long process, promulgated by historian Salo W. Baron in New York as part of his "anti-lachrymose conception of Jewish history"[15] and then by art historian Kurt Weizmann at Princeton.[16] Sardis became the model diaspora community. Together with Dura Europos, it was a place where Jews and Christians, scarred by pogroms and the Holocaust, imagined a happy late antiquity—Weimar Berlin by the Aegean and post war America on the sunny Mediterranean. Is it any surprise that the American Jewry of the 1960s flocked to support Harvard's reconstruction of this distant synagogue? A commemorative plaque within the reconstructed synagogue lists eighty-five donor units. These range from Rabbi Edgar Magnin and his Wilshire Boulevard Temple in Los Angeles, to the patron of American modern Orthodox *Bildung*, Ludwig Jesselson. All are commemorated prominently with a small number of (approximately ten) Christian supporters interspersed, including Ernest Gallo of Gallo Winery and Harvard professor and later Bishop of Stockholm, Krister Stendahl. One prominent philanthropist, who happens not to have been Jewish, appears in her own name ("Miss Alice Tully"), while numerous women appear together with their husbands, most referred to by the formula "Mr. and Mrs." In two cases "Mrs." is followed by the names of their apparently deceased husbands. This inscription is a snapshot of an elite community asserting an elite *convivencia* and by implication, celebrating an ancient one. As late as 1999 John S. Crawford asserted that "among ordinary people away from the capital[17] there was an attitude of tolerance, demonstrated by reciprocal respect for Jewish and Christian religious symbols. The tolerance between Jews and Christians lasted at least until the early seventh

---

15   Salo W. Baron, "Ghetto and Emancipation," *The Menorah Journal* 14 (1928): 515–26.
16   See Margaret Olin, *The Nation Without Art: Examining Modern Discourses on Jewish Art* (Lincoln: University of Nebraska Press, 2002), 127–156; I discuss this phenomenon in *Art, History and the Historiography of Judaism in the Greco-Roman World* (Leiden: Brill, 2013), 200–9. See also Yitzchak Schwartz, "An Anti-Anti Lachrymose Approach to Jewish History?", https://jhiblog.org/2017/02/22/an-anti-anti-lachrymose-approach-to-jewish-history/.
17   Referring to Constantinople.

century, when Sardis was destroyed."[18] Living in our own less secure and historiographically less naive age, this picture seems far too rosy (even cosy), leaning too heavily on the "anti-lachrymose" tendencies of the previous generation of (mostly American) scholars and the communities that supported them.[19] We have, after all, just a small sampling of the furnishings, and most importantly, none of the communal newsletters—no "shul alerts," and no remains of the speeches and whispers that took place here over its 300 year history.[20] We do not know how Jews at Sardis responded to the accelerating Christian menace, as their response to the rising tide of imperial Christian pressure was not expressed explicitly in brick and mortar.[21] Barring evidence of an arson fire or rampant destruction—an ancient Kristallnacht—how could they be?[22]

It would be easy to suggest that over time the Jews of Sardis—like many moderns—saw their synagogue project in part as a kind of self-defence action. It was, after all, built in a most prominent place, reflecting what even imperial legislation of the 5th century was forced to admit, the well-established position of the synagogue in late Roman culture.[23] This would not be the last time in Jewish history when the construction of large and impressive buildings in the public square has masked defensive and insecure realities. I am thinking of the great synagogue in Rome, the Doheny Synagogue in Budapest and Congregation Emanuel in New York—to mention just three "cathedral synagogues" that survived the German onslaught against Jews and Judaism that burst forth starting in 1938. I am not convinced, though.[24]

---

18   John S. Crawford, "Jews, Christians and Polytheists in Late Antique Sardis," in *Jews, Christians and Polytheists in the Ancient Synagogue: Cultural Interaction During the Greco-Roman Period*, ed. Steven Fine (London: Routledge, 1999), 190–200 (190).

19   See Fine, *Art, History*, 200–9; David Engel, *Historians of the Jews and the Holocaust* (Stanford, CA: Stanford University Press, 2009).

20   On the value of synagogue bulletins in undoing a very different elite myth regarding Holocaust commemoration, see Hasia Diner, *We Remember with Reverence and Love: American Jews and the Myth of Silence after the Holocaust, 1945–1962* (New York: NYU Press, 2009).

21   The best statement of this perilous situation is still James Parkes, *The Conflict of the Church and Synagogue: A Study in the Origins of Anti-Semitism* (London: Soncino, 1934).

22   Leonard V. Rutgers, *Making Myths. Jews in Early Christian Identity Formation* (Leuven: Peeters, 2009).

23   Amnon Linder, *Jews in Roman Imperial Legislation* (Detroit: Wayne State University Press, 1988), 73–74 and *passim*.

24   See Jess Olson, "Reimagining the Synagogue in the Nineteenth and Twentieth Centuries," in *Jewish Religious Architecture*, ed. Steven Fine (Leiden: Brill, forthcoming); Saskia Coenen Snyder, *Building a Public Judaism: Synagogues and Jewish Identity in Nineteenth-Century Europe* (Cambridge: Harvard University Press, 2013).

A. Thomas Kraabel, the first to approach historical implications of the Jews of Sardis, compared the synagogue to the writings of the second century Church Father, Melito of Sardis.[25] Melito is particularly vehement in his disdain for Judaism, being the first to invoke the charge of deicide. To do this, Kraabel was forced to posit that Melito behaved as "the mouse that roars" against a powerful second century synagogue—which was so strong as to eventually build the monumental synagogue. Kraabel is certainly looking for an "ideological confrontation," but alas, his sources fall short.

Another "ideological confrontation" invoked by scholars—including myself—to somehow contextualize the extant evidence is John Chrysostom's *Discourses against Judaizing Christians*, a series of fourteen homilies delivered in not-so-distant Antioch in 386–387.[26] Chrysostom regaled his community with warnings against attending synagogues during the fall holidays and against believing that the synagogue is a "holy place." To cite just a bit of his fifth homily:

> In short, if you believe the place is holy because the Law and the books of prophets are there,... Look at it in another way. What sort of ark is it that the Jews now have, where we find no propitiatory, no tables of the law, no holy of holies, no veil, no high priest, no incense, no holocaust, no sacrifice, none of the other things that made the ark of old solemn and august? It seems to me that the ark the Jews now have is no better off than those toy arks which you can buy in the marketplace. In fact it is much worse. Those little toy arks cannot hurt anybody who comes close to them. But the ark which the Jews now have does great harm each day to those who come near it.[27]

Chrysostom indeed knew quite a bit about synagogues, and his community seemingly knew that much more. These include blowing the ram's horn on Rosh Hashanah, walking barefooted and fasting on Yom Kippur (known also

---

25   A. Thomas Kraabel, "Melito the Bishop and the Synagogue at Sardis: Text and Context," in *Studies Presented to George M.A. Hanfmann*, ed. David G. Mitten, John G. Pedley, and Jane A. Scott (Cambridge: Fogg Art Museum, 1971), 77–85, and the secondary literature cited there.

26   *Adversus Judaeos*, especially discourses 1 and 6. Translation by Paul W. Harkins, *Saint John Chrysostom: Discourses against Judaizing Christians* (Washington, D.C.: The Catholic University of America Press, 1979). See Robert L. Wilken, *John Chrysostom and the Jews: Rhetoric and Reality in the Late Fourth Century* (Berkeley: University of California Press, 1983); Fine, *This Holy Place*, 138–39.

27   *Adv. Jud.* 6.7, trans. Harkins, *Discourses against Judaizing Christians*, 80–83.

from rabbinic literature), lulavim for Sukkot, and incubation in hope of healing in synagogues. He also knew that Jews and non-Jews considered synagogues to be "holy places." The sanctity of the place being construed as deriving from the presence of Biblical scrolls and the application of Jerusalem Temple metaphors. Chrysostom suggests that the reading of Psalms was important to synagogue liturgy.[28]

The focus on the Torah shrines, the reading table and likely the reading platform in the Sardis synagogue suggests a building carefully "branded" in Jewish terms that Chrysostom and his community would well recognize. It reflects a surprisingly international vocabulary. Most significant is a small marble relief from the entablature of the southern wall showing an open Torah ark. While images of Torah shrines are common across the Mediterranean, the open door motif appears elsewhere only in Rome, and an actual shrine that rivals in size those of Sardis was uncovered at Ostia.[29] Books and bookcases as symbols of pagan, then Christian, paideia are well-known in late antique art, but most particularly from Jewish contexts.[30] Similarly, images of the menorah with curls under the branches, reflect a type known widely in Asia Minor—but nowhere else. It was a distinct local variant.[31] Did this imagery develop in "response" to Christian visual culture? Likely in part, but this totalizing assertion, which I have called the "Christianity-first" approach found in so much of recent scholarship, is only a part of the answer—which includes a larger visual culture that framed both Judaism and Christianity, internal Jewish development, local development and in Palestine, Samaritan fellow-travellers.[32]

---

28 Wilken, *John Chrysostom and the Jews*; Steven Fine, "The Complexities of Rejection and Attraction," in *Partings: How Judaism and Christianity Became Two*, ed. Hershel Shanks (Washington D.C.: Biblical Archaeological Society, 2013), 237–54 (249–51).

29 Steven Fine and Miriam Della Pergola, "The Synagogue of Ostia Antica and its Torah Shrine," in *The Jews of Ancient Rome* (Jerusalem: Bible Lands Museum, 1994), 42–57; Fine, "The Open Torah Ark."

30 Roberto Meneghini and Rossella Rea, eds., *La biblioteca infinita: I luoghi del sapere nel mondo antico* (Rome: Electa, 2014).

31 Steven Fine and Leonard V. Rutgers, "New Light on Judaism in Asia Minor During Late Antiquity. Two Recently Identified Inscribed Menorahs," *JSK* 3 (1996). 1–23.

32 See Steven Fine, "'He Entered and Removed a Golden Menorah': On the Treason of Yosef Meshita (*Genesis Rabba* 65, 26)," in *Text, Tradition and the History of Second Temple and Rabbinic Judaism: Studies in Honor of Professor Lawrence H. Schiffman*, ed. Stuart S. Miller et al. (Leiden: Brill, forthcoming), n. 57; Alon Goshen-Gottstein, "Jewish-Christian Relations and Rabbinic Literature—Shifting Scholarly and Relational Paradigms: The Case of Two Powers," in *Interaction between Judaism and Christianity in History, Religion, Art and Literature*, ed. Marcel Poorthuis, Joshua Schwartz, and Joseph Turner (Leiden: Brill, 2009), 15–43 (17–20). I plan to return to this issue more expansively in the near future.

Was Chrysostom responding to a magnificent synagogue in Antioch on a par with the Sardis synagogue,[33] or one like the nearby edifice in Apamea, or the many synagogue buildings that survive or do not?[34] The stress and "urgency" in his "golden voice" suggest that synagogues were imagined to be a spiritual threat. Is the fact that so little relating to the Jewish presence in Antioch has been discovered archaeologically related to a Christian response to this threat (an argument from lack of evidence, of course, is not evidence). Was this the case at Sardis? Were the "god-fearers" of Sardis Christians who somehow had gone over to the Jewish "dark side"? What was the inter-communal conversation like at Sardis? So far, churches that pale in comparison with the synagogue have been discovered in this city.[35] Does this reflect the power differential between Judaism and Christianity? Were Jews so powerful as to be untouchable? Without evidence of what really went on in late antique Sardis between Jews and Christians, who knows? Key to me is the fact that "paganism" continued strongly until the destruction of the city. My sense is that Judaism did the same, in a city where the traditional elite maintained itself longer than we are accustomed to imagining.

Close to Sardis, we have considerable evidence of Christians attacking synagogues during late antiquity, disputing their sanctity with their hands. Recently I collected a large number of examples of Christian reuse of Jewish artefacts as spolia, beginning with a large ashlar from a Jewish building reused in a baptistry in Nicaea, first reused in the city wall, then on the interior of a baptismal pool.[36] A menorah screen was removed from a synagogue screen, turned upside down and reused as paving in the Priene cathedral,[37] a capitol with menorahs and a synagogue inscription were disposed of on a trash heap at Corinth,[38] two well-carved synagogue screens with menorahs were used

33   Bernadette J. Brooton, "The Jews of Ancient Antioch," in *Antioch: The Lost Ancient City*, ed. Christine Kondoleon (Princeton, NJ: Princeton University Press, 2000), 29–37; David Noy and Hanswulf Bloedhorn, *Inscriptiones Judaicae Orientis: III: Syria and Cyprus* (Tübingen: Mohr Siebeck, 2004), 116–19.

34   On the Apamea synagogue see Eleazar L. Sukenik, "The Mosaic Inscriptions in the Synagogue at Apamea on the Orontes," *HUCA* 23 (1950–1951): 541–51; Noy and Bloedhorn, *Inscriptiones Judaicae Orientis: III: Syria and Cyprus*, 84–115.

35   Hans Buchwald, with a contribution by Anne McClanan, *Churches EA and E at Sardis* (Cambridge: Harvard University Press, 2015).

36   Fine and Rutgers, "New Light"; Fine, *Art, History*, 211–13; Ameling, *Inscriptiones Judaicae Orientis: II: Kleinasien*, no. 153.

37   Fine, *Art, History*, 209.

38   Robert Lorentz Scranton, *Medieval Architecture in the Central Area of Corinth* (Princeton: The American School of Classical Studies at Athens, 1957), 116; Fine, "The Complexities of Rejection and Attraction," 245.

to raise the floor of a flooded building at Limyra,[39] and menorahs were partially erased from Jewish spaces in Aphrodisias and Trailles.[40] A large column drum from Laodicea is particularly significant.[41] It shows a menorah, flanked by a lulav bunch and shofar. Haphazardly carved atop of this standard Jewish icon, a large cross was chiselled, banishing the Jewish demon, using the violent method known from Christian iconoclasm across the empire.[42] At Sardis itself, the magnificent Temple of Artemis was indeed literally blanketed by such crosses.[43] Not a single such cross, however, appears in the synagogue. In fact, the Sardis synagogue shows no evidence of this sort of desecration. A mosaic in the apse was subjected to iconoclastic activity, but this likely had nothing to do with Christians.

3   Concluding Remarks

In short, the Sardis synagogue reflects the limits of historical reconstruction. We have no positive evidence for "ideological confrontation" with Christians within this structure. This situation is significant in light of the widespread literary and archaeological evidence for Christian pressure on Jewish life close by in Asia Minor. My sense is that the very size of the synagogue, and the well-connectedness of the Sardis Jewish community, may have protected the synagogue. Does this mean that Jews did not sense the kinds of "ideological confrontation" over the long history of this structure? Does this mean that life in Sardis was one long and happy ecumenical and multi-generational love-fest? Absolutely not. Rather, it is my sense that we simply do not have enough evidence for the life of this community to judge. What is clear, however, is that whatever problems did come along down the road, the Jewish community at Sardis—with its "cathedral synagogue"—withstood them, and that the decline

---

39   Steven Fine, "The Menorahs of Limyra in Jewish Art and Visual Culture," *JAJ* 5 (2014): 217–22.

40   Joyce M. Reynolds and Robert F. Tannenbaum, *Jews and God-Fearers at Aphrodisias: Greek Inscriptions with Commentary: Texts from the Excavations at Aphrodisias Conducted by Kenan T. Erim* (Cambridge: Cambridge Philological Society, 1987). Angelos Chanitotis, "The Conversion of the Temple of Aphrodite at Aphrodisias in Context," in *From Temple to Church: Destruction and Renewal of Local Cultic Topography in Late Antiquity*, ed. Johannes Hahn, Stephen Emmel, and Ulrich Gotter (Leiden: Brill, 2008), 243–73; Fine, *Art, History*, 213.

41   Fine, *Art, History*, 213; Celal Şimşek, "A Menorah with a Cross Carved on a Column of Nymphaeum A at Laodicea Ad Lycum," *JRA* 91 (2006): 343–46.

42   Eberhard Sauer, *The Archaeology of Religious Hatred in the Roman and Early Medieval World* (London: Tempus, 2003).

43   Fine, *Art, History*, 198–99.

of this distinctly Jewish "holy place" was part and parcel of the destruction of Sardis by the invading Sasanians in 616.

Acknowledgments

This essay is preparatory to my forthcoming article, "The Sardis Synagogue and the History of Judaism in the Aegean Basin," which will appear in the final report of the Sardis synagogue excavations. Many thanks to Leah Bierman Fine; to Andrew Seager and Bahadir Yildirim of the Archaeological Exploration of Sardis for their insights and helpfulness; and to Mark Wilson for his assistance on site. This contribution is dedicated in memory of Paul Laderman (1934–2015).

References

Ameling, Walter. *Inscriptiones Judaicae Orientis: II: Kleinasien*. Tübingen: Mohr Siebeck, 2004.

Baron, Salo W. "Ghetto and Emancipation." *The Menorah Journal* 14 (1928): 515–26.

Brooton, Bernadette J. "The Jews of Ancient Antioch." Pages 29–37 in *Antioch: The Lost Ancient City*. Edited by Christine Kondoleon. Princeton: Princeton University Press, 2000.

Buchwald, Hans, with a contribution by Anne McClanan. *Churches EA and E at Sardis*. Cambridge: Harvard University Press, 2015.

Chanitotis, Angelos. "The Conversion of the Temple of Aphrodite at Aphrodisias in Context." Pages 243–73 in *From Temple to Church: Destruction and Renewal of Local Cultic Topography in Late Antiquity*. Edited by Johannes Hahn, Stephen Emmel, and Ulrich Gotter. Leiden: Brill, 2008.

Coenen Snyder, Saskia. *Building a Public Judaism: Synagogues and Jewish Identity in Nineteenth-Century Europe*. Cambridge: Harvard University Press, 2013.

Crawford, John S. "Jews, Christians and Polytheists in Late Antique Sardis." Pages 190–200 in *Jews, Christians and Polytheists in the Ancient Synagogue: Cultural Interaction During the Greco-Roman Period*. Edited by Steven Fine. London: Routledge, 1999.

Cross, Frank M. "The Hebrew Inscriptions from Sardis." *HTR* 95 (2002): 3–19.

Diner, Hasia. *We Remember with Reverence and Love: American Jews and the Myth of Silence after the Holocaust, 1945–1962*. New York: NYU Press, 2009.

Engel, David. *Historians of the Jews and the Holocaust*. Stanford, CA: Stanford University Press, 2009.

Feldman, Louis H. "Proselytes and 'Sympathizers' in the Light of the New Inscriptions from Aphrodisias." *RÉJ* 148 (1989): 265–305.

Fine, Steven. *Art, History and the Historiography of Judaism in the Greco-Roman World.* Leiden: Brill, 2013.

Fine, Steven. "The Open Torah Ark: An Iconographic Type in Late Antique Rome and Sardis." Pages 121–34 in *Viewing Ancient Jewish Art and Archaeology: VeHinnei Rachel—Essays in Honor of Rachel Hachlili.* Edited by Ann Killebrew and Gabriel Faßbeck. Leiden: Brill, 2015.

Fine, Steven. *This Holy Place: On the Sanctity of the Synagogue During the Greco-Roman Period.* Notre Dame: University of Notre Dame Press, 1997.

Fine, Steven. "The Complexities of Rejection and Attraction, Herein of Love and Hate." Pages 237–54 in *Partings: How Judaism and Christianity Became Two.* Edited by Hershel Shanks. Washington D.C.: Biblical Archaeological Society, 2013.

Fine, Steven. "The Menorahs of Limyra in Jewish Art and Visual Culture." *JAJ* 5 (2014): 217–22.

Fine, Steven. "'He Entered and Removed a Golden Menorah': On the Treason of Yosef Meshita (*Genesis Rabba* 65, 26)." Forthcoming in *Text, Tradition and the History of Second Temple and Rabbinic Judaism: Studies in Honor of Professor Lawrence H. Schiffman.* Edited by Stuart S. Miller, Steven Fine, Naomi Grunhaus, Alex Jassen, and Michael Swartz. Leiden: Brill.

Fine, Steven, ed. *Sacred Realm: The Emergence of the Synagogue in the Ancient World.* New York: Oxford University Press and Yeshiva University Museum, 1996.

Fine, Steven, and Miriam Della Pergola. "The Synagogue of Ostia Antica and its Torah Shrine." Pages 42–57 in *The Jews of Ancient Rome.* Jerusalem: Bible Lands Museum, 1994.

Fine, Steven, and Leonard V. Rutgers. "New Light on Judaism in Asia Minor During Late Antiquity: Two Recently Identified Inscribed Menorahs." *JSR* 3 (1996): 1–23.

Goshen-Gottstein, Alon. "Jewish-Christian Relations and Rabbinic Literature— Shifting Scholarly and Relational Paradigms: The Case of Two Powers." Pages 15–43 in *Interaction between Judaism and Christianity in History, Religion, Art and Literature.* Edited by Marcel Poorthuis, Joshua Schwartz, and Joseph Turner. Leiden: Brill, 2009.

Harkins, Paul W. *Saint John Chrysostom: Discourses against Judaizing Christians.* Washington, D.C.: The Catholic University of America Press, 1979.

Kraabel, A. Thomas. "Melito the Bishop and the Synagogue at Sardis: Text and Context." Pages 77–85 in *Studies Presented to George M.A. Hanfmann.* Edited by David G. Mitten, John G. Pedley, and Jane A. Scott. Cambridge: Fogg Art Museum, 1971.

Kraabel, A. Thomas. "The Diaspora Synagogue: Archaeological and Epigraphic Evidence since Sukenik." Pages 95–126 in *Ancient Synagogues: Historical Analysis and Archaeological Discovery*. Edited by Dan Urman and Paul V.M. Flesher. Leiden: Brill, 1995.

Kroll, John H. "The Greek Inscriptions of the Sardis Synagogue." *HTR* 94 (2001): 5–55.

Linder, Amnon. *Jews in Roman Imperial Legislation*. Detroit: Wayne State University Press, 1988.

Magness, Jodi. "The Date of the Sardis Synagogue in Light of the Numismatic Evidence." *American Journal of Archaeology* 109 (2005): 443–75.

Meneghini, Roberto, and Rossella Rea, eds. *La biblioteca infinita: I luoghi del sapere nel mondo antico*. Rome: Electa, 2014.

Noy, David, and Hanswulf Bloedhorn. *Inscriptiones Judaicae Orientis: III: Syria and Cyprus*. Tübingen: Mohr Siebeck, 2004.

Olin, Margaret. *The Nation Without Art: Examining Modern Discourses on Jewish Art*. Lincoln: University of Nebraska Press, 2002.

Olson, Jess. "Reimagining the Synagogue in the Nineteenth and Twentieth Centuries." Forthcoming in *Jewish Religious Architecture*. Edited by Steven Fine. Leiden: Brill.

Parkes, James. *The Conflict of the Church and Synagogue: A Study in the Origins of Anti-Semitism*. London: Soncino, 1934.

Reynolds, Joyce M., and Robert F. Tannenbaum. *Jews and God-Fearers at Aphrodisias: Greek Inscriptions with Commentary: Texts from the Excavations at Aphrodisias Conducted by Kenan T. Erim*. Cambridge: Cambridge Philological Society, 1987.

Rutgers, Leonard V. *Making Myths: Jews in Early Christian Identity Formation*. Leuven: Peeters, 2009.

Sauer, Eberhard. *The Archaeology of Religious Hatred in the Roman and Early Medieval World*. London: Tempus, 2003.

Schwartz, Yitzchak. "An Anti-Anti Lachrymose Approach to Jewish History?", https://jhiblog.org/2017/02/22/an-anti-anti-lachrymose-approach-to-jewish-history/.

Scranton, Robert Lorentz. *Medieval Architecture in the Central Area of Corinth*. Princeton: The American School of Classical Studies at Athens, 1957.

Seager, Andrew, and A. Thomas Kraabel. "The Synagogue and the Jewish Community." Pages 168–90 in *Sardis from Prehistoric to Roman Times: Results of the Archaeological Exploration of Sardis, 1958–1975*. Edited by George A. Hanfmann, William E. Mierse, and Clive Foss. Cambridge: Harvard University Press, 1983.

Şimşek, Celal. "A Menorah with a Cross Carved on a Column of Nymphaeum A at Laodicea Ad Lycum." *JRA* 91 (2006): 343–46.

Sukenik, Eleazar. "The Mosaic Inscriptions in the Synagogue at Apamea on the Orontes." *HUCA* 23 (1950–1951): 541–51.

Wilken, Robert L. *John Chrysostom and the Jews: Rhetoric and Reality in the Late Fourth Century*. Berkeley: University of California Press, 1983.

CHAPTER 6

Psalm 47 as a Song of Zion: Nationalistic and Universalistic Tendencies

David Frankel

One of the most central and controversial texts in the modern study of the Psalms is Ps 47.[1] This psalm plays a major role in Sigmund Mowinckel's famous and controversial hypothesis concerning the existence of an ancient Israelite New Year festival of divine enthronement. Both supporters and critics of Mowinckel's theory cannot avoid attending to this psalm, for it contains the key proclamation of verse 5—"God has ascended amid shouts of joy, the Lord amid the sounding of trumpets"—which, to a great extent, rests at the centre of the controversy.[2] The disagreement surrounding Ps 47 does not begin or end, however, with the question of whether or not the psalm reflects an enthronement festival. Rather, it goes back to the oft-contentious ways in which the psalm was appropriated and interpreted in the early religious traditions of Judaism and Christianity. In the modern period as well, differences in Jewish and Christian sensibilities have, at least covertly, animated conflict with regard to the psalm. While modern Christian interpreters have largely tended to interpret the psalm as an expression of "religious universalism," Yehezkel Kaufmann, unquestionably one of the most important Jewish biblical scholars of modern times, has advocated, in line with much of Jewish tradition and in pointed contrast with the Christian one, a strongly nationalist reading of the psalm. The present study seeks to break the impasse between these two readings by suggesting that the antithesis that many interpreters posit between "nationalism" and "universalism" reflects a modern way of thinking that is alien to the conceptual world of the text. The psalm, it will be argued, centres

---

1 In Hebrew texts Ps 47:1–9 is numbered 47:2–10. As the text citations will be in English, the verse numbering will follow the English format.

2 For reviews and evaluations of Mowinckel's theory see David J.A. Clines, "The Evidence for an Autumnal New Year in Pre-exilic Israel Reconsidered," *JBL* 93 (1974): 22–40; John Day, *Psalms* (Sheffield: JSOT Press, 1990), 68–87; J.J.M. Roberts, "Mowinckel's Enthronement Festival: A Review," in *The Book of Psalms: Composition and Reception*, ed. Peter W. Flint and Patrick D. Miller (Leiden: Brill, 2005), 97–115; Alexander Rofé, *Introduction to the Literature of the Hebrew Bible*, transl. Harvey N. Bock and Judith H. Seeligmann, Jerusalem Biblical Studies 9 (Jerusalem: Simor, 2009), 471–77.

© DAVID FRANKEL, 2021 | DOI:10.1163/9789004437210_008

on Zion and must therefore be understood within the context of the Zion tradition. An analysis of the psalm within the context of this tradition shows that it combines a strong sense of political nationalism together with a robust and inclusive universalistic impulse.

1   Psalm 47 in Early Jewish and Christian Interpretation

Before proceeding with a critical analysis of the psalm, it will be instructive to note some of the early meanings that were attached to it. In the Jewish tradition, the prominence of Ps 47 is reflected in the role it plays in the liturgy of the New Year, Rosh Hashanah. The psalm is recited just before the blowing of the shofar, and many of its passages are cited in the musaf service (the "additional" service that follows the morning service on Sabbaths and holidays), particularly within the context of the *malkhuyot* section, the section that highlights the universal kingship of YHWH.[3] This datum, as is well known, played a key role in bolstering Mowinckel's thesis that the psalm belonged to an enthronement ceremony from the very outset. The psalm has also been the subject of various "historical" interpretations. In Pirqe Rabbi Eliezer we read:

> On the first day of the month of Elul God said to Moses, "Come up to me on the mountain" (Exod 24:12). They sounded the blast of the shofar throughout the camp indicating that Moses went up the mountain, so that they would not veer off into idolatry again, and God was elevated by that shofar blast, as it says, "God went up with a teruah, the Lord with the blast of the shofar."[4]

The midrash here subtly interprets Ps 47:5 as referring to two ascensions, corresponding to the two-fold structure of the verse, and the fact that "Elohim" is employed in the first stich while YHWH is mentioned in the second stich. The first ascension is indicated by the opening words, "Elohim went up with a teruah." The word "Elohim" is taken as a reference to Moses, who went up Mount Sinai to seek the forgiveness of the people after their apostasy with the golden calf. The Israelites blew the shofar at that time so as to prevent a repetition of the making of the calf. The second, parallel ascension is indicated

---

3   See Philip Birnbaum, *High Holiday Prayer Book* (New York: Hebrew Publishing Company, 1951), 335–37.

4   The translation is mine. For the Hebrew text see Gerald Friedlander, *Pirke De Rabbi Eliezer* (New York: Sepher-Hermon Press, 1981), 360.

by the second half of the verse, "YHWH with the sound of the shofar." This is understood as indicating that God was elevated in heaven as a result of Moses's ascension up the mountain and Israel's blowing of the shofar.[5]

In patristic exegesis, this same verse is seen as a reference to Jesus's ascension to heaven. Augustine's commentary on Psalms reads:

> When it says, *Went up*, where was he going? We know very well. He went to a place where the Jews did not follow him, even with their eyes, for they had mocked him when he was raised up on the cross, but could not see him as he was lifted up to heaven.[6]

Jesus's ascension to heaven, unseen by "the Jews," was joyously witnessed by his disciples. It is in accordance with this understanding of the words "Elohim rose up" that the entire psalm is read, in Christian tradition, on the fortieth day after Easter, on Ascension Day, when the resurrected Christ was said to have been taken up to heaven (Acts 1:1–11).

Of course, these readings of the psalm in terms of past events in sacred history in no way interfered with the desire to find in it references to the eschatological future as well. Thus, we find in Midrash Tehilim:

> "May He subdue peoples under us, and nations under our feet" (Ps 47:4)— When will this happen? At the time that "He will choose our inheritance for us, the excellence of Jacob whom He loves" (Ps 47:5). And when will he choose and give us our inheritance? When he "sits on his throne" [cf. Ps 47:9, "God sat on his holy throne"] ... And when will he sit [on his throne]? "Then saviors shall come up to Mount Zion, to judge Mount Esau, and the kingdom shall be the Lord's" (Obad 1:21).[7]

In this reading, the words of the psalm express a prophetic vision of the future. When, then, will God subdue the nations under our feet, give us back our land

---

5   The interpretation of "Elohim" as referring to Moses's ascension to God may reflect a Jewish appropriation of the Christian motif of the ascension of Jesus. Cf. also Oded Yisraeli, "'Moses Didn't Die': A Rabbinic Tradition in the Zohar," in *Moses the Man—Master of the Prophets*, ed. Moshe Hallamish, Hannah Kasher, and Hanokh Ben-Pazi (Ramat-Gan: Bar-Ilan University Press, 2010), 381–406 (Hebrew).

6   Maria Boulding, *Expositions of the Psalms: Volume 2*, vol. 3/16 of *The Works of Saint Augustine: A Translation for the 21st Century*, ed. John E. Rotele (Hyde Park, NY: New City Press, 2000), 329.

7   The translation is mine. For the Hebrew text see Solomon Buber, *Midrash Tehillim* (also) *Called Shoher Tov* (Vilna: Rom, 1891; repr., New York: Om, 1947), 273.

and sit on his throne? When he punishes "Mount Esau," that is, the Christian Roman Empire.[8]

As is to be expected, Augustine's understanding of the eschaton reflected in the psalm is radically different. Following the Septuagint and Vulgate, the words עם אלוהי אברהם of verse 9 are taken to mean "*unto* the God of Abraham" rather than "the people of the God of Abraham." The "God of Abraham" refers to the God of the Jews who, "took pride in their father's name and wore his flesh, but did not hold fast to his faith." In contrast, the "princes of the peoples," that is, "not the princes of one people, but the princes of all people" will be gathered together "unto the God of Abraham."[9] Augustine points to the centurion of Matt 8:5–13 and Luke 7:1–10 as an example of one of these "princes of the peoples" that was "gathered together unto the God of Abraham," insofar as he displayed a measure of Abrahamic faith greater than could be found in all of Israel. Augustine interweaves the words of Jesus in the story of the centurion with the words of the psalm:

> *In truth I tell you*, he said, *many will come from the east and the west*, people who are no kin of Israel. Those crowds will come, to whom the psalm says, *All nations, clap your hands*. And they *will sit down with Abraham in the kingdom of heaven*. By what right? Not by being born from his flesh, but by following his example of faith. *But the children of the kingdom—* the Jews, that is—*will be thrown into the outer darkness, where there will be weeping and gnashing of teeth* (Mt 8:12). Those who were born of Abraham's flesh will be condemned to the darkness outside, while those who have imitated Abraham's faith will dine with him in the kingdom of heaven.[10]

Thus, Ps 47 looks forward to a time when "all the nations," to the exclusion of the Jews, will be gathered to the God of Abraham. In sum, while many Jews understood the psalm as stating that God would punish the Christians and vindicate the Jews,[11] many Christians found in it a confirmation of the universal triumph of Christianity and the casting out of the Jews.

---

8   On Esau as symbol of the Roman Empire see Gerson D. Cohen, "Esau as Symbol in Early Medieval Thought," in *Studies in the Variety of Rabbinic Cultures* (Philadelphia: The Jewish Publication Society, 1991), 243–70.

9   See Boulding, *Expositions of the Psalms*, 332–33.

10   Boulding, *Expositions of the Psalms*, 332–34.

11   The commentary of Rashi is particularly interesting insofar as it offers a stark anti-Christian interpretation, in the wake of the Rhineland massacres of 1096. Rashi identifies the "nobles of the peoples" of the psalm with "those that offered themselves for slaughter

2 The Tension between Nationalism and Universalism in the Psalm

Let us now move on to the modern study of the psalm. A major issue that has occupied scholarly attention is the question of the relationship between nationalism and universalism within the psalm. The psalm is seemingly animated by contrary tendencies. On the one hand, we find strong nationalist sentiments in verse 3: "He subdued nations under us, peoples under our feet." In verse 4, the subjugation of nations is interpreted as a reflection of God's preferential love: "He chose our inheritance for us, the pride of Jacob, whom he loved." On the other hand, a universalist chord seems to be struck at the very beginning of the psalm (verses 1–2): "Clap your hands, all you nations; shout to God with cries of joy. For the Lord *Elyon* is awesome, the great King over all the earth." A similar mood pervades verses 8–9: "God reigns over nations; God is seated on his holy throne. Princes of peoples assemble, the people of the God of Abraham, for the shields of the earth belong to God; he is greatly exalted." Of particular significance is the reference to the "princes of peoples" as the "people of the God of Abraham." Since Abraham is presented in Genesis and other biblical sources as the father of the Israelites, the unique reference to the nations as constituting the people of the God of Abraham strikes many as expressing a conception according to which all the nations of the world stand together under a single, unifying religious rubric. How have commentators dealt with these seemingly contrary tendencies?

One rather typical treatment of this issue from within the Protestant tradition can be found in the highly influential Psalms commentary of the German theologian Artur Weiser.[12] Weiser extols the universalism of Ps 47, placing it on a higher level than that of the prophets, and setting it on par with the New Testament teachings:

> What the prophets proclaim in their prophecies of salvation, namely that the Gentiles will one day join the people of God (Isa. 49.14 ff.; 56.6 ff.; 60.3 ff.; Zech. 8.22 f.), is here even surpassed; the nations become themselves the "people of the God of Abraham." The Psalm is in harmony with

---

and killing in the sanctification of the name." These martyrs will be restored to Jerusalem in the end of days. God's wrath will be spent on the nations and this will allow Israel to survive. For a discussion of this text within the context of Rashi's anti-Christian polemics see Avraham Grossman, *Rashi*, transl. Joel A. Linsider (Oxford: Littman Library of Jewish Civilization, 2012), 201–2.

12   It is not very well known that Weiser was a Christian supporter of the Nazi party. See Horst Junginger, *The Scientification of the "Jewish Question" in Nazi Germany*, Numen Book Series 157 (Leiden: Brill, 2017), 132.

the eschatological teaching of the NT in so far as both hold the view that there will be one flock and one Shepherd ... It regards all distinctions to be annulled in the sight of God and ungrudgingly classes the converted Gentiles with the people of the God of Abraham.[13]

The psalm, in this reading, represents an eschatological reality in which all national and social distinctions are annulled and humanity as a totality stands united under the kingship of the God of Abraham. In contrast with Augustine, who excludes the Jews from the eschaton, Weiser implicitly includes them, but only, it must be noted, as individuals. Their national-religious singularity is destined to be dissolved within a single, undifferentiated "flock" of believers. It is in this sense that the psalm is seen as surpassing the theology of the biblical prophets so as to arrive at the greater heights of New Testament theology. How, then, does Weiser make sense of the psalm's strongly nationalist sentiments, particularly as expressed in verses 3 and 4? Weiser takes verses 3 and 4 as referring to the conquest of Canaan of the *Heilsgeschichte*. This nationalist beginning sets the stage for the "forward look to the consummation of the *Heilsgeschichte* in Yahweh's enthronement as King of the whole world" when "all distinctions will be annulled." In other words, Israel's special status in the divine economy belongs to the past but not to the future. Weiser also takes pains to emphasize that the psalm's belief in God's dominion over the world is to be found "exclusively in the religious sphere" and is not "prompted by the pursuance of power politics."[14]

The tension between nationalism and universalism in the psalm has also been noted more recently by the prominent French-American Protestant theologian and Bible scholar Samuel L. Terrien. Terrien points in particular to the conflict between verses 3–4 and the religious universalism expressed in the MT of verse 10 ("as the people of the God of Abraham"). With regard to the latter Terrien asserts: "Against the synagogal trends of Talmudic Judaism, the MT clearly maintains that the chiefs of the goyim will become the goy of Abrahamic expectancy (Gen 12:3)."[15] In other words, according to Terrien, the MT of Ps 47 (the text of which he clearly regards as original) understands the promise of Genesis 12:3 that Abraham will become "a great nation" as referring to "the chiefs of the goyim." Whether or not this includes the Israelites/Jews is

---

13   Artur Weiser, *The Psalms*, transl. Herbert Harwell, Old Testament Library (Philadelphia: Westminster Press, 1962), 378.

14   Weiser, *Psalms*, 377.

15   Samuel Terrien, *The Psalms: Strophic Structure and Theological Commentary*, Eerdmans Critical Commentary (Grand Rapids: Eerdmans, 2003), 378.

not entirely clear—Terrien does not state that the chiefs of the goyim will *join* the people of Abraham, but become it. In any event, the straightforward, nationalist understanding of the promise to Abraham is attributed to "Talmudic Judaism," which, by implication, misses the mark. Terrien, as we have noted, admits that verses 3 and 4 appear to contradict this "universalist" expectation and inconclusively wonders if it "persists only as a nationalistic foil to the universalistic ideal that explodes in the second strophe (verses 9–10)?"[16]

It is against the backdrop of the strongly anti-nationalist tendencies reflected in so much of the scholarly literature on Ps 47—the above is only a small sampling of this—that we must situate the reading offered by Yehezkel Kaufmann, who was, among other things, a strong proponent of Jewish nationalism:[17]

> In Psalm 47 we find the prayer: "May He subdue nations under us and nations under our feet. May He choose our inheritance for us" ... (4–5). As in other psalms, the nations are called upon to cheer for Israel's victories (1). The nations will be subdued under Israel, but it is not stated that they have a share together with Israel in God's grace. The "princes of peoples" of verse 10 are not the officers of the nations, but of the Israelite tribes, they are the "people of the God of Abraham." ... It is almost impossible to understand how, in spite of verses 4–5, it was possible to find prophetic universalism, the idea of a world religion that "shatters the boundaries of race and nation."[18]

For Kaufmann, Ps 47 is strongly nationalistic. The initial verses do not recall the subjugation of the Canaanites in the historical past. Rather, as in the reading of Midrash Tehilim cited above, they express a wish or prayer for Israel's future. As such, the nationalism these verses express can hardly be understood as passing or penultimate. Kaufmann further argues that verse 1 amounts to little more than a call to the nations to praise YHWH for Israel's national victories. Thus, the verse which is so often construed as an expression of universalism is actually thoroughly Israel-centred. While God is clearly thought of as king of the world (verses 2, 7–9), his special grace remains eternally focused on and constricted to Israel. Thus, the "princes of peoples" who make up the "people of the God of Abraham" are the Israelite tribal leaders alone (or,

---

16   Terrien, *Psalms*, 378.

17   See Avinoam Barshai, "The Nationalist Outlook of Yehezkel Kaufmann," in *Yehezkel Kaufmann: Selected Writings on Jewish Nationality and Zionism* (Jerusalem: Bialik, 1995), 13–59 (Hebrew).

18   Yehezkel Kaufmann, *History of Israelite Religion from Its Beginnings until the End of the Second Temple Period*, 4 vols. (Tel Aviv: Bialik, 1937–1956), 2:718–19 and n. 109 (Hebrew).

alternatively, the Israelite chieftains who have been appointed as rulers over the conquered nations).[19]

Kaufmann presents his interpretation of Ps 47 within the broad context of a discussion of the universalism reflected in the Psalter as a whole. One of his major concerns in this context is to distinguish the eschatology and universalism of the book of Psalms from those of the literary prophets.[20] Whereas the literary prophets propounded an historical vision of a future era in which the nations would acknowledge the God of Israel as the only true God and thereby acquire a share in the divine grace initially designated for Israel, the Psalter did not. Though the Psalter does reflect a belief in a universal deity whose dominion encompasses the entire universe, this universal dominion is strictly of an abstract, theoretical nature. Human history is not expected to change in any fundamental way. Though many psalms present the nations as acknowledging YHWH's kingship, this belongs to the realm of poetic imagery, much like the acknowledgment of YHWH that the Psalter often attributes to the forces of nature. The acknowledgment of the nations is presented neither as a present, concrete reality nor a real, future expectation. It merely gives expression to the idea of God's universal kingship.

Most telling for Kaufmann is the fact that there is no intimation in the psalms of the theme that appears rather prominently in prophetic literature—the eschatological end of idolatry among the nations (e.g., Isa 2:18–20; 17:7–8; 30:19–22; 31:6–7; Zeph 2:11; Jer 10:11, 14–15; 16:19–20). In the psalms in general and in Ps 47 in particular, the nations are poetically imagined acknowledging the supremacy of YHWH, but they are at the same time thought of as remaining pagan idolaters in actual reality. Consequently, they are granted no share in Israel's divine grace.

How are we to evaluate these contrary readings of the psalm? Is Ps 47, with Kaufmann, a thoroughly nationalistic psalm, with no significance for the nations in terms of divine grace or, to the contrary, a thoroughly universalistic psalm in which "[t]he nations and their rulers belong to God in the same special sense as does Israel!"?[21] In the following, an attempt will be made to critique both of these extreme positions and to suggest a third, moderating understanding.

---

19 See also Ben C. Ollenburger, *Zion, the City of the Great King: A Theological Symbol of the Jerusalem Cult*, JSOTSup 41 (Sheffield: JSOT Press, 1987), 182–83.

20 Kaufmann, *History of Israelite Religion*, 2:512–18, 711–25.

21 Geoffrey W. Grogan, *Psalms*, The Two Horizons Old Testament Commentary (Grand Rapids: Eerdmans, 2008), 102.

3   Post-Exilic Monotheism or Early Cultic Pluralism?

Let us begin with the question of "monotheism" in relation to the psalm. Most scholars who interpret Ps 47 as an expression of a robust universalism associate it with the monotheistic and universalistic rhetoric that comes to the fore in exilic and post-exilic texts, most conspicuously in the second half of the book of Isaiah.[22] Typical of this material are passages such as Isa 45:22–23: "Turn to me and be saved, all you ends of the earth; for I am God, and there is no other. By myself I have sworn, my mouth has uttered in all integrity a word that will not be revoked: Before me every knee will bow; by me every tongue will swear." Israel's God, as the one and only true God, is determined to be acknowledged and worshipped by all of humanity. The salvation of all the ends of the earth is concomitant upon this. But is Ps 47 "monotheistic" and concomitantly "universalistic" in the same sense? Verse 6, זמרו אלהים זמרו, זמרו למלכנו זמרו, would seem to indicate otherwise. Though the verse is usually rendered, "Sing praises to God, sing praises; sing praises to our King, sing praises," this understanding is somewhat difficult since there is no indication, following this reading, as to who is being addressed. Since there is no explicit "to" before the word אלוהים, it is preferable to follow J.J.M. Roberts in rendering the verse, "Sing praises ye gods, sing praises; sing praises to our King, sing praises."[23] The call to the gods in verse 6 would then parallel the call to the nations in verse 1. This reading of verse 6 is reminiscent of passages such as Ps 29:2: "Ascribe to the Lord, you heavenly beings, ascribe to the Lord glory and strength." Passages from the psalms such as this are generally seen as reflecting a relatively early period in Israelite history, when the gods of foreign nations were seen as both real and legitimate objects of worship, at least for those nations.[24] The fact that passages like these were carefully reworked to fit a more monotheistic outlook in post-exilic times (cf. Ps 96:7: "Ascribe to the LORD, you family of nations, ascribe to the Lord glory and strength" with Ps 29:1[25]) further underscores the theological gap separating Ps 47:6 from Isaiah 40–66 and similar late, prophetic texts.

---

22   See, e.g., Claus Westermann, *The Praise of God in the Psalms*, transl. Keith R. Crim (Richmond, VA: John Knox, 1965), 142–51.

23   J.J.M. Roberts, "The Religio-Political Setting of Psalm 47," *BASOR* 221 (1976): 129–32. Contra Erhard S. Gerstenberger, *Psalms: Part 1: With an Introduction to Cultic Poetry*, FOTL 14 (Grand Rapids: Eerdmans, 1988), 196.

24   See, for example, E. Theodore Mullen, *The Divine Council in Canaanite and Early Hebrew Literature*, HSM 24 (Chico, CA: Scholars Press, 1980); Mark S. Smith, *The Origins of Biblical Monotheism: Israel's Polytheistic Background and the Ugaritic Texts* (Oxford: Oxford University Press, 2001), 41–53.

25   See on this Jeffrey H. Tigay, *Deuteronomy*, The JPS Torah Commentary (Philadelphia: The Jewish Publication Society, 1997), 516.

This understanding of verse 6, which Kaufmann himself would not have endorsed,[26] nonetheless bolsters his claim that the nations, in spite of the call to them to acknowledge YHWH, are still thought of as committed to the worship of their ancestral gods. After all, the psalmist acknowledges these gods and calls upon them to sing to YHWH. The nations are thus hardly thought of as eschewing their gods. Rather, they are expected to acknowledge the subordinate status of their gods to YHWH. Thus, the acknowledgment of YHWH by the nations in Ps 47 hardly indicates the achievement of a "united humanity." National, ethnic and religio-cultic differences continue to stand between the clans, cities, and nations of the world, even if they acknowledge YHWH as the supreme deity.

In light of this, there is little reason to assume that the psalm relegates Israelite nationalism to the bygone realm of early history. Even if verses 3–4 refer to the past, it is a foundational past relived in the present, as Weiser himself most cogently argued.[27] If so, however, it can hardly serve as a mere foil to an eschatological future that undermines and supersedes it. As Kaufmann correctly emphasizes, the psalm evinces no expectation of a radical eschatological transformation. Finally, Weiser's attempt to identify within the psalm a purely "religious" expectation for the world that is devoid of any relation to power politics reflects an anachronistically modern conception of "religion" as encompassing a pure "spiritual" sphere, distinct from the "secular" sphere, that did not pertain in the world of antiquity.[28] If the psalmist speaks of YHWH's dominion over nations, this dominion must surely encompass the political realm.

4   A Critique of Kaufmann

Having found the radically universalistic, eschatological reading of Ps 47 wanting, we turn to a consideration of Kaufmann's nationalistic reading of the psalm. Kaufmann's most decisive assertion with regard to Ps 47 is that the "people of the God of Abraham" are the Israelites alone. We will discuss this presently, but first we must briefly consider some of Kaufmann's less central claims. First, his assertion that the words ידבר עמים תחתינו ולאמים תחת רגלינו (verse 3)

---

26   Kaufmann's conservative view regarding the relationship between biblical literature and mythology is well-known. For a good critique see Jon D. Levenson, *Creation and the Persistence of Evil: The Jewish Drama of Divine Omnipotence* (Princeton: Princeton University Press, 1994), 3–50.

27   Weiser, *Psalms*, 377.

28   For a fine treatment of this subject see the recent work of Brent Nongbri, *Before Religion: A History of a Modern Concept* (New Haven: Yale University Press, 2013).

constitute a prayer for future national conquests is highly questionable. The fact that these verses follow the call of verse 1 to the nations to enthrone YHWH and lead into his actual enthronement at verse 5 strongly indicates that they refer to the salvific acts of the past upon which the deity's claim to kingship is founded. In fact, since verse 4, which speaks of God's election of the national inheritance, concerns an event that occurred in the past, the conquest of the nations mentioned in verse 3 must also refer to an event in the past. Kaufmann thus seems to exaggerate the nationalistic quality of the psalm here. This is not to say that the psalmist would frown upon future national conquests. Of this there is hardly testimony. It does mean, however, that this is not the explicit focal point of the verses in question.

More important are Kaufmann's attempts to qualify the universalistic import of the opening call to the nations to clap and shout for YHWH (verse 1). As we have seen, Kaufmann argues that this call focuses on YHWH's acts of national salvation on behalf of Israel and that it consists of little more than a poetic image that expresses the abstract idea of YHWH's universal kingship. Concerning the first issue, Kaufmann's point is well-taken. Kaufmann aptly points to similar passages in which the nations are called upon to extol YHWH for his acts of national salvation, such as Ps 117: "Praise YHWH all you nations, extol him, all you peoples, for great is his love toward us and his faithfulness endures forever, Hallelujah." Thus, the universal call can hardly be said to undermine the national aspect of the psalm. On the other hand, it must be noted that the phrase תקעו כף, with which Ps 47:1 begins, refers to enthronement, as, for example, in 2 Kgs 11:12, ויכו כף ויאמרו יחי המלך. There should be little doubt, then, that the psalm calls upon the nations not just to extol YHWH and sing his praises, but to join Israel in enthroning him as the great king of all the earth (Ps 47:1–2, 7–9). The representation of the nations enthroning YHWH surely implies that they acknowledge his kingship and accept their subordination to his authority. The more pressing question, then, becomes whether or not this representation amounts to little more than poetic imagery that is completely unrelated to the psalm's view of reality. Even if this understanding is possible with regard to verses 1–2, there is nothing particularly unrealistic about verse 9's representation of "nobles of peoples" participating in the enthronement ceremony. These are not, it must be emphasized, "*the* nobles of *the* peoples" that gather at the ceremony site, as most renditions would have it, which indeed might be taken as referring unrealistically to the nations of the world as a whole, but simply נדיבי עמים—a contingency of nobles.[29] Now, if this group

---

29   Similarly, Ps 47:3 states ידבר עמים תחתינו and not העמים, since the victory referred to was over several peoples but not the world. In contrast, Ps 47:1 constitutes a call to all the nations and therefore we read כל העמים תקעו כף.

of nobles or princes is made up of or includes non-Israelites, and if they and the peoples they represent are indeed referred to as "the people of the God of Abraham," then there is no reason to deny, as Kaufmann most emphatically does, that these peoples are thought of as gaining a share in the divine grace bestowed on Israel. After all, they actively participate in the ceremony of enthronement of YHWH.

This brings us to the heart of Kaufmann's thesis regarding Ps 47—the claim that the "nobles of peoples" are the Israelite tribal leaders, who alone make up the "people of the God of Abraham" (verse 9a). In support of this claim, Kaufmann points to several biblical passages in which עמים or גוים refer to the Israelite tribes.[30] That נדיבי עמים can refer to Israel's tribal leaders is indeed beyond question. What is open to doubt, however, is whether it in fact refers to them, and to them alone, in the passage at hand. Here, the context would seem to indicate otherwise. For the continuation of the verse reads, "for the leaders of the earth are God's; he is highly exalted" (verse 9b). This final clause makes little sense if verse 9a refers exclusively to Israel and her tribal leaders. If, on the other hand, verse 9a refers to a contingency that consists of or includes outsider leaders, the continuity with verse 9b is most understandable. The several nobles that participate in the enthronement of YHWH demonstrate, following the principle of *pars pro toto*, that the leaders of the earth as a whole are his, at least in theory. Further, the word עמים that comprises the phrase נדיבי עמים appears already at the outset of the psalm (verses 1 and 3) with reference to "outsider" nations. If, then, נדיבי עמים signifies or includes world leaders, the "people of the God of Abraham" must signify something beyond the tribal league of Israel. Ps 47 thus expresses a conception of divine kingship and grace that is broader than Kaufmann would have us believe. In sum, Kaufmann's strictly nationalistic reading of Ps 47 does not adequately address the genuine, supranational tenor of the psalm.

5   The Divine "Inheritance" and "Pride of Jacob"—Land or City?

I believe that a major key to unlocking the ideological world of the psalm is the recognition that it is rooted in the city of Jerusalem. This city embodied national and international qualities that did not undermine but, on the

---

30   For עמים he cites Gen 28:3; 48:4; Deut 33:19; for גוים he cites Gen 35:11; Ezek 35:10. See
        Kaufmann, *History of Israelite Religion*, 2:719 (n. 109).

contrary, reinforced one another.[31] The rootedness of the psalm in Jerusalem is indicated, first of all, by the setting of the psalm between two psalms that clearly highlight the centrality of the city. Thus, in Ps 46:4–5 we read: "There is a river whose streams make glad the city of God, the holy place where Elyon dwells." Correspondingly, Ps 48 opens with the joyous declaration: "Great is the Lord, and most worthy of praise, in the city of our God, his holy mountain." The setting of Ps 47 between these psalms testifies, at the very least, to the sense of the early editors of the book that it is rooted in Jerusalem. As for the substance of Ps 47, the Zion-Jerusalem background is reflected, first of all, in verse 4: "He chose our inheritance for us, the pride of Jacob, which he loved." Nearly all modern scholars interpret the phrases, "our inheritance" and "the pride of Jacob" as references to the land of promise. God's "choosing" of this inheritance is then taken as a reference to the conquest of the land of the *Heilsgeschichte*, reflecting God's special love for Israel in contrast with the nations.[32] This, however, does not appear to be correct. First of all, we do not find the language of divine "choosing" (בח"ר) with reference to the land of promise, but we do find it with reference to Zion. Thus, Ps 132:13 states: "For the Lord has chosen Zion, he has desired it for his dwelling." Similarly, in Ps 78:68–69 we read: "But he chose the tribe of Judah, Mount Zion, which he loved. He built his sanctuary like the heights, like the earth that he established forever." Here God chooses Judah, Zion and the sanctuary of Jerusalem as his capital from which he rules over "Israel" as a whole.[33] It should further be noted that the phrase "Mount Zion, which he loved" corresponds with "the pride of Jacob, which he loved" of our verse, indicating that "the pride of Jacob" in our Psalm refers to the city of Jerusalem and its temple. Indeed, God is never said to bear a special love for the land of Canaan. This coincides with the observations of Joel S. Burnett, who noted that the phrase "the pride of Jacob" generally refers to a temple city.[34] This is most apparent in Amos 6:8, where we find YHWH declaring in oath: "I abhor the pride of Jacob and detest its fortresses; I will deliver up the

---

31 For the international character of pre-exilic Jerusalem see John T. Willis, "Isaiah 2:2–5 and the Psalms of Zion," in *Writing and Reading the Scroll of Isaiah: Studies of an Interpretive Tradition*, ed. Craig C. Broyles and Craig A. Evans, VTSup 70 (Leiden: Brill, 1997), 295–316; John Eaton, *The Psalms* (London: Continuum, 2008), 33–34.

32 See, e.g., Weiser, *Psalms*, 375; Albert A. Anderson, *The Book of Psalms*, The New Century Bible Commentary (Grand Rapids: Eerdmans, 1981), 363.

33 For the position of Zion within the context of Israel as a whole see also Pss 76:2–3; 87:2; 114:2; 122:4.

34 Joel S. Burnett, "The Pride of Jacob," in *David and Zion: Biblical Studies in Honor of J.J.M. Roberts*, ed. Bernard F. Batto and Kathryn L. Roberts (Winona Lake, IN: Eisenbrauns, 2004), 319–50.

city and everything in it." Here, the "pride of Jacob" is apparently applied to the temple city of Samaria, whereas in our psalm it is applied to Jerusalem. This is further indicated by the parallel between the "pride of Jacob" and "our inheritance," which, following the LXX and Peshitta, should probably be read as "his inheritance."[35] That this phrase can refer to Jerusalem and its temple is clearly indicated by passages such as Ps 79:1: "O God, the nations have invaded your inheritance; they have defiled your holy temple, they have reduced Jerusalem to rubble." And Moshe Weinfeld has gathered various pieces of evidence that indicate that the phrase "inheritance of YHWH," in its most fundamental sense, refers to a city with a YHWH temple.[36] Ps 47:4, then, speaks of Jerusalem as the "pride of Jacob," that is, the capital city and choice delight of all of Israel. This accords with the statement of Ps 87:2: "The Lord loves the gates of Zion more than all the other dwellings of Jacob."[37]

6   The "God of Abraham" as the Deity of Davidic Jerusalem

The Jerusalem setting of Ps 47 is further indicated by the phrase of verse 9, "the people of the God of Abraham," for there is a special connection between the figure of Abraham and the city of Jerusalem.[38] This connection is attested to in the story of the binding of Isaac of Gen 22. In Gen 22:14 we read: "Abraham

35   This reading is accepted by many. See, e.g., Choong-Leong Seow, *Ark Processions in the Politics of the Monarchy* (Ann Arbor: University Microfilms, 1985) 181.

36   Moshe Weinfeld, *Social Justice in Ancient Israel and in the Ancient Near East* (Jerusalem: Magnes, 1995), 239–40.

37   Christl M. Maier's treatment of this Psalm is reminiscent of Weiser's approach to Ps 47. The psalm, which she situates in the post-exilic period, is "unheeded in the rest of the Hebrew Bible because it disregards all boundaries between Israel and the nations and denies any prerequisite for joining with Israel in its faith in YHWH. Depicting Zion as the ultimate place of God's election and proclaiming the foreign nations to be the children of Jerusalem, Psalm 87 exceeds all expectations of salvation." Ps 87, unheeded in the Hebrew Bible, finally wins a hearing in the New Testament. See Christl M. Maier, "Psalm 87 as a Reappraisal of the Zion Tradition and its Reception in Galatians 4:26," *CBQ* 69 (2007): 473–86 (480–81). In my view, Maier's estimation of the nature and late date of the psalm is highly questionable. The psalm's use of kinship language to describe foreign pilgrims is actually quite similar to the reference to the "family of the God of Abraham" in Ps 47.

38   This connection is intimately related to the connection between Abraham and David. On this see Moshe Weinfeld, "The Davidic Empire: Realization of the Promise to the Patriarchs," in *Avraham Malamat Volume*, ed. Shmuel Ahituv and Baruch A. Levine, Eretz Israel 24 (Jerusalem: Israel Exploration Society, 1993), 87–92 (Hebrew); Walter Dietrich, "Die David-Abraham-Typologie im Alten Testament," in *Verbindungslinien: Festschrift für Werner H. Schmidt zum 65. Geburtstag*, ed. Axel Graupner, Holgert Delkurt, and Alexander B. Ernst (Neukirchen-Vluyn: Neukirchener, 2000), 41–55.

called that place 'YHWH Yireh.' And to this day it is said, 'On the mountain of YHWH it will be provided.'" Most scholars agree that the "mountain of YHWH" that is spoken of "to this day" is probably Jerusalem.[39] The connection is evinced most clearly, however, in the famous passage of Gen 14:18–20:

> Then Melchizedek king of Salem brought out bread and wine. He was priest of El Elyon, and he blessed Abram saying, "Blessed be Abram by El Elyon, Creator of heaven and earth. And praise be to El Elyon, who delivered your enemies into your hand." Then Abram gave him a tenth of everything.

This text presents Abram as paying a tithe of his battle spoils to the king-priest of El Elyon, the deity of Jerusalem, in gratitude for the victory that this deity bestowed upon him over his enemies, presented in the larger narrative as great kings. The implication of the text is that Abram was fulfilling a vow that he had made at the sanctuary of Jerusalem before embarking on his military venture. The text thus evinces Abraham's strong connection not only with Jerusalem and its king, but also with its deity, El Elyon, who supports him in battle (compare "YHWH Elyon" in Ps 47:2). As is well known, this passage in Genesis is closely related to Ps 110:1–4, which speaks of the Davidic king in Zion as a Melchizedek-like figure. Here, too, the context is a military one in which the deity bestows victory over kings:

> The Lord said to my Lord, "Sit at my right hand, till I make your enemies your footstool." The Lord shall send the rod of your strength out of Zion. Rule in the midst of your enemies ... The Lord has sworn and will not repent: "You are a priest forever, in the order of Melchizedek." The Lord is at your right hand; he will shatter kings on the day of his wrath.

The "God of Abraham" of Ps 47:9 must thus be identified with the God of Jerusalem, who is a God of military conquest. In accordance with this, we should probably understand the reference in verses 3–4 to the subjection of nations under "our feet" and the concomitant "choosing" of the divine inheritance as a Judean "foundation narrative" of sorts for the city of Jerusalem.[40] It

---

39   See Jon D. Levenson, *The Death and Resurrection of the Beloved Son: The Transformation of Child Sacrifice in Judaism and Christianity* (New Haven: Yale University Press, 1993), 111–24. See also Archibald van Wieringen's contribution to this volume.

40   The same must be said for other texts in the Psalter such as Ps 76 (cf. verses 1–2) and Ps 78 (esp. verses 60–72). The precise details of the presumed narratives are, unfortunately, difficult to determine due to the poetic nature of the texts. On foundation traditions of

is surely not coincidental that the Davidic warrior-king of Ps 18 praises YHWH
with the words וידבר עמים תחתי, a praise which echoes Ps 47:3: ידבר עמים תחתנו.
In this context, the collective "we" of the psalm would most likely be, at least
primarily, the Judeans. YHWH delivered peoples under their feet and "chose"
Jerusalem for himself (and for them) as his capital. In the broad sense, then,
the psalm may be linked to the "Songs of Zion."[41] The close connection between Abraham, the Davidic Jerusalem and the theme of the defeat of enemies
again makes it highly unlikely that Ps 47 envisions a dissolution of all nationalist sentiment in a spiritualized, religious universalism. At the same time, it
should be recognized that the "nationalism" expressed in Ps 47 centres directly
on "Zion" and only secondarily on "Jacob."

7   The World-Empire of David/Zion and the Figure of Abraham

The recognition that Ps 47 is rooted in the Zion tradition allows us to suggest a
resolution to the tension that is so often seen as existing between the psalm's
nationalism, particularly as reflected in the glorification of the subjugation of
nations under "our feet" and its universalism, particularly as reflected in the
reference to the gathering of "princes of peoples" as the "people of the God
of Abraham." As is well known, the Zion tradition promoted an ideology of
empire under the auspices of the deity of Zion and his Davidic king.[42] Typical
is the statement of Ps 72:8: "May he rule from sea to sea and from the River to
the ends of the earth." What is important to emphasize is that this Zion ideology may be said to reflect a unique and harmonious kind of coalescence of
particularistic and universalistic impulses. On the one hand, the glorification
of previous military conquests and aspirations toward expansive dominion are
fervently nationalistic. In Gen 49:8–10 we read:

> Judah, your brothers will praise you; your hand will be on the neck of your
> enemies; your father's sons will bow down to you … You are a lion's cub,
> Judah; you return from the prey, my son … The sceptre will not depart

---

cities, clans, and nations see most recently Guy Darshan, "The Origins of the Foundation
Stories Genre in the Hebrew Bible and Ancient Eastern Mediterranean," *JBL* 133 (2014):
689–709.

41   For an extensive listing of psalms that enter this category and that does not include Ps 47
see Jon D. Levenson, "Zion Traditions," in *The Anchor Bible Dictionary*, ed. David Noel
Freedman, 6 vols. (New York: Doubleday, 1992), 6:1098–1102 (1099).

42   See the illuminating treatment of J.J.M. Roberts, "God's Imperial Reign According to the
Psalter," *HBT* 23 (2001): 211–21.

from Judah, nor the ruler's staff from between his feet forever,[43] for tribute will come to him and the obedience of peoples is his.

Judah's violent victories over his external enemies will win him the praise and admiration of his "brethren." The Judean leader will be acknowledged not only as king over the "sons of his father," but, further, as emperor over "peoples" from afar, who will bring him "tribute." His successes near and far bring glory to the national deity, YHWH. And in Ps 2:8–9, YHWH tells his anointed son on Mount Zion: "Ask of me, and I will give you nations for an inheritance, and the ends of the earth for your possession. You shall break them with a rod of iron; You shall dash them to pieces like a potter's vessel."[44] On the other hand, kingship over brethren and imperial dominion over additional peoples has a universalistic quality to it. Thus, we read in Ps 72:11–14 with regard to the Davidic king:

> May all kings fall down before him, all nations give him service. For he delivers the needy when they call, the poor and those who have no helper. He has pity on the weak and the needy, and saves the lives of the needy. From oppression and violence he redeems their life; and precious is their blood in his sight.

The kings of the nations joyously accept the authority of the Davidic emperor and his divine sponsor because of the king's passion for universal justice, which derives from the national God (verse 2: "your people"), the God of justice (verse 1). Closely related to this is the broadly attested association of the deity of Jerusalem with justice (צדק).[45] Of course, the king and his deity will still have their ungrateful enemies, who will be condemned to "lick the dust" (verse 9). The rebellious kings who plot against "YHWH and his anointed one" in Ps 2 are similarly condemned, as we have seen above. Yet this psalm, too, ends on a universalistic note: "Happy are all those who take refuge in him" (Ps 2:12).

---

43 For an insightful analysis of this verse see Richard C. Steiner, "Poetic Forms in the Masoretic Vocalization and Three Difficult Phrases in Jacob's Blessing: יתר שאת (Gen 49:3), יצועי עלה (49:4) and יבא שילה (49:10)," *JBL* 129 (2010): 209–35.

44 While it is true that Ps 47 does not mention the Judean king, this is because it seeks to highlight the divine king. The psalm's speaker, nonetheless, speaks in the name of "we," the conquerors of nations, and may well be the king, who, as in the case of Melchizedek, may also have played the role of cultic leader. For the king as speaker in various psalms see Steven J.L. Croft, *The Identity of the Individual in the Psalms*, JSOTSup 44 (Sheffield: JSOT Press, 1987), 73–132.

45 See Bernard F. Batto, "Zedeq," in *Dictionary of Deities and Demons in the Bible*, ed. Karel van der Toorn, Bob Becking, and Pieter W. van der Horst (Leiden: Brill, 1995), 929–34. Cf. Pss 15:1–2; 101:8; Isa 1:21.

As some scholars have noted, the figure of Abraham is closely connected
to these themes.[46] The idea of the vast empire is expressed at Gen 15:18: "On
that day the Lord made a covenant with Abraham saying, I grant this land
to your offspring, from the river of Egypt to the great river, the Euphrates."
Furthermore, the land of this Abrahamic covenant is similar to the land attributed to Solomon in 1 Kgs 5:1: "Solomon ruled all the kingdoms from the
Euphrates River to the land of the Philistines, as far as the border of Egypt."
The universalist interpretation of "the people of the God of Abraham" fits most
naturally, of course, with the divine covenant that was made with Abraham in
Gen 17, according to which Abraham would be someone from whom "kings
will issue forth," and a "father of a multitude of nations" (Gen 17:4–6). This
text unites these nations through the bonds of kinship. Most important, according to Gen 17:7, God makes an everlasting covenant with Abraham,
להיות לך לאלהים ולזרעך אחריך, "to serve as deity to you and your seed after
you." This implies that these multitudinous nations and kings are also bound
together in Abraham's God. And it is surely not irrelevant that, according to
Gen 14:13, 24, Abraham was joined in battle against the four invading kings by
his Amorite covenant partners Aner, Eshcol and Mamre. These texts indicate
that the figure of Abraham can be linked with covenants of a sacred character
that bind "insider" and "outsider" leaders in a common coalition. This, then,
is the probable signification of "the people of the God of Abraham." It refers
not to all the peoples of the world nor to the tribal leaders of Israel, but to the
kingdoms that have entered into covenant with Jerusalem.[47] These add to the
glory of Jerusalem and her deity. The kingdoms also gain a share in the divine
blessings that are bestowed on those that bless Abraham. There is no reason,
however, to see them as undermining the special status of "Jacob." After all,
as noted above, these "outsider" peoples are still subject to their local gods,
whereas the people of Jacob are under YHWH's direct and exclusive authority,
at least theoretically. Thus, the "people of the God of Abraham" are not completely on a par with the people of Israel.

The dual aspect of Abraham as a nationalistic figure and a universalistic
one, as one that brings evil to the nations but also blessing, comes to clearest
expression in the famous passage of Gen 12:2–3: "I will make of you a great nation, and I will bless you, and make your name great, so that you will be a blessing. I will bless those who bless you, and those who curse you I will curse; and in
you all the families of the earth shall be blessed." Abraham will become a great

---

46   Weinfeld, "The Davidic Empire."

47   Although one cannot exclude the possibility that Israelite tribal leaders are included as
      well, this seems less likely.

nation and he will impinge variously upon the families of the earth. Those that bless Abraham will be blessed and those that curse him will be cursed. This parallels that which we have seen in Ps 2—the kings that plot against "YHWH and his anointed one" suffer defeat and humiliation whereas those that take refuge in him are happy. It also parallels that which we have seen in Ps 72—the enemies of the king will lick the dust of the earth, but those kings who submit to his rule will enjoy the blessings of his divinely given justice and righteousness. The same duality appears in Gen 18:18–19: "Abraham shall become a great and mighty nation, and all the nations of the earth shall be blessed in him. For I have chosen him, that he may charge his children and his household after him to keep the way of the Lord by doing righteousness and justice; so that the Lord may bring about for Abraham what he has promised him." Again, Abraham's destiny is to become a great and mighty nation that will impinge positively upon "all the nations of the world." This positive universal effect is directly related to Abraham's (and his kingly dynasty's)[48] pursuit of a life of righteousness, which constitutes the "way of YHWH."

8   Conclusion

Many Christian interpreters who come to the text with a contemporary, confessional orientation, understand Ps 47 as an eschatological vision of a united humanity that dislodges the position of Israel as YHWH's special people.[49] The psalm relegates Israel's special status to the past and looks forward to the realization of the universal ideal in which all peoples unite under YHWH. The "people of the God of Abraham" thus refers to all the people of the world. Yehezkel Kaufmann presented a sustained critique of this interpretation and suggested, instead, that the psalm was thoroughly nationalistic in orientation. The "people of the God of Abraham" refers, in his view, to the Israelites alone. In this study I have subjected both interpretations to criticism. I suggest that Ps 47 rehearses the history of the foundation of Jerusalem as YHWH's city and that, as such, it combines nationalistic and universalistic impulses in a single vision. Those who oppose Jerusalem are doomed to destruction while those who support it and join in the enthronement of its deity are thought of as blessed. The nations that join in covenant with Jerusalem are referred to as the

---

48   For this interpretation see Weinfeld, *Social Justice*, 215–17.

49   For a notable, ecumenically sensitive exception see Walter Brueggemann, *The Message of the Psalms: A Theological Commentary*, Augsburg Old Testament Studies (Minneapolis: Augsburg, 1984), 150.

"people of the God of Abraham." They add to Jerusalem's glory and have a share in the blessedness that is associated with its deity, but they do not thereby undermine the unique position of Jacob/Israel.

References

Anderson, Albert A. *The Book of Psalms*. The New Century Bible Commentary. Grand Rapids: Eerdmans, 1981.

Barshai, Avinoam. "The Nationalist Outlook of Yehezkel Kaufmann." Pages 13–59 in *Yehezkel Kaufmann: Selected Writings on Jewish Nationality and Zionism*. Jerusalem: Bialik, 1995. (Hebrew).

Batto, Bernard F. "Zedeq." Pages 929–34 in *Dictionary of Deities and Demons in the Bible*. Edited by Karel van der Toorn, Bob Becking, and Pieter W. van der Horst. Leiden: Brill, 1995.

Birnbaum, Philip. *High Holiday Prayer Book*. New York: Hebrew Publishing Company, 1951.

Boulding, Maria. *Expositions of the Psalms: Volume 2*. Vol. 3/16 of *The Works of Saint Augustine: A Translation for the 21st Century*. Edited by John E. Rotele. Hyde Park, NY: New City Press, 2000.

Brueggemann, Walter. *The Message of the Psalms: A Theological Commentary*. Augsburg Old Testament Studies. Minneapolis: Augsburg, 1984.

Buber, Solomon. *Midrash Tehillim (also) Called Shoḥer Tov*. Vilna: Rom, 1891. Repr., New York: Om, 1947.

Burnett, Joel S. "The Pride of Jacob." Pages 319–50 in *David and Zion: Biblical Studies in Honor of J.J.M. Roberts*. Edited by Bernard F. Batto and Kathryn L. Roberts. Winona Lake, IN: Eisenbrauns, 2004.

Clines, David J.A. "The Evidence for an Autumnal New Year in Pre-exilic Israel Reconsidered." *JBL* 93 (1974): 22–40.

Cohen, Gerson D. "Esau as Symbol in Early Medieval Thought." Pages 243–70 in *Studies in the Variety of Rabbinic Cultures*. Philadelphia: The Jewish Publication Society, 1991.

Croft, Steven J.L. *The Identity of the Individual in the Psalms*. JSOTSup 44. Sheffield: JSOT Press, 1987.

Darshan, Guy. "The Origins of the Foundation Stories Genre in the Hebrew Bible and Ancient Eastern Mediterranean." *JBL* 133 (2014): 689–709.

Day, John. *Psalms*. Sheffield: JSOT Press, 1990.

Dietrich, Walter. "Die David-Abraham-Typologie im Alten Testament." Pages 41–55 in *Verbindungslinien: Festschrift für Werner H. Schmidt zum 65. Geburtstag*. Edited by Axel Graupner, Holgert Delkurt, and Alexander B. Ernst. Neukirchen-Vluyn: Neukirchener, 2000.

Eaton, John. *The Psalms*. London: Continuum, 2008.

Friedlander, Gerald. *Pirke De Rabbi Eliezer*. New York: Sepher-Hermon Press, 1981.

Gerstenberger, Erhard S. *Psalms: Part 1: With an Introduction to Cultic Poetry*. FOTL 14. Grand Rapids: Eerdmans, 1988.

Grogan, Geoffrey W. *Psalms*. The Two Horizons Old Testament Commentary. Grand Rapids: Eerdmans, 2008.

Grossman, Avraham. *Rashi*. Translated by Joel A. Linsider. Oxford: Littman Library of Jewish Civilization, 2012.

Junginger, Horst. *The Scientification of the "Jewish Question" in Nazi Germany*. Numen Book Series 157. Leiden: Brill, 2017.

Kaufmann, Yehezkel. *History of Israelite Religion from Its Beginnings until the End of the Second Temple Period*. 4 vols. Tel Aviv: Bialik, 1937–1956. (Hebrew).

Levenson, Jon D. "Zion Traditions." Pages 6:1098–1102 in *The Anchor Bible Dictionary*. Edited by David Noel Freedman. 6 vols. New York: Doubleday, 1992.

Levenson, Jon D. *The Death and Resurrection of the Beloved Son: The Transformation of Child Sacrifice in Judaism and Christianity*. New Haven: Yale University Press, 1993.

Levenson, Jon D. *Creation and the Persistence of Evil: The Jewish Drama of Divine Omnipotence*. Princeton: Princeton University Press, 1994.

Maier, Christl M. "Psalm 87 as a Reappraisal of the Zion Tradition and its Reception in Galatians 4:26." *CBQ* 69 (2007): 473–86.

Mullen, E. Theodore. *The Divine Council in Canaanite and Early Hebrew Literature*. HSM 24. Chico, CA: Scholars Press, 1980.

Nongbri, Brent. *Before Religion: A History of a Modern Concept*. New Haven: Yale University Press, 2013.

Ollenburger, Ben C. *Zion, the City of the Great King: A Theological Symbol of the Jerusalem Cult*. JSOTSup 41. Sheffield: JSOT Press, 1987.

Roberts, J.J.M. "The Religio-Political Setting of Psalm 47." *BASOR* 221 (1976): 129–32.

Roberts, J.J.M. "God's Imperial Reign According to the Psalter." *HBT* 23 (2001): 211–21.

Roberts, J.J.M. "Mowinckel's Enthronement Festival: A Review." Pages 97–115 in *The Book of Psalms: Composition and Reception*. Edited by Peter W. Flint and Patrick D. Miller. Leiden: Brill, 2005.

Rofé, Alexander. *Introduction to the Literature of the Hebrew Bible*. Translated by Harvey N. Bock and Judith H. Seeligmann. Jerusalem Biblical Studies 9. Jerusalem: Simor, 2009.

Seow, Choong-Leong. *Ark Processions in the Politics of the Monarchy*. Ann Arbor: University Microfilms, 1985.

Smith, Mark S. *The Origins of Biblical Monotheism: Israel's Polytheistic Background and the Ugaritic Texts*. Oxford: Oxford University Press, 2001.

Steiner, Richard C. "Poetic Forms in the Masoretic Vocalization and Three Difficult Phrases in Jacob's Blessing: יתר שאת (Gen 49:3), יצועי עלה (49:4) and יבא שילה (49:10)." *JBL* 129 (2010): 209–35.

Terrien, Samuel. *The Psalms: Strophic Structure and Theological Commentary*. Eerdmans Critical Commentary. Grand Rapids: Eerdmans, 2003.

Tigay, Jeffrey H. *Deuteronomy*. The JPS Torah Commentary. Philadelphia: The Jewish Publication Society, 1997.

Weinfeld, Moshe. "The Davidic Empire: Realization of the Promise to the Patriarchs." Pages 87–92 in *Avraham Malamat Volume*. Edited by Shmuel Ahituv and Baruch A. Levine. Eretz Israel 24. Jerusalem: Israel Exploration Society, 1993. (Hebrew).

Weinfeld, Moshe. *Social Justice in Ancient Israel and in the Ancient Near East*. Jerusalem: Magnes, 1995.

Weiser, Artur. *The Psalms*. Translated by Herbert Harwell. Old Testament Library. Philadelphia: Westminster Press, 1962.

Westermann, Claus. *The Praise of God in the Psalms*. Translated by Keith R. Crim. Richmond, VA: John Knox, 1965.

Willis, John T. "Isaiah 2:2–5 and the Psalms of Zion." Pages 295–316 in *Writing and Reading the Scroll of Isaiah: Studies of an Interpretive Tradition*. Edited by Craig C. Broyles and Craig A. Evans. VTSup 70. Leiden: Brill, 1997.

Yisraeli, Oded. "'Moses Didn't Die': A Rabbinic Tradition in the Zohar." Pages 381–406 in *Moses the Man—Master of the Prophets*. Edited by Moshe Hallamish, Hannah Kasher, and Hanokh Ben-Pazi. Ramat-Gan: Bar-Ilan University Press, 2010. (Hebrew).

CHAPTER 7

Where Shall Wisdom Be Found? Identity, Sacred Space, and Universal Knowledge in Philostratus and Acts of the Apostles

Pieter B. Hartog

This article explores the connection between sacred spaces, the cultural and religious identities of their visitors, and ideals of universal knowledge in the early Roman Empire. Taking my point of departure in a social-scientific approach to identities as "global mélanges" (a concept I will explain below), I will argue that visits to sacred spaces activated aspects of the multi-faceted identities of their visitors that would not, or less easily, be activated elsewhere. These aspects often appeal to an ideal of universal knowledge, as literary works from the early Roman Empire could represent sacred spaces as loci of universal wisdom.[1] As a result, these sacred spaces obtained a transformative potential that stimulated their visitors to embrace global wisdom and to construct a glocalised cultural or religious identity for themselves.[2]

1　The observations in this article are relevant, therefore, for the study of encyclopaedism in writings from the Hellenistic and Roman periods. Recent studies on this topic have shown that many writers from these periods presented their works as providing complete knowledge, either on a specific topic or on as many topics as possible. As a result of these universalist claims, encyclopaedic rhetoric could serve useful purposes in contexts of cultural competition. Generally on encyclopaedism see Jason König and Greg Woolf, eds., *Encyclopaedism from Antiquity and the Renaissance* (Cambridge: Cambridge University Press, 2013). For a case study of encyclopaedic rhetoric in the early Jewish book of Jubilees see Pieter B. Hartog, "Jubilees and Hellenistic Encyclopaedism," *JSJ* 50 (2019): 1–25. Cf. also how Verity Platt speaks of the "encyclopaedic range" of Philostratus's *Life* ("Virtual Visions: *Phantasia* and the Perception of the Divine in *The Life of Apollonius of Tyana*," in *Philostratus*, ed. Ewen Bowie and Jaś Elsner, GCRW [Cambridge: Cambridge University Press, 2009], 131–54 [131]).

2　See John Elsner, "Hagiographic Geography: Travel and Allegory in the *Life of Apollonius of Tyana*," *JHS* 117 (1997): 22–37. Though Elsner does not make explicit reference to glocalisation terminology, his study of Philostratus's project persuasively illustrates the interaction between the global and the local which the concept of "glocalisation" seeks to capture. See, e.g., Elsner's remark that "Philostratus presents us with a living continuation of the sacred culture and identity of ancient Greece through the sacred character of Apollonius who surpasses all holy men past and present, *and whose travels take him, take his Greece, further than any countryman of his has yet journeyed, beyond Achaea, and through the whole empire*" (36; my italics). On the development of glocalisation terminology and its application in the

To illustrate this I concentrate on two episodes in travel narratives from the early Roman Empire, in which the protagonist visits a sacred space. The first, in Philostratus's *Life of Apollonius of Tyana*, describes how Apollonius travels to India in order to visit the Brahmins who live on a hill near the city Paraca. In Philostratus's account, the sacredness of this hill is evident from the well it houses, which contains mysterious and powerful water; from its crater, where Indians would visit to purify themselves; and from its plenitude of deity statues (3.14). What is more, Philostratus explicitly labels both the inhabitants of the hill (2.33) and their abode (3.33) as "our sacred house" (τὸν ἱερὸν οἶκον). The second episode I discuss is Paul's visit to the Areopagus in Athens, as described in Acts 17:16–33. Though Acts does not expressly portray the Areopagus as sacred, its association with Mars and the abundant presence of altars and deity statutes that triggered Paul's emphasis on the cult in his speech (17:22–23) do allow viewing the Areopagus as a sacred space. Focusing on these two passages, I will explore how Apollonius's visit to the hill of the sages and Paul's visit to the Areopagus tie in with how Philostratus and Luke portray their cultural and/or religious identities.

1   Identity as Global Mélange

As one of the main characteristics of our modern, globalised world several scholars have pointed to the compression of time and space.[3] This means that individuals are able to travel ever greater distances in ever smaller amounts of

---

study of the ancient world see Pieter B. Hartog, *Pesher and Hypomnema: A Comparison of Two Commentary Traditions from the Hellenistic-Roman World*, STDJ 121 (Leiden: Brill, 2017), 16–28 (with references); Pieter B. Hartog, "Contesting *Oikoumenē*: Resistance and Locality in Philo's *Legatio ad Gaium*," in *Intolerance, Polemics, and Debate in Antiquity: Politico-Cultural, Philosophical, and Religious Forms of Critical Conversation*, ed. George van Kooten and Jacques T.A.G.M. van Ruiten, TBN 25 (Leiden: Brill, 2019), 205–31 (206–13).

3   The concept of time-space compression was formulated by David Harvey, *The Condition of Postmodernity: An Enquiry into the Origins of Cultural Change* (Cambridge: Blackwell, 1990) and has made a profound impact in the study of geography and space. See, e.g., Doreen Massey, *Space, Place and Gender* (Cambridge: Polity, 1994); Barney Warf, *Time-Space Compression: Historical Geographies* (Oxford: Routledge, 2008). Globalisation theorists adopting the concept include Roland Robertson, "Glocalization: Time-Space and Homogeneity-Heterogeneity," in *Global Modernities*, ed. Mike Featherstone, Scott Lash, and Roland Robertson, TCS (London: Sage, 1995), 25–44; Timothy W. Luke, "Identity, Meaning and Globalization: Detraditionalization in Postmodern Space-Time Compression," in *Detraditionalization: Critical Reflections on Authority and Identity*, ed. Paul Heelas, Scott Lash, and Paul Morris (Cambridge: Blackwell, 1996), 109–33; George Ritzer and Paul Dean, *Globalization: A Basic Text* (Chicester: Wiley Blackwell, 2015), 238–40.

time and that information between individuals can be shared more and more quickly. As a result, individuals and the groups to which they belong become increasingly interconnected. This interconnectedness has an impact on how individuals connect to and construct the spaces in which they find themselves and how they formulate their cultural and religious traditions and identities.

As scholars have increasingly come to realise, such processes of time-space compression are not unique to our modern world. The Roman world in particular has, in the past two decades or so, been intensively and fruitfully studied from a globalisation perspective.[4] As they united the Mediterranean under their rule and set up a vast network of roads and waterways, the Romans facilitated the transfer of people, goods, and ideas between the various groups that inhabited their empire. As a result of these increases in mobility and intercultural interaction, many cultural expressions in the Roman world assumed a "glocal" shape, in which local tendencies and traditions merged in an ongoing interplay with global ones. These processes of what some have dubbed "glocalisation"[5] affected the various cults in the Roman era—and the sacred spaces associated with them—as they did other cultural elements. A telling example is the Roman veneration of gods originating from Egypt, such as Isis, which were adopted into the Roman pantheon. As the cult of Isis spread across the empire and yet was not detached completely from its Egyptian roots, it developed into a glocalised Roman-Egyptian cult.[6]

---

4   On the application of globalisation theories in the study of the Roman world see Martin Pitts and Miguel John Versluys, "Globalisation and the Roman World: Perspectives and Opportunities," in *Globalisation and the Roman World: World History, Connectivity and Material Culture*, ed. Martin Pitts and Miguel John Versluys (Cambridge: Cambridge University Press, 2015), 3–31. In addition to the contributions in this volume see Robert Witcher, "Globalisation and Roman Imperialism: Perspectives on Identities in Roman Italy," in *The Emergence of State Identities in Italy in the First Millennium BC*, ed. Edward Herring and Kathryn Lomas (London: Accordia Research Institute, 2000), 213–25; Richard Hingley, *Globalizing Roman Culture: Unity, Diversity and Empire* (London: Routledge, 2005); Andrew Gardner, "Thinking about Roman Imperialism: Postcolonialism, Globalisation and Beyond?" *Britannia* 44 (2013): 1–25; Miguel John Versluys, "Understanding Objects in Motion: An *Archaeological* Dialogue on Romanization." *Archaeological Dialogues* 21 (2014): 1–20; Tamar Hodos, ed., *The Routledge Handbook of Globalization and Archaeology* (London: Routledge, 2017).

5   Roland Robertson, *Globalization: Social Theory and Global Culture* (London: Sage, 1992); Roland Robertson, "Glocalization"; also Erik Swyndegouw, "Neither Global nor Local: 'Glocalization' and the Politics of Scale," in *Spaces of Globalization: Reasserting the Power of the Local*, ed. Kevin R. Cox (New York: Guilford Press, 1997), 137–66.

6   See, e.g., Miguel John Versluys, "Isis Capitolina and the Egyptian Cults in late Republican Rome," in *Isis en Occident: Actes du IIème Colloque international sur les études isiaques, Lyon III 16–17 mai 2002*, ed. Laurent Bricault, RGRW 151 (Leiden: Brill, 2004), 421–88.

But glocalisation should not be taken merely as an interplay between two traditions—one global, the other local. In most cases, a range of global and local tendencies is at play in determining the shape and presentation of a given cultural expression. Focusing on the construction of cultural identities in particular, Jan Nederveen Pieterse attributes this complex interplay between global and local tendencies in the formation of identities to an *"increase in the available modes of organization*: transnational, international, macro-regional, national, microregional, municipal, local."[7] This "increase in the available modes of organization" leads to the establishment of new connections on various levels and the construction of multiple and multi-levelled identities. In Nederveen Pieterse's words:

> Multiple identities and the decentering of the social subject are ground-ed in the ability of individuals to avail themselves of several organiza-tional options at the same time. Thus globalization is the framework for the diversification and amplification of "sources of the self."[8]

Most important for my purposes are Nederveen Pieterse's notions of "the de-centering of the social subject" and the "diversification of 'sources of the self'." Whilst these terms run the risk of remaining somewhat abstract, Nederveen Pieterse offers a helpful illustration of how they play out in practice:

> An English Princess (Princess Diana) with an Egyptian boyfriend, uses a Norwegian mobile telephone, crashes in a French tunnel in a German car with a Dutch engine, driven by a Belgian driver, who was high on Scottish whiskey, followed closely by Italian Paparazzi, on Japanese motorcycles, treated by an American doctor, assisted by Filipino para-medical staff, using Brazilian medicines, dies![9]

The gist of this example is that it challenges the categorisation of Princess Diana as quintessentially "English." In view of Nederveen Pieterse's theory, she can instead be understood as a social subject decentred from its particularly English context and assuming a more diversified shape as it incorporates a wide range of different sources or traditions. The result is a "global mélange": an intricate and multi-levelled identity of which particular aspects can be

---

7 *Globalization and Culture: Global Mélange*, 3rd ed. (Lanham, MD: Rowman & Littlefield, 2016), 71–72 (italics original).
8 *Globalization and Culture*, 74.
9 *Globalization and Culture*, 150 (n. 15).

activated in particular circumstances. The reason why we would normally think of Princess Diana as an English lady, therefore, is not that she was unequivocally English, but rather that the circumstances surrounding her would in most instances activate and bring about her Englishness.

In my analysis of Philostratus and Luke, the concepts of the decentring of the social subject and the diversification of sources of the self work together to challenge scholarly classifications of Philostratus's Apollonius as quintessentially "Greek" and Luke's Paul as straightforwardly "Christian."[10] As a result of the processes outlined by Nederveen Pieterse and the complexity of cultural identity-formation in the Roman world, I intend to show that Apollonius's Greekness can be emphasised within a specific context (i.e., Apollonius's visit to the Brahmins), but is at the same time challenged and incorporated in a larger, glocalised identity that is promoted in the *Life of Apollonius* as a whole. Similarly, Luke portrays Paul's cultural/religious identity in a thoroughly glocalised way by making Paul's self-identification depend on the specific context in which Paul finds himself.

2 Apollonius among the Brahmins

Apollonius's journey to India occupies books 2 and 3 in the *Life of Apollonius* and can be considered a key episode in Philostratus's biography. In his portrayal of India, Philostratus displays a remarkable blend of exoticism and familiarity. In *Vit. Apoll.* 2,[11] Apollonius crosses the Indus river only to find reliefs in a temple in the Indian city Taxila (now in Pakistan) that depict the acts of Alexander the Great and Poros, king of India. Philostratus adds that Poros was a faithful satrap of Alexander and so claims Taxila for the sphere of influence of the Hellenistic kings (2.20–21[12]). He goes on to liken the city to Athens (2.23) and writes that Taxila housed a Helios temple with golden statues of Alexander and Poros in it (2.24). What is more, king Phraotes of Taxila turns out to speak

---

10   My point here reacts to a tendency amongst some New Testament scholars to read Acts as describing the road to victory of Christianity in the Roman Empire. In addition to the fact that "Christianity" is an anachronistic term in the time Acts was written, my argument is that the book does not testify to a unified, well-delineated cultural/religious identity of its protagonists (whether we call it "Jewish," "Christian," or something different), but rather shows that the central message of Acts is continuously being formulated anew in new circumstances. The result is a glocalised identity, according to which followers of "the Way" constitute a global whole whilst upholding their local customs and traditions.

11   On Apollonius's journey to India see Christopher P. Jones, "Apollonius of Tyana's Passage to India," *GRBS* 42 (2001): 185–99.

12   References in this section are to Philostratus, *Vit. Apoll.* Translations follow C.P. Jones (LCL).

perfect Greek, practices sports "in the Greek way" (τὸν Ἑλληνικὸν τρόπον; 2.27), and offers a meal in the shape of a Greek symposium (2.27–28).[13] Yet the source for his wisdom does not lie in the Greek world, and Phraotes makes this quite clear: he apologises for having been born a barbarian (2.27), criticises the laws of the Greeks, and sings the praise of the Indian rather than the Greek approach to philosophy (2.29). Instead, Phraotes attributes his knowledge of the Greek language and Greek customs to the wise men (σοφοί) who live across the Hyphasis river—i.e., the Brahmins Apollonius was travelling to visit (2.31–32).

In book 3, Apollonius crosses the river Hyphasis to reach his final destination in India. This is a symbolic move, as the Hyphasis famously represented the eastern border of Alexander's empire.[14] Crossing it, Apollonius leaves the Greek world behind. And yet Philostratus's India remains strange and familiar at the same time. To begin with, all inhabitants of Paraca speak Greek, just like the king in Taxila (3.12). The hill on which the Brahmins live is said to resemble the Acropolis (3.13) and is replete with statues of all kinds of gods (including Greek ones), which are venerated "with Greek rites" (Ἑλληνικοῖς ἤθεσι; 3.14). The Indian sages speak Greek, and their leader Iarchas even surpasses Apollonius in his formulations (3.36). Finally, Philostratus draws a comparison between the hill of the Brahmins and Delphi: in 3.14 he applies the term "navel" (ὀμφαλός)—which was widely regarded as a reference to Delphi—to the Brahmins' living place,[15] in 3.10 he remarks that the king of India consults the wise men "like those who send to a god for advice," and in 3.43 he compares Iarchas's predictions to those of Delphia and Dodona. From these references it appears

---

13   On the symposium as a trope in Philostratus's *Life* and the Acts of Thomas see Kendra Eshleman, "Indian Travel and Cultural Self-Location in the *Life of Apollonius* and the *Acts of Thomas*," in *Journeys in the Roman East: Imagined and Real*, ed. Maren R. Niehoff, CRPG 1 (Tübingen: Mohr Siebeck, 2017), 183–201 (185–88).

14   See Arrian, *Anabasis* 5.28.1–29.1 on how Alexander's troops mutinied at the Hyphasis, forcing their commander to withdraw. See also Philostr., *V A* 2.43, which describes a bronze stele near the Hyphasis, which is inscribed with the text: "Alexander stopped here" (Ἀλέξανδρος ἐνταῦθα ἔστη).

       On the symbolism of Apollonius's crossing the Hyphasis see Roshan Abraham, "The Geography of Culture in Philostratus' *Life of Apollonius of Tyana*," *CJ* 109 (2014): 465–80 (469–70); T.J.G. Whitmarsh, "Philostratus," in *Space in Ancient Greek Literature*, ed. Irene J.F. de Jong, MnS 339 (Leiden: Brill, 2012), 463–79 (464).

15   For *omphalos* as a reference to Delphi see, e.g., Euripides, *Medea* 666; Pindar, *Pythian* 6.3–4. In the Hellenistic and Roman period, the term was often used in contexts of cultural competition; cf., e.g., how the book of Jubilees applies it to Mount Zion (8:19) and see Philip S. Alexander, "Jerusalem as the *Omphalos* of the World: On the History of a Geographical Concept," *Judaism* 46 (1997): 147–58.

as if we are back in Greece[16]—and yet we are not quite. For Philostratus, India remains an exotic and distant country. In 3.11–12, for instance, Philostratus's mention of the fact that the inhabitants of Paraca all speak Greek is contextualised within a description of exotic features of these same inhabitants:

> [T]hey saw a young man running towards them, blacker than any Indian, but with a crescent-shaped mark gleaming on his forehead ... The Indian also carried a golden anchor, they say, which is a customary symbol of messengers in India since it "secures" everything. He ran up to Apollonius and greeted him in Greek, which was not in itself surprising since everybody in the village talked Greek.

Just as Phraotes, the Paracans and the Brahmins may speak Greek, but refuse to be identified as Greeks and reject Greek wisdom. When, for instance, Apollonius assumes that Iarchas, the head of the Brahmins, "would think self-knowledge something hard to achieve" just as the Greeks do (3.18), Iarchas responds that self-knowledge is, instead, the basis of the wisdom of the Indian sages. Moreover, Iarchas engages in cultural competition by comparing his own former body, which he identifies with the Indian king Ganges, to that of Achilles. The comparison turns out favourable for Iarchas/Ganges as he, unlike the Greek hero, founded cities rather than destroying them—and, as Iarchas adds, "there is nobody who thinks sacking cities is more glorious than building them" (3.20). In short, true wisdom is Indian wisdom—even if that wisdom unmistakably exhibits traits of Greek knowledge.[17]

This ambiguous characterisation of India and its inhabitants reflects a broader issue: the wisdom of the Indians is not merely Indian wisdom, but incorporates the knowledge of other peoples. The cult of the Brahmins, for instance, is an intricate assemblage of Greek, Egyptian, and Indian gods (3.14). And in 3.20, Iarchas informs Apollonius that the Ethiopians used to live in India and so presents the wisdom of the Indian sages as the basis for that of the Ethiopians. The repeated references to the Indians "living on the earth and not on it, walled without walls, owning nothing and owning everything" (3.15) or being gods (3.18) and their wisdom as showing those who obtain it "a path

---

16 Even if this Greece is located at the end of the known world. On centre and periphery in Philostratus see Abraham, "Geography of Culture."

17 Cf. Whitmarsh's remark that "the *narration* of space [in *Life*] is filtered through the archival resources of the Greek literary tradition ... [T]here is a recurrent ethnocentrism in the description of non-Greek spaces, which requires that the narrator should measure exotic features and architecture against criteria drawn from, if not always Greece itself, then the world familiar to the Greeks" ("Philostratus," 468; italics original).

through heaven" (3.51) also emphasises that the wisdom of the Indians encompasses the entire earth and goes beyond it. Thus, the Indians in Philostratus's account assume a glocal shape. They remain Indians, but not straightforwardly so: their wisdom, and hence their cultural affiliations, transcend clear ethnic denominators such as "Indian" or "Greek," as the Indians incorporate all kinds of knowledge in a global mélange. On this perspective, it is not surprising that the Indian sages are familiar with the best that Greek wisdom has on offer and yet do not identify their knowledge as Greek per se. Their ability to speak Greek, for instance, is less a sign of their Greek character than of their universal, or glocalised, wisdom.[18]

This glocalised portrayal of India contrasts somewhat with how Philostratus characterises Apollonius in *Vit. Apoll.* 3. During his stay with the Brahmins, Apollonius is repeatedly portrayed as a "Greek" who espouses Greek knowledge. When arriving in Paraca, Apollonius is greeted in Greek by an inhabitant of the city and takes the language this Indian uses to reflect his Pythagorean inclinations; as a result, he follows his guide joyfully, expecting to acquire profounder *Greek* wisdom from the Indian wise men than he had ever found elsewhere. As soon as Apollonius enters into conversation with Iarchas and the other Brahmins, however, it becomes clear that the wisdom of the Indian sages is not Greek wisdom: Iarchas refutes the Greek claim that self-knowledge is difficult, telling Apollonius instead that "we know everything because we begin by knowing ourselves. None of us would embark on this kind of philosophy without first knowing himself" (3.18). Similarly, Iarchas criticizes Greek views of righteousness (3.25)[19] and speaks ill of the Greek fascination with heroes recorded in the *Iliad* and the *Odyssey*. As we have just seen, Iarchas, taking Achilles as a prime example of the Greek heroes, sings the praise of the Indian king Ganges, who founded rather than destroyed cities (3.20). To drive his point home, Iarchas points Apollonius to an Indian young man who has every ability to become a good philosopher, and "yet with these gifts he is an enemy of philosophy" (3.22). The reason is that he is an incarnation of Palamedes, one of the Greek heroes that fought against Troy and the one who cunningly forced Odysseus to join the Greek expedition against Troy, who found his death after

---

18   This is evident from the passage in 3.26–33, where Apollonius can talk to the king of Paraca only with the help of a translator. Apparently this king, whom Philostratus denounces as having no philosophical inclination, did not speak Greek, whereas (most of) the other individuals Apollonius encounters on his journeys do.

19   Erkki Koskenniemi's remark that righteousness is "dealt with in III 24–25 and VI 21" ("The Philostratean Apollonius as a Teacher," in *Theios Sophistes: Essays on Flavius Philostratus' Vita Apollonii*, ed. Kristoffel Demoen and Danny Praet, MnS 305 [Leiden: Brill, 2009], 321–34 [333]) obscures the fact that Iarchas *criticises* the Greek point of view.

Odysseus took revenge, and is famously absent from the *Iliad*. For that reason, says Iarchas, "his two greatest enemies are Odysseus and Homer ... The wisdom he had brought him no advantage, he got no praise from Homer ... and he fell victim to Odysseus despite having done him no wrong. So he is an enemy of philosophy and bewails his ill-treatment" (3.22). With this example, Iarchas shows how two embodiments of Greek wisdom—Odysseus as a symbol of Greek cunning and the *Iliad* as a basis for Greek education and cultural memory[20]—can, in fact, hinder those with a talent for philosophy from acquiring wisdom.

This portrayal of Apollonius as a Greek fits in with his presentation in the first chapters of the *Life* as a perfect embodiment of philosophy and Greekness, who surpasses even his teacher Pythagoras (1.2) and is repeatedly called a "divine man" (θεῖος ἀνήρ).[21] Yet it seems that in *Life* 2 and 3, Philostratus depicts Apollonius as a Greek only to criticize Greek wisdom, contrasting it with the universal knowledge of the Indians.[22] Staying with the Brahmins, Apollonius

---

20   On which see Henri I. Marrou, *A History of Education in Antiquity*, trans. George Lamb (London: Sheed and Ward, 1956), 162–63; Willem J. Verdenius, *Homer, the Educator of the Greeks*, MKNAWL 33/5 (Amsterdam: North-Holland, 1970); Teresa Morgan, *Literate Education in the Hellenistic and Roman Worlds*, CCS (Cambridge: Cambridge University Press, 1998; repr., 2000); Raffaella Cribiore, *Gymnastics of the Mind: Greek Education in Hellenistic and Roman Egypt* (Princeton: Princeton University Press, 2001), 194–97.

21   See *Vit. Apoll.* 2.17 ("a man who was a Greek and divine"), 2.40.

22   Cf. Janet Downie, "Palamedes and the Wisdom of India in Philostratus' *Life of Apollonius of Tyana*," *Mouseion* 13 (2016): 65–83, who argues convincingly that "one of the central concerns of the *Life of Apollonius* [is]: what is the nature and value of Hellenism in a cosmopolitan, imperial world?" and writes: "Apollonius' encounter with Palamedes in India situates Greek *paideia* in the context of a wider geography of wisdom and exposes it to critique. In the story of Palamedes' tumulus, Philostratus explores the possibility of revising Hellenic cultural memory" (both quotations from the summary at 65). For Downie, Philostratus's reference to Palamedes in 3.22 offers a critique of Greek cultural memory, shaped to a large extent by the *Iliad*, and invites Philostratus to adopt a more cosmopolitan outlook—which he does when he restores the cult of Palamedes in *Vit. Apoll.* 4.

        Downie's reading of *Life* contrasts with that of scholars who hold that in his representation of India Philostratus defends rather than criticises Greek wisdom. As one example of this view see Roshan Abraham, "Magic and Religious Authority in Philostratus' *Life of Apollonius of Tyana*" (PhD diss., University of Pennsylvania, 2009), 34, https://repository.upenn.edu/dissertations/AAI3363239/ (last accessed 21 October, 2019): "Apollonius becomes an arch-Hellenist during his stay in Paraca, where Greek culture is preserved, unaltered and undefiled by the realities of the Roman Empire ... Philostratus transforms the Indian land into a Greek utopia both temporally, by harkening to the culture and religion of the Hellenistic past, and spatially, through his descriptions of the land and the city itself." Similarly also Koskenniemi, "The Philostratean Apollonius."

        It seems to me that the very categories "Greek" and "Indian" are being problematised in Philostratus's *Life*. So even if we conclude that Philostratus promotes "Greek culture,"

undergoes a transformation from a Greek to a more cosmopolitan sage.[23] This transformation begins with Iarchas telling that Apollonius's Greek wisdom is worthwhile, but still lacking (3.16):

> In amazement Apollonius asked [Iarchas] how he knew, and he replied, "You have come with a part of this wisdom, but not of all" (καὶ σὺ μέτο-χος, ἔφη, τῆς σοφίας ταύτης ἥκεις, ἀλλ' οὔπω πάσης). "Will you let me learn it all, then?" (διδάξῃ οὖν με, ἔφη, τὴν σοφίαν πᾶσαν) Apollonius asked. "Unstintingly," Iarchas replied.

An allusion to this conversation occurs in 3.50, where Philostratus writes that Apollonius only leaves the Brahmins after having acquired "all their doctrines, both avowed and secret" (λόγους φανερούς τε καὶ ἀπορρήτους πάντας).[24] In the letter that accompanies the camels Apollonius sends back to Iarchas (3.51), Apollonius testifies again to his transformation by stressing the universal appeal of the wisdom of the Indians ("you also shared your special wisdom with me, and showed me a path through heaven") and implying the difference

---

this culture assumes a notably cosmopolitan shape and incorporates the wisdom of many other groups besides the Greeks. I also take this to be the import of the statement "to a wise man Greece is everywhere, and he will not consider or believe any place to be deserted or uncivilized" (Philostratus, *Vit. Apoll.* 1.35). Cf. Adam Kemezis's observation on the paradoxical nature of Philostratus's Hellenic wisdom: "For all their remoteness ..., it is in these locales that Apollonius will encounter the wisdom of the Indians, which he embraces as the truest and, paradoxically, the most Hellenic" (*Greek Narratives of the Roman Empire under the Severans: Cassius Dio, Philostratus and Herodian* [Cambridge: Cambridge University Press, 2014], 169). Cf. also Jaap-Jan Flinterman's remark that Greekness, for Philostratus, "more or less coincides with wisdom or a philosophical frame of mind" and hence "is neither exclusively nor primarily a racial category, but a moral and cultural one" (*Power, Paideia & Pythagoreanism: Greek Identity, Conceptions of the Relationship between Philosophers and Monarchs and Political Ideals in Philostratus' Life of Apollonius* [Amsterdam: J.C. Gieben, 1995], 91).

23   I do not discuss the visit of the king of Paraca here (see 3.26–33). During this visit, Iarchas presents Apollonius as a Greek (3.28), but in this case Apollonius's Greekness is a sign of his wisdom in comparison to the folly of the visiting king (cf. 3.23: "And Iarchas replied: 'Let [the king] come, for he too will go away all the better for making the acquaintance of a man of Hellas'."). The point of the story seems to be that due to his Greek wisdom Apollonius surpasses the king; yet it is not yet full wisdom as the Indians possess it.

24   Translation slightly adapted. LCL has "all sorts of lore both profane and mysterious," but in my impression the point is that Apollonius makes all the knowledge of the Indians his own rather than that he is confronted with a wide variety of knowledge. Cf. the Dutch translation by Simone Mooij-Valk, *Philostratus: Het leven van Apollonius van Tyana* (Amsterdam: Athenaeum—Polak & Van Gennip, 2013): "[H]ij maakte zich alle wijsheid eigen, openbare en geheime" (135).

between this universal wisdom and Greek knowledge ("I will recall all this to
the Greeks"). In the remainder of the *Life*, Apollonius represents this ideal of
glocalised wisdom, in which the traditions of various peoples interact.[25] In
4.16, for instance, Apollonius tells his followers how he used Indian prayers to
approach Achilles.[26] And in 4.7, Apollonius compares Pheidias's statue of Zeus
and Homer's depiction of the Greek god in order to praise the wisdom of travellers that acquaint themselves with the wisdom of many cultures:

> Seeing how eagerly the Smyrneans pursued every kind of knowledge, he
> encouraged them and added to their eagerness. They must put more pride
> in themselves, he told them, than in the appearance of their city; even if
> it was the most beautiful beneath the sun, with the sea at its command
> and always supplied with a west wind, still it had a pleasanter crown in
> its true men than in its colonnades, pictures, and excess of gold. Buildings
> stayed in one place, never seen anywhere except in the part of the world
> where they were, while good men were seen everywhere and spoken of
> everywhere, and they made the city of their origin larger in proportion
> to the number of them that could travel the world. Cities as beautiful as
> this one, he said, were like the statue of Zeus made by Phidias at Olympia.
> It was seated where the artist wished, whereas good men went every-
> where, and were no different from Homer's Zeus, who in his many forms
> is a more marvelous creation of Homer than the ivory Zeus, for this Zeus

---

25   As Eshleman aptly notes: "These claims anchor Apollonius's authority for the rest of
      the work: his unique blend of Greek paideia with esoteric Indian wisdom equips him to
      correct the teachings, customs, and religious practices of everyone else he encounters,
      whether Greek, Roman, or barbarian" ("Indian Travel," 186). See also Elsner, "Hagiographic
      Geography," 29–30 (and cf. more broadly 28–32): "Philostratus uses the travels as a reflec-
      tion of Apollonius' spiritual progress. Here the very range of ethnographic topoi experi-
      enced by the sage suggests the depth and universality of wisdom which is mastered
      and with which he is equipped to teach … While the journey to India takes Apollonius to
      self-knowledge and full philosophic maturity, the trip to Egypt … is the occasion for his
      demonstration of mastery."
26   Downie, "Palamedes and the Wisdom of India" describes the implications of this refer-
      ence to Indian customs: "The encounter with Achilles that leads to the restoration of
      Palamedes' cult site, then, depends upon the wisdom that Apollonius has gained from his
      encounter with the Indian sages. His conversation with the revenant hero follows (and
      parodies) the pattern of traditional Greek *Homerkritik*, in which Palamedes' absence was
      a long established *topos*. However, in his description of his ritual actions at Achilles' tu-
      mulus, Apollonius makes it clear that he engages with the heroes not simply according
      to the forms of Greek culture but also with a broader view: his perspective on the Greek
      tradition has changed since his visit to India" (80).

was visible on earth, while the other could be sensed in every corner of the universe.

In Philostratus's account, therefore, the sacred space that houses the Indian sages acquires a transformative potential. It is on this hill that Apollonius encounters the zenith of wisdom and learns about the partiality of the Greek wisdom with which he had been familiar. As a result, he transforms from a Greek to a glocalised sage, whose wisdom encompasses and incorporates that of other cultures. What is more, Philostratus's depiction of these events seeks to instil a similar glocalised ideal in his readers. As Janet Downie has observed, Philostratus's portrayal of Apollonius's journeys invites his readers "at every turn to weigh Apollonius' claims to wisdom against those of his interlocutors."[27] By so doing, the episode reviewed here invites Philostratus's readers to undergo a transformation similar to Apollonius's and to embrace a glocalised ideal of wisdom.

3   Paul at the Areopagus

As we turn to Luke's portrayal of Paul in Acts 17:16–34, we find a similar dynamics at play. Here, however, it is not the visitor to a sacred space who learns of its global appeal from those who live there. Rather the reverse: when visiting the Areopagus, Paul points out its global appeal to the Athenians. Presenting his message in glocalised terms, Paul encourages his Epicurean and Stoic interlocutors to accept the God he proclaims.

The peg for Paul's exposition is the altar devoted to an unknown god, which Paul encountered in Athens (17:23[28]). Praising this altar as a sign of the Athenians' religiosity (17:22), Paul claims that the unknown god the Athenians revere is, in fact, the God of the Judaeans, who "now ... commands all people everywhere to repent" (τὰ νῦν παραγγέλλει τοῖς ἀνθρώποις πάντας πανταχοῦ μετανοεῖν) and will judge the entire world (οἰκουμένη) through Jesus (17:31).[29] In his speech Paul adopts a universal tone, incorporating the local aspects of his arguments (his god being the God of the Judaeans who revealed himself in Jesus Christ) with claims about all of humankind. In so doing, he appropriates

---

27   "Palamedes and the Wisdom of India," 72.

28   References in this section are to the book of Acts. Translations follow the ESV.

29   On the "unknown god" see Pieter W. van der Horst, "The Altar of the 'Unknown God' in Athens (Acts 17.23) and the Cults of 'Unknown Gods' in the Graeco-Roman World," in *Hellenism—Judaism—Christianity: Essays on Their Interaction* (Kampen: Kok Pharos, 1994), 165–202 (with references).

Greek and Stoic traditions. To begin with, Paul famously quotes the fifth line of Aratus's *Phaenomena* (17:28) to argue that God is the source of all life on earth. The Aratus quotation puts Paul's earlier comments on the omnipresent God of the Judaeans in perspective: by claiming that the god Paul proclaims is "the God who made the world and everything in it" (ὁ θεὸς ὁ ποιήσας τὸν κόσμον καὶ πάντα τὰ ἐν αὐτῷ; 17:24) and "made from one man every nation of mankind to live on all the face of the earth" (ἐποίησέν τε ἐξ ἑνὸς πᾶν ἔθνος ἀνθρώπων κατοικεῖν ἐπὶ παντὸς προσώπου τῆς γῆς; 17:26) and by subsequently quoting Aratus, Luke subtly equates the Judaean God with Zeus as Aratus describes him. Moreover, when he speaks about the final judgement in 17:31, Paul's use of *oikoumene* is reminiscent of the cosmopolitan ideals propagated by Stoics in the Roman period.[30] Paul's twist is that he portrays the inhabitants of this *oikoumene* as originating from one God—that of the Judaeans—who will judge the *oikoumene* at his time.

By incorporating Greek and Stoic knowledge in his message, Luke's Paul provides his interlocutors with a message similar to the one Iarchas delivered to Apollonius: you are indeed wise, but your wisdom remains lacking. Paul's message, like Iarchas's, presents glocalised knowledge, which incorporates the claims of various groups.[31] Thus, instead of a "new teaching" (ἡ καινὴ αὕτη ... διδαχή), "strange things" (ξενίζοντα ... τινα), or "foreign divinities" (ξένων δαιμονίων),[32] Paul presents the Athenians with knowledge that surpasses their Greek wisdom by being more universal. The purpose of Paul's speech is similar to that of Iarchas's conversations with Apollonius: the Athenians are called to transform their particular Greek convictions and integrate them within the global message Paul presents.

---

30   On the intellectual background of Paul's speech see David L. Balch, "The Areopagus Speech: An Appeal to the Stoic Historian Posidonius against Later Stoics and the Epicureans," in *Greeks, Romans, and Christians: Essays in Honor of Abraham J. Malherbe*, ed. David L. Balch, Everett Ferguson, and Wayne A. Meeks (Minneapolis: Fortress, 1990), 52–79; J. Daryl Charles, "Engaging the (Neo)Pagan Mind: Paul's Encounter with Athenian Culture as a Model for Cultural Apologetics (Acts 17:16–34)," *Trinity Journal* 16 (1995): 47–62 (54–60).

31   I pay less attention to the Judaean elements in the message Luke's Paul proclaims at the Areopagus. These find expression not just in what Paul says about the God he proclaims, but also in how he says it. On intertextual connections between the Areopagus episode and the Jewish Scriptures see Kenneth D. Litwak, "Israel's Prophets Meet Athens' Philosophers: Scriptural Echoes in Acts 17,22–31," *Bib* 85 (2004): 199–216.

32   17:18–19.

The glocal outlook of Acts 17 corresponds with the remainder of the book of Acts.[33] The universal scope of the book is evident already in 1:8, where Jesus tells his disciples: "[Y]ou will be my witnesses in Jerusalem and in all Judea and Samaria, and to the end of the earth (ἕως ἐσχάτου τῆς γῆς)." The reference to the "end of the earth" may carry a double entendre: it refers both to the global scope of the message of the risen Christ and to the end of time which Luke expected in the near future.[34] Yet this universal ideal does not negate local customs. The story of Pentecost demonstrates this: rather than all learning to speak in the same language, Judaeans from various regions all hear the same universal message in their local language (2:1–13). This glocal perspective pervades the book of Acts: in each place where the message is proclaimed, Luke's Paul finds words fitting to the occasion, sometimes stressing his Judaean ancestry (e.g., Acts 21:37–40), sometimes calling attention to his Roman citizenship (e.g., Acts 22:22–29), sometimes (as in Acts 17) presenting himself in the guise of a Greek philosopher.[35] Thus, Acts presents Paul as an individual at home at the crossroads of cultures,[36] and his message as glocalised wisdom that incorporates Judaean, Roman, Greek, and presumably other traditions into a universal whole.

In sum, Paul's presentation of the message of Christ at the Areopagus reflects the circumstances in which Paul speaks and addresses his audience in terms familiar to them. Incorporating Greek knowledge within a universal argument, Paul seeks to confront the Stoics and Epicureans with the partiality of their knowledge: their views may contain much wisdom, but are not complete unless these Stoics and Epicureans embrace Paul's global message. Just as the hill near Paraca described by Philostratus, therefore, the Areopagus in Luke's account becomes a place of transformation from wisdom attached to

33   On Acts's universalistic agenda see Ben Witherington III, *The Acts of the Apostles: A Socio-Rhetorical Commentary* (Grand Rapids: Eerdmans; Carlisle, PA: Paternoster, 1998), 68–76 and *passim* (also *ad* 17:16–34); also Daniel Marguerat, *The First Christian Historian: Writing the 'Acts of the Apostles'*, SNTSMS 121 (Cambridge: Cambridge University Press, 2004 [French original 1999]), 231–56.

34   On the central position of 1:8 within the narrative structure of Acts see Marguerat, *The First Christian Historian*, 49, 93. Note that for Marguerat Acts provides an open ending: "Rome did not coincide with the ἔσχατον τῆς γῆς (the end of the earth) of Acts 1. 8 and the programme of the resurrected Jesus was not accomplished at 28. 31" (208).

35   On Luke's Socratic presentation of Paul in the Areopagus episode see Eckhard Plümacher, *Lukas als hellenistischer Schriftsteller: Studien zur Apostelgeschichte* (Göttingen: Vandenhoeck & Ruprecht, 1972), 19; Dean Zweck, "The *Exordium* of the Areopagus Speech, Acts 17.22, 23," NTS 35 (1989): 94–103 (103): "[Paul] is portrayed in a Socratic role."

36   Cf. Kathy Ehrensperger, *Paul at the Crossroads of Cultures: Theologizing in the Space Between*, LNTS 456 (London: T&T Clark, 2013).

a local cultural identity to a glocalised and universal kind of wisdom that is the basis of a cultural identity as a global mélange, as it incorporates a wide range of local traditions. Yet whereas in Philostratus's story the visitor—i.e., Apollonius—undergoes the transformation, in Acts it is those who are at home at the Areopagus whom Paul encourages to be transformed—though seemingly with little success, as only some of his listeners (τινὲς δὲ ἄνδρες; 17:34) embraced his message.

4   Conclusion

Apollonius's visit to the Indian sages near Paraca and Paul's visit to and speech on the Areopagus turn sacred spaces into loci of transformation. What is at stake is the scope of knowledge to which these spaces give access; and, by implication, the cultural and religious identities of their visitors and inhabitants. When he arrives in India, Apollonius is depicted as a Greek and in conversations with the Indian sages he consistently represents and defends the Greek point of view. Yet as he is exposed to the glocalised wisdom of the Indians—which includes many Greek elements, but is never explicitly referred to as "Greek"—Apollonius's own knowledge takes on a more universal shape. Thus, Philostratus's Apollonius embodies a cosmopolitan, rather than a straightforwardly Greek, ideal. In Acts 17, Paul challenges the particularly Greek knowledge of the Stoics and Epicureans by presenting them with the message of Christ in glocal terms. This message of Christ, Paul makes clear, incorporates Greek statements about their gods (Aratus) as well as the Stoic cosmopolitan ideal and integrates these within Judaean views on God. By so presenting his case, Paul aims to bring about a transformation amongst his hearers and convince them to accept his message.

The results of this study and the theoretical framework it adopts challenge the distinction between "Judaean," "Christian," "Greek," and other groups and the apologetic readings that imply such distinctions.[37] For Luke's Paul, Stoic philosophy and the message of Christ are compatible within the framework of a glocalised body of knowledge. The point here is not that by integrating some aspects of Greek philosophy Paul wishes to show its lack of validity in favour of "Christianity,"[38] but rather that the message of Christ as Luke's Paul

---

37   For another challenge of apologetic readings of Philostratus, though from a different angle, see Kemezis, *Greek Narratives of the Roman Empire under the Severans*, 160–64.

38   This is sometimes the tenor in studies that take the Areopagus episode as a blueprint for missionary endeavours. See, e.g., Dean Flemming, "Contextualizing the Gospel in Athens:

formulates it is a multi-layered and context-dependent global mélange that takes up elements from a wide range of other traditions in the Roman empire without implying that these other traditions have become invalid with the advent of Christianity, even if they have now been revealed to provide only partial wisdom.

Acknowledgments

I am grateful to the participants in the Jewish and Christian Perspectives conference and the members of the Graeco-Roman Society and the New Testament group in the European Association of Biblical Studies for their feedback on presentations in Jerusalem and Helsinki.

References

Abraham, Roshan. "Magic and Religious Authority in Philostratus' *Life of Apollonius of Tyana*." PhD diss., University of Pennsylvania, 2009. https://repository.upenn.edu/dissertations/AAI3363239.

Abraham, Roshan. "The Geography of Culture in Philostratus' *Life of Apollonius of Tyana*." *CJ* 109 (2014): 465–80.

Alexander, Loveday. "Mapping Early Christianity: Acts and the Shape of Early Church History." *Interpretation* 57 (2001): 163–73.

Alexander, Philip S. "Jerusalem as the Omphalos of the World: On the History of a Geographical Concept." *Judaism* 46 (1997): 147–58.

Balch, David L. "The Areopagus Speech: An Appeal to the Stoic Historian Posidonius against Later Stoics and the Epicureans." Pages 52–79 in *Greeks, Romans, and*

Paul's Areopagus Address as a Paradigm for Missionary Communication," *Missiology* 30 (2002): 199–214. My problem with this approach is that it implies a fixed "gospel" which must be "contextualised." I would argue that Acts presents us with a gospel that includes certain local claims (e.g., Jesus's resurrection), but is at the same time of a thoroughly translocal and context-dependent nature. Hence, the gospel and its context merge: every formulation of the gospel is a contextualised one. Cf. Loveday Alexander's conclusion that "wherever we can get behind these later models [of the church], we see the first-century church as much more fluid, more open to local variation, and harder to configure in terms of an overarching global or regional structure" ("Mapping Early Christianity: Acts and the Shape of Early Church History," *Interpretation* 57 [2001]: 163–73 [172]). Alexander quotes Wayne A. Meeks, *The First Urban Christians* (New Haven: Yale University Press, 1983), 139 with agreement; see also more recently Joshua W. Jipp, "Paul's Areopagus Speech of Acts 17:16–34 as Both Critique and Propaganda," *JBL* 131 (2012): 567–88.

Christians: Essays in Honor of Abraham J. Malherbe. Edited by David L. Balch, Everett Ferguson, and Wayne A. Meeks. Minneapolis: Fortress, 1990.

Charles, J. Daryl. "Engaging the (Neo)Pagan Mind: Paul's Encounter with Athenian Culture as a Model for Cultural Apologetics (Acts 17:16–34)." *Trinity Journal* 16 (1995): 47–62.

Cribiore, Raffaella. *Gymnastics of the Mind: Greek Education in Hellenistic and Roman Egypt*. Princeton: Princeton University Press, 2001.

Downie, Janet. "Palamedes and the Wisdom of India in Philostratus' *Life of Apollonius of Tyana*." *Mouseion* 13 (2016): 65–83.

Ehrensperger, Kathy. *Paul at the Crossroads of Cultures: Theologizing in the Space Between*. LNTS 456. London: T&T Clark, 2013.

Elsner, John. "Hagiographic Geography: Travel and Allegory in the *Life of Apollonius of Tyana*." *JHS* 117 (1997): 22–37.

Eshleman, Kendra. "Indian Travel and Cultural Self-Location in the *Life of Apollonius and the Acts of Thomas*." Pages 183–201 in *Journeys in the Roman East: Imagined and Real*. Edited by Maren R. Niehoff. CRPG 1 (Tübingen: Mohr Siebeck, 2017).

Flemming, Dean. "Contextualizing the Gospel in Athens: Paul's Areopagus Address as a Paradigm for Missionary Communication." *Missiology* 30 (2002): 199–214.

Flinterman, Jaap-Jan. *Power, Paideia & Pythagoreanism: Greek Identity, Conceptions of the Relationship between Philosophers and Monarchs and Political Ideals in Philostratus' Life of Apollonius*. Amsterdam: J.C. Gieben, 1995.

Gardner, Andrew. "Thinking about Roman Imperialism: Postcolonialism, Globalisation and Beyond?" *Britannia* 44 (2013): 1–25.

Hartog, Pieter B. *Pesher and Hypomnema: A Comparison of Two Commentary Traditions from the Hellenistic-Roman World*. STDJ 121. Leiden: Brill, 2017.

Hartog, Pieter B. "Jubilees and Hellenistic Encyclopaedism." *JSJ* 50 (2019): 1–25.

Hartog, Pieter B. "Contesting *Oikoumenē*: Resistance and Locality in Philo's *Legatio ad Gaium*." Pages 205–31 in *Intolerance, Polemics, and Debate in Antiquity: Politico-Cultural, Philosophical, and Religious Forms of Critical Conversation*. Edited by George van Kooten and Jacques T.A.G.M. van Ruiten. TBN 25. Leiden: Brill, 2019.

Harvey, David. *The Condition of Postmodernity: An Enquiry into the Origins of Cultural Change*. Cambridge: Blackwell, 1990.

Hingley, Richard. *Globalizing Roman Culture: Unity, Diversity and Empire*. London: Routledge, 2005.

Hodos, Tamar, ed. *The Routledge Handbook of Globalization and Archaeology*. London: Routledge, 2017.

Horst, Pieter W. van der. "The Altar of the 'Unknown God' in Athens (Acts 17.23) and the Cults of 'Unknown Gods' in the Graeco-Roman World." Pages 165–202 in *Hellenism—Judaism—Christianity: Essays on Their Interaction*. Kampen: Kok Pharos, 1994.

Jipp, Joshua W. "Paul's Areopagus Speech of Acts 17:16–34 as Both Critique and Propaganda." *JBL* 131 (2012): 567–88.

Jones, Christopher P. "Apollonius of Tyana's Passage to India." *GRBS* 42 (2001): 185–99.

Kemezis, Adam. *Greek Narratives of the Roman Empire under the Severans: Cassius Dio, Philostratus and Herodian.* Cambridge: Cambridge University Press, 2014.

König, Jason, and Greg Woolf, eds. *Encyclopaedism from Antiquity and the Renaissance.* Cambridge: Cambridge University Press, 2013.

Koskenniemi, Erkki. "The Philostratean Apollonius as a Teacher." Pages 321–34 in *Theios Sophistes: Essays on Flavius Philostratus' Vita Apollonii.* Edited by Kristoffel Demoen and Danny Praet. MnS 305. Leiden: Brill, 2009.

Litwak, Kenneth D. "Israel's Prophets Meet Athens' Philosophers: Scriptural Echoes in Acts 17,22–31." *Bib* 85 (2004): 199–216.

Luke, Timothy W. "Identity, Meaning and Globalization: Detraditionalization in Postmodern Space-Time Compression." Pages 109–33 in *Detraditionalization: Critical Reflections on Authority and Identity.* Edited by Paul Heelas, Scott Lash, and Paul Morris. Cambridge: Blackwell, 1996.

Marguerat, Daniel. *The First Christian Historian: Writing the 'Acts of the Apostles'.* SNTSMS 121. Cambridge: Cambridge University Press, 2004. French original 1999.

Marrou, Henri I. *A History of Education in Antiquity.* Translated by George Lamb. London: Sheed and Ward, 1956.

Massey, Doreen. *Space, Place and Gender.* Cambridge: Polity, 1994.

Meeks, Wayne A. *The First Urban Christians.* New Haven: Yale University Press, 1983.

Mooij-Valk, Simone. *Philostratus: Het leven van Apollonius van Tyana.* Amsterdam: Athenaeum—Polak & Van Gennip, 2013.

Morgan, Teresa. *Literate Education in the Hellenistic and Roman Worlds.* CCS. Cambridge: Cambridge University Press, 1998. Repr., 2000.

Nederveen Pieterse, Jan. *Globalization and Culture: Global Mélange.* 3rd ed. Lanham, MD: Rowman & Littlefield, 2016.

Pitts, Martin, and Miguel John Versluys. "Globalisation and the Roman World: Perspectives and Opportunities." Pages 3–31 in *Globalisation and the Roman World: World History, Connectivity and Material Culture.* Edited by Martin Pitts and Miguel John Versluys. Cambridge: Cambridge University Press, 2015.

Platt, Verity. "Virtual Visions: *Phantasia* and the Perception of the Divine in *The Life of Apollonius of Tyana.*" Pages 131–54 in *Philostratus.* Edited by Ewen Bowie and Jaś Elsner. GCRW. Cambridge: Cambridge University Press, 2009.

Plümacher, Eckhard. *Lukas als hellenistischer Schriftsteller: Studien zur Apostelgeschichte.* Göttingen: Vandenhoeck & Ruprecht, 1972.

Ritzer, George, and Paul Dean. *Globalization: A Basic Text.* Chicester: Wiley Blackwell, 2015.

Robertson, Roland. *Globalization: Social Theory and Global Culture.* London: Sage, 1992.

Robertson, Roland. "Glocalization: Time-Space and Homogeneity-Heterogeneity." Pages 25–44 in *Global Modernities*. Edited by Mike Featherstone, Scott Lash, and Roland Robertson. TCS. London: Sage, 1995.

Swyndegouw, Erik. "Neither Global nor Local: 'Glocalization' and the Politics of Scale." Pages 137–66 in *Spaces of Globalization: Reasserting the Power of the Local*. Edited by Kevin R. Cox. New York: Guilford Press, 1997.

Verdenius, Willem J. *Homer, the Educator of the Greeks*. MKNAWL 33/5. Amsterdam: North-Holland, 1970.

Versluys, Miguel John. "Isis Capitolina and the Egyptian Cults in Late Republican Rome." Pages 421–88 in *Isis en Occident: Actes du IIème Colloque international sur les études isiaques, Lyon III 16–17 mai 2002*. Edited by Laurent Bricault. RGRW 151. Leiden: Brill, 2004.

Versluys, Miguel John. "Understanding Objects in Motion: An *Archaeological* Dialogue on Romanization." *Archaeological Dialogues* 21 (2014): 1–20.

Warf, Barney. *Time-Space Compression: Historical Geographies*. Oxford: Routledge, 2008.

Whitmarsh, T.J.G. "Philostratus." Pages 463–79 in *Space in Ancient Greek Literature*. Edited by Irene J.F. de Jong. MnS 339. Leiden: Brill, 2012.

Witcher, Robert. "Globalisation and Roman Imperialism: Perspectives on Identities in Roman Italy." Pages 213–25 in *The Emergence of State Identities in Italy in the First Millennium BC*. Edited by Edward Herring and Kathryn Lomas. London: Accordia Research Institute, 2000.

Witherington III, Ben. *The Acts of the Apostles: A Socio-Rhetorical Commentary*. Grand Rapids: Eerdmans; Carlisle, PA: Paternoster, 1998.

Zweck, Dean. "The Exordium of the Areopagus Speech, Acts 17.22, 23." NTS 35 (1989): 94–103.

CHAPTER 8

"Holy Mokum"—a Case Study: the Dynamics of Sacred Place at Kastanjeplein, Amsterdam on National Remembrance Day

Willem Jan de Hek

Every year on National Remembrance Day[1] a public ritual takes place in the heart of the Oosterpark neighborhood in Amsterdam. Since 2012 this ritual has annually been designed and organized for this particular location and its historical context. The organizer, local artist Ida van der Lee, has ambitious plans with it. During the Second World War, 2,800 Jewish citizens were deported from the neighborhood to internment camps and never came back. Van der Lee is seeking reconciliation with this terrible past by orchestrating a commemoration ritual that allows residents of the area to "bring them back" personally and one by one.[2] The ritual takes place annually at Kastanjeplein, a public square hidden in this quiet neighborhood and named after its chestnut trees. On an average weekday one can see some elderly people sitting on a bench and a few kids playing on the square. But on this particular day of the year, the area takes on a totally different appearance as a public ritual unfolds, and passers-by are invited to participate. As I enrolled myself for the ritual on 4 May 2018, one of the hosts told me from her experience how the atmosphere at the square changes dramatically every year "from just ordinary to almost sacred."

The event attracted my attention since Kastanjeplein is part of an urban area that I have been researching for some time now.[3] Having been educated as both an architect and a theologian, I am searching for sacredness in public

---

1   This day on 4 May is set apart in the Netherlands to commemorate all Dutch civilians (and soldiers) who have died in wars since the Second World War. The official text of the Memorandum for Remembrance Day on 4 May states: "During the national commemoration of Remembrance Day we remember all Dutch victims—civilians and soldiers—who have been killed or murdered in the Kingdom of the Netherlands or anywhere else in the world in war situations or during peacekeeping operations since the outbreak of the Second World War." See https://www.4en5mei.nl/english/4-may.

2   For more information on this event, named "Commemorating Names and Numbers," including a video impression, see http://namenennummers.eu.

3   Parts of this research project, including method and data analysis, were presented at the World Congress of the International Union of Architects in Seoul, South Korea. See Willem

environments, asking questions like: How, where and when do citizens of late-modern western cities experience the sacred? And what exactly makes a place a sacred place? In this contribution I will use the public ritual at Kastanjeplein as a case study to illustrate how sacredness can be seen as a dynamic concept. My main aim is to show that sacredness in fact happens—and that it can happen everywhere and at any moment. Such a dynamic understanding of the concept of sacredness fits well within our late-modern western world: a society that can best be characterized as fluid,[4] which also means that the boundaries between the sacred and the profane are porous.

Sensing the sacred in our everyday world is related to the experience of emotive human desires being fulfilled. This particular experience results in the attribution of otherworldly meaning and value to the environment in which the experience happens. Over the course of this article, I will argue that sacredness happens in a dynamic and complex interaction involving two key-elements. On the one hand, the attribution of otherworldly meaning and value to a specific place in the urban environment. On the other hand, the physical encounter with certain situational "typologies of sacred place" in the city. In order to do this, I will first describe the public ritual at Kastanjeplein in greater detail. Second, I will reflect on three notions that play an important part in my argumentation: that of place and place making, sacredness, and city-souls. Third, I will look at the role that desire plays in our confrontation with the urban environment in which we live. I will show how place and place making, city-souls, and desire work together in three distinguishable and overlapping "typologies of sacred place," all recognizable at the square on 4 May. I will end this article with some concluding remarks.

1   Case Study

The case study brings us to a charming square in a relatively peaceful neighborhood in the eastern part of Amsterdam (fig. 8.1). But it has not always been like that. During the Second World War this exact neighborhood was the scene of terrible razzias. From the Kastanjeplein many Jewish children, women and men were deported to the concentration camps. Amsterdam has a well-known Yiddish nickname: Mokum. The word מָקוֹם is used in the Hebrew Bible as a

---

Jan de Hek, "Place-Making in Mokum: Searching for the Souls of Amsterdam" (paper presented at the World Congress of the International Union of Architects, Seoul, 5 September 2017).

4   Zygmunt Bauman, *Liquid Times: Living in an Age of Uncertainty* (Cambridge: Polity, 2007).

FIGURE 8.1   Bird's eye view of the Oosterpark neighborhood looking in a northwestern
direction. Kastanjeplein can be seen in the centre, with Vrolikstraat on the far left
side and the Oosterpark city park on the far right side.

generic word for any place, but also to designate particular sacred places.[5] For
example, in the story of the sacrifice of Isaac, he and his father Abraham followed God's command and walked for three days. Then, Abraham lifted up his
eyes and saw the place (מָקוֹם) far off.[6] Reflecting on Mokum as a nickname
for Amsterdam in light of this story and of what happened during the Second
World War, one is struck by the irony and paradox of this name. Has the city
ever been further away from being a sacred place for its citizens than during
this dark era, which is commemorated annually on 4 May?

When I reach Kastanjeplein at around 3 PM, the square has been set up as a
temporary memorial place. It accommodates a carefully arranged route along
various stages of reflection, contemplation and interaction. A large map made
of wooden planks has been laid out over the square, projecting the Oosterpark
neighborhood. Apart from long wooden planks representing the linear street
pattern, I also see numerous smaller decorated planks with colourful names
on them. One of the hosts explains that these are names of Jewish residents,
deported from the area during the Second World War. They never made it back

---

5   Sunhee Kim, "Sacred Space," in *Lexham Theological Wordbook*, ed. Douglas Mangum et al.
(Bellingham, WA: Lexham Press, 2014).

6   Gen 22:4.

FIGURE 8.2   Participants walk a circular course over the square. The route is indicated by railroad tracks chalked on the street curb, marking the porous border between ritual space in the square and the public area on the city street.

as they were murdered in the concentration camps. Am I willing to commemorate one of them, by participating in a ritual route, the lady asks? I agree to enroll in the ritual, starting with a short briefing in a so-called "time office." Another host-volunteer tells me that I will now step into "*kairos* time," which according to her can be translated as "ritual time." I accept her invitation to enter into another "realm," and the ritual route first brings me to a cabinet.

From a booklet with names of deported Jews, I choose the name of a teenage boy: Jacob Hijman Frank, the youngest son of a family with three children. At one of the long tables further down the ritual route, I decorate a sign and write Jacob's name on it. I am not the only one. Some fellow participants work in silence at the table. It takes some time to finish the nameplate and I muse about who this boy might have been. Would he still be alive if he had not been deported from the area? After finishing my nameplate, I take it with me on a walk following a predetermined circular course over the square. The route is indicated by railroad tracks chalked on the street curb, marking the porous border between the ritual space in the square and the public area on the city-street (fig. 8.2). Several names of internment camps are written on the pavement slabs: Auschwitz, Bergen-Belsen, Theresienstadt. At the end of this pilgrimage I lay the inscribed plank in the map, somewhere along the projected Vrolikstraat. There is violin-playing in the background (fig. 8.3). Then a bell

FIGURE 8.3 A large map of planks is laid out over the square, projecting the street pattern of the neighborhood. Participants lay their decorated plank, with the name of a victim on it, in the map, while a violin plays in the background.

rings and I say out loud: "Jacob, I bring you home."[7] After a moment of silence, suddenly the ritual is over, and I am invited for a cup of tea to share my experiences and thoughts with others: "What do *you* think is ripe for change now?" One of the hosts talks to me about "*kairos* time" again and I start to understand why. Is the basic sense of *kairos* not that this notion points to a decisive or crucial place or point in time, whether spatially, materially or temporally? Rather than being merely "ritual time," *kairos* could also be described as "a decisive moment in time." The ritual seems to be organized in such a way that it ends with a discussion among the participants on issues in our current society that really need change—perhaps even a discussion about our desire for "the good life," for justice in our everyday world, and for reconciliation with the past.

---

7   According to the organizers, the public ritual is designed as a customized experience, in which the participants are invited to personally identify with a Jewish victim. The inner process of commemoration is addressed in different ways. The participants get the time to stand still and let go of the rat-race of city life. They undergo the ritual in several steps, whereby their creativity is addressed and human feelings are touched upon. Writing the name by oneself and using one's creativity to make something beautiful gives the participant the feeling that he or she can really do something for the victims. The attention that is paid to the victim's personal background gives something back to the victim, and by bringing someone symbolically home, the participant takes this unique person into his or her heart. If more and more participants do so, the street monument will grow with more names every year. See http://namenennummers.eu.

2   The Dynamics of Place and Place Making

The first time I walked across Kastanjeplein was in April 2017. I had just started the fieldwork for my research project on urban theology. At its core lay a relatively simple method: a stroll with respondents through the contemporary city of Amsterdam, using a method called "photo-walking with the city." This research method aims to provide an effective way of studying late-modern western cities. The challenge of dealing with these urban environments is often their enormous complexity: they are multicultural, multilayered, multifunctional and so forth. But, according to urban and educational scholars—and some practical theologians now follow in the same line of thinking[8]—simply walking through town can help to get a grip on it. After all, examining the city is also a social matter, since it is related to our experience of participating in daily life. Hence, peer groups could play an important role in perceiving the city and group-interaction is fundamental. The participants in this method will reflect on their urban experiences and bring in several perspectives. Stephen Dobson, who wrote about this method, argues that this strategy of urban exploration goes back to Walter Benjamin. He famously spoke of the *flâneur*: the walker who has time on his hands and who saunters, strolls, wanders and promenades. In doing so, the *flâneur* is able to reap uncharted and unexpected experiences.[9] By combining walking with photography, participants will be even more aware of the urban environments through which they walk, as they are forced to pay extra attention to what they see. This might help to make the familiar unfamiliar, and to reflect on everyday practices and places, since learning can be approached as a process of rethinking the world. Learning happens during an encounter with the world and should be seen as a relational and multidirectional event, where sensing and knowing happens with the human and the non-human world, as stated by Noora Pyyry.[10]

For my fieldwork I asked various peer groups to accompany me on a number of photo-walks in search for sacred places. The walk consisted of a six-kilometer course, whose route was determined by simply drafting a straight line from the Oude Kerk in the inner city of Amsterdam into a southeastern direction. Walking the route exposed the participants to an urban environment that is all about variety and dynamics. The participants walked the

---

8   Elaine Graham and Stephen Lowe, *What Makes A Good City? Public Theology and the Urban Church* (London: Darton, Longman and Todd, 2009), 51–54.

9   Stephen Dobson, "Urban Pedagogy: A Proposal for the Twenty-First Century," *London Review of Education* 4 (2006): 99–114.

10   Noora Pyyry, "Learning with the City via Enchantment: Photo-Walks as Creative Encounters," *Discourse: Studies in the Cultural Politics of Education* 37 (2016): 102–15.

route in three separate stages, with a discussion intermezzo after every leg. The transcriptions of these group-discussions formed the major source for my empirical data-analysis, together with my own memos and the almost 1,000 photographs that were taken by the participants during the walks. These pictures of the urban environment reflect the respondents' understanding of the notions of place making, sacredness and city-souls. What urban environments would they consider "sacred" and why? A particular place along the route that was photographed quite often turned out to be Kastanjeplein. This was an important motivation for me to participate and analyze the public ritual at this square on 4 May.

One of the more general outcomes of my research project[11] has been that place is experienced as a dynamic reality. This idea is strongly supported by recent literature on space and place. Every place is unique. Chinese-American geographer Yi-Fu Tuan, for example, stresses the importance of distinguishing place from space: "What begins as undifferentiated space becomes place as we get to know it better and we start endowing it with value."[12] The work of Tuan and other scholars caused a complete change in the way space and place were conceived in several disciplines, particularly in the humanities—an event that can be summarized as "the spatial turn."[13] It emphasized, as Tim Cresswell has pointed out, that place is not just a thing in the world, but rather a way of understanding the world. We should look at the world as a world of places. Each of these places are worlds of meaning and experience in their own rights.[14] Places are constantly changing, never finished and always becoming.[15] Places are made on a daily basis through people living their everyday life, as Jane Jacobs stated in her groundbreaking study on American cities.[16] Ultimately it is the people—with their unique stories, distastes, desires, relations, histories and faiths—that can make or break a place. Place making indeed is everywhere once you start noticing it. All over the world humans are engaged

<hr>

11 For this article the outcomes of a first round of data-analysis have been used (analyzing the 1,000 photographs taken by my respondents, the annotated group-discussions during the walk and my own memos). A more detailed description of the data-analysis will be published later on.

12 Yi-Fu Tuan, *Space and Place: The Perspective of Experience* (Minneapolis: University of Minnesota Press, 1977), 6.

13 Such as Edward W. Soja, *Thirdspace: Journeys to Los Angeles and Other Real-and-Imagined Places* (Malden, MA: Blackwell, 1996) and Edward S. Casey, *The Fate of Place: A Philosophical History* (Berkeley: University of California, 1998).

14 Tim Cresswell, *Place: An Introduction*, 2nd ed. (Chicester: Wiley Blackwell, 2015), 15–18.

15 Cresswell, *Place*, 71–74.

16 Jane Jacobs, *The Death and Life of Great American Cities* (New York: Random House, 1961), 50–52.

in place making activities—from homeowners who redecorate their houses to city governments that legislate for public buildings.[17] In most cases, their intention is to create a better world for themselves and for their fellow citizens. But what does that better world look like? Obviously, that depends on personality, culture and context. Yet every time someone starts dreaming of a place-as-it-can-be and starts to engage in bringing a certain place-as-it-is towards the place-dreamt-of, it is in fact place making in progress. For example, when a group of people organizes a public ritual at a square somewhere in the city.

3   The Dynamics of Sacredness

At Kastanjeplein the atmosphere changed during the ritual "from just ordinary to almost sacred," according to one of the hosts. But how to understand and value such an observation? The notion of the sacred has been highly debated over time. What definition of this concept fits best with our contemporary context? In a recent study on perceptions of the sacred at a sacred-music festival, Lieke Wijnia states that all theoretical approaches to the notion of the sacred share one common characteristic: a focus on the set-apart. Once non-negotiable or exceptional value is attributed to something, it is set apart and thus can be experienced as sacred. However, this valuation of a particular content is not set in stone: the being set apart can transform over time. Wijnia argues that the sacred needs to be regarded as dynamic—a continuous cycle of attribution and experience. This process of setting apart is not only a physical process, but equally so a mental process. The central role of the set-apart does not concern the things regarded as sacred, but rather the value that is given to these things and the relationship it enables. It is the meaning or the value that is attributed to a thing, a person or an idea, that is non-negotiable or unquestionable.[18]

When exploring how the notion of the sacred has been debated over the last century, Wijnia points to two fundamentally different approaches: one substantive, the other situational.[19] The substantive approach evolves around the question as to whether the sacred is something—a power that manifests itself and has a presence independent of other factors, being a mystery of

---

17   Cresswell, *Place*, 10–12.

18   Lieke Wijnia, "Making Sense Through Music: Perceptions of the Sacred at Festival Musica Sacra Maastricht" (PhD diss., Tilburg University, 2016), 41–42.

19   Wijnia, "Making Sense," 31.

predominantly experiential quality. One can think of Rudolph Otto's "holy,"[20] Gerardus van der Leeuw's "power,"[21] or of Mircea Eliade's "real."[22] The situational (or functional) approach regards the sacred as a concept used to describe the highest and collectively most cherished values within a particular semantic system, and the variety of practices that upholds these valuations and the system in general. The situational analysis can be traced back to the work of Émile Durkheim[23] and has located the sacred at the core of human practices and social projects.

A major difference between these two approaches is described by Arie L. Molendijk, who at the same time points at the interconnectedness between the two approaches:

> One could say that Durkheim, to some extent, substantialized the sacred by attributing "power" to it. The main difference, of course, is that Van der Leeuw and certainly Otto related the power of the sacred to the numinous or the sphere of the gods, whereas Durkheim related it to society and collective ideals. The first viewpoint implies an interest in religious experience or even the numinous itself, whereas the situational view focusses on human activity (ritual) and how place is sacralized.[24]

Molendijk recognizes the crucial position of specific religious experiential qualities when it comes to the notion of the sacred. Yet, he argues that these experiences are the consequences of human actions. It is the question whether this level of religious experience can be or should be conceptualized as independent manifestations, as is done in the substantive approach. This is main reason why Wijnia grants primacy to the situational approach in her study.[25] For my argumentation over the course of this contribution I will follow this line of thought, while briefly coming back to this issue in my concluding remarks.

---

20   Rudolph Otto, *The Idea of the Holy*, trans. John W. Harvey (Oxford: Oxford University Press, 1958).

21   Gerardus van der Leeuw, *Religion in Essence and Manifestation: A Study in Phenomenology* (Princeton: Princeton University Press, 1986).

22   Mircea Eliade, *The Sacred and the Profane: The Nature of Religion*, trans. William R. Trask (Orlando, FL: Harcourt, 1987).

23   Émile Durkheim, *The Elementary Forms of Religious Life*, trans. Karen E. Fields (New York: The Free Press, 1995).

24   Arie L. Molendijk, "The Notion of the 'Sacred,'" in *Holy Ground: Re-Inventing Ritual Space in Modern Western Culture*, ed. Paul Post and Arie L. Molendijk (Leuven: Peeters, 2010), 55–89 (84).

25   Wijnia, "Making Sense," 32.

4   The Dynamics of City-Souls

Before making a start with interpreting the public ritual at Kastanjeplein, we need to look briefly at a third concept that is relevant here, particularly since the ritual is related to a commemorative event. In contemporary urban discourse, more and more attention is being paid to the concept of city-soul. For example, the 2017 World Congress of the International Union of Architects in Seoul, chose "Soul of City" as its general theme. City-soul in this context is often understood as the characteristic identity marker of a particular city or municipality. It is however very much the question whether we can speak of soul (singular) at all when discussing cities. It probably makes much more sense to consequently speak of souls (plural), since contemporary cities consist of a multitude of different cultures.[26] Having said that, the increasing interest in city-souls shows a revival of what Durkheim wrote about the soul.

Durkheim argued that a society is a supra individual force, existing independently of the actors who compose it. Social integration in a society is rooted in a shared moral code that can sustain a harmonious order.[27] And it is exactly the soul that holds this society together. Souls are anonymous forces, essentially unstable and indefinite, changing from moment to moment to suit circumstances. But this does not mean that they are totally immaterial. Since they are holding societies together, souls materialize when a society reunites, assembles or meets at certain times and at certain places.[28] The working definition for "city-souls" that I use in my research project derives from Durkheim's ideas: city-souls are the anonymous forces that hold societies and cultures together, and that are somehow able to materialize in specific places. In the case of the public ritual at Kastanjeplein, one can think for example of a shared history that is commemorated annually, or of shared values in terms of equality and certain ideas about justice. Once these city-souls have materialized one way or the other, people that feel connected to the city or neighborhood could feel touched, possibly resulting in some form of engagement.

---

26   De Hek, "Place-Making."

27   Scott Appelrouth and Laura Desford Edles, *Classical and Contemporary Sociological Theory: Texts and Readings* (Thousand Oaks, CA: Sage, 2008), 85–93.

28   Durkheim, *Elementary Forms*, 22–26 and 242–44.

5   Urban Desires and a Theology of Place

Following the so-called spatial turn over the second half of the 20th century, a lot has been said about the dynamics of sacred place, as is proven by a growing amount of theologies of place that have seen the light.[29] The scope of this article does not allow me to reflect in great detail on these theologies. I will instead focus on one significant element that many of these theologies have in common: the notion of "desire." The American theologian Eric O. Jacobsen, for example, concludes his work on theology of the built environment with the plea for a "geography of rest." He argues that human goodness is rooted in the fact that people are created by a good and loving God. It is specifically the Sabbath that is given to the world as a day to enjoy being part of a good creation. A desire for rest is at the core of our human existence. According to Jacobsen, people can learn how to rest from Sabbath practices, but these lessons can be either supported or contradicted by the built environment that surrounds them.[30] Another theologian who incorporates the notion of "desire" into his theological thinking about the urban environment is Philip Sheldrake. He states that cities are meant to "civilize" us, by teaching us the arts of cooperation and creative living. In his book *The Spiritual City* he writes a chapter on "urban virtues." We can learn to shape our desires. Urban virtues help us to discern between different human desires and make the right choice in striving towards a city in which "the good life" can flourish. At the core of such a spirituality lies the desire for communion with others.[31]

The American Old Testament scholar Walter Brueggemann uses a biblical metaphor in order to describe the role of desire in our daily lives. In his landmark book *The Land: Place as Gift, Promise, and Challenge in Biblical Faith*, he talks about a landless people with the longing for a promised land. According to Brueggemann, the Hebrew Bible suggests that a sense of place is one of the primary categories of faith. He shows how being rooted is a central promise of God to his people. Parts of the Bible are about Israel as God's homeless people. But without a place to live, it is often on its way to a promised place. As a

---

29   For a comprehensive overview of theologians who are at work contributing to this discourse on theology and space/place, as well as for a mapping of some of many different topics that can be followed in this movement, see Sigurd Bergmann, "Theology in Its Spatial Turn: Space, Place and Built Environments Challenging and Changing the Images of God," *Religion Compass* 1 (2007): 353–79.

30   Eric O. Jacobsen, *The Space Between: A Christian Engagement with the Built Environment* (Grand Rapids: Baker Academic, 2012), 271–77.

31   Philip Sheldrake, *The Spiritual City: Theology, Spirituality, and the Urban* (Chichester: Wiley Blackwell, 2014), 185–99.

landless people, yearning for land, Israel is presented in several images derived from various experiences: from Abraham, Isaac and Jacob as sojourners to the exiled Jews in Babylon who were displaced and alienated.[32] What keeps the Israelites going is their desire for "a promised land." This is probably a fruitful metaphor when thinking about place-as-it-can-be. What is it that drives people in aiming for better places to live, work and relax?

Analyzing the data from my research project, photo-walking with Amsterdam, it turned out that the desires of my respondents could be best described by using two opposite categories of feelings. On the one hand, respondents expressed their distastes: for the commercial, for seclusion, indefiniteness, ugliness and chaos. On the other hand, however, they also expressed their desires, telling what they liked about a place or what they would dream of for a particular location. Some of these were clearly the antipodes of distastes mentioned above. But they also mentioned other desires; a desire for a social community, for instance—for being connected, engaged and in interaction with other people in a certain place, transcending the boundaries of generation, race, gender and cultural background—or a desire for symbolism, expressing their admiration for symbolic places that somehow point to immaterial, ideal, or otherwise intangible truths or states—places that bring to mind another domain that is distinct from the everyday city, like a sculpture in the park pointing at history, at myths or at religious narratives. In other words: they recognized a bit of the "promised land" in the worshipping places, commemorating places and enjoying-life places we came across.

In 2011, the International Academy of Practical Theology devoted a conference in Amsterdam to the theme of desire. In his introduction to a volume in which several authors explore the practical theological significance of desire, Ruard Ganzevoort argues that such explorations should always start by understanding desire as the conscious impulse towards something that promises satisfaction in its realization. It emerges from the connection made between a presently experienced lack or deficiency and a possible fulfillment.[33]

Characteristic for humankind might be the desire to attribute meaning to life and its experiences. Humans long to understand their life, and to give or find meaning to it. They want to be at home in themselves and in the world. Desire thus denotes the force of movement that resists being satisfied with the

---

32   Walter Brueggemann, *The Land: Place as Gift, Promise, and Challenge in Biblical Faith*, 2nd ed. (Minneapolis: Fortress, 2002), 3–7.

33   Ruard R. Ganzevoort, "Exploring Practical Theologies of Desire," in *City of Desires—A Place for God? Practical Theological Perspectives*, ed. Ruard Ganzevoort, Rein Brouwer, and Bonnie Miller-McLemore (Münster: LIT, 2013), 7–15 (7).

actual situation or experience. Instead of just asking "what is?" desire deals with the question "what if?" In other words: desire transcends the boundaries of our lives.[34]

In the same volume, Maaike de Haardt states that it is the urban environment that offers the most opportunities for survival or a better life. Hence the city can rightly be considered as being a place of desire and a place of hope.[35] And one could even add: a place of reconciliation. De Haardt argues that the city exists not only in the physical environment, but also, on another level, in how it is imagined and desired. In the messy actuality of both physical "place-as-it-is" and desired "place-as-it-can-be," one finds the dynamics of contest and struggle, of resistance and protest. Also, it is in this messy actuality that one can find hope, dreams and longings for a better life.[36] Theology should turn to actual cities, and search for the religious dynamics that can be found there. Between reality and metaphor are the so-called lived places.[37] This concept of place offers a model for reflecting on the city, desire and God. The status of lived place as provisional and elusive allows one to speak of the rootedness, the materiality and the particularity of the sacred, without any form of securing, saving or objectifying this.[38]

I would argue that Kastanjeplein on 4 May can be seen as a good example of such a lived place. Enrolling in the ritual, participants are invited to live out uncommon practices, and in doing so add a new layer of meaning to the way this square is normally perceived and conceived. The participants are invited to step into "*kairos* time," another dimension of time, but also of place. Material objects that physically make up this place (facades, trees and benches) and prescriptive symbols and regulations that give this square its obvious primary meaning (heart of the neighborhood, gathering place, play area) are challenged and transformed during the ritual. New meanings and values are attributed to Kastanjeplein, as people formerly knew it only as a charming place somewhere in the city. And it seems that the participants have one thing in common: the very reason they participate in the ritual in the first place. Driven by a desire for freedom, liberty and community they imagine Kastanjeplein as it has in fact

---

34   Ganzevoort, "Desire," 10.

35   Maaike de Haardt, "'It Don't Mean a Thing If It Ain't Got that Swing': City of Desires," in Ganzevoort, Brouwer, and Miller-McLemore, *City of Desires*, 29–38 (29).

36   De Haardt, "City of Desires," 30.

37   De Haardt compares "Lived places" to "Third spaces" as described by Edward W. Soja. This form of place transcends and reshapes both "First space" (the given reality) and "Second space" (the powerful prescriptive symbols and regulations). See also Soja, *Thirdspace*.

38   De Haardt, "City of Desires," 32–33.

not always been: as a safe haven for everyone, where justice prevails. And as a place where reconciliation with the past takes actual shape.

6   Typologies of Sacred Place

Does that mean the atmosphere at Kastanjeplein indeed changed "from just ordinary to almost sacred," as was observed by one of the hosts? I can imagine it did. Perhaps even in a number of different ways. In the following paragraph I will look at three "typologies of sacred place" by combining the different notions introduced above: place and place making, sacredness, city-souls, and urban desire. Places are layered and constantly changing. A more-or-less "static" approach of sacred place (as if some places are sacred and others are not) would leave out of the picture the very fact that our world is heavily influenced by connections we are incapable of understanding. Since sacredness and place are both dynamic concepts, identifying specific typologies of sacred place is not easy. It probably starts with recognizing certain patterns when studying place-as-it-is. When doing so, the concept of city-souls in a Durkheimian fashion can be of great help. Is it possible to recognize a pattern in the way city-souls materialize in a physical environment? Secondly, we should also look at place-as-it-can-be. Is there a pattern in the way people attribute otherworldly meaning and value to an urban environment, based on the desires or distastes that they bring to that place? Part of the data-analysis of my research project has been to search for patterns like the ones described above. Without aiming to be complete, I will identify three distinguishable typologies of sacred place. From the data, an overall pattern showed up concerning the potentialities of some urban environments to be experienced as sacred.

– Worshipping place. Even in late-modern western cities like Amsterdam, it is not at all difficult to encounter worshipping places such as synagogues, churches, and mosques when walking through town.[39] Besides, one can also find other types of worshipping places: locations where people with shared ideas or ideologies gather to celebrate whatever connects them. City-souls materializing into worshipping place can be described as religious or ideological ideas, traditions and constructs that are holding societies together. These references to "another world" might interact with desires that people bring into the built environment. From my research data it turned out that one can think of desires that relate to accessibility, community, and

---

39   Incorporated in the research data of this project (amongst others): Oude Kerk, Mozes en Aaronkerk, Portugese Synagoge, Hofkerk, De Bron, and Koningskerk.

symbolism. Worshipping places are seen as places where people connect, mostly based on a common object of worship that is represented in an environment full of symbolic references. When those meanings and values indeed get attributed to the place, the spatial environment might be perceived as sacred, at least from the perception of its visitors. Meanwhile, the lack of accessibility and of free entrance to these places of worship along the walking route clearly is often experienced as a disappointment.

– Commemorating place. Its rich history provides the city of Amsterdam with many cultural memorial sites at specific locations in town.[40] City-souls materializing into these commemorating places are often connected to the history of a city, culture and society. They can be stories and lessons from the past that symbolize the good and the bad and that can be remembered on a regular basis in order to keep them alive for future generations. As such they point at "otherworldly" realities that can interact with the desires a visitor brings to that place. When discussing commemorating places with my respondents, they expressed their desire for authenticity and symbolism and a longing for diversity. One can recognize in these desires certain values that, over time, have become more and more important in Amsterdam: such as the value of freedom and liberty for all and of a society that is inclusive and where everyone is welcome. Values like equality and connectivity are indeed deeply rooted in Amsterdam, "the world's most liberal city."[41] And again, we can argue that when values like these, as they are pointing at overarching and otherworldly realities, become attributed to a monument or artifact, this object and its context will be perceived as sacred.

– Enjoying-life place. The number of cafés, restaurants, and hotels is still growing in the city of Amsterdam. This partly has to do with the growing influx of tourists. But more and more citizens, too, are growing in enthusiasm to enjoy life in the public urban environment instead of their own homes. The city provides them with numerous locations where the good life can indeed be celebrated: terraces, squares, parks, canals.[42] City-souls materializing into enjoying-life place, can be described as contemporary trends that have an overarching and bonding function in order to hold societies together: such as food and sports culture, entertainment, and media-trends.

---

40   Incorporated in the research data of this project (amongst others): Nieuwmarkt, Wertheim Park, Hollandsche Schouwburg, Plantage Middenlaan, Oosterpark, and Kastanjeplein.

41   Russell Shorto, *Amsterdam: A History of the World's Most Liberal City* (New York: Vintage Books, 2013).

42   Incorporated in the research data of this project (amongst others): Nieuwmarkt, Jodenbreestraat, Hortus Botanicus, Artis, Plantage Middenlaan, Tropenmuseum, Kastanjeplein, Oostpoort, Middenweg, Transvaalkade, Elsa's Café, and Park Frankendael.

Moreover, "enjoying life" is a broad concept. Apart from food and beverage it involves leisure: visiting museums, expositions, or art-workshops. In fact, from my data analysis it turns out that enjoying-life places in particular are being connected to desires that somehow relate to a world that transcends everyday life. Think of the desire for community, but also for nature, diversity, and even beauty. When passing through urban environments that can be described as enjoying-life places, people start thinking about life-as-it-can-be, which is then expressed in the desires they start to share. One of these is the longing for interaction and personal connection, which expresses the underlying value of community and bonding. When this value is attributed to a certain place in this category, the location might be experienced by the visitor as sacred, with the potential of fulfilling a role that in fact until recently has been fulfilled by the more-or-less "traditional" places of worship.

Having listed these three typologies of sacred place, it is now important to note that multiple typologies can in fact co-exist in a hybrid way at the same physical location. Kastanjeplein on 4 May actually provides a good example (fig. 8.4). During the public event, the square can obviously be seen as a commemorating place. But in the meantime, it also functions as a worshipping place. By enrolling into the ritual, the participants agree to become part of a larger whole, sharing a common view on what happened years ago that somehow connects them. And the square can even be seen as an enjoying-life place. Its visitors are also willing to enroll in this event in order to celebrate how fortunate they are themselves when it comes to their personal freedom.

And thus, one can conclude that Kastanjeplein turns out to be a rich place. It is dynamic and constantly changing, and because of that the square is able to fulfill a wide range of human desires. This observation touches on the existence of what we might call rich and shallow places in the city when it comes to sacredness. Some places are simply richer than others, in the sense that multiple typologies of sacred place are able to appear in one and the same built environment. They can be connected to a multitude of stories, to a variety of different functions. Perhaps we might even say that the richness of a place determines the likelihood of sacredness happening in that particular environment.[43] Or, as the theologian John Inge observes: "We should recover a sense of *storied* place. *Sacred* places will be those which have been associated

---

43   De Hek, "Place-Making."

FIGURE 8.4 Kastanjeplein turns out to be a rich and storied place on 4 May. Multiple
"typologies of sacred place" appear at the same time: the square as worshipping
place, commemorating place, and enjoying-life place.

with sacred stories, places linked with divine disclosure. Surely the Lord is in
this place; and I did not know it."[44]

7   Conclusion

Kastanjeplein turned into a sacred place on National Remembrance Day,
at least according to one of the hosts I spoke to during the ritual. Apparently,
the place was able to fully accommodate in its role as worshipping, commemorating and enjoying-life place, thus providing its visitors with a feeling of
sacredness. This observation undergirds the claim that sacredness happens
in the dynamic and complex interaction between the attribution of otherworldly meaning and value to an urban environment on the one hand, and certain particular situational typologies of sacred place on the other. It illustrates
how sensing the sacred in the everyday world seems to relate to the experience of the fulfillment of emotive human desires, resulting in the attribution of

---

44   John Inge, "Towards a Theology of Place," *Modern Believing* 40 (1999): 42–50 (47), quoting
Gen 28:16.

otherworldly meaning and value to the environment in which the experience happened.

Throughout this contribution, I have consistently used the notion of sacredness. But what about the holy? Is there any difference between sacredness as described above and the holiness of sites that seem to be far more "static" and settled as a sacred place for a certain faith tradition, sometimes already for centuries? I raise this question because it seems to me that when discussing sacred places, holy sites, and religious buildings, the difference between the sacred and the holy as separate notions is often not clear, whereas distinguishing between the two could be of help when assessing our urban environment. I would argue that the sacred could be seen as an anthropological category, which is why I choose a situational approach when interpreting the events on Kastanjeplein. Perhaps the holy can then be seen as a theological category. It is interesting that Roy A. Rappaport makes a difference between the sacred, which for him is about the quality of a discourse, and the numinous, which he sees as a non-discursive experiential feature. Together, the sacred and the numinous constitute the holy.[45]

I have demonstrated in this contribution that it is not easy to demarcate sacred place in our fluid urban environment. Some places that are well known for their "holy" character are no longer perceived as such by the majority of the people coming across them. At other locations, such as Kastanjeplein, sacredness is suddenly perceived. It shows how in our contemporary society it seems that the sacred can happen everywhere. But if that is the case, does the concept of sacred place not lose its meaning? If every place has the potential to become sacred, should we not conclude that no place really is? This is an open question with which I will leave the reader and myself, and which begs further study. Distinguishing between the sacred and the holy as two separate categories might be a helpful first step. Having said that, one thing we know for sure is that, since place, sacredness, and city-souls are dynamic concepts, sacred place will be this as well. And the same is true of the holy. It can pop up everywhere. Perhaps even when and where we expect it the least. "When you see it ... you will know it."[46]

---

45 Roy A. Rappaport, *Ritual and Religion in the Making of Humanity* (Cambridge: Cambridge University Press, 1999), 371.

46 Joshua Schwartz, "The Land of Israel is Holier than All the Other Lands: What Makes the Land of Israel Holy?" (paper presented at the Jewish and Christian Perspectives conference, Jerusalem, 14–17 May 2018).

Acknowledgments

The author wishes to thank Marcel Barnard and the editors for their valuable comments on an earlier version of this contribution. He also wishes to thank the organizers of the JCP conference in 2018 for their invitation to participate in this conference on the topic of "Holy Places." It was a truly enriching experience.

References

Appelrouth, Scott, and Laura Desford Edles. *Classical and Contemporary Sociological Theory: Texts and Readings.* Thousand Oaks, CA: Sage, 2008.

Bauman, Zygmunt. *Liquid Times: Living in an Age of Uncertainty.* Cambridge: Polity, 2007.

Bergmann, Sigurd. "Theology in Its Spatial Turn: Space, Place and Built Environments Challenging and Changing the Images of God." *Religion Compass* 1 (2007): 353–79.

Brueggemann, Walter. *The Land: Place as Gift, Promise, and Challenge in Biblical Faith.* 2nd ed. Minneapolis: Fortress, 2002.

Casey, Edward S. *The Fate of Place: A Philosophical History.* Berkeley: University of California, 1998.

Cresswell, Tim. *Place: An Introduction.* 2nd ed. Chicester: Wiley Blackwell, 2015.

Dobson, Stephen. "Urban Pedagogy: A Proposal for the Twenty-First Century." *London Review of Education* 4 (2006): 99–114.

Durkheim, Émile. *The Elementary Forms of Religious Life.* Translated by Karen E. Fields. New York: The Free Press, 1995.

Eliade, Mircea. *The Sacred and the Profane: The Nature of Religion.* Translated by William R. Trask. Orlando, FL: Harcourt, 1987.

Ganzevoort, Ruard R. "Exploring Practical Theologies of Desire." Pages 7–15 in *City of Desires—A Place for God? Practical Theological Perspectives.* Edited by Ruard Ganzevoort, Rein Brouwer, and Bonnie Miller-McLemore. Münster: LIT, 2013.

Graham, Elaine, and Stephen Lowe. *What Makes A Good City? Public Theology and the Urban Church.* London: Darton, Longman and Todd, 2009.

Haardt, Maaike de. "'It Don't Mean a Thing If It Ain't Got that Swing': City of Desires." Pages 29–38 in *City of Desires—A Place for God? Practical Theological Perspectives.* Edited by Ruard Ganzevoort, Rein Brouwer, and Bonnie Miller-McLemore. Münster: LIT, 2013.

Hek, Willem Jan de. "Place-Making in Mokum: Searching for the Souls of Amsterdam." Paper presented at the World Congress of the International Union of Architects. Seoul, 5 September 2017.

Inge, John. "Towards a Theology of Place." *Modern Believing* 40 (1999): 42–50.

Jacobs, Jane. *The Death and Life of Great American Cities.* New York: Random House, 1961.

Jacobsen, Eric O. *The Space Between: A Christian Engagement with the Built Environment.* Grand Rapids: Baker Academic, 2012.

Kim, Sunhee. "Sacred Space." In *Lexham Theological Wordbook.* Edited by Douglas Mangum, Derek R. Brown, Rachel Klippenstein, and Rebekah Hurst. Bellingham, WA: Lexham Press, 2014.

Leeuw, Gerardus van der. *Religion in Essence and Manifestation: A Study in Phenomenology.* Princeton: Princeton University Press, 1986.

Molendijk, Arie L. "The Notion of the 'Sacred'." Pages 55–89 in *Holy Ground: Re-Inventing Ritual Space in Modern Western Culture.* Edited by Paul Post and Arie L. Molendijk. Leuven: Peeters, 2010.

Otto, Rudolph. *The Idea of the Holy.* Translated by John W. Harvey. Oxford: Oxford University Press, 1958.

Pyyry, Noora. "Learning with the City via Enchantment: Photo-Walks as Creative Encounters." *Discourse: Studies in the Cultural Politics of Education* 37 (2016): 102–15.

Rappaport, Roy A. *Ritual and Religion in the Making of Humanity.* Cambridge: Cambridge University Press, 1999.

Schwartz, Joshua. "The Land of Israel is Holier than All the Other Lands: What Makes the Land of Israel Holy?" Paper presented at the Jewish and Christian Perspectives conference. Jerusalem, 14–17 May 2018.

Sheldrake, Philip. *The Spiritual City: Theology, Spirituality, and the Urban.* Chichester: Wiley Blackwell, 2014.

Shorto, Russell. *Amsterdam: A History of the World's Most Liberal City.* New York: Vintage Books, 2013.

Soja, Edward W. *Thirdspace: Journeys to Los Angeles and Other Real-and-Imagined Places.* Malden, MA: Blackwell, 1996.

Tuan, Yi-Fu. *Space and Place: The Perspective of Experience.* Minneapolis: University of Minnesota Press, 1977.

Wijnia, Lieke. "Making Sense Through Music: Perceptions of the Sacred at Festival Musica Sacra Maastricht." PhD diss., Tilburg University, 2016.

CHAPTER 9

The Garden in Eden: a Holy Place?

Robin B. ten Hoopen

Non ignoro de paradiso multos multa dixisse[1]

∵

The Eden Narrative (Gen 2:4–3:24)[2] does not contain explicit references to a temple, sacredness or holiness. It might thus come as a surprise that both ancient and more recent interpretations of this narrative attest that the Garden in Eden[3] is a sanctuary, a depiction that implies concerns about holiness and purity.[4] These interpretations are not only remarkable in light of the silence of

---

1 Augustine, *Gen. litt.* 8.1.

2 From a diachronic perspective, Gen 2–3 is part of a non-P layer that is at least present in Gen 1–11. While Gen 2–3 contains older traditions, I agree with Mettinger that no clear sources can be distinguished within the narrative. See Tryggve N.D. Mettinger, *The Eden Narrative: A Literary and Religio-Historical Study of Genesis 2–3* (Winona Lake, IN: Eisenbrauns, 2007), 5–41. A clear addition to the non-P narrative can, however, be seen in 2:4. In my view, the whole of Gen 2:4 should be seen as a heading created by a priestly editor, connecting Gen 1:1–2:3 and 2:5–3:24. On the redaction of Gen 1–11 see Robin B. ten Hoopen, "Genesis 5 and the Formation of the Primeval History: a Redaction Historical Case Study," *ZAW* 129 (2017): 177–93.

3 Whereas some scholars use "Garden of Eden," I prefer the term "Garden in Eden" to emphasize that the Garden is not coterminous with Eden, but is in Eden (Gen 2:8). The Garden of Eden combines two motifs: Eden and a garden located within this larger area. See Arie van der Kooij, "The Story of Paradise in the Light of Mesopotamian Culture and Literature," in *Genesis, Isaiah, and Psalms: A Festschrift to Honour Professor John Emerton for His Eightieth Birthday*, ed. Katherine J. Dell, Graham Davies, and Yee Von Koh, VTSup 135 (Leiden: Brill, 2010), 3–22.

4 The best-known recent advocates of this view are Gordon J. Wenham, "Sanctuary Symbolism in the Garden of Eden Story," in *I Studied Inscriptions from Before the Flood: Ancient Near Eastern, Literary, and Linguistic Approaches to Genesis 1–11*, ed. Richard S. Hess and David T. Tsumura (Winona Lake, IN: Eisenbrauns, 1994), 399–404; Gregory K. Beale, *The Temple and the Church's Mission* (Downers Grove, IL: Apollos IVP, 2004), 66–80. For a critical view see Jacques T.A.G.M, Van Ruiten, "Visions of the Temple in the book of Jubilees," in *Gemeinde ohne Tempel/Community without Temple: Zur Substituierung und Transformation des Jerusalemer Tempels und seines Kults im Alten Testament, antiken Judentum und frühen*

Gen 2–3; the whole book of Genesis remains rather silent on the topic of holiness. The root קד"ש is nearly absent[5] and references to holy ground or a holy God do not occur.[6] There thus seems to be a tension, maybe even an ideological confrontation, between what the Eden Narrative explicates and how the passage is interpreted.

The current contribution discusses whether the idea of the Garden in Eden as a holy place was already part of the Eden narrative as it is found in the book of Genesis or if it should be seen as part of the reception history of the story, founded on a desire to connect the garden and the temple in Jerusalem. Particular attention is given to Ancient Near Eastern (ANE) sources that have been used to contextualize and interpret the Garden.

My contribution contains six sections. First, I set the stage by introducing the Garden. Second, I briefly reflect on the term holiness. Third, I introduce early voices who present the Garden in Eden as a holy place. Fourth, I take up recent voices who attest this position as well as reflect on some exegetical issues related to this position. Fifth, I carry out a comparison between several ANE gardens and the Garden in Eden. A short conclusion is found in the sixth and final section.

1   Setting the Stage

After God has created the first human being (אדם), the Eden Narrative tells that God planted a garden in Eden. Eden is a luxurious and fertile place,[7] rich in water and located in the east.[8] Gen 2:8–15 depicts Eden as near a source that

---

Christentum, ed. Beate Ego, Armin Lange, and Peter Pilhofer (Tübingen: Mohr Siebeck, 1999), 215–27; Daniel I. Block, "Eden: A Temple? A Reassessment of the Biblical Evidence," in *From Creation to New Creation: Biblical Theology and Exegesis*, ed. Daniel M. Gurtner and Benjamin J. Gladd (Peabody MA: Hendrickson, 2013), 3–29. The tension in the Eden Narrative between concerns for holiness and the presence of death and sexuality has been discussed by David P. Wright, "Holiness, Sex, and Death in the Garden of Eden," *Bib* 77 (1996): 305–29.

5   Besides the reference to a shrine attendant/prostitute (Gen 38:21–22) and Kadesh (Gen 14:7; 16:14; 20:1), Gen 2:3 is the only occurrence of the root קד"ש.

6   See Stuart Lasine, "Everything Belongs to Me: Holiness, Danger, and Divine Kingship in the Post-Genesis World," *JSOT* 35 (2010): 31–62.

7   The root עד"ן has the connotation of "abundance," "fertility," and "luxury." The attention for etiologies in non-P narratives shows the importance of this meaning. See Terje Stordalen, *Echoes of Eden: Genesis 2–3 and Symbolism of the Eden Garden in Biblical Hebrew Literature*, CBET 25 (Leuven: Peeters, 2000), 257–61.

8   In my view, מקדם refers to a location. The Vg. and the *recentiones* (but not LXX) translate the term as "of old." See Stordalen, *Echoes*, 261–70. Although this could solve the apparent discrepancy between Gen 2:8 and 3:22–24, all other occurrences of קדם in Gen 1–11 imply

later turns into four rivers.[9] This picture reminds one of (1) glyptic art containing deities and cult,[10] (2) temple imagery,[11] and (3) ANE locations where gods
and immortals dwell.[12] While some of these involve cult, all contain motifs of
blessing and abundance provided by a deity. Thus, both the name Eden and
its ancient context reveal that Eden is not a regular place, but a place of abundance filled with blessings and related to a deity.

The location of Eden was probably perceived by the author as locatable
as well as mythical and unreachable for regular humans.[13] While the former
two are illustrated by the reference to countries and the well-known Tigris
and Euphrates (2:10–15),[14] the latter are manifested by YHWH's placing of the
אדם in the garden (2:8, 15),[15] the cherubim that guard the road to the tree of

---

the meaning "eastward" (2:14; 4:16; 10:30; 11:2). Since locations in the east are well known
from Mesopotamian sources as places where immortals and deities dwell, a spatial location is to be preferred for Gen 2:8. See for the Mesopotamian material Christopher
Woods, "At the Edge of the World: Cosmological Conceptions of the Eastern Horizon in
Mesopotamia," *JANER* 9 (2009): 183–239.

9   The Hebrew signifies a place where water exits the ground. See Ziony Zevit, *What Really
      Happened in the Garden of Eden?* (New Haven: Yale University Press, 2013), 97–103.

10   See the collection in Terje Stordalen, "Heaven on Earth—Or Not? Jerusalem as Eden in
      Biblical Literature," in *Beyond Eden: The Biblical Story of Paradise (Genesis 2–3) and Its
      Reception History*, ed. Konrad Schmid and Christoph Riedweg (Tübingen: Mohr Siebeck,
      2008), 28–57 (55–57).

11   See Manfred Dietrich, "Das biblische Paradies und der babylonische Tempelgarten:
      Überlegungen zur Lage des Garten Eden," in *Das Biblische Weltbild und seine altorien-
      talischen Kontexte*, ed. Bernd Janowksi and Beate Ego (Tübingen: Mohr Siebeck, 2001),
      281–324 (290–99).

12   One could think of distant locations in the east such as Dilmun, the "mouth of the riv-
      ers" (*pî nārāti*) in Gilgamesh Epic (GE) 9.205–206, as well as of the residence of Ilu at
      the source of the rivers (*mbk nhrm*) in KTU 1.3 V 13–16. According to Wyatt, the Ugaritic
      material (and Gen 2–3) refers to a location at the cosmic centre. However, as noted by
      Niehr, Ilu resides in the east, at the borders of the world. Nicolas Wyatt, "A Royal Garden:
      The Ideology of Eden," *SJOT* 28 (2014): 1–35; Herbert Niehr, "Die Wohnsitze des Gottes El:
      Ein Beitrag zu ihrer Lokalisierung," in Janowski and Ego, *Das biblische Weltbild*, 325–60
      (341). See also John Day, *From Creation to Babel: Studies in Genesis 1–11* (London: T&T Clark
      International, 2013), 27–32.

13   Unreachable does not imply unlocatable, although Eden was outside the regular world.
      This contra Mettinger, *Eden Narrative*, 16; Ronald S. Hendel, "Other Edens," in *Exploring
      the Longue Durée: Essays in Honor of Lawrence E. Stager*, ed. David Schloen (Winona Lake,
      IN: Eisenbrauns, 2008), 185–89. Stordalen, "Heaven on Earth," argues that Eden is a uto-
      pia. However, as the Ugaritic Mount Zaphon is both a real mountain and the mountain of
      Baal, the Garden in Eden is also locatable and beyond the regular world.

14   These verses are not to be seen as an addition. They fit the meaning of the term Eden
      very well.

15   Gen 2:15 is not a doublet, but should be read in line with GE 9.205–206 where the flood
      hero is taken away and placed at the *pî nārāti*. See Van der Kooij, "Paradise," 11–14. The root

life (3:24), and the location in the east near the source of the rivers.[16] While some have argued that Eden should be located in the cosmic centre,[17] both the fact that the אדם is taken there and the location in the east (2:8) argue against such a view.[18] As noted above, Mesopotamian and Levantine sources[19] attest similar whereabouts of gods and immortals in the east, beyond or near the borders of the ordinary world.[20] The Garden in Eden should be seen as a similar location.[21] The fact that the Garden contains a tree of life (2:9), is guarded by cherubim (3:24) and is depicted as a place of possible immortality does not exclude but actually argues for a location at the border of the world. Such a mythical space does, however, not exclude a place on the map: either Mesopotamia[22] or more likely Armenia.[23]

Finally, the Garden was probably assumed to be close to a mountain on which the residence of YHWH was located. In contrast to Ezek 28, Gen 2–3 does not refer to a mountain. However, its presence might be assumed on the basis of two elements. First, the Tigris and Euphrates originate in the mountains. The source of these rivers should thus likely be sought there. Second,

---

נו"ח in Gen 2:15 might have been used to create a connection between Adam and Noah. For the connection between this passage and the taking away of Enoch see Robin B. ten Hoopen, "Where Are You, Enoch? Why Can't I Find You? Genesis 5.21–24 Reconsidered," *JHS* 18 (2018): 1–23.

16   While in English the "mouth of the river" assumes the end of the stream, Akkadian *pî nārāti* refers to the source. See William F. Albright, "The Mouth of the Rivers," *AJSL* 35 (1919): 161–95 (167, 172–74).

17   Pirqe R. El. 11.78; Michael A. Fishbane, "The Sacred Center," in *Texts and Responses: Studies Presented to Nahum N. Glatzer on the Occasion of his Seventieth Birthday by His Students*, ed. Michael A. Fishbane and Paul R. Flohr (Leiden: Brill, 1975), 6–27; Jon D. Levenson, *Sinai and Zion: An Entry into the Jewish Bible* (New York: HarperCollins, 1985), 128–35; Wyatt, "Royal Garden." The idea of a centre is also based on the interpretation that all four rivers encompass the earth. But see Zevit, *What Really Happened*, 107 for a critique on the latter.

18   An eastern location for the Garden in Eden or Garden of Righteousness is found in Jub. 8:16; 1 En. 28–32; 2 En. 42:3; 65:10.

19   See Woods, "At the Edge" and note 12.

20   In Gen 2:8 the east does not imply the utmost east, but a location related to the eastern horizon. In a similar way, the Jewel Garden in GE is related to the eastern horizon without being at the utmost east.

21   In this instance, I follow but adjust the view of Van der Kooij. Eden is a place *like* Dilmun (contra Van der Kooij, "Paradise," 12–14). I also emphasize that Levantine sources mention the idea of a source of the rivers.

22   Dietrich, "Paradies," but many before him.

23   Day, *From Creation*, 27–32; Marjo C.A. Korpel and Johannes C. De Moor, *Adam, Eve, and the Devil: A New Beginning*, 2nd enl. ed., HBM 65 (Sheffield: Sheffield Phoenix Press, 2015), 29–44.

several ANE texts show that a connection between the source of the rivers, the east, and a mountain was broadly shared.[24] In sum, Eden is located in the east on a mountain in a real, but unreachable place. It should be seen as a place of divine blessing and possible immortality.

The description of the Garden is not that extensive. It may be assumed that the Garden had one entrance and was enclosed.[25] It contains trees that are pleasing to the eye and good for food, and mentions two trees in particular (2:9, 16–17). The אדם is called to work and guard the garden (2:15). While the working of the ground continues outside the garden (3:22–24), the task of guarding has to be handed over to the cherubim and the sword (3:24).

The presence of the cherubim and the sword, the walking of God in the garden (Gen 3:8), the notion of divine blessing, and the reference to the presence of YHWH near Eden in Genesis 4:16 make it likely that the Garden is God's garden and was near his domain.[26] Although the garden and Eden are thus distinguished,[27] they are also related.

Finally, the presence of a tree of which one is not allowed to eat (the tree of knowledge of good and evil), as well as the presence of the serpent, show that although Eden and the Garden function as a place of blessing, danger and evil are not far away.

2   Holiness

From an ANE perspective, the holiness of a place is grounded in an assumed relationship between a place and the divine presence in that place as well as by a connection between place and cult, and from there the notions of purity and impurity.[28] The divine imparts holiness to a place, but because a place

---

24   The mountain of Ilu and the *mbk nhrm*, but also Akkadian and Sumerian sources attest a mountain at the borders of the world. See Day, *From Creation*, 28–29; Woods, "At the Edge," 186–90, 203–4; Korpel and De Moor, *Adam, Eve, and the Devil*, 29–44. Royal Neo-Assyrian gardens also attest a garden and a mountain. See Stephanie Dalley, *The Mystery of the Hanging Garden of Babylon: An Elusive World Wonder Traced* (Oxford: Oxford University Press, 2013), 43–63, 129.

25   The reference to the guarding of the way to the tree of life in 3:24 suggests this. The root גנן, could also imply an enclosed area as does the rendering of the LXX as παράδεισος, although the latter could also attest a later interpretation.

26   Gen 13:10; Isa 51:3; Ezek 28; 31 show evidence for a connection between Eden and the domain of God.

27   See Van der Kooij, "Paradise," 14.

28   See David P. Wright, "Holiness (OT)," in *The Anchor Bible Dictionary*, ed. David Noel Freedman, 6 vols. (New York: Doubleday, 1992), 3:237–49.

is marked holy, the divine will enter there.[29] Having noted above that God's presence is to be found in the Garden in Eden, the Garden might contain some degree of holiness.[30] Since the Hebrew Bible, does, however, not speak univocally about holiness,[31] and the book of Genesis remains rather silent on this topic, no clear-cut concept of holiness can be deduced from Gen 2–3. One may doubt whether we can even assume the larger ANE perspective as set out above. Although I remain reticent to do so, two pointers for this view could be found in the Eden Narrative. Firstly, Eve states that the couple is not allowed to touch the tree (Gen 3:3). This might assume that, at least in Eve's view, the tree has some element of holiness to it (see Num 4:15).[32] Secondly, the fact that the garden is enclosed and has to be guarded shows that it is intentionally separated from other places. In an ancient Israelite worldview, this seperation could also point to a degree of holiness. While one must be careful to assume too much, some degree of holiness, although explicitly not expressed in this terminology, can likely be assumed for the garden.

The next question to take under consideration is whether this concept of holiness assumes cult and concern for purity.[33] In light of the absence of explicit cultic concerns in Gen 2–3, a concern for holiness without assuming cult seems to be preferred. Both Sinai (Exod 19:12–13, 23) and the Ugaritic Mount Zaphon (KTU 1.3 III 30; 1.16 I 7) are examples of holy places without clear attestation of cult. Should such a perspective also be assumed for Gen 2–3? A closer examination of arguments for the presence of cult in the Garden in Eden must be carried out before conclusions may be drawn.

3   The Garden in Eden as a Holy Place: Ancient Exegesis

One of the earliest representatives of the position that the Garden in Eden can be considered a holy place is found in the book of Jubilees.[34] Here the

---

29   Mark S. Smith, *The Origins of Biblical Monotheism: Israel's Polytheistic Background and the Ugaritic Texts* (New York: Oxford University Press, 2001), 93–94.

30   See Wright, "Holiness," 237, for the notion of degrees of holiness. In contrast to for example Isa 6 and Ezek 1–2, the couple hides from YHWH because they are naked (3:10), not because of his holy presence.

31   See Moshe Weinfeld, *Deuteronomy and the Deuteronomic School* (Oxford: Clarendon, 1972), 225–32.

32   A connection between touching, holiness, and death also occurs in Exod 19:12, 13, 23.

33   See for a positive answer Wright, "Sex and Death."

34   4Q265 11–17 shares this interpretation. See Florentino García Martínez, "Man and Woman: Halakah Based upon Eden in the Dead Sea Scrolls," in *Qumranica Minora II: Thematic*

garden is seen as the "Holy of Holies and dwelling of the Lord" (3:12; 8:19).[35] Jubilees, moreover, presents Adam as a priest burning incense at the gate of the Garden. Finally, Jubilees connects the Garden to both Sinai and Zion, emphasizing that cult goes back to the first human (8:19). Although such explicit references to the Garden as holy are rare,[36] a larger corpus of texts does relate the Garden to the eschatological temple or the future residence of God, thus also comparing and connecting Eden and Jerusalem (e.g., Isa 51:3;[37] Ezek 36:35; Joel 2:3;[38] Rev 2:7; 21–22; 1 En. 25; 2 En. 8; T. Levi 18:6–11; T. Dan 5:12; Apoc. Mos. 13). While these passages do not imply that Eden was seen as a holy place, they do relate Eden and Jerusalem by comparing *Urzeit* and *Endzeit*. Jerusalem or a new Jerusalem will be as Eden. In contrast, several passages from rabbinic literature could imply the holiness of Eden. These describe the garden as a sanctuary (Gen. Rab. 16:5), refer to YHWH dwelling in Eden, relate the exile from the garden to the ascent of the Shekinah,[39] and refer to Adam as a priest (Gen. Rab. 34:9; Lev. Rab. 2:7).[40] Ephrem the Syrian and the author of *Syrian Cave of Treasures* are amongst the Christian authors who designate the Garden as holy. In both cases, holiness is intimately connected to the figure of Christ and the tree of life.[41]

In sum, only a handful of texts describe the Garden as holy. A larger corpus compares Eden to the holy place par excellence, the temple, or depicts

          Studies on the Dead Sea Scrolls, ed. Eibert J.C. Tigchelaar, STDJ 64 (Leiden: Brill, 2007), 57–76 (71–76).

35   See Jacques T.A.G.M. Van Ruiten, "Adam in the Book of Jubilees," in *The Adam and Eve Story in the Hebrew Bible and in Ancient Jewish Writings including the New Testament*, ed. Antti Laato and Lotta Valve, SRB 7 (Turku: Åbo Akademi University; Winona Lake, IN: Eisenbrauns, 2016), 143–75 (161–66).

36   Zoharic tradition also relates the Holy of Holies to Eden. See Rachel Elior, "The Garden of Eden is the Holy of Holies and the Dwelling of the Lord," *Studies in Spirituality* 24 (2014): 63–118 (75–76).

37   Note also Isa 65:17–25, which uses Eden imagery to describe a new Jerusalem.

38   The presence of shared imagery between the temple (1 Kgs 6–8) or future temple (Ezek 41:17–25; 47:1–12; Joel 4:18; Zech 14:8–11) and Eden is often used to show that the temple is a new Eden or Eden a temple. These similarities could, however, also be explained by assuming shared imagery for temples and divine gardens.

39   Gen. Rab. 19:7 connects Gen 3:8 to the ascent of the Shekinah from the earth. In contrast, 3 En. 5:1–3, 10–14 reports how the Shekinah descended in Eden after Adam was exiled. See Christfried Böttrich, "The Figures of Adam and Eve in the Enoch Tradition," in Laato and Valve, *The Adam and Eve Story*, 211–51 (246–47).

40   See also Tg. Ps.-J. 8:20 and Apoc. Mos. 29. Sir 49:16–50:1 (Hebrew) relates Adam to the high priest. See for a broader discussion Gary A. Anderson, *The Genesis of Perfection: Adam and Eve in Jewish and Christian Imagination* (Louisville: Westminster John Knox, 2001), 121–34.

41   Ephrem, *Hymn. Parad.* 3.14–16; 4.2–4; *Cave of Treasures* (W) 3–4. See Anderson, *The Genesis of Perfection*, 55–58, 79–80.

a new Jerusalem in Eden imagery. Within the Hebrew Bible, the comparison between Eden and Jerusalem focuses especially on fruitfulness (Isa 51:3; Ezek 36:35; Joel 2:3), not on cult. Only Ezek 28, to be discussed in the next section, might point in another direction.

4   The Garden in Eden as a Holy Place: Recent Exegesis

A still-growing group of exegetes argues that the intimate connections between Eden, temple, and cult are already found in Gen 2–3. In their view, the Garden in Eden should be seen as a prototype of a sanctuary or an actual sanctuary.[42] The arguments for such a position are at least fourfold:

– Gen 2–3 contains "sanctuary symbolism."[43] Scholars refer to the use of the *hitpael* of הל״ך (Gen 3:8; Lev 26:12; Deut 23:14), the cherubim (Gen 3:24), and the description of the task of the אדם (Gen 2:15).
– The river Gihon in Gen 2:13 should be related to the Jerusalem river Gihon (1 Kgs 1:33, 38, 45; 2 Chr 32:30; 33:14).[44]
– Gen 2–3 resembles so-called cosmic mountain ideology and/or relates Zion and the temple. This shows that the Garden is a pre-figuration of tabernacle and temple.[45]
– The Garden should be interpreted as a sacred or holy place on the basis of Mesopotamian temple gardens.[46]

Criticizing this position, others have emphasized that the "sanctuary symbolism" is read into the story,[47] the garden cannot be located in Jerusalem,[48] the whole cosmic mountain theory cannot carry the weight attributed to it, and the Edenic Garden should not be seen as a temple garden.[49] The two camps

---

42   See note 4. More scholars might be mentioned, e.g., Mircea Eliade, *Patterns in Comparative Religion*, trans. Rosemary Sheed (Lincoln: University of Nebraska Press, 1979), 282; Fishbane, "The Sacred Center"; L. Michael Morales, *The Tabernacle Pre-Figured: Cosmic Mountain Ideology in Genesis and Exodus*, BTS 15 (Leuven: Peeters, 2012).

43   Wenham, "Sanctuary," 400.

44   Levenson, *Sinai and Zion*, 129–31.

45   Levenson, *Sinai and Zion*, 129–31; Morales, *The Tabernacle*.

46   Dietrich, "Paradies." See also John H. Walton, *The Lost World of Adam and Eve: Genesis 2–3 and the Human Origins Debate* (Downers Grove, IL: IVP Academic, 2015), 104–27.

47   See Day, *From Creation*, 31–32; Robert P. Gordon, "Evensong in Eden: As It Probably was *Not* in the Beginning," in *Leshon Limmudim: Essays on the Language and Literature of the Hebrew Bible in Honour of A.A. Macintosh*, ed. David A. Baer and Robert P. Gordon, LHBOT 593 (London: Bloomsbury, 2013), 17–30.

48   Hendel, "Other Edens."

49   Van der Kooij, "Paradise," 9–14.

illustrate different approaches to the text. Proponents of a holy Eden are often interested in larger themes and/or argue for a more theological or canonical reading. Also those who assume a broadly shared ANE symbolism are amongst the proponents of a holy Garden in Eden. Opponents of this view emphasize the lack of evidence in Gen 2–3 as well as the absence of a concern for holiness in non-P literature. Although I am amongst those who are critical of the idea of Eden as a temple, the current contribution also intends to build a bridge between the two camps.

The scope of this contribution prohibits me from discussing all of the four arguments mentioned above. The focus will be on the fourth issue: comparative traditions concerning gardens. Before I discuss these, I will briefly lay out my view on three aspects related to the second and third argument.[50]

4.1   *Genesis 2–3 and Other Passages That Refer to the Garden in Eden*

The Hebrew Bible contains several passages that identify the Garden in Eden as the Garden of God (Ezek 28:11–19; 31:8–9) and Garden of YHWH (Gen 13:10; Isa 51:3). While Gen 13:10 and Isa 51:3 (as well as Ezek 36:35 and Joel 2:3) resemble a concept of the Garden that is similar to Gen 2–3,[51] Ezek 28 and 31 show some explicit differences to Gen 2–3. Ezek 28 is of particular interest here. This oracle not only contains a recasting of a myth about Adam or a divine being,[52] but could also be seen as the clearest illustration of "the figurative field 'Zion-is-Eden'."[53] The connection between Eden and Jerusalem is especially pertinent in the LXX version of Ezek 28, which depicts the King of Tyre as the high priest and locates him with the cherub.[54] The MT version of Ezek 28 is more reluctant to relate the King of Tyre to Jerusalem. While it primarily speaks of Tyre, it subtly echoes Jerusalem and criticizes its establishment.[55] This criticism of Tyre and the Jerusalem establishment is visible in the use of the cultic language (28:7, 9, 16, 18). Some scholars also interpret the holy mountain and fiery stones (28:14) as references to Zion. Although these elements probably suggest the use of an older myth about a mountain of the

---

50   For a critique on Wenham's work see Block, "Eden: A Temple?"; Gordon, "Evensong."

51   Gen 13:10 does not contain a different concept. Contra Stordalen, *Echoes*, 321–29.

52   See Day, *From Creation*, 47–49.

53   Stordalen, *Echoes*, 332, 352–54

54   See Stordalen, *Echoes*, 335–56 for an extensive discussion of the differences between LXX and MT.

55   See Lydia Lee, *Mapping Judah's Fate in Ezekiel's Oracles against the Nations*, ANEM 14 (Atlanta: SBL Press, 2016), 89–95.

gods (see Ezek 28:2),[56] the choice for the term "holy" could have been read by Ezekiel's contemporaries as a reference to Zion. However, Ezek 28 does not identify Eden and Zion (so also Ezek 36:35), it rather subtly relates the two domains or fields. So, while it comes as no surprise that Ezek 28 was one of the impetuses for linking Eden and Jerusalem,[57] a direct connection between the two is not attested in this text.

The exegesis of Ezek 28 is of more importance since some hold Gen 2–3 to be dependent on Ezek 28. In their view, the cultic symbolism used in Ezek 28 can also be found in Gen 2–3.[58] Such a view should, however, be refuted. First, Ezek 28 and Gen 2–3 show related traditions, but one does not depend on the other.[59] Second, as seen above, the cultic motifs primarily criticize Tyre and hint at the Jerusalem establishment. They should not be seen as evidence for a cultic Garden in Eden. In sum, while Ezek 28 was an impetus for relating Eden and the temple, neither Ezek 28[60] nor Gen 2–3 attests a cultic Garden in Eden.

4.2 Eden and Jerusalem

As noted above, I do not assume a cosmology in which the references to the Tigris and Euphrates are not seen as geographical pointers. It is only in such a reading that the Gihon can refer to the spring in Jerusalem. The geography of Gen 2–3 locates this river, however, near Cush (Kassite Mesopotamia or Nubia).[61] Although later readers might have perceived the name Gihon as an echo to the river in Jerusalem (or the other way around), Eden is not in Jerusalem.[62]

I also disagree with those who see the Garden's alleged pre-figuration of the land of Israel (based on Num 24:5–7; Isa 5:1–7 and Ps 80:9–17) as an argument for the view that Jerusalem is implied in Gen 2–3.[63] Garden imagery and exile are found throughout the Hebrew Bible and ANE in different contexts.[64] Their presence in the Eden Narrative neither implies a direct connection between the location of Eden and Jerusalem nor a post-exilic date for the Eden

---

56　Korpel and De Moor, *Adam, Eve, and the Devil*, 166–71. The term "holy mountain" was a flexible term used for different mountains in different periods: Zaphon, Horeb, Sinai, Zion, and maybe even a mountain in Tyre.

57　But see Stordalen, *Echoes*, 352–56, 394–97, for a different view.

58　See for example Wyatt, "Royal Garden."

59　See Day, *From Creation*, 47–49.

60　LXX is more explicit in linking the high priest and Eden, however, even here Eden is not in Jerusalem.

61　See Hendel, "Other Edens," 186; Day, *From Creation*, 29.

62　The LXX renders Gihon as Γηων, likely the Nile. It does not relate the two Gihons.

63　See for example Wyatt, "Royal Garden."

64　For the first see Ezek 31 and the ANE texts in section 5. For the second see Gen 4:11 and 11:8.

Narrative.[65] While it would have been very likely for an Israelite scribe to locate the Garden in Eden in Jerusalem, this scribe does not do so.

4.3 *Eden as a Cosmic Mountain*

A final argument to relate Eden and temple is to perceive the alleged mountain in Gen 2–3 as an *omphalos* and cosmic mountain.[66] I remain unconvinced of this larger cosmic mountain theory. While the motifs of creation, temple, and mountain were related throughout the ANE, a passage containing a mountain near a water source does not necessarily imply cult. What connects a mountain of the gods and cult is the motif of divine presence. It is only from either a phenomenological perspective[67] or from a particular canonical perspective[68] that the assumed mountain of Eden in Gen 2–3 can be seen as a cosmic mountain. Moreover, Gen 2–3 clearly differentiates between the place of creation (Gen 2:7) and the garden (2:8ff). This differs from what is presented in Ezek 28 and Ezek 31. In Gen 2–3, the two motifs are distinguished, implying that even when a cosmic mountain theory is assumed, the garden cannot be the temple.[69]

5   To What Should One Compare the Garden in Eden?

Both in the Hebrew Bible and throughout the ANE, gardens symbolize fertility and cultivation, but also hold a symbolic function.[70] They function as cultic, royal, mythical, or even divine spaces.[71] It has often been noted that the Garden in Eden has much in common with other ANE gardens. Four main suggestions have been proposed to contextualize the Garden in Eden:[72]

---

65 See Day, *From Creation*, 46–9. I currently remain unconvinced of an exilic or post-exilic date for Gen 2–3.

66 See Morales, *Tabernacle*, 2, 7–20.

67 Eliade, *Patterns*.

68 Morales, *Tabernacle*, 1.

69 Note that Clifford does not find the cosmic mountain in Gen 2–3. Richard J. Clifford, *The Cosmic Mountain in Canaan and the Old Testament*, HSM 4 (Cambridge: Harvard University Press, 1972), 98–103.

70 See for an overview Donald J. Wiseman, "Mesopotamian Gardens," *Anatolian Studies* 33 (1983): 137–44.

71 Most scholars focus on Mesopotamian parallels. See for the Egyptian material Izak Cornelius, "The Garden in the Iconography of the Ancient Near East: A Study of Selected Material from Egypt," *Journal for Semitics* 1 (1989): 204–28.

72 I will limit myself to the gardens that are most referred to in scholarly literature, being aware that I will leave out promising material such as erotic/love gardens and gardens in Egyptian graves.

- The garden is a garden of God/the gods[73]
- The garden is a temple or cultic garden[74]
- The garden is a royal garden[75]
- The garden is a numinous or mythological garden[76]

The final part of this contribution will contain a comparison of these four types of gardens to the one in Eden.[77] In the following, I will limit myself to a horizontal comparison as set out in William Hallo's contextual method.[78] Differences and similarities between texts are noted, but no direct dependence is assumed. The section aims to show that a broad contextualization of sources prevents scholars from too easily assuming cultic symbolism to be present in the Edenic Garden.

In almost all cases,[79] the comparative material is reconstructed from multiple texts rather than from just one source. Another complicating factor is that the material stems from different periods: from the Old Babylonian to the Persian. Moreover, the distinction between gardens is not always clear-cut. For example, it is often difficult to distinguish between temple and royal gardens. In sum, the next section contains a daunting exercise and is part of an ongoing discussion in light of new evidence.

5.1 Numinous or Mythological Gardens

Two "gardens" found in the Gilgamesh Epic (GE) have been presented as parallels to the Garden in Eden.[80] The first is the Cedar Forest.[81] This forest

---

73 Howard N. Wallace, *The Eden Narrative*, HSM 32 (Atlanta: Scholars Press, 1985); Korpel and De Moor, *Adam, Eve, and the Devil*.

74 Dietrich, "Paradies"; Walton, *Lost World*.

75 Wyatt, "Royal Garden"; Van der Kooij, "Paradise."

76 Stordalen, *Echoes*.

77 I will limit myself to the garden and not discuss the similarities and differences in protagonists, plots, or motifs.

78 William W. Hallo, "Introduction: Ancient Near Eastern Texts and their Relevance for Biblical Exegesis," in *The Context of Scripture: Canonical Compositions from the Biblical World*, ed. William W. Hallo and K. Lawson Younger Jr., 4 vols (Leiden: Brill, 2002), 1:xxii–xxviii.

79 Except the numinous gardens and the one reconstructed by Korpel and De Moor, *Adam, Eve, and the Devil*.

80 Stordalen, *Echoes*, 146–55. See for text and translation Andrew R. George, *The Babylonian Gilgamesh Epic: Introduction, Critical Edition and Cuneiform Texts*, 2 vols. (Oxford: Oxford University Press, 2003).

81 GE 2.217–229, 274–300; 5.1–9, 182–184 (George, *Gilgamesh*, 566–71, 602–3, 610–11). According to Dalley, the forest contained pines, not cedars. Stephanie Dalley, *Myths from Mesopotamia: Creation, The Flood, Gilgamesh, and Others*, rev. ed., Oxford World's Classics (Oxford: Oxford University Press, 2000), 61.

is presented as a dangerous place,[82] located on a mountain described as "the dwelling of the gods, the throne-dais of the goddesses."[83] It includes high trees and one cedar standing at its top, reaching to heaven.[84] The forest is guarded by Ḫumbaba who is appointed by Enlil "to keep the cedars safe."[85] The similarities and differences between this passage and Gen 2–3 are the following:

Similarities	Differences
Domain of gods	Forest (GE)—garden (Genesis)
Guard(s)	No mention of trees as food in GE
Alleged mountain	No presence of water in GE
Reference to a particular tree (cedar)	No task/work in the garden in GE
In the East?[86]	Forest is a place of danger in GE, but
Presence of animals[87]	garden is a place of blessing in Genesis
	No creation motif in this passage of GE

The second garden is the so-called Jewel Garden. This "garden" is located at the exit of Mount Mashu, a mountain guarded by a scorpion-man and his mate. Unfortunately, the text is highly fragmentary. It describes trees that are full of gemstones or are made of gemstones and bear fruit.[88] The conjecture that the trees are "trees of the gods" seems likely and suggests that this is a place in which divine presence is found.[89] It is, however, not clear whether the trees imply a garden or a forest. The similarities and differences are the following:

---

82   GE 2.274–300 (George, *Gilgamesh*, 568–71).

83   GE 5.6 (George, *Gilgamesh*, 602–3). The OB version depicts this forest as the dwelling of the Annunaki. George, *Gilgamesh*, 466. Stordalen, *Echoes*, 150–51 argues that the Cedar Forest is not a divine abode, but a place where chthonic forces dwell. This interpretation is rarely followed.

84   GE 5.293–294 (George, *Gilgamesh*, 612–15).

85   GE 2.227–228 (George, *Gilgamesh*, 566–67).

86   According to some traditions it was located in the east. See George, *Gilgamesh*, 496.

87   Both the LV version as well as the recently found SB fragment report the presence of animals in the forest. See Farouk N.H. Al-Rawi and Andrew R. George, "Back to the Cedar Forest: The Beginning and End of Tablet V of the Standard Babylonian Epic of Gilgameš," *JCS* 66 (2014): 69–90; Dalley, *Myths from Mesopotamia*, 71–72.

88   The presence of gemstones in both Gen 2–3 and GE is often emphasized. The gemstones in Gen 2:11–12 are, however, not in the garden (in contrast to Ezek 28) and do thus not contribute to the description of the garden.

89   See GE 9.172 (George, *Gilgamesh*, 497, 672–75). Note, however, the different translation in Dalley, *Myths*, 99.

Similarities	Differences
Trees are depicted as beautiful	No animals in GE
Beautiful place	No water in GE
Trees contain fruit[90]	No task/work in the garden in GE
Garden?	No creation motif in GE
Domain of gods	
Alleged mountain	
In the East[91]	
Guards	

5.2   Temple or Cultic Gardens

Temple or cultic gardens were known throughout the ANE, but have been es-
pecially attested in Mesopotamia. They were mostly found in the courtyard
of the temple, near a spring and emphasized the fertility given by the deity.
Both garden and temple were seen as a representation of the deity's abode.
The most extensive reconstruction of temple gardens has been proposed by
Geo Widengren.[92] His study has, however, rightly been criticized as over-
interpreting the material.[93] A more nuanced argument for the idea that the
Garden in Eden is a temple garden has been set out by Manfred Dietrich.[94] The
similarities and differences are the following:

Similarities	Differences
Garden	No mention of cult (altar/sacrifice/statue) in
Water	Genesis
Creation Motif	The depiction of trees as beautiful and good for
Domain of gods	food is rare in comparative material[95]

---

90   Whether the fruit from the trees in the Jewel Garden could be eaten or not is unclear. It
partly depends on whether one assumes that the fruit is compared to gemstones or actually consisted of gemstones.

91   George, *Gilgamesh*, 492–96.

92   Geo Widengren, *The King and the Tree of Life in Ancient Near Eastern Religion* (Uppsala:
Lundequistska bokhandeln, 1951).

93   See Stordalen, *Echoes*, 140.

94   See Dietrich, "Paradies." To be able to make such a comparison Dietrich argues that the
אדם was created in the garden. This, however, contradicts Gen 2:8, 15. Another argument
for a cultic garden has been set out by Schüle. See Andreas Schüle, "Made in the Image of
God: The Concepts of Divine Images in Gen 1–3," *ZAW* 117 (2005): 1–20.

95   An exception might be Sennacherib's garden next to the Akitu temple; see Dietrich,
"Paradies," 290–91. In temple gardens, however, the food was primarily used as an offering
to the deity and not, as in Gen 2–3, as food for humans.

Alleged mountain?[96]   No animals in comparative material[97]
Guard(s)
Reference to a particular tree[98]
Work in the garden[99]

5.3   *Royal Gardens*

While the Hebrew Bible reports a Garden of the King,[100] especially Assyrian
and Persian kings were known for their orchards.[101] Located adjacent to the
palace, these gardens were full of beautiful trees, well-watered, and often contained animals. As set out by Stephanie Dalley, royal gardens came in different
versions.[102] All gardens, however, showed that the king ruled over his empire,
guarded creation, and made it prosper as a true gardener.[103] While most scholars distinguish royal gardens from temple gardens, at least in the Neo-Assyrian
period royal gardens contained aspects of cult and sacredness.[104] Neo-Assyrian
kings were seen as high priests and several depictions of gardens combine cultic and royal aspects.[105] The following differences and similarities between
royal gardens and Gen 2–3 may be noted:

Similarities	*Differences*
Garden	Royal garden is not the domain of the
Trees that are pleasing to the eye	gods
and for food	It is not a king, but YHWH who plants

---

96   Some scholars relate temple garden and mountain, but the mountain is not found in
      Dietrich, "Paradies."

97   Animals might be assumed for cultic gardens, but are not referred to by Dietrich. They
      would, moreover, have served for the cult.

98   See for example the Kiškanu-tree passage. Mark J. Geller, *Evil Demons: Canonical Utukkû
      Lemnûtu Incantations*, SAACT 5 (Helsinki: Neo-Assyrian Text Corpus Project, 2007), 169–
      71, 245–46.

99   In temple gardens this task is cultic, while in Gen 2–3 it is primarily related to the ground.

100   2 Kgs 25:4; Jer 39:4; 52:7; Neh 3:15; Qoh 2:5 (both גן and פרדס); Esther 1:5; 7:7–8 (גנה).

101   Wiseman, "Mesopotamian Gardens"; Dalley, *The Mystery*; Oded Lipschits, Yuval Gadot,
      and Dafna Langgut, "The Riddle of Ramat Raḥel: The Archaeology of a Royal Persian
      Period Edifice," *Transeuphratène* 41 (2012): 57–79.

102   Dalley, *The Mystery*, 172–4.

103   Dietrich, "Paradies," 287.

104   Anastasia Amrhein, "Neo-Assyrian Gardens: A Spectrum of Artificiality, Sacrality and
      Accessibility," *Studies in the History of Gardens & Designed Landscapes* 35 (2015): 91–114
      (96–97).

105   See for pictures Dalley, *The Mystery*, 44. The Nineveh garden has a statue of the king and
      an altar. Sargon's garden in Khorsabad also has an altar. The Garden Party depicts a priest
      and might be associated with the cult of the dead.

Guard (cherub-king)	the garden in Genesis
Animals	No reference to particular trees in the
Beautiful and abundant place	royal garden
Water	
Alleged mountain?[106]	
Work in the garden	
Creation motif?[107]	

5.4 Garden of the Gods

The view that Eden is a divine garden has been posited in two different ways. A first reasoning connects the Levantine mountain of the gods, Ezek 28; 31, the Zion tradition, and Hebrew Bible passages that depict Eden as the Garden of YHWH (Gen 13:10; Isa 51:3).[108] This argument is often complemented by a larger cosmic mountain theory. If we follow the position as set out by Howard Wallace, the following similarities and differences appear:

Similarities	*Differences*
Domain of gods	No trees as food in comparative material
Garden of the gods?[109]	No animals in comparative material
Alleged mountain	No clear work/task in comparative
Beautiful and abundant place	material
Reference to particular tree	
Guard(s)	
Creation motif	
Presence of water	
Exile	

The second reasoning has been set out by Marjo Korpel and Johannes de Moor. On the basis of their reconstruction of an Ugaritic myth,[110] they argue that the vineyard of the great gods in KTU 1.100 and 1.107 is similar to the Garden in Eden. Their reconstructed myth also contains a tree of death (and life?), a serpent, and a protagonist called 'adammu. The similarities and differences are the following:

---

106   Present in some sources. See Dalley, *The Mystery*, 43–63, 129.

107   The royal garden illustrated the king's ability to create in a similar way as the gods did.

108   See primarily Wallace, *Eden Narrative*, 76–83.

109   Most Levantine sources do not attest a garden of the gods, this in contrast to Ezek 28 and 31.

110   Korpel and De Moor, *Adam, Eve, and the Devil*.

Similarities	Differences
Particular tree (tree of life/death)	Vineyard-garden
Domain of gods	No other animals in KTU
In the East	Creation motif in KTU?
Alleged mountain	No guard(s) in KTU
Tree as food	
Beautiful and abundant place	
Exile	
Work/task[111]	

5.5   *Summary*

The similarities and differences between the various options are shown in Table 9.1.

TABLE 9.1   Features of ANE gardens

	Cedar forest	Jewel garden	Temple garden	Royal garden	Divine garden (Wallace)	Korpel/ De Moor
Garden	–/?	?	X	X	X	–/?
Particular tree	X	–	X	–	X	X
Trees for food	–	?	–	X	–	X
Beautiful trees	X	X	X/?	X	X	?
Beautiful place/blessing	–	X	X	X	X	X
Domain of gods	X	X	X	–	X	X
In the East	?	X	–	–	–	X
Alleged mountain	X	X	–	X/?	X	X
Creation motif	–	–	X	X/?	X	?
Guarding	X	X	X	X	X	–
Water	–	–	X	X	X	X
Exile/removal	–	–	–	–	X	X
Animals	X	–	–	X	–	–
Work/task	–	–	X	X	–	X

---

111   *'Addamu* takes up/is given the task of going to the vineyard.

Both the table and the comparison set out above illustrate that the garden of Gen 2–3 resembles many of the motifs found in gardens throughout the ANE. While a more thorough study should consider the possibility that the author(s) had one of these gardens in mind when drafting his Garden in Eden, my purposes here are more limited: to see whether the comparative evidence shows that the Garden in Eden should be seen as a cultic garden. It does not. While the cultic or temple garden has some specific similarities to Gen 2–3, the similarities to other gardens are as large or even larger.

The royal garden, for example, seems a better possibility, especially because of the shared double function of the trees (food and beauty), its abundant status, and the presence of animals. However, the planting of the garden by God and his walking in the garden, as well as the presence of two particular trees and a serpent show that the Edenic garden is more than a regular royal garden. In this royal-divine garden, YHWH is King.[112]

The numinous gardens could be linked to the divine garden, as both are referred to as domain of the gods. Especially the presence of particular trees shows similarity to the Eden Narrative. However, while the comparison to the Jewel Garden seems promising at first, the similarities are not that extensive compared to other options. The Cedar Forest resembles more elements found in Gen 2–3. However, the dangerous atmosphere as well as the absence of creation motifs clearly differs from Gen 2–3.

While the divine garden seems to come closest, the proposals of Wallace and Korpel and De Moor do not close the case yet. Although the vineyard of KTU texts shares the most specific elements with Gen 2–3, Korpel and De Moor's reconstruction of the Ugaritic texts has not been reviewed extensively by others. Wallace's reconstruction is not found in a single text. In addition, Gen 2–3 locates the garden nearby the divine dwelling, not at the same place. God does not live in the garden.

In sum, the presence of particular trees, water, and a creation motif does not have to imply a cultic garden, but could suggest a divine garden or royal garden. Moreover, the most pressing similarity, cult, has to be assumed for Gen 2–3. In my view, seeing Eden as a cultic garden is thus the least convincing option. The comparison set out above, God's planting of and walking in the Garden, as well as other passages in the Hebrew Bible (Isa 51:3; Gen 13:10; Ezek 28; 31), show rather that the garden is God's own garden, located near his

---

112   The presence of both royal and divine elements should not be surprising since royal gardens were likely based on divine gardens. See Dalley, *Mystery*, 156–57.

domain. In contrast to Ezek 28 and 31, Gen 2–3 uses elements known to us from royal gardens to depict this divine garden in Eden.[113]

6   Conclusions

Although Gen 2–3 locates the garden near the place where God resides and likely assumes a degree of holiness for the garden, it is not concerned with cult or sacrifice. Especially in recent scholarship, this has led to an ideological confrontation between those assuming cult to be implicitly present and Eden functioning as prefiguration of the temple and those arguing against such a position. In my contribution, I have tried to show that Eden can contain a form of holiness without being cultic. I argued that the depiction of Eden as a pre-figuration of the temple in Jerusalem is not found in the book of Genesis, but was part of a later tradition.

Three elements have contributed to seeing Eden as a temple:
– While prophetic literature mainly compared Jerusalem to Eden (Isa 51:3; Ezek 36:35) some prophetic, but primarily early Jewish and Christian, sources depicted a new Jerusalem in Eden imagery (e.g., Isa 65:17–25; Rev 2:7; 21–22; 1 En. 25). This identification of *Urzeit* and *Endzeit* led later interpreters to read backwards and see Eden as a prefiguration of the temple. The reception of Ezek 28 and the presence of the Gihon in Gen 2:13 might have contributed to this view.
– As noted above, temple and divine dwelling were closely related in the minds of Ancient Near Eastern people. Some early Jewish and Christian interpreters were aware of this (e.g., Ephrem the Syrian). The use of similar imagery for Eden and the temple likely led them to identify the two.
– The book of Jubilees, rabbinic literature, and Zoharic tradition illustrate a desire to relate the issues of cult and/or purity to the book of Genesis, a book that remains silent about these issues.

These three elements contributed to the idea of the Garden in Eden as the holy place par excellence, an idea not found in Gen 2–3. The fact that some of my colleagues will disagree with me not only shows the ongoing fascination for the Eden Narrative, but also illustrates how this holy place has become a metaphorical place of ideological confrontation. This confrontation is not one

---

113   Other aspects of royal imagery are present in Gen 2–3. See Stordalen, *Echoes*, 312–14. The אדם was, however, no king. The royal imagery rather illustrates his special status and relationship to YHWH.

between Jewish and Christian interpreters, but one between different views on what may be assumed to be present in Gen 2–3 as well as on which comparative material best illuminates the biblical text. Or in the words of Augustine: *Non ignoro de paradiso multos multa dixisse.*

Acknowledgments

Thanks are due to Marjo C.A. Korpel, Christopher B. Hays, John Day, and the editors of this volume for their valuable suggestions.

References

Albright, William F. "The Mouth of the Rivers." *AJSL* 35 (1919): 161–95.

Al-Rawi, Farouk N.H., and Andrew R. George. "Back to the Cedar Forest: The Beginning and End of Tablet V of the Standard Babylonian Epic of Gilgameš." *JCS* 66 (2014): 69–90.

Amrhein, Anastasia. "Neo-Assyrian Gardens: A Spectrum of Artificiality, Sacrality and Accessibility." *Studies in the History of Gardens & Designed Landscapes* 35 (2015): 91–114.

Anderson, Gary A. *The Genesis of Perfection: Adam and Eve in Jewish and Christian Imagination.* Louisville: Westminster John Knox, 2001.

Beale, Gregory K. *The Temple and the Church's Mission.* Downers Grove, IL: Apollos IVP, 2004.

Block, Daniel I. "Eden: A Temple? A Reassessment of the Biblical Evidence." Pages 3–29 in *From Creation to New Creation: Biblical Theology and Exegesis.* Edited by Daniel M. Gurtner and Benjamin J. Gladd. Peabody, MA: Hendrickson, 2013.

Böttrich, Christfried. "The Figures of Adam and Eve in the Enoch Tradition." Pages 211–51 in *The Adam and Eve Story in the Hebrew Bible and in Ancient Jewish Writings including the New Testament.* Edited by Antti Laato and Lotta Valve. SRB 7. Turku: Åbo Akademi University; Winona Lake, IN: Eisenbrauns, 2016.

Clifford, Richard J. *The Cosmic Mountain in Canaan and the Old Testament.* HSM 4. Cambridge: Harvard University Press, 1972.

Cornelius, Izak. "The Garden in the Iconography of the Ancient Near East: A Study of Selected Material from Egypt." *Journal for Semitics* 1 (1989): 204–28.

Dalley, Stephanie. *Myths from Mesopotamia: Creation, The Flood, Gilgamesh, and Others.* Rev. ed. Oxford World's Classics. Oxford: Oxford University Press, 2000.

Dalley, Stephanie. *The Mystery of the Hanging Garden of Babylon: An Elusive World Wonder Traced.* Oxford: Oxford University Press, 2013.

Day, John. *From Creation to Babel: Studies in Genesis 1–11*. London: T&T Clark, 2013.

Dietrich, Manfred. "Das biblische Paradies und der babylonische Tempelgarten: Über-legungen zur Lage des Garten Eden." Pages 281–324 in *Das biblische Weltbild und seine altorientalischen Kontexte*. Edited by Bernd Janowksi and Beate Ego. Tübingen: Mohr Siebeck, 2001.

Eliade, Mircea. *Patterns in Comparative Religion*. Translated by Rosemary Sheed. Lincoln: University of Nebraska Press, 1979.

Elior, Rachel. "The Garden of Eden is the Holy of Holies and the Dwelling of the Lord." *Studies in Spirituality* 24 (2014): 63–118.

Fishbane, Michael A. "The Sacred Center." Pages 6–27 in *Texts and Responses: Studies Presented to Nahum N. Glatzer on the Occasion of his Seventieth Birthday by His Students*. Edited by Michael A. Fishbane and Paul R. Flohr. Leiden: Brill, 1975.

García Martínez, Florentino. "Man and Woman: Halakah Based upon Eden in the Dead Sea Scrolls." Pages 57–76 in *Qumranica Minora II: Thematic Studies on the Dead Sea Scrolls*. Edited by Eibert J.C. Tigchelaar. STDJ 64. Leiden: Brill, 2007.

Geller, Mark J. *Evil Demons: Canonical Utukkû Lemnûtu Incantations*. SAACT 5. Helsinki: Neo-Assyrian Text Corpus Project, 2007.

George, Andrew R. *The Babylonian Gilgamesh Epic: Introduction, Critical Edition and Cuneiform Texts*. 2 vols. Oxford: Oxford University Press, 2003.

Gordon, Robert P. "Evensong in Eden: As It Probably was Not in the Beginning." Pages 17–30 in *Leshon Limmudim: Essays on the Language and Literature of the Hebrew Bible in Honour of A.A. Macintosh*. Edited by David A. Baer and Robert P. Gordon. LHBOT 593. London: Bloomsbury, 2013.

Hallo, William W. "Introduction: Ancient Near Eastern Texts and Their Relevance for Biblical Exegesis." Pages 1:xxii–xxviii in *The Context of Scripture: Canonical Compositions from the Biblical World*. Edited by William W. Hallo and K. Lawson Younger Jr. 4 vols. Leiden: Brill, 2002.

Hendel, Ronald S. "Other Edens." Pages 185–89 in *Exploring the Longue Durée: Essays in Honor of Lawrence E. Stager*. Edited by David Schloen. Winona Lake, IN: Eisenbrauns, 2008.

Hoopen, Robin B. ten. "Genesis 5 and the Formation of the Primeval History: A Redaction Historical Case Study." *ZAW* 129 (2017): 177–93.

Hoopen, Robin B. ten. "Where Are You, Enoch? Why Can't I Find You? Genesis 5.21–24 Reconsidered." *JHS* 18.4 (2018): 1–23.

Kooij, Arie van der. "The Story of Paradise in the Light of Mesopotamian Culture and Literature." Pages 3–22 in *Genesis, Isaiah, and Psalms: A Festschrift to Honour Professor John Emerton for His Eightieth Birthday*. Edited by Katherine J. Dell, Graham Davies, and Yee Von Koh. VTSup 135. Leiden: Brill, 2010.

Korpel, Marjo C.A., and Johannes C. De Moor. *Adam, Eve, and the Devil: A New Beginning*. 2nd enl. ed. HBM 65. Sheffield: Sheffield Phoenix Press, 2015.

Lasine, Stuart. "Everything Belongs to Me: Holiness, Danger, and Divine Kingship in the Post-Genesis World." *JSOT* 35 (2010): 31–62.

Lee, Lydia. *Mapping Judah's Fate in Ezekiel's Oracles against the Nations.* ANEM 14. Atlanta: SBL Press, 2016.

Levenson, Jon D. *Sinai and Zion: An Entry into the Jewish Bible.* New York: HarperCollins, 1985.

Lipschits, Oded, Yuval Gadot, and Dafna Langgut. "The Riddle of Ramat Raḥel: The Archaeology of a Royal Persian Period Edifice." *Transeuphratène* 41 (2012): 57–79.

Mettinger, Tryggve N.D. *The Eden Narrative: A Literary and Religio-Historical Study of Genesis 2–3.* Winona Lake, IN: Eisenbrauns, 2007.

Morales, L. Michael. *The Tabernacle Pre-Figured: Cosmic Mountain Ideology in Genesis and Exodus.* BTS 15. Leuven: Peeters, 2012.

Niehr, Herbert. "Die Wohnsitze des Gottes El: Ein Beitrag zu ihrer Lokalisierung." Pages 325–60 in *Das Biblische Weltbild und seine altorientalischen Kontexte.* Edited by Bernd Janowksi and Beate Ego. Tübingen: Mohr Siebeck, 2001.

Ruiten, Jacques T.A.G.M. van. "Visions of the Temple in the book of Jubilees." Pages 215–27 in *Gemeinde ohne Tempel/Community without Temple: Zur Substituierung und Transformation des Jerusalemer Tempels und seines Kults im Alten Testament, antiken Judentum und frühen Christentum.* Edited by Beate Ego, Armin Lange, and Peter Pilhofer. Tübingen: Mohr Siebeck, 1999.

Ruiten, Jacques T.A.G.M. van. "Adam in the Book of Jubilees." Pages 143–75 in *The Adam and Eve Story in the Hebrew Bible and in Ancient Jewish Writings including the New Testament.* Edited by Antti Laato and Lotta Valve. SRB 7. Turku: Åbo Akademi University; Winona Lake, IN: Eisenbrauns, 2016.

Schüle, Andreas. "Made in the Image of God: The Concepts of Divine Images in Gen 1–3." *ZAW* 117 (2005): 1–20.

Smith, Mark S. *The Origins of Biblical Monotheism: Israel's Polytheistic Background and the Ugaritic Texts.* New York: Oxford University Press, 2001.

Stordalen, Terje. *Echoes of Eden: Genesis 2–3 and Symbolism of the Eden Garden in Biblical Hebrew Literature.* CBET 25. Leuven: Peeters, 2000.

Stordalen, Terje. "Heaven on Earth—Or Not? Jerusalem as Eden in Biblical Literature." Pages 28–57 in *Beyond Eden: The Biblical Story of Paradise (Genesis 2–3) and Its Reception History.* Edited by Konrad Schmid and Christoph Riedweg. Tübingen: Mohr Siebeck, 2008.

Wallace, Howard N. *The Eden Narrative.* HSM 32. Atlanta: Scholars Press, 1985.

Walton, John H. *The Lost World of Adam and Eve: Genesis 2–3 and the Human Origins Debate.* Downers Grove, IL: IVP Academic, 2015.

Weinfeld, Moshe. *Deuteronomy and the Deuteronomic School.* Oxford: Clarendon, 1972.

Wenham, Gordon J. "Sanctuary Symbolism in the Garden of Eden Story." Pages 399–404 in *I Studied Inscriptions from Before the Flood: Ancient Near Eastern, Literary, and Linguistic Approaches to Genesis 1–11*. Edited by Richard S. Hess and David T. Tsumura. Winona Lake, IN: Eisenbrauns, 1994.

Widengren, Geo. *The King and the Tree of Life in Ancient Near Eastern Religion*. Uppsala: Lundequistska bokhandeln, 1951.

Wiseman, Donald J. "Mesopotamian Gardens." *Anatolian Studies* 33 (1983): 137–44.

Woods, Christopher. "At the Edge of the World: Cosmological Conceptions of the Eastern Horizon in Mesopotamia." *JANER* 9 (2009): 183–239.

Wright, David P. "Holiness, Sex, and Death in the Garden of Eden." *Bib* 77 (1996): 305–29.

Wright, David P. "Holiness (OT)." Pages 3:237–49 in *The Anchor Bible Dictionary*. Edited by David Noel Freedman. 6 vols. New York: Doubleday, 1992.

Wyatt, Nicolas. "A Royal Garden: The Ideology of Eden." *SJOT* 28 (2014): 1–35.

Zevit, Ziony. *What Really Happened in the Garden of Eden?* New Haven: Yale University Press, 2013.

CHAPTER 10

Rituals of Holy Places in the 11th Century: the Circling of the Gates of Jerusalem and Pilgrimage to the Cave of Machpelah

Tamar Kadari and Gila Vachman

Midrash Song of Songs Rabbah (ShirR) is the oldest and largest of the midrashim on the Song of Songs.[1] It was redacted at the end of the sixth or beginning of the seventh century in the land of Israel, and comprises Tannaitic and Amoraic interpretations of the scroll, verse by verse.[2] While working on the project of preparing a critical edition of ShirR, it stood out that MS Oxford Bodleian Library 102 preserves a short passage which is absent from all the rest of the textual witnesses.[3] These lines reveal interesting evidence regarding the circling of the gates of Jerusalem and pilgrimage to the Cave of Machpelah by Jews during the 11th century.

This paper is divided into three main parts. First we will discuss the content of the addition in MS Oxford Bodleian Library 102 and its context. Then we will determine its date, by examining distinct terminology and names that appear in the fragment. Finally, we will propose to clarify its contribution to our understanding of the importance of Jerusalem and Hebron as foci of pilgrimage during the early Islamic period.

---

1 Another midrash on the Song of Songs based on MS de Rossi 541 was published concurrently under two different names: Salomon Buber, *Shir ha-Shirim Zuta* (Berlin: Reem, 1894) and Solomon Schechter, *Agadath Shir ha-Shirim* (Cambridge: Bell, 1896). An additional midrash was published by Eliezer H. Greenhut, *Midrash Shir ha-Shirim* (Jerusalem: Hazvi, 1897); see Myron B. Lerner, "The Works of the Aggadic Midrash and the Esther Midrashim," in *The Literature of the Sages*, ed. Samuel Safrai et al., 2 vols. (Assen: Van Gorcum, 2006), 2:133–229 (141–42).

2 Despite its great importance there is as yet no critical edition available which offers a critical version of the text accompanied by an apparatus and a commentary. For a synoptic edition see https://www.schechter.ac.il/midrash/shir-hashirim-raba/.

3 MS Oxford, Bodleian Library Seld. Sup. 102 (Neubauer 164/1).

1   The Content and Context of the Addition

MS Oxford Bodleian Library 102 is a 16th-century manuscript written in
Sephardic handwriting.[4] Its importance lies in the fact that it is one of the
only four complete manuscripts that contain the entire midrash on the Song
of Songs. Moreover, it is the only manuscript which contains all five midrashim
on the five scrolls (118a–362a).[5]

The additional lines in MS Oxford Bodleian Library 102 (see fig. 10.1) read
as follows:

ואתם אחינו ⟨שבמערת המכפלה שקבלתם את אליהו וששה מן המערה

שביירושלם. ר׳ נתן ור׳ עמרם. ור׳ חלסון [חלפון?] ⟨ויצחק עני ירושלם⟩ על אחת

כמה וכמה שישלם לכם שכר טוב.

And you, our brethren ⟨in the Cave of Machpelah, who received Elijah
and six from the Cave in Jerusalem, Rabbi Nathan and Rabbi Amram and
Rabbi Halson [Halfon?] and Isaac, the poor [ones] of Jerusalem⟩ all the
more so will [He] pay you a good reward.[6]

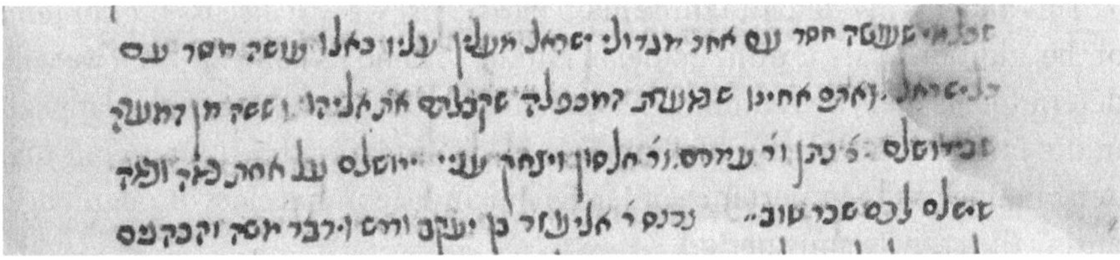

FIGURE 10.1   Detail from MS Oxford Bodleian Library 102, fol. 286v

4   The copying of the first section (segments of Yalqut Shimoni) ended at 1513; see Adolf D.
    Neubauer, *Catalogue of the Hebrew Manuscripts in the Bodleian Library and in the College
    Libraries of Oxford*, 3 vols. (Oxford: Clarendon, 1886–1906), 1:27; Malachi Beit-Arié, *Catalogue
    of the Hebrew Manuscripts in the Bodleian Library: Supplement of Addenda and Corrigenda
    to Vol. I* (Oxford: Clarendon, 1994), 22. According to Beit-Arié, the section including the mi-
    drashim on the five scrolls was copied by a different scribe on the same volume, around 1514.

5   On collections of midrashim on the five scrolls in medieval manuscripts see Marc Bregman,
    "Midrash Rabbah and the Medieval Collector Mentality," *Prooftexts* 17 (1997): 63–76; Lerner,
    "The Works of the Aggadic Midrash," 166–69.

6   ShirR 2:5,3. All midrash translations are based on H. Freedman and Maurice Simon, *Midrash
    Rabbah* (London: Soncino, 1939), with some adjustments.

The text indicates two very well-known holy places: the Cave of Machpelah (Cave of the Patriarchs) and the Cave in Jerusalem. We are able to understand that Elijah and a group of rabbis, Rabbi Nathan, Rabbi Amram, Rabbi Halson (probably Halfon) and Isaac, were hosted by their brethren in the Cave of Machpelah. The group is titled "the poor of Jerusalem." Although the text clearly reads "six from the Cave in Jerusalem," only four names are listed. The hospitality of the brethren in Machpelah is granted by a blessing: "All the more so will [He—God] pay you a good reward."

These additional lines appear in ShirR within a long sermon concerning the matter of hospitality, based on the verse: "Stay me with flagons, comfort me with apples, for I am sick of love" (Cant 2:5):[7]

"סַמְּכוּנִי בָּאֲשִׁישׁוֹת רַפְּדוּנִי בַּתַּפּוּחִים כִּי חוֹלַת אַהֲבָה אָנִי" (שה״ש ב,ה)
בשילפי השמד נכנסו רבותי׳ לאושא. ואלו הן ר׳ נחמיא ור׳ יהודה ור׳ מאיר ור׳ יוסי
ור׳ שמעון בן יאחי ור׳ אלעזר בנו של ר׳ יוסי הגלילי ור׳ אליעזר בן יעקב ... כיון שהגיע
זמנן להפטר אמרו מקום שנתקבלנו בתוכו אנו מניחין אותו ריקן?

"Stay me with flagons, comfort me with apples, for I am sick of love" (Cant 2:5). At the termination of the era of persecution, our rabbis assembled at Usha and they are Rabbi Nehemia and Rabbi Yehuda and Rabbi Meir and Rabbi Yossi and Rabbi Shimon ben Yoḥai and Rabbi Eliezer son of Rabbi Yossi of Galilee … When the time came for their departure, they said: Shall the place where we have been received be left empty-handed?[8]

The midrashic unit opens by describing the assembly at Usha during the end of the era of persecution. The connection of the story to the verse is a play on words with אשישות (ʾashishot, "flagons") and the name Usha (אושא). According to the midrashic narrative, seven Tannaim were gathered in the Galilean town of Usha, most likely after the Bar Kochba revolt, in order to teach Torah in public.

Several scholars considered this story as evidence of the actions taken by Rabbi Akiva's students in order to renew the activity of the Sanhedrin in Usha after the decrees of Hadrian and the Bar Kochba revolt.[9] According to Ephraim

---

7   All the biblical citations are based on the King James Version, with some adjustments.

8   ShirR 2:5,3.

9   See Gedalyahu Alon, *History of the Jews in the Land of Israel During the Period of the Mishna and the Talmud*, 2 vols. (Tel Aviv: Hakibuz Hameuchad, 1958), 1:69–71 (Hebrew); Aharon Oppenheimer, "The Restoration of Jewish Settlement in Galilee and Golan during the Third and Fourth Centuries," in *Eretz Israel from the Destruction of the Second Temple to the Muslim Conquest*, ed. Zvi Baras et al., 2 vols. (Jerusalem: Yad Ben Zvi, 1982), 1:75–92 (80–82) (Hebrew).

Urbach, Usha was not one of the main cities of the Galilee, so it did not arouse opposition on behalf of the Roman authorities, and was suitable for the establishment of leadership institutions in the first generation after the revolt. The purpose of the assembly was to encourage the local people and obtain their consent.[10]

The assembly at Usha ends with an Aftara, which was part of the ritual of leave-taking between the sage and his pupils or his audience after mutual learning.[11] The Aftara included a homily based on verses and ended with words of blessing including praise and appreciation, as well as wishes for the future. As a sign of gratitude for their warm reception, each of the seven sages gives a long sermon regarding the subject of hospitality and loving kindness. The structure is as follows:[12]

1.   Rabbi Yehuda entered and taught ...
2.   Rabbi Nehemia entered and taught ...
3.   Rabbi Meir entered and taught ...
4.   Rabbi Yossi entered and taught ...
5.   Rabbi Shimon ben Yoḥai entered and taught ...
6.   Rabbi Eliezer [son of Rabbi Yossi of Galilee] entered and taught ...
     ⟨additional lines MS Oxford Bodleian Library 102⟩
7.   Rabbi Eliezer ben Yaacov entered and taught ...

All seven sermons end with a repetitive formula which appears with some changes (and tends to shorten in some of the manuscripts), and is phrased as a blessing:

> And you, our brethren in Usha, since you received our rabbis with food and drink, all the more so will the Holy One, blessed be He, pay you a good reward.

The additional lines in the Oxford Bodleian Library manuscript are located at the end of the sixth sermon, that of Rabbi Eliezer son of Rabbi Yossi of Galilee.

---

10   Ephraim E. Urbach, "From Judaea to Galilee," in *Jacob Friedman Memorial Volume*, ed. Shlomo Pines (Jerusalem: Hebrew University, 1974), 66–70 (69–70) (Hebrew); Benjamin Isaac and Aharon Oppenheimer, "The Revolt of Bar Kokhba: Ideology and Modern Scholarship," in *The Near East Under Roman Rule: Selected Papers* (Leiden: Brill, 1998), 220–56 (243–45).

11   On the Aftarah see Uri Ehrlich, "Verbal and Non-Verbal Rituals of Leave-Taking in Rabbinic Culture: Phenomenology and Significance," *JSQ* 8 (2001): 1–26.

12   A few later Amoraic sayings were added to these Tannaitic sermons. Regarding the literary structure of this unit see Rella Kushelevsky, "Rabbinic Sage Stories in Midrashic Compilations: An Intertextual Reading of the Usha Synod Narrative in Song of Songs Rabbah 2:5 and Deuteronomy 27:9," *JJS* 65 (2014): 284–301.

These lines also mention the hospitality which the people of Jerusalem received while visiting the Cave of Machpelah, and they fit in well within the general context of the midrash. They also use a similar formula at the end: "All the more so will he pay you a good reward," exactly as we find at the end of the other sermons:

> *Repetitive formula ShirR 2:5, 3*
> And you, our brethren in Usha,
> since you received our rabbis with food and drink,
> all the more so will the Holy One, blessed be He, pay you a good reward.

> *Additional lines MS Oxford-Bodleian 102*
> And you, our brethren ⟨in the Cave of Machpelah,
> who received Elijah and six from the cave in Jerusalem ...⟩
> all the more so will [He] pay you a good reward.

Yet a few details give doubt as to whether these lines belong to ShirR. Some of the names mentioned in them, Rabbi Halson (or Halfon) and Elijah, are not familiar as names of rabbinic sages. Furthermore, the term "the poor of Jerusalem" is not found in rabbinic literature, nor do we hear of a place called "the Cave in Jerusalem" in the time of the Talmud. This evidence leads to great doubt as to whether these lines are an original version of the midrash, or rather an addition, an interpolation that was added at a relatively later time, during the transitions and copying of the midrash.

2   Determining the Date of the Addition

We shall now review the special terms and names that appear in the addition in the hope that they will help determine its date and shed light on its possible historical context.

2.1   *The Poor of Jerusalem*

The term "the poor of Jerusalem" does not exist elsewhere in rabbinic literature, but it does appear in letters found in the Cairo Genizah, published by Moshe Gil. In these documents, dated to the 11th century, residents of Jerusalem send their requests for help to Jewish communities in the diaspora. These letters demonstrate that the economic state of the residents of Jerusalem at this time was difficult and that they suffered from continuing drought and plagues. They complain about the heavy taxes and their ongoing challenges, both from the local Christians and the pilgrims on the one hand, and the Muslims on the other.[13] Special messengers carrying these letters were sent to different communities in order to organize fundraising for the residents of Jerusalem. Yet the financial support that the diaspora Jews gave to their brethren in Jerusalem derived first and foremost from religious motivations. In the letters published by Gil, the term "the poor of Jerusalem" is used as a general name for the city's residents, regardless of their economic status. They are also called "the poor of the holy city" (עניי עיר הקדש), "the remnants of the holy city" (פליטת עיר הקודש), and "the sect of the poor rabbis" (כת הרבנים העניים).[14] It is therefore most likely that this attribute does not describe a class or an economic situation (though these suffered from deprivation and poverty), but that it refers mostly to spiritual and religious dependence on God.[15]

Diaspora Jewry saw great importance in the continuation of a Jewish presence in Jerusalem. It safeguarded the site of the Temple and protected the communities in the diaspora. The funds delivered to Jerusalem and its residents had the same status as tithes (מעשר), fines and vows which were brought to the Temple while it existed. Halachically speaking, the rules of dedication (הקדש) applied to these funds; they were sacred and it was prohibited to change their purpose.[16] The donors received letters of appreciation and were granted great honours: their names were announced in front of all the pilgrims at the assembly on the Mount of Olives during Hoshana Rabbah.[17] In return for this

---

13   See Moshe Gil, *Palestine During the First Muslim Period (634–1099)*, 3 vols. (Tel Aviv: Tel
       Aviv University, 1983), 1:330–31 and 1:492–97 (Hebrew).

14   See Gil, *Palestine During the First Muslim Period*, 2:91 on Genizah fragment 52 (JTS ENA
       2804,3); Gil, *Palestine During the First Muslim Period*, 2:700 on Genizah fragment 383 (JTS
       ENA 2739,18); Gil, *Palestine During the First Muslim Period*, 2:52–53 on Genizah fragment 31
       (JTS ENA 2804,1); Gil, *Palestine During the First Muslim Period*, 2:273 on Genizah fragment
       154 (T-S NS 324, 6). Genizah fragments 33 and 420 are quoted below.

15   It is similar to the usage of the word in some of the Psalms and in Qumranic literature.
       See Yael Wilfand, *Poverty, Charity and the Image of the Poor in Rabbinic Texts from the
       Land of Israel* (Sheffield: Sheffield Phoenix Press, 2014), 36–40. A related term in Arabic
       is *fukraa*, meaning both poor in the material sense and a name for those who seek God's
       mercy; see Yaacov Lev, *Charity, Endowments, and Charitable Institutions in Medieval
       Islam*, (Gainesville: University Press of Florida, 2005), 8–9; Amy Singer, *Charity in Islamic
       Societies* (Cambridge: Cambridge University Press, 2008), 157–65. We would like to thank
       Dr Katia Cytryn-Silverman for drawing our attention to this matter.

16   See Gil, *Palestine During the First Muslim Period*, 1:494–96; Moshe Gil, *Documents of the
       Jewish Pious Foundations from the Cairo Geniza* (Leiden: Brill, 1976), 3–4.

17   Gil, *Palestine During the First Muslim Period*, 1:498; Marc Hirshman, "The Priest's Gate
       and Elijah ben Menahem's Pilgrimage," *Tarbiz*, 55 (1986): 217–27 (221) (Hebrew), and his
       references in note 8. For a description of the pilgrims, the circling of the gates, and the
       assembly on the Mount of Olives see Elchanan Reiner, "Jewish Pilgrimage to Jerusalem
       in Late Antiquity and the Middle Ages," in *Pilgrimage: Jews, Christians, Moslems*, ed. Ora

support, the poor of Jerusalem would pray for diaspora Jewry and maintain a Jewish presence in the Holy City.

One example of this interchange is a letter dated 1024 from the people of Jerusalem to Bishr ibn Ghalib of Fustat:

[...]היה לעניי ירושלם יד ומשען בחסדך הנאה [כ]די שנכפיל ברכותך מול היכל יי...
ושלומך [ו]שלום אחיך אנשי ירושלם מעצמים שלומך.[18]

... May you be a hand and support to the poor of Jerusalem in your love-ly gracefulness, so that we may multiply your blessings in front of the Temple of God ... your well-being, and the well-being of your brethren. And the people of Jerusalem empower your well-being.

The writer asks for financial aid and in return promises to double the prayers for the Parnas (donor) in front of the Temple of God (היכל ה'). The letter ends by saying that the well-being of the people of Jerusalem guarantees the well-being of diaspora Jewry.

A different letter written probably by Elijah HaCohen ben Shlomo Gaon to the community of Egypt in 1057, reads as follows:

ואתם אחינו בית ישראל, הנה יבואו אליכם ראויים ולא ראויים, הגונים ולא הגונים,
ותעשו עמהם כפי חסדכם. כל שכן שאנחנו אחיכם עניכם המתפללים עליכם בעיר
קודש אלוהים חיים ... חנונו חנונו עזרונו עזרונו. כי אנחנו שומרים לכם לכל אשר
יבוא. וראוי לכם לע[זור לנו בנדבותיכם] וצדקותיכם ומתנותיכם. ולא תמוש היתד
התקועה במקום נאמן.

And you our brethren the house of Israel, the worthy and the unworthy will come to you, the honest and the dishonest, and you will do with them according to your kindness. Even more so us, your brethren the poor, who pray for you in the Holy City of the eternal God ... mercy mercy upon us, help help us. For we are your guards to whoever might come. And you ought to assist us with your donations, your charity and your gifts. So that the peg that is stuck in a firm place, will not budge.[19]

Limor, Elchanan Reiner, and Miriam Frenkel (Raanana: The Open University, 2014), 72–89 (Hebrew).

18 Gil, *Palestine During the First Muslim Period*, 2:55–56 on Genizah fragment 33 (JTS ENA 4020, 19).

19 Gil, *Palestine During the First Muslim Period*, 3:14–18 on Genizah fragment 420 (RNL Evr. II).

The people of Jerusalem describe themselves as "your brethren the poor," "the peg that is stuck in a firm place." They pray for "the house of Israel" and are "your guards to whoever might come," probably describing the pilgrims. The first reference—"and you our brethren the house of Israel"—is especially noteworthy for its similarity to the opening of the addition in the Oxford manuscript: "and you our brethren in the Cave of Machpelah."

2.2   *The Cave in Jerusalem*

Another peculiar phrase that is mentioned in the addition to the Oxford Bodleian Library manuscript is "the Cave in Jerusalem." Dan Bahat pointed out that the name "the Cave" or "Al Magara" appears in documents from the Genizah between 1029–1070.[20] The place is first mentioned in a letter from Shlomo ben Yehuda, head of the Geon Yaacov Yeshiva in Jerusalem, to Ephraim ben Shemaria, head of the Shamean (Syrian) community in Fustat, dated 1029. He writes as follows:

ביום שני נכללנו במערה בקהל רב והוצאנו ספרי תורות והחרמנו על כל חוקק
חקקי און.

On Monday we gathered in the Cave as a big crowd and we took out the Torah scrolls and we censured all those who made unjust laws.[21]

The documents indicate that for the Jews of Jerusalem this was a site of assembly, which had Torah scrolls and was designated for sacred use, all of which leads Bahat to the conclusion that it served as a synagogue. In a different letter, written five years later, the Gaon describes the collapse of the wall located beside the synagogue:

[וראוי] להודיעך הנס הגדול [שעשה עמנו] אלהינו ביום טוב הראשון שלפסח ברוך
הוא אשר לא הסיר ברכתו מבית ישראל. כי היו התפילה [...] בירוש' העם בבית
הכנסת וטף ונשים באים ויוצאים. והם בו קורים בתורה בעוד אשר נפל הכתל אשר
על יד הבית [...] אמות על [...] עשרים נדבכים קרוב לחמש עשרה אמ[ות] ולא
הוזק אדם ...

And it is worth informing you of the great miracle [made by] our God on the first day of Pesach, blessed be him who has not left of his kindness and truth from the house of Israel. For they were praying [...] community

---

20   Dan Bahat, "Identification of the Gates of the Temple Mount and the 'Cave' in the Early Muslim Period," *Cathedra* 106 (2002): 61–86 (Hebrew).

21   Gil, *Palestine During the First Muslim Period*, 2:140 on Genizah fragment 79 (T-S 20, 102).

in Jerusalem were all in the synagogue and children and women coming and going. And they were reading the Torah when the wall near the house collapsed [...] amot on [...] twenty tiers that are approximately fifteen amot, but no one was hurt ...[22]

According to Shlomo ben Yehuda, the wall collapsed during the first day of the festival of Passover when the synagogue was full of people, but miraculously no one was hurt. These words most probably describe the result of the great earthquake of 1033, which caused the collapse of part of the Western Wall of the Temple Mount. Two other letters by the Gaon contain details about the restoration, the clearing of the stones and the soil from the street and the building of the foundations. It is understood from his letters that the renovation of the wall included about 18 meters of the Western Wall.

Following this information, Bahat tried to trace the exact location of the synagogue. He claims that there is a restored section of the Western Wall called "the patch" which is located at what is known today as Warren's Gate, about 30 meters north of Wilson's Arch. At the top of the entrance there is a carved arch in a style typical of gates renovated during the 11th century. These findings prove, according to Bahat, that this site is indeed the Cave synagogue.[23]

2.3   Elijah

Four rabbis are mentioned in the addition, besides Elijah: Rabbi Nathan, Rabbi Amram, Rabbi Halson (or Halfon) and Isaac. The name Halfon is very rare in rabbinic literature but it became quite common in later periods and was typical of Jews living in Islamic countries.[24] The identity of these four persons is quite difficult to determine. It may well be that the key for solving this problem lies in the name Elijah.

22   Gil, Palestine During the First Muslim Period, 2:215 on Genizah fragment 118 (TS NS J 172).

23   See Bahat, "Identification of the Gates." For other suggestions of identifying the Cave's location see Moshe Gil, "The Jewish Community," in The History of Jerusalem: Early Muslim Period, 638–1099, ed. Joshua Prawer and Haggai Ben-Shamma (Jerusalem: Yad Ben Zvi, 1996), 163–200 (175); Elchanan Reiner, "Concerning the Priest Gate," Tarbiz 56 (1986–1987): 279–90 (284) (Hebrew); Eyal Meiron, "On the Problem of the Location of the Jewish Neighborhood in Jerusalem on the Eve of the First Crusade," in New Studies on Jerusalem: Volume 20, ed. Eyal Baruch and Avraham Faust (Ramat-Gan: Bar Ilan, 2015), 279–304 (299–300) (Hebrew).

24   In the lexicon of Jewish names prior to the Muslim conquest the name Halfon does not appear. See Tal Ilan, Lexicon of Jewish Names in Late Antiquity, 4 vols. (Tübingen: Mohr Siebeck, 2002–2012). On the other hand, in Gil's book at least 15 people by this name are mentioned. See Gil, Palestine During the First Muslim Period, 3:674.

About 30 years ago, Marc Hirshman published two articles discussing four
additions inserted to midrash Ecclesiastes Rabbah and ShirR, in which the
name Elijah son of Menachem appears.[25] Hirshman found that there are no
rabbis by the name of Elijah and the name is not to be found in any talmudic
or midrashic work.[26] He identifies him as Rabbi Elijah son of Menahem, the
descendant of a Palestinian Gaonic dynasty, who lived in the second half of
the 11th century.[27]

The additions which Hirshman examined, like our addition, also deal with
holy places and rituals that are associated with them. One of these additions
has a special importance for our discussion:

כל ישראל אינן מתכנסין אלא לירושלם תבנה במהרה ועולי בפעמי רגלים שלש
פעמים בשנה כמו שזכרי בוראי ויוצרי וישעי וסברי הב״ה לי אני אליהו בר מנחם
ב״ר״ק׳ נ״ע׳ [בן ר׳ קלונימוס?] נוחו עדן] והעלני ג׳ פעמים בחג המצות ובחג השבועות
ובחג הסוכות ובחג הפסח שנית יתברך שמו לעולמי עולמי׳ ועשיתי הושענא רבה
בהר המשחה ושמחת תורה בירושלים עיר אלהינו הר קדשו. כשעמדנו בהר הזתים
בהושענא רב׳ אפילו שבאו מכל הקהלות שבעולם לא היו נראין אלא כמאתיים והן
היו יב׳ אלף משער חולדה עד שער הכהן ... יזכני אני ואחי בירושלים.

All of Israel do not gather but to Jerusalem, may it soon be built, and
they make pilgrimage on the festivals three times a year, just like my creator and savior blessed be he has remembered [granted?] me, Elijah son
of Menahem BRK NA [son of Rabbi Klonimus?, may he rest in heaven][28]
and brought me to pilgrimage three times: on the festival of Matzot and
on the festival of Shavuot and on the festival of Sukkot and on the festival of Pesach again, may his name be blessed forever and ever. And I
did Hoshana Rabbah in the Mount of Mishchah (Mount of Olives) and
Simhat Torah in Jerusalem the city of our God and his holy mountain.

---

25   Hirshman, "The Priest's Gate"; Marc Hirshman, "'Rabbi Elijah Interpreted the Verse
      Concerning Pilgrims' (ShirR 2:14, 7): Another Medieval Interpolation and Again Rabbi
      Elijah," *Tarbiz* 62 (1991): 275–76 (Hebrew).

26   Hirshman, "Rabbi Elijah," 275.

27   Hirshman, "The Priest's Gate," 225. Some scholars disagree with his identification and
      suggest that this is Rabbi Elijah the Elder of Le Mans, one of the most prominent rabbis
      of France in the 11th century. See Avraham Grossman, *The Early Sages of France: Their
      History, Their Way in the Leadership, Their Spiritual Work* (Jerusalem: Magnes, 1995),
      82–107 (Hebrew); Hananel Mack, "A Sermon of Rabbi Elijah the Elder in a Medieval
      Midrash," *Zion* 61 (1996): 209–13 (Hebrew); Reiner, "Jewish Pilgrimage to Jerusalem," 74.
      Jonah Fraenkel rejects Grossman's suggestion and supports Hirshman's identification; see
      Jonah Fraenkel, ed., *Machzor Shavuot* (Jerusalem: Koren, 2000), xlvii–xlviii.

28   On the abbreviations and their meaning see Hirshman, "The Priest's Gate," 224 (n. 31).

> When we stood on the Mount of Olives on Hoshana Rabbah even though people came from all the communities in the world, they seemed to be no more than two hundreds and there were twelve thousands from the Hulda Gate to the Priest (HaCohen) Gate … May he grant me and my brethren in Jerusalem.

In this text, the writer, Elijah son of Menahem, describes his pilgrimage to Jerusalem three times and then once more. Due to the fact that he made a pilgrimage to Jerusalem four times during his life, Hirshman assumes that he lived near the land of Israel or within it. Elijah tells of his participation in a ritual that took place on Hoshana Rabbah, the seventh day of Sukkot, in which he stood on the Mount of Olives, also named Mount of Mishchah, and of the powerful experience he had watching the large crowd that had gathered and circled around the gates of the city, from the Hulda Gate to the Priest's Gate. Although he claims that there were twelve thousand people there, it seemed like they were only two hundred. We shall discuss this ritual on the Mount of Olives and its relation to the Oxford addition in greater detail later on.

According to Hirshman's suggestion, Rabbi Elijah owned a copy of Ecclesiastes Rabbah and ShirR and added his notes in the margins of their sheets. A later copier, who got hold of this manuscript, thought these were glosses and integrated them into the midrashic text. And so, the words of Rabbi Elijah ben Menahem from the 11th century became an integral part of the midrashic text.

Hirshman's findings reveal an important phenomenon in the history of manuscripts and the midrashic texts, and could support our suggestion that the lines in the Oxford manuscript are also a later addition which was integrated into the midrash. We can conclude the second part of our paper by stating that all the various findings point in the same direction. Namely, the term "poor of Jerusalem" and the identification of the "Cave in Jerusalem" both lead to the assumption that the addition in MS Oxford Bodleian Library is from the 11th century. This concurs with Hirshman's additions, also dated to the 11th century. The Elijah appearing in our addition and the one from Hirshman's findings most probably refer to the same person.

3   The Cave of Machpelah and Jerusalem as Foci of Pilgrimage during the 11th Century

We will now turn to discusses the significance of the addition to our understanding of pilgrimage to holy places in the 11th century. The addition points to an interesting connection between two caves, the Cave of Machpelah in

Hebron and the Cave in Jerusalem. Aside from the holiness of Machpelah and Jerusalem, the two sites are known to be foci of pilgrimage. Hirshman's passages also deal with pilgrimages to Jerusalem and the rituals associated with them.

3.1   *Pilgrimage to the Cave of Machpelah*

Dating back to ancient times, the city of Hebron and the Cave of Machpelah have been regarded as holy places and destinations for pilgrimage. According to Elchanan Reiner, the Cave of Machpelah was the second most important pilgrimage site after Jerusalem. From the descriptions of several 12th-century Jewish pilgrims, Reiner concluded that the visit to Hebron took place as part of a complex route seemingly reproducing the lives of the patriarchs.[29] Among the most prominent sites in the writings of pilgrims from the 12th century he points out these: the house of Abraham, the Oak of Mamre and the stone on which the angels sat, the tree on which they leaned, Sarah's tent, her well, the stone on which Isaac was circumcised, the place where Adam was created and the spring of Hagar. Hebron and its environs were presented as a large sacred compound, in which the pilgrim advanced along its stations until reaching its heart, the Tomb of the Patriarchs. The status of the Cave of the Patriarchs in the consciousness of the pilgrim must therefore be compared to the status of the Temple Mount in the route of the pilgrimage to Jerusalem.[30]

The custom of pilgrimage to the Cave of Machpelah during the 11th century is documented in letters preserved in the Cairo Genizah. Among the pilgrims we find also residents of Jerusalem, whose custom it was to come to the cave of Machpelah and visit the graves of the patriarchs. In a letter written by Eli Hacohen ben Ezekiel of Jerusalem to Eli Hacohen ben Haim of Fustat (approximately 1060 CE) we read:

דע לך אדוני הפרנס, יגן עליך אלהים, כי הלכתי אל קברי אבות והיה עמי קהל, וחי ירושלים! אכן התפללתי למען אדוני החבר אבו זכרי ש״צ [שליח ציבור] ולמען בנו ולמען אחיו ולמען אדוני ורבי שר העדה ולמענך אדוני, בשעת פתיחת ספר התורה ואחרי כל תפילה. אלהים יקבל ממני את מיטב תפילותי למען כל ידיד.

> You should know, my lord the sustainer (פרנס), may God protect you, that I went to the graves of the patriarchs and there was a crowd (קהל) with me and in the name of Jerusalem! I prayed at the time of the scrolling the

---

29   Elchanan Reiner, "Overt Falsehood and Covert Truth: Christians, Jews, and Holy Places in Twelfth Century Palestine," *Zion* 63 (1998): 158–88 (177–78) (Hebrew).

30   Reiner, "Overt Falsehood and Covert Truth," 178 (n. 56).

Torah and after every prayer, for the sake of my lord the Haver (חבר) Abu Zakri the leader, and for his son and for his brother and for the sake of my master and teacher, the head of the community, and for you my lord. God will receive my finest prayers for the benefit of every friend.[31]

The letter indicates that a resident of Jerusalem travelled with a crowd of people to the Cave of Machpelah to visit the tomb of the patriarchs, quite similarly to the image deriving from our addition in ShirR, where Elijah and six from the Cave in Jerusalem visit the Cave of Machpelah.

A letter dated 1080 from Seadiah ben Abraham, living in Hebron, to Yeshua ben Yachin in Fustat, ends with the following words:

מני קרובו אוהבו ידידו, המתפלל תמיד בעדו, סעדיה החבר המשרת לאבות עולם, זכרם לברכה, בן אברהם בר נתן נב"ע [נשמתו בגן עדן].

From his loving relative, his friend who always prays for him, Seadiah the Haver, servant of the Patriarchs of the world, may their memory be of blessing, son of Abraham bar Nathan, may his soul rest in heaven.[32]

We can understand that there were people who settled in the Cave of Machpelah, took care of it and prayed for the well-being of their brethren. The role of the "servant of the Patriarchs" is similar to that of "the poor of Jerusalem."

Muslim sources can also teach us much about pilgrimage customs to the Cave of Machpelah and their implications. In Islamic tradition the Cave of Machpelah played a major role and was among the most sacred places in the land of Israel, second only to the mosques on the Temple Mount, and both were called Ḥaram al-Sharif (the sacred places).[33] During the beginning of the 11th century, Ibn al-Murajja wrote the first guide for the Muslim pilgrim. He praises the great virtues in combining a pilgrimage to Jerusalem with the visiting of the Tomb of Abraham in Hebron. Whoever accomplishes this

---

31 Originally in Judeo-Arabic, brought by Gil, *Palestine During the First Muslim Period*, 3:78 on Genizah fragment 452. Abu Zakri is Judah ben Seadiah and the head of the community is Abraham ben Isaac ben Furat: see Gil, *Palestine During the First Muslim Period*, 3:78 (nn. 3–4).

32 Gil, *Palestine During the First Muslim Period*, 3:550–51 on Genizah fragment 613.

33 Amikam Elad, "Pilgrims and Pilgrimage to Hebron (al-Khalīl) During the Early Muslim Period (638?–1099)," in *Pilgrims and Travelers to the Holy Land*, ed. Bryan F. Le Beau and Menachem Mor (Omaha: Creighton University Press, 1996), 21–62. The Oak of Mamre, where Abraham built an alter and dwelled, was also sanctified; see Elad, "Pilgrims and Pilgrimage to Hebron," 23–24.

and recites five prayers will be granted all his requests and all his sins shall be forgiven.[34]

The practice of Muslim pilgrimage to the Cave of Machpelah is found in the 10th-century writings of the famous Muslim geographer, al-Muqaddasī (946–1000?). Muḥammad ibn Aḥmad Shams al-Dīn al-Muqaddasī was born in Jerusalem to a family of Persian origins. His book, entitled *The Best Divisions for Knowledge of the Regions*, was written in 985 at the latest.[35] The book contains the most exhaustive review of the land of Israel and its cities, with Jerusalem at its centre. Here is his account of Hebron:

> (p. 172) Habrā (Hebron) is the village of Abraham Al-Khalīl (the Friend of God) on him be peace. Within it is a strong fortress[36] said to be of the building of the jinns, being of enormous squared stones. In the middle of this stands a dome of stone, built in Islamic times, over the sepulcher of Abraham ... facing each prophet lies his wife. The enclosure has been converted into a mosque, and built round about it are rest houses for the pilgrims ...
>
> (p. 173) In Hebron is a public guest house which is continuously open, with a cook, a baker and servants in regular attendance. These offer a dish of lentil and olive oil to every poor person who arrives, and it is set before the rich, too, should they wish to partake. Most people think the food is from Abraham; however it is, in fact, from the bequest of Tamim Al-Dārī [the owner of the ground] and others. In any case, it were better, in my mind, to abstain from eating it.[37]

Al-Muqaddasī's descriptions and observations are consistent, and among his generation's writers he is considered the most comprehensive geographer. His descriptions indicate that the pilgrimage phenomenon required a whole

---

34   Elad, "Pilgrims and Pilgrimage to Hebron," 27–30; Amikam Elad, *Medieval Jerusalem and Islamic Worship: Holy Places, Ceremonies, Pilgrimage* (Leiden: Brill, 1995), 68–71. On the merits of visiting Abraham's Tomb in Muslim popular beliefs see Iganz Goldziher, *Muslim Studies*, ed. and trans. C. Renate Barber and Samuel M. Stern, 2 vols. (London: Allen and Unwin, 1971), 2:87.

35   See Basil A. Collins, *Al-Muqaddasī: The Best Divisions for Knowledge of the Regions* (Lebanon: Garnet Publishing, 1994), ix–xxviii.

36   On the transition and expansion of the settlement of Hebron and the location of the Cave of Machpelah see Elad, "Pilgrims and Pilgrimage to Hebron," 21–23.

37   Collins, *Al-Muqaddasī, The Best Divisions for Knowledge of the Regions*, 156, with some adjustments.

institution of fixed hospitality, aimed at welcoming and taking care of the Muslim pilgrims and their needs. It included, among other things, people who were paid for to provide food to the visitors. The money came from a charity foundation (הקדש). According to Al-Muqaddasī, the pilgrims associate this hospitality with that of Abraham and viewed the food as coming from him. Al-Muqaddasī descriptions shed light on the reception of Muslim pilgrims in the 10th century.

Further indication of the hospitality offered to Muslim pilgrims is documented in the writings of Nāṣer Khusraw, a traveler of Persian origin. It is of exceptional importance, as it dates to the time of the addition in ShirR. Nāṣer Khusraw was a Persian poet and philosopher who lived in the 11th century (1004–1088 CE). His book, the *Safar Nāma*, is a record of his journey to the Mediterranean coast, Egypt, Arabia, and back.[38] He compiled his *Safar Nāma* in the latter half of the 11th century. Khusraw describes Hebron as follows:

> On the roof of the *maqsura* inside the shrine are cells to house guests who stop there. The revenues of this charity are considerable, being derived from villages and houses in the Holy City ... Pilgrims, travelers and other guests, are given bread and olives. There are also many gristmills where oxen and mules grind flour all day long. There are also young girls who bake bread every day, each loaf weighing one Mann (1.5 kg). Anyone who goes there is given a daily ration of one loaf of bread, a bowl of lentils cooked with olive oil, and raisins. This custom has been maintained from the time of Abraham (the Friend of the Merciful) himself down to the present. On some days there are five hundred pilgrims present, all of whom receive this hospitality.[39]

The descriptions of al-Muqaddasī and Nāṣer Khusraw draw a similar picture. We have no parallel evidence from the 11th century concerning the hospitality offered to Jewish pilgrims when arriving at the Cave of Machpelah, nor to their numbers. The passage that was added to midrash ShirR is therefore an important and vital indication of the existence of such hospitality offered by Jews in the Cave of Machpelah during the 11th century:

---

38   On Nāṣer Khusraw and *Safar Nāma* see Wheeler M. Thackston, *Nāṣer-e Khosraw's Book of Travel (Safarnāma)* (New York: Bibliotheca Persica, 1986), ix–xii.

39   Thackston, *Nāṣer-e Khosraw's Book of Travel*, 36–37, with some adjustments made from the translation by Guy Le Strange, *Palestine under the Moslems: A Description of Syria and the Holy Land from AD 650–1500* (London: Palestine Exploration Fund, 1890), 314–15.

And you, our brethren in the Cave of Machpelah, who received Elijah
and six from the Cave in Jerusalem, Rabbi Nathan and Rabbi Amram and
Rabbi Halson [Halfon?] and Isaac, the poor [ones] of Jerusalem, all the
more so [He] will pay you a good reward.

3.2   Customs of Pilgrimage to Jerusalem

Much has been written about the customs of pilgrimage to Jerusalem.
Therefore, we will focus on the information related to the addition in MS
Oxford Bodleian Library 102 in ShirR. According to the identification of Bahat,
there was a gate at the entrance to the Cave synagogue in Jerusalem from the
Second Temple period; this gate was renovated in the 11th century following
the great earthquake. This gate and its location had special significance as it
was located at the closest spot outside of the Temple Mount to the holy of holies. Bahat identifies this gate as Warren's Gate, or as it is called in the prayer of
the gates: "The Gate of Yehuda" (in Arabic: *bab-a sachina*).

The main ritual of the Jewish pilgrims to Jerusalem consisted of circling the
Temple Mount and praying at its gates.[40] Circling the gates served as a substitute for visiting the site of the Temple (העלייה למקום המקדש). The pilgrims
would circle the mountain from the outside, and the ancient gates served as
prayer stations along the path. This prayer was called "prayers of the gates" or
"circling of the gates" (in Arabic, *salat abab*). It is well-documented in piyyutim
from the early Muslim period. According to Reiner, the roots of this ritual are
in the ritual performed by the individual pilgrim when arriving at the city, regardless of a specific date or any public event. Even so, parts of this prayer were
weaved into public rituals that were performed by a large audience (ברוב עם)
during the pilgrimage seasons, especially on Hoshana Rabbah, the seventh day
of Sukkot. The gathering on Hoshana Rabbah was described in the addition
in Ecclesiastes Rabbah, where Elijah ben Menahem testifies that from where
he stood on the Mount of Olives he could see the crowd that gathered from
Hulda's Gate to the Priest's Gate and that there were twelve thousand people.
These three spots—the Mount of Olives, Hulda's Gate, and the Priest's Gate—
were part of the route that pilgrims took when circling the gates, alongside the
gate at the entrance to the Cave synagogue.

It is therefore possible that the Elijah mentioned in our addition came to
Jerusalem and circled the gates, including a visit to the gate at the entrance to
the Cave synagogue. If this is the same Elijah ben Menahem, he may have also

---

40   For a list of the main sources regarding this ritual see David Golinkin, "Jerusalem in
      Jewish Law and Custom: A Preliminary Typology," *Sidra* 16 (2000): 5–16 (13–14 and n. 45)
      (Hebrew).

participated in the ritual on the Mount of Olives. Afterwards he went on and made a pilgrimage to the Cave of Machpelah, together with some of the local residents, called "the poor of Jerusalem." In the Cave of Machpelah he received warm hospitality as was customary for all pilgrims. Days later, when he returned to his home, he added in his books descriptions of his experience. The description of Hoshana Rabbah was added to midrash Ecclesiastes Rabbah, traditionally associated with the festival of Sukkot, and in the margins of midrash Song of Songs Rabbah, associated with the festival of Pesach, he added a special blessing to his benefactors (גומלי טובתו) from the Cave of Machpelah, alongside the midrash speaking of hospitality.

4   Conclusion

In this paper, we pointed out the historical significance of a short fragment preserved in a manuscript of midrash ShirR. The name Elijah, the term "the poor of Jerusalem," as well as the mentioning of two holy places, the Cave in Jerusalem and the Cave of Machpelah, led us to conclude that this is an addition from the 11th century which made its way into ShirR.

It is interesting to see how a midrash redacted around the 6th or 7th century in the land of Israel preserves an addition from the 11th century, which appears in a 16th-century manuscript. This addition contains rare evidence of people, places and customs of an earlier era, and reveals important information regarding the historical-geographical reality in the land of Israel, as well as social aspects that arise from it.

In his paper on the Priest's Gate, Hirshman writes: "[T]he ability of a late scribe to copy bona fide a late tradition into the body of the midrash indicates, among other things, the natural way in which late experiences are integrated into ancient texts."[41] We are now able to add to these experiences another such case: the warm welcome that Elijah and the people of Jerusalem were given by their brethren, the people of Hebron, while visiting the Cave of Machpelah.

Acknowledgment

This study was made possible through the support of the Israel Science Foundation (Grant No. 1152/09).

---

41   Hirshman, "The Priest's Gate," 225.

References

Alon, Gedalyahu. *History of the Jews in the Land of Israel During the Period of the Mishna and the Talmud.* 2 vols. Tel Aviv: Hakibuz Hameuchad, 1958. (Hebrew).

Bahat, Dan. "Identification of the Gates of the Temple Mount and the 'Cave' in the Early Muslim Period." *Cathedra* 106 (2002): 61–86. (Hebrew).

Beit-Arié, Malachi. *Catalogue of the Hebrew Manuscripts in the Bodleian Library: Supplement of Addenda and Corrigenda to Vol. I.* Oxford: Clarendon Press, 1994.

Bregman, Marc. "Midrash Rabbah and the Medieval Collector Mentality." *Prooftexts* 17 (1997): 63–76.

Buber, Salomon. *Shir ha-Shirim Zuta.* Berlin: Reem, 1894.

Collins, Basil A. *Al-Muqaddasī: The Best Divisions for Knowledge of the Regions.* Lebanon: Garnet, 1994.

Ehrlich, Uri. "Verbal and Non-Verbal Rituals of Leave-Taking in Rabbinic Culture: Phenomenology and Significance." *JSQ* 8 (2001): 1–26.

Elad, Amikam. *Medieval Jerusalem and Islamic Worship: Holy Places, Ceremonies, Pilgrimage.* Leiden: Brill, 1995.

Elad, Amikam. "Pilgrims and Pilgrimage to Hebron (al-Khalīl) During the Early Muslim Period (638?–1099)." Pages 21–62 in *Pilgrims and Travelers to the Holy Land.* Edited by Bryan F. Le Beau and Menachem Mor. Omaha: Creighton University Press, 1996.

Fraenkel, Jonah, ed. *Machzor Shavuot.* Jerusalem: Koren, 2000.

Freedman, H., and Maurice Simon. *Midrash Rabbah.* London: Soncino, 1939.

Gil, Moshe. *Documents of the Jewish Pious Foundations from the Cairo Geniza.* Leiden: Brill, 1976.

Gil, Moshe. *Palestine During the First Muslim Period (634–1099).* 3 vols. Tel Aviv: Tel Aviv University, 1983. (Hebrew).

Gil, Moshe. "The Jewish Community." Pages 163–200 in *The History of Jerusalem: Early Muslim Period, 638–1099.* Edited by Joshua Prawer and Haggai Ben-Shammai. Jerusalem: Yad Ben Zvi, 1996.

Goldziher, Iganz. *Muslim Studies.* Edited and translated by C. Renate Barber and Samuel M. Stern. 2 vols. London: Allen and Unwin, 1971.

Golinkin, David. "Jerusalem in Jewish Law and Custom: A Preliminary Typology." *Sidra* 16 (2000): 5–16. (Hebrew).

Greenhut, Eliezer H. *Midrash Shir ha-Shirim.* Jerusalem: Hazvi, 1897.

Grossman, Avraham. *The Early Sages of France: Their History, Their Way in the Leadership, Their Spiritual Work.* Jerusalem: Magnes, 1995. (Hebrew).

Hirshman, Marc. "The Priest's Gate and Elijah ben Menahem's Pilgrimage." *Tarbiz* 55 (1986): 217–27. (Hebrew).

Hirshman, Marc. "'Rabbi Elijah Interpreted the Verse Concerning Pilgrims' (ShirR 2:14, 7): Another Medieval Interpolation and Again Rabbi Elijah." *Tarbiz* 62 (1991): 275–76. (Hebrew).

Ilan, Tal. *Lexicon of Jewish Names in Late Antiquity.* 4 vols. Tübingen: Mohr Siebeck, 2002–2012.

Isaac, Benjamin, and Aharon Oppenheimer. "The Revolt of Bar Kokhba: Ideology and Modern Scholarship." Pages 220–56 in *The Near East Under Roman Rule: Selected Papers.* Leiden: Brill, 1988.

Kushelevsky, Rella. "Rabbinic Sage Stories in Midrashic Compilations: An Intertextual Reading of the Usha Synod Narrative in Song of Songs Rabbah 2:5 and Deuteronomy 27:9." *JJS* 65 (2014): 284–301.

Le Strange, Guy. *Palestine under the Moslems: A Description of Syria and the Holy Land from AD 650–1500.* London: Palestine Exploration Fund, 1890.

Lerner, Myron B. "The Works of the Aggadic Midrash and the Esther Midrashim." Pages 2:133–229 in *The Literature of the Sages.* Edited by Samuel Safrai, Zeev Safrai, Joshua Schwartz, and Peter Tomson. 2 vols. Assen: Van Gorcum, 2006.

Lev, Yaacov. *Charity, Endowments, and Charitable Institutions in Medieval Islam.* Gainesville: University Press of Florida, 2005.

Mack, Hananel. "A Sermon of Rabbi Elijah the Elder in a Medieval Midrash." *Zion* 61 (1996): 209–13. (Hebrew).

Meiron, Eyal. "On the Problem of the Location of the Jewish Neighborhood in Jerusalem on the Eve of the First Crusade." Pages 279–304 in *New Studies on Jerusalem: Volume 20.* Edited by Eyal Baruch and Avraham Faust. Ramat-Gan: Bar Ilan, 2015. (Hebrew).

Neubauer, Adolf D. *Catalogue of the Hebrew Manuscripts in the Bodleian Library and in the College Libraries of Oxford.* 3 vols. Oxford: Clarendon, 1886–1906.

Oppenheimer, Aharon. "The Restoration of Jewish Settlement in Galilee and Golan during the Third and Fourth Centuries." Pages 1:75–92 in *Eretz Israel from the Destruction of the Second Temple to the Muslim Conquest.* Edited by Zvi Baras, Yoram Tsafrir, Samuel Safrai, and Menahem Stern. 2 vols. Jerusalem: Yad Ben Zvi, 1982. (Hebrew).

Reiner, Elchanan. "Concerning the Priest Gate." *Tarbiz* 56 (1986–1987): 279–90. (Hebrew).

Reiner, Elchanan. "Overt Falsehood and Covert Truth: Christians, Jews, and Holy Places in Twelfth Century Palestine." *Zion* 63 (1998): 158–88. (Hebrew).

Reiner, Elchanan. "Jewish Pilgrimage to Jerusalem in Late Antiquity and the Middle Ages." Pages 72–89 in *Pilgrimage: Jews, Christians, Moslems.* Edited by Ora Limor, Elchanan Reiner, and Miriam Frenkel. Raanana: The Open University, 2014. (Hebrew).

Schechter, Solomon. *Agadath Shir ha-Shirim*. Cambridge: Bell, 1896.

Singer, Amy. *Charity in Islamic Societies*. Cambridge: Cambridge University Press, 2008.

Thackston, Wheeler M. *Nāṣer-e Khosraw's Book of Travel* (*Safarnāma*). New York: Bibliotheca Persica, 1986.

Urbach, Ephraim E. "From Judaea to Galilee." Pages 66–70 in *Jacob Friedman Memorial Volume*. Edited by Shlomo Pines. Jerusalem: Hebrew University, 1974. (Hebrew).

Wilfand, Yael. *Poverty, Charity and the Image of the Poor in Rabbinic Texts from the Land of Israel*. Sheffield: Sheffield Phoenix Press, 2014.

CHAPTER 11

Church History and Archaeology on Holy Places in the Netherlands

Gert van Klinken

Compared to the Middle East, holy places in the Netherlands tend to be comparatively young. Quite a lot of local deities and shrines are known from the Roman era, but none of these cults survived the Christian advance. Even where the plot of a *fanum* (sanctuary) was actually taken over, as in Elst (Gelderland), only the church would matter. Paganism seemed to have left the landscape. Pre-Christian cults left precious few traces, until Roman documents were retrieved during the Renaissance era.[1] Only in the 20th century would their spiritual presence (numen) in the landscape be rediscovered by the wider public, due to the efforts of archaeology. The rebuilding of Nehalennia's temple at Colijnsplaat, where it is common to find floral offerings nowadays, exemplifies the trend.[2]

Carolingian holy places, from the 8th century, were inspired by Middle European and Mediterranean prototypes. Popular saints, such as the Frankish St. Martin of Tours, came from abroad. Holy places that sprung up around the memory of these men and women (and not necessarily at places they would have known during their lifetime) showed that an imported religion could successfully adapt to local needs and circumstances. Local cults in the Netherlands grew in number during the later Middle Ages—and apparently also in importance. The miracle of the sacrament of Amsterdam (1345) was ruthlessly exploited by magistrates. This mingling of commerce and holiness worried the *Devotio Moderna* movement.[3] A speedy abolition of holy places followed during the Reformation era. Protestants characteristically believed that any place, however humble, may become a receptacle of the light emanating from the divine word. Bible studies and homiletics in church became far more important than concepts of sacred space. Holy places, as foci for multi-religious and

---

1 Erich Heller and Manfred Furhmann, *P. Cornelius Tacitus: Annalen: Lateinisch und Deutsch* (Darmstadt: Wissenschaftliche Buchgesellschaft, 1997).

2 P. Stuart and J. Bogaers, *Nehalennia: Römische Steindenkmäler aus der Oosterschelde bei Colijnsplaat*, 2 vols. (Leiden: National Museum of Antiquities, 2001).

3 Thomas a Kempis, *De imitatione Christi* 1.22. Edition in *Libri Quatuor Auctore Ven. Thoma Hemerken a Kempis* (Haarlem: Gottmer, 1949), 18.

ideological confrontation, had to await their revival until the modern era, after the separation of church and state. The Kingdom of the Netherlands (1814) elevated toponyms like Waterloo to emblems of national pride. Emancipatory movements within a modernising national state followed a similar track. The Roman Catholics were finally allowed to again have access to their former holy places, such as Heiloo.[4] It was even possible to invent medieval traditions, as in Hasselt[5]—where a suitable placing on the map (as a well-placed meeting point of Roman Catholics from Gelderland, Overijssel and Frisia [Fryslân]) outbid any considerations of historical accuracy. An emerging Calvinist cult in Den Briel (victory of the Sea Beggars in 1572) sat uncomfortably close to the Roman Catholic cult of the clergy that had been hanged by those same Sea Beggars.

1   Secularisation

It would be a misconception to suppose that these holy places represented a distant past. Quite the contrary: most of them owed their existence to contemporary history, especially during the later decades of the 20th century. The staggering number of sites related to the memory of the Second World War surpasses any preceding presence of "holy places" not only by visual impact, but also by the number of visitors. The Netherlands went through a speedy process of secularisation. Membership of a religious community was no longer standard. Of those who still consider themselves religious in the 21st century, a substantial percentage no longer belong to the three main traditional denominations (Roman Catholicism, Protestantism or Judaism), but either to Islam or to evangelical communities from Africa or Asia.

If we define holiness as a shared experience of where we come from and where we might be going,[6] it is clear that most of the historical churches and synagogues in the Netherlands can no longer hope to fulfil these aims, at least not at the level of the national population. If not here, where then? Where do we find places that claim to offer holiness, defined as common experience and common expectation for the future, that can be discussed by members of Dutch society, irrespective of their specific backgrounds? Monuments

---

4   Marijke Mijboer, Peter Louwerse, Anton Sinke, and Marius van den Berg, *Wandelen langs heilige plaatsen: Dagtochten naar bedevaartsoorden in Nederland* (Zoetermeer: Meinema, 2008).

5   Willem Frijhoff, "Le pèlerinage dans la vie religieuse des Pays-Bas, forme de continuité religieuse: L'exemple du Lieu-Saint de Hasselt (Ov)" (MA Thesis, Paris University, 1970).

6   Karsten Wentink, *Ceci n'est pas une hache: Neolithic Depositions in the Northern Netherlands* (Leiden: Sidestone 2006).

relating to the Second World War may shed light on this. Even more important are the extensive efforts to cultivate the pre-literary ("prehistorical") elements in Dutch public space, and to link them to the perception of holiness in the national education system. Commemorations of the Second World War, on the evening of the 4th of May, have become a well-established feature of civil life. The celebrations are orchestrated by the secular authorities, though representatives of religious, political and ethnic subdivisions are encouraged to participate. However, whether this implies shared experience is not always clear. Archaeology offers an attractive alternative, a neutral ground for discussion about what religion is and is not. A similar trend is apparent in the United Kingdom.[7]

The extent to which holy places add to the dynamics of the social landscape in the Netherlands is not always clear. Knowledgeable appropriation of the traditions that are being represented at these sites, especially in their written forms, is limited to select (and dwindling) groups. The striking absence of major confrontations between Roman Catholics and Calvinists after 1960 may be connected to this trend. Whereas the church of the Heilige Stede ("Holy Site") in Amsterdam prompted vitriolic confrontations between Calvinists and Roman Catholics even in the early 20th century (the Calvinists preferring to tear the medieval monument down, rather than to sell it to the episcopate[8]), no such confrontations between Roman Catholics and Protestants are known to have erupted during the era of secularisation. However, another domain exists in which an attempt has been made to connect a concept of holiness (in the sense of awareness of common descent and common identity) to specific places. It aims to cement this perception of holiness by connecting it to the curriculum of Dutch education. This specialist field is relatively young, but nonetheless a viable factor in the shaping of the perception of the Dutch landscape: archaeology.

2   The Shift towards Archaeology

Connecting archaeology to a perception of holiness seems far-fetched. Yet in the Dutch context, there are good reasons to underline its importance. As was noted above, traditional perceptions of holy places seem to be losing plausibility, at least at the level of society as a whole. On the other hand, it seems that

---

7   Ronald Huston, *Pagan Britain* (New Haven: Yale University Press, 2013).
8   Charles Caspers and Peter Jan Margry, *Het mirakel van Amsterdam: Biografie van een betwiste devotie* (Amsterdam: Prometheus, 2017).

archaeology is benefitting from entrenchment in the educational system. The schools offer a set of common standards and knowledge, which is lacking at the level of separate religious and/or ethnic communities.

When it comes to the perception of holiness within the matrix of local topography, archaeology boasts some features that make this field especially attractive for a multicultural society. Archaeology lacks what, within the paradigm of *laïcité*, is perceived as a major offset of a traditional holy place. That is: the requirement that a religious commitment is presupposed for a "true" perception of what a holy place means to convey to the visitor. This would exclude major parts of the Dutch present-day population. The objection is also pertinent to WWII commemorations, though to a lesser extent: many of the people who have recently immigrated to the Netherlands may still have the feeling that the German occupation and the Holocaust belong to a history that is not theirs, even though the national education system stresses the importance of their attendance at these commemorations.[9]

Those who have left established religion behind will usually prefer a general cultural perception over commitment to in-group teachings. Migrant communities seem to perceive Dutch World War II history as not quite relevant for themselves. In contrast, the archaeological heritage of the Netherlands seems to possess many advantages. All living humans are connected to a common tree of life. Most importantly, from a perspective of *laïcité*, is the fact that it does not require mastering the written heritage of any specific religion—let alone consent to theological teachings—in order to evaluate its results. On the contrary, archaeological explanations both in museums and at the actual sites make it abundantly clear that they wish to operate from a detached and scientific view, not from a commitment to the claims of a religious faith.[10]

Prehistoric collections, museums and informative panels in the field offer the most widespread explanations of sacred space in the Netherlands. They aim at the general public, in the widest sense. Divisions in present-day society, such as the split between Jews, Roman Catholics, Muslims, and secularised liberals simply cease to be valid once applied to the Palaeolithic, Mesolithic, Neolithic, or even Bronze Age and Iron Age in northern Europe. There is a common heritage for all in Africa, the continent from where modern Homo

---

9   See https://www.4en5mei.nl/english/education.
10   Brent Nongbri, *Before Religion: A History of a Modern Concept* (New Haven: Yale University Press, 2013).

sapiens migrated between 200,000 and 100,000 years before the common era. Archaeology can be studied as part of a "big," non-denominational history.[11]

Non-denominational history of this given type, focusing on archaeology and the earlier stages of human history, is manifest in the history handbooks of Dutch secondary schools, thus establishing a link between archaeology, standard patterns of knowledge, and a modern appreciation of holiness as manifested in ancient sites. Many theologians, churches, mosques, and synagogues still tend to ignore the contents of current Dutch school textbooks. This neglect is to their disadvantage, given their importance for the curriculum of the average teenager. Marije Mazereeuw's investigation, carried out in her PThU MA thesis,[12] has led her to argue that the field of archaeology constitutes the first and perhaps most important moment at which the notions of holiness and religion are explained to the Dutch school public in general, apart from treatment of religion in its specific forms, such as Hinduism, Christianity, and so on. This introduction into the backgrounds of religion—and by extension, also into its essence—takes a dual didactic form: detached at the one level, and equally committed at another. Detached, in the sense that holiness is consistently discussed in terms of *do ut des*. Committed in the sense that people "invest" in religion, for the obvious reason that they expect to benefit from the process of exchange that religion essentially is. They connect to the ancestors, thus strengthening a communal sense of belonging, both to the group and to the place of residence. The right to inhabit that place, and to defend it against incursions of others, is derived from the ancestors and demonstrated by the presence of their tombs. Offerings are interpreted as a way of ensuring a successful hunt, fertility, faith healing. Holy places are thus connected to a magical, pre-modern worldview.

Study of this worldview requires detachment, non-commitment to any specific claim of truth, whether ethnic or religious.[13] Unlike catechesis, or explanation by a priest at a holy place, archaeology claims scientific reliability and relevance for all citizens, irrespective of their personal background. From this starting point, it becomes possible to define commitment and to invite the general public to participate in it. First of all, the archaeological legacy refers to mankind in its entirety (as all living human populations share a descent from

---

11   Cynthia Stokes Brown, *Big History: From the Big Bang to the Present* (New York: The New Press, 2007).

12   Marije Mazereeuw, "Donar en Wodan? 'Germaanse religie' in Nederland tussen 250 en 650 AD kritisch beschouwd" (MA Thesis, Protestant Theological University, 2015).

13   E. Fuller Torrey, *Evolving Brains, Emerging Gods: Early Humans and the Origins of Religion* (New York: Columbia University Press, 2017).

Homo sapiens), potentially bridging the gap between ethnic communities. Based on recent German expositions, such as the Schöningen Neanderthal site, we find a tendency to assert the common African background.[14] In other words: archaeology claims to offer a contemporary way to vindicate holiness in the sense of becoming aware of our background—irrespective of the credal and social divisions of our present-day society. And so, a new sense of holiness is on offer: no longer bound by tenets of traditional religion, but open for every individual. Even the magical element can be transformed, and so appropriated in modern contexts. The aims of ancient magic, of prayer and so on, have not become obsolete. We still need cohesion, a place under the sun, healing if necessary and an expectation of the future. All of this we share with the ancestors, ancestors of mankind instead of denominations. As such, archaeology offers a communal sense of origin and destiny for a multicultural society, and thus a very contemporary sense of holiness—embedded in the national system of education and thus accessible to the general population. Previously held conceptions are discussed within this new framework. I will offer an example: the ongoing discussion of the coming of Christianity to the Netherlands, related to the question whether the Christian worldview was preceded by a supposed Germanic cult of Wodenism.

3   Case Study: Discussing Pagan Holy Sites in the Netherlands

The historiography of the Christianisation of the Netherlands between 300 and 800 CE refers to the supposition, still present in recent literature on the subject, that a cult of Woden (Wodan) and Thor existed in this area prior to the coming of Christianity. This view is also reflected in Frank van der Pol's chapter on the conversion era in the *Handboek Nederlandse Kerkgeschiedenis*.[15] This handbook emphasizes the importance of the *Indiculus superstitionum et pagianarum* in the Codex Palatinus 577, now kept in Rome and written in Fulda about the year 800. The Carolingian codex not only mentions a short list of forbidden pagan behaviour (such as *dadsias*, "songs for the dead"), but also contains the famous Old-Saxon baptismal vow. Here we find the famous denial

14   Thomas Terberger et al., eds., *300.000 Jahre Spitzentechnik: Der altsteinzeitliche Fundplatz Schöningen und die frühesten Speere der Menschheit* (Darmstadt: Wissenschaftliche Buchgesellschaft, 2018).

15   Frank van der Pol, "De Middeleeuwen tot 1200," in *Handboek Nederlandse Kerkgeschiedenis*, ed. Herman J. Selderhuis (Kampen: Kok, 2010), 15–118.

of three specifically named non-Christian gods, to be rejected by the baptismal candidate: *ec forsacho allum diaboles uuercum and wordum, thunar ende uuoden ende saxnote* (I forswear all works and words of the devil, of Donar, Woden and Saxnot).[16] A translation with comments can be found in Joris van Eijnatten and Fred van Lieburg, *Nederlandse Religiegeschiedenis*.[17]

What follows in the handbook is a series of sweeping statements, unrelated to the very short text in the *Indiculus*, and yet presented as fact. Woden is presented as the equivalent of Odin, "the Lord of the World," after whom our Wednesday was named. Odin, who met with the bravest of the fallen in Valhalla, is also described as lord of "wisdom and poetry." Some proof is added to support the hypothesis that a Germanic set of beliefs, centred on a family of gods relating to Woden (Odin), actually existed in the Netherlands before the Carolingian era: toponyms like Woensberg near Blaricum (Woden's hill?), Donderberg near Rhenen (Thor's hill?),[18] a temple to the god Irmin that may have existed near Ermelo, an amulet with the runic inscription of the name Igwaz (identified with Tiwaz and Saxnot) in Wijnaldum, and finally tokens that have been interpreted as Thor (Donar)-amulets in Hogebeintum.[19] The suggestion, in accordance to the juxtaposition of Christian faith and pagan cult in the *Indiculus*, is that a developed pagan cult can be assumed to have existed in the Netherlands, equipped with a full set of temples (Ermelo), sacred texts (runic), ritual and mythology. Claudia Dekkers, Gaston Dorren and Rob van Eerden sketch a similar portrait of religion before the arrival of Christianity in their introduction to the archaeology of the coastal zone of the province of North Holland: cone-shaped pendants with some geometric decoration are once again interpreted as Donar-amulets and associated to a Woden-related shamanism. However, these authors admit that there is no way to retrieve any substance concerning native perceptions about these gods.[20]

---

16   Transcription after Lutz E. von Padberg, *Christianisierung im Mittelalter* (Darmstadt: Wissenschaftliche Buchgesellschaft, 2006), 76.

17   Joris van Eijnatten and Fred van Lieburg, *Nederlandse Religiegeschiedenis* (Hilversum: Verloren, 2005), 57.

18   For medieval links between the site and the memory of Redbad see Bert Huiskes, *Eeuwige rust op de Donderberg: Een groot vroegmiddeleeuws grafveld bij Rhenen* (Leiden: Sidestone, 2011), 13.

19   Van der Pol, "Middeleeuwen," 43–44.

20   Claudia Dekkers, Gaston Dorren, and Rob van Eerden, *Het land van Hilde: Archeologie in het Noord-Hollandse kustgebied* (Haarlem: Matrijs, 2006), 66–67.

4   Dutch Doubts and German Insistence

Recent interest in the figure of Redbodus (Redbod or Redbad), referred to as a
"king" in 7th-century Christian texts, shows that the fascination for this era is
not restricted to church historians. Redbod is an example of the way in which
Christian hagiographers ascribed heathen practices, including temples, to the
Frisians in the Dutch coastal area:

> *Sed quoniam gravi ingruente paganorum impetu hostilis exorta dissensio
> inter Carlum principem gloriosumque ducem Franchorum et Redbodum
> regem Fresonum populos ex utraque parte perturbabat maximaque iam
> pars ecclesiarum Christi, quae Franchorum prius in Fresia subiectae erant
> imperio, Redbodi incumbente persecutione ac servorum Dei facta expulsio-
> ne vastata erat ac destructa, idulorum quoque cultura extructis dilubrorum
> fanis lugubriter renovata, tum vir Dei perspecta perversitatis nequitia per-
> venit ad Trecht ...*

As the heathens came storming in during those days, and as enmity between Charles, the glorious prince and duke of the Francs, and the Frisian
king Redbod perturbed both peoples, also a major part of the churches
of Christ, that previously had been subjected to Francian rule over Frisia,
were plundered and destroyed by the impact of Redbod's persecution
and the repression of God's servants, while the idolatry in re-erected heathen temples had been infamously renewed, the man of God [Boniface]
moved to Utrecht, having noted this abomination ...[21]

Sven Meeder and Erik Goosmann stress the social importance of so-called
warlords in Redbod's coastal society. Any aspects of this paganism, however,
are simply unknown, apart from biased Christian descriptions. It is interesting
to note the absence of any reference to a cult of Woden or Thor.[22] The same can
be said of Luit van der Tuuk's book on Redbod, where the Frisian religion of the
time is connected to magic,[23] but again without reference to the Woden cult. It
seems that Dutch historiography is moving towards caution.

---

21   *Vita Bonifatii auctore Willibaldo* 4.15–22. Edition and translation in M. Tangl, Ph.H. Külb
      and Reinhold Rau, *Briefe des Bonifatius: Willibalds Leben des Bonifatius* (Darmstadt:
      Wissenschaftliche Buchgesellschaft, 2011), 476–77.
22   Sven Meeder and Erik Goosmann, *Redbad: Koning in de marge van de geschiedenis*
      (Houten: Unieboek Spectrum, 2018), 74.
23   Luit van der Tuuk, *Radbod: Koning in twee werelden* (Utrecht: Omniboek, 2018), 39.

On the other hand, German authors such as Arnulf Krause still defend the Woden hypothesis. In *Die Götter und Mythen der Germanen*, Krause maintains that a mythology with Odin at its centre played a vital role in Germanic religion before the advent of Christianity. We know about the contents of this mythology from Tacitus's *Germania* (2nd century) and from the Icelandic *Edda* (12th century). Krause is convinced of the plausibility of a continuous veneration of Odin/Woden and Thor/Donar during the millennium between Tacitus and Snorri Sturluson: "Die germanische Religion umfasst mit ihren Göttern und Mythen mehr als ein Jahrtausend."[24] In 2017, Thomas Höffgen, in a similar fashion, reflected on Iron Age masks, like the famous Middelstum example. According to Höffgen's interpretation, these masks are related to Woden in his function as a Germanic shaman's deity. "Das wichtigste Hilfsmittel bei diesen Kulten war naturgemäß die Maske, wie denn Odin in den Mythen selbst mannigfach in Maskerade auftritt: Ein Beiname des Odins ist Grímr, das heißt Maske (gríma)."[25]

5   Explaining Woden

Despite the efforts to link sites like Wijnaldum and Hegebeintum to a mythology of this kind, the evidence for Woden in the Netherlands is meagre to say the least. Elaborating on Mazereeuw's thesis, I propose an alternative view, in which the existence of a well-developed pagan cult was a requirement for Christian literary treatment of the conversion process. During the 7th century it also offered a viable legitimating alternative to Christianity for Anglo-Saxon warlords who aimed at leadership of larger entities than mere tribes. This is not the same as saying that such a cult ever existed "on ground," in the daily life that is reflected in material evidence.

"Well-developed" is taken here in the sense of endowment with ritual, sacred spaces, mythology (all of which, taken together, may be expected to exert an influence on later developments of culture and religion). Indications for the presence of at least a few of these markers can be found in earlier stages of religious history in the Netherlands. For instance, in the dolmens of the Neolithic, the Bronze Age elite burials and their astronomical orientations, the exotic provenance of stone and metal votive offerings from both these eras. Other examples are the elaborate and well-made votive altars in the early

---

24   Arnulf Krause, *Die Götter und Mythen der Germanen* (Wiesbaden: Marix, 2015), 63.
25   Thomas Höffgen, *Schamanismus bei den Germanen: Götter, Menschen, Tiere, Pflanzen* (Remda-Teichel: Roter Drache, 2017), 31–32.

Roman era. It should be noted that many native gods are invoked (Hludlana, Nehalennia, Magusanus), but neither their names nor their iconography show any convincing resemblance to Woden and Thor and their kin. As Thor Ewing rightly remarks: "Clearly, the religion of Roman Germania cannot have been identical with the religion of Viking Scandinavia. Indeed, it is in the nature of pre-Christian religion that no definition can be narrow enough to include only a single unified expression of the religion."[26]

If we compare them to these examples of a "well-developed cult," the alleged Woden amulets of Hegebeintum disappoint as rather simple artefacts. The existence of the supposed Ermelo temple (compare "Irminsul") has never been verified. The runic texts from the Netherlands, all of them very short, are basic at best. More promising for our investigation are the gold hoards of Wijnaldum and Wiewerd, with their expensive materials, exotic inlays that may even have come from India, and sophistication of design. Johan Nicolay has written extensively on the subject.[27] The parallels between the treasury-troves in Frisia and the contemporary Anglo-Saxon ship burial in Sutton Hoo (Suffolk) are obvious. For a discussion of a possible connection to Woden, it seems advisable that we turn our attention to England. How can we explain the literary allusions to the presence of Woden in pre-conversion societies bordering the southern coasts of the North Sea, while—quite unlike the situation in Scandinavia after 800—clear references to Woden in the sphere of religious ritual are almost completely lacking?

6   Ancestors

A clue comes from a well-known passage in the *Historia ecclesiastica gentis anglorum*, where Beda Venerabilis (673/674–735) writes about the relation between Anglo-Saxon kings and Woden:

> *Duces fuisse perhibentur eorum primi duo fratres Hengist et Horsa ... Erant autem filii Uictgisli, cuius pater Uitta, cuius pater Uecta, cuius pater Uoden, de cuius stirpe multarum provinciarum regium genus originem duxit.*

---

26   Thor Ewing, *Gods and Worshippers in the Viking and Germanic World* (Stroud: The History Press, 2008), 9.

27   Johan A.W. Nicolay, *The Splendour of Power: Early Medieval Kingship and the Use of Gold and Silver in the Southern North Sea Area (5th to 7th Century AD)* (Groningen: Barkhuis, 2014).

It is said that their first leaders were two brothers, Hengist and Horsa.... They were sons of Wihtgisl, whose father was Witta, whose father was Wecta, whose father was Woden; from which stock royal clans of many shires claimed their descent.[28]

Here at last we find a clear indication of what the importance of Woden in this age and society actually meant for the people of the age. It was not his belonging to a structured and accessible world of the gods that made him important, but his belonging to the world of the ancestors. This squares well with Dutch findings at Donderberg for instance, where the importance of social structure, family bonding and the maintenance of status in a martial society are very much more in evidence than religion of the kind that is attested in the Nehalennia cult during the Roman or in an early medieval Christian church.

A remarkable result of investigations by British archaeologists and historians is that the impact of what we might call Wodenism on Anglo-Saxon society actually increased during the pre-conversion era.[29] This finding demonstrates how far we have come since the 19th century. A Hegelian interpretation of history tends to qualify prehistoric societies—even in the Iron Age—as both static and relying on magic for their religion,[30] contrasting them to the societal and intellectual impetus of later and more modern times. Wodenism, if anything, was not static. The first depictions of Woden/Odin were adapted from coin portraits of Roman emperors, just as the runic scripts were adapted from Mediterranean prototypes. Wodenism did not precede Christianity, it coincided with it. Sutton Hoo and Wijnaldum both exemplify societies in which indications for religious cult are weak, while the markers for group status and family attachment are far stronger. It may be that our present-day secularisation is not as unique as we might think. It is quite possible that even societies in the later Iron Age went through periods in which relationships between human beings and gods (or God) were less important than relationships between humans and their families and/or group stratifications. It will not come

---

28 Beda Venerabilis, *Historia ecclesiastica gentis anglorum* 1.15. Edition and translation in Günther Spitzbart, *Beda Venerabilis: Historia ecclesiastica gentis anglorum* (Darmstadt: Wissenschaftliche Buchgesellschaft, 1997), 60–61.

29 Cf. Geoffrey Hindley, *A Brief History of the Anglo-Saxons: The Beginnings of the English Nation* (London: Yale, 2015), 13–19, 26–30.

30 "Volksfrömmigkeit" could be interpreted as a rudimentary legacy of this former stage of cultural entelechy. Cf. Hans-Martin Kirn: "In allen Bevölkerungsschichten blieben mythisch-magische Glaubens- und Wertevorstellungen sowie Praktiken lebendig, die sich nicht ohne weiteres konfessionskonform regulieren ließen" (*Geschichte des Christentums IV, 1: Konfessionelles Zeitalter* [Stuttgart: Kohlhammer, 2018], 82).

as a surprise that Rob Meens and others have argued that both ancestors and living kin were more important to Redbad's generation than transcendent gods.[31] However, once it became clear that state-building on a larger scale—such as Mercia, East Anglia, or even Frisia in Redbad's dreams—would benefit from a cohesive mythology, together with a literate class of clerics, there were options to consider. Christianity was one of them, but a developing Wodenism (as exemplified by Scandinavian proto-states in the Carolingian age) could act as a potential alternative. The Sutton Hoo ship offers a vivid portrayal of these coinciding options, literally side-to-side.

Hard evidence for the existence a cult of Woden and Thor, even within the sphere of tribal leadership, remains very hard to find in the Netherlands—which is a point of concern given the thoroughness of Dutch archaeological research during the previous decades. As the written accounts are solely written by Christian clerics, and mostly after 800, it is tempting to consider the possibility that their portrayal was modelled after the most powerful pagan presence during the Carolingian era, and even later—that is to say, the Scandinavian presence, the impact of which was felt from the North and clearly appealed to the popular imagination. Whether this also implies the presence of a Woden cult in the Netherlands before the Norse incursions in the 9th century is debatable.

7   Conclusions

Ongoing discussions on holy places in the Netherlands reflect the impact of secularisation. Even in the 20th century, church historians tended to analyse the subject from a Christian angle and by using Christian written sources. The limitations of this approach have become evident in recent years. Most members of the Dutch population no longer relate to a Christian church or creed. Their perspective of holy places relies on education in general, and on a wide variety of religious and philosophical preferences. The perception of holy places shows a shift away from Christianity, and towards forms that are closer to current school programs. A growing popular interest in archaeology fits into this pattern. The trend is reflected in material and immaterial sites of memory regarding the Christianisation of the Netherlands. An interest in paganism is not new. Innovative is the insistence on a secular interpretation of

---

31   Rob Meens, "With One Foot in the Font: The Failed Baptism of the Frankish king Radbod and the 8th-Century Discussion about the Fate of Unbaptized Forefathers," in *Early Medieval Ireland and Europe: Chronology, Contacts, Scholarship: Festschrift for Dáibhí Ó Cróin*, ed. Pádraic Moran and Immo Warntjes (Turnhout: Brepols, 2015), 577–96.

the phenomenon, in which a pre-Christian "Wodenism" is not a religion in the traditional sense, but rather a by-effect of group status, social stratification and early attempts at state-building. The interpretation of related sites is moving away from a Christian interpretation of holiness and towards a vindication of secular principles of human bonding. As this trend is reflected in the curriculum of secondary schools, a traditional exposition of Christianisation becomes hard to maintain. A modern treatment of the subject requires both a careful assessment of material (archaeological) data and a willingness to explore non-religious explanations of what was formally understood as a clash between two sets of religious beliefs (Christianity and paganism).

Acknowledgment

I thank Dr Bärry Hartog for his comments on the earlier draft of this paper.

References

Caspers, Charles, and Peter Jan Margry. *Het mirakel van Amsterdam: Biografie van een betwiste devotie*. Amsterdam: Prometheus, 2017.

De imitatione Christi libri quatuor auctore ven. Thoma Hemerken a Kempis. Haarlem: Gottmer, 1949.

Dekkers, Claudia, Gaston Dorren, and Rob van Eerden. *Het land van Hilde: Archeologie in het Noord-Hollandse kustgebied*. Haarlem: Matrijs, 2006.

Eijnatten, Joris van, and Fred van Lieburg. *Nederlandse Religiegeschiedenis*. Hilversum: Verloren, 2005.

Ewing, Thor. *Gods and Worshippers in the Viking and Germanic World*. Stroud: The History Press, 2008.

Frijhoff, Willem. "Le pèlerinage dans la vie religieuse des Pays-Bas, forme de continuité religieuse: L'exemple du Lieu-Saint de Hasselt (Ov)." MA Thesis, Paris University, 1970.

Heller, Erich, and Manfred Furhmann. *P. Cornelius Tacitus: Annalen: Lateinisch und Deutsch*. Darmstadt: Wissenschaftliche Buchgesellschaft, 1997.

Hindley, Geoffrey. *A Brief History of the Anglo-Saxons: The Beginnings of the English Nation*. London: Yale, 2015.

Höffgen, Thomas. *Schamanismus bei den Germanen: Götter, Menschen, Tiere, Pflanzen*. Remda-Teichel: Roter Drache, 2017.

Huiskes, Bert. *Eeuwige rust op de Donderberg: Een groot vroegmiddeleeuws grafveld bij Rhenen*. Leiden: Sidestone, 2011.

Huston, Ronald. *Pagan Britain*. New Haven: Yale University Press, 2013.

Kirn, Hans-Martin. *Geschichte des Christentums IV, 1: Konfessionelles Zeitalter*. Stuttgart: Kohlhammer, 2018.

Krause, Arnulf. *Die Götter und Mythen der Germanen*. Wiesbaden: Marix, 2015.

Mazereeuw, Marije. "Donar en Wodan? 'Germaanse religie' in Nederland tussen 250 en 650 AD kritisch beschouwd." MA Thesis, Protestant Theological University, 2015.

Meeder, Sven, and Erik Goosmann. *Redbad: Koning in de marge van de geschiedenis*. Houten: Unieboek Spectrum, 2018.

Meens, Rob. "With One Foot in the Font: The Failed Baptism of the Frankish king Radbod and the 8th-Century Discussion about the Fate of Unbaptized Forefathers." Pages 577–96 in *Early Medieval Ireland and Europe: Chronology, Contacts, Scholarship: Festschrift for Dáibhí Ó Cróin*. Edited by Pádraic Moran and Immo Warntjes. Turnhout: Brepols, 2015.

Mijboer, Marijke, Peter Louwerse, Anton Sinke, and Marius van den Berg. *Wandelen langs heilige plaatsen: Dagtochten naar bedevaartsoorden in Nederland*. Zoetermeer: Meinema, 2008.

Nicolay, Johan A.W. *The Splendour of Power: Early Medieval Kingship and the Use of Gold and Silver in the Southern North Sea Area (5th to 7th Century AD)*. Groningen: Barkhuis, 2014.

Nongbri, Brent. *Before Religion: A History of a Modern Concept*. New Haven: Yale University Press, 2013.

Padberg, Lutz E. von. *Christianisierung im Mittelalter*. Darmstadt: Wissenschaftliche Buchgesellschaft, 2006.

Pol, Frank van der. "De Middeleeuwen tot 1200." Pages 15–118 in *Handboek Nederlandse Kerkgeschiedenis*. Edited by Herman J. Selderhuis. Kampen: Kok, 2010.

Spitzbart, Günther. *Beda Venerabilis: Historia ecclesiastica gentis anglorum*. Darmstadt: Wissenschaftliche Buchgesellschaft, 1997.

Stokes Brown, Cynthia. *Big History: From the Big Bang to the Present*. New York: The New Press, 2007.

Stuart, P., and J. Bogaers. *Nehalennia: Römische Steindenkmäler aus der Oosterschelde bei Colijnsplaat*. 2 vols. Leiden: National Museum of Antiquities, 2001.

Tangl, M., Ph.H. Külb, and Reinhold Rau. *Briefe des Bonifatius: Willibalds Leben des Bonifatius*. Darmstadt: Wissenschaftliche Buchgesellschaft, 2011.

Terberger, Thomas, Utz Böhner, Felix Hillgruber, and Andreas Kotula, eds. *300.000 Jahre Spitzentechnik: Der altsteinzeitliche Fundplatz Schöningen und die frühesten Speere der Menschheit*. Darmstadt: Wissenschaftliche Buchgesellschaft, 2018.

Torrey, E. Fuller. *Evolving Brains, Emerging Gods: Early Humans and the Origins of Religion*. New York: Columbia University Press, 2017.

Tuuk, Luit van der. *Radbod: Koning in twee werelden*. Utrecht: Omniboek, 2018.

Wentink, Karsten. *Ceci n'est pas une hache: Neolithic Depositions in the Northern Netherlands*. Leiden: Sidestone, 2006.

CHAPTER 12

Seeing Jerusalem through Selected Jewish, Christian, and Islamic Collective Memory's Visualizations

Shulamit Laderman

Shalom Sabar and Dan Bahat note in their introduction to *Jerusalem Stone and Spirit*:

> No city has been the subject of such various, ideologically, disparate descriptions as Jerusalem. The city's long history, the different cultures which have ruled in it, and its central importance for the three major, monotheistic religions have accorded it an exceptional place in the history of art.[1]

To apprehend Jerusalem's exceptional place in the history of art I explore a selection of works of art that describe this special city in light of Maurice Halbwachs's theory of Collective Memory.[2] I trust that viewing these Jewish, Christian, and Islamic artistic images of cultural memories will help us understand the way Jerusalem has been visualized not as a reflection of how the city actually appeared in different periods, but rather as the way it was perceived by artists, especially during periods in which they had no physical access to the city.

According to Halbwachs, collective memory exists in the shared and private imagination of a group of people, as well as in their texts, their practices, and their artefacts. It concerns group recollections of the past constructed through the perspective of the present and interpreted to serve contemporary purposes. Halbwachs states that:

> The memory of groups contains many truths, notions, ideas and general propositions; the memory of religious groups preserves the recollection

---

1 Dan Bahat and Shalom Sabar, *Jerusalem Stone and Spirit: 3000 Years of History and Art* (Jerusalem: Matan Arts, 1997), 11.

2 Maurice Halbwachs, *On Collective Memory*, edited, translated, and with an introduction by Lewis A. Coser (Chicago: University of Chicago Press, 1992).

of dogmatic truths that were revealed to them in the beginning and that successive generations of believers and clergymen formulated. But if a truth is to be settled in the memory of a group it needs to be presented in the concrete form of an event, of personality or of a locality.[3]

The appeal to collective memory in analysing a historical work of art can be invoked when we view a work painted by Nicolas Poussin in 1625/1626 (fig. 12.1).[4]

Entitled *The Destruction and Sack of the Temple of Jerusalem*, it was commissioned by the artist's patron Cardinal Francesco Barberini, who was at the time the head of a papal legation that attempted in vain to negotiate an end to the bloody war between France and Spain, as a gift to Cardinal Richelieu, the French King Louis XIII's chief minister. In this work Poussin drew a parallel between his patron, the would-be peacemaker, and the enlightened pagan emperor Titus, who, according to Flavius Josephus's account, tried unsuccessfully

FIGURE 12.1   Nicolas Poussin, *The Destruction and Sack of the Temple of Jerusalem* (1625–1626)

---

3   Halbwachs, *On Collective Memory*, 200.
4   A gift from Yad Hanadiv in memory of Sir Isaiah Berlin. See Yigal Zalmona, ed., *The Israel Museum at 40: Masterworks of Beauty and Sanctity* (Jerusalem: Israel Museum, 2005).

to avert the ruin of Jerusalem and its Temple.[5] The narrative that guided Poussin was based on Josephus's *Jewish War*, which is the only complete historical account that has survived from the period of the destruction of the Temple. It was written by Josephus, an eyewitness of the fall of Jerusalem.

Josephus the author was a Jewish priest and a military commander who surrendered to Vespasian and went to Rome where he became the official Roman chronicler who accompanied Titus's army and witnessed the conquest and destruction of Jerusalem in the year 70 CE. The Jews did not trust his writings, fearing that he was eager to please Rome and not record the facts as they were. Poussin's painting follows Josephus's account as he describes it in *Jewish War* (6.254):

> A runner brought the news to Titus as he was resting in his tent after the battle. He leapt up as he was and ran to the Sanctuary to extinguish the blaze. His whole staff panted after him, followed by the excited legions ... Caesar shouted and waved to the combatants to put out the fire, but his shouts were unheard as their ears were deafened by a greater din, and his gesticulations went unheeded amidst the distraction of battle and bloodshed. As the legions charged in, neither persuasion nor threat could check their impetuosity: passion alone was in command.[6]

Yigal Zalmona notes that the events described by Josephus in the *Jewish War* were "a source of European artists over several centuries."[7] The accepted understanding is that Josephus's testimony—written originally in Greek and subsequently translated into many other languages—became the basis for the collective memory of the Christian view of the sack of Jerusalem. Poussin's portrayal was, in effect, a visualization of Josephus description of the fall of Jerusalem, the burning of the Temple and the reason for the menorah being taken to Rome. The picture reinforces the church's attitude that the Temple was

---

5 Yigal Zalmona et al., *Nicolas Poussin's* Destruction and Sack of the Temple of Jerusalem: *A Rediscovered Masterpiece* (Jerusalem: Israel Museum, 1999), 5–6 and note that Zalmona bases the discussion of the painting's history on the work of Denis Mahon, who was the first to identify the lost Poussin; see Denis Mahon, *Nicholas Poussin: Works from His First Years in Rome* (Jerusalem: Israel Museum, 1999).

6 Josephus, *J.W.* 6.254, trans. Geoffrey A. Williamson, *Josephus: The Jewish War*, rev. ed. with a new introduction, notes, and appendixes by E. Mary Smallwood (Harmondsworth: Penguin Classics 1981), 357–58.

7 Zalmona, "A Rediscovered Poussin," 5.

destroyed not by Titus who was a helpless bystander as his troops rampaged in violence, but by the will of God that was predicted by Jesus's prophecy.[8]

It seems that in order to make this collective memory more relevant, Poussin referred to a visual model of ancient classical Roman architecture and copied the facade of the Pantheon[9] and the relief of the menorah on the Arch of Titus (81 CE) to symbolize the Temple during that period.[10] All this enabled him to relate to both the narrative and the visual memory of the time. Josephus's narrative thus became the Christian collective memory by relating the fall of the Temple and of Jerusalem not to Titus but to the fulfilment of Jesus's promise that the Temple would be torn down as recorded in Matt 24:1–2 and in Luke 19:41–44.[11]

For the Jews, who were extremely traumatized by the destruction of the Temple and the subsequent exile from Jerusalem, there was an urgent need to prove to themselves as well as to the Christians that their collective memory of being God's chosen people had to be preserved and to reinforce the notion that Jewish life would continue to exist and even to prosper. The Jews viewed the destruction as a national catastrophe and mourned the loss of the Temple, but despite their deep sorrow and the harshness of their lives then, and throughout the ages, their collective memory of the Temple and of Jerusalem continued to play a major role and have presence for them.[12]

---

8   William den Hollander, "Jesus, Josephus, and the Fall of Jerusalem: On Doing History with Scripture," *HTS* 71 (2015), 9, https://repository.up.ac.za/bitstream/handle/2263/51005/DenHollander_Jesus_2015.pdf?sequence=1&isAllowed=y.

9   Commissioned by Marcus Agrippa during the reign of Augustus (27 BCE–14 CE), the Pantheon was built on the site of an earlier temple. The present building was completed by emperor Hadrian and was probably dedicated around 126 CE.

10   Zalmona et al., *Nicolas Poussin's* Destruction and Sack of the Temple of Jerusalem, 13–15.

11   Luke 19:41–44: "When he drew near, he saw the city and wept over it, saying, 'If you, even you, had known today the things which belong to your peace! But now, they are hidden from your eyes. For the days will come on you, when your enemies will throw up a barricade against you, surround you, hem you in on every side, and will dash you and your children within you to the ground. They will not leave in you one stone on another, because you did not know the time of your visitation'" (WEB).

12   Elisheva Revel-Neher, "An 'Encore' on the Bar Kokhba Tetradrachma: A Re-Vision of Interpretation," in *"Follow the Wise": Studies in Jewish History and Culture in Honor of Lee I. Levine*, ed. Zev Weiss et al. (Winona Lake, IN: Eisenbrauns, 2010), 189–205.

1   The Collective Memory of Jerusalem for the Jews

1.1   *Preserving the Memory of the Temple*

Zekher ha-miqdash (the memory of the Temple) was preserved by a tradition that mandated incorporating the Temple, using visual symbols, in the synagogue, which was called "a minor temple," (*miqdash meʿaṭ*) and directing the people's prayers and worship toward Jerusalem and the site where the Temple once stood.

Worshipers in the land of Israel as well as in the diaspora always turned toward the Temple in Jerusalem (after the destruction toward the site) as the locus of the Divine Presence.[13] The transfer of the functions of sacred worship, albeit modified, to the synagogue was possible through the development of the prayer service, the study of Torah, and the Torah scrolls themselves.[14] Steven Fine offers the view that the synagogue did not become a substitute for the Temple, but that it received the collective memory of the spirit of sanctity from the presence of the Torah scrolls and the prayers that were recited.[15] Thus the Torah Ark became the symbol of the Temple and of Jerusalem, and its placement in the synagogue mandated the way the worshippers should stand so as to be facing toward Jerusalem. This feature is clearly evident in many ancient synagogues, for example, the synagogue in Dura-Europos in Syria and the Hammath Tiberias and Bet Alpha synagogues in the land of Israel. It seems that referencing the Torah Ark and other visual symbols to sustain the collective memory of the Temple was an effective way to cope with the trauma of the destruction of the Temple and of Jerusalem.

In more recent studies, in an article entitled "Art and Remembering Traumatic Collective Events," the authors contend that: "Works of art are considered to be cultural artifacts, symbolic rituals of commemoration that allow social memory to have an external cognitive and affective frame."[16] As can be

---

13   Samuel Safrai, "The Temple and the Synagogue," in *Synagogues in Antiquity*, ed. Aryeh Kasher, Aharon Oppenheimer, and Uriel Rappaport (Jerusalem: Yad Ben Zvi, 1987) 31–51 (31–32, n. 4) (Hebrew) cites the following sources: m. Ber. 4:5; y. Ber. 4:5. Safrai contends that this approach is alluded to in the Bible: 1 Kgs 8:44 and parallel passages in 2 Chr 6:34; Dan 6:11.

14   Baruch M. Bokser, "Approaching Sacred Space," *HTR* 78 (1985): 279–99.

15   Steven Fine, *This Holy Place: On the Sanctity of the Synagogue during the Greco-Roman Period* (Notre Dame: University of Notre Dame Press, 1997), 94.

16   Juanjo Igartua and Darío Páez, "Art and Remembering Traumatic Collective Events: The Case of the Spanish Civil War," in *Collective Memory of Political Events: Social Psychological Perspectives*, ed. James W. Pennebaker, Darío Páez, and Bernard Rimé (Hillsdale, NJ: Lawrence Erlbaum, 1997), 79–101 (81).

seen in the following examples, the Jewish channels for collective memory involved both visual images and textual sources.

1.2   *The Dura-Europos Synagogue*

The painting above the Torah niche in the third-century Dura-Europos synagogue is an important visual example of the wish to pray in the direction
of Jerusalem (fig. 12.2). It reflects the symbolic image of Jerusalem based on
the collective memory of the Temple and of the biblical text regarding the

FIGURE 12.2
Torah niche (ciborium)
in the third-century
Dura-Europos
synagogue

importance of continuing God's worship by praying in the direction of the Holy City, as noted in 1 Kgs 8 and elaborated by the rabbis in Sifre Deuteronomy 29; Midrash Tana'im Deuteronomy 3; and b. Ber. 30a:

> Those who stood outside the land would turn their faces towards the land of Israel and pray as it says (1 Kgs 8:48): "And pray unto Thee toward their land"; those in the land of Israel would direct their faces toward Jerusalem (1 Kgs 8:44): "They pray unto the Lord toward the city which Thou hast chosen"; those who stood in Jerusalem would turn their faces toward the Temple (1 Kgs 8:33): "and pray and make supplication unto Thee in this house."

The Dura-Europos fresco features many visual representations of the Temple, including the two twisted columns and the two doors with decorated knobs, a seven-branched menorah with very tall branches that reflect the biblical description of "knop" and "flower" (*kaftor* and *perakh*) mentioned in Exod 25:31–40. Large images of a lulav[17] and an etrog[18] stand between the menorah and a depiction of the Temple. To the right of the Temple facade is a portrayal of Abraham about to sacrifice Isaac on Mount Moriah, an episode known as the aqedah, which, according to tradition, took place in Jerusalem on *har ha-Moria*, the place that was to be the site of the future Temple.

1.3   *The Hammath Tiberias and Bet Alpha Synagogues*

Viewing Jerusalem and the Temple as the foci of prayers is also evident in the mosaic floors of the fourth-century Hammath Tiberias (fig. 12.3)[19] and the sixth-century Bet Alpha[20] synagogues, both of which were built in the land of Israel during the Byzantine period and uncovered during archaeological expeditions in the twentieth century.

The Hammath Tiberias mosaic floor shows the symbols of the Temple in its top register pointing in the direction of Jerusalem. On the floor of Bet Alpha, the three registers all point toward Jerusalem and portray the Temple implements in a stylized Byzantine fashion. The uppermost of the two panels in the Hammath Tiberias floor shows the Ark/Temple image, which Moshe Dothan

---

17   Lulav—A shoot of a young palm branch, one of the *arba'at minim* used on the holiday of Sukkot.

18   Etrog—A citrus fruit, the "fruit of a goodly tree" (Lev 13:40), one of the *arba'at minim* used on Sukkot.

19   The synagogue was uncovered by Moshe Dothan between 1961 and 1963.

20   Nahum Avigad, "Bet Alpha," in *The New Encyclopedia of Archaeological Excavations in the Land of Israel*, ed. Ephraim Stern, 4 vols. (Jerusalem: Israel Exploration Society-Carta, 1993), 1:190–192.

FIGURE 12.3   The mosaic floors of the fourth-century Hammat Tiberias

described as "an *oikos* type of shrine consisting of two slender columns sur-
mounted by a triangular pediment or gabled roof."[21] The structure has three
schematically drawn steps that lead up to the base of two closed doors. A white
curtain, which hangs over the doors with its edges rolled inward and tied in
a knot, transforms the image of the Temple into a synagogue Ark, revealing
its centrality to Jewish worship in the House of God, even after the Temple's
destruction. The other implements—the menorahs, the lulav, and the etrog on
both sides of the Temple/Ark image—convey the same idea. The two seven-
branched menorahs are positioned on either side of the Ark, with the flames
from their candles all turned toward the central branch.

The mosaic floor in Bet Alpha is unique in that it has a dedicatory inscription on its narthex mosaic to the emperor Justinian, which dates it to the sixth
century CE.[22] The floor is divided into three panels. The uppermost depicts
the Tabernacle and its implements as if looking through an open curtain tied
on both sides (fig. 12.4). The architectonically structured Ark with a gabled top
has an eternal light within it and two heraldic birds standing on two horn-
like protrusions; there is also a single menorah on either side of the Ark with
the traditional ritual objects: shofar, lulav, etrog, and incense shovel. The ark
is flanked by two lions, symbols of the Kingdom of Judah, which was centred
in Jerusalem.

21   Moshe Dothan, *Hammath Tiberias: Early Synagogue and the Hellenistic and Roman
      Remains* (Jerusalem: Israel Exploration Society, 1983), 34.

22   This is the only synagogue in Israel that has an inscription with a date other than the one
      in the synagogue of Navoria, and that one refers to the renewed building.

FIGURE 12.4   The mosaic floor in the Bet Alpha synagogue

1.4   *Hebrew Illuminated Manuscripts with Illuminations of the Temple Implements*

The Temple implements portrayed in the ancient synagogues clearly allude to the city of Jerusalem being the only place where the *bet ha-miqdash* (Temple) could be built. These same images also appear in a large group of Sephardi Hebrew illuminated manuscripts dated to the thirteenth and fourteenth centuries, which served as mnemotechnics to help Jews relate to their collective memory of the Temple and Jerusalem. In a sense these depictions created a kind of "a spiritual space," which served as a substitute for the destroyed physical Temple.[23] For example, the Parma Bible[24] and the Perpignan Bible (fig. 12.5[25]) both depict many of the Temple implements on two matching pages with relevant titles identifying each of the vessels and visualizing its purpose. All of the implements, scattered haphazardly, seem to fit the term *memoria*

---

23   Jan Assmann, *Cultural Memory and Early Civilization* (New York: Cambridge University Press, 2011), 191–93.

24   The Parma Bible (Bibl. Palat 2668), executed around 1277, was the first manuscript produced in Spain to use these images on its frontispieces: Elisheva Revel-Neher, *Le témoignage de l'absence* (Paris: De Boccard, 1998), 61–95; Joseph Gutmann, "The Messianic Temple in Spanish Medieval Hebrew Manuscripts," in *The Temple of Solomon: Archeological Fact and Medieval Tradition in Christian, Islamic and Jewish Art*, ed. Joseph Gutman (Missoula, MT: Scholars Press, 1976), 125–45, n. 6.

25   Perpignan Bible Paris, Hebrew 7 BN, illuminated in Catalonia around 1299.

FIGURE 12.5A
Perpignan Bible. Paris,
Bibliothèque nationale,
Heb. 7, Bible, fol. 12v

rerum coined by Mary Carruthers,[26] who focuses on the schemes of memory created through "the use of the Tabernacle rendering as a mnemotechnical meditational *pictura*."[27] She also cites artistic examples that accord with the notion of *zekher ha-miqdash*, that is, "things" that help one remember the Temple, its sacrifices, and its rituals, which are essential parts of worshippers' collective memory of Jerusalem. Carruthers views the random displays of the Sanctuary implements on the frontispieces of these Bibles and the textual frames around them as "cues and links" to the Temple and to Jerusalem. They emphasize the association between *memoria rerum* (memory of objects) and *memoria verborum* (memory for exact words), which together allow for the collective memory of Jerusalem by combining the biblical and liturgical texts. This can be seen, for example, in the frame of the Perpignan Bible on folio

---

26   Mary J. Carruthers, *The Craft of Thought: Meditation, Rhetoric, and the Making of Images, 400–1200* (Cambridge: Cambridge University Press, 1998), 29, 31.

27   Carruthers, *The Craft of Thought*, 221–34.

FIGURE 12.5B
Perpignan Bible. Paris,
Bibliothèque nationale,
Heb. 7, Bible, fol. 13r

12v, where the verse from Num 8:4 delineates instructions for Aaron regarding the menorah in the Tabernacle, which also became the symbol of God's abode in both the First and Second Temples: "And this work of the candlestick was of beaten gold, unto the shaft thereof, unto the flowers thereof was beaten work according to the pattern which the Lord had showed Moses, so he made the candlestick."[28]

The framing text in the Perpignan Bible folio 13r, which was not taken from the Bible, reads as follows:

> All these existed when the *heikhal* [Temple, SL] stood on its place and its foundation. Happy was he who saw the grandeur of its glorious beauty and all its strength and power. Happy is he who awaits and will see it. May it be God's will that He will rebuild it soon in our day. May our eyes see and our hearts rejoice. Amen. Amen. Selah.

---

28   KJV.

The original source of this quotation is not known, but part of it is found in a piyyut[29] that describes the *seder ha-ʿavodah*[30] in the Temple on Yom Kippur composed by Shlomo Ibn Gabirol (c. 1020–c. 1060), which he introduced with the following words:[31] "All this took place when the Sanctuary was firmly established and the *miqdash ha-qodesh* [stood] on its foundation." The High Priest ministered; his generation watched and rejoiced. The following are selected verses from the piyyut, which describes the Temple and its sacred service:

> While the Ark was housed of the Holy of Holies
> While its staves were inserted in the rings of the Ark ...
> While the sprinkling of the blood was on the untainted altar
> While the cherubim spread their wings from above ...
> While the priests offered their incense
> While the stone tablets were in the Ark ...
> While the sweet smell of the daily sacrifice
> While the Most High dwelled in our midst ...

Thus, the text framing folio 13r in the Perpignan Bible as well as the Temple images within the frame symbolize the yearning that is expressed in the piyyut. Their purpose was to preserve the memory of the Temple through study of its sacred implements and the recitation of the *seder ʿavodah*, but it seems to convey a more profound message as well. The frontispieces of the thirteenth-century Parma and Perpignan Bibles as well as those of the fourteenth- and fifteenth-century Sephardi Bibles evidence efforts on the part of the contemporary rabbis to reaffirm faith in God's presence even after the destruction of the Temple. The artists who executed these frontispieces gave expression to what Rachel Elior refers to as the rabbinic shaping of "the Jews' collective memory, their perception of historical reality, their historiography and consciousness after the destruction of the Second Temple," which changed the priestly controlled hegemony of the Tabernacle/Temple to a rabbinic virtual "memory of Temple" and a symbol of Jerusalem.[32]

---

29   Piyyut (pl. piyyutim)—A liturgical hymn; a poetic embellishment recited by the prayer leader and the congregation in addition to the statutory prayer service.

30   *Seder ʿavodah*—From Rabbinic literature the Hebrew word *ʿavodah* used for the Temple sacrificial services is also used for the post-Temple liturgy, especially in the musaf service on Yom Kippur.

31   Daniel Goldschmidt, *Day of Atonement Prayer Book* (Jerusalem: Koren, 1970), 485 (Hebrew).

32   Rachel Elior, *The Three Temples: On the Emergence of Jewish Mysticism*, trans. David Louvish (Oxford: Littman, 2005), 6.

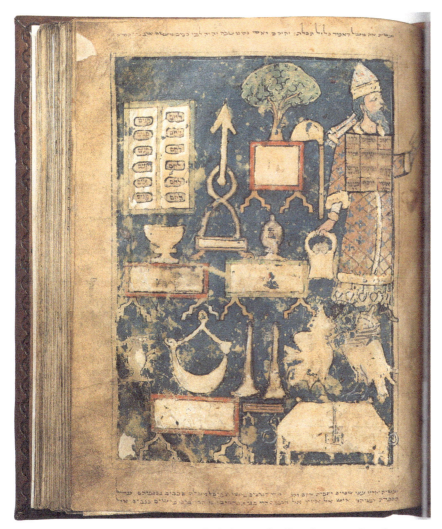

FIGURE 12.6   Regensburg Bible, Aaron the high priest kindling the menorah in the
                Tabernacle

Some fourteenth-century frontispieces also featured other images apart from
the Temple implements. A tree appears in many of them (fig. 12.6), which raises the question of why such an image was added to the display. We find an
explanation in a manuscript produced in Saragossa in 1404 (fig. 12.7), which
features a full-page illustration with an olive tree on a mound framed by a verse
from the book of Zech 14:4:

And His feet shall stand in that day upon the Mount of Olives, which is before Jerusalem on the east, and the Mount of Olives shall cleft in the midst thereof toward the east and toward the west, so that there shall be a very great valley; and half of the mountain shall remove toward the north, and half of it toward the south.[33]

The message is clear: The olive tree as well as the Temple implements symbolize Jerusalem and the hope that the Messiah will come and that the Temple will be rebuilt.[34]

FIGURE 12.7
Saragosa 1404: illustration of an olive tree on a mound, framed by Zech 14:4

---

33   ASV.
34   Revel-Neher, *Le témoignage de l'absence*, 79–80.

2   The Collective Memory of Jerusalem for the Christians

In 324 CE Constantine became the supreme ruler of the Roman Empire and declared Christianity to be the official religion, at which time Jerusalem began its ascent to an exalted status in Byzantine culture. The city was identified as the holy place where Jesus preached, was imprisoned, judged, and crucified; where he died and was buried; where Christians believe that he was resurrected and rose to heaven. Clearly, in Constantine's days Jerusalem became the focus of the religious yearnings of many worshippers within the Roman Empire, all of whom regarded the destruction of the Temple as a fulfilment of Jesus's prophesy.

According to Halbwachs's hypothesis, as the events connected to Jesus's life and his divine nature became more and more distant, Christian dogma modified his story and at times altered its geographical locations. The holy sites that were associated with Jesus's life and divine nature were hallowed in the collective memory of Christians to become the essential truths of Christianity and focused on Jerusalem, the great religious centre of the Jews.[35]

2.1   *The Madaba Map*

The new Christian symbol of Jerusalem was Jesus's sepulchre, which was commemorated by a magnificent church built in the fourth century by empress Helena, the mother of Constantine. Christian pilgrims followed in Helena's footsteps and came to Jerusalem. Churches were built in the places where Jesus had lived, preached, and taught, in order to commemorate his works and his miracles. The Madaba mosaic map (fig. 12.8), dated to 560–565 CE, which was discovered in a church in the northern part of the city of Madaba in Jordan,[36] has become an important graphic source for studying the land of Israel with its cities, villages, and holy places. Jerusalem appears in the centre of the map as a large ellipse ten times the size of the other cities represented. Eusebius's fourth-century *Onomasticon* seems to have been the source for the map, but the centrality and the size of Jerusalem clearly suggest that the artist regarded the city as the centre not only of the Holy Land but of the entire world.[37]

---

35   Halbwachs, *On Collective Memory*, 200–201.

36   Michael Avi-Yonah, *Madaba Map: Its Translation and Commentary* (Jerusalem: Israel Exploration Society, 1954) (Hebrew); Herbert Donner, *The Mosaic Map of Madaba: An Introductory Guide* (Kampen: Kok Pharos, 1992); Yoram Tsafrir, "The Topography and Archaeology of Jerusalem in the Byzantine Period," in *The Roman and Byzantine Periods (70–638 CE)*, ed. Yoram Tsafrir and Shmuel Safrai (Jerusalem: Yad Ben Zvi, 1999), 281–352 (Hebrew).

37   Avi-Yonah, *Madaba Map*, 28.

FIGURE 12.8   Madaba mosaic map in Jordan

The collective memory of the Christian pilgrims viewed Jerusalem as the hub of the universe and the Church of the Holy Sepulchre as its centre. To emphasize its importance, the church was portrayed in a way that seems to be a reversal of the classical perspective for figuring such architecture, which generally offers a clear view of all of the various parts of a structure. On the church's facade we can see the entrance stairs and the front atrium, with the stairs leading to the three golden gates of the basilica, called the "martyrium." The courtyard between the basilica and the rotunda (the rear atrium), with the Golgotha stone in one corner, appears in a somewhat reduced form from the west of the basilica, and the golden rotunda known as the place of the grave and the resurrection (the *anastasis*) rises behind the atrium.

The Church of the Holy Sepulchre is situated at the centre of the *cardo maximus* (north/south), which is the street that extends the length of the city from north to south and appears on the Madaba map as if wide open as seen from a bird's-eye view. The mosaicist emphasized the *cardo maximus* and tried to present it in all its glory, with two colonnades and the red roofs of the church buildings on both sides. This visualization is in contrast to the image of the secondary *cardo* (east/west), which shows only one row of pillars in a naive perspective so as to allow the viewing of other buildings between the two streets.[38]

It is generally agreed that the city plan seen on the map refers to the Roman city Aelia Capitolina with some additional details from the Byzantine period.[39] However, according to Nahum Avigad,[40] the *cardo* should not be regarded as the reconstruction of a Roman street, but rather as a Byzantine construction ordered by emperor Justinian,[41] who wanted to demonstrate a connection between the New Church, called the "Neah," and the Church of the Holy Sepulchre.[42] From the description of the architectonic buildings it appears that the artist of the Madaba mosaic sought to perpetuate the Christian tradition and the Christian collective memory of Jerusalem by visualizing the Church of the Holy Sepulchre, which replaced the destroyed Jewish holy site as the symbol of Jerusalem.

2.2 Santa Maria Maggiore in Rome

The lofty status of Jerusalem in the collective memory of Byzantine Christians was expressed in many contemporary schematic descriptions of the city, such as on the wall mosaic in the Church of Santa Maria Maggiore in Rome, which depicts a walled city with a central gate and side towers.[43] Above the wall we can see the roofs of the city's houses drawn in the style of the period—gabled roofs resting on pillars. The mosaic depicts a cross hanging over the gate to the city and six sheep standing before it. There is little doubt that here Jerusalem represents the Christians' church and faith and that the sheep are personifications of the believers. As in Jewish art this and similar pictorial designs do not reflect the true appearance of the city, but rather bear witness to the importance assigned to Jerusalem in the collective memory of contemporary Christian consciousness in the fifth and sixth centuries.[44]

---

38   Yoram Tsafrir, "Jerusalem in the Map of Madaba, Eretz Yisrael in the Map of Madaba," *Ariel* 116 (1996): 67–73, esp. 68 (Hebrew).

39   Nahum Avigad, *The Upper City of Jerusalem* (Jerusalem. Shikmona, 1980), 211 29 (Hebrew).

40   Avigad, *The Upper City of Jerusalem*, 225.

41   It was during Justinian's reign (527–565 CE) that the city of Jerusalem reached the apex of its growth.

42   The church was built in Jerusalem by order of Constantine in 326–335 CE.

43   See the 9th picture in this link: https://romeonrome.com/2015/03/byzantine-treasures -of-rome/.

44   Rehav Rubin, *Image and Reality: Jerusalem in Maps and Views* (Jerusalem: Magnes, 1999), 17.

2.3   The Sacra Parallela

In order to show the biblical roots of Jesus's prophecy about the destruction of the city, the Christian collective memory of Jerusalem was linked to the Old Testament. This can be seen in a ninth-century Byzantine manuscript called the Sacra Parallela in which an illumination shows the prophet Jeremiah sitting and weeping near the city wall. The painting, which visualizes Jerusalem from the perspective of its forthcoming destruction, illustrates Jer 6:6:

> For thus hath the LORD of hosts said: hew ye down her trees, and cast up a mound against Jerusalem; this is the city to be punished; everywhere there is oppression in the midst of her. Be thou corrected, O Jerusalem, lest My soul be alienated from thee, lest I make thee desolate, a land not inhabited. (KJV)

2.4   The loca sancta

The many pilgrims arriving in Jerusalem wanted souvenirs of *loca sancta* to bring back with them, which led to the creation of small flasks known as ampullae decorated with these kinds of mementos, such as images of the Church of the Holy Sepulchre.[45] The symbolic decorations on these objects reflect the development of the subjects of Christian collective memory around the death and resurrection of Christ. These sixth-century ampullae from Jerusalem, which contained holy oil or holy water, were often adorned with images depicting the cross at Golgotha and the Holy Sepulchre.[46] The mass pilgrimage from the West, was mostly made up of ordinary people (not only of prominent clergymen as earlier), who were eager to feel part of the history of salvation and to own tangible objects decorated with images alluding to the life of Christ or his resurrection, among them: the Adoration of the Magi, the Annunciation of the Shepherds, and Christ's Baptism, Crucifixion, and Ascension.[47]

2.5   The Map of Arculf

Other important visualizations of Jerusalem in Christian art are maps that were abstracted conceptual representations of the city and its holy places. The

---

45   Bianca Kühnel, "Jewish Symbolism of the Temple and the Tabernacle and Christian Symbolism of the Holy Sepulcher and the Heavenly Tabernacle," *Jewish Art* 12/13 (1986/1987): 147–68 (151).

46   Sixth-century ampullae from Jerusalem, which contained holy oil or holy water, often adorned with the cross at Golgotha and the Holy Sepulcher. A flask from Bobbio, with the women at the empty tomb. From https://en.wikipedia.org/wiki/Monza_ampullae.

47   Andre Grabar, *Les ampoules de Terre Sainte* (*Monza-Bobbio*) (Paris: Klincksieck, 1958), plates ix, xi, xxii, xxiv, xxxiv, xxxv, xxxvi, xlv.

seventh-century map of Arculf (670–697 CE) is evidence as to how Christian collective memory was able to reconstruct the past with the aid of materials that traced rites, texts, and traditional thinking to shape the virtual reality seen on such maps.[48] Arculf, the first Christian traveller to tour the Near East following the Muslim conquest, was for many generations considered to be an important source of information on Jerusalem and various holy sites.[49] His recollections were recorded by Adomnán, the abbot of Iona, in an essay entitled *De locis sanctis* (Of the Holy Places), which marked the Latin-speaking community's interest in the Holy Land. This work is not a pilgrim account of "an assemblage of geographical information it is a virtual visit to the Holy Places for those who, such as his own monks on Iona, cannot go there themselves but whose lives are intimately linked through the liturgy, through their study and reflection, and in their hopes and fears for the future with sacred lands that stand close to the center of their world."[50] Arculf's description of Jerusalem and the Church of the Holy Sepulchre was based on the martyria of Christ and various saints and the places associated with their legends.

Arculf traced the shapes of the Church of the Holy Sepulchre, the Church of Zion, and the Church of the Ascension on the Mount of Olives[51] onto a waxed tablet, which was a standard medieval trope for memoria.[52] Thus, the illustrations that Adomnán inserted in *De locis sanctis* constitute a chart-like "mental map" that functioned in the context of memory.[53] In connection with Adomnán's work, Halbwachs notes:

> Long before the Middle Ages, beginning with the constructions by Constantine and Helena in the early fourth century, what was to occupy the forefront of Christian memory would be the scenes of the Passion and the Resurrection. One need only read the account of Arculf that

48 Nachman Ran, ed., *Tracks to the Promised Land: The Land of Israel, Ancient Maps, Prints and Travelogues through the Centuries* (Tel Aviv: Terra Sancta Arts, 1987), 46–47, Michael Ish-Shalom, *Christian Travels in the Holy Land* (Tel Aviv: Am-Oved, 1979), 17–18 (Hebrew).

49 Arculf was a French bishop from Gaul who travelled to the Holy Land and resided in Jerusalem for nine months. On his way back home, his ship was swept ashore onto the isle of Iona in Scotland, where he recounted the tales of his travels to Adomnán, the abbot of the local monastery.

50 Thomas O'Loughlin, *Adomnán and the Holy Places: The Perceptions of an Insular Monk on the Locations of the Biblical Drama* (London: T&T Clark, 2007), 204.

51 John Wilkinson, *Jerusalem Pilgrims before the Crusades* (Jerusalem: Ariel, 1977), 193–97.

52 Delano Smith, "Geography or Christianity? Maps of the Holy Land before AD 1000," *JTS* 42 (1991): 143–52.

53 Adomnan, *De locis sanctis*, drawing of the Holy Sepulchre, Vienna. See https://www.flickr.com/photos/quadralectics/7438679760.

opens with a detailed description of the Basilica of the Holy Sepulcher ... There are twenty-eight pages on Jerusalem. A chapter is dedicated to the stone that closed the tomb, which is to be found in two fragments in the church. Another chapter is devoted to the Church of the Discovery of the Cross, [and] still another to the chalice and the sponge that were placed in an exedra etc.[54]

In his book on Adomnán's mental maps, Thomas O'Loughlin analyses Arculf's ideas, writing:[55]

> Adomnán's work is fundamentally a work of theological literature; its "picture" of the Holy Places is the product of a library and the questions that came to monks arose from their imaginative interaction with that distant land in reading and prayer. It has very little information on seventh-century Palestine, but much about the monasticism of which it was a product ... [I]n fact, it does tell us of its own time: how those in its place of composition *imagined Palestine* at that time. Palestine is a religious landscape and as such is an icon. And this icon of "the Holy Land" organizes all space around it and provides a key to the landscape the monks on Iona sought for themselves.[56]

During the period from 638 (when the Arabs conquered Jerusalem) until 1099 when the Crusaders returned to regain control over the city, there was no contact with the real city of Jerusalem and the works of art describing it emphasized its ideal. The image of the city was rooted in the Gospels and further based on the testimony and descriptions of pilgrims who had visited Jerusalem and like Arculf had recorded their memories, which, in some measure, reflected the real look of the city.

2.6   *The Capture of Jerusalem by the Crusaders*

A painting titled *Capture of Jerusalem by the Crusaders in 1099* by an unknown artist is another pictorial example that demonstrates how visual representations of Jerusalem reflect the Christian collective memory of the city (fig. 12.9).[57] The work portrays an architectural structure that resembles a

---

54   Halbwachs, *On Collective Memory*, 229; Ran, *Tracks to the Promised Land*.

55   Thomas O'Loughlin, "The View from Iona: Adomnán's Mental Maps," *Peritia* 10 (1996): 98–122.

56   O'Loughlin, *Adomnán and the Holy Places*, 210.

57   From the *History of William of Tyre*, 14th century, Paris, Bibliothèque nationale de France, MS Fol. 352, fol. 52v. Painting from Ran, *Tracks to the Promised Land*, 59.

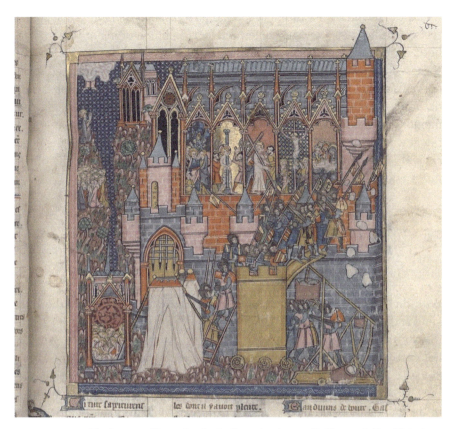

FIGURE 12.9   *The Capture of Jerusalem by the Crusaders in 1099.* Guillaume de Tyr, *Historia*

Gothic cathedral and visualizes the scenes of the passion of Jesus before his death in Jerusalem on the upper level of the church.[58] The depiction includes Jesus's betrayal by being kissed by Judas, his arrest, his passage with the cross on his shoulder along what is known as the Via Dolorosa, his crucifixion, and his burial as recorded in the Gospels.

Observing this picture carefully, we can see another epoch portrayed in the foreground of the same church-like structure. This second visualization depicts the Crusaders attacking Jerusalem using a siege engine and trebuchet to allow them to set up ladders in order to scale the walls and take the city. In this picture, the artist has conflated the end of Jesus's life with the image of

---

58   The passion (from Late Latin: *passio* "suffering, enduring") as described in the Gospels that deal with the final period in the life of Jesus, including his arrest and his crucifixion on Calvary, which defines the climactic event central in the Christian doctrine of salvation history.

the battle in which the Crusaders conquered Jerusalem so many years later. It seems that he chose to visualize Jerusalem as a church of major importance, both historically and theologically. What remains unclear is whether the scenes of the passion and entombment should be read as historical narratives of events that took place in the city or be perceived as having been copied from decorative stained-glass windows that were designed to foster the collective memory of the worshippers in a fourteenth-century church. If the latter, the intent was to educate Christians to accept Jerusalem as part of their theological and religious lives wherever they happened to live. The ambiguity of the image encourages overlapping and complementary readings.

3   The Collective Memory of Jerusalem for Muslims and Its Jewish Influences

3.1   *The Dome of the Rock*

With the rise of Islam in the seventh century and the conquest of the Holy Land and Jerusalem by caliph Umar, a third religion joined in contributing to the city's architectonic development and its visual symbols.[59] The Dome of the Rock was built in 691 by the Umayyad caliph Aba al-Malik over the Foundation Stone (*'even ha-shtiya*), which was known as the site of the Holy of Holies in the First and Second Temples. Although Jerusalem is not explicitly mentioned in the Qur'an, later traditions ascribed various events to the city.[60] Some of these episodes were attributed to the Foundation Stone—such as it being the site of King Solomon's Temple and the place where Muhammad rested his foot when he ascended to heaven.

The original reference to the *'even ha-shtiya*—the *omphalos* or "navel of the earth"—is found in Ezek 38:12 and later in other Jewish sources such as in m. Mid. 5:2; y. Yoma 5:3; b. Yoma 54b. The rabbinic commentary from the talmudic period as well as later midrashim note specifically that the *'even ha-shtiya* was in the Holy of Holies and was the centre of the world from where the entire creation was wrought. We read in Midrash Tanhuma:

59   Andreas Kaplony, "635/638–1099: The Mosque of Jerusalem (Masijid Bayt Al-Maqdis)," in *Where Heaven and Earth Meet: Jerusalem's Sacred Esplanade*, ed. Oleg Grabar and Benjamin Z. Kedar (Jerusalem: Yad Ben Zvi, 2009), 101–31, esp. 106. See also the contribution of Katia Cytryn-Silverman in this volume.

60   Rachel Milstein, "Jerusalem in Islamic Painting: An Object in Narrative Space," in *Jerusalem as Narrative Space: Erzählraum Jerusalem*, ed. Annette Hoffmann and Gerhard Wolf (Leiden: Brill, 2012), 463–75.

FIGURE 12.10   Sayyid Ali's *Kitab shawq nameh* (Pilgrimage Guide), which illustrates
Muhammad's apocalyptic journey from the Dome of the Rock up
to heaven

Just as the navel is in the center of a person, so the land of Israel is the
navel of the earth, as it is said, "those who live at the navel of the earth"
[Ezek 38:12] ... The land of Israel sits in the center of the world, Jerusalem
in the center of the land of Israel, the Temple in the center of Jerusalem,
the Sanctuary in the center of the Temple, the Ark in the center of
the Sanctuary, and the foundation stone—from which the world was
formed—sits in front of the Sanctuary.[61]

The Islamic theological conceptions and collective memory of Jerusalem were
strengthened by the Sufi mystical order, which regarded the Ḥaram al-Sharif
(literally: the Noble Sanctuary; the Temple Mount) as a space both earthly
and heavenly and a junction between the corporeal and the transcendental
worlds. This was the notion that inspired the illumination *bayt al-maqdis* (the

---

61   *Qedoshim* 10 (ed. Buber 39b). See John T. Townsend, *Midrash Tanḥuma* (*S. Buber
Recension*), 3 vols (Hoboken: Ktav, 1989).

Temple) in Sayyid Ali's *Kitab shawq nameh* (Pilgrimage Guide), which illustrates Muhammad's apocalyptic journey from the Dome of the Rock up to heaven (fig. 12.10).[62] Sayyid Ali described the pilgrimage places:

> Indeed of all its marvels are the *sakhra*, the Rock of God, which stands hanging between Heaven and Earth and the Rock, around which a dome is now built ... At the time that the city wall of al-Quds was built a dome and windows were installed too [for the Dome of the Rock, SL]. In this place are ... the gates of Hell and Paradise.[63]

The *bayt al-maqdis* illumination depicts imagined monuments of heavenly Jerusalem and the *sakhra-ye-allah* (Rock of God) at the centre of a schematic diagram of the Dome of the Rock encircled by a high platform and free-standing arcades. Among the sites labelled in the painting, Rachel Milstein discerned those related to the eschatological narration of the Last Judgement at the End of Days: *dar-e-dawzakh* (Gate of Hell), *dar-e-bihisht* (the Gate of Paradise), *dar-e-takht* (the Gate of the Throne), the *mizan al-a'mal* (Scales of Acts), and the *khawd-e kawthar* (Pool of Paradise).[64] It is worthy of note that a domed rectangular structure that implied the Ark of the Covenant, the Temple, the throne of God, and the cosmos in Byzantine imagery has the same import in Islamic art, which also shared a reverence for the biblical heritage of Solomon's Temple and Jerusalem.[65]

Influenced by their collective memory, when the Crusaders saw the octagonal structure of the Dome of the Rock they called it "the Temple of the Lord" (*templum domini*), and that image eventually became the most widespread stereotypic symbol of the Temple and of Jerusalem in both Christian and Jewish art.[66]

---

62   Oleg Grabar, "The Islamic Dome: Some Considerations," in *Islamic Arts and Beyond: Constructing the Study of Islamic Art, Volume III* (Hampshire: Ashgate, 2006), 87–102; Rachel Milstein, "*Kitab Shawq Nameh*: An Illustrated Guide to Holy Arabia," *Jerusalem Studies in Arabic and Islam* 25 (2001): 275–345.

63   Grabar, "The Islamic Dome," 317.

64   Grabar, "The Islamic Dome," 318.

65   Rachel Milstein, "The Evolution of a Visual Motif: The Temple and the Ka'ba," *Israel Oriental Studies* 19 (1999): 23–48; Milstein, "Jerusalem in Islamic Painting," 464–67.

66   Halbwachs, *On Collective Memory*, 231.

3.2   *The* Mishne Torah

The edition of Rambam's fourteen-volume work that was illustrated in northern Italy in the fifteenth century is known as the Frankfurt *Mishneh Torah.*[67] We find an historiated title panel for the eighth book, the Book of Sacrifice, where the Hebrew word *'avodah* appears above the image of two priests performing a sacrifice outside the Temple. Here the Temple is not represented symbolically by its vessels and implements, but rather by an octagonal domed building that resembles the Dome of the Rock. Thus, in constructing the dome above the *'even ha-shtiya*, the Muslims created their own image of the ancient Solomonic Temple, an image that became part of the Crusaders' collective memory as *templum domini*. Upon their return to Europe they circulated this image, which was then used in many medieval paintings, including the one in the Frankfurt *Mishneh Torah.*[68] Above the historiated title panel is a verse from the book of Psalms (122:6): "Pray for the peace of Jerusalem," thus associating Jerusalem with peace and tranquillity.

4   The Collective Memory of Jerusalem for Palestinian and Israeli Artists[69]

To conclude, I turn to the concept of collective memory in connection with more contemporary evidence regarding Jerusalem in art as seen in both Palestinian and Israeli artistic works created toward the end of the twentieth century.

In an article titled "Finding Meaning in Memory: A Methodological Critique of Collective Memory Studies," Wulf Kansteiner expresses ideas about collective memory that might well be relevant to the collective memory seen in works of Palestinian artists discussed here:

> [A]lthough collective memories have no organic basis, and do not exist in any literal sense, and although they involve individual agency, the term

---

67   Frankfurt *Mishneh Torah*, North Italy, 15th century, New York Private Collection. See https://jewishbusinessnews.com/2013/02/02/sothebys-to-auction-judaica-from-stein hardt-collection/.

68   Bianca Kühnel, *The Holy City in Christian Art of the First Millennium* (Freiberg: Herder, 1987), 138–41; Pamela Berger, *The Crescent on the Temple: The Dome of the Rock as Image of the Ancient Jewish Sanctuary* (Leiden: Brill, 2012), 73, 76–77; Robert Schick, "Christian Identifications of Muslim Buildings in Medieval Jerusalem," in *Jerusalem as Narrative Space: Erzählraum Jerusalem,* ed. Annette Hoffmann and Gerhard Wolf (Leiden: Brill, 2012), 367–92.

69   William J.T. Mitchell, *Holy Landscape*, ed. Larry Abramson (Tel Aviv: Ressling, 2009), 17–23 (Hebrew).

"collective memory" is not simply a metaphorical expression. Collective memories originate from shared communications about the meaning of the past that are anchored in the life-worlds of individuals who partake in the communal life of the respective collective. As such, collective memories are based in a society and its inventory of signs and symbols.[70]

In a 1984 oil-on-canvas painting entitled *Jerusalem*, Nabil Anani figured the city as a large circle painted primarily in green and yellow. In the very centre is a green tree and around it are small houses in yellow. People are shown standing outside of the circle. According to Gannit Ankori, this painting reflects the Palestinian collective memory of when they were displaced in 1967. The painting features the symbolic Tree of Life surrounded by houses with their people standing outside—refugees who are excluded from Jerusalem's embrace. The round shape of the city is conceptually related to the Crusader maps of earlier times.[71]

Another oil-on-canvas painting entitled *Song of Jerusalem* done by Silman Mansur in 1970 portrays a Palestinian woman sitting and playing her mandolin with the image of the Dome of the Rock and the city of Jerusalem seen behind her within a ball-like configuration hovering over an undefined space. Her reserved pose, as well as the painting's blue colour scheme and the coastal location of the scene all evoke the tragic mood of Picasso's Blue Period and reflect a feeling of sadness about the city. Jerusalem is not shown realistically, but rather as a supernatural place that seems distant and unrealistic.

An untitled 1985 painting by Samir Salamec also depicts Jerusalem as an ideal city situated in a round space in the sky. Inside the top part of the circle are images of small houses within a city wall, which is marked by Arabic lettering. The picture creates a conflation between the small realistic houses and the Arabic calligraphy that represents the Islamic collective memory, which attributes great importance to words and letters as representatives of the word of God revealed to Muhammad.

4.1   *Mordechai Ardon*
Finally, I come to Mordechai Ardon's work that portrays the wall of Jerusalem using images of parchment from the Dead Sea Scrolls to visualize Isaiah's

---

70   Wulf Kansteiner, "Finding Meaning in Memory: A Methodological Critique of Collective Memory Studies," *History and Theory* 41 (2002): 179–97 (188).

71   Gannit Ankori, "Behind the Walls: The Real and Ideal Jerusalem in Contemporary Palestinian Art," *Jewish Art* 23/24 (1997–1998): 575–85 (577).

prophecy about Jerusalem (Isa 2:3–4; fig. 12.11).[72] Kansteiner's words on collective memory seem to be pertinent here:

> Memories are at their most collective when they transcend the time and space of the event's original occurrence. As such they take on a powerful life of their own, "unencumbered" by actual individual memory, and become the basis of all collective remembering as disembodied, omnipresent, low-intensity memory.[73]

The left-hand panel shows the roads taken by the nations on their way up to Jerusalem. Each road is marked with the verse "Come let us go up to the mountain of the Lord" inscribed in various languages and alphabets, including Latin, Greek, and Arabic. The intertwined paths represent the people who will go up to "the house of the God of Jacob; and He will teach us of His ways, and we will walk in His paths. For out of Zion shall go forth the law and the word of the Lord from Jerusalem" (Isa 2:3).

In the lower section of the central panel we see the walls of the city visualized, as already noted, as parchment from the Dead Sea Scrolls, of the book of Isaiah. Above the walls are motifs from the Kabbalah, including blue circles and lines and the Tree of Sefirot as well as other images from the Zohar (the Kabbalistic Book of Splendour). All of these images reflect the hope for redemption.

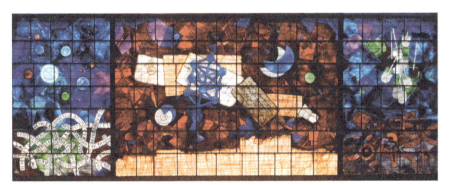

FIGURE 12.11	Mordechai Ardon, stained glass triptych of Isaiah's prophecy about Jerusalem, Hebrew University of Jerusalem National Library 1980–1984

72	Mordechai Ardon's stained-glass triptych was executed in 1980–1984 and set in the National and University Library on the Givat Ram Campus of the Hebrew University of Jerusalem.

73	Kansteiner, "Finding Meaning in Memory," 189.

The panel on the right illuminates the fulfilment of Isaiah's prophetic vision: "And He shall judge between the nations, and they shall beat their swords into ploughshares, and their spears into pruning hooks; nation shall not lift up sword against nation, neither shall they learn war any more" (Isa 2:4).

Ardon's portrayal of Jerusalem does not portray the real city of mortar and stone. The stone wall that actually surrounds the city is transmuted into a spiritual wall and the earthly Jerusalem seems to blend with the universal collective memory of the promise of worldly redemption.

5   Summary

Jan Assmann's words on cultural memory help to sum up this study of selected art works of Jerusalem:

> Just as thinking may be abstract, remembering is concrete. Ideas must take on a form that is imaginable before they can find their way into memory, and so we have an indissoluble merging of idea and image. But if a truth is to be settled in the memory of a group it needs to be presented in the concrete form of an event, of a personality or of a locality.[74]

It seems that observing the collective memory of Jerusalem for Jews, Christians, and Muslims verifies this statement. The collective memory of Jerusalem in Jewish artistic works is based on the destruction of the Temple and of Jerusalem, and the desire to preserve the memory of the Temple as a symbol of God's presence. The collective memory of Jerusalem for Christians is grounded in the events surrounding Jesus's life and death that became signs of his divine nature, and, in time, were hallowed, with Jerusalem being thought of as the hub of the universe and the Church of the Holy Sepulchre as its centre. The collective memory of Jerusalem for Muslims is influenced by such concepts as the *'even ha-shtiya*, upon which the Dome of the Rock was built. Most of the specific episodes attributed to Islamic collective memory are related to this site including the binding of Isaac and Muhammad resting his foot when he ascended to heaven. The Islamic collective memory of Jerusalem was strengthened by the Sufi mystical order, which regarded Ḥaram al-Sharif as the Temple Mount.

Finally, the collective memory of Jerusalem for Palestinian works of art is summed up by Ankori:

---

74   Assmann, *Cultural Memory*, 23–24.

Jerusalem has become a dominant symbolic motif in Palestinian art, a metonym for the entire lost homeland ... Composed of memories of the past formed into nostalgic images of yearning, constructed from hopes for the future that combine personal and collective aspirations it is by definition never real but forever an idealized paradise lost.[75]

The last work discussed in the article is the stained-glass triptych by the Israeli artist Mordechai Ardon. This work gives visual expression to the prophecy of Isaiah for Jerusalem. It is part of a universal, long-term, collective memory of peace that is to be shared by all groups and all people.

References

Ankori, Gannit. "Behind the Walls: The Real and Ideal Jerusalem in Contemporary Palestinian Art." *Jewish Art* 23/24 (1997–1998): 575–85.

Assmann, Jan. *Cultural Memory and Early Civilization*. New York: Cambridge University Press, 2011.

Avi-Yonah, Michael. *Madaba Map: Its Translation and Commentary*. Jerusalem: Israel Exploration Society, 1954. (Hebrew).

Avigad, Nahum. *The Upper City of Jerusalem*. Jerusalem, Shikmona, 1980. (Hebrew).

Avigad, Nahum. "Bet Alpha." Pages 1:190–92 in *The New Encyclopedia of Archaeological Excavations in the Land of Israel*. Edited by Ephraim Stern. 4 vols. Jerusalem: Israel Exploration Society-Carta, 1993.

Bahat, Dan, and Shalom Sabar. *Jerusalem Stone and Spirit: 3000 Years of History and Art*. Jerusalem: Matan Arts, 1997.

Berger, Pamela. *The Crescent on the Temple: The Dome of the Rock as Image of the Ancient Jewish Sanctuary*. Leiden: Brill, 2012.

Bokser, Baruch M. "Approaching Sacred Space." *HTR* 78 (1985): 279–99.

Carruthers, Mary J. *The Craft of Thought: Meditation, Rhetoric, and the Making of Images, 400–1200*. Cambridge: Cambridge University Press, 1998.

Donner, Herbert. *The Mosaic Map of Madaba: An Introductory Guide*. Kampen: Kok Pharos, 1992.

Dothan, Moshe. *Hammath Tiberias: Early Synagogue and the Hellenistic and Roman Remains*. Jerusalem: Israel Exploration Society, 1983.

Elior, Rachel. *The Three Temples: On the Emergence of Jewish Mysticism*. Translated by David Louvish. Oxford: Littman, 2005.

---

75   Ankori, "Behind the Walls," 575.

Fine, Steven. *This Holy Place: On the Sanctity of the Synagogue During the Greco-Roman Period*. Notre Dame: University of Notre Dame Press, 1997.

Goldschmidt, Daniel. *Day of Atonement Prayer Book*. Jerusalem: Koren, 1970. (Hebrew).

Grabar, André. *Les ampoules de Terre Sainte (Monza-Bobbio)*. Paris: Klincksieck, 1958.

Grabar, Oleg. "The Islamic Dome: Some Considerations." Pages 87–102 in *Islamic Arts and Beyond: Constructing the Study of Islamic Art, Volume III*. Hampshire: Ashgate, 2006.

Gutmann, Joseph. "The Messianic Temple in Spanish Medieval Hebrew Manuscripts." Pages 125–45 in *The Temple of Solomon: Archeological Fact and Medieval Tradition in Christian, Islamic and Jewish Art*. Edited by Joseph Gutmann. Missoula, MT: Scholars Press, 1976.

Halbwachs, Maurice. *On Collective Memory*. Edited, translated, and with an introduction by Lewis A. Coser. Chicago: University of Chicago Press, 1992.

Hollander, William den. "Jesus, Josephus, and the Fall of Jerusalem: On Doing History with Scripture." *HTS* 71 (2015). https://repository.up.ac.za/bitstream/handle/2263/51005/DenHollander_Jesus_2015.pdf?sequence=1&isAllowed=y.

Igartua, Juanjo, and Darío Páez. "Art and Remembering Traumatic Collective Events: The Case of the Spanish Civil War." Pages 79–101 in *Collective Memory of Political Events: Social Psychological Perspectives*. Edited by James W. Pennebaker, Darío Páez, and Bernard Rimé. Hillsdale, NJ: Lawrence Erlbaum.

Ish-Shalom, Michael. *Christian Travels in the Holy Land*. Tel Aviv: Am-Oved, 1979. (Hebrew).

Kansteiner, Wulf. "Finding Meaning in Memory: A Methodological Critique of Collective Memory Studies." *History and Theory* 41 (2002): 179–97.

Kaplony, Andreas. "635/638–1099: The Mosque of Jerusalem (Masijid Bayt Al-Maqdis)." Pages 101–31 in *Where Heaven and Earth Meet: Jerusalem's Sacred Esplanade*. Edited by Oleg Grabar and Benjamin Z. Kedar. Jerusalem: Yad Ben Zvi, 2009.

Kühnel, Bianca. "Jewish Symbolism of the Temple and the Tabernacle and Christian Symbolism of the Holy Sepulcher and the Heavenly Tabernacle." *Jewish Art* 12/13 (1986/1987): 147–68.

Kühnel, Bianca. *The Holy City in Christian Art of the First Millennium*. Freiberg: Herder, 1987.

Mahon, Denis. *Nicholas Poussin: Works from His First Years in Rome*. Jerusalem: Israel Museum, 1999.

Milstein, Rachel. "The Evolution of a Visual Motif: The Temple and the Ka'ba." *Israel Oriental Studies* 19 (1999): 23–48.

Milstein, Rachel. "Kitab Shawq Nameh: An Illustrated Guide to Holy Arabia." *Jerusalem Studies in Arabic and Islam* 25 (2001): 275–345.

Milstein, Rachel. "Jerusalem in Islamic Painting: An Object in Narrative Space." Pages 463–75 in *Jerusalem as Narrative Space: Erzählraum Jerusalem*. Edited by Annette Hoffmann and Gerhard Wolf. Leiden: Brill, 2012.

Mitchell, William J.T. *Holy Landscape*. Edited by Larry Abramson. Tel Aviv: Ressling, 2009. (Hebrew).

O'Loughlin, Thomas. "The View from Iona: Adomnán's Mental Maps." *Peritia* 10 (1996): 98–122.

O'Loughlin, Thomas. *Adomnán and the Holy Places: The Perceptions of an Insular Monk on the Locations of the Biblical Drama*. London: T&T Clark, 2007.

Ran, Nachman, ed., *Tracks to the Promised Land: The Land of Israel, Ancient Maps, Prints and Travelogues through the Centuries*. Tel Aviv: Terra Sancta Arts, 1987.

Revel-Neher, Elisheva. *Le témoignage de l'absence*. Paris: De Boccard, 1998.

Revel-Neher, Elisheva. "An 'Encore' on the Bar Kokhba Tetradrachma: A Re-Vision of Interpretation." Pages 189–205 in *"Follow the Wise": Studies in Jewish History and Culture in Honor of Lee I. Levine*. Edited by Zev Weiss, Oded Irshai, Jodi Magness, and Seth Schwartz. Winona Lake, IN: Eisenbrauns, 2010.

Rubin, Rehav. *Image and Reality: Jerusalem in Maps and Views*. Jerusalem: Magnes, 1999.

Safrai, Samuel. "The Temple and the Synagogue." Pages 31–51 in *Synagogues in Antiquity*. Edited by Aryeh Kasher, Aharon Oppenheimer, and Uriel Rappaport. Jerusalem: Yad Ben Zvi, 1987. (Hebrew).

Schick, Robert. "Christian Identifications of Muslim Buildings in Medieval Jerusalem." Pages 367–92 in *Jerusalem as Narrative Space: Erzählraum Jerusalem*. Edited by Annette Hoffmann and Gerhard Wolf. Leiden: Brill, 2012.

Smith, Delano. "Geography or Christianity? Maps of the Holy Land before AD 1000." *JTS* 42 (1991): 143–52.

Snodgrass, Klyne. *Stories with Intent: A Comprehensive Guide to the Parables of Jesus*. Grand Rapids: Eerdmans, 2008.

Townsend, John T. *Midrash Tanḥuma (S. Buber Recension)*. 3 vols. Hoboken: Ktav, 1989.

Tsafrir, Yoram. "Jerusalem in the Map of Madaba, Eretz Yisrael in the Map of Madaba." *Ariel* 116 (1996): 67–73. (Hebrew).

Tsafrir, Yoram. "The Topography and Archaeology of Jerusalem in the Byzantine Period." Pages 281–352 in *The Roman and Byzantine Periods (70–638 CE)*. Edited by Yoram Tsafrir and Samuel Safrai. Jerusalem: Yad Ben Zvi, 1999. (Hebrew).

Wilkinson, John. *Jerusalem Pilgrims before the Crusades*. Jerusalem: Ariel, 1977.

Williamson, Geoffrey A. *Josephus: The Jewish War*. Rev. ed. with a new introduction, notes, and appendixes by E. Mary Smallwood. Harmondsworth: Penguin Classics 1981.

Zalmona, Yigal, ed. *The Israel Museum at 40: Masterworks of Beauty and Sanctity*. Jerusalem: Israel Museum, 2005.

Zalmona, Yigal, Francesco Solinas, Avraham Ronen, and Judith Spitzler. *Nicolas Poussin's Destruction and Sack of the Temple of Jerusalem: A Rediscovered Masterpiece*. Jerusalem: Israel Museum, 1999.

CHAPTER 13

From Church to Synagogue: the Bankras Church (Amstelveen, the Netherlands) as a Case from the Responsa

Leon Mock

In the three monotheistic religions communal worship is concentrated on a specific, designated physical area—the church, mosque or synagogue. It is there where most communal festivals, celebrations or religious rituals are performed or celebrated. This grants these physical compounds and their spaces a religious importance, and even a dimension of holiness, which enhances communal identity and reinforces/makes possible segregation from rival religious community identities. This raises the question as to whether and how a religious building can be re-used by another religion/religious tradition. In this article I will describe a recent case of converting a church building into a synagogue in Amstelveen, the Netherlands. This case was described by two authors of orthodox rabbinic responsa, one rabbi of the orthodox Dutch Jewish Community, the other from Israel. I will analyse their arguments to see what their perspectives are on Christianity from a halakhic standpoint, and whether the environment/cultural background has some influence on the discourse—a diaspora setting versus a rabbi from Israel. Furthermore it will be interesting to see whether the discourse shows some influences of "bridging the gap" between the two religions, in the wake of the changed relations between them over the last 50 years, and the intensive religious dialogue between Judaism and Christianity.

1   The Bankras Church

The Bankras Church was built in 1970 and inaugurated in April 1971. It was a Protestant Church in which two denominations were combined: the "Gereformeerden" and the "Hervormden." In 2008, the Protestant church council decided to close the church and to offer it for sale.[1] In January 2009, the Bankras Church building was purchased by the Jewish community of Amsterdam, as a synagogue for its community in Amstelveen (a suburb of

---

1   http://www.amstelveenweb.com/fotodisp&fotodisp=2305.

Amsterdam).[2] The reason for the acquisition of a church building instead of building a new synagogue from scratch seems to have been an economical one: it is cheaper to buy an existing building and renovate and renew it as a synagogue than building a new synagogue from scratch. Hence the halakhic question whether a church may be used as a synagogue for permanent use.

On 9 December 2012, the new synagogue was inaugurated in the presence of the chief rabbi of Amsterdam, Aryeh Ralbag, the mayor of Amstelveen, other prominent guests and local residents—both Jewish and non-Jewish.[3] The transfer of the church building to the Jewish community took place in a harmonious atmosphere without signs of negative emotions or antisemitism. On the contrary, the Jewish community opened its doors for residents from the neighbourhood—Jewish and non-Jewish—on 27 January 2013 and questions were asked of the rabbi of the synagogue by interested non-Jewish people.[4]

It was not the first time that a Jewish community in the Netherlands bought a church building and converted it into a synagogue. In 1807, the Jewish community of Naaldwijk bought a church in the Heilige Geesthofje and used it as a synagogue until 1920. A wooden house in Amstelveen (built in 1932), previously used as a protestant church, was used by the Jewish community of Amstelveen as a synagogue from 1938 until May 1942 when, due to Nazi oppression, Jewish prayer-services became impossible. In 1972, the Jewish orthodox community of Amsterdam (NIHS) bought the church building of the Vrije Gemeente (built in 1966) and has used it as a synagogue and Jewish community centre up to the present day. In 1974, the Jewish orthodox community of The Hague bought the Goede Vrijdagkerk (Protestant) and used it as a synagogue until 1985.[5]

2   The Acquisition

The rabbinate of Amsterdam approved the acquisition of the church building in the Bankras by the end of 2008/the beginning of 2009. However, prior to their decision on this acquisition, the rabbinate of the Jewish community of

---

2   On 20 January 2009, the website of the NIK (the umbrella organisation of Dutch Orthodox Communities in the Netherlands) reports that the Jewish community of Amsterdam (NIHS) has bought the building: http://www.nik.nl/2009/01/amstelveen-kerk-wordt-sjoel/.

3   https://www.nik.nl/2012/12/nieuwe-sjoel-in-amstelveen-opent-haar-deuren/.

4   http://www.amstelveenweb.com/fotodisp&fotodisp=2316.

5   www.nik.nl/2009/01/amstelveen-kerk-wordt-sjoel/; www.historischamstelveen.nl/9-uncate gorised/112-behoud-voormalige-synagog-randwijcklaan-13; https://www.monumentaal westland.nl/monumenten/het-heilige-geesthofje/; Joseph Michman, Hartog Beem, and Dan Michman, *Pinkas: Geschiedenis van de joodse gemeenschap in Nederland* (Amsterdam: Kluwer, 1992), 390.

Amsterdam (NIHS) consulted Rabbi Yitshak Shechter (Netanya, Israel) on the matter.[6] Rabbi Shechter wrote a responsum on this matter to the Amsterdam rabbinate in November 2008. Another rabbi who was consulted on this matter was Rabbi Raphael Evers, who was employed as a rabbi by the umbrella organization of Dutch Jewish Orthodox Communities (NIK), from 1990 until the summer of 2016. In an undated responsum of Rabbi Evers—written probably in the spring of 2011—he states his opinion on the acquisition and use of the church building as a synagogue for the Amstelveen community. In an addendum to Evers's own responsum, a responsum of Rabbi Shechter to Rabbi Evers is attached with his answer on the matter.[7] The original responsum and addendum were printed in volume four of Evers's responsa *Weshav weRafeh* (no. 4). In the following analysis, Evers's responsum and the addendum of Shechter will be analysed and compared.

The reason why the question was addressed to Rabbi Shechter may raise some surprise—he does not live in the Netherlands and has a more Haredi-Chassidic signature. He is a well-known rabbi in Haredic circles, though, and a pupil of the Tzanzer Rebbe Yekutiel Jehudah Halberstam (1905–1994), author of the famous responsa series entitled *Divrei Yatsiv*. Shechter himself is the author of the responsa series *Yashiv Yitshak* with more than ten volumes. Rabbi Evers has consulted Shechter on halakhic questions since at least 2006, on both communal (apparently addressed to the Beit Din of Amsterdam) and personal questions posed by Evers to Shechter.[8] Some of Shechter's answers are sent to Evers by the intermediary of Rabbi Eliezer Wolf, rabbi of the Beth Din of Amsterdam and at that time of Marseille (France). So there was already since at least 2006 an established halakhic communication between the rabbinate of Amsterdam (Rabbi Wolf), Rabbi Evers of the NIK (the united Dutch Orthodox Communities) and Shechter on other matters.[9]

---

6 This information comes from Rabbi S. Katz, the secretary of the rabbinate of Amsterdam.

7 The question is interestingly enough addressed in the Hebrew plural: "Concerning your question that you wrote" (שאלתכם שכתבתם), although the Amsterdam rabbinate already approved the acquisition two years earlier. From the opening of the question it seems that there was an opposition to the original acquisition (and decision of the Amsterdam rabbinate?): "because of the protests for different reasons" (מפני המעוררין מכמה סיבות).

8 See Raphael Evers, *Weshav weRafeh*, 4 vols. (Jerusalem: Fisher, 2008–2014), 3:nos. 4, 82, 112, 117, 120, 122, 147, 157, 193, 218, 228, 242. Some of the questions that were asked to the Beit Din of Amsterdam (for example nos. 112, 147 on kashrut matters and family purity) open with the phrase "your question" in the plural and are of a communal nature.

9 In a personal conversation, Rabbi Evers explained his choice for Shechter as a halakhic source: "He is a famous *posek* [halakhic decisor] with a lot of experience, who answers questions relatively fast. He wrote 60 works [?] of responsa and is easy to approach and has an open eye for practice."

3   *Shituf*: Association, Fusion

Evers begins by stating that Protestant churches do not contain physical idols (צלמים), only a cross, and that some do not have even a cross. From this he moves to a discussion of the halakhic concept of *shituf*, which can be translated as "association(ism)," "syncretism," "participation," "combination," or "fusion." This is based on a discussion in b. Bek. 2b as to whether it is permissible to do business with a heathen:

> Has not the father of Samuel said: One must not form a partnership with a heathen lest he [the heathen] will be bound to take an oath to him and he will swear in the name of his idol and the Torah says [Exod 23:13]: "[And make no mention of the name of other gods.] neither let it be heard out of thy mouth?"[10]

On this the Tosafot comment:

> Rabenu Tam explained [it as permitted because] nowadays all [Christians] swear by [the name of] Saints and they do not consider them to be divine. And although they mention (together with them = [the Saints]) the name of Heaven, and their intention is (towards "something else"), in any case this is not (a name of) idolatry, for their minds is for the sake of the Maker of Heaven and Earth. And although he fuses the name of Heaven with "something else," [in this case] there is not [a prohibition of] "putting a stumbling block before the blind" [Lev 19:24, i.e., causing someone to transgress a prohibited action], for a Noahide is not commanded about this. And for us [= Jews] we do not find a prohibition for causing "fusion" [by others, by a Noahide].[11]

These words of Tosafot are somehow ambiguous (what is this "something else," for example), and can be interpreted in a narrow and broader perspective.[12]

---

10   All the Talmud and Mishnah translations are taken from the Soncino editions, the responsa from the CD-ROM Bar-Ilan Responsa Project, version 26 unless otherwise stated.

11   CD-Rom Bar-Ilan Responsa Project, version 26:
עוד פר״ת בזמן הזה כולן נשבעים בקדשים ואין תופסין בהם אלהות ואף על פי שמזכירין
[עמהם] שם שמים וכוונתם [לד״א מ״מ] אין זה [שם] עבודת כוכבים כי דעתם לשם עושה
שמים וארץ ואף על גב **שמשתתף ש״ש ודבר אחר** אין כאן לפני עור לא תתן מכשול דבני נח
לא הוזהרו על כך ולדידן לא אשכחן איסור בגרם שיתוף.

12   See Alan Brill, *Judaism and Other Religions: Models of Understanding* (New York: MacMillan, 2010), 178–80; Alon Goshen-Gottstein, *Same God, Other God: Judaism, Hinduism, and the Problem of Idolatry* (New York: MacMillan, 2016), esp. 93–95. See also

In the narrower understanding, Rabbenu Tam does not make any theological claim on the permissible status of Christianity. He only states that in the specific context of taking an oath, a Jew may accept an oath of a Christian—even with a clear Christian content—and this is not considered a prohibition for the Jew or Christian. In the broader contextual understanding, the Tosafot seem to make a theological statement on Christianity as a permissible monotheistic religion for a non-Jew.[13] Evers gives a summary of some rabbinic authors on the subject of *shituf* and the status of Christianity. In these sources the following positions can be found:[14]

– Christianity is not idolatry, and henceforth even their idols or prayer houses are permissible.
– Christianity is not idolatry, but their images in a religious-cultic setting are forbidden so therefore also their prayer-houses, if they contain images.
– Christians are not idolaters, but Christianity is idolatry.
– Christianity is idolatry (according to some: even without idols—as long as clear religious actions are performed, like kneeling, bowing down, burning of candles, praying).

4   *Shituf* and Dutch Protestantism

In his technical discussion of the halakhic sources, Evers seems to have a (slight?) preference for a stricter standpoint, which limits the applicability of *shituf* as a permissible category for Christianity.[15]

On the other hand he writes in a more positive way on the services in Protestant churches:

Judah David Bleich, "Entering a Non-Jewish House of Worship," *Tradition* 44 (2011): 73–102 (74–77).

13   The parallel version of Rabenu Tam's words in Tosafot on b. Sanh. 63b though seem to support a broader approach:
מ״מ בזמן הזה כולן נשבעים בקדשים שלהן ואין תופסין בהם אלהות ואף על פי שמה שמזכי־
רין עמהם ש״ש וכוונתם לדבר אחר מ״מ אין זה שם עבודת כוכבים גם דעתם לעושה שמים
ואף על פי שמשתתפין שם שמים ודבר אחר לא אשכחן דאסור לגרום לאחרים לשתף ולפני
עור ליכא דבני נח לא הוזהרו על כך.

14   Evers, *Weshav weRafeh*, 4:no. 4, 37–41.

15   Evers, *Weshav weRafeh*, 4:no. 4, 41 writes that according to the stricter views on *shituf*, believers in the Trinity would be violating the prohibition of idolatry, that consists "most of the Christian sects [כתות]."

[M]ost of the Christians in our country are called Protestants, in their [various] denominations. And there are some (as in this case) that do not possess any remembrance of any idol [צלם] or image [דמות] in their prayer houses, and their custom is only to pray there and to utter the psalms in their language and translation. And afterwards somebody stands up and preaches to them on the verses of Tenach or a biblical story, or from their New Testament. And he preaches to them highly on that man [= Jesus] (and they do not prostrate themselves there at all).[16]

5   Arguments for Permission

The more subtle religious service in Dutch protestant churches is not sufficient reason to permit the use of its buildings for the precinct of a synagogue. For this purpose other halakhic reasons/arguments are necessary, according to Evers. The following arguments are brought up by him:

– Church buildings are often used for non-religious purposes, like the selling of non-religious books, a coffee corner, musical performances, and lectures. Sometimes the location is rented to others for various purposes. In this way one can argue/say that it is not a universally sacral/holy/sanctified space that is designated only for religious worship.[17]
– The building itself—because there are no visible idols or images—can be considered as serving the visitors mainly, and is therefore not a place of idol worship in a direct way.[18]
– Converting a house of idol-worship into a Jewish place of worship is a "sanctification of the Holy Name," and a foretaste of the messianic era in which all people serve the One God.[19]
– The halakhic precedent of re-using a house in which idols were worshiped as a place of prayer.[20]

---

16   Evers, *Weshav weRafeh*, 4:no. 4, 39.
17   Evers, *Weshav weRafeh*, 4:no. 4, 39.
18   Evers, *Weshav weRafeh*, 4:no. 4, 40.
19   The argument of the *Sho'el uMeshiv* (Joseph Saul Nathansohn, *Sho'el uMeshiv*, 3 vols. [Lemberg: Uri Zeev Wolf Salat, 1865–79]); Evers, *Weshav weRafeh*, 4:no. 4, 39.
20   Evers, *Weshav weRafeh*, 4:no. 4, 39 and 41.

6   Reusing a Church Building: Halakhic Precedents

This last argument is based on the words of the *Magen Avraham* (Gombiner, 17th century); on the *Shulkhan Arukh*, OH 154:17, one which is based on earlier sources; the *Knesset Hagedolah* (Benvenishti, 17th century); and the *Re'em* (Eliyahu Mizrahi, 15–16th century). The commentary of the *Magen Avraham* is made in the context of the text of the *Shulkhan Arukh* (OH 154:11):

> Wax candles that were donated by pagans for idol worship—if the attendant has extinguished them and gave them, or sold them to an Israelite, then these are forbidden for lighting in the synagogue. Gloss [of M. Isserliss]: although they are permitted for the layman.[21]

On this paragraph the *Magen Avraham* writes:

> And the same law applies to any light that is a precept [מצוה] and for anything that is a religious precept—we don't make it from anything that was made for idolatry ... and the *Knesset haGedolah* wrote in name of the *Re'em* ... that even when an idol was worshipped in a house on a regular basis, it is permitted to pray in it. And perhaps his argument is that something attached [to the ground] is different. And although usually a house has the status of something "detached" [תלוש], it is similar though to something attached [to the ground] ... and in this case it is different because the house itself was not worshipped.[22]

This permission to pray in a house where an idol had been worshipped could be understood in more than one way. The *Eliyahu Rabbah* (Eliyahu Shapira, 17th century) understood this as permission for praying in such a house

---

21   *Shulkhan Arukh* OH, Laws of the Synagogue §154:11:
נרות שעוה שנותנם כותי לעובדי אלילים, וכיבן שמשן ונתנם או מכרן לישראל, אסור להדלי־
קם בבהכ״נ.
הגה: אף על פי שמותרים להדיוט.

22   Magen Avraham (subpar 17) on *Shulkhan Arukh* OH, Laws of the Synagogue §154:11:
וה״ה לכל נר מצוה וה״ה לכל מילי דמצוה אין עושין מדבר שנעשה לע״א עסי׳ י״א סעיף ח׳
וסי׳ תקפ״ו סעיף ג׳ ובכ״ה כתב בשם הרא״ם ח״א סי׳ ע״ט דאפי׳ נעבד בבית ע״א בקבע מותר
להתפלל בתוכו ואפשר דס״ל דמחובר שאני ואף על גב דבית דינו כתלוש מ״מ דמי למחובר
וצ״ע בע״א דף מ״ו מ״ז והכא שאני דלא עבד הבית עצמו.

occasionally, but not on a regular basis.[23] Others understood this as referring to praying on a regular basis, and hence this constituted permission to use a church and turn it into a synagogue.[24] This practice—which seems to have become popular in the second half of the 19th century[25]—is endorsed by the *Mishneh Berurah* of Kagan (19th–20th century), which has an important role in the post-Shoah discourse on orthodox halakha, although in a more prag-matic way: "[A]nd it seems that people used to be lenient in the matter."[26] In the same glossary of Kagan he refers to his more in-depth commentary *Bi'ur Halakha* (*ad loc.*), in which he states that this leniency is restricted to houses of worship without images—even if these were taken out afterwards and the building was sold. However, a church in which images were once placed can-not be re-used as a synagogue.[27] Although, when even only a "likeness" (דמות)[28] was present in the building during its use for religious worship, then only a thorough change and renovation of the building permits its use as a synagogue, so that its former use is not in any way visible.[29] After the renovation—and not before this stage—the building should be consecrated as a synagogue.[30]

---

23   *Eliyahu Rabbah* OH 154:15. See on the interpretation of the *Magen Avraham* also Evers, *Weshav weRafeh*, 4:no. 4, 39. Although this halakhic discussion is discussed in more detail by Shechter in the addendum; see Evers, *Weshav weRafeh*, 4:no. 4, 43–44.

24   See for example the responsum of Nathansohn, *Sho'el uMeshiv*, 3:no. 72.

25   The original responsum of the *Sho'el uMeshiv* that both Evers and Shechter use is from the original question sent by Rabbi Judah Mittelman from New York.

26   *Mishneh Berurah* on OH. 154:11, subpar. 45: "... וכמדומה שהעולם נוהגים להקל ..." See also Evers, *Weshav weRafeh*, 4:no. 4, 41.

27   Evers, *Weshav weRafeh*, 4:no. 4, 41:

     עיין בביה"ל שבירררנו דדוקא כשאין דרכן להעמיד שם אליליהם אבל אלו שמעמידין שם אליליהם אף שהוציאום משם ומכרו הבית לישראל דאז מותר הבית להדיוט מטעם שכבר נתבטל עי"ז

     משם משמשי אליל כדאיתא ביו"ד קמ"ה ס"ג עכ"פ לביהכ"נ אסור...

28   It is not clear what Evers or his sources exactly mean with the different words used in their discourse: דמות, צלם, צורה.

29   Based on Moshe Feinstein's *Iggrot Moshe* OH, no. 49; see Evers, *Weshav weRafeh*, 4:no. 4, 41.

30   At the end of his conclusion, Evers gives a very brief summary of the decision of the rab-binate of Amsterdam that permits the acquisition of the church building under certain conditions. I will not discuss this extensively because I was not presented with the origi-nal text by the rabbinate of Amsterdam. Their conditions are:
- Before or during the transfer of the building the seller has to remove every symbol, table, plate or inscription that is a reminder of its former use.
- The acquired building should be appointed as a Jewish cultural centre in order that the building will not conceive the holiness of a synagogue (!).
- Inside the building the Jewish character of the building should be emphasized clearly.

This element of renovating the building as a way for permitting the use of the church—mentioned by both Evers and Shechter—and the importance of the moment of consecration, are both based on a responsum of Rabbi Feinstein (OH, V. 1, nr. 49). This responsum deals with the question of using a church building for a synagogue. Interestingly enough, although Evers and Shechter refer to Feinstein's responsum, both omit the author's negative stance on the custom of converting a church into a synagogue. The original responsum of Feinstein (dated 1952) starts with stating his disapproval:

> Now, in fact on the custom in America of making from "their" houses of prayer a synagogue as I saw in many synagogues—they rely in this matter on the *Magen Avraham* in the name of the *Re'em* ... and I saw this also in the *Mishneh Berurah* ... that the custom is to be lenient—but I do not feel good about that. Because it is evident that it is a disgrace [to use it] for a religious precinct ... and therefore, although I do not come to forbid those synagogues that have already been made according to the Sages' instructions, and even in retrospect we do not forbid it ... anyway out of my mouth such a leniency will not come.[31]

More interesting though is the fact that the original responsum of Feinstein refers to a Catholic church building that was destroyed by a fire, then rebuilt as a school, and then again destroyed (נחרב), so that only its walls remained. The whole argument of renovation and change in the building is not only halakhic, but also practical—the building is not fit for use at all without first renovating

---

    – The rabbinate will be involved in the process of the renovation, reshaping, and furnishing of the inner space of the building because of the halakhic aspects of the process.

    – The section for the women will be built as a balcony. It would be interesting to speculate whether this condition has anything to do with the former Christian character of the building or is a separate halakhic issue on the Mechitzah.

31   Iggrot Moshe OH, V. 1, no. 49:

והנה בעצם מה שנהגו בפה אמעריקא /אמריקה/ לעשות מבית תיפלה שלהם לבית הכנסת כאשר ראיתי בהרבה בתי כנסיות והוא מחמת שסומכים על המג״א /או״ח/ בשם הרא״מ בסי׳ קנ״ד ס״ק י״ז, וכן ראיתי במ״ב שם ס״ק מ״ה שכתב וכמדומה שהעולם נוהגין להקל עין שם. אין דעתי נוחה מזה דפשוט שמאוס זה למצוה וכן מבאר שם בבאור הלכה שבאלו שהעמידו שם אליליהם יש לאסור. ולכן אף שלא באתי לאסור את אלו בתי כנסיות שכבר נעשו ע״פ הוראת חכמים, וגם בכלל בדיעבד אין לאסור כדחזינן בלולב שיצא בדיעבד אחר בטול, אלמא דטעם מאיס למצוה הוא רק דין דלכתחלה וא״כ אפשר שאחרי שהוציאו כבר הוצאה גדולה ועשוהו לביהכ״נ נחשב כדיעבד גם להתפלל בו לכתחלה אח״כ, אבל עכ״פ מפי לא תצא היתר לזה.

and rebuilding it![32] Both authors ignore the original context of Feinstein's responsum and explain it in a more lenient way.

7   A Discourse of Later Decisores

If we take a closer look at the sources that are used by Evers in his responsum, it is striking that hardly any discussion takes place on the classical rabbinic texts like Mishnah and Talmud on *'abodah zarah*. Although both do refer specifically to the status of houses of pagan worship and the re-using of stones and the like. For example we find the following mishnah in m. 'Abod. Zar. 3:7:

> There are three types of shrines:[33] A shrine originally built for idolatrous worship—behold this is prohibited. If a man plastered and tiled [an ordinary house] for idolatry and renovated it, one may remove the renovations. If he had only brought an idol into it and taken it out again, [the house] is permitted.[34]

But there are at least two other possible mishnayot and their talmudic discussions relevant for the question on the reusing of a church building as a synagogue.[35] However, actually no thorough discussion takes place on relevant medieval sources, either on the status of pagan buildings, their stones and the subject of *shituf.* Most of Evers's responsum—and especially its conclusion—seems to be based on the sources of the later decisores of the previous 300–400 years. It is possible to explain this phenomenon by referring to (some)

---

32   Iggrot Moshe OH, V. 1, no. 49:

בדבר בית תיפלה של נוצרים קתולים **שנחרב ע"י שרפה** זה יותר מכ"ו שנה, ואח"כ תקנו אותה
לבית ספר, ולפני ג' שנים **נחרב עוד הפעם ונשארו רק הכותלים שהם מלבנים וצריך גם לתקן
הכותלים שאין ראוין כמו שהן** וכן בנין שהיה סמוך נחרב גם הוא, ולא ניכר שם שום דבר
מעניני הע"ז אם יש להתיר לקנותם לעשות מהבנינים בית הכנסת אחרי שיתקנום לזה.

33   Better: "houses."

34   B. 'Abod. Zar. 47b.

35   M. 'Abod. Zar. 3:6 and 3:8 (b. 'Abod. Zar. 47a–b and 47b): "If [an Israelite] has a house adjoining an idolatrous shrine [בית] and it collapsed, he is forbidden to rebuild it. How should he act? He withdraws a distance of four cubits into his own ground and there builds. [If the wall] belonged to him and the shrine [בית] it is judged as being half and half. Its stones, timber and rubbish defile like a creeping thing." And: "There are three kinds of [idolatrous] stones: a stone which a man hewed originally to serve as a pedestal [for an idol]—behold this is prohibited. If a man [merely] plastered and stuccoed [a stone] for idolatry, one may remove the plaster and stucco, and it is then permitted. If he set an idol upon it and took it off behold [the stone] is permitted."

other contemporary authors of orthodox responsa that share this same feature with Evers's responsum: a focus on the halakhic discourse of the last 300–400 years, at the expense of a deeper discussion on the talmudic sources (or even medieval commentaries), as I stated elsewhere.[36]

Another possible explanation in the specific context of this responsum is that Evers (and perhaps other contemporary authors that he uses) does not really consider Christianity as paganism in the same way that the Talmud and Mishnah perceived the Graeco-Roman world. In focusing mainly on later post-medieval sources, the question arises whether it is possible to claim a clear continuum, in this case between the classic rabbinic sources and contemporary reality. On the other hand, Evers's responsum does not show a clear knowledge or acquaintance with contemporary Christian theology and its themes.

8   The Addendum of Rabbi Shechter

In the addendum we find the responsum of Rabbi Shechter on the same matter, which is more extended than Evers's own responsum (seven pages A4 in total). Rabbi Shechter is a member of the rabbinate of Kiryat Sanz in Netanya and author of his own responsa collections *Yashiv Yitshak*. In general, Shechter uses the same sources as Evers and comes to the same conclusion that permits the acquisition of the church building. But there are some interesting differences that are striking.

Shechter introduces b. Meg. 6a into the discourse, which is not discussed by Evers. He discusses this Talmud text—mainly the commentary of Tosafot *ad loc.* and the possible explanations of it. B. Meg. 6a states:

> R. Jose b. Hanina said: What is meant by the text [Zech 9:7], *And I will take away his blood out of his mouth and his detestable things from between his teeth, and he also shall be a remnant for our God?* "And I will take away his blood out of his mouth": this refers to their sacrificial shrines. "And his detestable things from between his teeth": this refers to their oracles. "And he also shall be a remnant for our God": these are the synagogues and houses of learning in Edom. "And he shall be as a chief in Judah, and Ekron as a Jebusite" [Zech 9:7]: these are the theatres and circuses

---

36   See Leon Mock, "Het begrip 'Ruach Ra'a' in de rabbijnse responsliteratuur van na 1945: Een casestudy in de relatie tussen kennis over de fysieke wereld en traditionele kennis" (PhD diss., Tilburg University, 2015), 10–12.

in Edom in which one day the chieftains of Judah shall publicly teach
the Torah.

In its commentary, Tosafot deals with "theatres and circuses in Edom"
(תראטריות וקרקסיות). The first possible explanation brought by Tosafot states
that these are places of pagan worship, and if so, he suggests that a pagan
building will in the future be reused for holy matters (Zech 9 is a clearly eschatological chapter): the chieftains of Judah shall publicly teach there the Torah!
Tosafot finds this a difficult explanation—it would be better that these pagan
places would be desolate in the messianic future.[37] In his second explanation,
Tosafot sees in these "theatres and circuses in Edom" places of gathering for
the council of pagan worshipers—but not a clear place of religious worship.

9   Differences between Shechter and Evers

Other striking differences between the responsum of Shechter and Evers are:
–   Shechter does not discuss the whole matter of *shituf*—it is only superficially
    dealt with in the discussion. Evers, on the other hand, delves deeply into this
    halakhic theme.
–   Shechter seems to emphasize more the issue of destruction, renovation and
    changing the interior of the building as fitting into the concept of *bitul*, nul-
    lifying pagan cultic utensils or structures by a deed of destruction that is
    found in the Mishnah[38] and Talmud, and in fact continues the Deuteronomic
    theme of the destruction of idols in a more sublimated way.[39] Shechter also
    suggests changes in the exterior of the building, along with the renovation
    and changes that are made in the interior of the building.[40] This transition
    in status, through an action of destruction or renovation,[41] is a halakhic con-
    cept and less a psychological one. It marks the transition of an object or
    space from a prohibited and idolatrous status to a profane and permitted

---

37   Tosafot on b. Meg. 6a:

וקשה לומר שאותן מקומות מטונפות יכול
ללמוד שם תורה אלא ודאי לשממה יהא במהרה בימינו.

38   See m. 'Abod. Zar. 3:7, 10; 4:4–5.

39   Evers, *Weshav weRafeh*, 4:no. 4, 45–46. See also Christine E. Hayes, *Between the Babylonian
      and Palestinian Talmuds: Accounting for Halakhic Difference in Selected Sugyot from
      Tractate Avodah Zarah* (New York: Oxford University Press, 1997), 57.

40   Evers, *Weshav weRafeh*, 4:no. 4, 49.

41   Or other intentional actions that show a change in the perception and intention
      (*kavana*) of the owner from an idolatrous function of the object towards profane uses.

one, in a way similar to the concept that actions (and intentions) create a shift from the profane state of objects and spaces towards the sacred realm and vice versa.[42] In fact there are different opinions on the sanctity of a synagogue—whether it is a biblical or a rabbinic level of holiness—and the Talmud and codices know also of the possibility of diminishing the sacred status of a synagogue from the beginning by "making a condition" (על תנאי), although this is almost exclusively applied to the diaspora.[43]

– Shechter dwells more deeply on the prohibition of entering a church,[44] and expands this prohibition to entering a mosque. Entering the church building would be forbidden even if this is done by members of the Jewish community to see whether the building meets their requirements to serve as a synagogue, and how the rebuilding of the interior should be done. As long as the church building is not sold, it is strictly forbidden to enter it, according to Shechter, and the Jewish community should use technological means like film and video to make images of the interior and decide on the acquisition of the building. After the church building is sold to the Jewish community, Shechter prefers that the renovation should be done by non-Jews.[45]

– Shechter's responsum shows some signs of a dualistic worldview in which forces of holiness and impurity are striving with each other. This is visible in his addition to the original responsum of the *Sho'el uMeshiv* which permits—while referring to b. Meg. 6a—the use of a church building for a Beth Midrash and considers it a *Kiddush Hashem* (Sanctification of the

---

42   See for example m. Parah 2:3: "If one had ridden on it, leaned on it, hung on its tail, crossed a river by its help, doubled on its leading rope, or put one's cloak on it, it is invalid. But if one had only fastened it by its leading rope or made for it a sandal to prevent it from slipping or spread one's cloak on it because of flies, it remains valid. This is the general rule: wherever anything is done for its own sake, it remains valid; but if for the sake of any other, it becomes invalid." See also b. B. Meṣ. 57a: "We learnt elsewhere: 'If the consecrated [animal] was blemished, it becomes *hullin*, but its value must be assessed.' R. Johanan said: It becomes *hullin* by Biblical law, but its value must be assessed by Rabbinic law." On the role of intention see for example m. Naz. 5:1: "Beth Shammai say that consecration in error is [effective] consecration, but Beth Hillel say that it is not effective. For example, if someone says, 'the black bull that leaves my house first shall be sacred,' and a white one emerges, Beth Shammai declare it sacred, but Beth Hillel say that it is not sacred."

43   B. Meg. 28b: "R. Assi said: The synagogues of Babylon have been built with a stipulation, and even so they must not be treated disrespectfully. What [for instance] is this?—Doing calculations [for business purposes] in them." See also *Shulkhan Arukh* OH 151:11.

44   Evers also dwells on the prohibition of entering a church, but he seems to address the specific issue whether the community leaders are permitted to enter the building in order to decide on the acquisition; see Evers, *Weshav weRafeh*, 4:no. 4, 38–39. On the prohibition of entering a church see also Bleich, "Entering a Non-Jewish house of Worship."

45   Evers, *Weshav weRafeh*, 4:no. 4, 49.

Name of God). Shechter adds: "[A] Kiddush Hashem to take out of the region [רשות] of the *Sitra Akhra* [the Other Side][46] and transfer it to Holiness." In this light the end of Shechter's responsum is interesting—he concludes his responsum with:

> And may the words of Zecharia 9 be fulfilled: "And I will take away his blood out of his mouth ... and he also shall be a remnant for our God"— that in the future they will be changed into Houses of Study [there]as stated in Talmud Megilla 6 and in Tosafot [there].[47]

10   Conclusions

Both responsa do not reflect influences from the changed/altered relationship between Judaism and Christianity in the West over the last fifty years, and the ongoing religious dialogue between them. We do not find, for example, a discussion on the positive evaluation of the Meiri (13th century) of Christianity by either author.[48] Both responsa are heavily text-oriented—no references are made to (the many) precedents from the diaspora of using a church building for a synagogue. In fact, Shechter does refer to a real case from the diaspora (Montreal), but does so only in a very general way.[49] It is remarkable that Evers does not refer to precedents from the Netherlands of using a church building for a synagogue, although they do exist. The heavy textual orientation of contemporary orthodox responsa I discussed more extensively in my PhD-thesis.[50] In this specific case, this textual orientation leads to an interesting phenomenon: from a picture on the internet (fig. 13.1)[51] it is clear that the Bankras Church did have a cross on its wall, although Evers does not seems to be interested whether in this specific case a cross was or was not hanging on the wall. This could of course easily be checked in "real life" and could make the case perhaps

---

46   A concept in Kabbalah and the Zohar that refers to the demonic, evil side of existence.

47   Evers, *Weshav weRafeh*, 4:no. 4, 49.

48   See for example Bleich, "Entering a Non-Jewish house of Worship," 77–84; Moshe Halbertal, "'Ones Possessed of Religion': Religious Tolerance in The Teachings of The Me'iri," *Edah* 1 (2000): 1–24; David Berger, "Jews, Gentiles, and the Modern Egalitarian Ethos: Some Tentative Thoughts," in *Formulating Responses in an Egalitarian Age*, ed. Marc D. Stern (Lanham, MD: Rowman & Littlefield, 2005), 83–108.

49   Evers, *Weshav weRafeh*, 4:no. 4, 44.

50   Mock, "Het begrip 'Ruach Ra'a' in de rabbijnse responsliteratuur van na 1945."

51   http://www.amstelveenweb.com/fotodisp&fotodisp=2305.

FIGURE 13.1   Interior of the Bankras Church

more problematic[52]—in the same way that a close reading of the original responsum of Feinstein would make it less useable as a lenient source (in fact
the contrary).

Although both authors use the same sources, there are some remarkable
differences between them. Evers dwells much more on the halakhic discussion
on *shituf* than Shechter. It would be possible to argue that for Evers, a rabbi
(with an academic degree) of a modern-orthodox diaspora community, who
was frequently involved with Christian clergy, it is less clear that Christianity
is idolatry, in the same way that pagans in the Graeco-Roman world were for
the authors of the Mishnah and Talmud. For Shechter on the other hand, as
an ultra-orthodox rabbi of a Haredi-community in Israel, the whole subject
of *shituf* is less relevant for his image of Christianity. It seems for him more
evident that Christianity is idolatry and may explain his emphasizing the explicitly stated prohibition for the community leaders to enter the church, even
for the purpose of checking whether it is suitable for use as a synagogue, and
the more extended role of destruction and *bitul* (annihilation/nullification) in
his discourse. Shechter's discourse seems to reflect the more traditional view,

52   Evers himself starts his responsum with a reference to Isserlis (JD 141:1) who states that
        a figure (צורה) that is worshipped (prostrating) has the same status as a moulded idol
        (צלם).

in which the different religions are at odds with each other—hence he emphasizes the prohibition of entering a mosque—and this religious tension is only resolved in messianic times.

Finally, the fact that the question arises in a diaspora setting may add to explain the different attitude of both rabbis. Already in the Bible, idolatry is more problematic in the Holy Land—the war against idolatry and its servants is explicitly connected to crossing into the land of Israel.[53] The Talmud too seems to adopt a more lenient view on idolatry in the diaspora as exemplified by the dictum: "The gentiles outside the land [of Israel] are not idolaters; they only continue the customs of their ancestors."[54] Using church buildings and turning them into a permanent synagogue has been practiced in the diaspora, at least on a larger scale, since the 19th century. On the other hand, in the land of Israel the presence of idolatry and places of worship are more problematic from the traditional halakhic point of view. The revival of the halakhic notion that Christianity is idolatry in the traditional sense is also present in some halakhic questions on entering a church of contemporary Israeli rabbis and in (popular) rulings on the Internet.[55] Unfortunately we have witnessed in the last decades in Israel several negative incidents concerning churches and Christian clergy by extremists.[56] Applying halakhic categories that were formed in the past—shaped also by the tense relationships between paganism and Judaism in antiquity and Christianity and Judaism in the Middle Ages—to the modern situation could pose a challenge for orthodox Judaism in Israel.

---

53 See Deut 11:29–12:4.

54 B. Ḥul. 13b. See also Hayes, *Between the Babylonian and Palestinian Talmuds*, 127–43.

55 See for example the responsa *Tzitz Eliezer* of Rabbi Waldenberg, v. 14, no. 91; Bleich, "Entering a Non-Jewish House of Worship." See also Rabbi Shlomo Aviner (dated 30 May 2016) on attending the Festival of Light in the Old City of Jerusalem. Aviner forbids this, because churches are illuminated with coloured lights and presume that Jerusalem is holy for Christians and Muslims too (https://www.srugim.co.il/149632 -%D7%94%D7%A7%D7%95%D7%90%D7%9C%D7%99%D7%A6%D7%99 %D7%94-%D7%A9%D7%9C-%D7%94%D7%A0%D7%99%D7%90%D7%95 -%D7%A8%D7%A4%D7%95%D7%A8%D7%9E%D7%99%D7%9D-%D7%95%D7%9 4%D7%A9%D7%9E%D7%90%D7%9C-%D7%94%D7%93%D7%AA) See also the answer of Rabbi R. Arusi on the question whether one is allowed to mention the Christian festivals by their names (http://shut.moreshet.co.il/shut2.asp?id=187492).

56 Avi Lewis, "Vatican: Anti-Christian Violence Crosses 'Red Line' in Israel," *Times of Israel*, 10 August 2015, https://www.timesofisrael.com/vatican-anti-christian-violence-crosses -red-line-in-israel/; Larry Derfner, "Mouths Filled with Hatred," *Jerusalem Post*, 26 November 2009, http://www.jpost.com/Magazine/Mouths-filled-with-hatred.

References

Berger, David. "Jews, Gentiles, and the Modern Egalitarian Ethos: Some Tentative Thoughts." Pages 83–108 in *Formulating Responses in an Egalitarian Age*. Edited by Marc D. Stern. Lanham, MD: Rowman & Littlefield, 2005.

Bleich, Judah David. "Entering a Non-Jewish House of Worship." *Tradition* 44 (2011): 73–102.

Brill, Alan. *Judaism and Other Religions: Models of Understanding*. New York: MacMillan, 2010.

Derfner, Larry. "Mouths Filled with Hatred." *Jerusalem Post*, 26 November 2009. http://www.jpost.com/Magazine/Mouths-filled-with-hatred.

Evers, Raphael. *Weshav weRafeh*. 4 vols. Jerusalem: Fisher, 2008–2014.

Goshen-Gottstein, Alon. *Same God, Other God: Judaism, Hinduism, and the Problem of Idolatry*. New York: MacMillan, 2016.

Halbertal, Moshe. "'Ones Possessed of Religion': Religious Tolerance in The Teachings of The Me'iri." *Edah* 1 (2000): 1–24.

Hayes, Christine E. *Between the Babylonian and Palestinian Talmuds: Accounting for Halakhic Difference in Selected Sugyot from Tractate Avodah Zarah*. New York: Oxford University Press, 1997.

Lewis, Avi. "Vatican: Anti-Christian Violence Crosses 'Red Line' in Israel." *Times of Israel*, 10 August 2015. https://www.timesofisrael.com/vatican-anti-christian-violence-crosses-red-line-in-israel/.

Michman, Joseph, Hartog Beem, and Dan Michman, *Pinkas: Geschiedenis van de Joodse gemeenschap in Nederland*. Amsterdam: Kluwer, 1992.

Mock, Leon. "Het begrip 'Ruach Ra'a' in de rabbijnse responsliteratuur van na 1945: Een casestudy in de relatie tussen kennis over de fysieke wereld en traditionele kennis." PhD diss., Tilburg University, 2015.

Nathansohn, Joseph Saul. *Sho'el uMeshiv*. 3 vols. Lemberg: Uri Zeev Wolf Salat, 1865–79.

CHAPTER 14

The "Inn of the Good Samaritan": Religious, Civic and Political Rhetoric of a Biblical Site

Eric Ottenheijm

The Inn of the Good Samaritan is a site, known to pilgrims and tourists, that localizes the parable from the Gospel of Luke (Luke 10:25–37). This paper traces the site's spatial settings in relation to the parable and its history of interpretation. The guiding question is to how text and space become intertwined in negotiations of religious, as well as secular identities. The argument follows three stages. First, It discusses Luke's parable in its inner Jewish dimension and in early Christian interpretation. Secondly, it surveys the history of the physical site and its connection to the story. Finally, it traces the choreography of the present-day museum at the site in the way it relates to the history of Luke's parable.

Two notions, a theory of textual interpretation and spatial theory, underlie the analyses of the data offered here. First, sacred texts propel trajectories of explanation that unwind potentials of meaning of the text, intended or unintended, and this history of interpretation (*Wirkungsgeschichte*) becomes part of the text itself.[1] This shift from text to interpretation even extends to the way subsequent cultures understand themselves, and in their modes of interpretation come to (re)produce Biblical texts as discursive objects or as media of cultural identification.[2] Moreover, these processes not only involve cognition, but also emotional regimes, stable forms of apprehension and perception as dominant in a given social and cultural reality.[3] Second, spaces, beyond their

---

1   Hans G. Gadamer, *Wahrheit und Methode* (Tübingen: Mohr Siebeck, 1960) locates any individual's self-understanding as part of a text's history of interpretation. The hermeneutic taking into account the history of a text's "horizon" criticizes historicistic claims of intended, original meaning as being definite. Cf. Alexander J. Jensen, *Theological Hermeneutics* (London: SCM, 2007), 139–41; Jean Grondin, *Einführung in die philosophische Hermeneutik*, 3rd ed. (Darmstadt: Wissenschaftliche Buchgesellschaft, 2012), 152–72, esp. 161.

2   Timothy Beal, "Reception History and Beyond: Toward the Cultural History of Scriptures," *BibInt* 19 (2011): 357–72.

3   Emotional scripts are supra-individual, culturally as well as socially produced schemata that engrain the individual's emotions and responses to it in a social, cultural, and political realm. Ole Riis and Linda Woodhead, *A Sociology of Religious Emotion* (Oxford: Oxford University Press, 2010), 47: "We have argued that 'emotion' is a label for a range of coordinated

physical dimensions, carry meaning as imbued with social and cultural practices, including religious mapping.[4] In modernity, this involves politically guided constructions of religious and secular regimes labelled as "choreography."[5]
Where these "choreographies" are informed by texts, these in turn produce
modes of perception of the text and signal new appropriation and performance of the text. As such, sacred spaces in their modern "choreography" become intertwined with the history of textual interpretation and production.

1   The Story: the Parable of the Good Samaritan

In Luke 10:25–37, Jesus tells a parable of a certain man who went down from
Jerusalem to Jericho and was attacked and wounded by robbers, who left him
"half dead" at the side of the road. A passing priest did not help him, neither
did a passing Levite. A Samaritan, however, was touched deeply, tended his
wounds with wine and oil, loaded the man onto his donkey and transported
him to an Inn. There, he left him in the care of the Innkeeper, paying in advance and with the promise that he would return and pay for any further care
needed. The story is an example-story, a variant of the parables. Indeed, any
metaphorical operation of its motifs presupposes a well-known social or historical meaning or context for the first readers, and the exemplary behaviour
is spelled out as well in the story.[6] Part of its spatial and emotional rhetoric

---

psychophysical elements, in and through which we relate to other beings and symbols, and
in terms of which they relate to us. By virtue of group processes, societal structures, and
cultural symbols, emotions also attain intersubjective and supra-individual status, and can
be analysed at a range of social scales. Far from being merely inner, private states of the individual, they are generated in interactions between self, society, and objects."

4   Henri Lefebvre, *The Production of Space*, trans. Donald Nicholson-Smith (Oxford: Basil
    Blackwell, 1991).

5   Elazar Barkan and Karen Barkey, "Introduction," in *Choreographies of Shared Sacred Sites:
    Religion, Politics, and Conflict Resolution*, ed. Elazar Barkan and Karen Barkey (New York:
    Columbia University Press, 2014), 1–32 (1): "choreographies" connotes "the politics of the
    'choreography of sacred spaces' within the framework of state-society relations."

6   Adolf Jülicher, *Die Gleichnisreden Jesu* (Darmstadt: Wissenschaftliche Buchgesellschaft,
    1976), 112–14 qualifies our parable as an exemplary story (*Beispielserzählung*), all four of
    which appear in Luke (Luke 12:16–21; 16:19–31; 18:9–14). The exemplary story in its his-
    torical realism resembles Rabbinic *ma'aseh* or Roman *exemplum*. Cf. Darrell L. Bock, *Luke
    9:51–24:53* (Grand Rapids: Baker Books, 1996), 1021; Klyne Snodgrass, *Stories with Intent: A
    Comprehensive Guide to the Parables of Jesus* (Grand Rapids: Eerdmans, 2008), 350–52. Ruben
    Zimmermann, *Puzzling the Parables of Jesus: Methods and Interpretation* (Minneapolis:
    Fortress Press, 2015), 112–17 criticizes this classification since the story still requires meta-
    phoric operation to disclose its full meaning. François Bovon, *Luke 2: A Commentary on the
    Gospel of Luke 9:51–19:27* (Minneapolis: Fortress, 2013), 56 points out that the parable has a
    "mobilizing function" beyond being illustration or proof.

is the mentioning of the Inn.[7] Greek *pandocheion* (πανδοχεῖον, Luke 10:34) is etymologically related to Arab *khan*, and the equivalent of the Vulgate *stabula*.[8] Scholars have assessed Luke's story of the Inn as derived from a local Palestinian tradition, and the excavations of Yitzhak Magen at the present-day Museum of the Good Samaritan have added some argumentative force to this view, even if its identification as the Inn of the parable is not buttressed by any evidence.[9] The site features cisterns from the Second Temple Period, a large Byzantine cistern, and one constructed in the era of the Crusades. No findings predate Herodian times.[10] All of this indeed points to its use as a temporary or permanent wayfarers' "inn" during the latter half of the Second Temple Period.[11] Luke stresses known features such as the Roman road connecting Jerusalem and Jericho, the man "going down" (Luke 10:30), and the presence of robbers.[12] However, even though the narrative reflects a known reality, the story barely needs historicity to convey its message. Moreover, Luke's story was inspired by 2 Chr 28:9–15, a passage about Samaritans taking care of Israelite captives, and

---

7   Lukan redaction is visible in verse 26: "how do you read?" (πῶς ἀναγινώσκεις;), and verse 30: "half dead" (ἡμιθανῆ), a *hapax legomenon*, cf. Joachim Jeremias, *Die Gleichnisse Jesu*, 6th rev. ed. (Göttingen: Vandenhoeck & Ruprecht, 1962), 190–93.

8   In Philo, *pandocheion* denotes a socially dubious place of residence; see Hans Klein, *Das Lukasevangelium* (Göttingen: Vandenhoeck & Ruprecht, 2006), 393. This might be related to the presence of female innkeepers; see Roger David Aus, *Weihnachtsgeschichte, barmherziger Samariter, verlohrener Sohn: Studien zu ihrem jüdischen Hintergrund* (Berlin: Institut Kirche und Judentum, 1988), 68–69. The inn of the parable is not related to the inn (Luke 2:7, κατάλυμα) of Jesus's birth.

9   Jeremias, *Gleichnissreden*, 201–2: "Die Geschichte … wird, zum mindesten in szenischen Rahmen, an eine tatsächliche Begebenheit anknüpfen." Yitzhak Magen, *The Samaritans and the Good Samaritan* (Jerusalem: Civil Administration for Judea and Samaria, 2008), 294.

10   Magen, *Samaritans*, 297. Yitzhak Magen, Staff Officer of Archaeology for Judea and Samaria, who conducted excavations on the site of the present-day Inn of the Good Samaritan, found dwelling caves as well as fireplaces, all dated to the Second Temple period. Object findings included a key, dating to the Herodian age, and a chalkstone cup, usually interpreted with respect to purity practices.

11   The finds of coins are quite compelling for his view that the site was functioning as a wayfarers' Inn during the latter Second Temple period: a peak in the Herodian age is followed by some coins of the Great Revolt (66–70 CE), after which a steep decline follows which will only peak again in the Byzantine era; Magen, *Samaritans*, 295; Yitzhak Magen, *The Good Samaritan Museum* (Jerusalem: Israel Antiquities Authority, 2010), 61. The identification of a wall structure as a Herodian palace, which he thinks could have been used as an inn, is conjectural.

12   Both first-century writers Josephus, *J.W.* 4.8.3 [474]; Strabo, 16.2.40–41 (c. 763), commenting on Pompey, as well as the fourth-century Eusebius and Jerome report on robbers in the area. A rabbinic example-story (m. Yebam. 16:7) tells about Levites leaving a sick person in the care of a female innkeeper between Jerusalem and "Zoar" (probably Jericho); on its connection with the parable see Aus, *Barmherziger Samariter*, 63–68.

even bringing them back to Jericho on donkeys.[13] Biblical hermeneutics, social and spatial reality, as well as biblical intertextuality form the background of Luke's parable, and any realistic features only serve to add to its metaphoric and rhetoric force.

This rhetoric, in Luke, bears on a dialogue between Jesus and an expert in the law of Moses (νομικός τις, Luke 10:25) on how to gain eternal life (Luke 10:25), and comments on the meaning of neighbour in the biblical verse "You shall not take vengeance or bear a grudge against any of your people, but you shall love your neighbor as yourself: I am the LORD" (Lev 19:18).[14] This question, as well as Jesus's reply in verse 26 "how do you read?" (πῶς ἀναγινώσκεις;) gains hermeneutical as well as historical relief in light of early Jewish discussions on the meaning of רֵעֲךָ ("your neighbour") in Lev 19:18, and despite the polemical tone in Luke's redaction, it still reflects the Jewish phase of the early Christian movement.[15] The application reorients the question as one of self-reflection: one has to become a neighbour first. Being or not being a neighbour follows from looking, since the acts of the Samaritan are initiated by his way of looking, resulting in feeling moved and acting accordingly. Therefore, the parable's rhetoric is not just to convey that "anyone" is a neighbour, a broad misunderstanding of the parable, but reorients any definition of neighbour to looking at a person's actions, especially one's reaction to a person in dire need of help.[16] It is no coincidence that "seeing" recurs three times, and it is the resulting action that makes all the difference (Table 14.1).

---

13   Bock, *Lukas*, 1020; Snodgrass, *Stories with Intent*, 358; Isaak Kalimi, "Episoden aus dem Neuen Testament und ihr Ursprung in der Hebräischen Bibel/dem Alten Testament," *SNTSU* 36 (2011): 93–110 (102–9).

14   The typically Lukan term νομικός, "lawyer," a scholar in the law, occurs only in Matt 22:35; Bock, *Lukas*, 1022. All Bible translations follow the NRSV, unless otherwise indicated. The story most probably circulated independent of the Lawyer's question.

15   A unity of the parable and dialogue is stressed in Snodgrass, *Stories with Intent*, 349. Most scholars, however, distinguish between a traditional source underlying the parable itself and Luke's inserting it into the dialogue with the lawyer: Shemaryahu Talmon, "Good Samaritan or Good Israelite?" *Qathedra* 80 (1996): 19–30 (22) (Hebrew); Thomas Kazen, "The Good Samaritan and a Presumptive Corps," *Svens exegetisk årsbok* 71 (2006): 131–44 (133). The parable is unique in its framing of the early Jewish discussions concerning the double love commandment: Serge Ruzer, *Mapping the New Testament: Early Christian Writings as a Witness for Jewish Biblical Exegesis* (Leiden: Brill, 2007), 69 concludes other synoptic traditions do not share the "universalistic" versus "particularistic" stress as offered in this parable.

16   Cf. Bock, *Lukas*, 1018. Grammatically, seeing combined with action is regular: Friedrich Blass, Albert Debrunner, and Friedrich Rehkopf, *Grammatik des neutestamentlichen Griechisch*, 18th ed. (Göttingen: Vandenhoeck & Ruprecht, 2001), 344. Rabbinic voices explain רֵעֲךָ as a term of legal exclusion, emphasizing that particular obligations are limited

TABLE 14.1   Acts of seeing in the parable of the Good Samaritan

Priest (v. 31)	"saw him" (ἰδὼν αὐτὸν)	"he passed by on the other side" (ἀντιπαρῆλθεν)
Levite (v. 32)	"saw" (ἰδὼν)	"he passed by on the other side" (ἀντιπαρῆλθεν)
Samaritan (v. 33)	"saw" (ἰδὼν)	"he was moved with pity" (ἐσπλαγχνίσθη)

In the story, both the priest and the Levite "saw" the man lying on the ground but "passed by the other side." The Samaritan, however, "saw" the man and this was followed by an emotional response, as well as by actions (v. 34) that depict the reversal of what the robbers did to the man.[17] The response "he was moved with pity" (ἐσπλαγχνίσθη, Luke 10:33), literally signifying being moved in one's bowels, employs a verb used rarely in Luke, but significantly to indicate the reaction of Jesus when looking (ἰδὼν, Luke 7:13) at a suffering widow.[18] The act of looking receives a rhetorical ring given the geographical setting of the narrative, evoking the dreadful dangers lurking in desert surroundings, and teeming with robbers. Moreover, passing priests and Levites may be historically plausible in light of the road mentioned, which ran between Jericho, a well-known residence of priests in late Second Temple times, and the Temple in Jerusalem.[19] However, its rhetorical force is more important, since "priest and Levite" arouses the expectation of a common Israelite to be the third party.[20] The unexpected appearance of a Samaritan causes the surprise ele-

---

to specific categories within Israel. "Looking" at actions underlies a Rabbinic discussion of the verse as well. Alluding to Isa 43:7, one voice comments as follows "Has it not been said: 'and you shall love your neighbor as yourself?' So what then is the reason (of this verse)? I created him and if he performs the works of your people he is your friend, and if not, he cannot be your friend" (כי אני בראתיו ואם עושה מעשה עמך אתה אוהבו ואם לאו אי אתה אוהבו; 'Abot R. Nat. a, 16).

17   Brad Young, *The Parables: Jewish Tradition and Christian Interpretation* (Peabody, MA: Hendrickson, 2007), 107. Oil and wine are medicinal: Klein, *Lukasevangelium*, 389 (n. 48). It may be that Luke knew about Lev 19:34. The notion of performing acts of benevolence is traditional as well: "but act mercifully towards your neighbor as to yourself (וְתִרְחֲמֵיהּ לְחַבְרָךְ כְּוָתָךְ), I am the Lord" (Tg. J. Lev 19:18).

18   Henry G. Liddell and Robert Scott, *Greek—English Lexicon*, new ed. (Oxford: Oxford University Press, 1973), 1628. Luke uses σπλαγνεύω in the reaction of the father in the Prodigal Son (Luke 15:20).

19   Priests lived in the surroundings of Jericho: Bock, *Lukas*, 1030; Bovon, *Luke*, 57.

20   E.g., Ezra 2:70; Neh 10:37–40; m. Pe'ah 8:6; m. Ta'an. 4:2. Other Biblical patterns of "three" occur as well, see Talmon, "Good Samaritan or Good Israelite?" 25.The rhetorical

ment of the parable, especially given the Samaritans' tense relations with Jews.[21] It is, in this light, the Samaritan's way of looking and his resulting actions that yet define him as a neighbour for the man on the ground, and, concomitantly, for the reader of the parable.[22] Finally, seeing what others do not see is a motif in the passage preceding the parable, when Jesus teaches his disciples how to deal with refusal: "Blessed are the eyes that see what you see. For I tell you that many prophets and kings desired to see what you see, but did not see it (ἰδεῖν ἃ ὑμεῖς βλέπετε καὶ οὐκ εἶδαν), and to hear what you hear, but did not hear it" (Luke 10:23–24). Adducing the verb ὁράω, the parable connects this saying to a narrative inculcating a mode of looking at a person's actions, thus transcending social and religious barriers.[23]

2   The Parable and Christian Theology

Departing from Luke's spatial and hermeneutical rhetoric, with the Samaritan as the unexpected "practical" teacher of the law, Christian interpretation, from the second century CE onwards, reads the parable as an allegorical story of salvation through Christ.[24] This transition is smooth in its metaphoric reading, but has a crucial difference. Luke's parable alluded, in its narratology, to the Samaritan as carrying out a similar emotional regime as Jesus, in taking pity on

---

importance of the Samaritan in the story, as a "close" example given them being object to early Christian mission, is correctly stated by Talmon, "Good Samaritan or Good Israelite?" 20, but his theory (26) that Luke, or a later copyist, was unaware of this tripartite division but knew of the self-designation of Samaritans as "benei Israel" is unconvincing as it overlooks Luke's knowledge of Scripture as well as the element of surprise of parables.

21   Bock, *Lukas*, 1031; Bovon, *Luke*, 59. Talmon, "Good Samaritan or Good Israelite?" 27 correctly doubts the connection of Samaritans with the site, or with the historical Jesus. The story (23) reflects Luke's literary style and theological rhetorics.

22   The status of Samaritans in rabbinic sources oscillates between outright hostility and having legal status in between Jew and gentile (e.g., m. Ber. 7:1); cf. Snodgrass, *Stories with Intent*, 345–47. Crucial is factual behaviour, e.g., m. Ber. 8:8. Politically, relations could be tense, especially after John Hyrcanus destroyed the Temple at Mount Gerizim in 111–110 BCE; Snodgrass, *Stories with Intent*, 345–47.

23   Notice how the disciples ask Jesus whether they should pray for fire to destroy a Samaritan village that refused to accept them (Luke 9:54–55; cf. 2 Kgs 1:10), but how Acts 8:14, by the same author as Luke's Gospel, tells about Samaritans being the first non-Jews to convert to the Jesus movement.

24   Riemer Roukema, "The Good Samaritan in Ancient Christianity," *VC* 58 (2004): 56–74 shows how elements of this interpretation appear in the second-century gnostic Gospel of Philip, in Clement of Alexandria as well as in the anti-gnostic interpretation of Irenaeus of Lyon.

people in need. In allegorical interpretations, the parable itself does not teach the tenets of the law, but Christian theology and, therewith, Christian identity. The Caesarea-based, third-century theologian Origen offers a classic explanation of the parable story, which will be followed by later church fathers. Origen ascribes it to an unknown presbyter:

> The man who was going down is Adam, Jerusalem is paradise, Jericho the world, the robbers are the hostile powers, the priest is the law, the Levite represents the prophets, the Samaritan is Christ, the wounds represent disobedience, the beast the Lord's body, the inn should be interpreted as the church, since it accepts all that wish to come in. Furthermore, the two denarii are to be understood as the Father and the Son, the innkeeper as the chairman of the church, who is in charge of its supervision. The Samaritan's promise to return points to the second coming of the Saviour.[25]

Origen interprets the motifs of the parable as spiritual metaphors of a metaphysical plot, and now the parable is about a new spiritual phase in humanity, and about Christianity as surpassing the spiritual phase of Judaism.[26] It tells about Adam, understood as mankind, going down from Paradise before the Fall to the world after the Fall and becoming trapped in sin, which explains the motif of "robbers" on the way. The priest and the Levite symbolize Judaism, embodied in the law and the prophets respectively, and both unable to rescue man from his sinful state. The Samaritan is Christ, as representative for Christianity, who has come to cure the man's wounds. Origen probably depended here on a play on the Hebrew שומרון, *shomron*, meaning "Samaritan," associated with the participle שומר, *shomer*, "guardian," in the Hebrew text of Ps 121:4: "See, the guardian of Israel neither slumbers nor sleeps."[27] This wordplay illustrates both the proximity to rabbinic midrash and the way he employs it to buttress his own exegesis. The inn is the church, and the innkeeper is the keeper of the church, either bishop or priest. Given the aforementioned dubious nature of the Greek and Latin words for inn, the association with church comes unexpectedly easily: are we to associate the church as a safe, intermediate, lodging for the night, awaiting a new day?[28] Origen ends with the notion of

---

25   Origen, *Hom. Luc.* 34.3. Translation by Roukema, "Good Samaritan," 62.

26   Origen applies his typological reading of spiritual phases both to the Old Testament and the New Testament; see Grondin, *Einführung*, 48–49.

27   JPS. See Roukema, "Good Samaritan," 64.

28   Note the associations with the story of Moses in Exod 4:23–26; thanks to Leon Mock for this notion.

a second coming of the Samaritan, i.e., Christ. This reading reflects a religious identity centred around the figure of Christ, and the parable as buttressing a Christian religious identity rooted in faith, ritual practice, and contemplation. Equally important is the motif of substitution: the priest and the Levite representing the failing law and prophets, and the inn as the salvific church, convey notions of religious supremacy, since Judaism, embodied in law and prophets, is being superseded by Christianity.[29] In this reading, the visual rhetoric of the parable remains but shifts from an ethical (interpretation of the Law) to one of a history of redemption: the Samaritan seeing the victimised traveller becomes divine regard for humanity, and for the reader "looking" at the act of the Samaritan the story becomes a reminder of his newly acquired religious identity. Nevertheless, the ethical meaning of the story also remained valid in patristic interpretations of the parable. Augustine for example (*Doctr. chr.* 1.30.31), elaborates Origen's reading but also emphasises that, like the Samaritan, we should help those who are in need, and, like Christ, we should consider anyone a neighbour who shows compassion towards us.[30] Both the ethical and the doctrinal-ecclesiastical dimensions of the story appear during the Byzantine and Medieval period.[31]

3   The Byzantine Inn

The visual rhetoric of the parable gains a new ring when Luke's parable becomes associated with the area during the Byzantine era. It is Jerome who in his edition of Eusebius's *Onomasticon* (24:10; 25:9–16) identifies the name Adumim as a "lieu de memoire":

> this blood defiled place was mentioned by the Lord in his parable concerning the man who descended from Jerusalem to Jericho,

---

29   Note the following in Augustine's *Quaest. ev.* 2.19: "But the priest and the Levite who saw him and passed him by signify the priesthood and the ministry of the Old Testament which could not be of benefit toward salvation." Quoted in David B. Gowler, *The Parables After Jesus: Their Imaginative Receptions across Two Millennia* (Grand Rapids: Baker Academic, 2017), 43. Roukema, "Good Samaritan" stresses, however, the anti-Marcionite context and continuing ethical tendencies of patristic readings.

30   Roukema, "Good Samaritan," 70; Gowler, *Parables after Jesus*, 34–35 (Origen), and 42 (Augustine) comments on the ethical purport of the parable as *imitatio Christi*.

31   Note, e.g., Gowler, *Parables after Jesus*, 97, on Bonaventura.

and, in a further gloss, he notices how the name derived from the blood that was spilled there.[32] Additionally, in his account of his travels with Paula to the Holy Land in 385–386 CE, Jerome adds an interesting remark:

> She went directly down the hill to Jericho as she thought about the wounded man in the Gospel, who was passed by the Priest and the Levite, with a cruel mind (*mentis feritate*). The merciful Samaritan, which means "guardian," took him, near death, on his mule to the Inn of the Church (*ad stabulum ecclesie deportavit*). And she went through the place called Adumim, which is translated "blood," because so much blood was spilled there on account of robbers, and the tree of Zachaeus, which means the repentance of good works.[33]

Travelling and seeing the landscape becomes a way of memorising, "reading" the text. But what text, and what landscape?[34] Jerome's *Epitaphium Sanctue Paulae* is a rhetorically styled spiritual journey through a sacred, Christianized, landscape, staging Paula as an idealized pilgrim. In Jerome's account, biblical references are fused with allegorical interpretations, and so the landscape becomes a reminder of Christian truth.[35] This is also the case for Jerome's gloss on Paula's journey: her memories are not aroused through seeing an inn, or a church, but by traversing a biblical landscape. The mention of Adumim as blood-stained is not related to the parable, but to the biblical strife between Juda and Benjamin.[36] And the meaning of Samaritan as "guardian" (*clementiam Samarite, id est, custodis*) reflects patristic identification of the Samaritan as Christ. Moreover, the designation *stabulum ecclesie* is ambiguous. Magen

---

32 Susan Weingarten, *The Saint's Saints: Hagiography and Geography in Jerome* (Leiden: Brill, 2005), 252 (n. 216); Andrew Caine, *Jerome's Epitaph on Paula: A Commentary on the Epitaphium Sanctae Paulae* (Oxford: Oxford University Press, 2013), 259.

33 *Epit. Paulae* 12.3. The journey actually took place; Weingarten, *Saint's Saints*, 236. Paula (347–404 CE) was an aristocratic Roman woman who met Jerome in 382 CE and accompanied him to the Holy Land to establish a monastery herself; Caine, *Epitaph*, 3–6. My translation, based on Arnold A.R. Bastiaensen, Jan W. Smit, and Christine Mohrmann, *Vita di Martino: Vita di Ilarione: In memoria di Paola* (Rome: Fondazione Lorenzo Valla, 1975), 174, is close to Caine, *Epitaph*, 59 and differs from Magen, *Samaritans*, 288.

34 Magen, *Samaritans*, 288: "Hieronymus was the first to identify the site with the inn mentioned in the parable. Most likely, he did not invent this identification, and was presenting a Christian tradition that had its basis in the Second Temple period." There is no proof for either parts of this statement.

35 Weingarten, *Saint's Saints*, 194–95, 218.

36 Magen, *Samaritans*, 288. Jerome recounts subsequent spiritual moments of her travel to Jericho, separated by "and" (*et*), such as the tree of Zachaeus, which follows immediately.

reads it as the twofold function of the Byzantine site, but Jerome refers to the allegorical interpretation of Luke's inn as church, as we noticed with Origen.[37] Nonetheless, a church and inn were built here, but at the beginning of the fifth century CE, not long after Paula's pilgrimage. Its remains form a square complex measuring 26.6 × 24.4 meters. The combination of a Church and a pilgrims' inn is, however, no coincidence in the region. Besides the increase in monasteries all over the Judean desert, pilgrimage became a practice from the fourth century CE onwards, as testified by the anonymous Pilgrim of Bordeaux (333/334 CE), and by Egeria's travels in 381 and 384 CE.[38]

4   The Museum of the Good Samaritan's Inn

The present-day Museum of the Good Samaritan is located halfway between Jerusalem and Jericho, along the 26 km long Route 1 winding down from the Mount of Olives (826 metres above sea level) to Wadi Qelt (258 metres below sea level). In close proximity to Jerusalem, and situated between the Jewish settlements of Kfar Adumim and Ma'aleh Adumim, its location makes it a politically contested area. The region is related to the biblical Ma'aleh Adumim, "the Ascent of Reds," a topographical marker (Josh 15:7; 18:17) referring to the redness of the rocks.[39] The name continues in the Latin *Turris Rubea* and the Arabic *Tala'at et Dam* and in the 4 kilometers west of the Inn situated Palestinian village of Khan al Aḥmar, the Red Khan, built close to the remains of the fifth-century CE monastery of St. Euthymius, which also functioned as an inn.[40] The present-day Inn of the Good Samaritan is situated along the ancient track of the Roman road connecting Jerusalem to Jericho.

After the disruption of the Persian conquest in 614 CE, the site came into use again during the era of the Crusades, when a fortress was added to the east of the site, guarding the winding road before it heads downwards to Jericho. Probably during the reign of the 19th-century CE Egyptian ruler Ibrahim

---

37   Cain, *Epitaph*, 274 on the allegorical instead of the ethical meaning.
38   Caine, *Epitaph*, 16: the Land became a "tourists' draw" after Constantine and Helena.
39   Pekka Pitkänen, *Joshua* (Nottingham: Apollos, 2010), 288. The red colour is due to iron-oxide in the limestone formations. It should be noted that more sites in this area are referred to with this name.
40   Jerome Murphy O'Connor, *Oxford Archaeological Guides: The Holy Land*, 4th ed. (Oxford: Oxford University Press, 1998), 294–96 identifies the name as this Byzantine monastery, but Magen limits it to the present-day Ottoman structure built over the remains of the Crusader and Byzantine caravanserai and Byzantine church. Magen, *Samaritans*, 281; Magen, *Good Samaritan*, 15, 52.

Pasha, a rectangular Ottoman inn was built over the southern part of the former Byzantine and Crusader structure, and the present-day main building (built in 1903) was used as a police station during the period of the British mandate.[41] The church gradually disappeared, its mosaic floors being discovered only in 1934, after which pilgrims started to take out mosaics as a souvenir or a relic. The present-day museum was initiated by Magen and his team and erected under the umbrella of the Civil Administration of Judea and Samaria. It was funded by the Israel Government Tourist Corporation and the Israel Antiquities Authority. The aim was to attract tourists and pilgrims.[42] A decision was made to use the space for the exhibition of mosaics of Jewish and Samaritan synagogues and of church mosaics, all found in Israel, Gaza, and the West Bank.[43] The Ottoman inn, however, has been beautifully restored and is furnished as a museum dedicated to the parable. So are a Second-Temple cave and the remains of the fifth-century Byzantine church. In the cave, visitors are able to watch a video scene showing a fragment of a 1925 silent movie, re-enacting the parable in the very same surroundings (see below). The few remains of the mosaic floor of the church led to a second, interesting, decision. Using old photographs, a project was carried out to reconstruct the floor by means of manually fabricating 1.7 million tesserae, employing old, Roman techniques or cutting and fixing the stones in old-recipe cement. A permanent wooden structure provides roofing and demarcates the church's original space (approximately 20 × 10 meters). Seating arrangements, a sober pulpit, and the roofing facilitate both touristic and religious practices. Through these, the construction exudes the semi-sacral atmosphere of the former Church.

5   Textual Interpretation and Emotional Regime

In discussing the parable, we have dealt with the rhetorical notion of how to look at and respond to people's needs. Thus, the parable inculcates an emotional regime of positively responding to ethnic or religious outsiders.[44] By

---

41   Magen, *Good Samaritan*, 79; Katja Cytryn-Silverman, "The Road Inns (Khāns) in Eretz Israel during the Mamluk Period," *Qadmoniot* 7 (2006): 66–77 (74–75) (Hebrew).

42   Magen, *Good Samaritan*, 19 explicitly mentions the touristic aim, but both the layout of the Church and the dominance of the parable in the museum suggest an intention to include Christian pilgrims.

43   Magen, *Good Samaritan*, 19.

44   The relative efficacy of its rhetoric has been traced in psychological research where people actually helping others were more keen in legitimizing their response with an appeal to the parable story than people who did not do so: John M. Darly and C. Daniel Batson,

employing media such as objects and movies, the museum stages a spatial performance of the story that also evokes and channels the visitor into a specific emotional regime, one departing from a Christian allegorical interpretation.[45]

The museum's performance of the parable is most clearly visible in the former Ottoman khan. It is rectangular and consists of six chambers. The east side of the building has been extended with a modern construction of steel and glass, adding an extra room. The use of steel and glass distinguishes and accentuates the original structure. The building houses an entrance and three sections of two rooms, each dedicated to a monotheistic religion associated with the history of the site: Judaism, Christianity, and the Samaritans. This last choice echoes the parable's rhetoric, since there are no historical reasons to link Samaritans with this place, especially in its capacity as linking Jericho with the Temple in Jerusalem.[46] Each section exhibits religious heritage, including the remains of nearby Byzantine monasteries, and other cultural sites.

6   Movies

The museum's media performance of the parable is found in two short movies shown in the museum complex. The first is a scene from a silent movie on the historical Jesus, shot in 1925, also shown in the aforementioned Second-Temple-period cave. It is an uncut scene as part of a planned movie on the life of Jesus, titled *The Man Nobody Knows* (figs. 14.1 and 14.2).[47] This was a "non-theatrical movie picture," staged until the end of the thirties. The reels were distributed for 30 dollars, which shows a large audience was expected.[48]

"'From Jerusalem to Jericho': A Study of Situational and Dispositional Variables in Helping Behavior," *Journal of Personality and Social Psychology* 27 (1973): 100–8.

45   Riis and Woodhead, *Sociology of Religious Emotion*, 33: "Obedience to emotional scripts allays guilt, deflects disapproval, and sustains a positive self-image."

46   Cf. Bock, *Lukas*, 1032. The choice may also be motivated by Magen's interest in Samaritan archaeology and history, as visible in Magen, *Samaritans*.

47   The scene is accessible on YouTube: https://www.youtube.com/watch?v=UZglOW-iRWo. The director mentioned is Errett Leroy Kenepp, an American filmmaker who prepared documentaries for Sunday schools: Alessandro Falcetta, *The Daily Discoveries of a Bible Scholar and Manuscript Hunter: A Biography of James Rendel Harris (1852–1941)* (London: T&T Clark, 2018), 411. It is remarkable that his name is not mentioned on the movie posters; see https://www.imdb.com/title/tt0016074/?ref_=nv_sr_3.

48   The movie was completed and shown for some years, for a relatively high entrance price, in several places in the USA, which suggests success. I thank Prof. Frank Kessler for this information (email d.d. June 2018).

FIGURE 14.1   Still of the 1925 Good Samaritan scene, featuring Samaritan High Priest Yitzhaq ben 'Amram

FIGURE 14.2   Still of the 1925 Good Samaritan scene: two "Jews" in Yemenite (right) and Chassidic (left) attire, and Yitzhaq ben 'Amram

The scene lasting approximately 11 minutes features a re-enactment of the parable, shot on location: the walls of old Jerusalem and the inn itself are visible. The actors were probably recruited from Jerusalem, but the prime hero, the Samaritan, is a historical figure, the Samaritan High Priest Yitzhaq ben 'Amram

(1855–1932). It bears some irony, in view of the vilified priest and Levite in the parable, that the key character in the movie is staged by a High Priest, albeit of Samaritan descent (fig. 14.1).

He is the hero, and his proud looks seem to underline his awareness of this. The scene also features robbers dressed like Bedouins, and a priest and a Levite dressed in garments of Chassidic and Yemenite Jews (fig. 14.2), visually inscribing religious stereotyping through Christian interpretations of the parable.

The scene and the movie were based on the best-selling book *The Man Nobody Knows*, written by Bruce Fairchild Barton. Barton (1886–1967) was a pioneer in advertising; he came up with the names of General Motors and General Electric.[49] Barton was also active in politics: in 1937 and 1939 he ran for the vacant seat of senator for the City of New York, as representative for the Republican Party, a seat he lost in 1940. The book is very well-written, in a vital, naturalistic and clear style, and with some knowledge of historical critical exegesis. It was a huge success.[50] Barton presents Jesus as a vital and strong person and as a teacher of values underlying modern-day capitalism as well: having psychological wisdom; being very healthy, equipped with a strong will, and authentic; and using excellent means of communication. Jesus established a "business" that would last for thousands of years and conquer all the world. The introduction leaves no doubt about the book's aim: "'Someday,' said he, 'someone will write a book about Jesus. Every businessman will read it and send it to his partners and his salesmen. For it will tell the story of the founder of modern business.'"[51] Jesus exudes vitality and a certain lust for life, not inhibited by weakness or effeminate behaviour.[52] When Pilate presents the tortured Jesus, known as the "*ecce homo*" scene in the Gospel of John, Barton has him exclaim: "Behold, the man!"[53]

---

49   Unfortunately, Richard M. Fried, *The Man Everybody Knew: Bruce Barton and the Making of Modern America* (Chicago: Ivan H. Dee, 2005), quoted in the Wikipedia lemma (https:// en.wikipedia.org/wiki/Bruce_Fairchild_Barton), was not available in libraries covered by Worldcat.

50   By 1956 the book had sold more than a million copies. See Edrene S. Montgomery, "Bruce Barton's *The Man Nobody Knows*: A Popular Advertising Illusion," *The Journal of Popular Culture* 19 (1985): 21–34 (26).

51   Bruce Barton, *The Man Nobody Knows: A Discovery of the Real Jesus*, 6th ed. (New York: Pocket Books, 1944), 9.

52   Montgomery, "Advertising Illusion" shows how Barton's "outdoor man" (21) portrayal of Jesus sparked controversy but responded to spiritual and social needs among the economically thriving, middle class readership of his generation (28). Barton, who developed political campaigning, can be qualified as a "conservative modernist"; so Douglas Carl Abrams, review of Richard M. Fried, *The Man Everybody Knew: Bruce Barton and the Making of Modern America*, *The American Historical Review* 112 (2007): 216–17 (216).

53   Barton, *The Man Nobody Knows*, 45.

Barton wanted to deal with his puritan pietistic upbringing, where Jesus is a meek and humble person, not outgoing but inward and sensitive, and negating worldly matters. The parables are the best examples of effective advertising for the business Jesus founded, with "crisp, graphic language, and a message so clear that even the dullest cannot escape it."[54] Barton lists four qualities, derived from the Jesus parables, that advertising should adhere to: condensed stories, simple language and without qualifying words, sincere, and with the force of repetition. Both in the book and in the movie-scene performed in the museum, the Good Samaritan is tantamount to public ethics in any society or social environment, be it secular or religious. In the words of Barton: "It (i.e., the parable, EO) condenses the philosophy of Christianity into a half dozen unforgettable paragraphs. The parable of the Good Samaritan is the greatest advertisement in the world."[55] The book's message recurs in the last shot, the parable being a lesson on "universal brotherhood" "regardless of creed, colour or race." It is this message that is shown to the public, and remains, like an advertisement statement, as the parable's core meaning.

A second performance, immediately following the 1925 movie, reinforces this idea of the parable as inducing civic ethos. It is a video display of a short, comic scene from the television show *Seinfeld* (1998), ironically addressing the "bystander effect." In it, Seinfeld and his friends watch the robbery of a fat man. All four talk about what they are going to do next, even filming the scene. However, in turn all four are arrested by a policeman.[56] To the astonished exclamations that they were not guilty of robbery, the policeman retorts that the town Latham keeps a law called the Law of the Good Samaritan. This law compels any bystander not to remain passive but to act on behalf of victimised others. It is especially the first part of the parable, the "watching" but inactive priest and Levite, who are transformed into Seinfeld and his friends being passive commentators, and the parable becomes a satirical form of self-criticism on modern consumerism and neutrality.[57]

---

54   Barton, *The Man Nobody Knows*, 95.
55   Barton, *The Man Nobody Knows*, 95.
56   *Seinfeld*, season 9, episode 23/24.
57   Albeit as a protective law for people trying to help others, Good Samaritan laws are operative in 50 states of the USA: "Good Samaritan laws offer legal protection to people who give reasonable assistance to those who are, or whom they believe to be, injured, ill, in peril, or otherwise incapacitated" (https://en.wikipedia.org/wiki/Good_Samaritan_law).

7   Choreography

Two aspects of the museum's choreography deserve discussion: its religious heritage and the museum's staging of religious and civic ethos in its political context. Culture is the first aim of the museum's outfit. Its spatial division creates a dialogue between three religious heritages, centred around the parable. Thus, a "Christian" tradition is used to shed light on Jewish and Samaritan heritage, and Jewish tradition serves to highlight the parable's background. This choreography departs from Byzantine interpretation and its tenets of Christianity as substituting Judaism: the museum reclaims the parable as part of Jewish culture. In this dialogical staging, the museum approaches religious traditions as part of local cultural heritage. Samaritan religious heritage as well as the Samaritan High Priest in the movie serve as the "outsider," breaking cultural and ideological boundaries as well as the binary opposition of Christianity and Judaism, and extending the parable's negotiation of who is "inside" or "outside" in modern-day cultural and religious reality. The 1925 movie stages him as the religious hero, teaching the proper fulfilment of Mosaic law.[58] In this choreography of the parable, the museum extends the parable's rhetoric as transcending borders of social and religious belonging and as emphasizing

FIGURE 14.3   Former Byzantine church with modern roofing. Background: the Crusader Fortress

---

58   Of course, Samaritans share the canonical Mosaic law of Lev 19:18.

the notion of "seeing" correctly. However, the museum's relative neglect of the Muslim stage of the site's history and the concomitant omission of a dialogue with Islamic heritage and religion raises questions. Is the Muslim history not considered part of its cultural display and civic ethos politics? Moreover, the only Muslims visible are the actors staged as robbers in the 1925 silent movie, scenes that reflect prejudices current in those days.

Noticeable as well is the way the reconstructed Byzantine church space facilitates Christian pilgrim practice (fig. 14.3). Its demarcation of the mosaic floor, the newly constructed wooden roof and seating arrangements mark this as a potential sacred space, to be inhabited and defined by ritual. Its space remains part of the museum's secular outline, nonetheless, and the site is not purely dedicated to pilgrimage. Telling is the absence of a cross or any other Christian symbol, like a fish. Moreover, the boundary markers of the Byzantine church's mosaic floor do not hamper visitors in moving around freely, and no religious or symbolic division is present. The exhibited mosaics remind pious pilgrims of Jewish and Samaritan contexts, and looking at all these cultures suggests religion not to be a dividing but rather an inspiring and binding force in society, and teaching values of pity and practical care.[59]

Nevertheless, while facilitating religious practices in a museum is not unique, here it acquires a political meaning as well, given the contested nature of the site as part of the Oslo II defined C areas and still awaiting a final status.[60] This political dimension gains weight given the nearby presence (4 kilometers west of the Inn) of the Palestinian village Khan Al Ahmar, occupied since 1952 by Bedouins of the Jahalin tribe.[61] Since May 2018, the village faces threat of demolition through a decision by the Israeli High Court of Justice. This site has become one of political struggle, starting with an Israeli High Court decision in 2014 to defer an order for demolishment of the village from military jurisprudence to the political realm. International organizations

---

59   Cf. Riis and Woodhead, *Sociology of Religious Emotion*, 46: "Fear, shame, pity, and so on are culturally contingent words with which we try, with varying degrees of inadequacy, to capture aspects of shifting social and material relationships and associated image-schema that always exceed the capacity of our words."

60   The C area is partly ruled by Israel's Defense Ministry (infrastructure, safety), through the Coordinator of Government Activities in the Territories, and partly (education, medical and social care) by the Palestinian National Authority in Ramallah. The site is, however, part of the disputed plans on the so called E1 area, the Jewish settlements east of Jerusalem, and of heated legal processes underlying these politics: Alice M. Panepinto, "Jurisdiction as Sovereignty Over Occupied Palestine: The Case of Khan-Al-Ahmar," *Social and Legal Studies* 26 (2017): 311–32.

61   The Inn's site is identical with Arab Khan al Hatruri. However, the name Khan al Ahmar is sometimes used as well for the Inn on internet, which causes confusion.

like the United Nations, the International Criminal Court, the European Parliament and Amnesty International have criticized this decision, and the Israeli Government seeks to negotiate a deal.[62] Given its location between the Jewish settlements of Ma'aleh Adumim and Kfar Adumim, and its proximity to the site of the museum, it is noteworthy that no attention is given to the history of this homonymous site. Thus, the museum's performance of the parable connects it both to its historical context and to a secular ethos. However, its displays of religious and cultural heritage gain political rhetoric as it becomes mingled willy-nilly among claims from local historical and religious memory. Given this entanglement of archaeology, religious memory, civic ethos and politics, the museum still is a contested site, despite its careful ways of displaying religious heritage. Indeed, the *Seinfeld* comedy suggests the parable to offer a "law" valid for any society, breaching the boundaries of religious ethics and secular ethos, and transcending ethnic affiliations. Moreover, the attention dedicated to Samaritans gives weight to a neglected ethnicity in the present-day tourism industry. Nonetheless, whenever religion comes into view it is limited to Christianity, Judaism, and the Samaritans, the last of whom have no historical links to the site apart from the fictive parable in Luke. Only the walls of the Ottoman khan, fitted with wall-irons used for stabling horses, as well as the building itself are reminders of the Islamic period. Clearly, the site, not initiated as a shrine or cultic place, became entangled in a negotiation between the religious and the secular through the parable. However, referring to former functions and religious practices is not worked out for the Ottoman khan, nor for its Mamluk predecessor, nor for their history of facilitating travel and Muslim pilgrimage to Jerusalem.[63]

8   Conclusions

The parable of the good Samaritan is a story that transcends ethnic and religious boundaries to teach about the fulfilment of the law. The Samaritan, the

---

62   The Israeli Government decided to postpone the demolition until, as the Israeli High Court preferred in its decision of May 2018, a negotiated decision would be reached (Tovah Lazaroff, "Israel Delays Demolition of West Bank Bedouin Village Khan Al-Ahmar," *Jerusalem Post*, 20 October 2018, https://www.jpost.com/Arab-Israeli-Conflict/Israel -delays-demolition-of-West-Bank-Bedouin-village-Khan-al-Ahmar-569861). Panepinto, "Jurisdiction" argues how the case shows a juridical shift in Israeli ruling of the C area and its political ramifications.

63   Cytrin-Silverman, "Road Inns," 74–75 discusses the inn as part of the Mamluk infrastructure in the land.

supposed "other" party in early Judaism, becomes the hero through his way of looking and acting, but in later Christian interpretation, the priest and the Levite become the "other," as a negative foil for Judaism, and as opposed to Christ embodied in the Samaritan. In the museum's staging of the parable, these processes of "othering," either of the Samaritans or the Jews, are debunked. Samaritan, Christian, and Jewish culture is visibly presented in such ways as to create a multi-religious context buttressing the parable's message of how to become a neighbour. Moreover, the performance of the parable in the museum reclaims it as local culture and as part of early Jewish heritage, abandoning notions of theological supremacy. The site also continues the parable's negotiation of the secular and the sacred, and its historical choreography is probably unique in the history of Jewish and Christian sacred landscapes: first, a travellers' station in the desert of Judea became wound up with a parable addressing an intra-Jewish debate on the law. After the parable turned into a canonical text, it imbued the location with an aura of sanctity through the text's interpretation in Christianity. In moving from Christian to Muslim regional dominance, it regained its former, "secular," status, but in its final phase, under the current Israeli government, the museum has embraced aspects of both secular and sacred functions. The museum in a way produces its version of the parable, within the context of Israeli society. In Luke, the space staged a story of looking at the victimised traveller which arouses fulfilment of the law, in Byzantine Christianity looking at the landscape arouses the memory of the parable as a guide for a pilgrim's spiritual quest to salvation. The museum stages an impressive choreography of plurality of cultures and religions, inculcating civic ethos with an alleged local story.

The museum even facilitates Christian worship connected with the parable's landscape, but in dialogue with other religious cultures and with secular society, with the movies performing the parable as a "billboard" for civic ethos. Tellingly, the Muslim dimensions of the site's history have become somewhat obfuscated in all dimensions of this choreography (fig. 14.4).[64] Since the museum, by its location on the West Bank, is entangled in the Palestinian-Israeli conflict, as well as in current Israeli society's identity politics, its choreography cannot escape new contestations, halfway between Jerusalem and Jericho.[65]

---

64   The museum may not be an isolated case: Yitzhak Reiter, "Tolerance versus Holiness: The Jerusalem Museum of Tolerance and the Mamilla Muslim Cemetery," in Barkan and Barkey, *Choreographies*, 299–355.

65   Thanks to Rob Nelisse for pictures taken during a field trip (summer 2017) with Lieve Teugels and Marcel Poorthuis. Thanks as well to Boaz Zissu for discussing archaeological aspects, Pooyan Tamimi Arab for discussing choreography, and to Marcel Poorthuis and the editors for their helpful and critical comments.

FIGURE 14.4   Postcard picture of the Ottoman inn, 1906

References

Abrams, Douglas Carl. Review of Richard M. Fried, *The Man Everybody Knew: Bruce Barton and the Making of Modern America*. *The American Historical Review* 112 (2007): 216–17.

Aus, Roger David. *Weihnachtsgeschichte, barmherziger Samariter, verlohrener Sohn: Studien zu ihrem jüdischen Hintergrund*. Berlin: Institut Kirche und Judentum, 1988.

Barkan, Elazar, and Karen Barkey, eds. *Choreographies of Shared Sacred Sites: Religion, Politics, and Conflict Resolution*. New York: Columbia University Press, 2014.

Barton, Bruce. *The Man Nobody Knows: A Discovery of the Real Jesus*. 6th ed. New York: Pocket Books, 1944.

Bastiaensen, Arnold A.R., Jan W. Smit, and Christine Mohrmann. *Vita di Martino: Vita di Ilarione: In memoria di Paola*. Rome: Fondazione Lorenzo Valla, 1975.

Beal, Timothy. "Reception History and Beyond: Toward the Cultural History of Scriptures." *BibInt* 19 (2011): 357–72.

Blass, Friedrich, Albert Debrunner, and Friedrich Rehkopf. *Grammatik des neutestamentlichen Griechisch*. 18th ed. Göttingen: Vandenhoeck & Ruprecht, 2001.

Bock, Darrell L. *Luke 9:51–24:53*. Grand Rapids: Baker Book, 1996.

Bovon, François. *Luke 2: A Commentary on the Gospel of Luke 9:51–19:27*. Minneapolis: Fortress, 2013.

Caine, Andrew. *Jerome's Epitaph on Paula: A Commentary on the Epitaphium Sanctae Paulae*. Oxford: Oxford University Press, 2013.

Cytryn-Silverman, Katia. "The Road Inns (Khãns) in Eretz Israel during the Mamluk Period." *Qadmoniot* 7 (2006): 66–77. (Hebrew).

Darly, John M., and C. Daniel Batson. "'From Jerusalem to Jericho': A Study of Situational and Dispositional Variables in Helping Behavior." *Journal of Personality and Social Psychology* 27 (1973): 100–8.

Falcetta, Alessandro. *The Daily Discoveries of a Bible Scholar and Manuscript Hunter: A Biography of James Rendel Harris (1852–1941)*. London: T&T Clark, 2018.

Fried, Richard M. *The Man Everybody Knew: Bruce Barton and the Making of Modern America*. Chicago: Ivan H. Dee, 2005.

Gadamer, Hans G. *Wahrheit und Methode*. Tübingen: Mohr Siebeck, 1960.

Gowler, David B. *The Parables After Jesus: Their Imaginative Receptions across Two Millennia*. Grand Rapids: Baker Academic, 2017.

Grondin, Jean. *Einführung in die philosophische Hermeneutik*. 3rd ed. Darmstadt: Wissenschaftliche Buchgesellschaft, 2012.

Jensen, Alexander J. *Theological Hermeneutics*. London: SCM, 2007.

Jeremias, Joachim. *Die Gleichnisse Jesu*. 6th rev. ed. Göttingen: Vandenhoeck & Ruprecht, 1962.

Jülicher, Adolf. *Die Gleichnisreden Jesu*. Darmstadt: Wissenschaftliche Buchgesellschaft, 1969.

Kalimi, Isaak. "Episoden aus dem Neuen Testament und ihr Ursprung in der Hebräischen Bibel/dem Alten Testament." *SNTSU* 36 (2011): 93–110.

Kazen, Thomas. "The Good Samaritan and a Presumptive Corps." *Svens exegetisk årsbok* 71 (2006): 131–44.

Klein, Hans. *Das Lukasevangelium*. Göttingen: Vandenhoeck & Ruprecht, 2006.

Kugel, James L. *The Bible as it Was*. Cambridge: Harvard University Press, 1997.

Lazaroff, Tovah. "Israel Delays Demolition of West Bank Bedouin Village Khan Al-Ahmar." *Jerusalem Post*, 20 October 2018. https://www.jpost.com/Arab-Israeli-Conflict/Israel -delays-demolition-of-West-Bank-Bedouin-village-Khan-al-Ahmar-569861.

Lefebvre, Henri. *The Production of Space*. Translated by Donald Nicholson-Smith. Oxford: Basil Blackwell, 1991.

Liddell, Henry G., and Robert Scott. *Greek—English Lexicon*. New Edition. Oxford: Oxford University Press, 1973.

Magen, Yitzhak. *The Samaritans and the Good Samaritan*. Jerusalem: Civil Administration for Judea and Samaria, 2008.

Magen, Yitzhak. *The Good Samaritan Museum*. Jerusalem: Israel Antiquities Authority, 2010.

Montgomery, Edrene S. "Bruce Barton's *The Man Nobody Knows*: A Popular Advertising Illusion." *The Journal of Popular Culture* 19 (1985): 21–34.

Murphy O'Connor, Jerome. *Oxford Archaeological Guides: The Holy Land.* 4th ed. Oxford: Oxford University Press, 1998.

Panepinto, Alice M. "Jurisdiction as Sovereignty Over Occupied Palestine: The Case of Khan-Al-Ahmar." *Social and Legal Studies* 26 (2017): 311–32.

Pitkänen, Pekka. *Joshua.* Nottingham: Apollos, 2010.

Reiter, Yitzhak. "Tolerance versus Holiness: The Jerusalem Museum of Tolerance and the Mamilla Muslim Cemetery." Pages 299–355 in *Choreographies of Shared Sacred Sites: Religion, Politics, and Conflict Resolution.* Edited by Elazar Barkan and Karen Barkey. New York: Columbia University Press, 2014.

Riis, Ole, and Linda Woodhead. *A Sociology of Religious Emotion.* Oxford: Oxford University Press, 2010.

Roukema, Riemer. "The Good Samaritan in Ancient Christianity." *VC* 58 (2004): 56–74.

Ruzer, Serge. *Mapping the New Testament: Early Christian Writings as a Witness for Jewish Biblical Exegesis.* Leiden: Brill, 2007.

Snodgrass, Klyne. *Stories with Intent: A Comprehensive Guide to the Parables of Jesus.* Grand Rapids: Eerdmans, 2008.

Talmon, Shemaryahu. "Good Samaritan or Good Israelite?" *Qathedra* 80 (1996): 19–30. (Hebrew).

Weingarten, Susan. *The Saint's Saints: Hagiography and Geography in Jerome.* Leiden: Brill, 2005.

Young, Brad. *The Parables: Jewish Tradition and Christian Interpretation.* Peabody, MA: Hendrickson, 2007.

Zimmerman, Ruben. *Puzzling the Parables of Jesus.* Minneapolis: Fortress, 2015.

CHAPTER 15

A Sense of Place and the Jewish Temple: from the Book of Psalms to the Temple Scroll

Eyal Regev

The Jerusalem Temple in the monarchic period and the Second Temple period was a holy place. But what is the exact meaning of "place"? What makes a place holy in the minds of believers and worshipers, not in relation to holy traditions and practices, but in the sense of perception of the place? In this paper I address the subject of holy places not from the perspectives of history, religion, or cultural anthropology, but from that of humanistic geography—a theory of place. I will discuss two texts which deal with the Temple and sacredness—the biblical book of Psalms and the Temple Scroll found in cave 11 in Qumran.

The songs in Psalms that are being put in the mouth of the worshipers and the rules about the construction of a new Temple in the Temple Scroll are two separate genres that posit very different concepts of place pertaining to the Temple in Jerusalem. Despite their common belief that the Temple is the house of God, the sacredness reflected in these holy places points to the diversity of holy places.

What, then, are the basic ideas in the theory of place that are relevant to both Psalms and the Temple Scroll? Unlike space, place is not a given object. Place is a space with meaning and value. In humanistic geography place is both an object and a way of looking at it. It is space where a person is involved.[1] The meaning and essence of place do not come from locations or the trivial functions that places serve. Place is a matter of human experience.[2] It is a concept

---

1   Tim Cresswell, *Place: A Short Introduction* (Oxford: Blackwell, 2004), 7, 10, 15, 20. See already Yi- Fu Tuan, *Topophilia: A Study of Environmental Perception, Attitudes and Values* (Englewood Cliffs: Prentice-Hall, 1974). On the distinction between space and place see Edward S. Casey, "Smooth Spaces and Rough-Edged Places: The Hidden History of Place," *Review of Metaphysics* 51 (1997): 267–96. This is somewhat similar to Soja's concept of Thirdspace. See Edward W. Soja, *Thirdspace: Journeys to Los Angeles and Other Real-and-Imagined Places* (Cambridge: Blackwell, 1996), esp. 56–57, 68. Thirdspace is comprised of three spatialities—perceived, conceived and lived. It interrupts the distinction between objective and spatiality, between spatial practices and perceptions. On the study of space and place and their application in recent biblical studies see Patrick Schreiner, "Space, Place and Biblical Studies: A Survey of Recent Research in Light of Developing Trends," *CBR* 14 (2016): 340–71.
2   Edward Relph, *Place and Placelessness* (London: Pion, 1976), 8, 43.

of space which is socially constructed, a product of society and culture. Thus, what is experienced is shaped by the social milieu that dominates it.[3]

Place is a concept that relates to power relations. Each society has certain expectations about the concept of place. Place is used to structure a normative landscape for living—the author's representation of the world. In order to make ideological beliefs effective, they must be connected through location. Place, insofar as it is the material context of our lives, forces us to make interpretations and act accordingly. Place thus contributes to the creation and reproduction of action-oriented (ideological) beliefs.[4]

"All widely practiced forms of religion are, in the final analysis, attempts at establishing places that answer human needs."[5] Thus, it is interesting to compare different notions of place that relate to the same site. In what follows I will examine the meaning of the Temple as a place in the eyes of the psalmist: How is it approached and how is it sensed? What ideas are linked to this spatial location? With regard to the Temple Scroll I intend to explore how the place of the Temple is constructed and how the architecture and laws ordained by the Scroll create a very different sense of holy place than that of the psalms, a place experienced through walls and boundaries.

1   The Enthusiastic Pilgrim: the Temple as a Sacred Place in Psalms

1.1   *Introducing Psalms*
In Psalms, worship in the Temple and offering sacrifices are not presented from the perspective of the priest or the Temple institutions and rulings, but from the perspective of the individual worshiper. The songs do not describe rules and in many cases they do not even refer to ritual practice, but rather to the sensibilities of the pilgrim. Reading these psalms in retrospect, they demonstrate the religious experience of visiting the Jerusalem Temple and offering

---

3   Cresswell, *Place*, 29–33, following David Harvey, *Justice, Nature and Geography of Difference* (Cambridge: Blackwell, 1996), esp. 292–94. The phenomenological approach to place is interested in the essence of human existence which is "in-place." The place is primarily a construction of meaning and society. The social construction depends on the structure of the place. See Jeff E. Malpas, *Place and Experience: A Philosophical Topography* (Cambridge: Cambridge University Press, 1999), 35–36. See also Edward S. Casey, *The Fate of Place: A Philosophical History* (Berkeley: University of California, 1998).

4   Tim Cresswell, *In Place/Out of Place: Geography, Ideology, and Transgression* (Minneapolis: University of Minnesota Press, 1996), 8, 161, following Pierre Bourdieu, *Outline of Theory and Practice* (Cambridge: Cambridge University Press, 1977), 163.

5   Yi-Fu Tuan and Martha A. Strawn, *Religion: From Place to Placelessness* (Chicago: Center for American Places at Columbia College, 2010), 15.

sacrifices.[6] The approach to God is described in words of praise and astonishment, not by commands and restrictions.[7] These psalms enable us to uncover the religious experience of lay Israelites in the Temple in Jerusalem during the late First and early Second Temple period. In a sense, I regard them as a data base similar to the anthropologist's field work—the psalms presume to reflect the perspective and the religious attitude of the individual visiting the Temple, in a manner which may (with some reservations) lead to certain conclusions about Israelite society as a whole.

The Jewish cult in the book of Psalms has been studied quite extensively. Among the subjects that have already drawn attention are the various types of sacrifices[8] as well as the history and Ancient Near Eastern background of the rites reflected in the psalms.[9] In a previous article I have discussed the attitudes towards sacrifices and the concept of sacrifices implied in many of the psalms. I suggested that animal sacrifice is seen as a gift and aims to achieve a connection with the divine.[10] In the present paper I would like to complement my study of Temple worship in Psalms and explore the meaning of the Temple itself as a place, the intersection of the pilgrim and God, and how it is formulated in the words and thoughts of the psalmist.

The liturgical context of the following literary evidence is praise of God, thanksgiving and requests, wherein the person puts himself before God, approaching God with words. The manner in which these contexts are linked

---

6   Hans-Joachim Kraus, *Theology of the Psalms*, trans. Keith Crim (Minneapolis: Fortress, 1986), 67–71, 84–100. I am aware that the fact that many of the psalms were sung in the Temple by the Levites may indicate that the personal language is only a literary genre, perhaps even a sham, and these are institutional liturgical works. Nonetheless, the fact that such Levites ascribed these ideas to the lay Israelites visiting the Temple appropriates these psalms as historical and cultural evidence.

7   Gary A. Anderson, "The Praise of God as A Cultic Event," in *Priesthood and Cult in Ancient Israel*, ed. Gary A. Anderson and Saul M. Olyan (Sheffield: JSOT Press, 1991), 15–33; Kraus, *Theology of the Psalms*, 101–6.

8   R.J. Thompson, *Penitence and Sacrifice in Early Israel outside the Levitical Law: An Examination of the Fellowship Theory of Early Israelite Sacrifice* (Leiden: Brill, 1963), 137–60; Rolf Rendtorff, *Studien zur Geschichte des Opfers im alten Israel* (Neukirchen-Vluyn: Neukirchener, 1967), 63–66, 85, 133–44.

9   Sigmund Mowinckel, *The Psalms in Israel's Worship* (Oxford: Blackwell, 1962); John H. Eaton, "The Psalms and Israelite Worship," in *Tradition and Interpretation: Essays by the Members of the Society for Old Testament Study*, ed. Gary A. Anderson (Oxford: Clarendon, 1979), 238–73.

10   Eyal Regev, "Sacrifices of Righteousness: Visiting the Temple and Bringing Sacrifices as Religious Experience in Psalms," *Tarbiz* 73 (2004): 365–86 (Hebrew).

to the holy place is the main subject of this paper.[11] When the speaker refers to the Temple and the cultic activities, they are not ornamental, nor are they relegated to the background.[12] They are actually the spiritual highlight of approaching God more closely and serving Him.

In studying the various songs in the book of Psalms as a whole I am not denying that each one of them is an independent unit. Examining them in relation to one another, as if they were created by one school of thought, is mainly a methodological step for finding common or interrelated characteristics. Furthermore, one may argue that the conclusions reached here do not reflect the individual pilgrim in a given song but rather the institutional editors of the entire book, which may hold an official role in the Temple or the religious establishment. But I leave this difficult question to experts in the book of Psalms. I will now turn to psalms which relate to the Temple as a place from several different aspects.

1.2   *The Temple as God's Dwelling Place*

Not only do the psalms repeatedly refer to the Temple, but at times they explicitly relate to it as a "place" (מָקוֹם). The psalmist declares that he loves it, probably in order to show his love of God: "LORD, I love the house in which you dwell, and the place where your glory abides" (Ps 26:8). Here it is emphasized that the Temple is the dwelling of God. It is both מִשְׁכָּן and מָעוֹן. The presence of God in the sanctuary is paralleled by His throne in heaven: "The Lord is in His holy temple; the Lord's throne is in heaven" (Ps 11:4).[13] There is a polar relationship between heaven and earth (axis mundi), quite like the one in Jacob's dream in Bethel: "How awesome is this place! This is none other than the house of God, and this is the gate of heaven" (Gen 28:17).[14]

---

11   The liturgical and spiritual context of the cult in Psalms is explored in James L. Kugel, "Topics in the History of the Spirituality of the Psalms," in *Jewish Spirituality: From the Bible through the Middle Ages*, ed. Arthur Green (New York: Crossroad, 1986) 113–44, esp. 122–25, 127–29, who follows Claus Westermann, *Praise and Lament in the Psalms* (trans. Keith R. Crim and Richard N. Soulen; Atlanta: Knox, 1981).

12   As in Ps 100:1–2, in which the thanksgiving sacrifice (תּוֹדָה) is the official context of the song. Cf. also Pss 38:1; 70:1, which refer to לְהַזְכִּיר, perhaps the offering of the incense (Lev 2:2; 6:8).

13   Compare the role of God's throne and the altar in heaven in Isa 6:1, 6.

14   On this phenomenon see Mircea Eliade, *The Myth of the Eternal Return: Or, Cosmos and History*, trans. William T. Trask (Princeton, Princeton University Press, 1971), esp. 12–17.

Moreover, in many cases in Psalms the Temple or Zion are regarded as the center of creation.[15] For example, in Ps 24:7, 9, the gates of the Temple are called פִּתְחֵי עוֹלָם, literally, "the everlasting openings," and certain scholars maintain that this reflects the belief that the Temple is the gate to heaven.[16] This relates to other traditions of the Temple as chosen by God's angel when the plague was halted (2 Sam 24:16–25; 1 Chr 21:15–22:1) and its identification with Mount Moriah where the binding of Isaac took place (2 Chr 3:1).

1.3 Praising God in the Temple

The Temple is not only a location where God is praised, it is a place which is indirectly praised when God is praised. Being there is a source of bliss: "Happy are those who live in your house, ever singing your praise" (Ps 84:5). Those who enter God's gates and courts do so in thanksgiving and praise, blessing God's name (100:4). The Lord's servants stand in his house, blessing him while lifting their hands in His house, and they believe that there, from Zion, God blesses them in return (Ps 134). Ps 96 praises the Lord and his wondrous deeds and speaks out against the fallacy of idols. God's glory is reflected in the Temple: "Honor and majesty are before him; strength and beauty are in his sanctuary" (Ps 96:6). The most basic act of honoring God is offering a sacrifice in his sanctuary. The psalmist urges the people to do so: "Ascribe to the LORD the glory due His name, bring an offering, and come into His courts. Worship the LORD in holy splendor" (Ps 96:8–9). The song ends by announcing that God judges nations on justice.

Acknowledging and honoring God through sacrifice, whether it is a personal or a public offering may seem rather like paying something, either a debt, a tribute, or a gift to the Lord.[17] Nonetheless, we should note that the ecstatic passion in these psalms attests to genuine religious sensibilities. In the course of the rite of offering a sacrifice, the lay pilgrim who brings it senses God's greatness in quite a direct manner and feels closer to the divine realm. This person experiences some of God's kingdom, abode, power and glory.

---

15 Richard J. Clifford, *The Cosmic Mountain in Canaan and the Old Testament* (Cambridge: Harvard University Press, 1972); Jon D. Levenson, *Sinai and Zion: An Entry into the Jewish Bible* (Minneapolis: Winston, 1985), 111–76.

16 Othmar Keel, *The Symbolism of the Biblical World: Ancient Near Eastern Iconographies and the Book of Psalms*, trans. Timothy J. Hallett (New York: Seabury, 1978), 172–74; Hans-Joachim Kraus, *Psalms 1–59: A Commentary*, trans. Hilton C. Oswald (Minneapolis: Fortress, 1988), 315 and references. The NRSV translation "O gates!" is flawed.

17 Compare Isa 60:7–8; Pss 56:11; 86:31; 2 Chr 17:5, 11.

1.4   *Thanking God by Sacrificing in the Temple*

Not only do sacrifices in the Temple convey the praise of God, they also thank Him. The most common sacrifices are those of repaying a vow (נֶדֶר), usually as an act of thanksgiving following rescue from danger, trouble, or strife. A well-known example is Ps 27, in which David declares: "I will offer in His tent sacrifices with shouts of joy; I will sing and make melody to the LORD" (Ps 27:6).[18] The courts of God's house are the place of thanksgiving when the psalmist refers to the vow and the offering after being saved: "I will pay my vows to the LORD in the presence of all His people ... I will offer to You a thanksgiving sacrifice and call on the name of the LORD; I will pay my vows to the LORD in the presence of all His people; in the courts of the house of the LORD, in your midst, O Jerusalem. Praise the LORD!" (Ps 116:14, 17–19).

1.5   *The Temple as a Place of Righteousness*

Not only is the Temple regarded as a place of ritual and worship, it is also a fortress of social justice and righteousness.[19] Its gates are the gates of righteousness (שַׁעֲרֵי־צֶדֶק) through which only the just shall enter: "Open to me the gates of righteousness, that I may enter through them and give thanks to the LORD. This is the gate of the LORD; the righteous shall enter through it" (Ps 118:19–20).[20] On the holy mountain only just people can dwell: "O LORD, who may abide in your tent? Who may dwell on your holy hill? Those who walk blamelessly, and do what is right, and speak the truth from their heart" (Ps 15:1–2).

The author of Ps 24 asks a question and provides his own answer in a sort of Temple liturgy: "Who shall ascend the hill of the LORD? And who shall stand in his holy place? Those who have clean hands and pure hearts, who do not lift up their souls to what is false, and do not swear deceitfully" (Ps 24:3–4). One may assume that the official view is that only those who meet these moral criteria are permitted to see the place of the King of Glory who is referred to later in this psalm (Ps 24:7–10). In any event, these psalms argue that people of immoral conduct should be restricted from closeness to God. They are unworthy

---

18   The sacrifices alluded to here as זבחי תרועה are sacrifices of joy. See Thompson, *Penitence and Sacrifice*, 145.

19   Eckart Otto, "Kultus und Ethos in Jerusalemer Theologie: Ein Beitrag zur theologischen Begründung der Ethik im Alten Testament," *ZAW* 98 (1986): 161–79. Some see the origins of this perception in incidents in which the psalmist is accused in the Temple and pleads his innocence. See Walter Beyerlin, *Die Rettung der Bedrängten in den Feindpsalmen der Einzelnen auf institutionelle Zusammenhänge untersucht* (Göttingen: Vandenhoeck & Ruprecht, 1970). For the Temple as the place of the righteous see Ps 92:1–14. On the Temple or Jerusalem as the eschatological place of righteousness see Jer 31:22.

20   On the symbolism of the gate as representing the entire Temple (cf. Ps 122:1–3) in light of ancient Near Eastern parallels see Keel, *Symbolism of the Biblical World*, 120–27.

of access to the sacred.[21] The basis for this requirement is the idea that God is righteous.[22]

Thus, when a person enters the Temple, this person feels that he is counted among the just and he is entitled to encounter the sacred. The altar itself is a place where the pilgrim feels righteous. "I wash my hands in innocence, and go around your altar, O LORD" (Ps 26:6). The very act of his standing there signifies closeness to God: "My foot stands on level ground; in the great congregation I will bless the LORD" (26:12). The person's presence in the Temple precincts makes him feel even more righteous.

The experience of visiting the Temple therefore relates not only to thoughts about God and his glory, but also to the pilgrim's self-perception of his status before God and society. Being counted among those who enter the sacred domain leads to spiritual empowerment, a feeling of self-value due to the experience of the holy place.[23]

1.6 *The Temple as a Place of Redemption and Salvation*

Another belief linked to the call to bring sacrifices is that God sends deliverance from the Temple and Zion: "May He send you help from the sanctuary, and give you support from Zion. May he remember all your offerings, and regard with favor your burnt sacrifices" (Ps 20:3–4). The Temple is therefore a center of deliverance and the pilgrim's offering may serve as a condition for divine intervention on his behalf.

1.7 *Living in the Temple—in Proximity to God*

Fulfilling his vow and giving thanks to God become permanent for the author of Ps 61. He was saved from his enemies and consequently he dwells in the Temple to sing His praise day by day: "Let me abide in your tent forever, find

---

21 An inscription in temples in ancient Egypt and Asia Minor forbids entry to those who commit social felonies. See Moshe Weinfeld, "Instructions for Temple Visitors in the Bible and in Ancient Egypt," in *Egyptological Studies, Scripta Hierosolymitana* 28, ed. Sarah Israelit-Groll (Jerusalem: Magnes, 1982), 224–50. On the relationship between cult and morality in ancient Greek see Robert Parker, *Miasma: Pollution and Purification in Early Greek Religion* (Oxford: Oxford University Press, 1983), 94 143, 322 24.

22 E.g., Pss 5:4–5; 37:28; 92:16; 98:2; 146:7. One may even assume that a person who is well aware of his evil deeds would be terrified by a divine punishment upon entering God's holy dwelling.

23 An interesting term in this respect is זִבְחֵי־צֶדֶק "sacrifices of righteousness" (NSRV: "right sacrifices") in Pss 4:6; 51:21. It shows that morality is not merely in the background of the cult but an integral part of the sacrificial rite. See also: "Let your priests be clothed with righteousness, and let your faithful shout for joy" (Ps 132:9). See the discussion in Regev "Sacrifices of Righteousness," 371–73.

refuge under the shelter of your wings ... For you, O God, have heard my vows; you have given me the heritage of those who fear your name" (Ps 61:4–5).[24] While these words may be seen as an exaggeration, a kind of metaphor for worshiping God passionately, some individuals actually lived in the Temple although they had no formal role in the cult. Luke mentions Anna who "never left the Temple but worshiped there with fasting and prayer night and day" (Luke 2:37).

1.8   *Yearning for God's Place*

The Temple is a place that people wish to attend. In a time of trouble and distress, David confesses his one and only aspiration: "One thing I asked of the LORD, that will I seek after: to live in the house of the LORD all the days of my life, to behold the beauty of the LORD, and to inquire in His Temple. For He will hide me in His shelter in the day of trouble; He will conceal me under the cover of His tent; He will set me high on a rock" (Ps 27:4–5).

Similarly, the author of the psalm in the book of Jonah thinks about the Temple in his darkest hour and grieves because he is far from it. He is eager for the moment when he will be able to thank God by offering the sacrifices which he vowed to bring in gratitude for being saved: "Then I said, 'I am driven away from your sight; how shall I look again upon your holy Temple?' ... My prayer came to you, into your holy Temple" (Jonah 2:4, 7b).[25]

The subject of Pss 42 and 43 (which were merged into one in the Septuagint) is the yearning for closeness to God and a longing to attend the Temple: "My soul thirsts for God, for the living God. When shall I come and behold the face of God? ... [H]ow I went with the throng, and led them in procession to the house of God" (42:2, 4b). The holy mountain, the dwelling of God, and His altar are the subjects of happiness and joy when the speaker thanks God: "O send out your light and your truth; let them lead me; let them bring me to your holy hill and to your dwelling. Then I will go to the altar of God, to God my exceeding joy; and I will praise you with the harp, O God, my God" (43:3–4). Although the chorus (42:6, 12; 43:5) about the quest for God and His presence does not

---

24   Some see here a plea for shelter in the Temple. See Hans-Joachim Kraus, *Psalms 61–150: A Commentary*, trans. Hilton C. Oswald (Minneapolis: Fortress, 1989), 9–10, and for the background to Pss 26:6; 27:4–5 see Kraus, *Psalms 1–60*, 326, 333, 335. For the parallel in ancient Greece see Ulrich Sinn, "Greek Sanctuaries as Places of Refuge," in *Greek Sanctuaries: New Approaches*, ed. Nanno Marinatos and Robin Hägg (London: Routledge, 1993), 88–109.

25   On Jonah's prayer and its secondary place in the literary history of the book see James S. Ackerman, "Satire and Symbolism in the Song of Jonah," in *Traditions and Transformation: Turning Points in Biblical Faith*, ed. Baruch Halpern and Jon D. Levenson (Winona Lake, IN: Eisenbrauns, 1981), 213–46.

refer to the Temple, its context in relation to the above verses attests that this can be realized only be attending the Temple and the altar.

The aspiration to visit the Temple stems from the divine inspiration that the psalmist finds in this particular place: "My soul longs, indeed it faints for the courts of the LORD; my heart and my flesh sing for joy to the living God. Even the sparrow finds a home, and the swallow a nest for herself, where she may lay her young, at your altars, O LORD of hosts, my King and my God. Happy are those who live in your house, ever singing your praise ... For a day in your courts is better than a thousand elsewhere. I would rather be a doorkeeper in the house of my God than live in the tents of wickedness" (Ps 84:2–4, 10; cf. 26:8). Here, in this very place, the pilgrim senses that he beholds God's glory in the sacred domain: "So I have looked upon you in the sanctuary, beholding your power and glory" (Ps 63:2). The source of attraction to the Temple as a place is therefore the access to God's glory, the possibility of becoming close to the divine. This may also be the result of regarding the Temple as the dwelling place of God, or at the very least God's glory or abode.

1.9 *Praying towards the Temple*

The effect of the Temple as a place extends beyond the actual geographical site or structure. It continues throughout the world. Jews practice ritual worship towards the Temple by paying attention to it. In Ps 138:2, the speaker bows down towards the holy Temple to show his thanksgiving and love. In Ps 28:2, his prayers and entreaties are directed to the holy of holies: "Hear the voice of my supplication, as I cry to you for help, as I lift up my hands towards your most holy sanctuary". Here it is difficult to ascertain whether this prayer was practiced far from the Temple, or in the outer court of the Temple in the direction of the דְּבִיר, the holy of holies.[26]

In fact, the phenomenon of praying from afar in the direction of the Temple is known from other sources, especially Solomon's prayer at the inauguration of the First Temple in 1 Kgs 8. Here, the king himself, the lay Israelite and even the foreigner pray towards the Temple which is designated "this place" (1 Kgs 8:29–30, 35) or "this house, the place of which you said, 'My name shall be there'" (1 Kgs 8:29).[27]

---

26   Artur Weiser, *The Psalms*, trans. Herbert Hartwell (London: SCM, 1962), 257 adheres to the second possibility. Following Mesopotamian parallels, Kraus, *Psalms 1–60*, 340, compares the verse to bowing to God's Sanctuary (Ps 5:10), while entering the gate, and assumes that the lifting of the hands is a gesture of seeking protection.

27   For dating this part of Solomon's prayer to the early Second Temple period see Jon D. Levenson, "From Temple to Synagogue: 1 Kings 8," in Halpern and Levinson, *Traditions and Transformation*, 143–66.

Regardless of precisely where the prayers alluded to by Solomon take place,[28] the point is that prayer needs to be mediated by the Temple. To be effective, the prayer does not go directly from the worshiper to God, but needs to go through the Temple. The mediation is of course more powerful if the prayer is uttered inside the Temple's domain. The Temple is therefore not merely a place where sacrifices are offered, but also a house of prayer (Isa 56:7) in at least two senses: prayer from within and without.[29]

1.10   The Psalms' Notion of the Temple as a Place

When the authors of the psalms shape the meaning and experience of the Temple, they actually form the identity of the pilgrim in relation to this place. Like any concept of place, their notion of the Temple as a holy place reflects a mental sense, a special way of being in the world. It relates to activities and situations, whether explicitly or implicitly.[30]

What is striking in the concept of the Temple as a holy place is that it does not merely relate to memory and myth as God's dwelling and encountering the sacred. In most of the psalms we have discussed, the pilgrim is called upon to take an active part in the holy center. The pilgrim enthusiastically praises, thanks, offers sacrifices, confesses his righteousness along with God's, and prays towards the Temple. Even when the pilgrim is actually passive, he is emotionally overwhelmed by God's dwelling, or longs to arrive there once again. This proactive concept of place focuses on the person reacting to the place rather than describing the place and its features. It relates to the question: what should one do in this place? How should one experience it?

There are two ways in which space is experienced by the self. The first and more obvious one is outgoing. The living body encounters the place-world by going out to meet it, through the body and in accessing a given space. The place shapes the bodily experience and vice versa. The second and more complex one is incoming, in which place is internalized within the body/self and

---

28   For indications for prayer within the Temple precincts see Ps 134. Note that Solomon mentions the prayer of the foreigner who comes to the Temple. See Regev, "Sacrifices of Righteousness," 375 n. 38.

29   On prayers directed towards, but outside the Temple, or the time of the sacrificial rite see Dan 9:21 (cf. 6:11); Jdt 9:1; cf. also Ezra 9:4–5.

30   On these functions of place see Relph, *Place and Placelessness*. Relph asserts that "we are never without emplaced experiences. It signifies as well that we are not only *in* places but *of* them" (19). Place is not a product or portion of space, but the perception that gives access to it. Yi-Fu Tuan, *Space and Place: The Perspective of Experience* (Minneapolis: University of Minnesota Press, 1977) discusses the bond between people and place. For Tuan, space turns into place by turning attachments, associations, and memories into place.

shapes the self. The body not only goes out to access places; it also bears the traces of the places it has known. These traces are continually laid down in the body. A body is shaped by the places it has come to know by a special kind of "placial incorporation" that is just as crucial to the human self as is the interpersonal incorporation. The reverse is also true: places are themselves altered by our having been in them. This persistence of place in the body relates to the manner in which a person feels in the presence of a certain place, and also how the self/body is subjected to the place.[31]

In Psalms we can see both ways of experiencing place. Most of the relevant passages relate to the outgoing experience of place: the spatial experience of being present in the Temple and the atmosphere of praise, gratitude and righteousness. The impact of the place is deep and lasts long after the visit. The incoming experience of place features the yearning for the Temple and the sense of missing it, and also praying towards it (if it was practiced from afar and not inside the Temple). Here the sense of encountering God's dwelling is internalized even when the person no longer stands within it.

In fact, I suggest that one intention of all the Temple psalms is to convey the sense of being in the Temple even when they are recited from afar. The authors wish the Israelites/Judeans/Jews to feel and express the sense of visiting God's dwelling even if they have not yet been there. Indeed, I assume that this is one of the functions of singing the Hallel (Pss 113–118) during the festivals in later Jewish liturgy. Thus, the psalms generate placial incorporation of the Temple. Those who recite them shape their own concept of the holy place, relating the concept or their memory of the Temple to the sensibilities mentioned in these songs. The worshipers whose perception of the Temple relies on the contents of the psalms do not contemplate its architecture or practical rites, but focus on coming closer to God.

2   Constructing the Temple as a Sacred Place in the Temple Scroll

2.1   *The Plan of the Temple Complex: Graded Holiness*
The Temple Scroll is a long and detailed halakhic manifest attributed to God speaking to Moses. It originated as a pre-Qumranic text from the mid-second century BCE. Its main theme is a reform of the plan of the Temple structure

---

31   Edward S. Casey, "Between Geography and Philosophy: What Does It Mean to Be in the Place-World?" *Annals of the Association of American Geographers* 91 (2001): 683–93 (688).

and the sacrificial cult according to very stringent principles of holiness.[32] A substantial part of the scroll contains instructions on how to construct the Temple precincts. The Temple Scroll describes a very detailed plan of the Temple courts, one that was influenced by the division of camps during Israel's wanderings in the desert as well as Ezekiel's vision of the Temple.[33]

The author begins the instructions with the building of the Sanctuary, its vessels and structures, including the veil, the holy of holies and the כרובים (keruvim), the Menorah, and the inner altar of incense (cols. 2–12), and proceeds to laws of sacrifices of the festivals (cols. 13–29). He then introduces other structures and spaces near the Sanctuary, such as the altar, the house of the laver (כיור, kior), and the porches (פרבר, parvar), their courts, gates and measurements (cols. 30–39), situating every ritual act in its appropriate place.

The plan of the Temple is divided into three circumferential courts. The inner court contains the Temple building (parallel to the Greek naos) and the altar on which the animal sacrifices were offered. It may be paralleled to the priestly court in rabbinic terminology or the fourth court in Josephus terminology.[34] This inner court is designated for holy vessels that must not be taken outside, in contrast to the pharisaic/rabbinic view, which also required the purification of the Menorah after certain festivals due to the suspicion that it had been defiled by the touch of lay people.[35] In this court, the priestly cult and priestly meals of sacrifices and cereal-offerings took place. They did not partake of them outside the inner court since their priestly share of the

---

32   Yigael Yadin, *The Temple Scroll*, 3 vols. (Jerusalem: Israel Exploration Society, 1977), vol. 1 (Hebrew). On the idea of holiness in this scroll see Eyal Regev, "Reconstructing Qumranic and Rabbinic Worldviews: Dynamic Holiness vs. Static Holiness," in *Rabbinical Perspectives: Rabbinic Literature and the Dead Sea Scrolls: Proceedings of the Eighth International Symposium of the Orion Center for the Study of the Dead Sea Scrolls and Associated Literature, January 7–9, 2003*, ed. Steven D. Fraade, Aharon Shemesh, and Ruth A. Clements (Leiden: Brill, 2005) 87–112; Eyal Regev, *Sectarianism in Qumran: A Cross-Cultural Perspective* (Berlin: Walter de Gruyter, 2007), 133–161.

33   Yadin, *Temple Scroll*, 1:146–48. The fact that the authors also anticipated a different eschatological Temple that God would bring down from the sky (Yadin, *Temple Scroll*, 1:141–44) indicates that the detailed plan of the Temple was considered to be realistic and obligatory. The following description of the courts and their function as well as "the city of the Temple" (עיר המקדש) is based on Yadin, *Temple Scroll*, 1:154–247; Lawrence H. Schiffman, "Exclusion from the Sanctuary and the City of the Sanctuary in the Temple Scroll," *Hebrew Annual Review* 9 (1985): 301–20.

34   For the distribution of the Temple courts see in general m. Mid. 2:1–6; 5:1; Josephus, *Ag. Ap.* 2.103–104. Cf. Josephus, *J.W.* 5.190–206; *Ant.* 15.416–419.

35   Temple Scroll 3:10–12; m. Ḥag. 3:8. The Pharisees and the Sadducees were debating this issue according to t. Ḥag 3:35 (ed. Leiberman 394).

sacrifices and offerings must be spatially separated from those of the laity that are eaten in the middle court (37:4–12).

The middle court, the size of which may be paralleled to the whole Temple Mount in Josephus and tractate Middot, was designated for eating sacrificial food by the lay males (its function parallels the court of Israel in Middot). Women, children and proselytes (until the fourth generation) were not allowed to enter (39:4–9). Wearing priestly garments was forbidden in the middle court (40:1–4), since it was not as holy as the inner court. The wall of the middle court was divided into chambers and contained twelve gates named for the tribes of Israel. The fabrics with which the gates were decorated and their exact measurements were also specified.

The size of the outer court was 1600 square cubits, much larger than the whole city of Jerusalem in the Hasmonean period (when the scroll was written). This was the court of the laity (quite like the court of women in Middot), but proselytes until the third generation were forbidden to enter (40:6–7). The outer court was designated for the religious activities of the laity, such as building tabernacles (42:7–17) and eating *shelamim* sacrifices during the feast of Sukkot (21:2–4; 22:11–13). It contained dozens of rooms and chambers for the chiefs of the tribes, priests and Levites, and many porticos (*parvarim*). The tabernacles of the lay people were to be built on the roofs of the chambers. The collaboration of all the people of Israel in the Temple ritual was symbolized by the twelve gates to and from the outer courts, each of which was also named for one of Jacob's twelve sons.

This spatial organization should be characterized as "graded holiness." Its main aim is to separate between the realms of the priests and the laity. However, the lay people have a significant hold on the Temple Mount, although they are physically located far from the altar, the holy vessels, and the atoning rituals.[36]

Another spatial sphere discussed in the Temple Scroll is "the City of the Temple" (עיר המקדש, *'ir ha-miqdash*), which seems to overlap the total area of all the three courts and generally extends beyond the whole city of Jerusalem (termed in MMT as "the camps of holiness").[37] Entrance is forbidden to males with skin diseases as well as those who have had a seminal discharge and are

---

36 See also Lawrence H. Schiffman, "Architecture and Law: The Temple and Its Courtyards in the Temple Scroll," in *From Ancient Israel to Modern Judaism: Intellect in Quest of Understanding: Essays in Honor of Marvin Fox*, ed. Jacob Neusner, Ernest S. Frerichs, and Nahum M. Sarna, 3 vols. (Atlanta: Scholars Press, 1989), 2:267–84.

37 I follow Schiffman's view that עיר המקדש (*'ir ha-miqdash*) refers to the whole sacred *temenos*, as opposed to Yadin, *Temple Scroll*, 1:222–23, who interpreted it as the city around the outer court. See Lawrence H. Schiffman, "Ir Ha-Miqdash and its Meaning in the Temple Scroll and Other Qumran Texts," in *Sanctity of Time and Space in Tradition and*

therefore defiled. This category also includes males after intercourse with women, in which case the purification process lasts three days (45:7–15). All defiled persons are restricted to three special areas located three thousand cubits from the "City of the Temple" (45:15–46:2). Yadin also believes that there are no interdictions pertaining to women in the City since women are completely prohibited from entering.[38] There are also strict restrictions in place regarding excretions in the City. They must be limited to a special place three thousand cubits outside the city (46:13–16). Impure food and drink must not be brought in (47:3–7). Non-sacral slaughtering is forbidden, as is bringing the hides and bones of such animals into the City (47:7–18; 52:14–53:4).

2.2 Boundaries Make a Place: the Mapping of the Temple in the Temple Scroll

I will now interpret the general plan of the Temple in the Temple Scroll in light of geographic theories of place. My question is: How do the author or readers experience the Temple not physically or halakhically, but as if they are visiting it? I suggest that the division into courts, the emphasis on their boundaries, and the restrictions regarding the function of these spaces create a specific concept of place.

In the phenomenology of place, a hierarchic structure such as that of courts and walls is an act of transgression. Space is sometimes imagined as a political geography of location, an act of resistance or differentiation.[39] This walling in and walling out, the relation between fence and offence, structures the normative place/world, but also questions it. It provides an alternative. The Temple and its restrictive borders and taboos construct a spatiality of otherness and map the author's ideology of resistance onto place,[40] thus reacting to the reality in Jerusalem or Judea. It is set against the dominating power. Since sacred places become markers and constitutes of identity,[41] the Temple's notion of

---

Modernity, ed. Dineke Houtman, Marcel J.H.M. Poorthuis, and Joshua Schwartz (Leiden: Brill, 1998), 95–109.

38   Yadin, Temple Scroll, 1:224, 237.

39   Steve Pile and Michael Keith, eds., Geographies of Resistance (London: Routledge, 1997), esp. 5, 28.

40   Cresswell, In Place/Out of Place, 9. According to Fernand Braudel, The Mediterranean and the Mediterranean World in the Age of Philip II, 2 vols. (London: Collins, 1972) 1:18, to draw a boundary around anything is to define, analyze and reconstruct it. However, the theory of place implies that this definition and analysis is a secondary reaction to a more "open" concept of place that is revised.

41   Jacob N. Kinnard, Places in Motion: The Fluid Identities of Temples, Images, and Pilgrims (New York: Oxford University Press, 2014), 4.

place in the Temple Scroll shapes the worldview of its later readers among the Qumran sects.

The Temple Scroll certainly reacts to the plan of the Temple in the second century CE, perhaps before Hasmonean independence.[42] Nonetheless, the focus on boundaries and rules with no hint of religious experiences or acts of worship that are not directly related to regulations and taboos is striking. In a sense, it seems that the author wishes to limit the religious sensibilities of the lay pilgrim. The sacredness of the Temple builds on the divisions within the hierarchy of different grades of holiness and their exact location.

3   Conclusions: Comparing the Psalms with the Temple Scroll

We have seen two very different ways in which Jews experience the Temple as a holy place. While the genre and purpose of the book of Psalms and the Temple Scroll are the main reason for these differences, they both relate to the very same Temple, at the same location, with similar sacrifices being offered. The psalms convey a more abstract approach without getting into legal and spatial details, but they nonetheless reflect a more direct approach to God.[43] While it is quite certain that the pilgrim encountered walls, courts, boundaries and taboos in the Temple, the songs are not at all concerned with them. The pilgrim feels he is entering the house of God. The fact that the Temple Scroll hardly involves feelings, but centers on mapping boundaries and restrictions results from its interest in sacred space and not place. Nevertheless, the author's approach does reflect how sacred space becomes an incoming experience as a placial incorporation. When one enters the Temple, one must beware not to transgress the boundaries of sacredness.

Drawing on Edward Relph's concept of identity of place, we may conclude that these are two very different identities of the Temple, pertaining to (1) its setting, (2) activities, situations, and events, and (3) the meanings created through people's experiences and intentions with regard to that place.[44] These differences demonstrate that place is a subjective concept. Place, in our case

---

42   Regev, *Sectarianism in Qumran*, 158–60.

43   On direct and abstract ways of experiencing place see Edward S. Casey, "How to Get from Space to Place in a Fairly Short Stretch of Time: Phenomenological Prolegomena," in *Senses of Place*, ed. Steven Feld and Keith H. Basso (Santa Fe: School of American Research Press, 1997), 13–52 (19).

44   Relph, *Place and Placelessness*, 45.

the Jerusalem Temple, is a space shaped by sensory, cognitive and behavioral capacities.[45]

In this paper, I have employed two very extreme approaches to the Temple as a place. They pertain to different times and different plans and structures, although both relate to the same site and the same sacrificial rite of the God of Israel in Jerusalem. Nonetheless, my point is that different people with different ideologies or agendas may experience the same geographical sacred space in very different ways. A holy place is not merely a site to which people ascribe sacred traditions and rites; it is a space to which people attach meaning in various ways, even within the same religious tradition.

References

Ackerman, James S. "Satire and Symbolism in the Song of Jonah." Pages 213–46 in *Traditions and Transformation: Turning Points in Biblical Faith*. Edited by Baruch Halpern and Jon D. Levenson. Winona Lake, IN: Eisenbrauns, 1981.

Anderson, Gary A. "The Praise of God as A Cultic Event." Pages 15–33 in *Priesthood and Cult in Ancient Israel*. Edited by Gary A. Anderson and Saul M. Olyan. Sheffield: JSOT Press, 1991.

Beyerlin, Walter. *Die Rettung der Bedrängten in den Feindpsalmen der Einzelnen auf institutionelle Zusammenhänge untersucht*. Göttingen: Vandenhoeck & Ruprecht, 1970.

Braudel, Fernand. *The Mediterranean and the Mediterranean World in the Age of Philip II*. 2 vols. London: Collins, 1972.

Bourdieu, Pierre. *Outline of Theory and Practice*. Cambridge: Cambridge University Press, 1977.

Casey, Edward S. "How to Get from Space to Place in a Fairly Short Stretch of Time: Phenomenological Prolegomena." Pages 13–52 in *Senses of Place*. Edited by Steven Feld and Keith H. Basso. Santa Fe: School of American Research Press, 1997.

Casey, Edward S. "Smooth Spaces and Rough-Edged Places: The Hidden History of Place." *Review of Metaphysics* 51 (1997): 267–96.

Casey, Edward S. *The Fate of Place: A Philosophical History*. Berkeley: University of California, 1998.

Casey, Edward S. "Between Geography and Philosophy: What Does It Mean to Be in the Place-World?" *Annals of the Association of American Geographers* 91 (2001): 683–93.

---

45   Jeff E. Malpas, *Place and Experience: A Philosophical Topography* (Cambridge: Cambridge University Press, 1999), 52–53.

Clifford, Richard J. *The Cosmic Mountain in Canaan and the Old Testament*. Cambridge: Harvard University Press, 1972.

Cresswell, Tim. *In Place/Out of Place: Geography, Ideology, and Transgression*. Minneapolis: University of Minnesota Press, 1996.

Cresswell, Tim. *Place: A Short Introduction*. Oxford: Blackwell, 2004.

Eaton, John H. "The Psalms and Israelite Worship." Pages 238–73 in *Tradition and Interpretation: Essays by the Members of the Society for Old Testament Study*. Edited by Gary A. Anderson. Oxford: Clarendon, 1979.

Eliade, Mircea. *The Myth of the Eternal Return: Or, Cosmos and History*. Translated by William T. Trask. Princeton, Princeton University Press, 1971.

Harvey, David. *Justice, Nature and Geography of Difference*. Cambridge: Blackwell, 1996.

Keel, Othmar. *The Symbolism of the Biblical World: Ancient Near Eastern Iconographies and the Book of Psalms*. Translated by Timothy J. Hallett. New York: Seabury, 1978.

Kinnard, Jacob N. *Places in Motion: The Fluid Identities of Temples, Images, and Pilgrims*. New York: Oxford University Press, 2014.

Kraus, Hans-Joachim. *Theology of the Psalms*. Translated by Keith Crim. Minneapolis: Fortress, 1986.

Kraus, Hans-Joachim, *Psalms 1–59: A Commentary*. Translated by Hilton C. Oswald. Minneapolis: Fortress, 1988.

Kraus, Hans-Joachim, *Psalms 61–150: A Commentary*. Translated by Hilton C. Oswald. Minneapolis: Fortress, 1989.

Kugel, James L. "Topics in the History of the Spirituality of the Psalms." Pages 113–44 in *Jewish Spirituality: From the Bible through the Middle Ages*. Edited by Arthur Green. New York: Crossroad, 1986.

Levenson, Jon D. "From Temple to Synagogue: 1 Kings 8." Pages 143–66 in *Traditions and Transformation: Turning Points in Biblical Faith*. Edited by Baruch Halpern and Jon D. Levenson. Winona Lake, IN: Eisenbrauns, 1981.

Levenson, Jon D. *Sinai and Zion: An Entry into the Jewish Bible*. Minneapolis: Winston, 1985.

Malpas, Jeff E. *Place and Experience: A Philosophical Topography*. Cambridge: Cambridge University Press, 1999.

Mowinckel, Sigmund. *The Psalms in Israel's Worship*. Oxford: Blackwell, 1962.

Otto, Eckart. "Kultus und Ethos in Jerusalemer Theologie: Ein Beitrag zur theologischen Begründung der Ethik im Alten Testament." *ZAW* 98 (1986): 161–79.

Parker, Robert. *Miasma: Pollution and Purification in Early Greek Religion*. Oxford: Oxford University Press, 1983.

Pile, Steve and Michael Keith, eds. *Geographies of Resistance*. London: Routledge, 1997.

Regev, Eyal. "Sacrifices of Righteousness: Visiting the Temple and Bringing Sacrifices as Religious Experience in Psalms." *Tarbiz* 73 (2004): 365–86. (Hebrew).

Regev, Eyal. "Reconstructing Qumranic and Rabbinic Worldviews: Dynamic Holiness vs. Static Holiness." Pages 87–112 in *Rabbinical Perspectives: Rabbinic Literature and the Dead Sea Scrolls: Proceedings of the Eighth International Symposium of the Orion Center for the Study of the Dead Sea Scrolls and Associated Literature, January 7–9, 2003.* Edited by Steven D. Fraade, Aharon Shemesh, and Ruth A. Clements. Leiden: Brill, 2005.

Regev, Eyal. *Sectarianism in Qumran: A Cross-Cultural Perspective.* Berlin: De Gruyter, 2007.

Relph, Edward. *Place and Placeness.* London: Pion, 1976.

Rendtorff, Rolf. *Studien zur Geschichte des Opfers im alten Israel.* Neukirchen-Vluyn: Neukirchener, 1967.

Sack, Robert D. *Human Territoriality: Its Theory and History.* Cambridge: Cambridge University Press, 1986.

Schiffman, Lawrence H. "Exclusion from the Sanctuary and the City of the Sanctuary in the Temple Scroll." *Hebrew Annual Review* 9 (1985): 301–20.

Schiffman, Lawrence H. "Architecture and Law: The Temple and Its Courtyards in the Temple Scroll." Pages 2:267–84 in *From Ancient Israel to Modern Judaism: Intellect in Quest of Understanding: Essays in Honor of Marvin Fox.* Edited by Jacob Neusner, Ernest S. Frerichs, and Nahum M. Sarna. 3 vols. Atlanta: Scholars Press, 1989.

Schiffman, Lawrence H. "Ir Ha-Miqdash and Its Meaning in the Temple Scroll and Other Qumran Texts." Pages 95–109 in *Sanctity of Time and Space in Tradition and Modernity.* Edited by Dineke Houtman, Marcel J.H.M. Poorthuis, and Joshua Schwartz. Leiden: Brill, 1998.

Schreiner, Patrick. "Space, Place and Biblical Studies: A Survey of Recent Research in Light of Developing Trends." *CBR* 14 (2016): 340–71.

Sinn, Ulrich. "Greek Sanctuaries as Places of Refuge." Pages 88–109 in *Greek Sanctuaries: New Approaches.* Edited by Nanno Marinatos and Robin Hägg. London: Routledge, 1993.

Soja, Edward W. *Thirdspace: Journeys to Los Angeles and Other Real-and-Imagined Places.* Cambridge: Blackwell, 1996.

Thompson, R.J. *Penitence and Sacrifice in Early Israel outside the Levitical Law: An Examination of the Fellowship Theory of Early Israelite Sacrifice.* Leiden: Brill, 1963.

Tuan, Yi-Fu. *Topophilia: A Study of Environmental Perception, Attitudes and Values.* Englewood Cliffs: Prentice-Hall, 1974.

Tuan, Yi-Fu. *Space and Place: The Perspective of Experience.* Minneapolis: University of Minnesota Press, 1977.

Tuan, Yi-Fu, and Martha A. Strawn. *Religion: From Place to Placelessness.* Chicago: Center for American Places at Columbia College, 2010.

Weinfeld, Moshe. "Instructions for Temple Visitors in the Bible and in Ancient Egypt." Pages 224–50 in *Egyptological Studies, Scripta Hierosolymitana 28*. Edited by Sarah Israelit-Groll. Jerusalem: Magnes, 1982.

Weiser, Artur. *The Psalms*. Translated by Herbert Hartwell. London: SCM, 1962.

Westermann, Claus. *Praise and Lament in the Psalms*. Translated by Keith R. Crim and Richard N. Soulen. Atlanta: Knox, 1981.

Yadin, Yigael. *The Temple Scroll*. 3 vols. Jerusalem: Israel Exploration Society, 1977.

CHAPTER 16

Remnants of Jewish Holiness in the Al Aksa Mosque in The Hague: Emotions, Rules, and "Iconic Fields"

Lieve M. Teugels

1 Synagogues in the Netherlands

Synagogue buildings are scattered over the cities and villages in the Netherlands: monumental ones in the big cities such as Amsterdam, Rotterdam, and The Hague, and often smaller but not always inconspicuous ones in the villages. After the Shoah, many Dutch synagogues were badly damaged or stood empty because there was no longer a viable Jewish community to maintain them. Many were demolished immediately after the war, or in the more recent years. Often the now smaller Jewish communities have moved to different buildings.

Nowadays about 150 synagogue buildings are preserved in a more or less recognizable way. These are described in the book *Synagogen van Nederland* by Edward van Voolen and Paul Meijer, with photographs by Willy Lindwer.[1] Several of these buildings have been restored and have received the status of protected monument. The choice for restoration and protection often depends on the architectural value of the building in the city-scape (or village-scape). Many of these buildings are no longer in use as synagogue, but have received other functions, as will be discussed in this paper.

Jewish communities, with synagogues, existed in the Netherlands in the Middle Ages, but none of the medieval buildings have been preserved because of heavy persecutions of Jews in the 14th century, as well as the anti-Jewish policies of the Habsburgs in the 16th century. But at the end of the 16th century this changed with the coming of many so-called *marranos* (Jews who forcibly, or through necessity, converted to Catholicism) from the Iberian Peninsula, who fled to the Dutch regions that became independent from Spain. These were relatively rich immigrants who were not only tolerated but also welcomed by the municipalities because of their value for the Dutch economy and trade. Many of these settled in Amsterdam, where they built synagogues. Of these, only the famous Portuguese Synagogue, built in the 1670s, still stands. These

---

1 Edward van Voolen, Paul Meijer, and Hans van Agt, *Synagogen van Nederland* (Zutphen: Walburg Pers, 2006).

Sephardim were soon followed by Ashkenazi Jews who fled from Germany and eastern Europe. The Large Synagogue of Amsterdam that now constitutes part of the Jewish Historical Museum is the oldest remaining Ashkenazi *shul*, also from the end of the 17th century.

Amsterdam has always been the heartland of Dutch Jewry. It is for a good reason that Amsterdam's most famous nickname is "Mokum" (from the Hebrew מָקוֹם, meaning "place"). The Jewish communities outside Amsterdam are called the "Mediene" (from the Hebrew מְדִינָה, one of whose meanings is "province"). Rotterdam and The Hague hold a position in between: these are large cities with significant Jewish communities, even today.

When civil equality was consolidated in the first Dutch constitution in 1798, Jews were allowed to settle all over the Netherlands. The result was that many new synagogues were built in cities and villages in the 19th century. The great Ashkenazi synagogue of The Hague, also called the Wagenstraat *shul*,[2] is one such 19th-century building. The adventures of this synagogue building are the topic of the present paper.

The Wagenstraat *shul* was built in 1842–1844 after a plan by architect Arend Roodenburg. It was conceived in neo-classicist style like many Dutch synagogues built in 19th century. The exterior contains classicist elements such plastered pilasters, horizontal cornices, and triangular frontons. Usually these classicist synagogues had a simple rectangular plan, with the *aron* (Torah shrine) on one short side and the women's gallery at the other short end. The synagogue of The Hague is an exception. Here the *aron* was placed on the long eastern wall, because a proper orientation of the building in its location was not possible.[3] Also the interior contained some special architectural features. There were galleries for the women at the two short ends of the room, set with neo-classicist columns all the way up to the ceiling.

2   Repurposing of Religious Buildings: Methodology and Questions

Many former synagogues in the Netherlands, as elsewhere, are being used for different purposes. Profane repurposing includes everything from stables to

---

2   The Yiddish word for synagogue, which literally means "school," because a traditional synagogue usually contains both a prayer hall, *beit knesset*, and study house, *beit midrash*, or serves both functions.

3   See van Voolen, Meijer, and van Agt, *Synagogen van Nederland*, 87. This orientation, with the *mihrab* in the long wall, has been preserved in the present mosque, into which the building was converted in 1979.

stores to private housing. In this contribution, I will focus on religious repurposing of synagogues. In most cases in the Netherlands, this means that the synagogues were used as churches or for other activities related to Christian religious communities. In the case of the great synagogue of The Hague, the synagogue was converted into a mosque.

My methodology draws from two disciplines: first, anthropology, and second, the study of halakhic sources. My main point of attention will be how holiness is perceived in these two fields. As we will see, in halakha, holiness is (mostly) defined in terms of rules. In anthropology, on the other hand, holiness is something people perceive at an emotional level. These two do not necessarily coincide: it is conceivable that people, Jews and others, perceive a certain (Jewish) holiness in a repurposed synagogue whereas, halakhically, that holiness has been removed. On the other hand, sometimes some of the "anthropological" feeling of holiness seems to have crept into the halakhic sources, as we will see. I will also introduce the notion of "iconic field," equally from the field of anthropology, as a tool to grasp the various factors at work in the emotional reactions of old and new congregants, and neighbours, with respect to the repurposing of religious buildings.

Although this contribution is based on anthropological research, it is not a proper comprehensive ethnographic analysis, as I did not engage in the typical participatory research that is central to anthropological study. This is, rather, an explorative study of a topic that is relevant for historians and scholars of religion. For the theoretical framework, I based myself on studies of Daan Beekers and Pooyan Tamimi Arab about the repurposing of churches in Amsterdam.[4] Indeed, a similar development as with synagogues, but on a much larger scale, is going on with churches in the Netherlands, many of which are becoming repurposed as stores, exhibit spaces, apartments, and so on, because of the increasing lack of congregants. Some churches are, interestingly, even converted into synagogues, as we can read in the contribution of Leon Mock in this volume. The studies of Beekers and Tamimi Arab on the repurposing of churches focus on the emotional reactions of the previous congregants, "neighbours," and new occupants. The studies of Beekers also draw on the rules of Catholic and Protestant Churches with respect to the repurposing of their former

---

4   See Beekers's contributions in Oskar Verkaaik, Daan Beekers, and Pooyan Tamimi Arab, *Gods huis in de steigers: Religieuze gebouwen in ontwikkeling* (Amsterdam: Amsterdam University Press, 2017), 161–92 ("De waarde van verlaten kerken"), 193–218 ("Rode burcht, jezuïetenkerk, moskee"); Daan Beekers and Pooyan Tamimi Arab, "Dreams of an Iconic Mosque: Spatial and Temporal Entanglements of a Converted Church in Amsterdam," *Material Religion* 12 (2016): 137–64.

religious buildings. These studies will serve as my model for the interpretation of the reactions to the repurposing of the synagogue in The Hague as a mosque,[5] as well as the relation between these emotional reactions and the official rules, which are, in the case of synagogues, set out in halakha.

For the analysis of the case of the repurposed synagogue in The Hague, I base myself on the television documentary *Facing East* ("Met het Gezicht naar het Oosten"), broadcast on Dutch television in 2013.[6] The presenter of this documentary, Naeeda Aurangzeb, interviewed members of the three communities directly involved: the new, Turkish Muslim community, user of the building; a representative of the Jewish community; and people living or working in the immediate neighbourhood, some of whom have known both the old and the new situations (I will call them "neighbours"). It needs to be added that not just the synagogue, but the neighbourhood as a whole, has changed drastically since the Second World War: whereas it was first a mainly Jewish area around a busy artery of the city, it is now a very mixed neighbourhood, part of which has become The Hague's "Chinatown."

As to the anthropological scope of my study, I will focus on the emotions of the various groups involved vis-à-vis the repurposing of this building as demonstrated in the documentary. With respect to the halakha, I will refer to the main halakhic stances about what makes a synagogue building holy; whether any of that holiness remains after the building ceases to be a synagogue; and whether it matters for what purpose the synagogue building will be reused.

---

5 Other contributions in *Gods huis in de steigers* focus on the fate of old synagogues and on the construction of new synagogues, but not specifically on religious repurposing. Chapters 4 and 5 (by Verkaaik) deal with newly built synagogues in Germany and synagogues in the Netherlands that had been abandoned but are now again used by Jewish communities. On the internet, several newspaper articles and similar items about repurposed synagogues in the US and Europe can be found. See e.g. https://www.washingtonpost.com/news/worldviews/wp/2016/04/28/a-french-synagogue-is-being-repurposed-as-a-mosque-after-local-jews-left-the-neighborhood/?utm_term=.b3b274e9114b; www.haaretz.com/world-news/europe/MAGAZINE-from-a-place-of-worship-to-a-bakery-synagogues-changing-their-role-1.5849108.

6 The full documentary can be watched here: https://www.npo.nl/met-het-gezicht-naar-het-oosten/12-07-2013/NPS_1228830.

3   Repurposing of Christian Churches in the Netherlands:
         Congregants and Authorities

From Beekers's study "De waarde van verlaten kerken,"[7] I extracted the main elements that serve as my model to interpret the documentary about the synagogue-
turned-mosque in The Hague. These elements can be summarized as follows.

    Because of the progressive secularization in former Christian communi-
ties in the Netherlands, many, often large, church buildings need to close.
Another factor is demographic change: since the 1950s, neighbourhoods have
been changing and becoming more "mixed." For example, in the case of the
Chassé-church, studied by Beekers, non-Catholics moved from other parts
of Amsterdam to this previously Catholic neighbourhood. Later, these were
joined by Turkish and Moroccan immigrants. Not only Catholics, who mourn
the loss of the churches, where they celebrated "landmarks" in their lives, such
as the holy communion, or marriage, but also neighbours, who consider "their"
church as a landmark or historical heritage, are deeply concerned with the fate
of these buildings. Beekers writes:

> There seems to be a wide consensus that the value of Church buildings
> surpasses their function as places of Christian religious congregation ...
> [I]n existing studies and official documents about the closing of church-
> es it is systematically mentioned that this is accompanied with "a lot of
> emotion."[8]

The Chassé-church was eventually transformed into a dance studio. Some aspects of the transformation were problematic for the former congregants, such
as the location of bathrooms in the former confessionals, and the conversion
of the holy water fonts to planters. Other aspects of the conversion were problematic for the Catholic church officials. An example of the latter is a splendid
wall mosaic, depicting Mary and John the Baptist, which the new owner would
have liked to keep visible because "it might inspire the children that come to
dance here."[9] The former parish board, however, demanded that it be covered,
because no religious symbolism should be left in this repurposed building. The
same holds for crucifixes chiselled in the walls and on objects: they have all
become unrecognizable.

---

7 In Verkaaik, Beekers, and Tamimi Arab, *Gods huis in de steigers*, 161–92, see note 4.
8 Verkaaik, Beekers, and Tamimi Arab, *Gods huis in de steigers*, 164.
9 Verkaaik, Beekers, and Tamimi Arab, *Gods huis in de steigers*, 179.

For an official Catholic perspective on the repurposing of church buildings, Beekers refers to a guidance paper by the Dutch Conference of Bishops, published in 2008.[10] The main points of this document can be listed as follows. The repurposing needs to be "dignified" for a church and needs to conserve as much as possible the original character of the building. If this is not possible, demolishment is preferred. The repurposed building should ideally remain testimony to the Christian tradition and culture. It can be sold to another Christian church community, but it should not be used for non-Christian religions.[11] If a Christian religious purpose is not feasible, then social and cultural repurposing is preferred above commercial exploitation.

For the official Dutch Protestant (PKN)[12] stance, Beekers cites a similar document from 2009.[13] This long "discussion paper" mentions the following important points: use by other Christian Churches in the ecumene[14] is applauded, as is use by the Jewish community. Use by "oppositional or controversial" Christian churches and by non-Christian religions (apart from Judaism) is not evident. Nevertheless, religious repurposing is always still better than profane. Cultural repurposing is preferred above commercial. Most important is that the "image" of the Church is maintained and that its original function can be remembered. The "emotions" of the original congregants are mentioned explicitly as a factor to be reckoned with.

---

10   Verkaaik, Beekers, and Tamimi Arab, *Gods huis in de steigers*, 179. See Nederlandse Bisschoppenconferentie, "Het kerkgebouw als getuige van de christelijke traditie: Uitgangspunten van beleid voor kerkgebouwen" (2008), https://www.rkdocumenten.nl/rkdocs/index.php?mi=600&doc=6509.

11   This does not mean that this never happens or happened: chapter 8 in *Gods huis in de steigers*, also by Daan Beekers, deals with the former Jesuit Church "De zaaier" (The Sower) in Amsterdam that has been converted into a mosque (Fatih mosque on the Rozengracht), after it had first been used as a carpet hall. Beekers cites a representative of the diocese who is of the opinion that the repurposing of the church as a mosque was only possible because of this "illegal intermediate step." See Verkaaik, Beekers, and Tamimi Arab, *Gods huis in de steigers*, 206. Interestingly, on the location of the former church first stood a famous socialist community centre that was converted into a chapel. The latter however, was demolished to make room for a newer, bigger church.

12   Protestantse Kerk in Nederland (Protestant Church in the Netherlands).

13   Verkaaik, Beekers, and Tamimi Arab, *Gods huis in de steigers*, 206. See Protestantse Kerk in Nederland, "Een Protestantse visie op het kerkgebouw met een praktisch theologisch oormerk: Discussienota van de Protestantse Kerk in Nederland" (2009), http://www.kerkelijkwaardebeheer.nl/wp-content/uploads/protestantse-visie-op-het-kerkgebouw.pdf. The important points listed here are found on pp. 28–31.

14   This includes all the members of the Council of Churches in the Netherlands, which are listed here: https://www.raadvankerken.nl/pagina/27/lidkerken.

So much for the official Church positions on the matter. But "what about the ordinary congregants?" Beekers asks with respect to the repurposing of the Chassé-church.[15] Some former congregants that were interviewed by him would have preferred that the church building be demolished rather than re-purposed as a dance studio, because entering the place in its new function "makes it too painful because of the memories."[16] Despite official "profana-tion" of the building "they still experience it as holy … the incense has been absorbed into the walls … the consecration sits between their ears. It remains a holy place in the memory of the people."[17]

We can conclude from the survey by Beekers that the official stances of the main Christian churches in the Netherlands (PKN and Catholic Church) display some differences, most notably that the PKN makes an exception for Judaism, which it treats on a par with Christian religions. But otherwise the perspectives of both churches are quite similar. Both Churches agree that, when church buildings need to be repurposed, it is important that the new purpose is "dignified" and that the original purpose can be remembered. Both agree that, if profane repurposing cannot be avoided, a new destiny in the so-cial or cultural sphere is preferred above commercial exploitation. In certain cases, demolition is preferred over "unworthy" new purposing. In the Catholic Church, a building can be "deconsecrated" by, among other things, removing religious objects and making its previous religious function as unrecognizable as possible (e.g., by covering up the mosaic and the crosses, as in the case of the Chassé-church).[18] However, the emotions of former congregants, and even of "neighbours," do not necessarily coincide with official church rules: they may still feel a certain "holiness" after the building has been repurposed. For some former congregants, the memories are so strong that they would rather see every trace of the building removed than that it be used for something else than the religious function it had for them.

---

15   Verkaaik, Beekers, and Tamimi Arab, *Gods huis in de steigers*, 180.
16   Verkaaik, Beekers, and Tamimi Arab, *Gods huis in de steigers*, 180.
17   Verkaaik, Beekers, and Tamimi Arab, *Gods huis in de steigers*, 181.
18   It needs to be mentioned that there are differences in opinion, even among official repre-sentatives of the Churches. Beekers interviewed a priest of another church in Amsterdam who is of the opinion that the mosaic should have remained visible, and that it could bear meaning precisely in its new context. The same holds for churches that are repurposed, even commercially, because they can invoke curiousness, inspire and "keep the memory of God" even in a secular context (Verkaaik, Beekers, and Tamimi Arab, *Gods huis in de steigers*, 191).

4 The Repurposed Synagogue: Halakha

The main rabbinic halakhic discussion about what should happen to a synagogue when it needs to be abandoned as a place of Jewish worship, and the ensuing discussion about its proper repurposing, is found in m. Meg. 3:1–3 and the Gemara in b. Meg. 26a–29a.[19] Below is the Mishnah in its entirety,[20] and the relevant sections of the Gemara.[21] I have italicized the sections that are particularly relevant for our discussion.

> (1) Inhabitants of a town who have sold the open place of the town, may buy for that money a synagogue. The proceeds of the sale of a synagogue, they may apply to the purchase of an ark; for the proceeds of the sale of such an ark, cloaks or wrappers may be purchased; for the proceeds of the sale of such wrappers, sefarim may be purchased; for the proceeds of the sale of sefarim, a Torah may be purchased; but if they had sold a Torah, it will not be lawful to apply the proceeds to the purchase of sefarim, nor wrappers for the proceeds of sefarim, nor an ark for the proceeds of wrappers, nor a synagogue with the proceeds of an ark, nor an open [or market] place with the money obtained by the sale of a synagogue, and even so in respect to any surplus fund. According to Rabbi Meir[22] it is unlawful to sell sacred public property to private individuals, *because its sanctity becomes thereby lowered*: but the Sages replied, "If so, it would be also prohibited for a large town to sell sacred things to a smaller one."
>
> (2) A synagogue may, according to Rabbi Meir, only be sold on condition that it may at any time be repurchased by the original owners; but the sages permit it to be sold permanently, only it may not be sold to be applied to the following occupations: namely, as a bathing-house, as a tanning place, as a diving-bath, and as a laundry. Rabbi Yehudah says, "It

---

19   About this topic see among others Lee I. Levine, *The Ancient Synagogue: The First Thousand Years* (New Haven: Yale University Press, 2000), 185–86; Steven Fine, *This Holy Place: On the Sanctity of the Synagogue during the Greco-Roman Period* (Notre Dame: University of Notre Dame Press, 1997).

20   The Mishnah text and English translation are taken from Sefaria.org, with some adaptations.

21   Translation of the Babylonian Talmud, with some adaptations, from Isidore Epstein, *The Babylonian Talmud* (London: Soncino Press, 1978).

22   Certain textual witnesses of the Mishnah read here "R. Yehudah." According to Michael Krupp, *Megilla: Rolle*, Die Mischna: Textkritische Ausgabe mit deutscher Übersetzung und Kommentar (Jerusalem: Lee Achim, 2002), 16 (n. 94), "R. Meir" is probably correct, because usually R. Meir brings the heavier argument and R. Yehudah the lighter. Attribution to R. Meir also fits better with mishnah 2. The Gemara (b. Meg. 27b) also reads "R. Meir."

may be sold on the condition that it be made an open court, and then the purchaser is at liberty to turn it to what purpose he pleases."

(3) Rabbi Yehudah teaches also, that no funeral orations may be delivered in a synagogue which had become ruinous, nor may it be used as a rope-walk, nor to spread nets therein, nor to spread fruit on its roof, nor to use it as a short cut, as it is said (Lev 26:31), "I will bring your sanctuaries into desolation," that is, *they remain sanctuaries even in their desolation.* If grass spring up therein, it may not be pulled up, that the view may contribute to the affliction [of the beholder].

b. Meg. 26a–29a (selection):

ad mishnah 1

(26a) "Inhabitants of a town who have sold the open place of the town." Rabbah b. Bar Hanah said in the name of R. Johanan: This is the view of R. Menahem b. Jose the anonymous author, *but the Sages say that no sanctity attaches to the square.*

(26b) Raba said: A synagogue may be exchanged or sold [for secular purposes], but may not be hired or pledged. What is the reason? *Its holiness is still adhering to it.*

(26b) [With regard to a synagogue which has been made] a gift, there is a difference of opinion between R. Aha and Rabina, one forbidding [it to be used for secular purposes] and one permitting. The one who forbade did so on the ground *that there is nothing to which its holiness is transferred,* while the one who permitted it argued that if he [the giver] did not derive some benefit from the act he would not give it, so that in the end the gift is equivalent to a sale.

(27b) That was a sound objection raised by the Rabbis against R. Meir, [was it not]? What says R. Meir to this?—[To sell] from a large town to a small one [is unobjectionable], *because if it was holy to begin with, it is still holy now.* But if it passes from a community to an individual, *there is no holiness left.*

ad mishnah 2

(27b) "Rabbi Yehudah says, 'It may be sold on the condition that it be made an open court, and then the purchaser is at liberty to turn it to what purpose he pleases.'" And even the Rabbis did not forbid save in the synagogue itself, *since its sanctity is permanent,* but for the four adjoining cubits, the sanctity of which is not permanent, they did not make such a rule.

ad mishnah 3

(28a–b) Our Rabbis taught: *Synagogues must not be treated disrespectfully.* It is not right to eat or to drink in them, nor to dress up in them, nor to stroll about in them, nor to go into them in summer to escape the heat and in the rainy season to escape the rain, nor to deliver a private funeral address in them. But it is right to read [the Scriptures] in them and to repeat the Mishnah and to deliver public funeral addresses.

(28b) R. Assi said: The synagogues of Babylon have been built with a stipulation, and even so *they must not be treated disrespectfully.* What [for instance] is this?—Doing calculations [for business purposes] in them.

This rabbinic source bears on the *selling* of a synagogue. The main rule in the mishnaic discussion of the sold synagogue is that "what is holy must be raised in honour and not be brought down."[23] Thus, with the proceeds of the sale of a synagogue one can buy an ark, or all kinds of attributes for a Torah scroll, and ultimately a Torah scroll, which contains the most holiness of all. It can also be inferred from this discussion that holiness gets transferred in the funds of the transaction.[24]

In his book *This Holy Place*, Steven Fine discusses how the synagogue building gradually obtained the status of "holy place."[25] The most important feature of a holy place according to rabbinic sources, Fine writes, is that it needs to be treated with respect. Holiness and dignity go hand in hand. Indeed, the concepts of holiness and dignity recur throughout the rabbinic discussion of the sale of a synagogue as indicated by the sections in italics, in the Mishnah and even more prominently in the Gemara. This is remarkably similar to what was brought up by the church authorities in the discussion about the reuse of church buildings in Beekers's study.

We can conclude that, from a halakhic point of view, a synagogue can be sold, that its holiness can get transferred to the monies of the sale, and that the main condition is that it is not lowered in holiness and that it receives

---

23   See also m. Shek. 6:4 and m. Men. 11:7: "What is holy must be raised in honor and not be brought down." Cf. Herbert Danby, *The Mishnah* (Oxford: Clarendon, 1933; repr., Oxford: Oxford University Press, 1991), 204 (n. 26).

24   In a recent conservative responsum by Rabbi David Fine, I found a similar argument, based on these Mishnaic sources. See "On the Sale of Holy Property" by Rabbi David J. Fine (OH 153:2.2005a), www.rabbinicalassembly.org/sites/default/files/public/halakhah/teshuvot/20052010/fine_holyproperty.pdf. See also the concurring responsum by Rabbi Aaron Mackler: www.rabbinicalassembly.org/sites/default/files/assets/public/halakhah/teshuvot/20052010/mackler_holyproperty.pdf.

25   Fine, *This Holy Place.*

a dignified new purpose. The latter point coincides with the stance of the PKN and Catholic Church on the reuse of church buildings. However, in the Mishnah, we also see that some authorities hold that synagogues "remain sanctuaries even in their desolation" (Rabbi Yehudah), and in the Gemara the opinions of several sages are quoted who object to hiring out or gifting synagogues in certain conditions and for certain purposes, because some holiness is still adherent. This is similar to what the former congregants of the Chassé-church in Beekers's study claim about the "incense that has been absorbed by the walls of the church building."

In the case of the Wagenstraat synagogue in The Hague, the sale was not directly to the Muslim community, but first to the municipality for a symbolic sum. Therefore the question whether the transformation of the building into a mosque was appropriate, was not a direct concern for the Jewish community at the time of the sale of the building.[26] Rather, one could argue that the sale to the town was "conditional," or that it was sold "as a courtyard" (m. Meg. 3:2).[27]

5   The Documentary *Facing East*

With the Talmudic texts, as well as Beekers's and Tamimi Arab's studies of the repurposed churches, in mind, I will now discuss the relevant sections of the documentary about the repurposed synagogue in The Hague.[28] I selected the fragments because they display the reactions of the various involved groups, i.e., the new (American) rabbi, who represents the official Jewish perspective; the neighbours, some of whom knew the old situation; and representatives of the new Muslim congregation. Surprisingly, no original Jewish congregants were interviewed. My special focus is on the way the interviewed

---

26   A similar situation was the case with the transformation of the Catholic "De zaaier" Church in Amsterdam, which was converted into a mosque after it had first been used as a carpet store. See note 11.

27   In a conservative responsum by Rabbi Eliott Dorff about whether a synagogue can be used by Christians for their services (which is answered affirmatively), the use by Muslims is also touched upon. Regarding this, it states: "All of these arguments would hold even more strongly if Jews were thinking of renting synagogue facilities to Muslims, for Islam's commitment to monotheism is even less questionable than Christianity's is." See https://www .rabbinicalassembly.org/sites/default/files/assets/public/halakhah/teshuvot/19861990/ dorff_christiangroup.pdf.

28   See note 6. The documentary is made and presented by Naeeda Aurangzeb. During the JCP conference in Jerusalem, where I first presented this paper, we watched some 12 minutes of the documentary, namely c. mins. 15–22, 25–28, and 43–45.

individuals relate to the "holiness" of the place, as well as on the new identity of the building as a Muslim landmark, as will be explained later.

Some introduction and contextualization of the discussed fragments will be helpful.[29] The synagogue was abandoned by the decimated Jewish community in 1975 and officially sold to the municipality for one guilder. The *aron* was moved to the Jewish Historical Museum in Amsterdam. From a different source I learned that it was later moved, by previous congregants of the Wagenstraat *shul*, to the *Beit Ezriel* synagogue in Jerusalem, nicknamed "The Dutch Shul," where it now has a prominent place in the modern interior.[30] The orthodox Jewish community moved to a smaller building in Bezuidenhout, a different part of town.[31] In the sections of the documentary that will be discussed, it is shown how, in 1978, a group of Muslim men squatted the building with the explicit purpose of converting it into a mosque. Since the Muslim community needed a mosque building, after long deliberations, the municipality offered them the building for sale, again for the symbolic sum of one guilder. This saved the now dilapidated building from possible demolition. The Muslim community collected money for a large-scale restoration and redesign campaign. The Hebrew signs marking the synagogue building were removed and new, Arabic signs were added to the facade. The interior was completely redecorated into a splendid Muslim prayer hall. Interestingly, and the likely reason for the title of the documentary, is that the *mihrab* was established along the same long eastern wall where the *aron* had stood. In 1987, two minarets were added in front of the building. The mosque was first called "Fatih" (the Conqueror), but in 1981 renamed "Mescidi Aksa" (the Al Aksa Mosque). A playground that includes engravings of the names of Jewish children who perished in the Shoah was erected on a nearby square in 2006 as a place of Jewish remembrance.

Now follows my English transcript/translation of the original Dutch interviews included in the relevant fragments of the documentary.[32]

---

29 For the history of the construction of the building, its original congregants, and the reduction of the Jewish community after the Second World War I refer to the beginning of this paper.

30 Corien Glaudemans, "Op zoek naar de ark: De geschiedenis van de Heilige Arke of Aron Hakodesj van de Grote Synagoge in de Wagenstraat," *Jaarboek Die Haghe 2015* (2015): 127–51. A short version can be consulted at https://www.joodserfgoeddenhaag.nl/de-heilige-arke-van-de-grote-synagoge-in-de-wagenstraat/.

31 Not mentioned in the documentary is that the Jewish community first moved temporarily to a former church building in Bezuidenhout before its new building was inaugurated in 1986. Thanks to Leon Mock, who pointed this out to me during the JCP conference.

32 This is a fairly literal translation. All mistakes, contradictions and particularities in the words of the speakers are original. I have not tried to change these.

Rabbi: The few people who returned (after the war) did their best to pick up life and revive the Jewish community. They held services in the synagogue. But in the sixties it became evident that it was no longer possible. And then the centre moved to Bezuidenhout. The synagogue at the Wagenstraat was left empty.

Representative of the mosque: Until 1975 this building served as synagogue. In 1976 the Jewish community sold the main building and the annexes to the city. After that it stood empty for about three years and it deteriorated fast, due to a lack of maintenance.

Owner of a previously Jewish-owned stamp store next to the building (Manuskowski): My previous owner tried to buy the building because he wanted to turn it into an auction hall.

Presenter: An auction hall in the synagogue?

Owner of the stamp store: Yes. This would be used once or twice a year for a stamp auction. But it never happened because they asked a gigantic amount of money.

Representative of the mosque: The Turkish Muslim organization of The Hague, that was founded in 1978, had been looking for a long time for a good mosque building. Official requests to the city to sell the synagogue building were to no avail.

Owner of the stamp store: Then it happened on a Friday afternoon that a lot of people of Turkish and Moroccan descent convened at the site with large wire-shears and they cut open the lock of the fence and squatted the building.

Representative of the mosque: The members of the community squatted the deserted building, this building.

Presenter: So the Turkish men squatted the building?

One of the original squatters (subtitled in Dutch because of strong accent): We came here with about thirty-five people. We squatted there and we squatted here. The police and the fire brigade came. They heard everything and they came. "Oh, what are you doing? Oh, squatting! Arrest those people." But the other policeman said: "Just wait a minute, let's make a phone call."

Representative of the mosque: But at that time squatting was a culture in the Netherlands. There was also a sort of law.

Presenter: If you squatted something and you stayed for a while you could keep it.

Representative of the mosque: It became legally yours.

Former squatter: Then we decided as Turkish community: "This we should buy, we are not leaving here."

Presenter: You decided that you would not leave? Even if someone would die?

Former squatter: No matter ... stay here.

Presenter: And if the riot police would have come?

Former squatter: No, no, we had really decided.

Presenter: You were not afraid?

Former squatter: No, we had decided that we would not return the building.

Presenter: Even if someone would die?

Former squatter: No. If people would die, or a few people would die, it doesn't matter. We stay here. The dead are dead, the living stay.

Photographer: That was a typical sight there, all of a sudden, all these Turks, with a broken open gate. I was there.

Presenter: And these were all the men?

Photographer: Yes, only men, no women, with those moustaches and so on. Long hair, in those days, even the Turkish men, and wide bottom pants. Even the Turkish men then followed the fashion of the day. I have always been surprised that Turkish people, of a different faith, enter a building, squatted, and accept it as their church building, whereas, when this building was built, a rabbi of sorts came and he [makes waving movements] declared the whole ground holy and Jewish, so that the building could be built there. Because it was built as a synagogue of course. And that has never changed. As far as I know, never a Turkish imam came [makes same movements] who said: "Woohoo, now it has become ours!"

Presenter: Did you know this was a synagogue?

Squatter: Yes of course.

Presenter: And did you not think, as a Muslim: "What am I going to do in a synagogue?"

Squatter: Make it a mosque!

Presenter: But didn't you find it strange?

Squatter: No, not at all. A building is a building. Whether it is Christian or Jewish or Muslim, doesn't matter. A building is a building. Also, when the building was 140 years old, when it became a monument, the Jews came to pray here. They congratulated us: "We are happy that this has become a mosque. We pray to God and you pray also to God." Everyone prays to God. It doesn't matter.

Representative of the mosque: We think, in fact, that God wanted that we received this building.

Presenter: God wanted that the Muslims got the synagogue ... ooh, that is ...?!

Representative of the mosque: This is what I heard from the people who were here at the time. It's remarkable, indeed.

Owner of the stamp store: What I thought about it? On the one hand I was very much against the way in which it happened. In fact you don't want that such a thing happens, but it simply happened. In the short time that

I worked here I developed a close relationship with many of the Jewish people and I saw a lot of misery. People, older men, were crying here in the store.

Now follows a section about how much the transaction cost. The "neighbours" are offended that the city sold the building for only one guilder ("and then they even demanded that the roof was fixed!"). But the Muslim congregants say they needed three years to collect all the money from their members ("the women even handed in their gold jewellery") in order to renovate the building and convert it into a mosque.

Presenter: What was the reaction in the street to the conversion?

Baker (owns former Jewish bakery Gordijn): Yes, there was a lot of re-action against it. And I also think—because this used to be a Jewish neighbourhood—I also think: Did they even have to take away their memory? They lost so much in the war. And now even the memory needs to disappear. It could have been a very nice monument, for tourists, as sight-seeing. There is nothing left. So little is left of the Jewish commu-nity; in fact nothing as far as I know.

Presenter: What do you think about the fact that the synagogue became a mosque?

Lamp store owner: I don't think much about it, but I can imagine that it must be hard to deal with, for people of Jewish descent.

Rabbi: What should happen with such a building? If it would have be-come a shopping centre or a nightclub, that would also not have been very good for the spirit of the building. So it is a fact of history with which we should have peace.

Presenter: You called the mosque "Mescidi Aksa?"

Former squatter: Yes, but only in 1981. In 1979 it was still called "Fatih." Because it was squatted, it was called "Fatih," the Conqueror. And then we changed the name into "Mescidi Aksa." Why Mescidi Aksa? Because the Jews have the Mescidi Aksa in their hands.

Presenter: You mean the Mescidi Aksa in Jerusalem?

Former squatter: Yes, yes, in Jerusalem. Therefore we have called the synagogue in the Netherlands "Mescidi Aksa."

Presenter: That is a political statement.

Former squatter: Yes, what can you do? They should not be the boss.

Presenter: Thus by calling this old synagogue the Mescidi Aksa you say that you don't agree with the politics in Israel?

Former squatter: Yes, yes, what can you do? They should not be the boss.

...

Presenter: I am a Muslim, but when I am here I always hear the voices from the Jewish past. I know so little about that past that entered my life through the diary of Anne Frank in High School. Then I only understood her yearning for love. I think about the Jewish men, women and children that, just like the Turkish Muslims now, found quiet, shelter, and peace here. It's surreal. A building is for us, humans, apparently a casing for a space that we can fill in as we wish.

When you are here—because you have been the president of the community for a long time, and you come here to pray—do you ever think about the Jewish people who also came here, praying to God with their face to the East?

Representative of the Mosque: I would lie if I would say that I think about this every day. But indeed, when the history of the building is mentioned, you think, indeed, the Jewish community has prayed here for more than a hundred years, to Allah. We have one God. Indeed. But usually I don't think about it.

Presenter: It is not so that you hear the spirits of the old Jewish people here?

Representative of the Mosque: [Laughs] No.

Presenter: [Laughs] I am the only one who hears them.

6 Iconic Field

In 2016, Beekers and Tamimi Arab coined the notion "iconic field"[33] to grapple the various aspects involved in the (religious) functions of a building, with respect to its temporal relations, i.e., its present and past functions, and its spatial relations with other iconic buildings in the nearby cityscape.[34] The technical, analytical use of the word "iconic" derives from the Iconic Religion project, in which Beekers was involved.[35] This project promotes the term "iconicity" as a tool to grapple with urban religious presence, including the complex of meanings carried by repurposed, or as they call it "converted" religious buildings. The notion "iconic field" is a suitable instrument to map the attitudes and reactions of the various involved groups discernible in the documentary *Facing East*.

Beekers and Tamimi Arab applied the notion "iconic field" to the Fatih mosque building in Amsterdam, which used to be the Catholic church "De zaaier" (The Sower). The latter, in its turn, came in the place of a socialist community building named "Constantia." The iconic field includes these two previous functions of the building (among other things). But it also covers the new meaning that is envisioned for the mosque by its younger congregants, who want to convert it into a Muslim landmark in that part of Amsterdam, which can compete as a tourist attraction and a public site with the nearby Westerkerk (Christian iconic place), the Anne Frank House (Jewish iconic place), and the Homo Monument. This involves coming out of the "hiddenness" behind the church facade, which has so far marked the mosque, and creating more visibility by the construction of a new entrance and more conspicuous signs that identify it as a mosque.

---

33 See Beekers and Tamimi Arab, "Dreams of an Iconic Mosque," esp. 141–42 and 160. The definition given in this study is: "We take 'iconic field' to refer to the distribution of, and interaction between, iconic places and buildings, giving shape to and co-constituting a particular space in both past and present" (141).

34 A similar concept, related to the managing of shared space by various religious groups, is that of "intersecting religioscapes" used by Robert Hayden and Timothy D. Walker, "Intersecting Religioscapes: A Comparative Approach to Trajectories of Change, Scale, and Competitive Sharing of Religious Spaces," *Journal of the American Academy of Religion* 81 (2013): 399–426. Beekers and Tamimi Arab, "Dreams of an Iconic Mosque," 141 quote from this study in which the authors ask attention for "intersecting religioscapes, referring to the ways in which different religious communities, and their physical manifestations, intersect in a particular geographical space and through time."

35 For the HERA research project "Iconic religion," see http://new.heranet.info/icorel/index.

Applying the notion of iconicity to interpret the religious repurposing of the synagogue of The Hague into the present Al Aksa Mosque, we notice a very similar pattern. Even more, the Al Aksa Mosque seems to have been conceived as an iconic building by the Muslim congregants from a fairly early stage in its "conversion" trajectory: the building, and the way it was acquired, is closely connected with the identity of the community, and with their visibility as a group. Using the two major aspects of "iconic fields" as coined by Beekers and Tamimi Arab, i.e., spatial and temporal relations, we can distinguish the following points in the documentary *Facing East*.

– The naming of the mosque involves relations within its (temporal) iconic field that span the history of the building, which includes its former function as a synagogue, the way the building was obtained (by squatting) and more recent developments in the self-perception of the mosque. The reason given in the documentary, by one of the original squatters, for the first name of the building when it became a mosque, i.e., "Fatih," was that it was called thus because it was "conquered" by the squatters. It must be remarked that many mosques in the Netherlands bear the name "Fatih," and that their example is probably the Fatih mosque in Istanbul which received that name after sultan Fatih who conquered Constantinople.[36] Therefore, the choice for this name would not necessarily bear much meaning, were it not that, in this particular case, the former squatter in the documentary mentions the conquering-by-squatting as the explicit rationale for the first naming of mosque.[37] A "conquering" of the building from the Jews is not mentioned, and would also not stand to reason as the building was owned by the municipality at the time of the squatting. However, the renaming of the building as "Mescidi Aksa" does imply a direct relationship to "the" Jews. This relationship reflects the present rather than the past. The name "Aksa" is explicitly argued for, by the same former squatter, as a political statement because "the Jews have our Al Aksa in Jerusalem,"[38] and "they should not

---

36   See Beekers and Tamimi Arab, "Dreams of an Iconic Mosque," 147.

37   In Beekers and Tamimi Arab, "Dreams of an Iconic Mosque," 161 (n. 4), in discussing the naming of the Fatih mosque in Amsterdam, a reference is made to the presently discussed documentary *Facing East*, and the reasons given by the former squatter (conquering by squatting, and the "revenge" on the Jews for the so-called possession of the Al Aksa Mosque in Jerusalem). When Tamimi Arab suggests that the name does not match the (Amsterdam) mosque's intercultural and interreligious outreach activities, the interviewed man replied that changing the name would mean "giving in to Dutch social pressure on mosques."

38   This is incorrect because the Temple Mount is governed by the Waqf, which is controlled by the Jordanian government, an arrangement which is usually referred to as the "Status Quo."

be the boss." Thus, this naming contains an explicit element of revenge, not so much on the former Jewish occupants of the building as on present-day Jewry, which is often, as here, conflated with the state of Israel.

– The representative of the mosque states that they think that "God wanted that we receive the building." Just before, we heard the "testimony" of the former squatter that "the Jews came to congratulate us," and the suggestion that the Jews are happy that the building will at least be devoted to the one God. The combination of exactly these two points is also found on the Turkish version of the website of the Fatih mosque in Amsterdam, according to the informant of Beekers and Tamimi Arab. Also there, "divine will" is mentioned and, in this case of conversion of a building from a church into a mosque, a priest of the former "De zaaier" (The Sower, i.e., the former St. Ignace-church) was allegedly honoured that the building was again "serving religion."[39] This combination of divine will and human approval is typically invoked when the legitimacy of the ownership threatens to be questioned by outsiders or by critical insiders. A sign that this might also be the case in The Hague is the answer of the representative of the mosque when Naeeda Aurangzeb, the maker of the documentary, questions his appeal to divine will: "This is what I have heard from the people who were here at the time." In terms of the iconic place of the building in the interplay of the two religions, it is obvious that the new Muslim users (or at least their representatives in the documentary) see their use of the building as a continuation (or replacement?) of its former Jewish religious function. Interestingly, even the new rabbi employs similar reasoning as he implies that the conversion of the building into a mosque is at least better than a commercial repurposing would have been.

– The conversion of the building from a synagogue into a mosque involved not only, as in the case of the Fatih Mosque in Amsterdam, an extensive refurbishing on the inside, but also the creation of a drastically different exterior. This included removing the Hebrew signs on the facade and replacing them by texts in Arabic, as well as the name of the mosque and the placement of Turkish and Dutch flags. Moreover, two minarets were

---

39   See Beekers and Tamimi Arab, "Dreams of an Iconic Mosque," 148 and n. 4. Beekers and Tamimi Arab quote an informant: "To clarify this, he quoted from the Turkish version of the mosque's website, which states that the purchase of The Sower was not only made possible by the initiative of the 'Turkish elders' but also by 'Divine Will.' The website recounts the story of a priest of the former The Sower who came to the mosque and said that he was honoured that the building was once again serving religion." Apparently the website has changed by the time of writing this paper, because I cannot find the referenced words.

erected. Since the latter were already part of the reconstruction plans from the beginning, it appears that the Mescidi Aksa in The Hague was construed as an iconic building by its new owners since the earliest stages of its conversion trajectory.

- The fact that the Mescidi Aksa seems to have been construed as a Muslim landmark in this neighbourhood from its very beginning may be related to the transformations in the entire neighbourhood since the 1950s. Indeed, this area evolved from a predominantly Jewish area into a culturally mixed shopping area, that also features, e.g., a newly erected Chinese gate. Also the latter can be identified as yet another "iconic shape" in this cityscape.

- The neighbours that are interviewed, none of them Muslim or Jewish, relate in different ways to the new iconicity of the building. Some refer to features of the building itself, mostly the minarets, others to the way it came to be a new, Muslim, icon in their neighbourhood. In a more or, often, less politically correct way they refer to the sound of the *adhan*, the Muslim call for prayer,[40] and the way the building was allegedly purchased for only one guilder ("and then they even demanded that the roof was fixed before"). Some seem to mourn the loss of the Jewish character of the street, but most disapprove of the general transformation of the neighbourhood by various immigrant groups, including the Turks and the Chinese.

- The construction of a playground that doubles as Jewish children's monument in the neighbourhood was not an initiative of the Muslims. It was designed by a Dutch and an Israeli artist and officially unveiled in 2006.[41] The square where the playground was erected, the Rabbijn Maarsenplein, is named after Isaac Maarsen, who was the chief rabbi of The Hague from 1925 to 1943, when he perished, as did his entire family, in a concentration camp in the Shoah. The square, which constituted the heart of the former Jewish quarter, contains several other Jewish memorial sites. The obvious reason for the erection of such monuments is to keep the Jewish memory of the place visibly alive. That this has its desired effect is proven by the testimony of the presenter that she always feels very sad when she walks by the playground, and cannot stop thinking about all those children who disappeared. Similarly, in a fragment at the end of the documentary not quoted above, the artist who designed the playground monument says: "Something needed to come back; this place has a history." About the present mosque

---

40   This is not found in the selected passages presented here. In the documentary, an elderly long-time inhabitant of the neighbourhood refers to the "racket" made by the call to prayer from the "towers," which was now fortunately "taken care of."

41   See http://www.joodskindermonument.nl/.

she says: "I cannot just enter there, it touches me." This monument too is a factor in the iconic interplay of the building, now a mosque, then a synagogue, with its environment, past and present.

- The making of the documentary is for Naeeda Aurangzeb a way of coping with the changed iconic field of the building, and of using this as a means to broadcast awareness, to teach history in the hope that people learn from it. At the end of the documentary she asks, rhetorically: "Is it a loss that we no longer know what was before us? ... Is it correct that I want to give a voice to the other story?"

7 Conclusions: Iconic Field and Holiness

Anthropological studies provide us with a broad concept of holiness that is related more to emotions than to rules. The notion of "iconic field," as used by Beekers and Tamimi Arab, serves as a valuable tool to grasp the various factors at work in the emotional reactions of old and new congregants, and neighbours, with respect to the repurposing of religious buildings, in the presently studied case from synagogue to mosque. The notion of persistent "holiness" mentioned by some with respect to repurposed religious buildings can also be seen as a factor in this iconic interplay which connects, in its temporal scope, past to present. This "lay" concept of holiness transcends the borders between religions. Thus a former congregant relates to a lingering Catholic sense of holiness, felt as "incense absorbed by the walls" in a dance studio established in a former church.[42] Naaeda Aurangzeb, who affirms in the documentary that she is a Muslim, feels the "ghosts of the Jewish people who came to pray here" in the present mosque.

Some of these emotional associations of holiness have also crept into halakhic texts, as is evident from the opinion of Rabbi Yehudah, recorded in the Mishnah, that even a desolated synagogue still contains holiness. From the

---

42 See Beekers and Tamimi Arab, "Dreams of an Iconic Mosque," 181. Beekers recalls similar remarks by a Muslim neighbour of the Fatih mosque in Amsterdam, a converted Catholic church: "It gave me a strange feeling ... As if you are praying and ... another god watches along. It made me wonder if I was busy *mosquisizing* the building. This felt as a kind of sacrilege. As if I was stealing something from the Christians." Beekers remarks that this negative experience was exceptional among the Muslim congregants of the Amsterdam Fatih mosque. The others, conversely, found it beautiful that the building remained a house of prayer. "But," Beekers writes, "what was often heard was the feeling that something of the previous use of the building lingers on." See Verkaaik, Beekers, and Tamimi Arab, *Gods huis in de steigers*, 197.

cases of the repurposed church in Beekers's study, and the repurposed synagogue in the documentary, it shows that emotions of people do not necessarily
coincide with official rulings: people, even "neighbours" that are not immediately connected to the history of the building, may feel holiness when the
Church officials or the Jewish authorities have in fact ruled that its holiness
has been removed.

References

Beekers, Daan, and Pooyan Tamimi Arab. "Dreams of an Iconic Mosque: Spatial and
Temporal Entanglements of a Converted Church in Amsterdam." *Material Religion*
12 (2016): 137–64.

Danby, Herbert. *The Mishnah*. Oxford: Clarendon, 1933. Repr., Oxford: Oxford University
Press, 1991.

Epstein, Isidore. *The Babylonian Talmud*. London: Soncino, 1978.

Fine, Steven. *This Holy Place: On the Sanctity of the Synagogue During the Greco-Roman
Period*. Notre Dame: University of Notre Dame Press, 1997.

Glaudemans, Corien. "Op zoek naar de ark: De geschiedenis van de Heilige Arke of
Aron Hakodesj van de Grote Synagoge in de Wagenstraat." *Jaarboek Die Haghe 2015*
(2015): 127–51.

Glaudemans, Corien. "De Heilige Arke van de Grote Synagoge in de Wagenstraat."
28 January 2017, https://www.joodserfgoeddenhaag.nl/de-heilige-arke-van-de-grote
-synagoge-in-de-wagenstraat/.

Hayden, Robert M., and Timothy D. Walker. "Intersecting Religioscapes: A Comparative
Approach to Trajectories of Change, Scale, and Competitive Sharing of Religious
Spaces." *Journal of the American Academy of Religion* 81 (2013): 399–426.

Krupp, Michael. *Megilla: Rolle*. Die Mischna: Textkritische Ausgabe mit deutscher
Übersetzung und Kommentar. Jerusalem: Lee Achim, 2002.

Levine, Lee I. *The Ancient Synagogue: The First Thousand Years*. New Haven: Yale
University Press, 2000.

Nederlandse Bisschoppenconferentie. "Het kerkgebouw als getuige van de christe-
lij-ke traditie: Uitgangspunten van beleid voor kerkgebouwen." 2008. https://www
.rkdocumenten.nl/rkdocs/index.php?mi=600&doc=6509.

Protestantse Kerk in Nederland. "Een Protestantse visie op het kerkgebouw met
een praktisch theologisch oormerk: Discussienota van de Protestantse Kerk in
Nederland." 2009. http://www.kerkelijkwaardebeheer.nl/wp-content/uploads/
protestantse-visie-op-het-kerkgebouw.pdf.

Verkaaik, Oskar, Daan Beekers, and Pooyan Tamimi Arab. *Gods huis in de steigers:
Religieuze gebouwen in ontwikkeling*. Amsterdam: Amsterdam University Press, 2017.

Voolen, Edward van, Paul Meijer, and Hans van Agt. *Synagogen van Nederland*.
Zutphen: Walburg, 2006.

CHAPTER 17

Sacred Stones: Literary and Folkloric Representations of the Remains of the Holy Temple

Vered Tohar

Stones play a central role in the three monotheistic religions in local legends whose theme is sacred space. The purpose of this article is to note some of the representations of the stone in sacred space in the Jewish narrative tradition, as well as to draw attention to some of its parallels in Islam and Christianity. In all these narrative traditions, both Jewish and non-Jewish, stones have a function in giving presence to the sanctity residual in a place, in the marking of the sacred place, and in creating a connection between the sacred place and other holy places in that culture.

In particular, I will focus on the three-way relationship between the stone—the city of Jerusalem—the Temple and their abstract manifestations in the stories that describe them, which can be defined as: sacred object—sacred space—sacred structure. The sacred structure is built of sacred objects and is located in the sacred space, and reciprocally: the sacred space makes the building sacred as well as the objects of which it is built.

This triangular connection exists in the Jewish narrative tradition, which describes two temporal states: the first state begins with the creation of the world until the construction of the Temple and the period when it stood. The second temporal state is from the time of the destruction of the Temple until the end of days. The crisis event between these two periods of time is the traumatic destruction of the Temple.

In all the narrative traditions, a clear distinction is made between what happened before the crisis and what happens after it, particularly with regard to the sacred object, i.e., the stone, which influences and is influenced by the structure and the space. Thus, for example, before the destruction the stone is stationary and located in Jerusalem on Mount Moriah. After the destruction, the stone is mobile and travels through many places along with the communities of the exiles. The characteristic of mobility that the stone takes on turns it into an emblem of the Jewish people wandering in exile. Likewise, before the destruction, the stone is of one piece. After the destruction, the single stone splits into many stones. The metaphor of this split also represents the fate of the Jewish people.

As for the genre, the narrative traditions that we describe here are, according to their type, place legends or "local legends." Local legends are a folkloric literary genre that indicates a narrative tradition created around a group's focus of interest that exists in space, is connected to this space, and is disseminated and preserved by the group living around this focus of interest. Local legends are created around a unique natural phenomenon or object that attracts attention in an unusual way. The most obvious example of local legends are etiological legends which explain the formation of an unusual phenomenon in nature, custom, or belief. Local legends are always tied to a certain tradition or culture, although their motifs can migrate from one narrative tradition to another.[1] The emergent local legends influence religious behaviour and perception. This suggests that local legends work in both directions: on the one hand, they are created out of religious perceptions, and on the other, they take part in the emergence of religious behaviour.[2]

1   Representations of the Stone before the Destruction of the Temple

Many Jewish texts link a stone to myths of creation and origin. The stone has a semiotic status as a sacred object in tradition as well as presence in central genesis legends: the creation of the world, the creation of man, the institution of the ancient Israelite monarchy, and the covenant between the people of Israel and God. In other words, the narrative traditions link the events of creation with central episodes in the life of the forefathers of the nation and with defining events in the history of the people. The traditions link all these events to the presence of one single stone from which everything came and to which everything will return. It is the stone that is located on Mount Moriah and is called "the Foundation Stone" (אבן השתיה, 'even ha-shtiya), inside which the entire land of Israel is folded up, and it is both the source of the world and its centre.[3]

We will deal here with some of these traditions, beginning with early rabbinic sources. According to the Mishnah, in the First Temple the ark of the covenant was placed on this foundation stone.[4] In the Second Temple, on

---

1 John Lindow, *Swedish Legends and Folktales* (Orlando: University of California Press, 1978), 27; Linda Degh, "What is a Belief Legend?" *Folklore* 107 (1996): 33–46.

2 Sabina Magliocco, "Religious Practice," in *A Companion to Folklore*, ed. Regina F. Bendix and Galit Hasan-Rokem (Malden MA: Wiley Blackwell, 2012), 136–53 (150).

3 In Hebrew, the term used for foundation, שתיה, also signifies absorption of liquids, as well as underpinning and basis.

4 m. Yoma 5:2.

Yom Kippur the High Priest would place the firepan with the incense on this stone and also sprinkled the blood of the sacrifices in front of the stone.[5] In the Babylonian Talmud it is written: "There was a stone from the days of the first prophets, and it was called 'foundation' [שתיה, *shtiya*, VT], and from it the world was founded."[6] In other words, the whole world was created from one stone. According to the Babylonian Talmud, the foundation stone is so named because this was the foundation place of the world, i.e., the creation of the world began from this place.[7]

Later texts from the Geonic period and onward also reflect a dominant presence of this myth in the Jewish ethos: Pirqe Rabbi Eliezer mentions that the great fish brings Jonah under the foundation stone and there he prays for salvation,[8] and also connects this place to the Garden of Eden and to Adam's grave.[9] The Zohar states that the foundation stone is located on Mount Moriah, and that it is the place where Jacob laid his head and dreamed of the ladder ascending heavenward, where the binding of Isaac took place, and where the Temple will be established one day.[10] This Zoharic tradition, therefore, links three defining events in the history of the nation with one stone located precisely in the same place where the three events transpired. Yalqut Shimoni connects the stone to the dream of Jacob: "It is written about Jacob: 'And he took the stone which he had placed under his head' ... Therefore, it is called the foundation stone, because it is the centre [navel, VT] of the land, and from there the entire land extends, and upon it is the sanctuary."[11] This tradition connects the place where Jacob had his dream of the ladder to the centre of the world—the ladder on which the angels climb begins in the kingdom of heaven and ends in the depths of the earth, a kind of transcendent opening to the higher worlds.

---

5   m. Yoma 5:2.

6   b. Yoma 53b–54a.

7   b. Yoma 54b. See also Shulamit Laderman, *Images of Cosmology in Jewish and Byzantine Art* (Leiden: Brill 2013), 221–22.

8   Pirqe R. El. 10. See also Rachel Adelman, "Midrash, Myth and Bakhtin's Chronotope: The Itinerant Well and the Foundation Stone in 'Pirke de-Rabbi Eliezer," *Journal of Jewish Thought & Philosophy* 17 (2009): 143–76.

9   See Adiel Kadari, "Interreligious Aspects in the Narrative of the Burial of Adam in Pirke de-Rabbi Eliezer," in *Religious Stories in Transformation: Conflict, Revision and Reception,* ed. Alberdina Houtman et al. (Leiden: Brill, 2016), 82–103 (95–96, nn. 42, 43).

10   Zohar on Vayeitze.

11   Yal. Shimoni to Gen 18:28.

In the Islamic tradition, too, there are very similar references to a stone as the source and origin of all, in keeping with Batsheva Garsiel's contention about the copying of religious motifs from Judaism to Islam precisely because they are familiar to the audience addressed by Muhammed.[12] The stone is called in Arabic "el Zahra," i.e., the centre of the world. All the rivers, clouds, and winds emerge from under the rock in Jerusalem, and everyone who prays is rewarded with absolution of all his sins and offenses. This is the place where Muhammad ascended to heaven. This is the place from which the four rivers of Paradise emerged, and it was there that Adam was created. On the Day of Judgment, the Foundation Stone and the Kaaba (كَعبَة) in Mecca will be united. The Foundation Stone is located today in the Al-Aqsa mosque. Another tradition calls this stone "the stone of ascent," referring to the rock on the Temple Mount where Islamic tradition states that Muhammad ascended to heaven and where the Jewish Temple was built. There is water under the rock.[13]

Another name for the stone in Hebrew is 'even ha-rosha (אבן הראשה, "key-stone") or 'even ha-pina (אבן הפינה, "cornerstone"), a term that indicates both the highest in the sense of importance and also the first, the beginning. It likewise refers technically to the most important stone which bears all the weight of the structure. In Zech 4:7 in the prophetic vision of the menorah, the prophet tells of a stone that he sees as the stone to be placed first in the Temple, and he calls it "the keystone." According to this vision, this is the most important stone of the structure.[14] The image of the cornerstone was also borrowed by Christianity, where Jesus accepts the metaphorical role of this stone.[15]

---

12 Batsheva Garsiel, *Bible, Midrash and Quran: An Intertextual Study of Common Narrative Materials* (Tel Aviv: Hakibbutz Hameuchad 2006) (Hebrew).

13 Aviva Schussman, *The Stories of the Prophets: Muhammad ibn Allah al-Kisai* (Tel Aviv: The Haim Rubin Tel Aviv University Press, 2013), 364 (Hebrew). I thank Dr Yoel Peretz for this reference.

14 One cannot ignore the other aspect of the cornerstone, which is the stone that was postponed, the stone which the constructors did not want, as in Ps 118:22. See also Michael Cahill, "Not a Cornerstone! Translating Ps 118,22 in the Jewish and Christian Scriptures," *RevB* 106 (1999): 345–57.

15 The expression is: "Christ the Cornerstone," and it is based on 1 Pet 2:6–7. See also Klyne Snodgrass, "1 Peter 2:1–10: Its Formation and Literary Affinities," *NTS* 24 (1977): 97–106. See also the rite called "the blessing of the foundation stone for building of a church": Thomas G. Simons, *Holy People, Holy Place: Rites for the Church's House* (Chicago: Liturgy Training Publications, 1999), 59–63.

According to Zech 3:9 God will guard this stone with special vigilance as well as the rest of the structure.[16]

However, both the Jewish and the Muslim tradition deal with one fixed stone located on what we now identify as the Temple Mount. It is important to note that this stone has been given many different names: the stone of drinking, the keystone, the centre of the world—and that these names indicate its sanctity and importance. It is the stone that precedes the structure. It marks out the sacred place and imbues it with its sanctity. It is the primal stone untouched by mortal hand and is the repository of all worlds. It is the interface between this world and the world beyond it. It is the stone that has accompanied all the important events in the life of the people ever since the creation of the world and the establishment of the nation.[17]

2   Representations of the Stone after the Destruction of the Temple

In the narrative traditions that deal with the time after the destruction, the stone changes. It is still perceived as a sacred object, but it undergoes a transformation in its function, in its physical properties, and in its placement. After the destruction of the Temple, its stones continue to accrue sanctity. Therefore, the second reason for the importance of the stone is the symbolic metonymic relationship of the stone with the Temple and Jewish fate.

A key development in the stories about the ruins of the Temple is the transformation of the role of the stone to become the foundation stone of a new synagogue. That is, one sacred structure is dismantled, and its holiness

---

16   There is also a connection associated with the specifically Jewish narrative tradition between "stone," "Jerusalem," and the number five. See, for example, Adonizedek, King of Jerusalem, and the five kings of the Amorites fighting Joshua, as God hurls great stones at them from the sky (Josh 10:11). David chooses five smooth stones, driving one stone into Goliath's forehead, and then David brings his severed head to Jerusalem (1 Sam 17:40–54). Rabbi Chanina ben Dosa brings a stone to Jerusalem with the help of five angels who take the shape of human beings (Eccl. Rab. 1; Song of Songs Rab. 1). There is also a connection between "stone" and the number 12: according to Targum Jonathan to parashat Tetzaveh, the twelve stones of the breastplate paralleling the twelve tribes of Israel were scattered and then united in the robe of the High Priest. The twelve stones of the tribes were brought together to erect the altar of Joshua.

17   See also the discussion by Mary Douglas about the cultural concepts of sanctity: *Purity and Danger: An Analysis of Concepts of Pollution and Taboo* (London: Routledge, 1966).

is dispersed by means of its stones.[18] Sanctity separates itself from the sacred space and moves out into new spaces, where it repositions itself.[19]

Here one can find two groups of stories. The first group is a small one, containing local legends about a stone from the Temple that travelled from its original site, Mount Moriah, to become the basis of a new synagogue within the land of Israel. The second, and larger, group comprises local legends about a stone from the Temple that wandered with the Jewish exiles and became the basis of a synagogue outside the land of Israel.[20]

As for the synagogues in the land of Israel, there are many known versions about the synagogue in Peqi'in (פקיעין). Zeev Vilnay cites one such story. The locals tell that close to the Holy Ark are two hewn stones lying on their side. Engraved on one are a menorah, lulav, etrog, and shofar; on the second is engraved the Holy Ark. According to the legend these stones are from the Temple that were brought there by the exiles and were deliberately placed on their side

---

18   The splitting of the stones of the Temple after the destruction is in contrast to the gathering of stones before the destruction; the twelve individual stones which represent the Twelve Tribes and form the breastplate of the High Priest: "And the stones were according to the names of the children of Israel, twelve, according to their names, like the engravings of a signet, every one according to his name, for the twelve tribes" (Exod 39:14), and the twelve stones of the tribes from which Joshua formed the first altar in the land of Israel: "And the children of Israel did as Joshua commanded, and took up twelve stones out of the midst of the Jordan, as the Lord spoke unto Joshua, according to the number of the tribes of the children of Israel; and they carried them over with them unto the place where they lodged, and laid them down there. Joshua also set up twelve stones in the midst of the Jordan, in the place where the feet of the priests that bore the ark of the covenant stood; and they are there unto this day" (Josh 4:8–9). The first example is already in Sinai, in Exod 24:4: "And Moses wrote all the words of the LORD and rose up early in the morning and built an altar under the mount and twelve pillars according to the twelve tribes."

19   In this regard, I would like to point out that there is an actual geological phenomenon known as "sailing stones," "walking rocks," "rolling stones," or moving rocks, which is observed in the Sahara Desert and in Death Valley in California. This refers to stones moving spatially, sometimes a very great distance, seemingly by themselves and without any external intervention. Although the phenomenon can be explained scientifically, it is still relevant here because the narrative traditions describe exactly the same phenomenon but clothe it in an aura of sanctity. It is also interesting that the geological phenomenon and the narrative traditions presented here are not common to the same cultural space.

20   Wandering stones appear also in rabbinic legends as part of the procedure of building. God sends Rabbi Hanina ben Dosa five angels in the form of human beings who will bring up a stone to Jerusalem for him (Eccl. Rab. 1; Song of Songs Rab. 1). And likewise Rabbi Berachia said "The verse does not say 'the house they were building' but rather 'the house while it was in building.' It was being built by itself" (Song of Songs Rab. 1). See also note 16 above.

as a sign of the destruction. The exiles ordered their descendants to turn the stones upright when the Temple is rebuilt.[21]

This trend of creating a link to stones in a building that no longer exists continues into the mid-20th century. Shmuel Zanvil Kahane, who was director-general of the Israeli Ministry of Religious Affairs after the Six-Day War and who dealt in particular with developing the holy sites in Israel, writes in his memoirs that when the Committee for Mount Zion began to deal with the mount, its members considered what to do with the huge piles of stones they found there. In the end, it was decided to use them as the foundation stones for new synagogues and houses of study in order to unite Torah institutions around Mount Zion, which would serve as a spiritual centre. This is a case of where it is the group that decides to disperse sacred stones from their original site in order to create sanctity for new places of worship but to maintain the original site as a spiritual centre.[22]

The second group of stories is a group of local legends which were created around synagogues outside the borders of the land of Israel. These legends were already documented in the 10th century and continued to be copied or printed throughout medieval and modern times and refer to synagogues in many different regions of Europe, North Africa, and the Middle East.

In the 10th century, Rav Sharira Gaon writes: "When Israel went into exile, Yehoyachin [Yechania, VT] and the craftsmen and the metalworkers and some prophets with them were brought to Nehardea, and Yehoyachin, the King of Judah and his faction built the synagogue and established its groundwork with stones and earth that they brought with them from the Temple."[23] Rashi, in his 11th-century commentary on the Talmud, shows that he is familiar with this narrative tradition by saying: "Yechania and his exile took with them of the stones and earth of Jerusalem and built it up there."[24]

We find a similar motif in the *Travels of Rabbi Petachia*, which is attributed to Rabbi Petachia of Ratisbon (Regensburg), one of the Jewish travelers in the Middle Ages. In the year 1180, Rabbi Petachia writes that in the city of Nisibis (Nusaybin) in Turkey on the Syrian border stands the synagogue built by Ezra the scribe with a red stone set on the wall of the synagogue; this is a stone that

21   Cited in Haim Schwarzbaum, "The Synagogue via Folk Legend," *Mahanayim* 95 (1965): 58–65 (61) (Hebrew).

22   *Kema'ayan ha-mitgaber* (ed. S.Z. Kahane).

23   Binyamin Menashe Levin, *The Letter of Rav Sharira Gaon* (Haifa: Golda Itzakovski, 1921), 72 (Hebrew).

24   Rashi to b. ʿAbod. Zar. 43b.

Ezra took with him from the stones of the Temple.[25] Then, in the 12th century, the traveller Benjamin of Tudela writes in his travelogue: "And there is the synagogue that Israel [the Jews, VT] built of the earth and stones of Jerusalem."[26]

Apparently the most famous legend, with the greatest number of documented versions, deals with the old synagogue of Prague, also known as "Altneuschul." Here is the text of the legend as it appears in Yehoshua Wolf Zikernik's anthology:

> After the destruction, the angels carried on their wings stones from the Temple and placed them in the Jewish quarter of Prague, and the synagogue was built upon them. The synagogue was named "Al Tnai Schule" [על תנאי, "on condition," VT] to note that when the Temple in Jerusalem will be rebuilt, this synagogue would no longer be necessary. In subsequent generations, the Hebrew phrase *Al Tnai* was garbled, and it became known as the *Alt Neu Schule* [the "old-new synagogue" in German, VT].[27]

Comparable legends are found about synagogues built in Arab countries. Nahum Slosatz documents a local legend of a synagogue on the island of Djerba in Tunisia, and the text is as follows: "The synagogue was built by a family of *kohanim* [כהנים, 'priests,' VT] who fled during the destruction of the First Temple and managed to save one of the Temple's doors from the flames. This door served as the door of the synagogue that was built on the island and then sank into the ground."[28] Another legend was documented in print in the 20th century about the synagogue in Baghdad: "In the Great Synagogue of Baghdad near the main entrance is a stone bearing the inscription: 'a stone from the land of Israel.'"[29]

Additional evidence of the relationship of the exiles to the sacred stones is also found in narrative traditions connected to the expulsion of Jews from Spain and Portugal. Those narratives emphasize the loyalty of the stones to the Jewish people, wandering with them from one exile to another, sharing

---

25   Rabbi Petachia of Regensburg, *Travels of Rabbi Petachia* (London: Jewish Chronicle, 1856), 8.

26   Rabbi Benjamin of Tuleda, *The Travels of Rabbi Benjamin of Tuleda* (Lemberg: Schneider, 1853), 46.

27   Yehoshua Wolf Zikernik, *Sippurim Nechmadim* (Zhitomer: Kesselman, 1903), 7. Also cited by Micha Joseph Bin Gorion (Berdichevsky), *Minekor Yisrael* (Tel Aviv: Dvir, 1938), 127.

28   Nahum Slouschz, *The Island of Wonders* (Tel Aviv: Dvir, 1957), 97 (Hebrew).

29   Cited by Zeev Vilnay, *Legends of the Land of Israel* (Jerusalem: Qiriyat Sefer, 1959), 116 (Hebrew). The tradition is based on the Babylonian Talmud; see Vilnay, *Legends*, 213 (n. 13).

the same destiny: "The exiles from Portugal, after being expelled from their country, remove stones from the synagogues and carry them with them to their new places of exile, where they sank those stones into the building of new synagogues."[30]

Tales about the Temple stone are also found in the oral folklore that was documented in the 20th century. A contemporary oral folktale tells about Rabbi Joseph Chaim of Baghdad, who emigrated to the land of Israel in 1868. After his aliyah, he returned to Baghdad for a visit, bearing stones and earth from the Holy Land which he placed at the entrance to the Great Synagogue of Baghdad. This synagogue was built by Yehoiakim, the last of the kings of Judah, from stones brought from the land of Israel.[31] This folktale, and other tales which incorporate the same theme, are based on rabbinic traditions about the holiness of the earth, any soil, from the Holy Land, called 'afar me-eretz yisrael (עפר מארץ ישראל), which is a variation on the motif of the stone from the land of Israel.[32] Indeed, the sanctity idea of the soil of the land of Israel, which serves as the basis for a sacred structure, already exists in the Bible: the prophet Elisha cures Naaman of leprosy, who in return takes two mules loaded with earth to build an altar to God: "And Naaman said: 'If not, yet I pray thee let there be given to thy servant two mules' burden of earth; for thy servant will henceforth offer neither burnt-offering nor sacrifice unto other gods, but unto the Lord'" (2 Kgs 5:17).

The idea of the stone that moves itself is also found in Song of Songs Rabbah in the context of the building of the Temple:

> Rabbi Berachia said: "The house that they build." The meaning here is "the house, while it was in building" (1 Kgs 6:7)—the house was built by itself, as it is written: "was built of stone made ready at the quarry" (1 Kgs 6:7). This teaches that the stone carried itself and placed itself on the layer [of stones, VT]. Rav said: "Do not be astonished at this. Regarding what it is written below: 'And a stone was brought, and laid upon the mouth of the den'" (Dan 6:18). And were the stones from Babylon? Rather, [they were] from the land of Israel.[33]

The author of Song of Songs Rabbah, therefore, links the story of the construction of the Temple to the stone that sealed the den in which Daniel was placed,

30   Shmuel Yosef Fin, *Kiria Neemana* (Vilna: Rom, 1860), 65.

31   The Israeli archive of folk literature no. 1680, told by Shimon Ernst from Iraq.

32   See, e.g., b. Meg. 29a.

33   See note 16 above.

which was also a sacred stone brought from Jerusalem, and it alludes to the rescue of Daniel.[34]

The concept of the transportability of buildings also has parallels in the repertoire of the world folk narrative; for example, in medieval folk narrative there is also a tale-type which is connected to the corner stone idea, as found in Tubach 4638: "Stones offered for foundation." This medieval legend tells about a citizen who offers great stones for the foundation of the church of the apostles.[35]

International folkloric indexes also contain parallels of this theme, but have a completely different flavour. I shall note here two main variations of the international tale-type. The first is AT 1325 B[36] (Uther 1325 B[37]), titled: "Moving the Church Away from the Dung." This tale-type's plot tells that on the way to church, a priest notices that one of his cows is relieving itself on the church wall. He runs to the municipal council, and they all decide to move the church away from the dirt. They tie a rope around the church and begin to pull the building. On the other side a boy secretly shovels the dirt away from the wall. The priest and the councilmen are sure that they have managed to pull the church away from the dirt, and everyone has done his duty. The second is AT 1326 (Uther 1326[38]), titled: "Moving the Church." This tale-type tells about fools who want to move their church. To mark their starting point, they put down a coat. While the fools are pushing together against the wall, the coat is stolen by a stranger. When the fools see that the coat has disappeared, they feel happy about how far they have moved the church (J 2328).[39] Those two tale-types are part of the chapter: "The wise and the foolish" and are told as humorous tales or jokes.

The humoristic approach is also dominant in the following Jewish legend, a very unusual legend in comparison to the local legends cited before. The tale is as follows:

---

34   Cf. Louis Ginzberg, *The Legends of the Jews*, trans. Henrietta Szold, 6 vols. (Philadelphia: The Jewish Publication Society, 1909–1938; repr., Jerusalem: Schechter Institute, 2009), 6:118.

35   Frederich Tubach, *Index exemplorum: A Handbook of Medieval Religious Tales* (Helsinki: Suomalainen Tiedeakatemia, 1969), 4638.

36   Antti Aarne, *The Types of the Folktale*, trans. Stith Thompson (Helsinki: Suomalainen Tiedeakatemia, 1961), 1325B.

37   Hans Jörg Uther, *The Types of International Folktales: A Classification and Bibliography based on the System of Antti Aarne and Stith Thompson* (Helsinki: Suomalainen Tiedeakatemia, 2004), 127.

38   Uther, *The Types of International Folktales*, 128.

39   Stith Thompson, *Motif Index of Folk Literature* (Bloomington: Indiana University Press, 1966), J2328 (p. 204).

The Eishishok synagogue was built without a floor to save money. Once a *darshan* [דרשן, "travelling preacher," VT] came to the town and saw the condition of the synagogue. After the prayers, he says: "You all should know that when the Messiah comes, when all the Jews are congregated in their synagogues, and the two archangels Raphael and Gabriel lift up all the synagogues on their shoulders, transferring all the Jews assembled in the synagogues to the Land of Israel, you, the Jews in the floorless synagogue, will stay on Lithuanian soil while the walls of your synagogue are lifted."[40]

This is a humoristic tale, with a double moralistic message. The first is, of course, about the pitiful condition of the synagogue. But the second moral is serious. It implies that the Jews who are not in the synagogue when the Messiah comes will not be saved. This message is directed to Jews who show disrespect towards the practice of regular prayer as a way of life. It shows that the exile is temporary, but it could become permanent as punishment for living a secular life. This humorous legend is, in fact, based on the following Midrash: "Legend recounts: 'When the Holy One, blessed be He, destroyed the Temple, tens of thousands of ministering angels came to the site of the Temple, took its stones and dispersed them all over the world'." But the Yiddish legend takes the idea of the angels carrying the synagogue and uses it, in effect, to rebuke the Jews in the community who stopped coming regularly to the synagogue.

3   The Symbolic and Archetypal Significance of the Wandering Stone: the Stone, the House, and the City

The stone usually teaches the human being what stability, durability, and endurance are.[41] Stones had become symbols of greatness and divinity by being so close and yet, so puzzling.

Often human beings were witnesses to rocks falling from the sky, which today we call meteorites, or rockfalls from great mountains, natural phenomena which they could not explain with the science available to them and therefore gave explanations for them based on faith and religion. Since stones were the raw material for early weapons and tools, they gained the status of possessing divine powers and knowledge. Moreover, stones were the source of fire, so

---

40   Haim Schwarzbaum, *Studies in Jewish and World Folklore* (Berlin: De Gruyter, 1968), 190.

41   Maria Leach, ed., *Standard Dictionary of Folklore, Mythology and Legend* (New York: Funk and Wagnalls, 1949).

they were further credited with the ability to create fire out of nothing, engaging human society with a whole range of possibilities in a world where they could use fire for heating, cooking, worshipping, and warfare.

Until mankind learned to use iron, stones were the hardest material known to them. Stones enabled human civilizations to build massive structures for worship and for permanent housing. The practice of building centres of worship from huge stones has been known for thousands of years. Megalithic monuments, stone circles, and stone altars created a connotative link between stones and sanctity. Like the various types of menhirs and Hünengräber ("giants' graves"), they were presumably intended to assure that the nation would continue to benefit from the presence of deceased culture heroes. They also were thought to protect the nation's territory, which is highlighted by their elevated geographical location. Sometimes they represent the axis mundi.[42] The stone is a symbol of the presence of God. The most precious stones are those that were not fashioned by human hands, and these have earned special prestige.

This view was also articulated by Erich Neumann, when he demonstrated the dispersal of an archetypal idea through many different tangible expressions.[43] This view is not unique to Judaism. In many cultures the stone is a symbol of divine powers because of its durability, which makes the stone appear immortal, timeless, and everlasting. Stones also seem to be infinite in number, because of their ability to split into fragments that have the same physiognomies as their source and become autonomous objects on their own.

Stone is non-representable. It represents a place that is a not a place, a structure that is not a structure, a structure that is actually a substitute for another structure. It is the concept of a sanctity that cannot be attained; it is not tangible but rather transcendental. The consciousness in these stories is one of a split: the ability to split the whole without damaging it while creating replicas of it. The stones split off from the whole creating an illusion of weakness, but this is in fact the quality of eternality, of eternal life, of immortality.[44]

This meaning is connected to the custom of placing stones on graves. Jewish visitors to cemeteries place small stones on the gravesite to symbolize their respect for the dead, as if they are taking part in the actual burial. While in Christianity there is a custom of putting flowers on the grave, in Jewish thought

---

42   Hans Biedermann, *Dictionary of Symbols: Cultural Icons and the Meaning Behind Them*, trans. James Hulbert (Meridian: New York, 1994), 217.

43   Erich Neumann, *The Great Mother: An Analysis of the Archetype*, trans. Ralph Manheim (London: Routledge, 1955).

44   This meaning is close to the meaning that stones are given also in Egyptian, Greek, Roman, Irish and Nordic mythologies, as well as others.

flowers are finite, but stone is immortal. There is also an etymological reason, because embedded in the word "stone" in Hebrew (אבן) are the letters of the words "father" (אב) and "son" (בן), and so the stone symbolizes the eternal circle of life and the grave is part of the endless chain of generations. It is also a symbol for the land of Israel. When Jewish visitors came to the land of Israel, they took small stones back with them to their countries of residence. Then when someone died, they would bury with him some of the stones of the land of Israel to symbolize the connection to the Holy Land. The stone adds weight to the grave, as it secures it to the ground. From here, a connection is created between the Temple, the synagogue, and the cemetery. A circle of life and death, the life of this world and the eternal life of the world-to-come. This view is manifested in the pre-destruction legends.

After the destruction, the narrative traditions relating to the stones of the holy temple created a contradiction of form and matter. Instead of representing what is fixed and permanent, the stone, paradoxically, became a wandering element that is a metonymy for the wandering of the Jewish people.

The wandering stone represents both the connection to the land of Israel, the weight and the solidness as well as the lightness of the transition from space to space in a miraculous manner. The stone is not an inert lump but rather contains divine qualities. It conveys a soul, consciousness, it sustains history and a secret. The Temple became the emblem of the house. Thus, the wandering Jew takes his home with him on his back during the years of exile. If he cannot be in the land of Israel, he takes the land of Israel with him.

From a phenomenological perspective, a contemplation of the rock already contains the fate of its shattering. The stone preserves within it the sadness of destruction. It bears the memory of the whole that was part of it in the past.[45] That is why the stone is invincible, because it faces its destruction, as history shows, yet comes out of it in the shape of little fragments. As for the returning of the stone from the exile to Jerusalem at the end of days, this idea is also represented by folktales which are connected to the sacred stone. The miraculous movement of the stone represented by the stone is a movement of return. From Jerusalem to the diaspora and back from the soil of the diaspora to the soil of Jerusalem. A temple that has become a pile of stones is the whole that becomes broken. A stone that has become a synagogue is a broken thing that has become whole. This is an imaginary landscape. The Jew goes to the synagogue, but in his imagination he is going to the Temple in Jerusalem. At the end of times, the cornerstones of all the synagogues will re-unite back in Jerusalem.

---

45   Gaston Bachelar, *La terre et les rêveries de la volonté* (Paris: José Conti, 1948), 176–77.

The synagogue is a synecdoche of the Temple. This is so on the abstract level. There are thousands of synagogues. Therefore, a process has transpired of making the abstract concrete and dispersing the sanctity. This is the "Big Bang" of the Temple, when thousands of buildings were miraculously scattered throughout the world and set down in a place where a Jewish community was destined to be built, with the synagogue at its centre.

It is a perspective that guides the dispersion and gives it direction. A Jew will live in a place where there is a stone from Jerusalem or soil from the earth of Jerusalem. This is the justification for the existence of a Jewish community in that place. The community protects the remnant of the Temple by maintaining Jewish life around it. In this way, Jerusalem remains the holy place; the land of the diaspora will never be sacred because the synagogue carries the sanctity of Jerusalem inside it. This is a way to establish sanctity in a place where, in reality, there is no sanctity as well as a way to preserve the connection with the holy place. The holy place is Jerusalem, and the memory of the holy place is the glue that connects the communities and the people.

It was written: "Come and see how beloved the people of Israel are before God, that wherever they were exiled, the Shechinah [שכינה, 'divine presence,' VT] went with them."[46] This statement teaches that the structure is a spatial representation of a transcendental essence. The structure does not stand on its own merit but rather because of the essence attributed to it. This is actually a reincarnation, a resurrection. The stone does not die with its structure but is reborn as an incarnation and continues to play a role in the world. The folk legend emphasizes that the synagogue is a branch of the Temple, not only conceptually but also physically, whether the synagogue is located in the land of Israel or outside it.

The stone is a product of nature, and it is connected in popular thinking to Jerusalem as a geographical designation and to the sacred structure of the House of God, which is also home to believers in the metaphorical sense of the word. The stone, the house, and the city are feminine, moreover maternal, representations that are supposed to mark the stable, permanent, and eternal foundation of life. The traditions about the wandering stone, which is a synecdoche of the wandering house—bringing a touch of Jerusalem to every Jewish community in the diaspora—is the pragmatic incarnation of the wish to return to the centre of the world, to the first stone in the Jerusalem on earth.

The development of the triangle: Jerusalem—stone—house in traditions that represent the situation before and after the destruction is as follows: The Foundation Stone → many stones; one Jerusalem → many exiles; one Temple →

---

46   b. Meg. 29a. Compare with note 32 above.

many synagogues. On the abstract level, the narrative traditions portraying the situation before and after the destruction depict the transition from the concrete to the abstract and from the existing to the imagined. In terms of time: fixed → temporary. In terms of movement in space: static → mobile. In terms of the representation of holiness: concrete → metaphorical. These narrative traditions confirm a primeval connection between the concepts of holiness, space, and symbolic object in Jewish culture. However, the efforts by so many local legends to explain the existence of holiness in exile on foreign land only emphasizes the sense of alienation and isolation of those communities.

References

Aarne, Antti. *The Types of the Folktale*. Translated by Stith Thompson. Helsinki: Suomalainen Tiedeakatemia, 1961.

Adelman, Rachel. "Midrash, Myth and Bakhtin's Chronotope: The Itinerant Well and the Foundation Stone in 'Pirke de-Rabbi Eliezer'." *Journal of Jewish Thought & Philosophy* 17 (2009): 143–76.

Bachelar, Gaston. *La terre et les rêveries de la volonté*. Paris: José Conti, 1948.

Biedermann, Hans. *Dictionary of Symbols: Cultural Icons and the Meaning Behind Them*. Translated by James Hulbert. New York: Meridian, 1994.

Bin Gorion (Berdichevsky), Micha Joseph. *Minekor Yisrael*. Tel Aviv: Dvir, 1938.

Cahill, Michael. "Not a Cornerstone! Translating Ps 118,22 in the Jewish and Christian Scriptures." *RevB* 106 (1999): 345–57.

Degh, Linda. "What is a Belief Legend?" *Folklore* 107 (1996): 33–46.

Douglas, Mary. *Purity and Danger: An Analysis of Concepts of Pollution and Taboo*. London: Routledge, 1966.

Fin, Shmuel Yosef. *Kiria Neemana*. Vilna: Rom, 1860.

Garsiel, Batsheva. *Bible, Midrash and Quran: An Intertextual Study of Common Narrative Materials*. Tel Aviv: Hakibbutz Hameuchad, 2006. (Hebrew).

Ginzberg, Louis. *The Legends of the Jews*. Translated by Henrietta Szold. 6 vols. Philadelphia: The Jewish Publication Society, 1909–1938. Repr., Jerusalem: Schechter Institute, 2009.

Kadari, Adiel. "Interreligious Aspects in the Narrative of the Burial of Adam in Pirke de-Rabbi Eliezer." Pages 82–103 in *Religious Stories in Transformation: Conflict, Revision and Reception*. Edited by Alberdina Houtman, Tamar Kadari, Marcel J.H.M. Poorthuis, and Vered Tohar. Leiden: Brill, 2016.

Laderman, Shulamit. *Images of Cosmology in Jewish and Byzantine Art*. Leiden: Brill, 2013.

Leach, Maria, ed. *Standard Dictionary of Folklore, Mythology and Legend*. New York: Funk and Wagnalls, 1949.

Levin, Binyamin Menashe. *The Letter of Rav Sharira Gaon*. Haifa: Golda Itzakovski, 1921. (Hebrew).

Lindow, John. *Swedish Legends and Folktales*. Orlando: University of California Press, 1978.

Magliocco, Sabina. "Religious Practice." Pages 136–53 in *A Companion to Folklore*. Edited by Regina F. Bendix and Galit Hasan-Rokem. Malden MA: Wiley Blackwell, 2012.

Neumann, Erich. *The Great Mother: An Analysis of the Archetype*. Translated by Ralph Manheim. London: Routledge, 1955.

Rabbi Benjamin of Tuleda. *The Travels of Rabbi Benjamin of Tuleda*. Lemberg: Schneider, 1853.

Rabbi Petachia of Regensburg. *Travels of Rabbi Petachia*. London: Jewish Chronice, 1856.

Schussman, Aviva. *The Stories of the Prophets: Muhammad ibn Allah al-Kisai*. Tel Aviv: The Haim Rubin Tel Aviv University Press, 2013. (Hebrew).

Schwarzbaum, Haim. "The Synagogue via Folk Legend." *Mahanayim* 95 (1965): 58–65.

Schwarzbaum, Haim. *Studies in Jewish and World Folklore*. Berlin: De Gruyter, 1968.

Simons, Thomas G. *Holy People, Holy Place: Rites for the Church's House*. Chicago: Liturgy Training Publications, 1999.

Slouschz, Nahum. *The Island of Wonders*. Tel Aviv: Dvir, 1957. (Hebrew).

Snodgrass, Klyne. "1 Peter 2:1–10: Its Formation and Literary Affinities." *NTS* 24 (1977): 97–106.

Thompson, Stith. *Motif Index of Folk Literature*. Bloomington: Indiana University Press, 1966.

Tubach, Frederich. *Index exemplorum: A Handbook of Medieval Religious Tales*. Helsinki: Suomalainen Tiedeakatemia, 1969.

Uther, Hans Jörg. *The Types of International Folktales: A Classification and Bibliography based on the System of Antti Aarne and Stith Thompson*. Helsinki: Suomalainen Tiedeakatemia, 2004.

Vilnay, Zeev. *Legends of the Land of Israel*. Jerusalem: Qiriyat Sefer, 1959. (Hebrew).

Zikernik, Yehoshua Wolf. *Sippurim Nechmadim*. Zhitomer: Kesselman, 1903.

CHAPTER 18

Jerusalem as an Aposiopesis in Old and New Testament Texts

Archibald L.H.M. van Wieringen

Jerusalem has a prominent role in the Bible. A grand overview of the Old Testament itinerary has Jerusalem as its final destination: the journey of God's people, from Egypt to the promised land, and from the Babylonian Exile back to the promised land, focuses on Jerusalem. In a way, all biblical stories can be read as revolving around, and eventually leading to, Jerusalem.

However, Jerusalem is often present in these biblical texts without the mention of its proper name. This is realised in two ways:

– Jerusalem is made present by using an alternative expression that alludes to Jerusalem.
– Jerusalem is present because it is an obvious part of a certain technical expression.

In this paper, I will use the term "aposiopesis" for both forms.[1] From a synchronic point of view, I would like to discuss various texts from both the Old and New Testament and reflect on the meaning of the use of these aposiopeses.

1 Jerusalem as an Aposiopesis in the Abraham Cycle

The best-known example of an aposiopesis for Jerusalem in the Torah is the story of Gen 14.[2] After having travelled to the promised land in chapters 12–13, Abraham encounters Jerusalem in chapter 14, but without Jerusalem being

---

1 The expression "aposiopesis" is used in various ways, and therefore I give my own definition here. For its use in literary studies see, e.g., the first division "Figures Involving Omission" of E.W. Bullinger, *Figures of Speech Used in the Bible* (London: Spottiswoode, 1898; repr., Grand Rapids: Baker Book, 1968), especially 151–54. For its use in musicological studies see, e.g., Eliel Almeida Soares and Diósnio Machado Neto, "A Aposiopesis em André da Silva Gomes," in *SIMA 2015: IV Simpósio Internacional de Música na Amazônia*, ed. Jefferson Tiago De Souza Mendes Da Silva et al. (Boa Vista: UFRR, 2016), 337–48.

2 See among others Benno Jacob, *Das erste Buch der Tora: Genesis* (Berlin: Schocken, 1934; repr., New York: Ktav, n.y.), especially 378; J.A. Emerton, "The Site of Salem, the City of Melchizedek (Genesis xiv 18)," in *Studies in the Pentateuch*, ed. J.A. Emerton, VTSup 41 (Leiden: Brill, 1990), 45–71.

mentioned. The text contains many proper names, which is very confusing, and most of them are not very well-known. Fortunately, the text explains some of them by connecting them to a more familiar name. בֶּלַע (Bela) appears to be the well-known צֹעַר (Zoar), which plays a prominent role in the subsequent stories about Lot (Gen 19:22, 23, 30; already in 13:10). This is the reason that Bela is even explained twice: in verse 2 and in verse 8. עֵמֶק הַשִּׂדִּים (Valley of Siddim) appears to be the well-known יָם הַמֶּלַח (Salt Sea; verse 3), which also plays a role in the destruction of Lot's place of abode Sodom and Gomorrah (Gen 19:26). In Gen 14:17, the explanation of an unknown toponym occurs once again: עֵמֶק שָׁוֵה (the Valley of Shaveh) turns out to be עֵמֶק הַמֶּלֶךְ (the Valley of the King). This toponym, however, is not very well-known either, because it is further mentioned only in 2 Sam 18:18. It is the valley close to Jerusalem, where Absalom built himself a mausoleum.

Next, the unknown toponym שָׁלֵם (Salem) is used in verse 18, however without any explanation, as was the case for Bela, the Valley of Siddim, and the Valley of Shaveh. Nevertheless, because שָׁלֵם (Salem) is mentioned directly after the Valley of the King, the identification of שָׁלֵם (Salem) with Jerusalem is obvious. The text contains many allusions to Jerusalem:

- The proper name שָׁלֵם (Salem) itself seems to be an abbreviation of the name יְרוּשָׁלַם (Jerusalem).
- The name שָׁלֵם (Salem) is semantically related to שָׁלוֹם (peace), which is meaningful in view of the war in which Lot and Abram have involuntarily been involved. The proper name יְרוּשָׁלַם (Jerusalem) is related to the word שָׁלוֹם (peace) as well (cf. also Ps 122:6; Isa 66:12).
- The King of Salem bears the meaning-laden proper name מַלְכִּי־צֶדֶק (Melchizedek), King of Justice. It is Jerusalem that should be the city of the just King (cf., e.g., Isa 32:1).
- Melchizedek's function is described as כֹהֵן לְאֵל עֶלְיוֹן (priest for God the High One; verse 18). Because Melchizedek is the only priest in the narrative, it is very tempting to interpret כֹהֵן לְאֵל עֶלְיוֹן as (the priest for God the High One), which means: the high priest. The high priest was of course connected to the temple in Jerusalem.
- Salem appears to be the place where the priest Melchizedek gives the divine blessing. The combination of blessing and Jerusalem occurs very often in the Hebrew Bible (cf., e.g., Ps 134).
- Furthermore, Salem is the place where the tithes are given by whoever has received this blessing. This combination of tithes and Jerusalem, is also well-known in the Hebrew Bible (cf., e.g., Num 18:20–32).

Why does the text of Gen 14 use an aposiopesis for Jerusalem? Abra(ha)m's itinerary, which is an itinerary on a small scale, and the itinerary of the entire people of God, which is an itinerary on a large scale, are parallel in biblical texts. Abraham already experiences what the entire people of God will experience— and the other way around: the entire people of God experiences what already happened to Abraham. Gen 14:1–22:19 describes Abraham's experiences in the promised land.[3] The first of them is the Jerusalem-encounter, but without the mentioning of Jerusalem, because the narrative still lies open for the experiences of God's people in the bigger story.

With regard to Abraham's experiences in the promised land, Gen 22:1–19 is also important, because it once again deals with a Jerusalem-encounter.[4] Again Jerusalem is not mentioned in the text. The location to which the Lord commissions Abraham to go together with his son Isaac, is called אֶרֶץ הַמֹּרִיָּה (the land of the Moriah; verse 2). In this land, the Lord will indicate a mountain on which Abraham can implement the assignment the Lord has given him. However, the name of this mountain is not revealed in the text. Apparently, the Lord must have spoken to Abraham at some moment after their dialogue in the verses 1–2. After all, Abraham is able to reach the place, but the text-internal reader has not come across its name in the text. He does, however, hear about the sacrifice on that anonymous peak, and in such an intensive way, that even in the days of the text-internal reader it is said: בְּהַר יְהוָה יֵרָאֶה (on the Lord's mountain there will be seen; verse 14).

This implies that, just as in Abraham's first experience in the promised land, Jerusalem is also present as an aposiopesis in his last experience in the land. The further use of the toponym מֹרִיָּה (Moriah) and the expression הַר־יְהוָה (the mountain of the Lord) make it clear that Jerusalem is intended. The proper name מֹרִיָּה (Moriah) is used only in 2 Chr 3:1, in combination with the toponym יְרוּשָׁלַם (Jerusalem). The expression הַר־יְהוָה (the mountain of the Lord) occurs in Isa 2:3; 30:29; Mic 4:2; Zech 8:3, each time in combination with the toponym יְרוּשָׁלַם (Jerusalem), indicating the Temple Mount.

---

3 Gen 22:20–25:11 contains the narratives about the transition from Abraham as the main character to Jacob as the main character, including the stories about the family tree of Terah in 22:20–24, about the death of Sarah in chapter 23, about finding a proper wife for Isaac in chapter 24, and, finally, about Abraham's death in 25:1–11. See in particular Willem A.M. Beuken, "De trektocht van Abraham," *Collationes* 21 (1991): 271–86.

4 See also Archibald L.H.M. van Wieringen, "The Reader in Genesis 22:1–19: Textsyntax— Textsemantics—Textpragmatics," *EstBib* 53 (1995): 289–304.

2   Jerusalem as an Aposiopesis in Deuteronomy and Kings/Chronicles

Jerusalem's presence via an aposiopesis is not limited to the Abraham cycle in Genesis. Jerusalem is not mentioned anywhere in the Torah. Even in the most obvious texts in which Jerusalem could be mentioned, i.e., the texts which deal with the future temple to be built in Jerusalem, the toponym Jerusalem is missing.

Instead of saying that the temple should be built in Jerusalem, Moses speaks about "the place that the Lord chooses to let his name dwell." These kinds of expressions are used many times in Deuteronomy.[5] This indirect identification of the place where God's house is to be built is also conveyed by using an indirect rendering of the Lord's view of his temple: it is not the Lord who speaks about the house for his name on a special spot, but Moses. Jerusalem is designated by using a double indirectness: an aposiopesis, and, above all, through a direct speech of Moses, instead of the Lord.

In the realization of the task of building a house for the Lord, the same expressions are used again. Solomon uses similar expressions when he dedicates the newly-built temple in Jerusalem, especially in 1 Kgs 8:16, 29, although using the verb הי״ה to be instead of the verbs שׂו״ם (to set; Deut 12:5, 21; 14:24) or שכ״ן (to dwell; Deut 12:11; 14:23; 16:2, 6, 11; 26:2).[6]

In reaction to Solomon's dedication prayer, the Lord confirms his presence in Jerusalem's temple in 1 Kgs 9:3. This reaction is remarkable. It is the first time in the biblical narrative the character "the Lord" directly speaks about the temple. Like Solomon, the Lord uses the same aposiopesis as found in Deuteronomy, by using the expression with the verb שׂו״ם (to set). However, he adds a temporal phrase to it: עַד־עוֹלָם (until in eternity).

When, in the same direct speech, the character "the Lord" discusses the pending exile, he no longer uses the aposiopesis-expression, but rather a direct indication of the temple built by Solomon by twice using the expression בַּיִת הַזֶּה (this house) in 9:7, 8. This means that, whereas the functioning temple is indicated by the aposiopeses, the destroyed and non-functioning temple is indicated by a direct identification with an indicative pronoun.

In Kings, this tension gradually increases. During the so-called schism dividing the land into a northern and southern kingdom, the prophet Ahijah tells Jeroboam the words of the Lord in which the Lord discontinues the aposiopesis by also mentioning the proper name Jerusalem: Jerusalem is the city chosen

---

5   Deut 12:5, 11, 21; 14:23–24; 16:6, 11; 26:2. See Eckart Otto, *Deuteronomium 12,1–23,15*, HThKAT (Freiburg: Herder, 2016), 1173–74.

6   See also Ernst Axel Knauf, *1 Könige 1–14*, HThKAT (Freiburg: Herder, 2016), 266.

as the dwelling place of the Lord's Name (1 Kgs 11:38). But from the twelve pieces into which Ahijah tears his garment, it is exactly the Jerusalem-piece which the Lord does not give to Jeroboam. The filling in of the aposiopesis, therefore, is not in favour of Jeroboam, although the Lord does give him ten tribes.

The intermezzo in 2 Kgs 23:26–27 maximizes the tension.[7] The Lord uses the aposiopesis again for both the city and the house, but fills in the aposiopesis concerning the city by mentioning the proper name Jerusalem as an apposition. The intermezzo is confusing for the text-internal reader. It is given at the end of King Josiah's activities related to the restauration of the temple and the reformation of the religious practices according to the instructions of the book of the Torah found in the temple. The text-internal reader is unexpectedly confronted with this doom-oracle as uttered by the Lord. The reason for the Lord's relinquishing of the city and the house of his presence, is King Manasseh, Josiah's predecessor, who is actually no longer on stage. Besides these semantic issues, the communicative setting raises more questions. The Lord's direct speech is introduced with a simple *wayyiqtol*: וַיֹּאמֶר יְהֹוָה (then the Lord said; verse 27), without mentioning to whom he is speaking. It therefore seems that the Lord is addressing the text-internal reader with his direct speech, instead of addressing King Josiah.

Chronicles is different. On the one hand, the same pattern can be seen in Chronicles; on the other hand, two differences occur in comparison to Kings.

Chronicles contains the same Jerusalem aposiopesis as is used in Deuteronomy and in Kings. While Solomon uses the expression (with the verb שׂו״ם, to set) in 2 Chr 6:20, the Lord uses these kinds of expressions in 7:16 (with the verb הי״ה, to be). Once again, the Lord's reaction contains the temporal phrase עַד־עוֹלָם (until in eternity) as a surplus.

Two new elements are, however, also present. First, the aposiopesis is filled in already at the beginning of Solomon's dedication prayer, by mentioning the toponym Jerusalem in an embedded direct speech of the Lord: Jerusalem is the place where the Lord's name is (2 Chr 6:6 contains the verb הי״ה, to be). By doing so at the beginning of his direct speech, the indirectness of the use of an embedded direct speech is continued, but the aposiopesis loses its strength. Only the connection with Deuteronomy and Kings is still there.

Secondly, the exilic experiences are clearly incorporated into the textual level of the dedication prayer. In contrast to the version in Kings, Solomon

---

7　This tension is well-known, but only discussed from a diachronic perspective, as by Norbert Lohfink, "Die Bundesurkunde des Königs Josias (Eine Frage an die Deuteronomiumsforschung)," *Bib* 44 (1963): 261–88, 461–98 (273).

explicitly mentions the exile by using the expression בְּאֶרֶץ שֹׁבֵיהֶם (in the land of their captivity twice; 6:37, 38).

Why is Jerusalem present in Deuteronomy as an aposiopesis? By using the aposiopesis, Deuteronomy avoids a direct identification of the commission to build a temple in Jerusalem and its realization. The biblical story is not simple: in the desert, after the exodus from Egypt, God asks the people to build a temple in Jerusalem; and in the promised land, Solomon, David's son, builds the temple God has asked for. A tension remains between the ideal God asks for on the way to the promised land and its realization after the journey into the promised land.

The tension between the addition עַד־עוֹלָם (until in eternity) in the Lord's reaction to the dedication of the temple, in both Kings and Chronicles, on the one hand, and the direct identification of the temple when the exile is discussed in the same reaction of the Lord, in both Kings and Chronicles, on the other hand, emphasizes the function of Jerusalem as an aposiopesis in Deuteronomy.

But Chronicles also discontinues the Jerusalem aposiopesis found in Deuteronomy. This discontinuation is related to the tension of the everlasting function of the house on the place the Lord has chosen and the loss of this function during the exile. Do the Lord's everlasting promise and Solomon's concrete building both really coincide? On the textual level of Chronicles, due to the mention of the so-called edict of Cyrus at the end of the book, the text is beyond the exile. This implies, on the one hand, that Solomon's words about the exile and the people's reconversion to the Lord have become reality, but, on the other hand, that his words are spoken in relation to the temple he built, but which no longer exists. In other words: Chronicles creates a new tension between past and present, in which the non-direct identification is continued, however not by using the aposiopesis found in Deuteronomy and Kings.

The Jerusalem aposiopesis as found in Deuteronomy is re-used at the beginning of the book of Nehemiah. Nehemiah's prayer in 1:4–9, still in Susa, contains the same expression in an embedded direct discourse of the Lord, directed to Moses: the Lord will bring back and gather his people again אֶל־הַמָּקוֹם אֲשֶׁר בָּחַרְתִּי לְשַׁכֵּן אֶת־שְׁמִי שָׁם ("at the place I have chosen to let my name dwell there"; 1:9).[8] In this way, the book of Nehemiah not only contains a connection to Deuteronomy, but also paves the way for the role of the edict of Cyrus at the end of Chronicles, which I will discuss below.

---

8   See, e.g., Terezija Snežna Večko, "Prayer at the Start of Action: Neh 1:5–11," *Bogoslovni vestnik* 65 (2005): 43–57 (50).

3   Jerusalem as an Aposiopesis in Prophetic Texts

The Jerusalem aposiopesis is not only present in narrative texts, but in prophetic texts as well, although its use varies in the various prophetic books.

Regarding the book of Isaiah, many main units contain a special aposiopesis.[9] In the first main unit, Isa 1:21, 24a–b (which are texts belonging to the text-immanent author) do not give any information about the spatial location of the direct speeches in verses 2–20, 22–23, 24c–26, and 27–31. Nevertheless, the town in verse 21 is directly identifiable as Jerusalem. Not only is the word קִרְיָה (town) used for Jerusalem elsewhere in the book of Isaiah (22:2; 29:1; 33:20[10]), but the words נֶאֱמָנָה (faithful), מִשְׁפָּט (righteousness) and צֶדֶק (justice) also evoke Jerusalem.

The location of the root of Jesse in chapter 11, which is part of the third main unit, the chapters 6–12, also functions as an aposiopesis. The identification with Jerusalem is not expressed, but nevertheless supposed in the phrase בְּכָל־הַר קָדְשִׁי (on all my holy mountain) in the Lord's direct speech in the verses 9a–b.

In the chapters 24–35, the second part of the fourth main unit, aposiopeses also play a role. The unnamed indication בָּהָר הַזֶּה (on this mountain) in 25:6, 7, 10 forms an aposiopesis for Jerusalem. The relation between this mountain and the Lord of hosts[11] makes it easy to identify this mountain.

In Isa 29:1, a city is addressed as אֲרִיאֵל (which is normally translated as "fireplace"). Only in verse 8 is the proper name צִיּוֹן (Zion) mentioned. The expression קִרְיַת חָנָה דָוִד (the town where David encamped; verse 1), however, already indicates that this identification has to be made. Its counterpart in chapter 32 is also represented as an aposiopesis. Isa 32:1–8 deal with a king; but where this king is king, is not mentioned. Again, the words צֶדֶק (justice) and מִשְׁפָּט (righteousness) make the aposiopesis understandable.

In a way, the chapters 36–39, the fifth main unit, also start with an aposiopesis. Isa 36:1 begins with כָּל־עָרֵי יְהוּדָה (all the fortified cities of Judah), in which the question whether Jerusalem belongs to these cities, remains unanswered. In verse 2, however, the movement, which has started from one of these cities, namely Lakish, appears to be directed towards Jerusalem.

---

9   Archibald L.H.M. van Wieringen, *The Reader-Oriented Unity of the Book Isaiah*, ACEBTS 6 (Vught: Skandalon, 2006), 79–83.

10   See also Ps 48:3; Lam 2:11; Mic 4:10.

11   Cf. the word הַר in Isa 2:2–3; 4:5; 8:18; 10:12; 11:9; 24:23; 27:13; 37:32; 40:9; 52:7; 65:11; 66:20.

The book of Amos is different.[12] On the one hand, Jerusalem and Zion are already mentioned in the second verse, rendering the first words of the character Amos. On the other hand, the proper names יְרוּשָׁלַם (Jerusalem) and צִיּוֹן (Zion) hardly occur in the book of Amos. The book of Amos creates the impression of being focussed on the northern kingdom Israel. The spatial decor consists of the sanctuary in Bethel, present as the toponym בֵּית־אֵל in verse 10 at the beginning of the narrative in chapter 7. This is the location of the well-known clash between the priest Amaziah and the prophet Amos in 7:10–17. The temple is described as a מִקְדַּשׁ־מֶלֶךְ (sanctuary of the king; verse 13). The king at issue here is King Jeroboam of the northern kingdom Israel, present in the preceding verses 10–11.

However, the expression בֵּית־אֵל can be understood as a description meaning "the house of God," which implies that the narrative takes place in the house of God instead of the city of Bethel. As a descriptive expression, בֵּית־אֵל indicates the temple in Jerusalem, as in 1 Kgs 8:6; 2 Chr 23:4, 15, 17–18. Furthermore, the expression מִקְדַּשׁ־מֶלֶךְ (sanctuary of the king; verse 13) is unique in the Hebrew Bible. The word מִקְדָּשׁ is never combined with the word מֶלֶךְ, but always with an expression indicating the Lord God.[13] This suggests that the word מֶלֶךְ can be understood as an indication for the Lord. The indication מֶלֶךְ for the Lord is very common in the Hebrew Bible,[14] especially in the book of Isaiah in which the Lord is called מֶלֶךְ (king) in 6:1 even before introducing any earthly king.

Against this background, it is possible that Amaziah's title כֹּהֵן בֵּית־אֵל can be translated both as "a priest of Bethel" and "the priest of the house of God." Due to this, a parallelism with the title הַכֹּהֵן (the high priest; Exod 31:10), used for the main priest in Jerusalem, arises. Due to these ambiguities, בֵּית־אֵל can also be understood as being an aposiopesis for Jerusalem.

The fifth vision in 9:1–4 can be considered as a continuation of the narration in 7:10–17, and consequently, as a continuation of the Jerusalem aposiopesis as well. Whereas the מִזְבֵּחַ (altar) indicates the liturgical centre of a sanctuary, the words כַּפְתּוֹר (capital) and סַף (threshold) form a merism, indicating the entire temple. The description of the anonymous altar and the supposed sanctuary runs parallel to the description of the sanctuary in the narration in 7:10–17.

---

12 Archibald L.H.M. van Wieringen, "The Triple-Layered Communication in the Book of Amos and Its Message of Non-Appropriation Theology," in *Multiple Teachers in Biblical Texts*, ed. Bart J. Koet and Archibald L.H.M. van Wieringen, CBET 88 (Leuven: Peeters, 2017), 89–106.

13 See Num 19:20; Josh 24:26; 1 Chr 22:19; Ps 73:17; Lam 2:20; Ezek 48:10.

14 See, e.g., 1 Sam 12:12; Pss 5:2; 10:16; 24:8, 10; 29:10; 44:4; 47:6–7; 48:2; 68:24; 84:3; 98:6; 145:1; Jer 10:10; 1 Chr 16:31; Ezek 20:33; Zeph 3:15; Zech 14:9; Mal 1:14.

This means that, instead of the sanctuary in Bethel, the temple can also be assumed. This idea is confirmed by the use of the words כַּפְתּוֹר (capital) and סַף (threshold) elsewhere in the Hebrew Bible. In Exod 25:31–40; 37:17–24, the word כַּפְתּוֹר is used for the lampstand in the tent-sanctuary in the desert/in the temple in Jerusalem. The word סַף occurs in the description of Solomon's temple (1 Kgs 7:50; 2 Chr 3:7), of Jehoash's restoration work at the temple (2 Kgs 12:13), of Josiah's reformation (2 Kgs 22:4; 23:4; 2 Chr 34:9), and of the entrance-guards (1 Chr 9:19, 22). In the prophetic literature, too, the word סַף is always connected to the Lord's temple in Zion/Jerusalem.[15]

More important is the fact that the only combination of seeing the Lord and a temple in the Hebrew Bible takes place in Jerusalem's temple, regarding the prophet Isaiah in chapter 6. Because of the role of the מִזְבֵּחַ (altar) in Isa 6:6, the characters Isaiah and Amos seem to be located at the same place. Whereas the prophet Isaiah sees the Lord sitting upon a throne (Isa 6:1), the prophet Amos sees the Lord standing upon the altar. Whereas the prophet Isaiah is aware of the fact that his vision could lead to destruction (Isa 6:5), the prophet Amos's vision is about the Lord planning and executing destruction.

4 The Jerusalem Aposiopesis as an Inclusion of the Tanakh

Jerusalem is not only an aposiopesis in the Abraham cycle and in Deuteronomy, but, as mentioned previously, the proper name יְרוּשָׁלַם (Jerusalem) is not present in the entire Torah, which is very remarkable.

The Jerusalem aposiopesis in the Torah deals with the exciting relation between the ideal Jerusalem the Lord has in mind and will choose, during the people's journey through the desert, and the realization of this ideal, when the people has finally arrived in the promised land. However, the aposiopesis in the Torah, the first part of the Tanakh, has to do with the concluding text of the Tanakh in Chronicles as well.

2 Chr 36:22–23 mentions the so called edict of Cyrus by quoting the text itself. Cyrus says that in Jerusalem in Judah a house has to be built for the Lord God. Then, he utters the wish that whoever belongs to his people, יְהוָה אֱלֹהָיו עִמּוֹ (the Lord his God be with him), using the preposition עִם (with) like in the famous Nathan prophecy (see 2 Sam 7). The text of the edict ends with an aposiopesis: וְיָעַל (that he go up), using the verb על"ה. The place to which he has to go up, is not mentioned, but for the technical verb על"ה Jerusalem, Zion, the temple is always meant. Moreover, the toponym יְרוּשָׁלַם (Jerusalem)

---

15   See Isa 6:4; Jer 35:4; 52:19, 24; Ezek 40:6–7; 41:16; 43:8; Zech 12:2.

was already used in the text of the edict. It is not difficult to know what the topographical goal of the עלֹ״ה-movement must be. Nevertheless, it is silenced; Jerusalem is present as an aposiopesis.

This implies that, at the end of the book of Chronicles, the same aposiopesis is used as in the Torah. Even more, just as the Jerusalem aposiopesis in Deuteronomy is shaped through an embedded direct discourse of the Lord within a direct discourse of Moses, the Jerusalem aposiopesis at the end of the Tanakh is also placed in an embedded direct discourse.[16]

By means of this aposiopesis, the text of the edict of Cyrus avoids the direct identification of the house that the Lord desires with the concrete temple-building that will be built in Jerusalem.

This also means that the ending of the Tanakh contains the same aposiopesis concerning Jerusalem as the beginning of the Tanakh in the Abraham narratives. The Jerusalem aposiopesis forms an inclusion for the Tanakh. If the text-internal reader wishes to know how the edict of Cyrus could be implemented, he should start (re-)reading again, beginning with the Torah.

5   The Non-Identification of Jerusalem in Old Testament Texts

The figure of speech "aposiopesis" facilitates the non-identification of the ideal, theological Jerusalem with the actual Jerusalem. In the process of realizing the implementation of the theological Jerusalem, the actual Jerusalem is never the final realization, but always "work-in-progress." It is on its way to become the ideal Jerusalem, only if everything goes well.

The aposiopesis is not the only figure of speech used to guarantee this non-identification. Other figures of speech are used as well, the "ellipsis" being the most important.[17] In my view, the book of Isaiah is the most intriguing example of the use of the ellipsis concerning Jerusalem.[18] It structures the entire book of Isaiah. The chapters 1–39 create a tension surrounding Jerusalem. At first, Jerusalem is threatened by the minor enemy Aram in 7:1–17. However, Aram is not even capable of waging war (verse 1). Next, Jerusalem is threatened by the major enemy Assur, especially in the chapters 36–38. It is true that Assur is capable of waging war against Jerusalem, but it is only an unsuccessful

---

16   Cf. Gregory Goswell, "Having the Last Say: The End of the OT," *JETS* 58 (2015): 15–30 (19–22).

17   See also Bullinger, *Figures of Speech*, 3–69.

18   Cf. also Ulrich Berges, *Das Buch Jesaja: Komposition und Endgestalt*, HBS 16 (Freiburg: Herder, 1998), 537.

siege, without the entering of the city. The climax is formed by Babel in the enigmatic narrative in chapter 39. The most remarkable point is that Babel enters Jerusalem. Nobody seems to stand in its way, not even King Hezekiah. Even more remarkable is the fact that nowhere in the narrative is mentioned that Babel leaves the city. Whereas Aram and Assur withdraw, Babel remains in Jerusalem—although it really seems to have a military goal, because King Hezekiah shows him his בֵּית־כֵּלָיו (armoury). How will this all end? The narrative does not tell. Chapter 40 continues beyond the crisis that started in the previous chapter. Words of comfort are spoken (verses 1–2), which implies that these are necessary, but the crisis itself is absent. The crisis of the Babylonian exile, including the destruction of Jerusalem and its temple, has to be situated somewhere between chapter 39 and chapter 40; but all this is only present as an ellipsis.

This major ellipsis in the book of Isaiah, concerning the decline of Jerusalem, is supported by the minor ellipsis created by the use of the word הֵיכָל as an indication of Jerusalem's temple.[19] In 6:1–13, the הֵיכָל (temple) is presented as filled. The described fullness is even greater than the temple can contain; the hems of the Lord's royal robe already fill the temple. In 66:6, too, the temple appears to be filled. The voice of the Lord is present in the temple and heard from there. Besides these two occurrences, the word הֵיכָל (temple) occurs only in 44:28, where the Lord mentions in a direct speech that the temple must be founded. In 66:6 the temple is indeed founded. However, from the viewpoint of 6:1, this statement is remarkable, because, in that verse, the temple has already been founded and exists. This implies that something has to have taken place concerning the temple, which makes the statement in 44:28 significant; but what this event is, is not given in the text; it is only present via an ellipsis.

It seems to me that biblical texts prefer using an "ellipsis" to describe something negative concerning Jerusalem, namely the decline of Jerusalem and its temple, but use an "aposiopesis" to describe something positive concerning Jerusalem, namely the way towards the realization of God's ideal Jerusalem.

This preference might be explained by the fact that an ellipsis does not mention anything at all, while an aposiopesis mentions something in a different form, hidden behind something else. In other words: the destruction of Jerusalem is rendered as a real absence, while, although the final realization of the ideal Jerusalem of the Lord has not yet occurred, the ongoing realization of this ideal Jerusalem can somehow already be seen.

In my view, the aposiopesis is a guarantee against a fundamentalist interpretation of Jerusalem. Jerusalem is in progress. Based upon biblical texts, the

---

19   Van Wieringen, *Reader-Oriented Unity*, 79–80.

actual Jerusalem and the ideal Jerusalem can never be equated. If this were to be done, the difference between the ideal Jerusalem and the actual Jerusalem, present in the aposiopesis, would be nullified. Based upon the same biblical texts however, it can also never be said that the actual Jerusalem has nothing to do with the ideal Jerusalem, which will someday be implemented and realized. If someone were to propose this, the same difference between the ideal and the actual Jerusalem, present in the aposiopesis, would also be nullified. Both views are sides of the same coin and held together by the use of the aposiopesis.

In my opinion, this double-view of Jerusalem, present in the use of the aposiopesis, is a solid textual basis for solving religious conflicts concerning Jerusalem (and mutatis mutandis for other sacred places), presuming that all parties involved are willing to acknowledge the non-fundamentalist impact of the aposiopesis.

The anti-fundamentalist aspect of the aposiopesis, which entails a Jerusalem theology that differs between the ideal Jerusalem of the Lord and the actual Jerusalem of God's people, could be understood in a broader context of both literary sciences and theology as well.

Literary sciences have shown that there is no one-to-one-relation between what occurs within a textual communication level and what occurs outside of it. Of course, there is a relation, but not simply a one-to-one-relation. In fact, texts are anti-fundamentalist in themselves. As soon as texts are not dealt with as texts, the danger of fundamentalism arises, and with all its consequences.

Theology using the help of modern literary methodologies has shown that the sacred text, in this case the (Hebrew) Bible, and divine revelation do not coincide: the text is the witness of the revelation, not the revelation itself. As soon as a sacred text is not dealt with as a witness of the revelation, the danger of fundamentalism arises, again, with all its consequences.

6   Jerusalem as an Aposiopesis and New Testament Texts

In the New Testament, the Jerusalem aposiopesis is not present as an overall structure like it is in the Tanakh.[20] Although the New Testament does not

---

20   An overall structure using the Jerusalem aposiopesis might be present in Luke-Acts. Luke starts and ends in the temple in Jerusalem (respectively 1:8–23 and 24:52–53). Acts starts in the temple in Jerusalem with the Petrine Pentecost (2:1–41), but the Pauline Pentecost is not realised at the end of Acts (it is alluded to in 20:15), although the parallels between Peter in the chapters 1–12 and Paul in the chapters 13–28 are numerous. See

contain many texts using an aposiopesis to evoke Jerusalem, a similar use of the Jerusalem aposiopesis can nevertheless be found in it. In fact, New Testament texts continue the Jerusalem aposiopesis from the Old Testament texts.

I would like to discuss two crucial texts in Matthew: 17:1–13 and 27:52–53. The first text marks the start of Jesus's journey to Jerusalem; the second one is related to Jesus's death on the cross.

The first text is Matt 17:1–13, the narrative of the so-called transfiguration.[21] Jesus and his disciples are located in the most northern part of the biblical land, in the region of Caesarea Philippi (16:13). Jesus has just begun to explain to his disciples that he has to go to Jerusalem, where he will suffer, even unto death, and where he will rise from the dead (16:21). Jesus then takes three intimate disciples with him, up onto a high mountain (17:1), where his appearance changes, and he appears clothed in a dazzling white garment, flanked by Moses and Elijah (verse 2). The name of this mountain is not mentioned in the text.

Some translations fill in this high mountain with Mount Tabor. Mount Tabor is an eye-catching mesa in the Galilean landscape, but is nowhere mentioned in the entire New Testament.[22]

Which biblical mountain is hidden in the ὄρος ὑψηλὸς (high mountain)? In my view, two mountains are possible, at the same time. The ὄρος ὑψηλὸς (high mountain) has characteristics of both the Sinai/Horeb in the desert and Mount Zion in Jerusalem. On the one hand, the narrative evokes Sinai/Horeb because of the apparition of Moses and Elijah. Both of them are connected to this mountain.[23] On the other hand, the narrative evokes Jerusalem by the glorification of Jesus, at his resurrection, which will take place in Jerusalem.

Both mountains play an important role in the journey of God's people from Egypt to the promised land. In a way, this "grand itinerary" can be described as being a journey from Sinai to Zion; from the place of the commission to build a house where the Lord's name can dwell, to the place where the implementation of this commission is initiated. By evoking both mountains, without mentioning them, Jesus's journey is made parallel to the journey of God's people, of which he is a member.

Archibald L.H.M. van Wieringen and Herwi W.M. Rikhof, *De zeven sacramenten*, ThPS 6 (Bergambacht: 2VM, 2013), 52.

21   See also Armand Puig i Tàrrech, "La gloire sur la montagne: L'épisode de la transfiguration de Jésus," *RCatT* 37 (2012): 203–45 (212–14).

22   In the Old Testament, תָּבוֹר (Mount Tabor) is mentioned in Josh 19:22; Judg 4:6, 12, 14; 8:18; 1 Sam 10:3; 1 Chr 6:77; Ps 89:12; Jer 46:18; Hos 5:1.

23   See respectively Exod 19:20; 24:16; 34:4, 29; Lev 7:38; 25:1; 26:46; Num 1:1; 3:1, 14; 9:1, 5; Deut 4:10; 1 Kgs 8:9; 2 Chr 5:10; Mal 4:4; 1 Kgs 19:8.

In the Lukan version of the narrative in Luke 9:28–36 this relation is intensified by Moses and Elijah talking with Jesus about his ἔξοδος (exodus), which he
is going to accomplish in Jerusalem (verse 31).

The three disciples wish to capture the event on the high mountain by making three tents, as if the resurrection, the final goal of Jesus's itinerary, can be
captured before its final implementation. But in fact, their reaction is a contradiction of the process of implementation hidden in the aposiopesis. They have
to bear the event in mind to understand what is going to happen in Jerusalem.
After Jesus's resurrection the event can be told and fully understood.

The second text is Matt 27:52–53.[24] As from chapter 21, Jesus is in Jerusalem.
This location is mentioned in 21:1, 10 concerning Jesus's entry into Jerusalem.
Furthermore, Jerusalem is mentioned for the last time in Matthew in 23:37.
Jerusalem is connected to the death of the prophets, just as Jesus's death will
soon take place in Jerusalem.

At Jesus's death, 27:52–53 tells that the graves of the saints who had passed
away, were opened, and that, at his death, even before Jesus's resurrection,
these saints already rise, but they only become visible after Jesus's resurrection, when entering into τὴν ἁγίαν πόλιν (the holy city). Within the context of
the chapters 21–28, this "holy city" must be Jerusalem, but Jerusalem is not
mentioned with its own proper name, but by using a description similar to the
"holy" (ἅγιος) people (the saints) involved.

The holy city of the resurrection is not simply equated with the actual
Jerusalem of the death of the saints. In this way, the use of the expression
ἁγία πόλις (holy city) for Jerusalem reflects the same tension as found in the
Jerusalem aposiopesis in the Old Testament texts.

Although the Jerusalem aposiopesis is hardly used in New Testament texts,
but is nevertheless present as an inclusion of Jesus's itinerary from Galilee, the
start of his journey, to the Jerusalem of his death and resurrection, the final
destination of his journey, the idea of a non-direct identification between the
actual and the ideal Jerusalem is prominently present in the New Testament.

As an illustration I would like to mention Revelation. The description of the
new Jerusalem in 21:9–22:5 makes clear that there is a difference between the
ideal and the actual Jerusalem. In the new Jerusalem, perfectly built with three
gates at each side of the square city, there is no temple, because the Lord and
the Lamb are the temple. This not only implies that the ideal Jerusalem is not

---

24   Archibald L.H.M. van Wieringen, "Descent into the Netherworld: A Biblical Perspective,"
       in *The Apostles' Creed: "He Descended into Hell"*, ed. Marcel Sarot and Archibald L.H.M. van
       Wieringen, STAR 24 (Leiden: Brill, 2018), 9–32 (27–28).

yet present, but also that the ideal Jerusalem is not made by the faithful, but comes from heaven, which means coming from God.[25]

The same tension can be observed in Jesus's speech about the coming of the Son of Man in Matt 24, which he delivers in Jerusalem. When Jesus discusses the question as to where the Messiah can be found (verses 23–28), the answer to which seems obvious, certainly if this question is asked in Jerusalem, he emphasizes that any answer which captures the place where the Messiah should be, is incorrect. There is only one proper answer: he is not here. It is exactly this statement which marks the place of the resurrection when the women discover the opened tomb, and the two men standing there say to them: "He is not here" (28:6).[26]

In the Lukan version of Jesus's speech on the coming of the Messiah (17:20–37), the question is elaborated with a second question regarding the place of the Kingdom of God (verses 20–21). In Luke this question is discussed on the way to Jerusalem. Nevertheless, the answer is not Jerusalem, although the way to Jerusalem, including Jerusalem itself, makes clear where the Kingdom of God and the Messiah must be searched for. Luke 19:11 makes this clear as well.[27] Jesus has just passed through Jericho, the last stop before Jerusalem (for both the people of God and for Jesus), when the crowds believe that the Kingdom will come immediately. By means of a parable Jesus has to explain that he is still on his way to Jerusalem, and that the ideal Jerusalem has therefore not yet come.

7   Concluding Remarks

The Jerusalem aposiopesis is used in various forms in both the Old Testament and the New Testament. In both, it has the function of avoiding a direct identification of the actual Jerusalem with the theologically ideal Jerusalem. Solomon's temple is not the final realization of the ideal Jerusalem, but does bring its realization a step closer. The destruction of the temple and the exile

---

25   For a detailed analysis of the text-passage see, e.g., Saji Joseph Kizhakkayil, "New Jerusalem as Bride of God, Holy of Holies and as Paradise. A Threefold Affirmation of God's Intimacy with his People (Rev 21:1–22:5)," in *Gottes Wort im Menschenwort: Festschrift für Georg Fischer SJ zum 60. Geburtstag*, ed. Dominik Markl, Claudia Paganini, and Simone Paganini, ÖBS 43 (Frankfurt: Peter Lang, 2014), 249–70.

26   See also Bas M.F. van Iersel, *Mark: A Reader-Response Commentary*, JSOTSup 164 (Sheffield: Sheffield Academic Press, 1998), 502.

27   See also Laurie Guy, "The Interplay of the Present and Future in the Kingdom of God (Luke 19:11–44)," *TynBul* 48 (1997): 119–37.

do not hinder the realization of the ideal Jerusalem. The coming of the Messiah and the place of his resurrection, too, do not coincide with the ideal Jerusalem, but, again, they do bring its realization a step closer.

Besides the Jerusalem aposiopesis, biblical texts contain other figures of speech expressing the tension between the actual and ideal Jerusalem, e.g., the ellipsis.

The biblical emphasis on the difference between the actual and ideal Jerusalem should always be understood as a mark of the intrinsic anti-fundamentalist character of the Bible.

In my view, the reception of the biblical tension, guaranteeing a non-fundamentalist interpretation of the text, expressed by using the Jerusalem aposiopesis (and the other various stylistic expressions) has often been nullified by choosing in favour of a filling in of the textual Jerusalem with either a historical Jerusalem or a theological Jerusalem. It seems to me that, in the post-biblical Christian reception, the historical Jerusalem is often absent, replacing Jerusalem with some heavenly place—which can be considered as a kind of theological fundamentalism. In a historical-fundamentalist view, whether this view be Jewish, Christian or Muslim, the textual Jerusalem is absent, equating the textual and historical Jerusalem. Further research into this anti-fundamentalist guarantee of the Bible for its reception would be very interesting.[28]

References

Berges, Ulrich. *Das Buch Jesaja: Komposition und Endgestalt.* HBS 16. Freiburg: Herder, 1998.

Beuken, Willem A.M. "De trektocht van Abraham." *Collationes* 21 (1991): 271–86.

Bullinger, E.W. *Figures of Speech Used in the Bible.* London: Spottiswoode, 1898. Repr., Grand Rapids: Baker Book, 1968.

Emerton, J.A. "The Site of Salem, The City of Melchizedek (Genesis xiv 18)." Pages 45–71 in *Studies in the Pentateuch.* Edited by J.A. Emerton. VTSup 41 (Leiden: Brill, 1990).

Goswell, Gregory. "Having the Last Say: The End of the OT." *JETS* 58 (2015): 15–30.

Guy, Laurie. "The Interplay of the Present and Future in the Kingdom of God (Luke 19:11–44)." *TynBul* 48 (1997): 119–37.

---

28   This research could further be enriched by using cultural theories regarding holy places and spaces as well. See, e.g., W.J.T. Mitchell, "Holy Landscape: Israel, Palestine, and the American Wilderness," in *Landscape and Power*, ed. W.J.T. Mitchell (Chicago: the University of Chicago Press, 2002), 291–317.

Iersel, Bas M.F. van. *Mark: A Reader-Response Commentary*. JSOTSup 164. Sheffield: Sheffield Academic Press, 1998.

Jacob, Benno. *Das erste Buch der Tora: Genesis*. Berlin: Schocken, 1934. Repr., New York: Ktav, n.y.

Kizhakkayil, Saji Joseph. "New Jerusalem as Bride of God, Holy of Holies and as Paradise: A Threefold Affirmation of God's Intimacy with his People (Rev 21:1–22:5)." Pages 249–70 in *Gottes Wort im Menschenwort: Festschrift für Georg Fischer SJ zum 60. Geburtstag*. Edited by Dominik Markl, Claudia Paganini, and Simone Paganini. ÖBS 43. Frankfurt: Peter Lang, 2014.

Knauf, Ernst Axel. *1 Könige 1–14*. HThKAT. Freiburg: Herder, 2016.

Lohfink, Norbert. "Die Bundesurkunde des Königs Josias (Eine Frage an die Deuteronomiumsforschung)." *Bib* 44 (1963): 261–88, 461–498.

Mitchell, W.J.T. "Holy Landscape: Israel, Palestine, and the American Wilderness." Pages 291–317 in *Landscape and Power*. Edited by W.J.T. Mitchell. Chicago: The University of Chicago Press, 2002.

Otto, Eckart. *Deuteronomium 12,1–23,15*. HThKAT. Freiburg: Herder, 2016.

Puig i Tàrrech, Armand. "La gloire sur la montagne: L'épisode de la transfiguration de Jésus." *RCatT* 37 (2012) 203–45.

Soares, Eliel Almeida, and Diósnio Machado Neto. "A Aposiopesis em André da Silva Gomes." Pages 337–48 in *SIMA 2015: IV Simpósio Internacional de Música na Amazônia*. Edited by Jefferson Tiago De Souza Mendes Da Silva, Gustavo Frosi Benetti, Francisco Zmekhol Nascimento de Oliveira, and Damían Keller. Boa Vista: UFRR, 2016.

Večko, Terezija Snežna. "Prayer at the Start of Action: Neh 1:5–11." *Bogoslovni vestnik* 65 (2005): 43–57.

Wieringen, Archibald L.H.M. van. "The Reader in Genesis 22:1–19: Textsyntax—Textsemantics—Textpragmatics." *EstBib* 53 (1995): 289–304.

Wieringen, Archibald L.H.M. van. *The Reader-Oriented Unity of the Book Isaiah*. ACEBTS 6. Vught: Skandalon, 2006.

Wieringen, Archibald L.H.M. van. "The Triple-Layered Communication in the Book of Amos and Its Message of Non-Appropriation Theology." Pages 89–106 in *Multiple Teachers in Biblical Texts*. Edited by Bart J. Koet and Archibald L.H.M. van Wieringen. CBET 88. Leuven: Peeters, 2017.

Wieringen, Archibald L.H.M. van. "Descent Into the Netherworld: A Biblical Perspective." Pages 9–32 in *The Apostles' Creed: "He Descended into Hell"*. Edited by Marcel Sarot and Archibald L.H.M. van Wieringen. STAR 24. Leiden: Brill, 2018.

Wieringen, Archibald L.H.M. van, and Herwi W.M. Rikhof. *De zeven sacramenten*. ThPS 6. Bergambacht: 2VM, 2013.

Index of Ancient Sources

Index of Modern Authors

Printed in the United States
By Bookmasters